Perennials

A Southern Celebration of Foods and Flavors

The Junior Service League of Gainesville, Georgia

The purpose of the Junior Service League of Gainesville, Georgia, is exclusively educational and charitable and is to promote volunteerism and to develop the potential of its members for voluntary participation in community affairs and to demonstrate the effectiveness of trained volunteers.

The proceeds from the sale of *Perennials* will be used to support community projects sponsored by the Junior Service League of Gainesville, Georgia.

First Printing . . . . . April, 1984

Second Printing . . . . . July, 1984

Third Printing . . . . . October, 1987

Fourth Printing . . . . . January, 1989

Fifth Printing . . . . . January, 1991

To order additional copies of

Perennials

use the forms provided in the back of the book or write to:

Perennial Publications
Post Office Box 32
Gainesville, Georgia 30503

Library of Congress Catalog Card Number 83-081825

ISBN 0-9612234-0-5

Printed in the USA by

WIMMER BROTHERS

A Wimmer Company

Memphis • Dallas • San Antonio

Introduction

Perennials in flowers and foods of the South are enduring, steadfast, predictable, renewing themselves throughout the years in familiar and comforting ways. Such are these gifts we bring to you of our favorite foods for many seasons. Their fragrance, flavor, and substance are as varied as the blossoms recurrent each year in Northeast Georgia. Some are exotic, intriguing, elusive. Others are hearty, lusty, dramatic. All of them you will want among your *Perennials*, your repertoire of recipes, to use again and again for years of family gatherings, quiet suppers, carefree cook-outs, holiday dinners; for times of gaiety, anniversary observances, neighborhood visits, and formal occasions.

For in the South, food is a part of the celebration of events and of feelings. It is central to all our gatherings. Food heralds a christening, welcomes a visitor, highlights an evening of revelry and fun, proclaims a New Year, sparks the merriment of a child's party, accents the statement of elegance for a traditional ceremony, offers tangible comfort and sustenance through times of sorrow, expresses caring and devotion in the ritual of daily meals.

Food has many meanings, and we are comfortable with its symbolism. The still-warm cookie placed in the hand of a child can become a memory to temper the chill of later heart-wounds. Good food shared with good friends is a perennial celebration we can count on for later restoration and renewal. Quotations from Southern literary figures throughout our book share insights into the significance of the preparation of food and its gracious serving within the customs and culture of the South. For food is basic to survival, but its symbolism touches also upon survival of thought, soul, and spirit.

The roots of our *Perennials* reach deeply into the rich and varied lore and loam of our South. We have not made our choices lightly. Each blossom, faithfully reproduced, represents a favorite, native to or naturalized in this area. These are our *Perennials* which have prevailed as things of beauty for centuries, surviving through changes to climate and ecology. Their flowering each year proclaims the return of a season, reminding us that they are trustworthy, dependable, and constant. So, too, you will find our recipes. They, also, have survived many testings. They will reassure with consistent results and familiar comforts. Comments introducing the recipes are an intimate sharing of our experiences with food, variations you may wish to try, combinations, accompaniments, and menus you may enjoy. Come join our celebration of foods and flavors! We hope they will become *Perennials* for you also.

...the time, the place, the company--indisputable seasoners of all good cooking.
Celestine Sibley, *A Place Called Sweet Apple*
Doubleday, Copyright 1967. Used with permission.

Cover Design and Color Illustrations
Gwen Newman

Gwen Newman, a native of Atlanta, Georgia, holds a Bachelor of Fine Arts Degree in Graphic Design from the University of Georgia. She is presently working as a free-lance illustrator.

Front Cover: *Daylily* (Hermerocallis fulva)
In early summer the daylily brings us the blaze of orange which edges our roadsides. It is unique as a wildflower in that at each stage of its yearly growth the daylily offers us food. Cut the young green shoots for salads in spring. In summer its blossoms may be battered and fried. In winter its tubers add crunch to salads or may be roasted as a snack.

Back Cover: *Japanese Honeysuckle* (Lonicera japonica)
Honeysuckle is a favorite wild treat of children in the South. Honeysuckle describes the pleasure of those who taste the sweet nectar trickling from the base of the corolla. Its fragrance, borne lightly on a warm breeze, awakens nostalgia for a Southern summer.

Cookbook Committee
1982 - 1984

Production Editor
Sally Butts Darden

Distribution Editor
Elaine Caras Waller

Recipe Committee
Jane Hix Oliver, Chairman

Diane Derrick Blalock
Judy Evans Harrison
Carolyn Hartford Mahar
Cathy McLanahan Nix

Jean Bennett Oliver
Ann Branch Smith

Flo Criss Smith
Debbie Jacobs Springle
Gail Adams Thomas
Carol Lynn Dobson Waggoner

Design-Format Committee
Susan Henson Frost, Chairman

Patti Jenkins Chambers
Connie Wallis Dixon

Susan Lynch Gilliam

Connie Kemp Goldfarb
Lynn Newman McCranie

Marketing Committee
Sherrie Nathan Schrage, Chairman

Beth Sullivan Copeland
Susan Bible Jessup
Betty Nichols Livingston

Joanne Portman McDonald
Darlene Cook Parrish
Cindy Collins Randolph

Flo Criss Smith
Debbie Jacobs Springle
Gail Adams Thomas

Office Manager - Treasurer
Kathy Reeves Mathis

Typists
Darlene Cook Parrish
Cathy Brown Wilson

Sustainer Advisors

Betty Ann Christopher Chambers
Kit Long Dunlap
Louise Hendrix Forrester
Mary Virginia McKibbon Harris
Carrie McClain Hatfield

Marian Martin Hosch
Martha Rand Jacobs
Melba Clark Jacobs
Evelyn Atwater Langston

Sissy Dunlap Lawson
Nell Whelchel Wiegand
Jane Eve Fair Wilheit
Mary Hart Keys Wilheit
Katherine Rogers Williams

Cookbook Chairmen

Jean Bennett Oliver	1985	Kathy Reeves Mathis	1989
Flo Criss Smith	1986	Julie Cottrill Ferguson	1990
Tina Byrd Burns	1987	Dee Ann Carter Benton	1991
Sue Dixey DeLong	1988	Regina Elzey Cochran	1992

The Cookbook Committee wishes to acknowledge the following persons without whose advice and expertise this book would not have been possible: Martin L. Curry and Nancy D. Story, Curry & Story, Consultants in the English Language; G. Harold DeLong, Jr., Graphic Designer; Suzanne Roberts Greene, Wine Consultant; Carlette H. Hammond, Microwave Consultant; Helen Scanling Hays and Ellen Robinson Rolfes, Hays, Rolfes & Associates, Community Cookbook Consultants; Betty N. Romberg, Typist; Jerald J. Rucker, Director of Northeast Georgia Small Business Development Center, Professor of Marketing, University of Georgia College of Business, Athens, Georgia; W. Woodrow Stewart, Attorney-at-Law; Lee S. Wenthe, Assistant Professor of Advertising, University of Georgia School of Journalism, Athens, Georgia; Katherine R. Williams, Introduction.

Perennials is a collection of over 700 triple-tested recipes. Our sincere appreciation to all who graciously contributed and tested the over 3500 recipes from which these were selected. Regretably, we were unable to incorporate all recipes due to similarity and lack of space.

Table of Contents

On using this book...

So that you may more easily prepare and enjoy the recipes from *Perennials*, the following clarifications should be noted. **Preparation** will certainly vary from cook to cook, but our assessments have been made in an attempt to denote the level of difficulty and/or the time involved in each recipe. **Oven Temperature** always refers to a preheated temperature unless otherwise specified. "Butter" refers to just that; margarine will be listed when optional. "Flour" refers to all-purpose white flour; all other types are specified. "Oil" refers to any cooking oil of choice; particular oils are specified when needed.

Micronote instructions are given for recipes when appropriate and/or when a significant time savings can be realized. These instructions assume the use of a 600-700 watt microwave oven. HIGH refers to 100% power; MEDIUM refers to 60% power; LOW refers to 30% power (or defrost setting). Space does not allow us to give basic microwave information; please refer to the manufacturer's instruction manual for your oven when basics are needed.

All entrées in *Perennials* are presented with a **Menu Suggestion** utilizing other recipes found in this book. Few of these suggestions form a complete menu; rather, they are intended as a starting point to stimulate your own creative selection. Food combinations and preferences are both very personal and very subjective; we hope to have offered you interesting and helpful ideas in menu planning, whether it be for a family supper or an elegant dinner party.

On wine...

When combined with other food, wine provides an enjoyable balance of flavors. Its acidity serves as a contrast to food, providing a pleasant and interesting sensation. A few basic guidelines can aid in the selection and serving of wine. As a very general rule serve: (1) white wines with seafood and cheese entrées, (2) full white and light red with chicken and Cornish hens, (3) Vin Rosé or a very light red with ham and pork, (4) red Bordeaux or California Cabernet with lamb, (5) red Burgundy or California Zinfandel with beef, pheasant, or game, and (6) the late harvest German wines, French Sauternes and Barsacs, and sweeter California Rieslings with fruit and dessert.

Usually, lighter wines go with lighter foods; heavier-bodied, fuller-flavored wines go with heavier, richer foods. The color of the wine can be deceptive, however. There are light reds, such as Beaujolais or Volnay, and heavier whites, such as Chardonnay. As the lighter foods in a meal precede the heavier, the wines should follow the same principle. Serve dryer wines with appetizers and main courses, and save the sweeter wines for dessert. In serving wine with food, it is important to contrast the simple with the complex. A fine wine is better enjoyed with elegantly but simply prepared food. When the food is heavily seasoned or features rich sauces, use a more basic wine, a generic wine, a vin ordinaire, or even an alternate beverage such as beer.

In cooking with wine, remember the adage, "Never cook with what you will not drink," and try to match in similarity the wine you are serving with that used in the accompanying dish. Also remember that vinegar is an enemy of wine; lemon juice can be substituted in a recipe to avoid a sour taste. In general a dessert wine is best when served with fruits and simply flavored sweets.

Cheese is always a complement to wine but, again, combine simpler, milder cheeses (Havarti, Port Salud) with more delicate wines and more flavorful cheeses (Roquefort, Stilton, sharp Cheddar) with more robust wines.

Be adventuresome in choosing wine, allowing your senses of taste, smell, and balance to guide you. Delightful and adequate selections can be purchased inexpensively if care and attention are given. Remember to store the bottle on its side. Always chill champagnes very cold and white wines medium cold before serving. Quality reds are served at cool room temperature and should be allowed a period of breathing. Generic and lighter reds can be very slightly chilled.

Included with each entrée is a **Wine** or **Beverage Suggestion**. We hope you will use the above suggestions as a guide to experiment for yourself, so that your selection will suit the occasion, the palate, and even the weather.

Beverages

Chicory

2 Beverages

Chicory (Cichorium intybus)

From two common names for chicory (coffee weed and wild endive), two of its culinary uses can easily be deduced. In the North Georgia mountains the roots of this naturalized wild herb are gathered and boiled for a coffee substitute. In early spring the young leaves of the chicory plant make fine salads when mixed with fresh spinach, fresh mushrooms, and tossed in a vinaigrette then topped with crisp bacon.

On Beverages

- To enhance the flavor of iced tea, add 1 (6-ounce) can frozen lemonade concentrate; garnish with fresh mint or lemon balm. For lemony ice cubes dissolve ½ cup sugar in ½ cup lemon juice and 3½ cups water. Pour into ice trays and freeze.
- To make coffee for a crowd, allow 1 pound ground coffee plus 2 gallons water for 40 servings.
- If milk begins to go a bit sour, no need to throw it away; it's fine for cooking. Use right away in cake batter or cookie dough (add ½ teaspoon baking soda to flour), or use it in any dish calling for buttermilk.
- As a cooking agent, beer can be used as a flavoring, a tenderizer, or a leavener.
- To keep punch from becoming diluted, prepare an ice mold or block from fruit juice and fresh fruit, or freeze a large cluster of grapes to use as garnish and "ice."
- Planning a party? Remember, there are 17 (1½-ounce) shots in a fifth of liquor; plan about 3 drinks per guest.
- Three tablespoons yield 1½ fluid ounces or 1 jigger.
- Serve coffee in mugs with a cinnamon stick stirrer; it adds a spicy, decorative touch to the beverage and is great as an after-dinner drink.
- Let a large punch bowl double as a cooler for beverages. Fill the bowl with ice, then put in your cans and bottles.
- To make exotic teas with unusual flavors: Pour loose tea leaves into a jar. Add small amounts of any combination of minced vanilla bean, whole cloves, cardamon seeds, anise, allspice, nutmeg, ginger, stick cinnamon, and dried orange or lemon rind. Store in tightly covered jar.

Hilltop Punch

An unbelievably simple punch which is loved by all ages.

Preparation: Easy

Equal Parts:
Ginger ale, chilled
Apple juice, chilled

Mix ginger ale and apple juice. Serve cold.

Mary Hart Keys Wilheit

Orange Blush

Preparation: Easy

Serves: 6
Must Partially Do Ahead

1 (6-ounce) can frozen orange juice concentrate, thawed
1 cup cranberry juice
¼ cup sugar
1 pint club soda
Orange slices (optional)
Mint sprigs (optional)

Combine undiluted orange juice, cranberry juice, and sugar. Mix and chill thoroughly. Just before serving, stir in club soda. Serve over crushed ice in individual glasses, or double recipe and serve from punch bowl. Orange slices or mint sprigs make a nice garnish.
Variation: Add 3 parts Chablis to 1 part orange juice concentrate.

Sherrie Nathan Schrage

Orange Julius

Preparation: Easy

Serves: 4
Must Serve Immediately

1 (6-ounce) can frozen orange juice concentrate
½ cup milk
½ cup water
¼ cup sugar
½ teaspoon vanilla extract
5-6 ice cubes
4 ounces vodka (optional)

Combine all ingredients in blender or food processor; process 30 seconds, or until smooth.

Gail Adams Thomas

Breakfast Milkshake

Nutritious, delicious, and ready in a jiffy. Serve with whole wheat cheese toast or cereal for a hearty breakfast.

Preparation: Easy

1 egg
Sugar or artificial
   sweetener to taste
1¼ cups milk
One or more of the
following:
   1 ripe banana
   ½ cup strawberries
   ½ cup blueberries
   1 teaspoon vanilla
     extract
   1 teaspoon strawberry
     extract

Serves: 2
Must Serve Immediately

Combine all ingredients in blender; blend until smooth.

Susan Henson Frost

Pineapple Punch

A good punch for showers, weddings, or any large gatherings.

Preparation: Easy

1 (46-ounce) can pineapple
   juice
1 (46-ounce) can water
1½ cups lemon juice
2-2¼ cups sugar
1 teaspoon almond extract
2 quarts ginger ale

Serves: 25

Mix all ingredients except ginger ale. Chill. Add ginger ale immediately before serving. (For a colorful Christmas punch add 1 quart cranberry juice cocktail. For other seasonal or decorative colors add 1 small package of appropriately colored fruit drink mix.)

Susan Byrd Smithson

Coffee Mocha Punch

Ideal for a summer morning coffee.

Preparation: Easy

1 gallon chocolate milk,
   divided
4 tablespoons instant coffee
2 teaspoons almond extract
1 gallon vanilla ice cream,
   softened and divided
Whipped cream or non-dairy
   whip (optional)
Nutmeg (optional)

Yield: 2 Gallons
Must Serve Immediately

Warm 1 cup chocolate milk; stir in coffee and almond extract. Blend well with remaining chocolate milk. In punch bowl place ½ gallon of vanilla ice cream. Pour milk over ice cream. Cover with scoops of remaining ice cream. Garnish with dollops of whipped topping and a sprinkle of nutmeg. (May be spiked with Kahlúa or Grand Marnier to taste.)

Muriel Halprin Nathan
Fort Valley, Georgia

Apricot Tea

Preparation: Easy

1 tea bag
2 cups boiling water
¼ cup sugar
1 tablespoon honey
1 tablespoon lemon juice
½ cup pineapple juice
½ cup apricot nectar
½ cup ginger ale
Mint sprigs (optional)
Lemon slices (optional)

Yield: 5 Cups
Partially Do Ahead

Steep tea bag in water 5 minutes; discard tea bag. Stir in sugar and honey, mixing well. Add lemon juice, pineapple juice, and apricot nectar. Just before serving, stir in ginger ale. Serve over ice. Garnish with mint sprigs or lemon slices.

Sally Butts Darden

On Methodists, Baptists, Church of Christ, Presbyterians, Catholics, and Episcopalians:
"The common denominator seems to be the iced tea. They almost all like it sweetened. I can therefore reach only one conclusion: if you like your tea unsweetened, you better get right with the Lord, 'cause on the evidence in question, I tend to think you're in a bunch of trouble."

Ludlow Porch, *A View from the Porch*
Peachtree Publications Ltd., Copyright 1981. Used with permission.

Golden Citrus Punch

Preparation: Easy

2 (6-ounce) cans frozen
   orange juice concentrate
2 (6-ounce) cans frozen
   lemonade concentrate
2 (6-ounce) cans frozen
   limeade concentrate
3 cups unsweetened pineapple
   juice
Water
Tonic water (optional)

Yield: 1 Gallon

Place orange juice, lemonade, limeade, and pineapple juice in a one-gallon container. Add enough water to fill the container; mix well. A splash of tonic water may be added just before serving.

Elaine Caras Waller

Cappuccino Coffee Mix

Keep some on hand for a gourmet treat at a moment's notice.

Preparation: Easy

  1 **cup instant coffee**
2¼ **cups nonfat dry milk (more or less depending on taste)**
1½ **cups sugar (or more depending on taste)**
  ½ **cup instant hot chocolate mix**
  2 **teaspoons ground cinnamon**
1½ **teaspoons ground orange peel**
   Brandy (optional)
   Whipped cream (optional)

Yield: 6-6½ Cups Mix

Mix all ingredients. Store in tightly sealed glass jar. To serve use 2 teaspoons of mixture per teacup. Fill with boiling water. To prepare in large quantity, use 4 teaspoons mix per 8 ounces water. To create an attractive after-dinner drink, add a splash of brandy and a dollop of whipped cream.

Sherrie Nathan Schrage

Supplies for the table - such as coffee, sugar, tea, salt, spices were gradually exhausted, and it was the province of the Southern woman to find substitutes for these and other indispensables. For coffee, - some families used parched wheat, others, toasted corn - bread crumbs, many like sweet potatoes cut in cubes the size of coffee beans. Dried blackberry leaves, and sassafras roots were substitutes for tea.

Mrs. Rebecca F. Green, Elizabeth Wiley Smith, *The History of Hancock County*
Wilkes Publishing Co., Inc., Copyright 1974. Used with permission.

Sugar and Spice Tea

Preparation: Easy

  4 **cups water**
  2 **teaspoons whole cloves**
  2 **sticks cinnamon**
  4 **tea bags**
1½ **cups sugar**
  1 **(12-ounce) can frozen orange juice concentrate**
  1 **cup pineapple juice**
  3 **tablespoons lemon juice**

Yield: 1 Gallon

Boil water with cloves and cinnamon for five minutes. Remove from heat. Add tea bags; steep 4 minutes. Pour over sugar. Add remaining ingredients and enough water to make 1 gallon. Heat thoroughly, but do not boil. Serve hot or over ice.

Carol Ann Alexander Armstrong

La Mansion del Rio Hot Chocolate

The traditional hot chocolate at the Mexican Christmas Festival in San Antonio, Texas.

Preparation: Easy

Serves: 10
Serve Hot

   3 **sticks cinnamon**
   ½ **cup water**
   ½ **cup cocoa**
   4 **cups milk, divided**
   2 **cups sugar**
   4 **cups half-and-half**

In small saucepan bring cinnamon sticks and ½ cup water to boil over high heat; boil until water is reduced to 3 tablespoons (about 3 minutes). Discard cinnamon sticks and set water aside. Dissolve cocoa in 1 cup milk; whisk until smooth. Add remaining 3 cups milk, sugar, and cinnamon-flavored water; stir until smooth. Place cocoa mixture in a large saucepan. Add half-and-half; cook over moderate heat, whisking frequently, until the chocolate is hot and frothy (about 5 minutes).

Diane Derrick Blalock

Winter Warmer

Preparation: Easy
Cooking Time: 15 Minutes

Serves: 16

   1 **quart apple cider**
   1 **pint cranberry juice**
   1 **cup orange juice**
   ¾ **cup lemon juice**
   ¼ **cup sugar**
   1 **teaspoon whole allspice**
   1 **teaspoon whole cloves**
   3 **whole sticks cinnamon**
   ¼ **cup dark rum or bourbon**
      (optional)

Combine all ingredients; simmer until thoroughly heated. For a large group make in electric percolator, putting spices in the basket.

Darlene Cook Parrish

Hot Buttered Lemonade

Preparation: Easy
Cooking Time: 5 Minutes

Serves: 6

   4½ **cups boiling water**
   ¾   **cup sugar**
   ¾   **cup lemon juice**
   1½ **teaspoons grated lemon
        rind**
   2   **tablespoons butter**
   6   **cinnamon sticks**

In saucepan combine water, sugar, lemon rind, and juice. Cook, stirring occasionally, until heated through. Pour into mugs; top with 1 teaspoon butter. Serve with cinnamon stick stirrers.

Jane Reynolds Hemmer

Creamy Strawberry Daiquiri

Preparation: Easy

Serves: 4-5
Must Serve Immediately

    4 ounces rum
    1 (3-ounce) can frozen pink
       lemonade concentrate
    1 cup strawberries, halved
    2 cups vanilla ice cream
    1 cup ice cubes
4-5 whole strawberries
      (optional)

Place all ingredients except whole berries in blender; process until creamy. Pour into stemmed glasses. Garnish with whole strawberries.

Elaine Matthews Ralston

Mai Tai

Preparation: Easy

Serves: 1

1½ ounces dark rum
1½ ounces light rum
  1 ounce Orgeat syrup (non-
     alcoholic almond syrup)
  2 ounces orange juice
     Pineapple juice
     Pineapple spears
     (optional)
     Orange slices
     (optional)
     Maraschino cherries
     (optional)

Pour rum, Orgeat syrup, and orange juice over ice in a 12-ounce glass. Fill glass with pineapple juice; stir vigorously. Serve with a spear of fresh pineapple and garnish with an orange slice and cherry on a cocktail pick.

Joan Driskell Hopkins

"Marinated" Bloody Marys

A wonderful "do-ahead" cocktail. It looks very seasonal at Christmas served in a clear glass pitcher with lime slices floating on the top.

Preparation: Easy

Serves: 15-20
Must Do Ahead

1 (46-ounce) can vegetable
   juice cocktail
1 (46-ounce) can tomato juice
1 cup lemon juice
2 tablespoons Worchestershire
1 teaspoon salt
3 cups vodka
   Lime slices for garnish

Combine all ingredients and mix well. Place in tightly covered container (a glass or plastic gallon jug works well). Refrigerate overnight. Serve over ice and garnish with lime slices.

Jane Hix Oliver

Brandy Bubbles

An excellent after-dinner drink. It can be made early in the day and kept in the freezer until needed.

Preparation: Easy

Serves: 4
Must Do Ahead

1 pint vanilla ice cream, softened
1 pint coffee ice cream, softened
3 ounces brandy
½ ounce coffee liqueur

Blend ice creams; add brandy and liqueur. Pour in silver pitcher and place in freezer for at least 4 hours. Remove from freezer 1 hour before serving. Pour into pretty, short glasses; eat with a spoon or sip.

Adelaide Gregory Norton

Brandy Alexander

Preparation: Easy

Serves: 3
Must Serve Immediately

6 ounces vanilla ice cream
3 ounces whipping cream
2 ounces brandy
1 ounce dark crème de cocoa
Nutmeg
Whipped cream
Shaved chocolate

Place vanilla ice cream, whipping cream, brandy, and crème de cocoa in blender. Process until smooth. Pour into stemmed glasses. Sprinkle with nutmeg. Garnish with dollop of whipped cream and sprinkle of shaved chocolate.

Knickers Restaurant
Gainesville, Georgia

Fuzz Buzz

Preparation: Easy

Serves: 4
Must Serve Immediately

2 large or 3 medium, fully ripe peaches
1 (6-ounce) can lemonade concentrate
6 ounces rum
12-15 ice cubes
Peach slices (optional)

Wash and peel peaches, leaving skin on at least one. Slice peaches into blender; purée. Add lemonade concentrate, rum, and ice cubes. Blend on high speed until thick and slushy. Pour into chilled glasses. Garnish with peach slice if desired. (May substitute vodka for rum, or omit alcohol for a children's beverage.)

Jayne Wilder Hardman

Amaretto Cooler

Preparation: Easy

Serves: 8

9 ounces Amaretto
27 ounces orange juice, very cold
13½ ounces club soda, very cold

Mix all ingredients; stir briskly. Serve over ice.

Sherrie Nathan Schrage

Tropical Fruit Freeze

Preparation: Average

6 ripe bananas
1 (12-ounce) can frozen orange juice concentrate
1 (6-ounce) can frozen lemonade concentrate
1 (46-ounce) can unsweetened pineapple juice
3 cups water
1 cup sugar
Vodka, bourbon, or rum (optional)
Ginger ale (optional)

Serves: 30

Place bananas, orange juice, and lemonade in blender. Process until smooth. Combine with all remaining ingredients; mix well. Pour into freezing container(s) and freeze. To serve: 1. As beverage: Place 1 cup frozen mixture in blender; add vodka, bourbon, or rum to taste (also splash of ginger ale if desired); process just until smooth but icy. Serve in stemmed glasses. Omit liquor to serve as children's drink. 2. As dessert: Leave at room temperature to slightly soften. Spoon into bowls or compotes; serve immediately. Accompany with ginger thins.

W. Jackson Thompson
Patsy Spiers Mercer

Piña Colada

Preparation: Easy

2 ounces light rum
2 tablespoons coconut cream
2 tablespoons crushed pineapple
Dash lemon juice
2 cups crushed ice

Serves: 3

Place all ingredients in blender in order listed. Process on high; stir once and serve.

Lynda Dickens Askew

Bourbon Slush

Preparation: Easy

1 cup sugar
6 cups water
2 cups strong tea
1½ cups bourbon
1 (12-ounce) can frozen lemonade concentrate
1 (6-ounce) can frozen orange juice concentrate
Ginger ale or lemon-lime carbonated drink
Orange slices (optional)
Maraschino cherries (optional)

Serves: 12
Must Do Ahead

Combine sugar, water, tea, bourbon, lemonade, and orange juice. Mix well. Freeze at least 24 hours before serving. To serve spoon mixture into glasses. Add carbonated beverage. Garnish with orange slices and cherries.

Mimi Luebbers Gerding

The General's Mint Julep

Preparation: Easy

18 mint leaves on stem, divided
2 teaspoons water
1 teaspoon sugar
   Finely crushed ice
2½ ounces 86 or 100-proof bourbon

Serves: 1

Partially tear 12 mint leaves, leaving them on the stem. Place leaves in large glass or silver julep mug with water and sugar. Stir slowly until sugar is dissolved. Fill with ice. Add bourbon. Add more ice to fill as bourbon melts original ice. Stir. Tear remaining mint leaves; place atop ice. Serve with a straw.

Carole Ann Carter Daniel

...a heritage of the Old South, an emblem of hospitality and a vehicle in which noble minds can travel together upon the flower strewn paths of a happy and congenial thought.
Richard Harwell, *The Mint Julep*
University Press of Virginia, Copyright 1977. Used with permission.

Château La Salle Wine Punch

Preparation: Easy

2 fifths Château La Salle wine (Christian Brothers)
1 (46-ounce) can grapefruit juice
1 (20-ounce) can pineapple chunks, undrained
1 (6-ounce) can frozen lemonade concentrate, thawed
1 (28-ounce) bottle club soda

Serves: 16

Combine all ingredients except club soda; chill. Add club soda immediately before serving.

Lynda Dickens Askew

Sangria

Preparation: Easy

3 cups Spanish dry red wine
2 tablespoons sugar
1 lemon, thinly sliced
½ orange, thinly sliced
1 (12-ounce) bottle club soda, chilled
¼ cup Cointreau
¼ cup Spanish brandy
2 cups ice cubes

Serves: 6
Must Partially Do Ahead

In large glass pitcher combine wine, sugar, lemon, and orange. Stir to dissolve sugar. Cover; refrigerate at least 6 hours. Add remaining ingredients. Let stand at least 15-20 minutes before serving. (If Spanish spirits are unavailable, substitute inexpensive domestic varieties.)
Variation: White Sangria - Substitute dry white wine and add strawberries or sliced peaches.

Elaine Caras Waller

Charity Ball Punch

Preparation: Easy

- 2 fifths champagne, chilled
- 16 ounces apricot brandy, chilled
- 8 ounces vodka, chilled
- 2 (32-ounce) bottles ginger ale, chilled
- 2 oranges, thinly sliced
- 1 lemon, thinly sliced

Serves: 25

Combine all ingredients immediately prior to serving.

A. Frank Wiegand, Jr.

We tasted the Cumberland Punch. It was not made on the one, two, three principle, but was even more simple. It was sugarless, lemonless, waterless. It was smokey, strong, and brought tears to the eyes. In short, it was white whiskey mixed with white whiskey.
Sherwood Bonner

Kir Champagne Punch

Serve in a crystal bowl with an ice ring filled with raspberries and orange slices - sophisticated and spectacular!

Preparation: Easy

- 2 (10-ounce) packages frozen raspberries, partially thawed
- 1 (32-ounce) bottle club soda, chilled
- 1 cup crème de cassis, chilled
- 3 (750 milliliters) bottles champagne, chilled

Serves: 30
Must Serve Immediately

Place one package raspberries in blender or food processor; process until smooth. Strain mixture to remove seeds. Pour raspberry purée into punch bowl with club soda and crème de cassis; stir gently to blend well. Break up remaining raspberries with fork; add to punch bowl. Resting champagne bottles on rim of bowl, slowly pour champagne down side of bowl. Stir gently with up and down motion to blend. Serve at once.

Evanda Gravitte Moore

Easy Eggnog

This recipe combines the goodness of old-fashioned Southern eggnog with ease of preparation. It can be assembled in the punch bowl.

Preparation: Easy

- 1 gallon vanilla ice cream
- 1 dozen eggs, beaten
- 2 cups bourbon
- 1 pint whipping cream, whipped

Serves: 18
Must Serve Immediately

Divide ice cream into medium chunks in large bowl. In separate bowl combine eggs and bourbon; beat well. Fold whipped cream into egg mixture; combine with ice cream. Let stand 20-30 minutes before serving.

Sue Hutchens Henson
Monroe, Georgia

Christmas Eggnog

For the traditionalist. Here is eggnog the way it has been made for generations.

Preparation: Average

Yield: Approximately 3 Quarts
Must Partially Do Ahead

12 eggs, separated
12 tablespoons whiskey
12 tablespoons dark rum (optional
     for strong flavor)
12 tablespoons sugar
3-4 cups whipping cream,
     whipped
     Vanilla ice cream
     (optional)
     Nutmeg (optional)

Beat egg yolks in large bowl until thick and lemon-colored. Add whiskey and rum; beat slowly at first and then more rapidly until thick. Cover; refrigerate at least one hour or until ready to serve. (May be done up to a day ahead.) Bring egg whites to room temperature. Thirty to forty minutes before serving, beat egg whites until foamy. Add sugar gradually, beating until stiff. Fold in egg yolk mixture and whipped cream. Place scoop of vanilla ice cream in bottom of each glass. Fill with eggnog. Sprinkle with nutmeg. May also serve from punch bowl with frozen ring made from 1 quart commercial eggnog, frozen in lightly oiled 4-cup ring mold.

Jane Sims Reynolds
Louise Sims Dukes

The tree was set up, and a fire lighted, and a bowl of eggnog on the table in the center of the hearth.

William Faulkner, *Sartoris*
Random House, Inc., Copyright 1966. Used with permission.

Hot Buttered Rum Mix

Preparation: Easy

Yield: 1 Quart Mix
Must Do Ahead

1 pound butter, softened
1 pound dark brown sugar
1 pound confectioners' sugar
1 quart vanilla ice cream,
    softened
1 teaspoon ground cinnamon
½ teaspoon ground nutmeg
½ teaspoon ground allspice
    Rum (1 jigger per serving)

Cream butter and sugars. Add ice cream and spices; blend well. Place in small freezer containers; freeze. To serve place 2-3 tablespoons of mixture in mug. Add 1 jigger rum. (Substitute bourbon for a less sweet drink.) Fill with hot water; stir. If desired, omit ground cinnamon and serve with a cinnamon stick.

Patty Nalley Wallis

Irish Coffee

A winter warmer.

Preparation: Easy

Serves: 1
Must Serve Immediately

1 teaspoon sugar
1-2 jiggers Irish whiskey
1 cup strong hot black coffee
1 tablespoon whipping cream

Warm serving mug or glass. Add sugar and whiskey. Fill to within an inch of brim with coffee; stir to dissolve sugar. Holding teaspoon curved side up across mug, pour cold cream slowly over spoon. Do **not** stir cream into coffee; it should float on top with hot, whiskey-laced coffee being drunk through cold cream.

Charlotte Morrow Dunlap

If foam and circles form around a cup of coffee, cream or tea, it is a sign you will get money.
Ronald G. Killion and Charles T. Walker, *A Treasury of Georgia Folklore*
Atlanta: Cherokee Publishing Company, 1983. Used with permission.

After-Dinner Coffee

Preparation: Easy

Serves: 1
Must Serve Immediately

Sugar
1 ounce crème de cacao
1 ounce Wild Turkey liqueur
1 ounce brandy
Hot coffee
Whipping cream (sweetened or
    unsweetened), whipped
Ground cinnamon (optional)
Ground nutmeg (optional)

Wet and sugar rims of Irish coffee mugs or stemmed glasses which have been wrapped with cloth napkins. Into each glass pour 1 ounce each of all three liqueurs. Fill to one inch of rim with hot coffee. Top with large dollop of whipped cream. Sprinkle with cinnamon or nutmeg, if desired.

Lucy Fokes Link

Café Brulot

Preparation: Average

Serves: 10

Grated rind of 2 oranges
Grated rind of 2 lemons
1 cinnamon stick
12 whole cloves
6 lumps sugar
8 ounces brandy
2 ounces Curaçao
1 quart black coffee

Blend rinds, cinnamon, cloves, and sugar. Add brandy and Curaçao; stir well. Pour into top of double boiler. Ignite brandy, stirring until sugar is dissolved. Add coffee slowly, mixing until flame is extinguished. Heat over boiling water until very hot. Strain. Serve in tall, thin brulot cups or demitasse cups.

Cindy Collins Randolph

Appetizers

Trumpet Creeper

Trumpet Creeper (Campsis radicans)

The trumpet creeper is a true survivor, belonging to a species of flower which bloomed on our planet before the time of man. The showy flowers of this vine are adapted to suit the nectar-seeking hummingbird which pollinates the blooms from July to September throughout North Georgia. These brilliantly colored flowers resemble trumpets in shape, hence the vine's common name.

On Appetizers

- To prevent darkening slice fruit (apples, pears, etc.) into orange juice. This will also prevent the tart taste when lemon juice is used.
- Pack cheese balls in a crock for easy picnic transport.
- Sturdy vegetables make delightful stuffed treats. Try stuffing beets, cucumbers, pickles, radishes, celery, peppers, tomatoes, artichokes, Brussels sprouts, or carrots with cheese or creamy spreads.
- To make quick work of shelling pecans: Cover them with boiling water for a few minutes. Drain and then crack on ends. Meats come out easily in halves.
- Turn marinated shrimp into a holiday centerpiece tree. Cover a styrofoam cone with foil. Spear shrimp on wooden picks; attach to cone. Fill around shrimp with fresh parsley, lemon balm, or other greens. Add bow on top if desired.
- To maintain white color of mushrooms, dip caps into lemon juice before stuffing.
- Hard-boiled eggs can be dressed up or down with stuffings. Try caviar, anchovies, pickles, crabmeat, cheese, dried beef, ham, minced celery, crumbled bacon, chopped chicken livers, mushrooms, or sardines.
- For quick sophistication: Prick a half wheel or wedge of Brie or Camembert with a fork; sprinkle with brandy and confectioners' sugar. Broil 1-2 minutes, until sugar is carmelized and top is golden. Serve immediately with crackers or fresh fruit wedges. (Also good for dessert.)
- One pound pecans in shells yields 1¼ cups chopped nuts.
- Ripe black olives keep longer if a few tablespoons of vodka are tossed with the olives. The vodka keeps the olives fresh and does not change the flavor.
- One-half pound fresh mushrooms yields 2½ cups sliced mushrooms.
- To test for ripeness in a pineapple: Pull off one of the inner leaves at the crown. If the pineapple is ripe, the leaf will come out easily. Also, the aroma of fresh pineapple should be apparent at the stem end.
- Use leftover pieces of roast or an overcooked steak for a homemade pâté. Cut meat into small chunks; feed into blender or food processor with some ·Worcestershire, a little mayonnaise, any spices you like, salt, and pepper.

Chicken Curry Mousse

An original recipe. The preparation takes some time, but it can be made several days ahead and refrigerated.

Preparation: Complex

Yield: 1 (5-cup) Mold
Must Do Ahead

¼ cup minced scallions,
    including green tops
¼ cup butter, melted
1 teaspoon curry powder
1½ cups raw (1-inch)
    chicken breast cubes
¼ cup Madeira or sherry
2 tablespoons unflavored
    gelatin, divided
2½ cups rich turkey or
    chicken broth, divided
⅓ cup Major Grey's Chutney
2 (3-ounce) packages
    cream cheese
⅔ cup sour cream
¼ cup mayonnaise
⅓ cup plain yogurt
¾ teaspoon salt
⅛ teaspoon white pepper
⅛ teaspoon cayenne
    Pecans (optional)
    Currants (optional)
    Green onions (optional)
    Rye toast or Swedish
    gingersnaps

Briefly sauté scallions in butter; add curry powder and chicken. Stir and cook until chicken turns white. Add Madeira or sherry; cook until alcohol has evaporated and chicken is done, being careful not to overcook. Remove chicken; cool and mince by hand, **not** in food processor. Soften 1 tablespoon gelatin in ¼ cup stock or water. Add 1 cup of stock to pan in which chicken was cooked; heat. Add gelatin, stirring until dissolved. Cool mixture in refrigerator. Purée chutney in blender or food processor; reserving 2 tablespoons. Add cream cheese to blender or processor; process a few seconds. Add sour cream and mayonnaise; process to blend. Add cold stock mixture and yogurt; process briefly. Return to refrigerator until mixture is thick but not set. Fold in minced chicken, salt, white pepper, cayenne, and more chutney if desired. To mold and decorate: Soften 1 tablespoon gelatin in ¼ cup stock. Heat remaining cup of stock; add softened gelatin, stirring until dissolved. Pour in enough stock to thinly cover a chilled oiled 5-cup mold. Arrange decorations of choice: pecans, currants, green onions. Chill to set, about ½ hour. Add stock to cover decorations; chill to set. Add 2 tablespoons reserved chutney to ½ cup stock. Add to mold; chill to set. Add chicken mixture; chill to set. Add remaining stock to seal mold; chill to set. To serve, unmold and accompany with rye toast or gingersnaps.

Paula Eubanks Smith

Polynesian Chicken Wings

Preparation: Easy
Cooking Time: 40 Minutes
Oven Temperature: 325°F

Yield: 36 Pieces
Must Partially Do Ahead

3 pounds chicken wings
1 cup soy sauce
½ cup orange juice
½ cup pineapple juice
¼ cup lemon juice
¼ cup Madeira wine
3 cloves garlic, crushed
1 tablespoon honey

Cut tips off wings and discard; cut each wing in half at joint. Place in baking dish. Combine remaining ingredients; pour over wings. Marinate 4-6 hours. Remove from marinade; place in large baking pan. Bake at 325°F for 40 minutes or until tender. Broil on both sides until crispy. Serve warm.

Linda Snelling Cobb

Chicken Nut Puffs

Preparation: Average
Cooking Time: 15-18 Minutes
Oven Temperature: 400°F

Yield: 7 Dozen
Must Serve Immediately

1 cup chicken broth
½ cup butter or margarine
2 teaspoons Worcestershire
1 cup flour
1 tablespoon chopped
   fresh parsley
2 teaspoons seasoned salt
¾ teaspoon celery seed
½ teaspoon paprika
⅛ teaspoon cayenne
   (optional)
4 eggs
1 (5-ounce) can boned
   chicken, drained
¼ cup chopped toasted
   almonds

Combine chicken broth, butter, and Worcestershire in saucepan; bring to boil. Combine flour, parsley, salt, celery seed, paprika, and cayenne. Add to boiling mixture all at once, stirring vigorously over low heat for approximately 1 minute or until mixture leaves sides of pan and forms smooth ball. Remove pan from heat; allow to cool slightly. Add eggs, one at a time, beating with a wooden spoon after each addition; beat until batter is smooth. Stir in chicken and almonds. (May be made ahead to this point and refrigerated until needed.) Drop by teaspoonfuls on ungreased baking sheet. Bake at 400°F for 15-18 minutes. Remove from pan immediately. Serve in cloth-lined basket or bun warmer to retain heat.

Jean Bennett Oliver

Almond-Chicken Balls

The ingredients in these tasty balls also make a good sandwich spread for whole wheat bread. Ham substitutes well for the chicken if you prefer.

Preparation: Average

Yield: 2
Must Partially Do Ahead

2 (8-ounce) packages cream
   cheese, softened
1 tablespoon steak sauce
1½ cups minced cooked
   chicken
⅓ cup minced celery
¼ cup minced green onions
¼ cup chopped pimiento
¼ cup chopped fresh
   parsley, divided
¼ cup chopped toasted
   almonds
Whole wheat crackers

Combine cream cheese, steak sauce, and chicken; blend well. Add celery, onions, pimiento, and 2 tablespoons parsley; mix well. Refrigerate remaining parsley. Shape chicken mixture into 2 balls. Wrap individually; chill 4 hours or overnight. Toss reserved parsley with almonds. Roll each ball in parsley mixture until well covered. Serve with whole wheat crackers.

Connie Kemp Goldfarb

Chicken Liver Pâté

A classic that is really not difficult to prepare.

Preparation: Average
Cooking Time: 5 Minutes

Serves: 10

> 1 **pound chicken livers**
> 1 **small onion,**
>   **finely chopped**
> ½ **cup butter, melted**
> 1½ **tablespoons brandy**
> 1½ **tablespoons dry sherry**
> 1 **teaspoon salt**
> ¼ **teaspoon nutmeg**
> ¼ **teaspoon pepper**
> ⅛ **teaspoon basil**
>   **Pinch of thyme**
>   **Pinch of marjoram**

Sauté liver and onion in butter until liver is brown on outside but still pink on inside. Remove to blender jar. Stir brandy and sherry into butter remaining in pan. Pour over livers. Add seasonings. Purée in blender until smooth. (To mold add 6 ounces softened cream cheese with seasonings; purée. Pour into oiled mold; chill until set.)

Sarah Markette Swoszowski

Variation: To 1 cup homemade or commercial mayonnaise, add ¾ teaspoon minced chives and ¾ teaspoon chopped fresh parsley. Spread herbed mayonnaise over pâté. Sprinkle with chopped, black olives and chopped, hard-boiled eggs.

W. Jackson Thompson

Oriental Kabobs

These miniature kabobs are just the thing when a more substantial appetizer is desired. Make them as large or small as your guests' appetites.

Preparation: Easy
Cooking Time: 30-40 Minutes
Oven Temperature: 350°F

Serves: 12
Must Partially Do Ahead
Must Serve Immediately

> 1 **(5-ounce) bottle soy sauce**
> ½ **cup white vinegar**
> 2 **tablespoons brown sugar**
> 1 **teaspoon garlic powder**
> 1 **pound boneless chicken**
>   **breasts, cut into**
>   **bite-sized pieces**
> 3-4 **green peppers, cut**
>   **into bite-sized pieces**
> 16 **or more fresh mushrooms**
>   **Small wooden skewers**

Mix soy sauce, vinegar, brown sugar, and garlic powder. Place chicken, green pepper, and mushrooms in bowl. Add marinade; let stand 1 hour. Arrange on small wooden skewers; place on roasting pan. Bake at 350°F for 10-20 minutes. Brush with marinade; cook 10 minutes more. Turn; brush again with marinade. Cook 10 minutes. Serve hot or warm.
Micronote: Follow above instructions for marinade. To assemble, place smaller cubes of chicken on center of skewer. Place skewers on oblong, glass casserole dish. Cook 6 minutes on HIGH per pound of chicken. Rotate dish twice during cooking. Baste with marinade while turning.

Cathy Turner Cleveland

Dippers Delight

The 1971 National Broiler Council - $10,000 Chicken Contest Winner.

Preparation: Average
Cooking Time: 30-45 Minutes

Serves: 12

12 chicken breast halves,
    boned and skinned
2 eggs, beaten
1 cup water
1 cup flour
3 tablespoons sesame seed
1½ teaspoons salt
2-3 cups cooking oil
    Sauces for dipping

Wash chicken and pat dry. Cut into bite-sized pieces. Set aside. Blend eggs and water. Add flour, sesame seed, and salt; blend well. Heat oil in heavy skillet over medium heat. Dip chicken pieces into batter; shake off excess. Fry 5 minutes or until golden brown and tender, being careful not to overcrowd skillet. Drain on absorbent toweling. Serve with one or more of the following sauces.

Pineapple Sauce

1 (12-ounce) jar pineapple
    preserves
¼ cup prepared mustard
¼ cup prepared horseradish

Combine all ingredients in saucepan. Cook over low heat, stirring for 5 minutes or until ingredients are thoroughly blended.

Dill Sauce

½ cup sour cream
½ cup mayonnaise
2 tablespoons finely
    chopped dill pickle
1 teaspoon dill weed

Combine all ingredients. Let stand at room temperature 1 hour to allow flavors to blend.

Royalty Sauce

1 cup catsup
6 tablespoons margarine
2 tablespoons vinegar
1 tablespoon brown sugar
½ teaspoon dry mustard

Combine all ingredients in saucepan. Cook over low heat for 5 minutes, stirring constantly.

Dee Lawson Morris

There was nobody like her for getting up a party, for the idea of food was inseparably connected in her mind with social occasions of a delightful nature, and though she loved to celebrate birthdays and holidays, still any day was quite good enough to her.
Katherine Anne Porter, *Collected Essays & Occasional Writings of Katherine Anne Porter*
Delacorte Press/Seymour Lawrence, Copyright 1973. Used with permission.

Sweet and Sour Chicken Wings

Allow your guests the pleasure of finger-licking while enjoying these. Not the neatest appetizer in the world, but without a doubt one of the best.

Preparation: Average
Cooking Time: 45-60 Minutes
Oven Temperature: 350°F

Yield: 30-36 Pieces
Must Partially Do Ahead

- 3 **pounds chicken wings**
  Garlic salt
  Monosodium glutamate
- 1 **cup cornstarch**
- 2 **eggs, well beaten**
  Oil
- ¾ **cup sugar**
- 1 **teaspoon monosodium glutamate**
- ½ **cup chicken stock or bouillon**
- ¼ **cup vinegar**
- 3 **tablespoons catsup**
- 1 **tablespoon soy sauce**

Cut tips off wings and discard; cut each wing in half at joint. Sprinkle pieces with garlic salt and monosodium glutamate. Let stand at least 1 hour. Coat pieces with cornstarch; dip in beaten eggs. Fry in hot oil until golden brown, but not done. Drain on absorbent toweling. Place in single layer in large, shallow baking pan. Combine all remaining ingredients in saucepan. Heat until sugar dissolves. Pour over chicken. Bake uncovered at 350°F for 45-60 minutes. Turn occasionally and coat with sauce. Wings are done when sauce is slightly thickened. Serve hot.

Judy Ferguson Field

Crab Mousse

Preparation: Easy
Cooking Time: 10-15 Minutes

Yield: 4½ Cups
Must Do Ahead

- 2 **(3-ounce) packages cream cheese**
- 1 **(10¾-ounce) can cream of mushroom soup**
- 1 **small onion, finely grated**
- 1 **tablespoon unflavored gelatin**
- ¼ **cup boiling water**
- 1 **(6-ounce) can crabmeat, drained**
- 1 **cup finely chopped celery**
- 1 **cup mayonnaise**
- 1 **tablespoon Worcestershire**
- ¼ **teaspoon Tabasco**
  Lemon wedges
  Fresh parsley

Heat cream cheese, mushroom soup, and grated onion in top of double boiler until thoroughly mixed and cream cheese is no longer lumpy. Dissolve gelatin in boiling water. Add gelatin mixture, crab meat (carefully checked for shells), celery, mayonnaise, Worcestershire, and Tabasco to soup mixture. Place in oiled 4½-cup mold; refrigerate 3 hours or overnight. Unmold; garnish with lemon wedges and fresh parsley. Serve with crackers.

Joan Driskell Hopkins

Cocktail Clam Puffs

Preparation: Average
Cooking Time: 45 Minutes
Oven Temperature: 400°F, 300°F

Yield: 6 Dozen
Must Partially Do Ahead

Clam Puff Pastry

1 cup clam broth or liquid
    from 10½-ounce can of
    clams + water
    to equal 1 cup
½ cup butter
1 cup flour
5 eggs at room temperature,
    divided
½ teaspoon milk
    Clam Filling or
    Shrimp Filling

Heat liquid in saucepan. Add butter; bring to boil. Add flour all at once, stirring vigorously with wooden spoon over low heat until mixture leaves sides of pan and forms smooth ball. Turn into mixing bowl; add 4 eggs, one at a time, beating after each addition until thick dough forms. Place level teaspoon of dough on lightly greased cookie sheet 1 inch apart. Beat remaining egg with milk. Brush tops of dough with egg mixture. Bake at 400°F for 10 minutes. Reduce heat to 300°F; bake 20-25 minutes. Do not open door during cooking. Remove from oven; cool completely. Cut pastry puffs in half. Fill with Clam or Shrimp Filling; replace tops. Place on lightly greased baking sheet. (Can be frozen at this point, then bagged in freezer bags.) Bake at 400°F for 15 minutes.

Clam Filling

3 (10½-ounce) cans
    minced clams
2 (8-ounce) tubs soft cream
    cheese with chives
6 dashes Tabasco
1 teaspoon salt or
    seasoned salt
½ teaspoon pepper

Combine all ingredients; blend well.

Shrimp Filling

2 (4½-ounce) cans tiny shrimp,
    drained
⅔ cup toasted slivered
    almonds
½ cup finely chopped celery
⅔ cup sour cream
2 tablespoons finely chopped onion
1 teaspoon prepared mustard
¼ teaspoon pepper

Combine all ingredients; mix thoroughly. Refrigerate if not using immediately.

Margaret Hutchens Henson
Huntsville, Alabama

Ceviche

Preparation: Average

2 pounds halibut or
   flounder fillets, cubed
2 cups lemon juice
2 cups chopped onion
3 firm tomatoes, peeled,
   seeded, chopped
2 small green chilies,
   chopped (1 tablespoon)
16 green olives, chopped
2 tablespoons chopped
   parsley
½ cup tomato purée
½ cup tomato juice
2 tablespoons Worcestershire
1 tablespoon salt
1 teaspoon Tabasco

Serves: 16-20
Must Do Ahead

Marinate cubes of fish in lemon juice for 6 hours in refrigerator. (The fish "cooks itself" in the lemon juice.) Combine all remaining ingredients for marinade. Pour off 1 cup lemon juice from fish. Add marinade to fish and remaining lemon juice; mix well. Refrigerate overnight. Serve in bowl with cocktail picks handy and crackers alongside. (Drain off portion of marinade before serving, if desired.)

Lynda Dickens Askew

Clam Canapés

Preparation: Easy
Cooking Time: 20 Minutes
Oven Temperature: 300°F

1 (8-ounce) package cream
   cheese, softened
1 (6¾-ounce) can minced
   clams, drained
Few drops Tabasco
⅛ teaspoon Worcestershire
⅛ teaspoon dried minced
   onion
Scant ¼ cup sherry
Melba rounds
1 (4-ounce) can sliced
   mushrooms
Melted butter (optional)
Paprika (optional)

Serves: 4-8
Must Serve Immediately

Mix cream cheese, clams, Tabasco, Worcestershire, onion, and sherry. Spread mixture on Melba rounds. Top with mushroom slice. Brush with melted butter and sprinkle with paprika if desired. Bake at 300°F for 20 minutes. Serve warm.

Flo Criss Smith

Shrimp Sea Island

The onions are as good as the shrimp, but do try it even if you aren't lucky enough to have access to our Vidalias.

Preparation: Average

Yield: 5 Pounds
Must Do Ahead

5 pounds medium shrimp
5 mild white medium
  onions, thinly sliced
  (Vidalias are the best.)
2 cups pure olive oil
¾ pint cider vinegar
1 large bottle capers
  and juice
¾ cup sugar
¼ cup Worcestershire
½-1 teaspoon Tabasco
1 teaspoon salt

Boil shrimp for 3 minutes, no more; drain immediately. Peel, devein, wash, and drain well. In deep, flat pan layer shrimp and onion rings repeatedly until all are used. Mix all remaining ingredients thoroughly; pour over shrimp and onions. Cover; refrigerate at least twelve hours. Stir (or flip marinator) at intervals. To serve, lift onions and shrimp from marinade; place in glass bowl or on large lettuce-lined platter. Accompany with cocktail picks. (If there are onions left over, refrigerate. Mix with mayonnaise to serve later as an hors d'oeuvre with saltine crackers.)

Lucy Fokes Link

Caviar Mousse

Caviar has always been the last word in elegance. Here it crowns a mousse - a lavish offering for that special occasion.

Preparation: Average

Serves: 10-12
Must Do Ahead

1½ envelopes unflavored
  gelatin
¼ cup cold water
1 cup sour cream
2 tablespoons grated onion
1 tablespoon lemon juice
½ teaspoon salt
1 cup whipping cream,
  whipped
  Bibb or Boston lettuce
1 (4-ounce) jar red or
  black caviar

Soften gelatin in cold water; dissolve over low heat. Cool slightly. Combine sour cream, onion, lemon juice, and salt; mix until well blended. Gradually stir in gelatin. Gently fold whipped cream into sour cream mixture. Spoon into oiled 4-cup mold. Chill until firm. Unmold onto bed of Bibb or Boston lettuce. Cover top with caviar.(If ring mold is used, place compote of finely minced onions and hard-boiled eggs in center of mold.)

Patricia Horkan Smith

Pickled Shrimp

Preparation: Average

1 (10¾-ounce) can tomato
soup
½ cup vinegar
¼ cup sugar
1 cup oil
Salt and pepper to taste
¼ teaspoon cayenne pepper
1 teaspoon Worcestershire
1 (0.18-ounce) box bay leaves
6 small onions, sliced
3 lemons, sliced
2 pounds shrimp, boiled
and shelled

Serves: 4-6
Must Do Ahead

Mix soup, vinegar, sugar, oil, salt, pepper, cayenne, and Worcestershire in blender; blend 10-15 seconds. Place one layer each of bay leaves, onion slices, lemon slices, and shrimp in large bowl. Pour dressing over layers; marinate 24 hours.

Mary Ross Ward Carter

Taramosalata

A Greek dish that is an inexpensive alternative to caviar - very good with champagne. Tarama can be purchased in a deli or Greek food shop.

Preparation: Average

4 ounces Tarama (cod roe)
8 slices day-old white
bread, trimmed and excess
moisture removed
1½ cups salad oil or
olive oil
Juice of 2 or 3 lemons
1 small onion, finely
grated

Yield: 2½ Cups
Must Partially Do Ahead

Place Tarama in bowl of electric mixer or food processor (use steel blade). Add small amount of oil and beat or process until smooth paste forms. Continue mixing and gradually alternate adding small amounts of bread, oil, and lemon juice until all have been added. Texture should be a smooth, cream-colored paste. Refrigerate in tightly closed container. Just prior to serving, add finely grated onion, mixing well. Serve with crisp crackers. (Use also as filling for hollowed cherry tomatoes, or for tiny pie shells topped with ½ slice of a green stuffed olive or almond.)

Elaine Caras Waller

Shrimp Party Mold

Preparation: Average

Yield: 4 Cup Mold
Must Do Ahead

1   envelope unflavored gelatin
2   tablespoons milk
1   (10¾-ounce) can cream of
    shrimp soup, undiluted
2   (3-ounce) packages
    cream cheese
1   cup finely chopped celery
1   (4⅓-ounce) can shrimp,
    drained and chopped
4   green onions, chopped
1   cup mayonnaise
1   tablespoon lemon juice
¼   teaspoon curry powder

Soften gelatin in milk. Heat soup and cream cheese over low heat until cheese is melted. Stir in softened gelatin. Add remaining ingredients. Pour into lightly greased 4-cup mold. Chill several hours, until firm. Serve with crackers. (May also mold in individual molds and serve as salad.)

Debbie Jacobs Springle

Sweet and Sour Sausage Balls

Preparation: Average
Cooking Time: 30 Minutes

Yield: 150

4   pounds bulk sausage
4   eggs, slightly beaten
1½   cups soft bread crumbs
3   cups catsup
¾   cup packed brown sugar
½   cup white wine vinegar
½   cup soy sauce

Combine sausage, eggs, and bread crumbs. Using palms of hands, shape mixture into balls the size of walnuts. Sauté in skillet until browned on all sides; drain. Combine catsup, brown sugar, vinegar, and soy sauce. Pour over sausage balls; simmer 30 minutes, stirring occasionally. Serve hot in chafing dish. (If made ahead, refrigerate or freeze balls in their sauce. To serve, reheat in oven at 350°F for 20 minutes.)

Joan Driskell Hopkins

Ham Puffs

Preparation: Easy
Cooking Time: 10-12 Minutes
Oven Temperature: 375°F

Yield: 24 Small Squares

1   (8-ounce) package cream
    cheese
1   egg yolk, beaten
1   teaspoon onion juice
½   teaspoon baking powder
¼   teaspoon horseradish
¼   teaspoon hot pepper sauce
    Salt to taste
1   (4½-ounce) can deviled ham
24   small bread squares

Blend cream cheese, egg yolk, onion juice, baking powder, horseradish, hot sauce, and salt. Spread deviled ham on each bread square; top with layer of cream cheese mixture. Place on ungreased baking sheet. Bake at 375°F for 10-12 minutes.

Jane Pattillo Lake

Cocktail Meatballs with Pizzazz

The sweet sauce makes these meatballs special.

Preparation: Average
Cooking Time: 15-20 Minutes
Oven Temperature: 350°F

Yield: 200

2-3 pounds ground beef
1 pound pork sausage
1 cup soda crackers
½ cup catsup
⅓ cup dried parsley flakes
2 tablespoons instant
   onion or 1 teaspoon
   garlic salt
2 eggs, slightly beaten
   Salt and pepper to taste

In a large bowl combine all ingredients. Form into walnut-sized balls. Place in shallow pan. Bake at 350°F for 15-20 minutes. Remove from pan; drain well. Transfer to crock pot or chafing dish. Pour Pizzazz Sauce over meatballs. Serve hot with cocktail picks.
Micronote: Combine ingredients; form into balls. Place ¼ of meatballs on glass tray or dish. Cover with waxed paper. Cook on HIGH 6-8 minutes, turning dish several times. Repeat until all meatballs are cooked.

Pizzazz Sauce

1 (1-pound) can cranberry
   sauce
½ cup catsup
4 ounces cherry preserves
2 tablespoons brown sugar
2 tablespoons soy sauce
1 tablespoon lemon juice
¼ teaspoon pepper

Combine all ingredients in saucepan. Simmer over moderate heat, stirring occasionally until smooth and cranberry sauce is melted.
Micronote: Combine and cook on HIGH 1 minute.

Mimi Jackson Fox

Bacon Roll-Ups

These crispy morsels are appropriate for any occasion - morning, noon, or night.

Preparation: Easy
Cooking Time: 30 Minutes
Oven Temperature: 350°F

Yield: 4 Dozen

1 (8-ounce) package soft
   cream cheese with
   chives and onion
1 tablespoon milk or
   mayonnaise
25 slices mixed grain
   sandwich bread, crusts
   removed; halved
25 slices bacon,
   halved crosswise
   Parsley sprigs (optional)

Combine cream cheese and milk, stirring until of spreading consistency. Spread 1 scant teaspoon cream cheese mixture on each slice of bread; roll tightly. Wrap each rollup with bacon; secure with wooden pick. Place on broiler pan. Bake at 350°F for 30 minutes, turning if necessary to prevent overbrowning. Garnish with parsley, if desired. (Roll-ups may be assembled ahead and frozen. To serve, thaw overnight in refrigerator; bake at 350°F for 30-40 minutes.)

Helen Helms Stewart

Bacon Wraps

Preparation: Easy

Angels on Horseback

Cooking Time: 10 Minutes
Oven Temperature: Broil

Serves: 6-8
Must Serve Immediately

1 pint fresh select oysters,
   well-drained
2-3 lemons
½ cup minced onion
½ cup minced parsley
   Bacon strips cut in half

Sprinkle each well-drained oyster with lemon juice, ½ teaspoon minced onion, and ½ teaspoon minced parsley. Wrap each oyster in ½ strip of bacon; secure with toothpick. Broil on each side just until bacon is crisp. Serve hot.

Ann Branch Smith

Rumaki with Sweet and Sour Sauce

Cooking Time: Rumaki: 20-30 Minutes
             Sauce: 15-20 Minutes
Oven Temperature: 300°F

Serves: 10
Must Do Ahead

1 pound bacon
   Brown sugar
1 pound chicken livers,
   quartered
1 (8½-ounce) can water
   chestnuts, halved
   Soy sauce
   Sweet and Sour Sauce

Spread bacon slices with brown sugar. Cut slices in half. Place water chestnut and 1 chicken liver on each bacon half. Roll up; secure with wooden pick. Marinate overnight in soy sauce in covered bowl. One hour prior to serving, drain Rumaki and place on baking sheet. Bake at 300°F until bacon is crisp, turning once. Place in chafing dish. Cover with Sweet and Sour Sauce. (Also excellent as a main dish served over rice.)

Sweet and Sour Sauce

½ cup brown sugar
6 gingersnaps, crumbled
1 teaspoon flour
1 cup hot water
¼ cup vinegar
1 teaspoon shortening
¼ cup raisins
1 slice lemon

In small saucepan blend all ingredients in order listed. Simmer 15-20 minutes.

Roxilea Jones Goble

Water Chestnuts Wrapped in Bacon

Cooking Time: 30 Minutes
Oven Temperature: 400°F

Yield: 16
Must Partially Do Ahead

1 (5-ounce) can water
   chestnuts, drained
   and halved
¼ cup soy sauce
¼ cup sugar
4 slices bacon, cut in half
   crosswise and lengthwise

Marinate water chestnuts 30 minutes in soy sauce. Roll each chestnut half in sugar. Wrap with bacon; secure with cocktail pick. Arrange on broiler pan. Bake at 400°F for 30 minutes. Drain on absorbent toweling. (May be made ahead and reheated at 350°F for 5 minutes.)

Sharon Hix Abernathy

Pineapple Roll-Ups

Cooking Time: 10 Minutes
Oven Temperature: Broil

Serves: 16-20

1 pound bacon,
   partially cooked
1 fresh pineapple or
   1 (20-ounce) can
   pineapple chunks,
   drained

Cut each bacon slice in half. Cut pineapple into bite-sized chunks. Wrap each pineapple chunk with half slice of bacon; secure with wooden pick. Place on broiler rack. Broil until bacon is crisp, turning once.
To grill: Thread wrapped pineapple chunks onto small skewers. Grill 3-4 inches from hot coals for 3-5 minutes, until bacon is crisp; turn once or twice.

Cookbook Committee

Bacon would improve the flavor of an angel.

Mark Twain

Parmesan Cheese Rounds

Preparation: Easy
Cooking Time: 5 Minutes
Oven Temperature: 400°F

Yield: 24
Must Serve Immediately

2 slices bacon, cooked
   and crumbled
½ cup grated Parmesan
   cheese
¼ cup evaporated milk
½ teaspoon Worcestershire
24 small toast rounds
   Pimiento-stuffed olives,
   sliced

Blend bacon, cheese, milk, and Worcestershire. Spread on toast rounds; top with olive slices. Bake at 400°F for 5 minutes. Serve hot.

Judy Mynatt Bush

Egg Rolls

Have fun creating your own version of this Chinese staple. Accompany with Mighty Mustard (page 289) or Sweet and Sour Sauce (page 40).

Preparation: Average
Cooking Time: 5 Minutes

Yield: 20

½ cup bean sprouts, chopped
½ cup chopped green
    onions with stems
¼-⅓ cup bamboo
    shoots, chopped
4 water chestnuts, minced
2 carrots, finely chopped
2 tablespoons sesame oil
2 tablespoons soy sauce
2 tablespoons oyster sauce
1-2 tablespoons cooking
    sherry
1 teaspoon garlic powder
½ pound ground beef,
    browned and drained
    (or ground pork or
    chopped shrimp)
2-3 eggs, beaten
    Egg roll wrappers
    Oil

Combine all ingredients except eggs and wrappers. Brush 2 corners of individual egg roll wrappers with egg. Place 2-3 tablespoons stuffing mixture in center of wrappers. Roll up and seal according to wrapper package directions. Cook in hot oil 5 minutes. Drain on absorbent toweling.

Variation: Vegetarian Egg Rolls - Omit meat from stuffing mixture. Add ¼ cup chopped cashews to other ingredients. Add 1-2 teaspoons cream cheese to stuffing for each egg roll before wrapping. Proceed as directed.

Nelson Hilty Carter

Ripe and Rye

Preparation: Easy
Cooking Time: 5-7 Minutes
Oven Temperature: 375°F

Yield: 36
Must Serve Immediately

1 (3 or 4-ounce) package
    sliced smoked beef,
    chopped
1 cup (4-ounces) shredded
    Cheddar cheese
1 (7¾-ounce) can pitted
    ripe olives, drained
    and sliced
1 cup mayonnaise
1 (8½-ounce) package
    RyKrisp crackers

Combine smoked beef, cheese, olives, and mayonnaise. Spread one tablespoon beef mixture on each RyKrisp. (May be frozen at this point.) Bake at 375°F for 5-7 minutes or until bubbly. Serve hot.

Carrie McClain Hatfield

Hot Cheese Bacon Rounds

Preparation: Easy
Cooking Time: 2 Minutes
Oven Temperature: Broil

Yield: Approximately 36 Rounds
Must Serve Immediately

1 loaf sandwich bread,
   toasted
8 ounces sharp Cheddar
   cheese, grated
12 slices bacon, fried
   and crumbled
1 (2½-ounce) package
   sliced almonds
2 medium green onions,
   finely chopped
1 cup mayonnaise
2 teaspoons Worcestershire
½ teaspoon salad seasoning
¼ teaspoon paprika

Cut 2 toast rounds from each slice of bread; set aside. Combine all remaining ingredients; mix until well blended. Spread mixture on each toast round; place on baking sheets. Broil until hot (approximately 2 minutes), taking care not to burn. (May also use spread on whole or half toast slices and serve open-faced for brunch.

Marilyn Murphy Doveton

Hunger is the handmaid of genius.
Mark Twain

Hot Cheese Tartines

Preparation: Average
Cooking Time: 10 Minutes
Oven Temperature: 450°F

Yield: 2 Dozen
Must Serve Immediately

6 slices firm white bread
3 tablespoons butter, melted
2 (3-ounce) packages cream
   cheese, softened
2 tablespoons whipping
   cream
2 tablespoons red wine
   vinegar
1 (2-ounce) jar diced
   pimiento
1 small green pepper,
   finely diced
   Salt
   Pepper

Trim crusts from bread; cut each slice into fourths. Dip both sides of each square into melted butter; place on baking sheet. Toast at 450°F until lightly browned, about 5 minutes. Blend cream cheese with cream and vinegar. Add pimiento, green pepper, salt, and pepper. Spread baked squares generously with cream cheese mixture. Return to oven; bake until lightly browned, about 5 minutes. (Toast and topping may be prepared ahead separately, then assembled just prior to serving.)

Lynda Dickens Askew

Tiropeta

Preparation: Average
Cooking Time: 45-60 Minutes
Oven Temperature: 325°F

Yield: 50 Triangles

4 **eggs**
1 **(8-ounce) package cream cheese, softened**
1 **pound Feta cheese**
1 **pound phyllo or strudel leaves**
½ **pound butter, melted**

Beat eggs with electric mixer until fluffy. Add cream cheese; blend well. Remove bowl from mixer. Crumble Feta with fork; add to egg mixture, stirring well. Prepare phyllo according to instructions for phyllo appetizer triangles on page 399. Place one tablespoon cheese mixture in bottom right-hand corner of each strip. Fold over flag-style into triangular shape, following diagrams on page 399. Brush top of each triangle **lightly** with melted butter. Place on ungreased cookie sheet. Bake slowly at 325°F for 45-60 minutes or until lightly browned. (May be frozen prior to baking. Pack and seal frozen triangles carefully until ready for use. Do not thaw; bake as directed.)

Variations: Spanokopita Appetizer - Use Spanokopita filling (page 269). Fold and bake as above.

Herbed Beef en Phyllo Appetizer - Use Herbed Beef en Phyllo filling (page 197). Fold and bake as above.

Ethel Martin Caras

Brie en Croûte

A very elegant look for a very small effort. Use pastry scraps to create seasonal decorations - holly leaves and berries for Christmas, a daisy for summer, etc. Amazing what wrapping cheese in pastry can do!

Preparation: Easy
Cooking Time: 20-25 Minutes
Oven Temperature: 450°F

Yield: 2 (6-inch) Pastries
Must Serve Immediately

4 **frozen Pepperidge Farm patty shells, thawed**
2 **(4½-ounce) cans Brie cheese rounds**
Apples and pears, sliced

Shape 2 patty shells into ball. On floured surface roll out to ⅛-inch thickness. Cut out an 8-inch circle. Place cheese in center. Wrap pastry around cheese; dampen and seal edges. Repeat with remaining shells and cheese. Decorate tops with pastry scraps. (Can wrap in waxed paper and refrigerate for 1-2 days at this point.) Place pastries on ungreased baking sheet. Place in 450°F oven; immediately reduce heat to 400°F. Bake 20-25 minutes or until pastry is lightly browned. Serve hot, surrounded by apple and pear wedges which have been pre-treated to prevent darkening (page 16). (May substitute Camembert cheese for Brie.)

Jane Hix Oliver

Cheese Brambles

Preparation: Average
Cooking Time: 8-10 Minutes
Oven Temperature: 350°F

Yield: 3 Dozen
Must Partially Do Ahead
Must Serve Immediately

13 **ounces cream cheese,**
    softened
½ **cup margarine, softened**
1 **cup flour**
¼ **teaspoon salt**
    Sharp Cheddar cheese,
    cubed

Blend cream cheese and margarine until smooth. Combine flour and salt; blend into cream cheese mixture until smooth. Chill dough. Roll on lightly floured surface to ⅛-inch thickness; cut into 2-inch rounds. Place small cube of cheese on half of each round. Fold over; crimp edges together with fork. Place on ungreased baking sheet. Cover; chill until time to bake. Bake at 350°F for 8-10 minutes, until puffed and slightly browned.

Ann Corry Collins
Cumming, Georgia

Cheese Straws

Preparation: Average
Cooking Time: 10-12 Minutes
Oven Temperature: 350°F

Yield: 3 Dozen

1 **pound New York sharp**
    Cheddar cheese, grated
1 **cup butter or margarine**
3 **cups sifted flour**
1 **teaspoon salt**
½ **teaspoon red pepper**

Cream cheese and margarine. Add dry ingredients; mix well. Pack into cookie press. Press onto ungreased baking sheet. Bake at 350°F for 10-12 minutes. Transfer to wire racks to cool or serve warm.

Darlene Cook Parrish

Brie Crisps

A nice change from Cheddar wafers or straws.

Preparation: Easy
Cooking Time: 10 Minutes
Oven Temperature: 400°F

Yield: 3 Dozen
Must Partially Do Ahead

4 **ounces Brie cheese,**
    room temperature
½ **cup butter, room**
    temperature
⅔ **cup + 2 tablespoons flour**
¼ **teaspoon cayenne pepper**
⅛ **teaspoon salt**
    Paprika

Combine cheese and butter in food processor. Mix until creamy. Add flour, cayenne, and salt. Mix, using on-off turns, until dough almost forms ball. Turn dough out onto large piece of plastic wrap. Shape into 2-inch diameter cylinder. Wrap tightly; refrigerate 30 minutes. Unwrap; roll dough into smooth even cylinder about 8 x 1½ inches. Rewrap dough in plastic. Refrigerate overnight. Slice cylinder into ¼-inch rounds. Place on ungreased baking sheets. Bake at 400°F for 10 minutes or until edges are nicely browned. Cool on rack. Sprinkle with paprika.

Cookbook Committee

Cheese Pineapple

Try your hand as a sculptor and create this impressive "show-off" appetizer. The results will be lovely to look at but even better to eat.

Preparation: Average

Yield: 3 Cups
Must Do Ahead

1½   **pounds sharp Cheddar cheese, grated**
½   **pound Swiss cheese, grated**
1   **(8-ounce) package cream cheese, softened**
¼   **pound blue cheese, crumbled**
½   **cup butter, softened**
½   **cup apple juice**
2   **tablespoons lemon juice**
1   **tablespoon Worcestershire**
  Sliced green olives
  Whole cloves
  Paprika
1   **leafy crown from large fresh pineapple**
  Wheat crackers

Combine cheeses with butter in large bowl. Slowly beat in juices and Worcestershire; blend well. Cover; chill until firm, several hours or overnight. Shape into a standing pineapple on serving plate. Flatten top; cover; chill until firm. Before serving mark cheese with wooden pick to resemble pineapple diamonds. In each diamond place olive slice and secure with a clove. Sprinkle lightly with paprika. Top with pineapple crown. Surround with wheat crackers.

Connie Kemp Goldfarb

Boursin McArthur

A nice blend of herbs and other flavors. This can be prepared in minutes and refrigerated for a week or more.

Preparation: Easy

Serves: 4-6
Must Do Ahead

1   **(8-ounce) package cream cheese, softened**
1   **clove garlic, crushed**
1   **teaspoon caraway seed**
1   **teaspoon basil**
1   **teaspoon chopped chives (may use onion)**
1   **teaspoon dill weed**
  Lemon pepper seasoning

Mix all ingredients. Shape into round ball; refrigerate at least 12 hours. Roll in lemon pepper. Serve with crackers.

Flo Criss Smith

Ginger Cheese Ball

Preparation: Easy

Yield: 1 (4-inch) Ball
Must Partially Do Ahead

3 (8-ounce) packages cream
   cheese, softened
1 cup preserved ginger,
   finely chopped
1 (5-ounce) can diced
   roasted almonds

Mix cream cheese and ginger in mixer or food processor until well blended. Chill in refrigerator until firm enough to handle. Shape into ball. Wrap in foil; refrigerate 4-24 hours. About 30 minutes before serving, roll in chopped almonds until completely coated. Let stand at room temperature. Serve with crackers.

Kaye Fairweather Mixon

Fruit and Cheese Spread

An interesting blend of flavors served beautifully in a pineapple shell.

Preparation: Average

Yield: 2½ Cups
Must Partially Do Ahead

1 (17-ounce) can fruit
   cocktail, drained and
   crushed
1 (8-ounce) package cream
   cheese, softened
2 tablespoons minced green
   onion tops
2 tablespoons mayonnaise
4 slices bacon, cooked
   and crumbled
1 medium pineapple
   Chopped fresh parsley

Combine fruit cocktail, cream cheese, green onions, mayonnaise, and bacon, mixing well; chill. Cut lengthwise slice from pineapple removing about ⅓ of pineapple. Scoop pulp from slice and discard rind. Scoop pulp from remaining portion of pineapple leaving shell of ½-¼-inch thickness; refrigerate pulp for another use. Spoon cream cheese mixture into pineapple shell; garnish with parsley. Serve with party-size slices of rye or pumpernickel or with slices of crisp apples or pears.

Sonya Wood Hancock

Jean Lee's Cheese Spread

Chutney and bell pepper give this spread an interesting and unusual flavor.

Preparation: Easy

Yield: 2 Cups
Must Partially Do Ahead

1 (8-ounce) package cream
   cheese, softened
½ bottle Major Grey's
   Chutney
2 tablespoons chopped
   bell pepper
2 teaspoons curry powder
½ teaspoon dry mustard
½ cup chopped pecans or
   almonds

Combine all ingredients, blending well. Pack into crock or serving bowl. Refrigerate. Serve with a variety of crackers.

Robert E.Lee
Hilton Head Island, South Carolina

Adrienne's Delight

Preparation: Easy

Serves: 35

12 ounces cream cheese,
    room temperature
½ cup butter, room
    temperature
½ cup sour cream,
    room temperature
½ cup sugar
1 envelope unflavored
    gelatin
¼ cup cold water
1 cup slivered almonds,
    toasted
½ cup white raisins
    Grated rind of 2 lemons
    Saltine crackers or
    gingersnaps

Combine cream cheese, butter, and sour cream; cream well. Mix in sugar. Soften gelatin in water. Place over hot water; stir to dissolve. Add to creamed mixture. Add almonds, raisins, and lemon rind. Turn into 1-quart mold; refrigerate until firm. Unmold; serve with saltine crackers or gingersnaps. May be frozen after unmolding; simply thaw when ready to use. Equally good as a dessert.

Lylla Crum Bowen

How Do You Do's

Preparation: Easy

Serves: 8-10
Must Serve Immediately

2 teaspoons flour
½ teaspoon salt
⅛ teaspoon cayenne pepper
1 cup grated sharp cheese
1 egg white, stiffly beaten
    Crushed nuts

Mix flour, salt, and cayenne. Blend with cheese. Fold flour mixture into egg white. Form into small balls; roll in crushed nuts. Fry in deep fat at 375°F until golden brown. Serve hot on toothpicks.

Mary Lou Sheridan

Fried Cheese Fondue

Great for a wine-tasting party.

Preparation: Easy
Cooking Time: 30 Seconds

Yield: Optional

    Assorted natural cheeses
    cut into ½-inch cubes
    (Suggested cheeses: Brie,
    Camembert, Cheddar,
    Edam, Gouda)
    Beaten egg(s)
    Fine dry bread crumbs
    Oil
1 teaspoon salt

Dip cheese cubes into egg, then crumbs; repeat again. (Thick coating helps keep cheese from leaking through.) Fill fondue pot half full of oil. Heat on range to 375°F. Add salt to oil. Move pot to burner. Spear cheese with fondue fork; fry in oil 30 seconds. Cool slightly before eating.

Patty Nalley Wallis

Cheese and Beer Fondue

Picture a bowl of chili and a blazing fire in the fireplace as accompaniments for this hearty fondue.

Preparation: Easy
Cooking Time: 10 Minutes

Serves: 6

8 ounces beer
3 teaspoons Tabasco
1 teaspoon garlic salt
1 pound sharp Cheddar
   cheese, grated
8 ounces Swiss cheese,
   grated
3 tablespoons flour, sifted
1 loaf French bread,
   cut into ¼-inch cubes

Pour beer into saucepan. Heat over low heat. Add Tabasco and garlic salt. Combine cheeses with flour. Gradually add cheese-flour mixture to beer mixture, stirring constantly. When well blended, transfer to fondue pot. Serve with bread cubes.

Micronote: In glass bowl mix flour and small amount of beer. Add remaining beer. Heat 2½-3 minutes on HIGH, stirring every 30-45 seconds. Add cheeses and seasonings. Cook on HIGH 1 minute longer or until cheese melts.

Susan Barker Young

Chili Con Queso

An appetizer that can be transformed into a main dish!

Preparation: Average
Cooking Time: 20-30 Minutes

Serves: 8-10

1 large onion, chopped
2 garlic cloves, minced
4 tablespoons butter, divided
1 (16-ounce) can tomatoes
1 (4-ounce) can chopped
   green chilies
2 tablespoons flour
1 cup milk
1 tablespoon Tabasco
1 teaspoon salt
2 pounds Velveeta cheese,
   cubed
½ pound Cheddar cheese,
   cubed
1½-2 pounds ground beef,
   browned and drained
   (optional)
   Corn chips

Sauté onion and garlic in 2 tablespoons melted butter until tender. Add tomatoes; simmer until thickened. Stir in green chilies. Make white sauce of remaining 2 tablespoons butter, flour, and milk. Add Tabasco and salt. Add both cheeses; stir over medium heat until cheese is completely melted. Combine cheese sauce, tomato mixture, and ground beef. Serve in chafing dish or fondue pot to dip with corn chips. (If ground beef is added, can be served over toasted buns or other "hearty" breads as a main dish.)

Micronote: In large casserole sauté onion and garlic in butter on HIGH for 1-2 minutes or until tender. Add tomatoes and cover; cook 6-8 minutes on HIGH. Add chilies. Prepare white sauce by melting butter 45 seconds; stir in flour and milk. Cook 3 minutes on HIGH, stirring every 30 seconds. Add cheeses. Reduce power to MEDIUM; cook 5 minutes or until cheese melts. Combine with tomato mixture. (If beef is added, cook on HIGH 8-10 minutes, stirring several times.)

Lucy Fokes Link

Chafing Dish Crab Dip

Preparation: Average
Cooking Time: 20 Minutes
Oven Temperature: 300°F

Yield: 2½ Cups

1 (8-ounce) package cream
   cheese, softened
½ cup mayonnaise
1 tablespoon lemon juice
½ teaspoon Worcestershire
1 teaspoon flour
   Salt
   Dash cayenne pepper
1 (7½-ounce) can white
   crabmeat, drained and
   shredded
½ cup slivered toasted
   almonds
   Toast rounds or patty
   shells

Beat cream cheese with electric mixer until smooth. Add mayonnaise, lemon juice, Worcestershire, flour, salt, and cayenne. Fold in crabmeat and nuts. Pour into greased baking dish. Bake at 300°F for 20 minutes. Turn into chafing dish; keep hot over boiling water. Serve with toast rounds or miniature patty shells.

Micronote: Soften cheese on MEDIUM, 5 minutes. Add other ingredients. Pour into dish; cook 3-5 minutes on MEDIUM.

Marilyn Woodberry McCarver

Sour Cream Crab with Mushrooms

Rich and luscious. Count on a crowd around the chafing dish when you serve this one.

Preparation: Average
Cooking Time: 30 Minutes

Serves: 40

1 pound fresh mushrooms
   or 1 (16-ounce) can
   sliced mushrooms
1½ cups water
1¼ cups butter
½ onion, chopped
5 tablespoons chopped
   fresh chives
5 tablespoons chopped
   fresh parsley
10 tablespoons flour
2½ pints sour cream
   Salt and pepper to taste
4 pounds crabmeat
   Sherry to taste
   Crackers or toast rounds

Wash mushrooms; remove stems and slice. Cook stems in water until tender. Drain, reserving stock; discard stems. (If using canned mushrooms, reserve liquid to use as stock, adding water to make 1½ cups.) Heat mushrooms, butter, onion, chives, and parsley. Simmer 3-4 minutes. Stir in flour gradually. Combine sour cream and mushroom stock; add to mushroom mixture. Season with salt and pepper. Add crabmeat; cook 5 minutes. Add sherry. Serve in chafing dish with crackers or toast rounds.

Johnnie Bowie Swetenburg

Hot Broccoli Dip

Preparation: Easy
Cooking Time: 15-20 Minutes

Yield: 2 Quarts

2 (10½-ounce) packages frozen chopped broccoli
¼ cup butter or margarine
2 large onions, chopped
2 cups chopped celery
2 cloves garlic, minced
1 (10¾-ounce) can cream of mushroom soup, undiluted
1 (4-ounce) can mushroom pieces, drained
1 (3-ounce) package cream cheese, softened
¼ teaspoon cayenne
Corn chips

Cook broccoli just until thawed; drain immediately. In large skillet melt butter; add onions, celery, garlic, and broccoli. Cook until onion is tender. Add remaining ingredients; cook and stir over low heat until smooth. Serve hot in chafing dish; accompany with corn chips. (Also delicious as side dish over hot baked potato.)

Micronote: Place broccoli in glass dish. Cook 5 minutes on HIGH; drain. Place broccoli and remaining ingredients in large casserole dish. Cook 5-6 minutes on HIGH.

Patricia Franklin Rauch

Hot Mushroom Dip

Preparation: Average
Cooking Time: 15 Minutes

Yield: 2½ Cups
Must Serve Immediately

4 slices bacon, fried
2 tablespoons bacon drippings
½ pound fresh mushrooms, sliced
1 medium onion, finely chopped
1 clove garlic, minced
2 tablespoons flour
¼ teaspoon salt
⅛ teaspoon pepper
1 (8-ounce) package cream cheese, cubed
2 teaspoons Worcestershire
1 teaspoon soy sauce
½ cup sour cream

Drain and crumble bacon; set aside. Heat bacon drippings in skillet. Add mushrooms, onion, and garlic; cook, stirring often, until liquid has evaporated. Stir in flour, salt, and pepper. Add cream cheese, Worcestershire, and soy sauce; cook, stirring constantly, until cheese melts. Stir sour cream and bacon into mushroom mixture; cook until thoroughly heated, stirring constantly. (Do not boil.) Serve warm with assorted crackers.

Micronote: Place bacon between layers of absorbent toweling; cook on HIGH 3½-4 minutes. Crumble; set aside. Sauté vegetables in 1 tablespoon bacon drippings 3-5 minutes on HIGH. Add flour, cheese. Reduce power to MEDIUM. Cook 1½ minutes or until cheese melts. Add sour cream and bacon. Cook on MEDIUM 1½-2 minutes or until heated.

Carolyn Hartford Mahar

Won-Ton Bows with Sweet and Sour Sauce

Preparation: Complex
Cooking Time: 20-30 Minutes
Oven Temperature: 400°F

Yield: 50 Bows

1 package won-ton skins
   (3-inch square)
Water
Oil
Sweet and Sour Sauce

Using finger or small brush, spread ½-inch strip water down center of each won-ton square. Crinkle center together to form bow shape; twist once to secure. Repeat with all squares. Pour oil to ½-inch depth in large skillet. Heat to 400°F. Fry won-ton in hot oil in single layer until golden. Drain on absorbent toweling. Store in airtight container. Before serving reheat in 400°F oven for 5-7 minutes. (Beware. These burn easily!) Place Sweet and Sour Sauce on serving tray. Surround with bows for dipping.

Sweet and Sour Sauce

¼ cup sugar
¼ cup white vinegar
¼ cup catsup
1 cup + 2 tablespoons water, divided
2 tablespoons cornstarch
½ cup chopped green pepper
3 tablespoons canned crushed pineapple, drained

In small pan bring 1 cup water, sugar, vinegar, and catsup to boiling. Mix cornstarch and remaining 2 tablespoons water until smooth. Add to sauce; return to boiling. Stir constantly until smooth and thick. Stir in green pepper and pineapple. **Micronote:** Mix 1 cup water, sugar, vinegar, and catsup; cook 3 minutes on HIGH. Mix cornstarch and 2 tablespoons water until smooth; add to catsup mixture. Cook 1½-2 minutes or until thick, stirring every 30 seconds. Stir in green pepper and pineapple.

Carol Dean Greene

Curry Dip for Raw Vegetables

Preparation: Easy

Yield: 1¼ Cups
Must Do Ahead

Mix all ingredients; chill. Serve with raw vegetables.

Flo Criss Smith

1 cup mayonnaise
2 tablespoons Durkee's Sauce
1 heaping tablespoon horseradish
1 teaspoon celery seed
1 teaspoon curry powder
1 teaspoon seasoned salt
½ teaspoon Worcestershire
⅛ teaspoon Tabasco
¼-½ clove garlic, minced
Pepper to taste

Nebraska Rye Boat Dip

A unique "eye-catcher." The serving bowl is the bread itself!

Preparation: Average

Yield: 2½ Cups
Must Partially Do Ahead

1⅓ cups salad dressing
1⅓ cups sour cream
 2 tablespoons minced onion
 2 tablespoons parsley
 2 teaspoons Beau Monde
 2 teaspoons dill weed
 2 (3-ounce) packages pressed
   corned beef, chopped
   into tiny pieces
 2 loaves unsliced rye
   bread (10 or 12-inch loaf)
   Fresh parsley
   Purple and green grapes

Combine salad dressing, sour cream, minced onion, parsley, Beau Monde, and dill; blend well. Stir in corned beef. Chill. Hollow out center of 1 loaf of bread to make serving bowl. Cut portion of bread removed and second loaf into bite-sized squares. Just before serving, pour dip into "bowl." Serve with bread pieces for dippers. Garnish with parsley and purple and green grapes.

Diane Derrick Blalock

The hostess must be like the duck--calm and unruffled on the surface, and paddling like hell underneath.

Anonymous

Water Chestnut Dip

Preparation: Easy

Yield: 2 Cups
Must Do Ahead

 1 (8-ounce) carton sour
   cream
 1 cup mayonnaise
 1 (8-ounce) can water
   chestnuts, drained and
   chopped
 ½ cup chopped parsley
 3 green onions (including
   tops), chopped
 2 tablespoons soy sauce
2-3 drops Tabasco or
   hot pepper sauce

Combine all ingredients. Process in blender or food processor until ingredients are fine but not puréed. Chill. Serve with chips or raw vegetables.

Linda Whatley Carter

Marinated Vidalia Onions

Preparation: Average

Yield: 3 Cups
Must Do Ahead

6 large Vidalia onions
2 cups boiling water
1 cup sugar
½ cup cider vinegar
1-1½ cups mayonnaise
2 teaspoons celery seed

Slice onions in thin, round slices. Separate into rings; place in shallow, covered container. Combine water, sugar, and vinegar; stir to dissolve sugar. Pour hot vinegar mixture over onions. Let stand, covered, overnight. Drain well, squeezing out excess marinade. Add mayonnaise and celery seed, tossing onions to coat well. Chill. Serve with crackers. Keeps in refrigerator, covered, for several weeks. **Variation: Gourmet Onion Sandwich -** Spread whole-wheat bread with cream cheese, top with tomato slice and onions.

Carolyn Hartford Mahar

Hold the mouth full of water while peeling onions and the onion juice will not get in the eyes.
A Treasury of Georgia Folklore by Ronald G. Killion and Charles T. Walker
(Atlanta: Cherokee Publishing Company, 1983.) Used by permission.

Sunburst Artichoke

An attractive dish to serve and always a big hit with those who have a taste for artichokes.

Preparation: Average
Cooking Time: 30 Minutes

Yield: 18

1 large artichoke
Water
1 teaspoon oil
Bay leaf
½ teaspoon salt
Lemon slices
1 (3-ounce) package cream
cheese, softened
1 tablespoon cream or
half-and-half
½ teaspoon garlic salt
½ teaspoon Worcestershire
2-3 drops Tabasco
18-20 small boiled shrimp,
peeled
Paprika

Trim artichoke 1 inch from top; cut off sharp tips. Cover artichoke with water; add oil, bay leaf, salt, and lemon slices. Cover tightly; simmer 30 minutes. Drain, cool, and remove leaves. Use only 18-20 fattest leaves; discard remainder. Place cream cheese, cream, garlic salt, Worcestershire, and Tabasco in blender or food processor; blend well. Spread ½-1 teaspoon cream cheese mixture on each leaf; top with shrimp and sprinkle with paprika. Arrange on platter in sunburst fashion. Serve immediately or refrigerate for later use.

Carol Dean Greene

Nacho Platter

If your guests will be formally dressed, provide bibs!

Preparation: Average

Serves: 20
Must Do Ahead

1 cup sour cream
½ cup mayonnaise
1 (1¼-ounce) package taco
   seasoning mix
3 medium avocados, peeled
2 tablespoons lemon juice
½ teaspoon salt
¼ teaspoon pepper
2 (10½-ounce) cans Jalapeño
   bean dip
1 cup chopped green onions
1 (4½-ounce) can chopped
   ripe olives
2 cups chopped tomatoes
8 ounces sharp Cheddar
   cheese, grated
   Nacho chips

Combine sour cream, mayonnaise, and taco mix. Refrigerate until chilled. Combine avocados, lemon juice, salt, and pepper in food processor or electric blender; process until smooth. Using large shallow serving dish or platter, layer in order: bean dip, avocado mixture, sour cream mixture, onions, olives, tomatoes, and cheese. Cover; chill thoroughly. (May be served without chilling, but flavors will not have had a chance to blend.) Serve accompanied by a basket of nacho chips for dipping.

Ann Couch Alexander

Bacon Stuffed Mushrooms

Preparation: Easy
Cooking Time: 20 Minutes
Oven Temperature: 350°F

Yield: 25-30 Mushrooms

25-30 medium mushrooms
2 tablespoons butter, melted
¼ cup minced onions
6 slices crisp cooked
   bacon, crumbled
1 cup sour cream
½ teaspoon salt
¼ teaspoon paprika
¼ teaspoon Worcestershire
⅛ teaspoon pepper

Remove stems from mushrooms and chop. Sauté stems and onion in butter until onion is tender. Combine onion mixture with remaining ingredients. Spoon into mushroom caps. Place in greased shallow baking dish. Bake at 350°F for 20 minutes.
Micronote: Sauté stems and onions in butter on HIGH for 1½ minutes or until tender. Stuff mushrooms as directed. Place in round baking dish. Cook on HIGH for 3½-4 minutes.

Judy Mynatt Bush

Crab Stuffed Mushrooms

Try these also as a vegetable side dish. You can vary the flavor by using sausage, bacon, or tuna in place of crabmeat.

Preparation: Average
Cooking Time: 20 Minutes
Oven Temperature: 350°F

Yield: 20 Mushrooms

20 **large mushrooms**
½ **cup seasoned bread crumbs**
½ **cup grated mild Cheddar cheese**
½ **cup sour cream**
1 **(4½-ounce) can of crabmeat or shrimp, drained**
2 **tablespoons chopped green onions**
1 **egg**
1 **tablespoon soy sauce**
2 **tablespoons margarine, melted**

Remove stems from mushrooms. With small spoon hollow out cap, reserving ¼ cup pulp. Wash caps well; drain on absorbent toweling. Mix all remaining ingredients (including reserved pulp) except margarine. Brush rounded tops of mushrooms with margarine; stuff with crab mixture. Place in ovenproof baking dish. Bake at 350°F for 20 minutes.
Micronote: Place mushrooms in round baking dish. Cook on HIGH for 3½-4 minutes.

Marilyn Murphy Doveton

Myra's Marinated Mushrooms

A great do-ahead dish for a cocktail party. Double the recipe and freeze half.

Preparation: Easy
Cooking Time: 8-11 Hours

Serves: 24
Must Do Ahead

4 **pounds extra large whole mushrooms**
1 **pound butter**
1 **quart Burgundy wine**
2 **cups boiling water**
4 **beef bouillon cubes**
4 **chicken bouillon cubes**
1½ **tablespoons Worcestershire**
1 **tablespoon monosodium glutamate**
1 **teaspoon dill weed**
1 **teaspoon ground pepper**
1 **teaspoon garlic powder**
Salt

Combine all ingredients in large pan. Bring to slow boil on medium heat. Reduce heat to simmer; cook covered 5-6 hours. Remove cover; simmer another 3-5 hours, until liquid reduces to barely cover mushrooms. Add salt to taste; allow to cool. Refrigerate overnight. Reheat. Serve hot in chafing dish.

Joan Driskell Hopkins

Mushroom Turnovers

Preparation: Complex
Cooking Time: 30 Minutes
Oven Temperature: 350°F

Yield: 30-35
Must Partially Do Ahead
Must Serve Immediately

1 cup margarine, slightly
    softened
1 (8-ounce) package cream
    cheese, softened
½ teaspoon salt
2 cups flour, unsifted
    Mushroom Filling
1 egg yolk
2 teaspoons milk

Cream margarine, cream cheese, and salt. Add flour; blend with electric mixer until smooth. Place dough on waxed paper; flatten to 8 x 6-inch rectangle. Wrap and chill overnight. Remove from refrigerator 10 minutes before rolling. Divide in half; roll each half into 9 x 6-inch rectangle. Fold over in thirds. Roll, fold over again, then roll to ⅛-inch thickness. Cut into 2½-inch circles. Place level measuring teaspoonful of filling in center of each circle. Moisten edges with water; fold double. Press edges with a floured fork. Place on ungreased baking sheet. Brush with mixture of egg yolk and milk. Chill 1-12 hours. Bake at 350°F for 25-30 minutes. Serve warm.

Mushroom Filling

2 (4-ounce) jars mushrooms
    or 16 ounces fresh
    mushrooms, minced
½ cup minced onion
2 tablespoons margarine,
    melted
2 teaspoons flour
1 teaspoon lemon juice
½ teaspoon salt
⅛ teaspoon pepper (optional)
½ cup light cream or milk
1 tablespoon sherry

Sauté mushrooms and onion in margarine for 5 minutes. Sprinkle with flour, lemon juice, salt, and pepper. Simmer 2 minutes longer. Stir in milk; simmer until thickened and smooth. Stir in sherry. Chill.
Micronote: Sauté fresh mushrooms in butter for 5 minutes. Combine remaining ingredients except for sherry; cook on HIGH 1½-2 minutes; stir every 30 seconds. Add mushrooms; stir in sherry.

Sandra Gilmer Souther

Pecan Stuffed Mushrooms

Preparation: Average
Cooking Time: 15 Minutes
Oven Temperature: 350°F

Yield: 2 Dozen

1 **pound large fresh mushrooms**
¼ **cup butter or margarine**
1 **clove garlic, minced**
½ **cup chopped pecans**
½ **cup fine bread crumbs**
½ **teaspoon salt**
¼ **teaspoon ground thyme**
¼ **teaspoon pepper**

Wash mushrooms; pat dry. Remove stems and chop. Place caps in shallow buttered baking dish. Melt butter in skillet. Sauté stems and garlic in butter. Add remaining ingredients; stir well. Stuff caps with mixture. Bake at 350°F for 15 minutes. Serve warm. (Also good as side dish with steak or London Broil.)
Micronote: Place mushrooms in round baking dish. Cook on HIGH 3½-4 minutes.

Dee Lawson Morris

Mini Microwave Mushroom Quiche

Preparation: Average
Cooking Time: 14 Minutes

Serves: 6

Pastry for 2 crust pie (page 339)
1 **medium onion, minced**
2 **cups fresh mushrooms, sliced**
2 **tablespoons margarine**
3 **tablespoons flour**
½ **cup milk**
2 **eggs, beaten**
¼ **cup evaporated milk**
¼ **teaspoon salt**
Black pepper to taste

Micronote: Roll pastry out to ¹⁄₁₆-inch thickness. Cut six circles 5½-6 inches in diameter. Lightly grease microwave muffin pan. Line each cup with dough. Trim and flute edges. Prick sides and bottom. Microwave on MEDIUM-HIGH for 4-6 minutes, or until flaky; rotate pan 2-3 times. Set aside. Combine onions, mushrooms, and margarine in 1-quart bowl. Microwave on HIGH for 2-3 minutes. Add flour; mix well. Stir in milk. Microwave on MEDIUM for 1-2 minutes or until mixture boils. Stir small amount of hot mixture into beaten eggs. Stir egg mixture, milk, salt, and pepper into hot mushroom sauce. Spoon mixture into baked shells. Microwave on MEDIUM for 4-6 minutes or until knife inserted in center comes out clean; rotate twice.

Polly Cross Moore

Spinach Quiche Squares

Preparation: Average
Cooking Time: 55 Minutes
Oven Temperature: 400°F

Yield: 60

½ cup butter or margarine
10 eggs, beaten
½ cup unsifted flour
1 teaspoon baking powder
1 teaspoon salt
1 bunch fresh spinach,
    chopped or 1 (10-ounce)
    package frozen chopped
    spinach, thawed
1 (8-ounce) can green
    chilies, seeded
    and chopped
2 cups fine curd cottage
    cheese
½ pound Cheddar cheese,
    shredded
½ pound Monterey Jack
    cheese, shredded

Melt butter in 13 x 9 x 2-inch pan in preheated oven, about 3 minutes. Mix eggs, flour, baking powder, and salt. (If using frozen spinach, squeeze very dry.) Add spinach, melted butter, chilies, and cheeses to egg mixture. Return mixture to baking pan. Bake at 400°F for 15 minutes. Reduce heat to 350°F; bake 35-40 minutes. Let stand 5 minutes to set. Cut into 60 squares. (May be served as vegetable side dish in larger squares.)

Diane Railey Curington

Honey Granola with Peanut Butter

A good breakfast cereal or snack.

Preparation: Average
Cooking Time: 40 Minutes
Oven Temperature: Lowest Setting

Serves: 16-20

3 cups quick oatmeal
1 cup wheat germ
1 cup pumpkin seeds
1 cup sunflower seeds
½ cup sesame seeds
1 cup All Bran
⅔ cup peanut butter
½ cup honey
2 tablespoons cooking oil

In large bowl combine oatmeal, wheat germ, pumpkin seeds, sunflower seeds, sesame seeds, and All Bran. In smaller bowl blend peanut butter, honey, and oil. Pour over cereal mixture; stir until well coated. Transfer mixture to ungreased 15 x 10 x 1½-inch pan or 2 (13 x 9 x 2-inch) pans. Bake at lowest oven setting for 40 minutes. Check often, stirring once during baking. Cool. Store in airtight container.

Lois Snyder Kenyon

Caramel Popcorn with Nuts

Perfect for a "take along" snack or for ball game munching. Be sure to make plenty, as this is one of those things people can't seem to stop eating! Packed in a decorative tin, it also makes a great gift.

Preparation: Average
Cooking Time: 1 Hour
Oven Temperature: 250°F

Yield: 4 Quarts
Must Do Ahead

3 quarts popped popcorn or puffed wheat cereal
1 cup blanched slivered almonds
1 cup pecan halves
1 cup cashews
½ cup butter or margarine
1 cup brown sugar
¼ cup honey
1 teaspoon vanilla extract

Combine popcorn and nuts in lightly greased 14 x 11 x 2-inch roasting pan. Set aside. Melt butter over low heat in medium saucepan. Add brown sugar and honey; bring to boil over medium heat. Boil 5 minutes without stirring. Add vanilla, stirring well. Pour syrup over popcorn mixture, stirring until popcorn is evenly coated. Bake at 250°F for 1 hour, stirring every 15 minutes. Cool completely, then break into pieces. Store in airtight container.

Carol Lynn Dobson Waggoner
Ann Rankin Vance

Georgia "Bulldawg" Food

Good for football game snacking. (Permission granted to change the name if, by some chance, you follow another team!)

Preparation: Easy

Yield: Variable

1 (12-ounce) package chocolate semi-sweet morsels
1 (12-ounce) package butter-scotch morsels
1 (12-ounce) package coconut morsels or peanut butter morsels
1 (8-ounce) package chopped dates
1 (8¼-ounce) jar dry roasted peanuts
1 (7-ounce) jar cashew nuts
1 (15-ounce) box raisins
1 (7½-ounce) can sesame sticks
1 (4-ounce) package sunflower seeds

Mix any or all ingredients, as desired. Store in airtight jar or plastic container.

Willia Beth Buquet Banks

Peanut Butter Sticks

A great snack - a favorite with both young and old. Be sure to store in a tightly covered tin, as they must stay crisp!

Preparation: Average
Cooking Time: 1 Hour
Oven Temperature: 200°F

Yield: 80-100 Sticks
Must Do Ahead

1 loaf sandwich bread
1 (8-ounce) jar smooth peanut butter
½ cup peanut oil

Trim crust from bread; cut into four fingers (or squares) per slice of bread. Place bread and crusts in separate pans. Bake at 200°F for one hour or until crisp, turning often. With rolling pin or food processor make crumbs from dry crusts. Mix peanut butter and oil. Dip bread fingers into peanut mixture, then roll in bread crumbs. Arrange in layers in airtight container; let stand overnight. (These may be made a week before serving.)

Alice Whitehead Paris

Roasted Pecans

A Southern favorite.

Preparation: Easy
Cooking Time: 30-40 Minutes
Oven Temperature: 300°F

Yield: 4 Cups

4 cups pecan halves
½ cup melted butter
Salt

Coat pecans with butter. Place in shallow roasting pan. Bake at 300°F for 30-40 minutes, stirring occasionally. Drain on absorbent toweling. Salt to taste. Cool. Store in airtight container.

Dee Lawson Morris

Sugar and Spice Pecans

Place in colorful tins or small jars, tie with yarn and add a sprig of holly to create a Christmas gift for friends and neighbors.

Preparation: Easy
Cooking Time: 20 Minutes
Oven Temperature: 300°F

Yield: 2 Cups
Must Do Ahead

1 tablespoon butter, melted
1 egg white, stiffly beaten
2 cups pecan halves
½ cup sugar
1½ teaspoons ground cinnamon
¾ teaspoon ground nutmeg
¾ teaspoon ground allspice
½ teaspoon salt

Mix butter and beaten egg white. Add nuts; coat thoroughly. Mix sugar and spices in separate bowl. Lightly cover the bottom of a baking sheet with a portion of sugar mixture. Coat pecans with remaining sugar mixture, doing a few at a time. Place on baking sheet; sprinkle with any remaining sugar. Bake at 300°F for 20 minutes. Separate with fork; cool.

Betty Garrett Mansfield

Strawberries in Rhine Wine

A great pick-up item for a brunch; or try these as an elegant dessert over ice cream in stemmed glasses or compotes.

Preparation: Easy

   1 **cup dry Rhine wine**
      Juice of 1 medium orange
  ½ **cup firmly packed light**
      brown sugar
  ½ **teaspoon almond extract**
  3 **pints fresh strawberries,**
      washed and hulled

Serves: 8
Must Do Ahead

Combine wine, juice, sugar, and extract. Mix well. Pour over strawberries. Cover and marinate in refrigerator at least 4 hours or overnight. (Berries will become too soft if left more than 24 hours.)
Variation: Substitute Christian Brothers Château La Salle wine for the Rhine wine and use either strawberries or fresh peach slices.

Sherrie Nathan Schrage

Nothing you ever ate in your life was anything like as delicate, as fragrant, as those wild white strawberries. You had to know enough to go where they are and stand and eat them on the spot, that's all.

Eudora Welty, *The Optimist's Daughter*
Random House, Inc., Copyright 1969. Used with permission.

Pickled Pineapple

Beautiful in a cut glass bowl with toothpicks for spearing. A most versatile tidbit for an appetizer, brunch item, meat accompaniment, or dessert garnish. Great to keep on hand in the refrigerator.

Preparation: Easy
Cooking Time: 10-12 Minutes

  2 **(20-ounce) cans unsweetened**
      pineapple chunks, well
      drained
  ½ **cup + 2 tablespoons**
      reserved pineapple juice
  ¾ **cup sugar**
  ¾ **cup white vinegar**
 15 **whole cloves**
  1 **cinnamon stick (broken**
      in half)
  ⅛ **teaspoon salt**

Yield: 1 Quart
Must Do Ahead

Place drained pineapple chunks in 1-quart jar; set aside. In medium saucepan combine pineapple juice with remaining ingredients. Simmer 10-12 minutes. Pour over pineapple chunks. When cool, cap jar and refrigerate a minimum of 3-4 days. Keeps refrigerated up to 8 weeks.

Hazel Richardson Jackson

Soups & Sandwiches

Passion Flower

Passion Flower (Passiflora incarnata)

This summer vine has one of the most unusual flowers of any of the wildflowers. Look closely at its floral parts, and you can see their resemblance to the suffering of Christ's crucifixion; hence one of its common names - the passion flower. Its yellow fruit, known as maypops, are edible and can be tasted in many a Southern jam. The leaves and blooms can also be brewed and chilled for a refreshing drink.

On Soups and Sandwiches

- For a quick soup: Place ½ cup leftover vegetables in blender or food processor. Add 1 cup boiling stock or bouillon while processing. Add butter or cream if desired.
- To thicken soup stir in a paste of 2 tablespoons melted butter, blended with 1 tablespoon flour for each quart of soup.
- Cream soups will thicken while standing or refrigerating. Reheat over low heat, whisking or stirring frequently. Gradually add 1-2 tablespoons cream, milk, broth, or water to thin to desired consistency.
- If soup or stew is too salty, drop in a peeled, raw potato; cook several minutes. Remove potato; check taste.
- To assemble a Bouquet Garni for seasoning: wrap several parsley sprigs, garlic cloves, fresh or dried thyme, and bay leaf in cheesecloth.
- No need to peel a garlic clove, just crush in press, peeling and all.
- A roux is a thickener for soups, sauces, and gravies made by blending equal parts melted butter or other fat with flour. Cook and stir over very low heat for 5 minutes for a white roux or longer for brown.

- A punch bowl or glass pitcher makes an attractive buffet server for cold fruit soups or gazpacho.
- Milk cartons make excellent freezing containers for stocks and soups. Plastic yogurt or sour cream containers are excellent for freezing 1-cup portions.
- Burned soup pots? Sprinkle powdered cleaner or baking soda over burned portion. Add enough water to moisten powder. Cover pot with plastic wrap; let stand several hours or overnight.
- For tea sandwiches: spread thin slices of bread with orange spread (3 ounces cream cheese blended with 1 tablespoon orange juice and 1 teaspoon grated orange rind) or almond spread (½ cup softened butter or margarine mixed with 1 tablespoon finely chopped almonds and ½ teaspoon almond extract). Also try a spread made from 3 ounces cream cheese blended with a favorite fruit jam or preserve. Be creative with bread selection; use date-nut bread, raisin bread, or other fruit breads in addition to white, wheat, and pumpernickel breads.

Crab Stew

Preparation: Easy
Cooking Time: 10 Minutes

Serves: 6

    2 medium onions,
          finely chopped
    6 tablespoons butter
    1 pint crab meat
    2 pints half-and-half
    3 drops Tabasco
    1 teaspoon salt
  ½ teaspoon cayenne

Sauté onion in butter on low heat until tender. Separate crab meat into small pieces with fork; add to onion. Stir in remaining ingredients. Simmer until thoroughly heated, but **do not boil**.
Micronote: Sauté onion in butter on HIGH 2 minutes or until tender. Add crab meat to onion; stir in remaining ingredients. Cook on HIGH 10 minutes, stirring frequently. Do not allow mixture to boil.

Knickers Restaurant
Gainesville, Georgia

Shrimp Chowder

Preparation: Average
Cooking Time: 30 Minutes

Serves: 6-8

    2 large onions, sliced
    2 tablespoons butter or
          margarine, melted
  ½ cup boiling water
    3 medium potatoes, peeled
          and cubed
    1 teaspoon salt
  ½ teaspoon black pepper
    1 cup milk
    1 cup half-and-half
    1 cup grated sharp
          Cheddar cheese
    1 pound raw shrimp, cleaned
          and shelled or 1 (12-ounce)
          package frozen raw whole
          shrimp
  ⅛-¼ teaspoon cayenne
  ¼ cup sherry
  ½ cup White Sauce
  1½ tablespoons chopped parsley

In Dutch oven or large kettle sauté onion in margarine until tender. Add boiling water, potatoes, salt, and black pepper. Simmer, covered, 20 minutes or until potatoes are just tender; stir occasionally to prevent sticking. In separate saucepan heat milk, half-and-half, and cheese; cook over low to moderate heat, stirring until cheese melts, but **do not boil**. Add raw shrimp to potato mixture; cook 3 minutes or until shrimp turn pink. Add milk-cheese mixture and heat. Add cayenne pepper, sherry, and White Sauce, stirring until thickened. Heat thoroughly, but **do not boil**. Garnish individual servings with parsley.
Micronote: In large casserole sauté onion in butter on HIGH 2-3 minutes. Add water, potatoes, salt, and black pepper. Cook, loosely covered, on HIGH 8-10 minutes. Combine milk, half-and-half, and cheese in large glass measure. Cook 5 minutes on HIGH; stir to blend. Cook shrimp in microwave on HIGH 3-5 minutes. Combine potato mixture, cheese mixture, and shrimp. Add cayenne, sherry, and White Sauce. Cook 1 minute longer.

White Sauce

    1 tablespoon butter, melted
    1 tablespoon flour
  ½ cup milk

In small saucepan blend butter and flour. Slowly add milk, stirring constantly. Cook over moderate heat until thick and smooth.
Micronote: Melt butter in microwave 30 seconds. Stir in flour; add milk. Cook on HIGH 1-1½ minutes, stirring every 30 seconds.

Melba Clark Jacobs

Easy New England Clam Chowder

Preparation: Easy
Cooking Time: 20 Minutes

Serves: 4

¼ **cup diced bacon**
¼ **cup minced onion**
1 **(10¾-ounce) can cream of potato soup**
¾ **cup half-and-half**
2 **(7-ounce) cans minced clams, undrained**
1 **tablespoon lemon juice**
⅛ **teaspoon pepper**

In large saucepan cook and stir bacon and onion until bacon is crisp and onion is tender. Stir in soup and half-and-half; heat through, stirring occasionally. Stir in clams, lemon juice, and pepper. Heat thoroughly.

Micronote: Cook bacon between absorbent toweling on HIGH for 1 minute per slice; crumble to make ¼ cup. Cook onions in large bowl on HIGH 2 minutes. Add bacon, soup, and half-and-half. Cook on HIGH 5 minutes. Stir in remaining ingredients. Cook on MEDIUM 5 minutes or until hot.

Patty Nalley Wallis

Murrell's Inlet Clam Chowder

This "Manhattan Style" chowder is much heartier and spicier than its Northern sister. It originated in Murrell's Inlet in the low country of South Carolina. Serve hot with rice or French bread and a salad for a light meal. It tastes even better the second day.

Preparation: Average
Cooking Time: 3 Hours

Serves: 8

8 **slices bacon**
3 **medium Irish potatoes, diced**
2 **medium onions, diced**
1 **(28-ounce) can tomatoes**
1 **(8-ounce) bottle clam juice**
½ **cup catsup**
1½ **tablespoons Worcestershire**
1½ **tablespoons Heinz 57 sauce**
1 **teaspoon salt**
1 **teaspoon pepper**
1 **teaspoon brown sugar**
½ **teaspoon vinegar (optional)**
¼ **teaspoon Tabasco**
2 **whole celery stalks**
3 **cups water**
3 **(6½-ounce) cans minced clams, undrained**

In large soup pot fry bacon; drain on absorbent toweling and crumble. Add potatoes and onions to bacon fat. Cook over medium heat 10 minutes, or until soft. In blender or food processor combine tomatoes, clam juice, catsup, Worcestershire, steak sauce, salt, pepper, bacon, brown sugar, vinegar, and Tabasco. Process 50 seconds or until tomatoes and other ingredients are well blended. Add to potatoes and onions; add celery and water. Simmer, stirring frequently, over low heat 45 minutes - 1 hour. Add clams; continue simmering 1-2 more hours, stirring frequently. Remove celery; discard. Adjust seasonings to taste.

Micronote: Cook bacon in microwave, 4 slices at a time, for 4 minutes on HIGH. Cover with absorbent toweling while cooking. Pour bacon drippings into large glass bowl; add potatoes and onions. Cook 10 minutes on HIGH, stirring several times. Purée ingredients as directed above. Add tomato mixture. Cook on HIGH until mixture boils, 12-15 minutes. Reduce power to MEDIUM; cook 12-15 minutes longer. (If mixture boils too much, reduce power further.) Add clams; cook on MEDIUM 12-15 minutes longer. Remove celery; adjust seasonings.

Jenny McGee Browning

Super Simple Crab Bisque

An easy way to transform canned soup into something special. Serve with citrus salad and hard rolls.

Preparation: Easy
Cooking Time: 3-5 Hours

Serves: 4

1 (10-ounce) package crab meat, slightly thawed or 2 (6-ounce) cans crab meat, undrained
1 (10¾-ounce) can tomato soup
1 (10¾-ounce) can cream of asparagus soup
1 cup half-and-half

Stir crab meat, soups, and cream into lightly buttered crock pot. Cover; cook on low setting 3-5 hours, stirring occasionally.

Micronote: Combine all ingredients in 2-quart casserole. Microwave on MEDIUM for 6-8 minutes, stirring several times.

Diana Dokken Anthony

Amelia's Cioppino

Fairly bursting with fabulous seafood and a wide array of subtle flavorings! A green salad and crusty French bread complete the meal.

Preparation: Average
(but time-consuming)
Cooking Time: 2½ Hours

Serves: 8-10

¼ cup olive oil
1 cup butter
2 medium onions, chopped
1 leek or 3 green onions, diced
2 green peppers, diced
4 cloves garlic, minced
2 (20-ounce) cans tomatoes
1 (6-ounce) can tomato paste
2 cups canned tomato sauce
1 bay leaf
¼ teaspoon dried oregano
¼ teaspoon thyme
¼ teaspoon basil
6 whole peppercorns
⅛ teaspoon cayenne pepper
Salt and pepper to taste
1¾ cups dry white wine
¼ cup Marsala wine
1 pound raw shrimp
2 medium lobsters (optional)
2 pounds flounder or red snapper
1 pound crab meat
1 pint oysters
1 (10-ounce) can minced clams

In large skillet or Dutch oven heat olive oil and butter. Add onions, leek, green peppers, and garlic; sauté until lightly browned. Add tomatoes, tomato paste, tomato sauce, bay leaf, oregano, thyme, basil, peppercorns, cayenne, salt, and pepper. Cover; cook **very slowly**, stirring frequently, for 2 hours. Add wines; cook 10 minutes more. While tomato mixture is cooking, cook shrimp and lobster in boiling salted water until tender. Cut fish into 2-inch cubes. Place seafood in layers in deep pot or kettle. Split lobsters in half and crack claws. Pour sauce over all. Simmer, covered, for 15-20 minutes.

Sally Butts Darden

Hearty Oyster Stew

Preparation: Average
Cooking Time: 10 Minutes

Serves: 6

2 pints oysters, fresh
 or frozen
2 slices bacon
⅓ cup chopped onion
1 (10¾-ounce) can cream of
 potato soup
3 cups half-and-half
1¼ teaspoons salt
⅛ teaspoon pepper
⅓ cup chopped parsley

Thaw oysters if frozen. Drain oysters, reserving liquor. Fry bacon until crisp. Remove bacon from fat; break into thirds. Cook onion in bacon fat until tender. Add soup, oyster liquor, half-and-half, and seasonings. Heat, stirring occasionally. Add bacon and oysters; heat 3-5 minutes longer or until edges of oysters begin to curl. Sprinkle with parsley.

Micronote: Place bacon on glass platter; cover with absorbent toweling. Cook 2-2½ minutes on HIGH. Drain bacon grease into large glass bowl; add onions. Cook on HIGH 1 minute. Add soup, oyster liquor, half-and-half, and seasonings. Cook on HIGH 6 minutes, stirring several times. Add bacon and oysters; cook on HIGH 3-5 minutes, stirring several times. Sprinkle with parsley.

Mary Ann Leathers Morrison

Chicken-Ham-Oyster Soup

Make this ahead of time, if possible, and allow the flavors to blend before serving.

Preparation: Average
Cooking Time: 45-50 Minutes

Serves: 10-12

4 (16-ounce) cans stewed tomatoes
4 chicken bouillon cubes
1 teaspoon salt
1 teaspoon whole basil
 leaves, crushed
½ teaspoon rubbed sage
 Hot sauce to taste (8-9 drops)
1 cup diced onion
1 cup diced green pepper
1 cup sliced mushrooms
¼ cup melted butter or
 margarine
2 (10¾-ounce) cans
 tomato soup
1½ cups water
1½ cups diced cooked
 chicken
1½ cups diced cooked ham
2 (12-ounce) cans FRESH
 oysters, drained
¼ cup dry white wine
½ cup sliced pimiento-
 stuffed olives

Combine tomatoes, bouillon cubes, salt, basil, sage, and hot sauce in a Dutch oven; stir well. Bring to boil; lower heat, simmer 30 minutes. Sauté onion, green pepper, and mushrooms in butter 5 minutes. Stir vegetables, soup, water, chicken, and ham into tomato mixture; simmer 5 minutes. Add oysters and wine; simmer 5-8 minutes or until edges of oysters curl. Stir in olives just before serving.

Joanne Moore Frierson

Rose's Cream of Chicken Soup

Preparation: Average
Cooking Time: 1 Hour 30 Minutes

Serves: 4-6

1 (3 to 4-pound) chicken
6 cups water
3 stalks celery
1 medium onion
1 teaspoon salt
1 teaspoon pepper
1 small onion, diced
2 tablespoons butter or
   chicken fat, melted
3 tablespoons flour
1½ teaspoons salt
1½ teaspoons pepper
1 cup milk
   Minced chives (optional)

Cook chicken in water with celery, onion, salt, and pepper for 1 hour or until tender. Strain stock and reserve. Remove chicken from bones; dice. In Dutch oven or soup kettle cook onion in butter until softened. Blend in flour, salt, and pepper. Cook over low heat, stirring constantly, until smooth. Remove from heat; add milk slowly, stirring constantly. Stir in 3 cups reserved chicken stock and diced chicken. Heat to serving temperature. Sprinkle individual servings with minced chives.

Micronote: Cook chicken conventionally as directed above. Place margarine in large bowl or crockery cooker; melt on HIGH 45 seconds. Blend in flour, salt, and pepper. Add milk and stock. Cook on HIGH 8-10 minutes, stirring several times. Add chicken; cook 2-3 minutes longer.

Ann Collins Hendrickson

Mulligatawny

This East Indian curried soup was very popular with British officers serving in India during the British colonial period, as it was easy to carry along flasks of the hot soup on winter forays into the hills.

Preparation: Average
Cooking Time: 2 Hours

Serves: 6-8

4 chicken breasts
2 quarts chicken broth or
   2 quarts water + 4
   tablespoons butter
2 carrots, sliced
1 onion, quartered
3 celery tops or 1 large
   celery stalk, chopped
3 sprigs parsley
1 bay leaf
7 whole cloves
2 tablespoons butter
1 onion, finely chopped
1 clove garlic, minced
¼ cup flour
2 teaspoons curry powder
2 tart apples, peeled
   and diced
½ teaspoon salt
½ teaspoon pepper
½ teaspoon ground thyme
   Lemon, thinly sliced (optional)
   Hot cooked rice (optional)

In large Dutch oven combine chicken breasts, broth, carrots, onion, celery, parsley, bay leaf, and cloves. Bring to boil; skim off foam. Lower heat; simmer, covered, for 1 hour or until chicken is tender. Remove chicken from broth; debone, dice, and set meat aside. Strain broth into large bowl; discard spices and vegetables. Rinse pot and dry. Melt butter in Dutch oven; add onions and garlic. Sauté 10 minutes. Whisk in flour and curry powder until well blended. Add broth slowly, stirring constantly. Add chicken, apples, salt, pepper, and thyme. Cook over low heat 25-30 minutes. Garnish with lemon slices; may be served over hot rice.

Nell Whelchel Wiegand

Peasant Soup

A meal in itself served with good homemade bread. Perfect for an after-the-game supper.

Preparation: Average
Cooking Time: 4-5 Hours

Yield: 5 Quarts
Must Partially Do Ahead

Veal or beef shank with
    2 pounds meat attached
2 quarts cold water
3 teaspoons salt, divided
½ teaspoon pepper, divided
¼ cup oil
½ cup chopped celery
½ cup chopped spinach
½ cup chopped green pepper
½ cup chopped onion
½ pound thinly sliced
    pepperoni (skin removed)
2 cups diced turnips
2 cups diced white potatoes
2 cups diced carrots
2 cups small macaroni shells,
    cooked according to
    package directions
1 (20-ounce) can tomatoes
1 (10-ounce) package frozen peas
3¾ cups beef broth
1 teaspoon garlic powder
¼ teaspoon basil
¼ teaspoon red pepper
Parmesan cheese

Place shank in 5-quart kettle; add water, 1 teaspoon salt, and ¼ teaspoon pepper. Cover; heat until boiling. Reduce heat. Simmer 2 hours or until meat is fork-tender. Allow meat to cool in broth. Remove meat and bones; cut meat into bite-sized pieces. Chill broth; remove fat from surface. Heat oil in skillet; sauté celery, spinach, pepper, and onion until onion is golden. Heat broth to simmering; add contents of skillet. Add pepperoni, turnips, potatoes, and carrots. Continue simmering until vegetables are almost cooked. Add well-drained macaroni shells, tomatoes, peas, and beef broth. Season with 2 teaspoons salt, garlic powder, basil, red and black pepper. Reheat until very hot. Sprinkle each serving with grated Parmesan cheese.

Sally Butts Darden

Vegetable Soup Forever

It's not much more trouble to make a lot of soup than it is to make a little. What could be a more welcome sight in your freezer on a winter day?

Preparation: Easy
Cooking Time: 3-4 Hours

Yield: 16 Quarts

2½-3 pounds stew beef
12 tomatoes, peeled
2 large onions, chopped
8 carrots, sliced
¼ head cabbage, thinly sliced
4 cups sliced okra
4 cups chopped celery
2 teaspoons sweet basil
1 tablespoon salt
1 teaspoon pepper
4 (29-ounce) cans tomato sauce

Place beef in large, heavy soup kettle or Dutch oven; add just enough water to barely cover. Simmer, covered, one hour. Add remaining ingredients; simmer until meat separates easily with fork, about 3-4 hours. Soup freezes well, so you can have vegetable soup forever!

Julia Warlick Cromartie

Oxtail Soup

Preparation: Average
Cooking Time: 4 Hours

Serves: 4-6
Must Partially Do Ahead

1 large oxtail,
    cut into pieces
3 ribs celery, chopped
1 carrot, sliced
1 small turnip, sliced
1 small onion, stuck with
    3 cloves
¼ cup butter or margarine, melted
1 teaspoon peppercorns
4 pints water
    Bouquet garni (2-3 sprigs
    parsley, sprig of thyme, bay
    leaf - tied with string in
    cheesecloth bag. One-fourth
    teaspoon dried thyme may
    be substituted for fresh.)
1 teaspoon salt
½ teaspoon pepper
2-3 ounces port wine
1 tablespoon flour (optional)

Brown oxtail and vegetables in butter. Transfer to large pot or Dutch oven; add peppercorns, water, bouquet garni, salt, and pepper. Bring to boil. Reduce heat; simmer, covered, 4 hours (or cook 30 minutes in pressure cooker). Strain liquid into bowl. Chill until fat solidifies; skim off fat. Remove all meat from bones; add to broth. Add wine. Heat thoroughly. If desired, thicken soup with 1 tablespoon flour blended with ½ cup broth.

Kim McElhenney Humphrey

French Onion Soup

Preparation: Average
Cooking Time: 30-45 Minutes
Oven Temperature: 500°F

Serves: 4-6
Must Serve Immediately

3 tablespoons butter
2 large onions (Vidalia or
    Bermuda), thinly sliced
1 clove garlic, minced
    Salt and pepper to taste
1 tablespoon flour
6 cups beef or chicken stock
¼ bay leaf
¼ teaspoon thyme leaves
1 cup dry white wine
    (optional)
4-6 (1-inch thick) slices
    toasted French bread
½ cup grated Swiss cheese

Melt butter in soup kettle. Add onions, garlic, salt, and pepper. Cook, stirring, 15 minutes or until onions become golden brown. Sprinkle with flour; cook 3 minutes more, stirring constantly. Add stock, bay and thyme leaves. Cover; simmer over very low heat 30-45 minutes. Stir in wine. Pour hot soup into individual ramekins; soup should come almost to top. Float 1 piece toast atop each; sprinkle with cheese. Place ramekins in foil-lined baking dish. Bake at 500°F until cheese is melted and golden brown.
Micronote: Preheat browning skillet. Add margarine and onions. Return skillet to oven; cook 3-4 minutes on HIGH. Add flour and stock, bay and thyme leaves. Place in large bowl; cook on HIGH until mixture begins to boil, stirring several times (approximately 10 minutes). Reduce power to MEDIUM; cook 10-12 minutes. Add wine; continue as directed above.

Elaine Caras Waller

Springtime Soup

Preparation: Average
Cooking Time: 1 Hour

Serves: 12

1 cup chopped scallions
    or onions
6 tablespoons margarine
5 (14½-ounce) cans chicken broth
2 cups non-dairy creamer
2 potatoes, thinly sliced
2 carrots, thinly sliced
¼ cup regular rice
1 teaspoon salt
1 (10-ounce) package frozen
    asparagus, thawed and diced
1 (10-ounce) package frozen
    chopped spinach

In large heavy pan sauté scallions in margarine. Add chicken broth and non-dairy creamer, beating with wire whisk to blend. Add potatoes, carrots, rice, and salt. Bring to boil; reduce heat and simmer 15 minutes, until rice is tender. Add asparagus and spinach. Simmer at least 45 minutes longer.

Mimi Luebbers Gerding

Cream of Artichoke Soup

Preparation: Average
Cooking Time: 30 Minutes

Serves: 8

½ cup finely chopped onion
½ cup finely chopped celery
6 tablespoons butter
6 tablespoons flour
6 cups strained chicken broth
¼ cup lemon juice
1 bay leaf
¼ teaspoon ground thyme
1 (7.5-ounce) can artichoke
    bottoms, drained and
    chopped
2 cups half-and-half
2 egg yolks, beaten
  Lemon slices
  Chopped parsley

In large saucepan sauté onions and celery in butter until tender. Add flour; cook, stirring constantly, 1 minute. Slowly add broth and lemon juice, stirring until blended. Add bay leaf, thyme, and artichokes. Cover; simmer 20 minutes, until thickened. Mix cream and egg yolks; blend into hot soup, stirring constantly. Garnish with lemon slices and parsley to serve. [If soup is not to be served immediately, keep hot over large saucepan of hot water. If smoother consistency is desired, soup may be processed in blender or food processor (removing bay leaf first) and reheated. Freezes well too.]

Micronote: Heat margarine in large glass bowl or browning skillet 30-45 seconds. Stir in onions and celery; cook uncovered on HIGH 2½-3 minutes. Add flour, broth, lemon juice, bay leaf, thyme, and artichokes. Cover; cook on HIGH 12-14 minutes, stirring several times during cooking. Continue as directed above.

Variation: Cream of Oyster and Artichoke Soup - Substitute 1 pint chopped oysters, plus enough milk and a little water to equal 6 cups for chicken stock. Do not purée.

Anne Warren Thomas

Mushroom Soup

A luxurious homemade taste. No one will ever suspect you used a can opener!

Preparation: Easy
Cooking Time: 30 Minutes

Serves: 14

4 (10¾-ounce) cans cream of
    mushroom soup, undiluted
2 cups half-and-half
2 cups milk
1 (8-ounce) carton sour cream
1 (8-ounce) package process
    cheese spread
⅛ teaspoon cayenne pepper
1 pound fresh mushrooms, sliced
¼ cup dry white wine

Combine soup, half-and-half, milk, sour cream, cheese, and pepper in large saucepan. Cook over low heat until cheese melts. Stir mushrooms into soup. Cook over very low heat 20-30 minutes, stirring frequently. Stir wine into soup just before serving.

Joan Driskell Hopkins

Spinach Soup

Preparation: Average
Cooking Time: 30 Minutes

Serves: 8-10

¾ cup chopped onion
¼ cup butter, melted
2 (10-ounce) packages frozen
    chopped spinach, thawed
¾ teaspoon salt
¼ teaspoon pepper
¼ teaspoon ground nutmeg
3 cups hot chicken broth
3 tablespoons flour
3 cups milk, divided
2 egg yolks
1 cup whipping cream
    Sour cream

Sauté onion in butter until tender. Add spinach, salt, pepper, and nutmeg. Simmer until spinach is tender. Stir in chicken broth. Simmer 15 minutes. Purée mixture in blender; pour into large pot or Dutch oven. Make smooth paste of flour and ¼ cup milk. Stir into purée. Add remaining milk; cook over medium-low heat until mixture thickens and begins to boil, stirring constantly. Simmer 10 minutes. Beat egg yolks with cream; gradually add to hot soup. Stir until smooth. Reheat, but **do not boil**. Top each serving with a spoonful of sour cream.
Micronote: Cook frozen spinach on HIGH for 5 minutes. In covered 2-3 quart casserole combine butter and onions. Cook on HIGH 3 minutes. Add spinach, salt, pepper, and nutmeg; cook on HIGH 4 minutes. Add broth; cook on HIGH 8 minutes. Purée mixture in small amounts in electric blender, placing each completed batch in large covered cooker. Add flour and milk as above. Cook on HIGH until mixture begins to boil and thicken, stirring occasionally. Beat eggs into cream; stir into hot soup. Cook on MEDIUM 10 minutes; **do not boil**. Serve as above.

Pamela K. Spivey

Collard Green Soup

Any child of the South knows that you must eat hog jowls (or other pork), greens, and black-eyed peas on New Year's Day for good luck. Be adventurous and try this unusual soup, rich in heritage of our region.

Preparation: Average
Cooking Time: 1 Hour

Yield: 2½ Quarts
Must Partially Do Ahead

- ½ cup dried Great Northern beans
- 2 quarts water
- 1 small ham bone
- 1 small ham hock
- ½ pound beef short ribs
- 1 bay leaf
- 1 teaspoon salt
- 2 potatoes, diced
- 1 bunch fresh collard greens, chopped or 2 (10-ounce) packages frozen collards
- ½ onion, chopped
- ½ green pepper, chopped
- 1 blood sausage (Morzilla) or any smoked sausage, sliced
- 3 tablespoons bacon drippings

Soak beans overnight. In large soup kettle combine water, ham bone, ham hock, short ribs, bay leaf, and salt. Bring to boil; skim off foam. Lower heat; simmer approximately 30 minutes. Add beans; cook until tender. Add potatoes and collard greens. In skillet sauté onion, green pepper, and sausage in bacon drippings until onion is tender; add to collard greens. Bring to boil; cook uncovered for 10 minutes (this eliminates bitterness from greens). Cover; simmer until potatoes and greens are tender.

Tracy Kelly Gaines

Cauliflower Cream Soup

Preparation: Average
Cooking Time: 20-25 Minutes

Serves: 6

- 1 small cauliflower, quartered
- 1 small onion, quartered
- 2½ cups hot water
- 1 heaping tablespoon instant chicken bouillon or 4 cubes chicken bouillon
- ½ teaspoon salt
- ¼ cup flour
- ¼ cup margarine, melted
- 2 cups milk
- ¼ teaspoon nutmeg
- ¼ teaspoon pepper
- ⅛ teaspoon dill weed
- Shredded Cheddar cheese

Place cauliflower, onion, water, bouillon, and salt in saucepan; cook until vegetables are tender. Process in blender or food processor until smooth. In large saucepan stir flour into margarine; cook over moderate heat, stirring constantly, for 1 minute. Gradually stir in milk and continue cooking and stirring until smooth and bubbly. Add spices and cauliflower mixture. Cook over low heat until hot. Sprinkle cheese over each serving. (May be served cold; sprinkle just before serving with chopped parsley or chives instead of cheese.)

Micronote: Combine first 5 ingredients; cook on HIGH for 10 minutes. Process in blender or food processor until smooth. Blend margarine and flour in large covered container until smooth. Cook on HIGH for 1 minute. Gradually stir in milk; cook on HIGH until thick and bubbly, approximately 6 minutes, stirring twice. Add spices and cauliflower mixture. Cook on MEDIUM until hot. Sprinkle cheese on each serving.

Jane Hix Oliver

Baked Potato Soup

Preparation: Easy
Cooking Time: 30 Minutes

Serves: 2-4

1 cup sliced celery
¾ cup chopped onion
2 tablespoons butter
2 tablespoons flour
2 cups half-and-half, divided
½ cup water
1 tablespoon chopped
    fresh parsley
1 teaspoon chicken granules
    or 1 chicken bouillon cube
½ teaspoon salt
¼ teaspoon pepper
4 large baking potatoes,
    baked and cubed
    Grated Cheddar cheese
    (optional)
    Sour cream (optional)
    Chopped fresh chives
    (optional)
    Bacon bits (optional)

Sauté celery and onions in butter until tender. Blend flour with ¼ cup half-and-half. Add to celery and onions, blending well. Add water, parsley, bouillon, salt, and pepper. Simmer until heated, but **do not boil**. Add remaining half-and-half; heat through, but **do not boil**. Stir in potatoes. Serve with garnishes of choice.

Micronote: Sauté celery and onions in butter on HIGH for 3-4 minutes, stirring once. Stir flour into vegetables. Add ¼ cup half-and-half, water, parsley, bouillon, salt, and pepper. Cook, covered, on HIGH 3 minutes. Add remaining half-and-half. Cook on HIGH for 3 minutes; stir. Reduce power to MEDIUM and continue cooking until heated through; **do not boil**. Stir in potatoes.

Carol Dean Greene

Bavarian Cheese Soup

A Bavarian family recipe.

Preparation: Average
Cooking Time: 30-45 Minutes

Serves: 10-12

6 tablespoons butter
6 leeks, white part only, chopped
4 celery stalks, finely chopped
6 tablespoons flour
5 cups chicken stock
3 cups water
1 teaspoon salt
1 pound cream cheese,
    slightly warmed in
    double boiler
1½-2 cups plain yogurt,
    slightly warmed
4 egg yolks, beaten
    White pepper
    Fresh chopped chives
    or parsley

Melt butter in Dutch oven over medium-high heat. Add leeks and celery; sauté until leeks are transparent. Stir in flour; cook additional 3 minutes. Add stock, water, and salt. Bring to boil, stirring occasionally. Reduce heat; simmer, partially covered, for 15 minutes. Whisk cream cheese, yogurt, and egg yolks in medium bowl until smooth. Gradually add 2 cups soup mixture, thoroughly blending. Add to chicken stock mixture; stir over low heat until soup is heated thoroughly, but **do not boil**. Season with white pepper. Garnish with chopped chives or parsley.

David S. Flanary
Houston, Texas

Cream Soup Base

Preparation: Average
Cooking Time: 35-40 Minutes

Serves: 8

4⅔ cups chicken stock
8 ounces finely chopped
  vegetables (spinach,
  celery, asparagus,
  or broccoli)
¼ cup + 2 tablespoons
  finely chopped onion
1⅔ cups milk
⅔ cup cream
2⅔ tablespoons butter, melted
2⅔ tablespoons flour

Bring stock to boil. Add desired vegetables and onions. Simmer 30 minutes (for broccoli, 1 hour). Heat milk and cream until hot but not boiling; add to stock mixture. Whisk together butter and flour to form roux. Cook 5 minutes over low heat; do not brown. Add roux to cream mixture, stirring until thickened and smooth; **do not boil**. Adjust seasonings; hold until ready to serve.

Rudolph's Restaurant
Gainesville, Georgia

Bean Pot Soup

This takes a bit of time to assemble, but is not difficult. Put it on in the morning, and forget it until dinner.

Preparation: Average
Cooking Time: 6-10 Hours

Serves: 8-10
Must Partially Do Ahead

2 cups dried pinto beans
1 pound ham, cubed
4 cups water
4 cups chicken stock
1 (22-ounce) can tomato juice
3 onions, chopped
¼ cup chopped green pepper
3 garlic cloves, minced
3 tablespoons chopped parsley
4 tablespoons honey
1 tablespoon (or more)
  chili powder
1 teaspoon salt
1 teaspoon crushed bay leaves
1 teaspoon oregano
½ teaspoon cumin
½ teaspoon rosemary
½ teaspoon celery seed
½ teaspoon thyme
½ teaspoon marjoram
½ teaspoon sweet basil
¼ teaspoon curry powder
4 whole cloves
1 cup sherry
  Chopped green onions
    (optional)

Soak cleaned beans in water overnight. Drain. Combine all ingredients except sherry in soup pot. Cook slowly until beans are tender. Add sherry. Serve in generous soup bowls. Top with green onions.

Kaye Fairweather Mixon

Iced Cucumber Soup

Wonderful to dress up a cold dinner on a hot summer evening.

Preparation: Easy

Serves: 4
Must Do Ahead

3 cucumbers, peeled and seeded
3 green onions, including tops
1 cup chicken bouillon
1 cup sour cream
2 tablespoons lemon juice
1 tablespoon Worcestershire
1 teaspoon dill weed
½ teaspoon celery salt
¼ teaspoon paprika
Salt and pepper to taste

Combine all ingredients in electric blender or food processor. Process just until smooth. Chill well. Extra dill and paprika may be sprinkled over each serving.

Jane Hix Oliver

Natural flowers add much to the appearance of a table, and often divert attention from a very short bill of fare.

Mrs. E. R. Tennent, *Housekeeping in the Sunny South*, 1885.

Gazpacho

Serve in chilled bowls topped with a dollop of sour cream and sprinkled with fresh parsley and/or dill. It may be served alone, with crackers, or as an accompaniment to cold meat salad. Create a delightful low-calorie salad simply by adding unflavored gelatin and congealing.

Preparation: Easy

Serves: 4
Must Do Ahead

1 clove garlic
½ small onion
1 stalk celery
½ small green pepper
3 large ripe tomatoes, peeled
1 medium cucumber, peeled
1-1½ cups tomato-
    vegetable juice
3 tablespoons wine vinegar
2 tablespoons olive oil
1½ teaspoons salt
½ teaspoon dried basil
¼ teaspoon pepper
Dash Tabasco

Place all ingredients in order listed into electric blender or food processor. Process on high speed until vegetables are desired consistency; do not purée. Chill.
Variation: Gazpacho Salad - Measure Gazpacho. For each 2 cups soup, use 1 envelope unflavored gelatin. Soften gelatin in ¼ cup cold water per envelope; heat over boiling water, stirring until dissolved. Stir into soup. Pour into oiled mold. Chill until set. [May use ring mold to congeal. Unmold onto lettuce leaves; fill center with Avocado Dressing (page 93).]

W. Jackson Thompson

Classic Vichyssoise

Preparation: Average
Cooking Time: 30 Minutes

Serves: 4-6
Must Partially Do Ahead

6 **leeks (or substitute any VERY mild onion)**
1 **quart homemade chicken stock (very rich)**
3 **medium potatoes, peeled and finely diced**
1 **cup sour cream or whipping cream**
Salt to taste
Nutmeg to taste
Chopped chives

Finely slice only white part of leeks. In saucepan combine leeks, chicken stock, and potatoes. Bring to boil; simmer, covered, for 30 minutes or until potatoes are well cooked. Strain broth. Purée vegetables in blender or food processor. Combine broth and purée; chill overnight. Just before serving stir in sour cream; add salt and nutmeg to taste. Serve in **chilled** cups; top with chives.

Micronote: Combine leeks, stock, and potatoes in large glass bowl. Cook on HIGH until mixture boils, 10-12 minutes. (Will vary according to temperature of stock.) Reduce power to MEDIUM; cook 10-12 minutes longer or until potatoes are cooked. Strain broth. Continue as directed above.

Sherrie Nathan Schrage

Cold Apple Soup

This can also be served in wine glasses as an appetizer. Garnish with sour cream or whipped cream and dust lightly with ground cinnamon or nutmeg.

Preparation: Easy
Cooking Time: 20-30 Minutes

Yield: 3 Quarts
Must Partially Do Ahead

8 **Golden Delicious apples**
2 **cups apple juice**
Juice from 2 lemons
1 **tablespoon sugar**
1 **cinnamon stick**
1 **teaspoon vanilla extract**
2 **cups whipping cream**
1 **cup orange juice**
3 **tablespoons Cointreau or Triple Sec liqueur**
Nutmeg (optional)

Peel, core, and quarter 6 apples. Combine apples, apple juice, lemon juice, sugar, and cinnamon in large saucepan. Cover; cook over medium heat until apples are very soft, about 20 minutes. Cool; add vanilla. Cover; refrigerate 24 hours. Remove cinnamon stick. Purée apple mixture in blender or food processor until smooth. Add whipping cream and orange juice. Shred remaining 2 apples (unpeeled); stir into soup along with liqueur. Pour into chilled tureen. Sprinkle with nutmeg.

Joan Sidelinger Rigel

Cold Strawberry Soup

An appealing appetizer for a spring or summer luncheon - also good as a different light dessert. Other berries may be substituted for strawberries.

Preparation: Easy

Yield: 4 Cups
Must Do Ahead

2 cups fresh strawberries, washed and hulled
2 cups unsweetened pineapple juice
⅓ cup sifted confectioners' sugar
½ cup rosé wine
½ cup sour cream
   Whipped cream, sweetened
   Sliced fresh strawberries
   Fresh mint leaves

Combine strawberries, juice, and sugar in blender; process until smooth. Add wine and sour cream. Blend 2 minutes more. Cover; chill several hours. Garnish with whipped cream, sliced berries, and mint leaves.

Pamela K. Spivey

In the preparation of food three grand objects ought to be kept in view; first, to retain all its nutritive and other valuable dietetic qualities; second, to make it healthful; third, to make it pleasant to the eye and agreeable to the taste.

Mrs. Hill's New Cookbook circa 1890.

Honeydew Lime Bisque

A delightfully cool refresher. Try it when delicious honeydews are in season.

Preparation: Easy

Serves: 4
Must Serve Immediately

½ large honeydew melon, peeled and cubed
1 cup lime sherbet
½ cup chilled Christian Brothers Château La Salle wine
   Juice of ½ lime
   Mint sprigs (optional)
   Sliced strawberries (optional)

Combine all ingredients in food processor or electric blender. Process until smooth. Serve immediately in chilled bowls or bowls placed over ice. Garnish with mint sprigs or sliced strawberries.

Cookbook Committee

Luncheon Sandwich

Perfect for a ladies' bridge luncheon.

Preparation: Easy
Oven Temperature: 350°F

Serves: 1
Must Partially Do Ahead

1 chicken breast half, cooked
1 slice rye or pumpernickel bread
Butter
Swiss cheese
Lettuce
Tomato
Avocado
Special Thousand Island Dressing

Remove chicken from bone in large pieces; place on slice of lightly buttered bread. Cover with Swiss cheese. Bake at 350°F until cheese melts. Layer other ingredients in order given. Top with desired amount of Special Thousand Island Dressing.

Micronote: Cook sandwich at MEDIUM until cheese melts. Continue as above.

Special Thousand Island Dressing

2 stalks celery, finely chopped
1 hard-boiled egg, chopped
¼ cup finely chopped onion
2 tablespoons finely chopped green pepper
½ cup mayonnaise
¼ cup sour cream
¼ cup chili sauce
¼ teaspoon Worcestershire
⅛ teaspoon salt
Pepper to taste

Combine all ingredients; chill. Keeps refrigerated up to 10 days.

Sue Boykin Henson
Columbus, Georgia

Hot Chicken Sandwich

Preparation: Easy
Cooking Time: 25 Minutes
Oven Temperature: 350°F

Serves: 2

1¾ cups diced cooked chicken
½ cup sliced pitted ripe olives
½ cup mayonnaise
4 slices bread
Butter
3 hard-cooked eggs, sliced
1 (10¾-ounce) can cream of chicken or cream of celery soup
1 cup sour cream

Combine chicken, olives, and mayonnaise. Trim crusts from bread; butter both sides. Place 2 slices bread in glass baking dish; spread with chicken mixture. Add egg slices. Top with remaining bread. Blend soup and sour cream. Pour over sandwiches. Bake at 350°F 25 minutes or until top is lightly browned.

Lillian Wheeler Robinson

Gourmet Turkey-Chutney Sandwich

It looks a bit like a club sandwich but is so much more elegant. Appropriate for lunch, brunch, or dinner.

Preparation: Easy

Yield: 1 Sandwich

3 slices white, wheat, or rye bread
1½ ounces sharp Cheddar cheese spread
1 tablespoon chutney
1 canned pineapple ring, sautéed in butter and halved
2 ounces turkey, thinly sliced
1 leaf of leaf lettuce

Trim crusts from bread. Toast on each side. Spread one bread slice with Cheddar cheese spread. Spread chutney over cheese spread. Top with second bread slice. Place pineapple halves on each half of sandwich. Add turkey and lettuce. Top with third bread slice. Cut sandwich in half.

Gail Adams Thomas

I can cook pretty well myself on an emergency, but don't fancy it as a regular job.

Bill Arp

Shrimply Delicious Sandwich

Preparation: Average

Serves: 6
Must Partially Do Ahead

2 (4½-ounce) cans shrimp, drained
½ cup mayonnaise
¾ cup chopped celery
2 tablespoons chopped onion
2 tablespoons chopped sweet pickles
2 hard-cooked eggs, chopped
⅛ teaspoon pepper
Cheese bread slices
Tomato wedges
Celery sticks
Carrot sticks
Pickle slices

Rinse shrimp in cold water; drain well. Save 6 whole shrimp for garnish; cut remaining shrimp in half. Combine cut shrimp with mayonnaise, celery, onion, pickles, eggs, and pepper; chill. Spread on sliced cheese bread. Garnish with tomato wedges, celery sticks, carrot sticks, and pickle slices.

Variations: Shrimp Salad - Spoon filling onto lettuce leaf or use to fill a tomato.

Shrimp Croissant - Substitute shrimp filling for Walnut-Cream Cheese Filling in croissants (page 114).

Cathy McLanahan Nix

Tuna Cheese Flips

Preparation: Easy
Cooking Time: 18-24 Minutes
Oven Temperature: 375°F

Serves: 10

2 (6½-ounce) cans tuna,
    drained and flaked
⅛ teaspoon lemon-pepper
2 ounces (½ cup) shredded
    Monterey Jack or Cheddar
    cheese
⅓ cup mayonnaise
2 tablespoons finely
    chopped celery
1 tablespoon finely
    chopped onion
1 (10-ounce) can refrigerated
    biscuits
1 egg, beaten
1 cup crushed potato chips

Combine tuna, lemon-pepper, cheese, mayonnaise, celery, and onion. Separate dough into 10 biscuits; press or roll each to 5-inch circle. Spoon about ¼ cup tuna mixture onto center of each biscuit. Fold dough in half over filling; press edges with fork to seal. Brush each sandwich with beaten egg on both sides; press in crushed chips to coat. Place on cookie sheet. Make 2 (½-inch) slits in each top crust. Bake at 375°F for 18 minutes or until golden brown. (Chopped cooked chicken may be substituted for tuna, if desired.) To reheat, wrap each in individual foil packet; heat at 350°F for 10-15 minutes.

Cookbook Committee

Extra Special Burgers

Hamburgers don't have to be ordinary. Dress them up with one of these stuffings or, for a group, make all three and let guests choose their favorite.

Preparation: Easy
Cooking Time: 15-20 Minutes

Serves: 4

1 pound ground beef
¼ teaspoon salt
¼ teaspoon garlic salt
⅛ teaspoon pepper
1 tablespoon soy sauce
1 (2½-ounce) jar mushroom
    stems and pieces, drained
¾ cup grated Cheddar cheese
6 slices bacon, fried,
    drained, and crumbled
1 tablespoon dried parsley

Thoroughly combine ground beef, salt, garlic salt, pepper, and soy sauce. Divide mixture into 8 equal patties (patties should be thin). Combine remaining ingredients; divide evenly atop 4 patties. Place another patty on top of each; seal edges (may be refrigerated at this point until ready to cook). Cook on grill or under broiler to desired doneness.
Variations: Reuben Burgers - Combine 1 cup shredded Swiss cheese and 6 tablespoons well-drained sauerkraut. Use as burger stuffing instead of mushroom mixture.
Blue Cheese Burgers - Combine ½ cup crumbled blue cheese, ¼ cup sour cream, and ¼ cup drained sweet pickle cubes. Use as burger stuffing instead of mushroom mixture.

Jean Bennett Oliver

Open Face Bacon-Cheese Sandwich

Preparation: Easy
Cooking Time: 10 Minutes

Serves: 4
Must Serve Immediately

4 tablespoons butter or
    margarine, melted
2-3 tablespoons flour
1½ cups milk
½ cup grated Cheddar cheese
    (sharp or mild)
8 slices wheat bread or split
    English muffins, toasted
1 pound bacon, fried and
    drained
2 tomatoes, thinly sliced

Blend butter and flour. Cook over low heat until mixture is smooth and thick. Remove from heat. Stir in milk. Heat to boiling, stirring constantly. Boil and stir 1 minute. Remove from heat; stir in cheese until melted. If necessary, return to heat to finish melting, but **do not boil**. On each piece of toast place 3-4 slices of bacon. Top with tomato slices. Spoon hot cheese sauce over each sandwich. Serve immediately. (For a quicker version top each sandwich with a slice of American cheese and broil until cheese melts instead of making cheese sauce.)

Micronote: Melt butter on HIGH for 45 seconds. Add flour and milk. Cook on HIGH 4 minutes, stirring every 30-45 seconds, until thick. Add cheese. Return to microwave 1 minute or until cheese melts. Continue as directed.

Carole Ann Carter Daniel

Hamelot

Preparation: Easy
Cooking Time: 10-15 Minutes
Oven Temperature: 400°F

Serves: 4
Must Serve Immediately

4 slices white or rye bread,
    toasted
4 slices Swiss cheese
4 slices baked ham
16 spears asparagus
1 cup mayonnaise
1 tablespoon horseradish

Layer bread, cheese, ham, and asparagus. Bake at 400°F for 10 minutes or until cheese is melted. Meanwhile blend mayonnaise and horseradish in small saucepan. Heat just until warm. Spoon desired amount of sauce over each sandwich.

Micronote: Heat sandwiches on MEDIUM until cheese melts. Heat sauce separately on HIGH until warm, 1-2 minutes.

Patti Jenkins Chambers

Cream Cheese Sandwiches

A rich, creamy luncheon or tea sandwich.

Preparation: Easy

- 1 (8-ounce) package cream cheese, softened
- 1 ripe banana, mashed
- ½ teaspoon fresh lemon or lime juice
- ½ cup raisins
- ½ cup toasted nuts, any kind
- 4 slices fresh or canned pineapple, chopped
- Chopped dates, pears, apples, or strawberries (optional)

Yield: 4 Large or 16 Finger Sandwiches

Combine cream cheese, banana, lemon juice, raisins, nuts, pineapple, and any optional ingredient. Spread on whole wheat bread, raisin bread, or date nut bread.

Susan Barker Young

Vegetable Sandwich Spread

A good and different spread. Nice for party sandwiches.

Preparation: Average

- 3 cucumbers, grated
- 2 carrots, grated
- 1 onion, grated
- 1 green pepper, grated
- 1 envelope unflavored gelatin
- 2 tablespoons cold water
- ½ cup boiling water
- 1 cup mayonnaise
- 2 tablespoons vinegar
- 1 tablespoon salt
- Whole wheat bread

Yield: 15 Large or 60 Finger Sandwiches
Must Partially Do Ahead

Combine grated vegetables. Soften gelatin in cold water; dissolve in boiling water. Add to vegetables, mixing well. Add mayonnaise, vinegar, and salt; chill several hours or overnight. Spread on whole wheat bread.

Georgia Darden Marsh
Raleigh, North Carolina

Little Reubens

These go quickly at a party. It is wise to have the next batch prepared ahead to go into the oven.

Preparation: Easy
Cooking Time: 6-8 Minutes
Oven Temperature: 400°F

- 1 loaf party rye bread
- 1 (8-ounce) bottle Thousand Island Dressing
- 1 (8-ounce) can sauerkraut, drained
- 4-6 ounces corned beef, very thinly sliced
- 1 (6-ounce) package Swiss cheese

Serves: 36
Must Serve Immediately

Spread bread slices with Thousand Island Dressing. Add very thin layers of sauerkraut, corned beef, and Swiss cheese. Bake at 400°F for 6-8 minutes. (May substitute pumpernickel for rye bread.)

Cathy Cox Miller

Salads

Wood Sorrel

Wood Sorrel (Oxalis montana)

Wood sorrel is a rich source of vitamin C, but use it sparingly to add its distinctive tartness to coleslaw or a summer salad. As a summer drink or iced tea substitute, steep a handful of fresh sorrel leaves for ten minutes, strain, and pour over ice. Sauté sorrel leaves in butter; add chicken broth, rice, and seasonings for a tasty pottage.

On Salads

- For easier release of gelatin molds, rinse mold with iced water or lightly coat mold with oil, shortening spray, or mayonnaise before filling.
- When making aspic use a metal mold for easier unmolding.
- Substitute fruit juice for water when preparing gelatin.
- To hollow out tomatoes, regular or cherry, use a melon baller or an infant feeding spoon.
- Mushrooms can be cleaned easily in a salad spinner. Place mushrooms and 1 cup water in spinner; set in motion. This quick method keeps mushrooms from becoming soggy.
- New potatoes are best for potato salad. Cook potatoes with a bay leaf and some onion for extra flavor.
- A 1-pound cabbage yields 5 cups shredded cabbage.
- For a flavor booster sprinkle caraway seeds over coleslaw; or toss tangerine, orange, or grapefruit sections into basic cabbage slaw.
- For a quick topping over cold artichokes or asparagus, combine mayonnaise and fresh lemon juice to taste.

- Carrot curls make a pretty garnish for a salad. Prepare these curls by slicing carrots lengthwise into wide, thin strips. Soak in iced water until strips curl. Drain; store in refrigerator until ready to serve.
- Prepare flavored vinegars by adding stems and trimmings of a favorite fresh herb to a jar of vinegar; try thyme, rosemary, basil, or tarragon. The herb will flavor the vinegar for months. Fresh vinegar can be added to the jar to replace whatever is used.
- For homemade croutons sauté diced bread crusts in oil or butter with herbs or spices of choice. See pages 400 - 401 for suggested herbs.
- For an unusual garnish: Peel a long, narrow strip of orange, lemon, or lime rind by cutting around the fruit with a circular motion. Tie the strip into a bow and trim ends. Use to garnish a salad, beverage, or dessert.
- Always wash strawberries before removing caps. Sweeten berries only a short time before serving to keep them from becoming too soft.

Green Salad Unique

Unusual and delightful in flavor and appearance. This salad is a winner!

Preparation: Easy

Serves: 20

- 1 **pound assorted lettuces**
- 1 **pound fresh spinach**
- 2 **medium avocados, sliced**
- 1 **pint strawberries, halved**
- 1 **cantaloupe, cut in balls**
- 1 **pint cherry tomatoes, halved**
- 2 **cucumbers, sliced**
- 8 **ounces fresh mushrooms, sliced**
  Poppy Seed Dressing

Tear lettuce and spinach into bite-sized pieces, add remaining ingredients. Toss with Poppy Seed Dressing just before serving.

Poppy Seed Dressing

Yield: 1¾ Cups

- 1 **cup vegetable oil**
- ½ **cup tarragon vinegar**
- ½ **cup sugar**
- 1 **tablespoon poppy seeds**
- 1 **teaspoon salt**
- 1 **teaspoon dry mustard**
- 1 **teaspoon grated onion**
- ¾ **teaspoon onion salt**

Combine all ingredients in covered jar; shake well. Refrigerate until ready to use. (May be prepared ahead.)

Cathy McLanahan Nix

He knew . . . the smell . . . of watermelons bedded in sweet hay, inside a farmer's covered wagon; of cantaloupe and crated peaches; and the scent of orange rind, bitter-sweet, before a fire of coals.

Thomas Wolfe, from *Look Homeward, Angel*.
Copyright 1929 Charles Scribner's Sons; copyright renewed 1957 Edward C. Aswell,
Administrator, C.T.A. and/or Fred W. Wolfe.
Reprinted with the permission of Charles Scribner's Sons.

Potato Fresh

Preparation: Average
Cooking Time: 20 Minutes

Serves: 10-12
Must Do Ahead

- 8 **medium potatoes**
- 1½ **cups mayonnaise**
- 1 **cup sour cream**
- 1½ **teaspoons horseradish**
- 1 **teaspoon celery seed**
- ½ **teaspoon salt**
- 1 **cup chopped fresh parsley**
- 2 **medium onions, finely minced**

Boil potatoes in their skins until just tender. Cool slightly; peel. Cut into ⅛-inch slices. Combine mayonnaise, sour cream, horseradish, celery seed, and salt; set aside. In separate bowl mix parsley and onion. In large serving dish layer one-third of each: potatoes, mayonnaise mixture, and parsley mixture. Repeat twice, ending with parsley mixture. **Do not stir.** Cover; refrigerate at least 8 hours.

Kathryn Hamilton Millikan

Puttin' on the Ritz

A delicious gourmet salad for that extra-special meal.

Preparation: Average

Serves: 20
Must Partially Do Ahead

3 **(14-ounce) cans hearts of palm, drained and sliced**
3 **(15-ounce) cans artichoke hearts, drained and quartered**
1 **(4½-ounce) can ripe olives, drained and chopped**
2 **(2-ounce) jars diced pimientos, drained**
1 **(4-ounce) can chopped mushrooms, drained**
1 **tablespoon Worcestershire**
2 **teaspoons French mustard**
1 **teaspoon salt**
½ **teaspoon pepper**
½ **cup olive oil**
½ **cup tarragon vinegar**
  Juice of ½ lemon
⅛ **teaspoon oregano**
⅛ **teaspoon basil**
  Red leaf lettuce (optional)

Combine hearts of palm, artichoke hearts, pimientos, olives, and mushrooms; chill. In covered jar, blend Worcestershire, mustard, salt, and pepper. Add remaining ingredients; shake well. Chill at least 2-3 hours. Pour dressing over salad just before serving. For individual salad plates, spoon onto red leaf lettuce. (Very tart dressing; do not marinate vegetables in it.)

Susan Barker Young

The Ritz and the Waldorf and such haunts also serve our most exotic vegetable. They call it hearts of palm, but to us at the Creek it is, simply, swamp cabbage.

Marjorie Kinnan Rawlings, from *Cross Creek*.
Copyright 1942. Charles Scribner's Sons.
Reprinted with permission of Charles Scribner's Sons.

German Potato Salad

This tangy salad is a natural for picnics, as it does not require refrigeration.

Preparation: Easy

Serves: 6-8
Must Do Ahead

8-10 **new** potatoes (must use **new** potatoes!)
¼ cup cider vinegar
3 tablespoons oil
2-3 tablespoons water
½ teaspoon salt
⅛ teaspoon white pepper
2-3 green scallions, sliced

Boil potatoes 15-20 minutes. Drain; cool completely. Peel and slice **thinly**. Combine vinegar, oil, water, salt, and pepper; bring to boil. Pour over potatoes. Gently mix scallions and potatoes. Do **not** refrigerate. Let stand at room temperature 1-2 days, stirring several times.

Ellen Hinterkopf Jones
Dunwoody, Georgia

Bavarian Sweet and Sour Salad

A colorful and tasty do-ahead dish, even for non-fanciers of kraut! Try it as a zippy alternative to coleslaw.

Preparation: Average

Serves: 10
Must Do Ahead

⅓ cup vinegar
⅓ cup oil
1 cup sugar
1 (16-ounce) can Bavarian Sauerkraut
1 cup finely chopped onion
1 cup finely chopped green pepper
1 cup finely chopped celery
1 cup grated carrot
1 (2-ounce) jar chopped pimientos

Combine vinegar, oil, and sugar in small saucepan. Heat to boiling; stir to dissolve sugar. Remove from heat; set aside to cool. Combine and toss remaining ingredients. Pour lukewarm liquid over vegetables. Cover; refrigerate 24 hours. Keeps well for 1-2 weeks.

Katherine Wallace Shannon

Layered Walnut-Herb Salad

Preparation: Average

Serves: 6
Must Do Ahead

1 cup walnuts, divided
1 teaspoon salad oil
¼ teaspoon garlic salt
⅛ teaspoon dill weed
4 cups finely shredded lettuce or mixed greens
6-8 cherry tomatoes, halved
1 cup shredded Cheddar cheese
1 (10-ounce) package frozen green peas, cooked and cooled or 1 (16-ounce) can tiny peas
Creamy Dressing

Place walnuts in rapidly boiling water; boil 3 minutes; drain well. Toss with oil, garlic salt, and dill. Place on shallow baking sheet; toast at 350°F for 10 minutes, stirring once; cool. Layer ingredients in large glass bowl in following order: 2 cups lettuce or greens, cherry tomatoes (cut sides against glass), cheese, peas, ¾ cup walnuts, and remaining greens. Top with 1 cup Creamy Dressing; seal to edges of bowl. Cover; chill several hours or overnight. Before serving, sprinkle with remaining walnuts. Pass remaining dressing if desired.

Creamy Dressing

Yield: 1½ Cups

¾ cup mayonnaise
½ cup sour cream
2 tablespoons chopped green onion
1 tablespoon lemon juice
2 teaspoons chopped parsley
1 teaspoon prepared mustard
½ teaspoon salt

Combine all ingredients; blend well.

Debbie Jacobs Springle

Chutney-Rice Salad

Preparation: Average

Serves: 8-10
Must Do Ahead

1 cup mayonnaise
1 cup celery, sliced
½ cup chutney
4 green onions, sliced
1 teaspoon curry powder
  Salt to taste
1 cup raw rice, cooked
  and cooled
1 cup frozen peas, cooked
  and chilled
  Lettuce (optional)
  Tomatoes (optional)

Combine mayonnaise, celery, chutney, onions, curry powder, and salt. Toss with rice and peas. Cover; refrigerate several hours or overnight. Serve on lettuce leaf or as a filling for hollowed fresh tomatoes.

Charlotte Sterchi Sneed
Marietta, Georgia

Salad Nicoise

Preparation: Easy

Serves: 6
Must Partially Do Ahead

1 (8-ounce) can small potatoes,
  rinsed and drained
1 cup + 2 tablespoons olive
  oil, divided
7 tablespoons + 1 teaspoon
  wine vinegar, divided
1 (.7-ounce) package Italian
  dressing mix
  Salad greens
1 (16-ounce) can whole green
  beans, rinsed and drained
2 (7-ounce) cans tuna, drained
2 (8-ounce) jars marinated
  artichoke hearts, drained
1 (14-ounce) can hearts of
  palm, drained
3-4 tomatoes, cut into wedges
6 hard-cooked eggs, quartered
1 (2-ounce) can anchovy fillets
1 red onion, thinly sliced
  into rings
  Black olives
1½ teaspoons salt
1 teaspoon dried basil
1 teaspoon parsley flakes
¼ teaspoon freshly ground
  pepper

Slice potatoes into bowl. Combine 6 tablespoons olive oil, 2 tablespoons vinegar, and dressing mix. Pour over potatoes; marinate 1 hour. Line large platter with salad greens. Place potatoes in center. Surround with beans, tuna, artichoke hearts, hearts of palm, tomatoes, and eggs. Top potatoes with anchovy fillets. Arrange onion rings and olives over all. Combine remaining oil and vinegar with salt, basil, parsley, and pepper. Serve in separate container to accompany salad.

Cookbook Committee

Majestic Layered Spinach Salad

Preparation: Easy

Serves: 6-8
Must Do Ahead

1 cup cubed Swiss cheese
4 cups torn fresh spinach
4 hard-cooked eggs, sliced
2 cups sliced fresh
   mushrooms
1 (8-ounce) container soft
   cream cheese
½ cup sour cream
3 tablespoons milk
1½ tablespoons lemon juice
2 teaspoons sugar
¼ cup sliced green onion
4 crisply cooked bacon
   slices, crumbled

In 2-quart bowl, layer Swiss cheese, spinach, eggs, and mushrooms. Combine cream cheese, sour cream, milk, lemon juice, and sugar; blend well. Stir in green onion. Spread over salad to seal. Cover; chill several hours or overnight. Top with bacon before serving.

Judy Seitz Black

Honeyed Citrus Nut Salad

Preparation: Average
Cooking Time: 5 Minutes

Serves: 3-4

1 bunch red leaf lettuce
1 (11-ounce) can mandarin
   oranges, drained
3 green onions, chopped
1 teaspoon chopped fresh
   parsley
2 tablespoons honey
1 (4-ounce) package slivered
   almonds or chopped pecans
Sweet and Sour Dressing

Gently toss lettuce, oranges, onions, and parsley. Heat honey in skillet; add nuts and toss until browned. Sprinkle nuts over salad. Toss with Sweet and Sour Dressing.

Sweet and Sour Dressing
¼ cup salad oil
2 tablespoons vinegar
2 tablespoons sugar
½ teaspoon salt

Blend all ingredients well.

Linda Portman Spencer
Cumming, Georgia

Artichoke-Rice Salad

The addition of chicken or shrimp makes this a good main dish for a luncheon.

Preparation: Average

Serves: 6-8
Must Do Ahead

2 cups chicken broth
1 cup rice
¼ cup diced green onion
¼ cup sliced pimiento-stuffed olives
2 (6-ounce) jars marinated artichoke hearts, sliced
½ cup mayonnaise
½ teaspoon curry powder or 1 teaspoon dill weed
1 (8-ounce) can sliced water chestnuts, drained (optional)

Bring chicken broth to boil; stir in rice. Simmer, covered, until done. Cool slightly. Combine with remaining ingredients; chill thoroughly. (One 8-ounce package prepared chicken-flavor rice mix may be used, omitting butter, instead of chicken broth and rice.)

Marsha Harris Meadows
Lake Jackson, Texas

West Coast Salad

Preparation: Easy

Serves: 6

8 cups mixed salad greens, bite-sized pieces
1 (8-ounce) package chopped dates
3-4 oranges, peeled and sectioned
1 small purple onion, thinly sliced
¼ cup salad oil
2 tablespoons lemon juice
2 tablespoons toasted sesame seeds
1 teaspoon salt
1 teaspoon Worcestershire
¼ teaspoon pepper
1 avocado, peeled and sliced

Combine greens, dates, oranges, and onion in large bowl. Combine remaining ingredients, except avocado, blending well. Toss dressing and avocado with salad just before serving. (Salad and dressing may each be made ahead; combine just before serving.)

Emily Warfield Thompson

Coleslaw Divine

A very different and delicious coleslaw for a change of pace.

Preparation: Average

Serves: 6-8
Must Do Ahead

    4 cups chopped cabbage
    1 cup chopped green pepper
    1 cup chopped celery
    1 (8-ounce) can crushed
         pineapple, drained
  1-2 cups sliced green
         seedless grapes
       Salt, Accent, or Beau
         Monde seasoning to taste
    ¼ cup prepared Italian
         dressing
    ¾ cup toasted almonds

Combine cabbage, green pepper, celery, pineapple, grapes, and seasoning. Chill thoroughly. Just before serving, toss lightly with dressing and almonds.

Elizabeth Martin Jennings

Southern Caviar

Preparation: Easy

Serves: 6-8
Must Do Ahead

    2 (15-ounce) cans blackeyed
         peas, drained
    ½ cup chopped red onion
    ½ cup chopped green pepper
    ½ clove garlic
    ¼ cup vinegar
    ¼ cup sugar
    ¼ cup oil
    ½ teaspoon salt
    ⅛ teaspoon pepper

Mix peas, onion, pepper, and garlic. Combine remaining ingredients; pour over pea mixture. Cover; refrigerate at least 12 hours. Remove garlic; discard. Drain before serving.

Patricia Franklin Rauch

Cucumbers in Sour Cream Dressing

A zesty, sweet-and-sour taste.

Preparation: Easy

Yield: 1¼ Cups
Must Partially Do Ahead

    4 cucumbers, thinly sliced
    2 green onions, thinly
         sliced
    1 cup sour cream
    3 tablespoons vinegar
    2 tablespoons sugar
    ⅛ teaspoon salt
       Coarse black pepper

Combine cucumbers and green onions. Let stand in iced water 2 hours. Drain. Combine sour cream, vinegar, sugar, and salt. Pour dressing over cucumbers and onions; top with coarse black pepper. (May toss vegetables with dressing mixture and chill for later use.)

Cathy McLanahan Nix

Marinated Vegetable Medley

Preparation: Easy

Serves: 8
Must Do Ahead

1 (16-ounce) can whole
   green beans, drained
1 (16-ounce) can whole
   baby carrots, drained
1 (6-ounce) jar marinated
   artichoke hearts, undrained
1 (3½-ounce) can pitted
   ripe olives, drained
1 medium purple onion,
   peeled and sliced
   into rings
¼ teaspoon chopped
   pimiento (optional)
1 (8-ounce) bottle Italian
   dressing
   Parmesan cheese (optional)

Layer all vegetables in flat, shallow serving dish. Top with sufficient dressing to marinate. Sprinkle with Parmesan cheese. Cover; refrigerate until ready to serve, 10 minutes or overnight.

Anne Adel Adams Moore

Party Pea Salad

Preparation: Easy

Serves: 10-12
Must Do Ahead

3 (17-ounce) cans Le Sueur
   peas, drained
1 (8-ounce) can sliced
   water chestnuts, drained
2 (4-ounce) cans sliced
   mushrooms, drained
¼ cup horseradish sauce
2 tablespoons mayonnaise
½ teaspoon pepper
⅛ teaspoon salt
1 cup diced, peeled
   cucumbers, (optional)
1 cup diced celery
   (optional)
½ cup diced pimiento
   (optional)
½ cup sliced black
   olives (optional)
⅓ cup crumbled Blue
   cheese (optional)

Combine peas, water chestnuts, mushrooms, and other chosen optional ingredients. Separately blend horseradish sauce, mayonnaise, pepper, and salt. Toss lightly with vegetables. Cover; chill six hours or overnight. Keeps well 2-3 days.

Sissy Dunlap Lawson

Herbed Tomatoes

It wouldn't be summer in the South without luscious, home-grown tomatoes. Try these with grilled chicken or for a cold buffet.

Preparation: Easy

Serves: 8
Must Do Ahead

- 8 small ripe tomatoes, peeled
- ⅓ cup minced fresh parsley, divided
- ⅓ cup minced chives
- 1¼ teaspoons salt
- ¾ teaspoon dried leaf thyme
- ¼ teaspoon pepper
- ½ cup oil
- ⅓ cup tarragon vinegar

Sprinkle tomatoes with parsley, chives, salt, thyme, and pepper. Combine oil and vinegar; pour over tomatoes. Chill, covered, for at least 2 hours, occasionally spooning dressing over tomatoes. To serve, drain tomatoes; sprinkle with additional parsley.

Note: These tomatoes are especially attractive served in pyramid fashion in a compote-type serving dish or served on a tray with Marinated Vidalia Onions (page 42) and Zesty Broccoli Spears (page 262).

Carolyn McManus
Newton, Pennsylvania

Many herbes in the Spring time are commonly dispersed throughout the woods--good for broths and sallets, as violets, pirslins, sorrel, etc.

John Smith, *Colonial Kitchens, Their Furnishings, and Their Gardens*

Broccoli and Cauliflower Salad

Preparation: Average

Serves: 10-12
Must Do Ahead

- 1 head cauliflower
- 3 bunches fresh broccoli
- ½ pound fresh mushrooms, thinly sliced
- 3 green onions, thinly sliced
- 1 cup mayonnaise
- ½ cup sour cream
- ¼ cup sugar
- 2 tablespoons vinegar
- 1 teaspoon Worcestershire
- 1 tablespoon dill weed (optional)
- ¼ teaspoon salt
- ¼ teaspoon pepper
- ⅛ teaspoon Tabasco

Wash and drain vegetables. Break cauliflower and broccoli tops into small flowerets. Slice tender parts of broccoli stalks very thin. Place all vegetables in large bowl. Combine remaining ingredients; pour over vegetables. Toss lightly to coat. Marinate in refrigerator for several hours.

Sheri Woods Johnson

Gourmet Artichoke-Mushroom Salad

Preparation: Average

Serves: 8-10
Must Do Ahead

1 (9-ounce) package frozen
   artichoke hearts
1 (.6-ounce) package Italian
   salad dressing mix
1 cup thinly sliced fresh
   mushrooms
1 (3-ounce) package lemon
   gelatin
1¾ cups water, divided
1 tablespoon diced pimiento
1 cup mayonnaise

Prepare artichokes according to package instructions; drain and cool slightly. Halve artichokes; set aside. Prepare salad dressing according to package instructions. In large bowl combine dressing, artichokes, and mushrooms. Refrigerate 1 hour. Drain artichoke mixture, reserving dressing. Dissolve gelatin in 1 cup boiling water; stir in ¾ cup cold water. Refrigerate until consistency of unbeaten egg whites. Fold in artichoke mixture and pimiento. Pour into oiled 4-cup mold. Cover and refrigerate until set. In small bowl combine mayonnaise and reserved salad dressing, blending well. Unmold salad; top with mayonnaise mixture or serve separately.

Cheryl Gibbons McElveen

Vegetable Aspic

Aspic is always a luncheon favorite. This one is pretty to serve and full of goodies.

Preparation: Average

Serves: 8
Must Do Ahead

1 (3-ounce) package lemon
   gelatin
1 cup boiling water
¼ cup cold water
¼ cup white vinegar
1 (8½-ounce) can small
   peas, drained
1 (8½-ounce) can artichoke
   hearts, drained and
   chopped
1 (8-ounce) can French style
   green beans, drained
¼ cup chopped parsley
2 tablespoons chopped ripe
   olives
1 tablespoon chopped onion
¼ teaspoon salt
⅛ teaspoon pepper
⅛ teaspoon Tabasco
   Horseradish Dressing

Dissolve gelatin in hot water; add cold water and vinegar. Chill. When partially set, add remaining ingredients; pour into oiled 4-cup mold. Chill until set. Unmold; spoon Horseradish Dressing over top.

Horseradish Dressing

½ cup mayonnaise
½ cup sour cream
1 teaspoon horseradish

Combine all ingredients; blend well.

Lylla Crum Bowen

Congealed Asparagus Salad

Preparation: Average

Serves: 8
Must Do Ahead

2 (14½-ounce) cans
  asparagus pieces
1 cup sugar
  Juice of ½ lemon
½ teaspoon salt
2 envelopes unflavored
  gelatin
½ cup white vinegar
1 cup chopped celery
¾ cup chopped pecans
1 (4-ounce) jar chopped
  pimientos
1 small onion, finely
  chopped
1 (8-ounce) can sliced
  water chestnuts, drained
  (optional)

Drain asparagus, reserving juice. Add water to juice to equal 1 cup. Combine asparagus liquid, sugar, lemon juice, and salt; bring to boil. Soften gelatin in vinegar; stir into hot mixture to dissolve. Add asparagus and all remaining ingredients. Mix well; pour into oiled 6-cup mold. Chill until set. (May be served with a dressing made from ½ cup sour cream combined with ½ cup mayonnaise.)

Guynelle Williams Rushin

Variation: Creamy Asparagus Salad - Reduce sugar to ¾ cup. Follow above instructions until gelatin is dissolved. Whisk into gelatin mixture 1 cup sour cream. Continue as directed.

Eleanor Gibson Nalley

Tomato Aspic

Serve it basic, use the optional ingredients, or personalize it with your own additions. Whatever you do with it, this aspic will be a hit.

Preparation: Average

Serves: 4
Must Do Ahead

1¾ cups tomato juice
  or V-8 juice, divided
1 envelope unflavored gelatin
1 tablespoon lemon juice
½ teaspoon sugar
½ teaspoon Worcestershire
½ teaspoon grated onion
¼ teaspoon salt
  Few drops Tabasco
1 cup tiny shrimp (optional)
1 cup diced celery
  (optional)
½ cup sliced water
  chestnuts (optional)
½ cup chopped artichoke
  hearts (optional)
¼ cup sliced olives
  (optional)
¼ cup chopped green
  pepper (optional)

Combine ½ cup tomato juice with gelatin in small saucepan. Cook over low heat, stirring constantly until gelatin dissolves. Remove from heat; add remaining ingredients. Pour into lightly oiled 2-cup mold; chill until firm.

Vee Vee Smith Blackshear

Sanford House Cucumber Mousse

Preparation: Average

Serves: 6
Must Do Ahead

1 tablespoon unflavored
  gelatin
¼ cup cold water
2 large cucumbers, peeled
4¼ cups boiling water,
  divided
  Juice of 1 lemon
½ cup mayonnaise
½ cup sour cream
¾ teaspoon salt
½ teaspoon pepper
1 teaspoon Worcestershire
  Green food coloring
  Lettuce
  Sanford House Dressing

Soften gelatin in cold water. Coarsely grate cucumbers. Soak cucumbers in 4 cups boiling water and lemon juice for 10 minutes. Drain liquid and discard. Combine mayonnaise, sour cream, salt, pepper, and Worcestershire. Add several drops of green coloring. Dissolve gelatin in remaining ¼ cup boiling water. Combine cucumbers, cream mixture, and gelatin. Mix thoroughly. Pour into 6 lightly oiled individual molds; chill until set. Serve on lettuce with Sanford House Dressing.

Sanford House Dressing

½ cup sugar
1 teaspoon salt
1 teaspoon paprika
1 teaspoon dry mustard
1 teaspoon celery seed
1 cup oil
¼ cup tarragon salad vinegar
½ teaspoon grated onion

Combine dry ingredients in bowl of electric mixer. Add oil and vinegar alternately. Beat well after each addition. Add onion last. Hold at room temperature. (If refrigerating, dressing may separate; whisk it "back together." Also good on fruit, spinach, or mixed green salads.)

Elizabeth Martin Jennings

Frozen Pineapple Salad

Give this salad a festive appearance for the holidays by garnishing with red and green candied cherries.

Preparation: Average

Serves: 12
Must Do Ahead

1 (8-ounce) package cream
  cheese, softened
¼ cup sugar
¼ cup light brown sugar
1 (20-ounce) can crushed
  pineapple, drained
2 cups pineapple yogurt
1 teaspoon ground ginger
  (optional)
2 tablespoons chopped pecans
6 maraschino cherries,
  halved

In small mixing bowl, beat cream cheese and sugars. Stir in pineapple, yogurt, and ginger (if desired). Spoon into 12 cupcake liners placed in muffin pans. Spoon some of nuts over each salad; garnish with cherry half. Cover; freeze. Let stand at room temperature 10 minutes before serving.

Marian Martin Hosch

Gourmet Fruit Salad with Creamy Ginger Dressing

Preparation: Average

Serves: 8
Must Do Ahead

    2 (3-ounce) packages cream
        cheese, softened
    ¼ cup maple syrup
    1½ cups drained diced
        pineapple
    ½ cup chopped dates
    ½ cup chopped nuts
    1 cup heavy cream, whipped
    2-3 tablespoons chopped
        crystalized ginger
        Lettuce
        Creamy Ginger Dressing

Blend cream cheese and syrup. Stir in pineapple, dates, and nuts. Fold in whipped cream. Spoon into 2-quart container. Sprinkle with ginger. Freeze overnight. Serve on lettuce with Creamy Ginger Dressing.

Creamy Ginger Dressing
    1 cup French vanilla ice
        cream, softened
    ¼ cup mayonnaise
    1½ tablespoons chopped
        crystalized ginger

Combine all ingredients just before serving.

Alice Whitehead Paris

Frozen Fruit Salad

A very forgiving recipe. Vary fruits according to availability. If fresh fruits are unavailable, use canned fruits or well-drained fruit cocktail.

Preparation: Easy

Serves: 16
Must Do Ahead

    6 ounces cream cheese,
        softened
    ½ cup mayonnaise
    ¼ cup sugar
    ¼ cup lemon juice
    1 cup whipping cream,
        whipped
    1 (16-ounce) can dark
        sweet pitted cherries,
        drained, juice reserved
    1 (16-ounce) can pineapple
        chunks, drained
    2 cups sliced fresh peaches
    1 cup sliced fresh
        strawberries
    1 cup fresh blueberries
    3 bananas, sliced crosswise
    1 cup chopped pecans
        Lettuce leaves

Blend cream cheese with ¼ cup reserved juice from cherries (discard remaining juice). Add mayonnaise, sugar, and lemon juice; blend well. Fold in whipped cream, fruits, and pecans. Turn into 16-ounce cans, quart milk cartons, or loaf pans. Freeze. Slice to serve; place on lettuce leaf. Let stand at room temperature 10-15 minutes to slightly soften.

Joanne Portman McDonald

Sour Cherry Salad

Preparation: Average

Serves: 8
Must Do Ahead

1 teaspoon unflavored gelatin
2 tablespoons cold water
1 (16-ounce) can sour
   cherries
1 (8-ounce) can crushed
   pineapple
¾ cup sugar
1 (3-ounce) package
   cherry gelatin
   Juice of 1 orange
   and 1 lemon
   Rind from 1 orange and
   1 lemon, finely grated

Soften unflavored gelatin in water. Drain cherries and pineapple, reserving juices. Combine juices and sugar in medium saucepan; bring to boil. Remove from heat; add cherry gelatin and plain gelatin. Stir until dissolved. Stir in orange juice, lemon juice, and grated rinds. Chill until slightly thickened. Fold in cherries and pineapple; pour into lightly oiled 4-cup mold; chill until set.

Carol Ann Alexander Armstrong

. . . I think of that Thanksgiving dinner, served out of the Sunday dishes, on the very best tablecloth, with a fire burning brightly on the hearth and a bowlful of apples our cousin sent from Virginia polished to a high sheen for a centerpiece . . . .

Celestine Sibley, *Especially at Christmas*
Doubleday, Copyright 1969. Used with permission.

Cranberry Salad Ring

The definitive holiday salad. With the aid of a food processor, it can be prepared in less time than you might imagine.

Preparation: Average

Serves: 18-20
Must Do Ahead

1½ cups sugar
2 cups boiling water
4 (3-ounce) packages
   raspberry gelatin
½ cup cold water
2 cups fresh cranberries,
   ground
2 oranges, unpeeled,
   seeded and ground
2 apples, unpeeled,
   cored and ground
1 (20-ounce) can crushed
   pineapple, undrained
1 cup chopped pecans
   Lettuce
   Mayonnaise
   Orange slices

Combine sugar and boiling water; add gelatin. Stir until dissolved. Stir in cold water. Chill until slightly thickened. Combine cranberries, oranges, apples, pineapple, and pecans. Fold fruit into gelatin. Pour into lightly oiled 8-cup ring mold. Chill until set. Unmold onto lettuce leaves. Fill center of ring with mayonnaise. Garnish with orange slices.

Julia Warlick Cromartie

Ambrosia Mold

Preparation: Average

1 envelope unflavored gelatin
½ cup cold water
1 (15½-ounce) can
    unsweetened pineapple
    chunks
2 (3-ounce) packages cream
    cheese, softened
⅓ cup sugar
    Juice of 1 lemon
1 orange, peeled, sectioned,
    and diced
½ cup chopped pecans
½ cup flaked coconut
    Lettuce (optional)
    Lemon slices (optional)

Serves: 6
Must Do Ahead

Soften gelatin in water; let stand 5 minutes. Drain pineapple, reserving juice; add water to juice to make 1 cup. Place juice in 2-quart saucepan; heat to boiling. Add gelatin mixture, stirring until dissolved. Remove from heat; stir in cream cheese, sugar, and lemon juice. Whisk until cream cheese is well blended. Chill until gelatin is partially set. Fold in fruits, nuts, and coconut. Spoon mixture into lightly oiled 1-quart mold; chill until set. Unmold onto bed of lettuce; garnish with twisted lemon slice.

Sally Butts Darden

Bridal Salad

Prepare this attractive luncheon salad the day before. It's not difficult, but takes a bit of time.

Preparation: Average
Cooking Time: 12 Minutes
Oven Temperature: 400°F

2 cups crushed extra
    thin pretzels
1 cup margarine, melted
¾ cup sugar, divided
1 (8-ounce) package cream
    cheese, softened
1 (9-ounce) container frozen
    whipped topping, softened
1 (6-ounce) package
    strawberry gelatin
2 cups boiling water
2 (10-ounce) packages
    frozen strawberries
    Lettuce (optional)

Serves: 10-12
Must Do Ahead

Combine pretzels, margarine, and 3 tablespoons sugar; press mixture over bottom of well-oiled 12 x 9-inch pan. Bake at 400°F for 12 minutes; cool. Beat cream cheese and sugar with electric mixer or food processor until light and fluffy; fold in whipped topping. Spread evenly over pretzel layer; chill until firm. Combine gelatin and water; stir to dissolve. Add strawberries; stir and break apart until berries are thawed. Chill, if necessary, to slightly thicken gelatin. Spoon gelatin mixture over cheese layer. Chill until set. Cut into squares; serve on lettuce leaf.

Carolyn Cathey Brinson

Apricot Mousse Salad

This creamy delight also makes a good summertime dessert, served in parfait glasses and topped with sweetened whipped cream.

Preparation: Average

$^2/_3$ cup boiling water
1 (6-ounce) package apricot
   gelatin
1 (8-ounce) can crushed
   pineapple, undrained
$^1/_2$ cup sugar
1 (8-ounce) package cream
   cheese, softened
2 (3-ounce) jars strained
   baby food apricots
1 (13-ounce) can evaporated
   milk, thoroughly chilled
$^2/_3$ cup chopped nuts (optional)

Serves: 15
Must Do Ahead

Dissolve gelatin in boiling water. Add pineapple; heat until mixture simmers. Blend sugar and cream cheese. Add apricots and cream cheese mixture to gelatin mixture. Continue heating, stirring occasionally, until cheese melts. Remove from heat; chill until mixture mounds when dropped from spoon. Whip evaporated milk until peaks form; fold into apricot mixture. Pour into lightly oiled 6-cup mold; chill until set. Unmold; top with chopped nuts.

Jane Pattillo Lake

Heavenly Lime Salad

Preparation: Average

1 (3-ounce) package lime
   gelatin
1 cup boiling water
1 cup miniature
   marshmallows
1 (3-ounce) package cream
   cheese, softened
1 (8-ounce) can crushed
   pineapple
1 cup chopped nuts
1 package dry whipped
   topping mix
$^1/_2$ cup cold milk

Serves: 6-8
Must Do Ahead

Dissolve gelatin in boiling water. Melt marshmallows in gelatin mixture. Place cream cheese in small bowl. Pour small amount of gelatin mixture over cheese; mix with hand mixer until blended. Add cheese mixture to gelatin; blend until smooth. Drain juice from pineapple; add water to make 1 cup. Stir into gelatin mixture. Fold in pineapple and nuts. Chill until mixture begins to thicken. Whip dry topping with milk, according to package directions. Add to gelatin; blend with hand mixer. Turn into lightly oiled 6-cup mold. Chill until set.

Susan Bible Jessup

Mincemeat Salad

A holiday favorite! Good with turkey, chicken, or beef.

Preparation: Easy

Serves: 8
Must Do Ahead

- 2 cups orange juice
- 1 (6-ounce) package lemon gelatin
- 1 (28-ounce) jar mincemeat
- 1 cup chopped celery
- 1 cup chopped nuts
- 1 (8-ounce) can crushed pineapple, drained
- 2 medium apples, diced

Heat orange juice. Add gelatin; stir until dissolved. Stir in remaining ingredients. Pour into lightly oiled 6-cup mold. Chill until set.

Nancy Martin Brewer

Banana-Pineapple Cloud

Rich and creamy. As the name suggests - a heavenly concoction.

Preparation: Easy

Serves: 6-8
Must Do Ahead

- ¾ cup boiling water
- 1 (3-ounce) package cream cheese, softened
- 14 large marshmallows
- 1 (3-ounce) package lemon gelatin
- 1 (8-ounce) can crushed pineapple, drained
- ½ cup evaporated milk
- ⅓ cup mayonnaise
- 1 large banana, sliced

Combine water, cream cheese, and marshmallows in large, heavy pan. Cook over medium heat, stirring frequently, until marshmallows and cream cheese melt and blend together. Add gelatin; stir until dissolved. Stir in remaining ingredients. Pour into oiled 3-cup mold. Chill until set.

Judy Evans Harrison

Sunshine Salad

Preparation: Average

Yield: 1 (2-quart) Salad
Must Do Ahead

- 1 (6-ounce) package lemon gelatin
- ⅔ cup boiling water
- 1 (8-ounce) can crushed pineapple, drained, reserving syrup
- ⅔ cup evaporated milk
- 1½ teaspoons vinegar
- 1 (8-ounce) package cream cheese, softened
- 2 large carrots, grated
- ½ cup golden raisins

Dissolve gelatin in boiling water. Add syrup, milk, and vinegar to gelatin; blend well. Add cream cheese; blend until smooth. Add carrots, pineapple, and raisins; mix thoroughly. Place in oiled 2-quart mold. Chill until set.

Ann Ash Hartness

Delicious Summer Fruit Salad

Preparation: Average

Serves: 6-8
Must Partially Do Ahead

1½ cups cantaloupe balls
1½ cups honeydew balls
1½ cups fresh pineapple
    chunks
1 (11-ounce) can mandarin
    oranges, drained
1 cup fresh strawberries
1 cup blueberries
1 cup Bing cherries, pitted
3 fresh peaches, peeled
    and sliced

Combine all fruits in large serving bowl. Cover; chill at least 2 hours. Proceed as directed with chosen dressing. (Fresh apples, pears, or bananas may also be added just prior to serving.)

Dressing I:
Cointreau Dressing

1 (6-ounce) can frozen
    lemonade concentrate,
    thawed
¼ cup orange marmalade
2 tablespoons Cointreau
    or other orange-
    flavored liqueur
    Mint sprigs (optional)

Yield: 1 Cup

Combine all ingredients; mix well. Pour over fruit; add mint sprigs; toss gently. Serve immediately or refrigerate. (Works equally well as an appetizer, a salad, or a dessert.)

Emily Warfield Thompson

Dressing II:
Microwave Mint-Anise Dressing

¾ cup water
½ cup sugar
2 tablespoons fresh
    lime juice
¼ teaspoon anise seed
⅛ teaspoon salt
    Sprig of mint

Yield: 1¼ Cups

Place all ingredients in 2-cup glass measure. Microwave on HIGH for 3½ minutes. Cover; steep 10 minutes. Uncover; cool. Pour over fruit; chill at least 2 hours.

Diane Hally O'Kelley

Dressing III:
Orange Cream Dressing

½ cup thawed orange juice
    concentrate
⅓ cup granulated sugar
2 egg yolks, beaten with
    fork
2 teaspoons vanilla extract
1 cup whipping cream,
    whipped

Yield: 1½ Cups

Combine all ingredients except cream; blend well. Fold in whipped cream. Refrigerate. Spoon over chilled fruit just prior to serving. (Also delicious served over angel food cake or pound cake.)

Patti Jenkins Chambers

Dressing IV:
Sesame Sour Cream Dressing

Yield: 1½ Cups

1 cup sour cream
2 tablespoons light brown
  sugar
2 tablespoons sesame seeds
2 tablespoons milk

Mix all ingredients and chill. Keeps up to 2 weeks in refrigerator.

Susan Barker Young

Amelia's Cranberry Pears

This is an attractive and different way to serve cranberries during the holidays.

Preparation: Average
Cooking Time: 20-30 Minutes

Serves: 6
Must Do Ahead

3 fresh pears
1 (6-ounce) can frozen
  lemonade concentrate
2 (6-ounce) cans water
1 cup sugar, divided
2 cups fresh cranberries

Peel, halve, and core pears.Combine lemonade concentrate, water, and ½ cup sugar in skillet. Add pears; simmer, covered, until pears are almost tender, add cranberries and ½ cup sugar. Simmer 5-10 minutes more, until cranberries are tender. Chill. Remove pears onto serving plate with slotted spoon; spoon some of cranberries into each pear half.
Micronote: Place lemonade, water, ½ cup sugar, and pears in glass bowl. Bring to boil on HIGH; cook on MEDIUM 5 minutes. Add cranberries and ½ cup sugar. Bring to boil on HIGH; cook on MEDIUM 2-3 minutes. Continue as above.

Lynda Dickens Askew

Guacamole Salad

Preparation: Easy

Yield: 2 Cups
Must Do Ahead

2 small ripe avocados,
  peeled and mashed
1 medium onion, minced
1 large tomato, peeled
  and finely chopped
1 small clove garlic,
  crushed
½ teaspoon salt
½ teaspoon chili powder
1 tablespoon lemon juice
⅛ teaspoon Tabasco

Combine all ingredients; blend well. Cover; chill thoroughly. Serve over salad greens. [May also be served as a dip with corn chips or as a dressing with Gazpacho Salad (page 65).]
Variation: Avocado Dressing - Omit tomatoes; reduce onion to 1-2 tablespoons. Combine remaining ingredients plus ⅓ cup mayonnaise. Purée in blender or food processor. (If preparing ahead, withhold mayonnaise. Place purée in narrow bowl. Spread mayonnaise over top, sealing to edges. Stir in just prior to serving.)

Marilyn Woodberry McCarver

Molded Tuna Salad

Preparation: Average

2 envelopes unflavored
   gelatin
½ cup cold water
1 cup hot water
2 (6½-ounce) cans tuna,
   drained
1 cup cottage cheese
1 cup chili sauce
1 cup mayonnaise
2 tablespoons grated onion
1 tablespoon lemon juice
½ teaspoon Worcestershire
   Sliced stuffed olives
      (optional)
   Lemon wedges (optional)
   Parsley (optional)

Serves: 8-10
Must Do Ahead

Soften gelatin in cold water. Add hot water; stir until gelatin is dissolved. Combine all remaining ingredients except olives. Add to gelatin; mix thoroughly. Pour into oiled 6-cup mold. Chill until set. Unmold; decorate with olive slices. To garnish as fish, use fish-shaped mold. Use olive slice for eye. Remove pimiento from other olives before slicing; use for lines on fish. Halve remaining olive slices and cluster along back to resemble scales. Garnish serving platter with lemon wedges and fresh parsley. (Chopped shrimp or flaked salmon may be substituted for tuna.)

Jean Howard
Atlanta, Georgia

Chicken Salad Supreme

Preparation: Average

2½ cups cold cooked diced
   chicken
1 cup finely chopped celery
1 cup sliced white grapes
½ cup slivered toasted
   almonds
1-2 tablespoons minced parsley
1 teaspoon salt
1 cup mayonnaise
½ cup whipping cream,
   whipped
   Lettuce (optional)
   Avocado (optional)
   Tomato (optional)
   Pineapple (optional)
   Stuffed olives (optional)
   Chicken slices (optional)

Serves: 8

Combine chicken, celery, grapes, almonds, parsley, salt, whipped cream, and mayonnaise; mix well. Serve on lettuce, avocado half, or in scooped-out tomato or pineapple half. Garnish with olives and chicken slices.
Variation: For a very special occasion, use this salad to fill elegant "swans." Use half a pineapple, scooped out, as the base. Fill with Chicken Salad Supreme. Insert sprigs of fresh dill or parsley to give arch to the tail. Use fanned-out apple or melon slices to form the wings. The head and neck about 4 inches tall must be prebaked from a stiff dough until firm and lightly browned. (Ornament Dough, page 397, could be used.) Dip a slivered almond in red food color for the beak; insert into dough before baking. Insert wooden pick halfway into base of neck before baking; use to anchor head to pineapple.
Wine Suggestion: A white Zinfandel. Its pale amber-pink color is always pretty at a luncheon.

Patricia Franklin Rauch

Chicken-Avocado Salad

Preparation: Average

1½   cups avocado, cut into
     chunks
1   cup chicken, cooked
     and diced
1   cup cooked white rice
½   cup chopped celery
2   tablespoons mayonnaise
2   tablespoons sour cream
4   teaspoons lemon juice
1   teaspoon grated onion
½   teaspoon salt
¼   teaspoon pepper
    Lettuce (optional)
    Tomatoes (optional)
    Paprika

Serves: 4
Must Do Ahead

Combine all ingredients; chill thoroughly. Serve on lettuce leaves or in hollow tomatoes. Sprinkle with paprika.

Flo Criss Smith

Rice Salad à la Nicole

Everything your heart could desire. Just reading the ingredients will make your mouth water!

Preparation: Complex

2   cups cooked rice
1   (6-ounce) package frozen
     crabmeat, cooked
2   pounds lobster meat
     or 2 pounds scallops,
     cooked
¾   pound shrimp, cooked
     and peeled
1   cup cooked diced ham
1   (8-ounce) can black
     olives, sliced
4   stalks celery, chopped
1   large tomato, chopped
2   hard-cooked eggs, chopped
    Maggi Sauce
    Parsley sprigs (optional)

Maggi Sauce
1½   cups mayonnaise
1   tablespoon spicy brown
     mustard
2   teaspoons lemon juice
⅛   teaspoon Tabasco

Serves: 8
Must Do Ahead

Combine all ingredients in large serving bowl; toss gently with Maggi Sauce. Chill thoroughly; garnish with parsley sprigs just before serving.

Combine all ingredients; blend well.
Wine Suggestion: An elegant dry white such as a German Schloss Vollrads.

Polly Rourke
Tuxedo, North Carolina

Chicken and Brown Rice Toss

An elegantly different chicken salad.

Preparation: Average
Cooking Time: 45 Minutes

Serves: 4-6
Must Do Ahead

3 cups cooked brown rice
2 cups cubed cooked chicken
½ cup sliced celery
¼ cup sliced pitted
   ripe olives
2 tablespoons sliced
   green onions
½ cup mayonnaise
¼ cup Italian salad dressing
½ cup coarsely chopped
   cashew nuts
   Lettuce leaves

In mixing bowl combine cooked rice, chicken, celery, olives, and green onion. Stir together mayonnaise and Italian dressing; add to chicken mixture, tossing gently to coat. Cover; chill. Just before serving, add cashews; toss again. Turn into lettuce-lined salad bowl.
Wine Suggestion: A fruity white wine such as a California Chenin Blanc.

Jane Byerly Allgood

Gourmet Chinese Salad

Preparation: Average

Serves: 10-12
Must Do Ahead

1 (10½-ounce) package frozen
   English peas, cooked and
   drained
1 (5-ounce) package yellow
   rice, cooked according to
   package
2½ pounds peeled, cooked shrimp
1½ cups diced celery
½ cup chopped onion
⅓ pound fresh mushrooms,
   sliced
1 (14-ounce) can artichoke
   hearts, drained and sliced
   Soy Almond Dressing
8-10 cherry tomatoes

Combine peas, rice, shrimp, celery, onion, mushrooms, and artichokes in large bowl. Add Soy Almond Dressing; toss to coat. Cover; chill 5 hours or overnight. Garnish with cherry tomatoes.

Soy Almond Dressing
½ cup salad oil
3 tablespoons cider vinegar
2 tablespoons soy sauce
2 teaspoons curry powder
1 teaspoon sugar
½ teaspoon celery seed
½ teaspoon salt
½ teaspoon monosodium
   glutamate
¼ cup sliced almonds

Combine all ingredients, mixing well.
Wine Suggestion: A crisp dry white such as a French Sancerre.

Pamela K. Spivey

Party Chicken Pie Salad

A good luncheon dish. Serve with fresh fruit or congealed fruit salad.

Preparation: Average

Serves: 12-14
Must Partially Do Ahead

2 cups diced cooked chicken
2 cups diced celery
1 (9-ounce) can pineapple chunks, drained, juice reserved
1 (3-ounce) can English walnuts or pecans
1 small onion, finely chopped
1 cup sour cream
⅔ cup salad dressing
½ teaspoon salt
2 (9-inch) pastry crusts, baked and cooled
1½ cups grated sharp Cheddar cheese
Sliced green olives

Combine chicken, celery, pineapple, nuts, and onion. In separate bowl combine sour cream, salad dressing, salt, and ¼-½ cup reserved pineapple juice. Add half dressing mixture to chicken mixture; refrigerate overnight. To serve, fill crusts with chicken salad mixture. Spread with remaining dressing mixture. Garnish with cheese and olives.

Carrie McClain Hatfield

Mediterranean Pasta Salad

Preparation: Average

Serves: 10-12
Must Partially Do Ahead

1 (14-ounce) can artichoke hearts, drained and quartered
8 ounces sliced Genoa salami, diced
¾ cup black pitted olives
¾ cup sliced fresh mushrooms
½ cup Italian dressing
1 (8-ounce) package macaroni, cooked
¾ cup coarsely diced celery
½ cup diced green pepper
1 cup cherry tomatoes, halved
Salt and pepper to taste
Curly leaf lettuce
Swiss cheese strips (optional)
Onion, sliced into rings (optional)

Combine artichoke hearts, salami, olives, mushrooms, and dressing; toss to coat. Chill, covered, 1 hour or longer. Rinse macaroni in colander until cold; drain well. Toss macaroni, celery, green pepper, tomatoes, salt, pepper, and marinated mixture. Turn into bowl or platter lined with lettuce. Garnish with cheese and onions to taste.
Wine Suggestion: A light red French generic or a Beaujolais.

Elaine Caras Waller

Rose's Blender Mayonnaise

Preparation: Average

1 **cup oil, divided**
1 **egg or 2 egg yolks**
1 **tablespoon cider vinegar**
1 **tablespoon lemon juice**
½ **teaspoon salt**
½ **teaspoon dry mustard**
¼ **teaspoon sugar**
⅛ **teaspoon white pepper**
⅛ **teaspoon cayenne**

Yield: 1½ Cups

Place ½ cup oil, egg, vinegar, lemon juice, salt, mustard, sugar, pepper, and cayenne into clean, dry blender container. Cover; blend 5-10 seconds. Continue blending while very slowly pouring remaining oil into the center of other ingredients. Store covered in refrigerator. (If mayonnaise should curdle, place additional egg into washed and dried container; start motor. Without stopping, gradually add mayonnaise, blend until smooth.)

Variations: Anchovy Mayonnaise - Blend 3-4 anchovy fillets with mayonnaise.

Chutney Mayonnaise - Add 2 tablespoons drained chutney. (Use with chicken salad.)

Cream Mayonnaise - Use lemon juice instead of vinegar. Add ¼ cup cream, whipped. (Use with fruit salad.)

Cucumber Mayonnaise - Blend ½ peeled cucumber, 3 mint leaves with mayonnaise. (Use with fish salad.)

Blue Cheese Mayonnaise - Add ½ cup each equal parts Blue Cheese and sour cream; blend until smooth. (Use with fish, tomato, cabbage, potato, macaroni salads.)

Garlic Mayonnaise - Blend 2 large minced cloves garlic, more if desired, with mayonnaise. (Use with fish and meat salads.)

Curry Mayonnaise - Blend 1 teaspoon curry powder, 2 tablespoons tomato paste, ½ clove garlic with mayonnaise. (Use with seafood and egg salads.)

Herb Mayonnaise - Blend ¼ cup firmly packed fresh herbs, stemmed, with mayonnaise. Use parsley, chives, tarragon in any combination. (Use with molded fish, seafood, and egg salads.)

Russian Dressing - Blend with mayonnaise 1 cup chili sauce, 1 slice onion, 1 teaspoon drained grated horseradish.

Thousand Island Dressing - Add ¼ cup chili sauce, 6 pimiento-stuffed olives, 2 teaspoons drained sweet pickle relish, 1 hard-cooked egg; blend.

Ann Collins Hendrickson

Mayonnaise had a mystique. Little girls were initiated into it by being allowed to stand at the kitchen table and help make it, for making mayonnaise takes three hands.

Eudora Welty, *The Eye of the Story: Selected Essays and Reviews.*
Random House, Inc., Copyright 1978. Used with permission.

Lemon-Mustard Dressing

Preparation: Easy

Yield: 1 Cup
Must Do Ahead

½ cup vegetable oil
1 egg
3 tablespoons lemon juice
2 tablespoons Dijon mustard
2 tablespoons minced fresh
    parsley
2 teaspoons Parmesan cheese
1 teaspoon Worcestershire
⅛ teaspoon Tabasco
    Salt and pepper to taste

Combine all ingredients in 1-pint jar; shake vigorously. Refrigerate. Serve on salad of fresh greens; particularly good on spinach.

Cookbook Committee

Lemon Thyme Salad Dressing

A light, refreshing dressing for a mixed green salad. The flavor is better if made a day or two ahead.

Preparation: Easy

Yield: 3½ Cups
Must Do Ahead

2 cups oil
1 cup lemon juice
1 cup chopped parsley
4 small garlic cloves,
    minced
5 tablespoons sugar
3 tablespoons thyme
2 tablespoons grated
    lemon peel
2 tablespoons salt
½ teaspoon pepper

Combine all ingredients; blend thoroughly. Chill.

Spring Street Restaurant
St. Helena, California

Kumback Salad Dressing

When homemade dressing is this easy, there's no reason to buy the bottled variety.

Preparation: Easy

Yield: 2 Cups

1 cup mayonnaise
½ cup oil
½ cup chili sauce
2 tablespoons water
1 teaspoon prepared mustard
1-3 teaspoons Worcestershire
1 teaspoon pepper
1 teaspoon paprika (optional)
1 teaspoon horseradish
⅛ teaspoon Tabasco
3 cloves garlic, minced

Combine all ingredients in 1-quart jar. Shake well; refrigerate.

Jacque May
Cherokee, North Carolina

Creamy Garlic Dressing

Preparation: Easy

Yield: 2 Cups

¾ cup salad oil
⅔ cup light cream
¼ cup lemon juice
2 cloves garlic
1 teaspoon salt
½ teaspoon sugar
½ teaspoon paprika
¼ teaspoon white pepper

Combine all ingredients in blender. Cover; process at low speed until blended. Refrigerate.

Jacqueline Mabry Frankum

Mama's French Dressing

Preparation: Easy

Yield: 3 Cups

1 cup sugar
1 cup chili sauce
⅔ cup oil
⅔ cup vinegar
2 tablespoons instant
   minced onion
2 teaspoons Worcestershire
2 teaspoons salt
1 teaspoon garlic powder

Combine all ingredients in tightly covered container. Shake well; refrigerate.

Mary Hart Keys Wilheit

Hot Bacon Dressing

Preparation: Average

Serves: 8-10

6 slices bacon, cooked
   and drained
½ cup vinegar
½ cup sugar
2 eggs
¼ cup sour cream

Crumble bacon into small pieces; combine with vinegar. Cream sugar, eggs, and sour cream; add to bacon mixture. Cook over moderate heat, stirring, until thickened. Cool slightly; pour over spinach or mixed green salad. Serve immediately. (May prepare ahead and warm just before tossing with greens.)

Carolyn Hartford Mahar

Blue Cheese Dressing

This classic salad dressing also makes a tasty dip for raw vegetables.

Preparation: Easy

Yield: 1⅔ Cups
Must Do Ahead

½ pint sour cream
½ cup mayonnaise
¼ cup crumbled blue cheese
1 tablespoon vinegar
¼ teaspoon garlic salt
⅛ teaspoon pepper
3 drops Tabasco

Combine all ingredients; refrigerate 1-2 days before serving. Keeps refrigerated 3-4 weeks.

Grace Hooten Moore

Breads

Jack-in-the-Pulpit

Jack-in-the-Pulpit (Arisaema triphyllum)

The unique shape and varying shades of green make jack-in-the-pulpit one of the most distinctive wildflowers in North Georgia. The Cherokee Indians named this plant wild turnip or Indian turnip. Although the plant contains calcium oxalate, which is an irritant, its roots may be used in making bread and herb cookies. When first collected the corms are intensely acrid and must be cut and dried for at least five months before grinding and using, as the Indians did, as a substitute for flour.

On Bread

- Always remove bread promptly from its pan to keep bottom and sides from becoming soggy. Wrap in or cover lightly with a towel until cool to prevent drying.
- Bread dough is easier to knead if hands are lightly oiled or floured first.
- Add a little sugar to bread dough to help it rise more quickly.
- Dough has been kneaded enough when it springs back quickly after denting it with a finger; "blisters" will also appear along surface.
- Any yeast roll dough which is fairly firm can be formed into fancy shapes before proofing; let rise as directed and bake. Form crescents by rolling dough into a 12-inch diameter circle, cutting into 12 wedges, and rolling each wedge from wide end. Form knots by tying ½-inch diameter ropes of dough. Form cloverleaf rolls by placing 3 small balls of dough into each greased cup of muffin pans. Prepare pan rolls by placing 1½-inch diameter balls of dough in greased round cake layer pans, leaving ½ inch between balls. After rolls have risen brush lightly with an egg white-water glaze and sprinkle with poppy seeds, sesame seeds, or herbs.
- Leftover pancake batter? Dip bread slices into batter; sauté as for French Toast. Marvelous with cinnamon-sugar, jam, preserves, or syrup.
- To speed proofing of yeast dough:
  - Place dough in oiled bowl; cover with plastic wrap and then a hot, wet towel.
  - Place covered bowl on top rack of oven. Place large shallow pan on bottom rack; fill with boiling water. Quickly close door.
  - Bring 1 cup water to boil in microwave; boil 1 minute. Turn on oven light. Add covered bowl of dough to oven; quickly close door, allowing as little as possible of warm moist air to escape.
- To thaw frozen bread or rolls, wrap in aluminum foil and heat at 325°F for 5 minutes.
- When making biscuits add liquid gradually and mix dough only long enough to moisten ingredients. If using food processor, add liquid last and process just until dough forms a ball.
- Out of baking powder? Make your own: sift together 2 tablespoons cream of tartar, 1 tablespoon baking soda, and 1 tablespoon cornstarch; store in airtight container.
- Refrigerate or freeze flour if not used frequently.
- Flour is sifted during milling, so there is no need to sift unless specified in recipe. When measuring flour stir lightly then spoon into measuring cup and level with straight edge.
- Mix grated citrus rind and honey with softened butter for a flavorful spread on muffins or toast.
- Use fresh orange juice in place of milk in egg batter for French toast.

Beech Island Bread

This bread was made by the cooks in Beech Island, South Carolina. The baking, which was done with a handful of this and a pinch of that, was carefully watched until measurements were correct.

Preparation: Average
Cooking Time: 35 Minutes
Oven Temperature: 400°F

Yield: 5 (7 x 4-inch) Loaves
Must Do Ahead

1	cup shortening
1	cup sugar
2	tablespoons salt
2	cups very warm milk
1	cup boiling water
2	packages dry yeast
¼	cup lukewarm water
1	teaspoon sugar, (optional)
8	cups flour
4	tablespoons butter, melted

Place shortening, sugar, and salt in large bowl. Add milk and boiling water. Beat with electric mixer until shortening is melted. Dissolve yeast in lukewarm water to which 1 teaspoon sugar has been added. Add 2 cups flour to shortening mixture; beat well at medium speed. When mixture is lukewarm, add yeast, continuing to beat. Add 2 more cups flour, beating at medium speed. When dough becomes too stiff for mixer, work remaining flour in thoroughly by hand. Add enough to make soft dough. Knead 5 minutes. Cover bowl with towel; let stand in warm, draft-free place for 2 hours or until doubled in bulk. Punch down; divide and place into greased 7 x 4-inch loaf pans. Cover; let rise again until doubled in bulk, approximately 2 hours. Bake at 400°F for 35 minutes. Turn onto racks. Brush tops of loaves with melted butter. Cover loosely with towel while cooling.

Jane Eve Fair Wilheit

The breaking of bread, the sharing of salt, is too ancient a symbol of friendliness to be profaned.

Marjorie Kinnan Rawlings, from *Cross Creek Cookery*.
Copyright 1942. Charles Scribner's Sons. Reprinted with permission of Charles Scribner's Sons.

Communion Bread

Preparation: Average
Cooking Time: 45 Minutes - 1 Hour
Oven Temperature: 350°F

Yield: 2 Large or 4 Small Loaves
Must Do Ahead

1	cup All-Bran cereal
¾	cup sugar or equal amount of honey
1	tablespoon salt
¾	cup oil
2	cups boiling water
2	packages dry yeast
6-6½	cups unbleached flour

Mix sugar, oil, All-Bran, and salt in large bowl. Add boiling water; mix well. When mixture is lukewarm, stir in yeast. Add flour; mix well. Turn onto floured surface; knead 10 minutes. Place in covered bowl; let rise until doubled in bulk. Punch down; form into 2 large (or 4 small) loaves. Place in greased loaf pans. Let rise until doubled in bulk. Bake at 350°F until golden brown (45 minutes for small, 1 hour for large loaves). Test with wooden pick for doneness. Remove from pan to wire rack to cool. Dough may be prepared late in the day. Allow to rise overnight. Punch down early next morning. Shape into loaves; continue.

Judy Stover Tritt

Honey Whole Wheat Bread

Wonderful for sandwiches or serve with soup and salad.

Preparation: Average
Cooking Time: 45 Minutes - 1 Hour
Oven Temperature: 350°F

Yield: 2 (8½ x 4½) Loaves
     3 (7½ x 3½) Loaves
Must Do Ahead

  2 packages dry yeast
1¾ cups warm water
    (105-115°F)
  ¼ cup firmly packed
    light brown sugar
  1 teaspoon salt
  ⅓ cup honey
  ¼ cup oil
2½ cups whole wheat
    flour
3-4 cups bread flour,
    divided

In large bowl dissolve yeast in warm water. Add sugar, salt, honey, and oil; mix thoroughly. Stir in whole wheat flour and 2⅓ cups bread flour; mix well. If using mixer with dough hooks, continue adding 1-1½ cups bread flour; mix until dough holds shape. If mixing by hand, turn dough out onto floured surface; work in remaining 1-1½ cups flour. Knead 10 minutes; place in a greased bowl; turn to coat all sides. Cover; let rise until doubled in bulk, 1-2 hours. Punch down; knead lightly. Let rest 15 minutes. Shape into loaves; place into 2 well-greased (8½ x 4½-inch) loaf pans. Cover; let rise until doubled in bulk, 1 hour. Bake in center of oven at 350°F for 45-60 minutes. Remove from pans; cool on wire racks.

Doris Porter Jones

Onion Bread

A delicious bread! It goes well with all foods. Try making into hamburger buns for a real treat!

Preparation: Average
Cooking Time: 15-25 Minutes
Oven Temperature: 400°F

Yield: 2-3 Loaves, 36 Rolls, or 2 Braids
Must Do Ahead

  ½ cup sugar
  ½ cup shortening
  2 teaspoons salt
  1 medium onion, chopped
  1 cup milk, scalded
  2 eggs
  2 packages dry yeast
  1 cup warm water
6-6½ cups flour, divided
1-2 egg whites

Place sugar, shortening, and salt in large bowl. Combine onion and milk; add to sugar and shortening. Stir to soften shortening; cool. Beat eggs into shortening mixture. Soften yeast in warm water; stir into shortening mixture. Add 4 cups flour; beat until smooth. Add enough remaining flour to make soft dough. Turn out onto floured surface; knead until smooth, 8-10 minutes. Place dough in greased bowl, turning once to grease surface. Cover; let rise in warm place 1 hour and 15 minutes or until doubled in bulk. Punch down; let rest for 10 minutes. Divide into halves or thirds. Shape into loaves; place in greased loaf pans. Let rise 45 minutes or until doubled. Bake at 400°F for 25 minutes.
Variations: Onion Rolls - After first rising, shape into 36 rolls. Place on greased pans; let rise 1 hour. Bake at 400°F 15-20 minutes.
Onion Braids - After first rising, divide dough into sixths and roll each into a 15-inch long rope. Shape into 2 braids. Let rise until double. Brush tops with unbeaten egg whites; bake at 375°F for 20-25 minutes.

Carol Lynn Dobson Waggoner

One-Bowl Wheat Germ Casserole Bread

This bread has a wonderful, "nutty" flavor. Serve with soup to make a complete meal.

Preparation: Average
Cooking Time: 45 Minutes
Oven Temperature: 375°F

Yield: 1 Loaf
Must Do Ahead

2¾ - 3¼ **cups unsifted flour,
      divided**
  ½ **cup wheat germ**
  2 **packages dry yeast**
  2 **teaspoons salt**
  2 **tablespoons margarine,
      softened**
1⅓ **cups very hot tap water**
  2 **tablespoons molasses
      (room temperature)**

In large bowl thoroughly mix 1 cup flour, wheat germ, undissolved yeast, and salt. Stir in margarine. Gradually add water and molasses. Beat with electric mixer 2 minutes at medium speed, scraping bowl occasionally. Blend in ½ cup flour. Beat at high speed 2 minutes, scraping bowl occasionally. Stir in enough remaining flour to make stiff batter. Cover; let rise in warm draft-free place until doubled in bulk, about 45 minutes. Stir batter down; beat vigorously 30 seconds. Turn into greased 1½-quart casserole. Bake at 375°F for 45 minutes or until done. Remove from casserole; cool on wire rack.

Jane Reynolds Hemmer

Our mothers were sans mixes, sans foil, sans freezer, sans blender, sans monosodium glutamate, but their ingredients were as fresh as the day; and they knew how to make bread.

Eudora Welty, *The Eye of the Story; Selected Essays and Reviews*
Random House, Inc., Copyright 1978. Used with permission.

Fan-Style Bread

The Cake Box, a Gainesville tradition, shares its most famous recipe.

Preparation: Average
Cooking Time: 15 Minutes
Oven Temperature: 425°F

Yield: 4 (9 x 4-inch) Loaves
Must Do Ahead

  8 **packages yeast**
  2 **cups lukewarm water**
  ¾ **cup lard or vegetable
      shortening**
  6 **cups bread flour**
  ½ **cup + 2 tablespoons cake flour**
  ¼ **cup + 1 tablespoon sugar**
  1 **tablespoon +
      ½ teaspoon salt**
    Melted butter

Place yeast and water in large mixing bowl; stir to dissolve. Add shortening; stir to soften. Add all remaining ingredients except butter. Mix until dough leaves sides of bowl. Cover; let rise until doubled in bulk, approximately 1 hour. Divide into 4 portions. Round up each portion; let rest. Cut each portion into 12 pieces; stand pieces on edge in four greased 9½ x 4½ x 3-inch baking pans. Brush with melted butter. Let rise until dough is even with top of pan. Bake at 425°F for 15 minutes or until golden brown. Brush with additional butter; turn out on cooling rack.

*Vern Sayre
The Cake Box Bakery
Gainesville, Georgia*

Rye Bread

Preparation: Average
Cooking Time: 35 Minutes
Oven Temperature: 350°F

Yield: 2 Loaves
Must Do Ahead

    3½ - 4½ cups white flour or
        All-purpose flour
    2 cups rye flour
    1 tablespoon salt
    1 tablespoon caraway seed
    2 packages dry yeast
    ¼ cup margarine, softened
    2 cups very warm
        water (120-130°F)
    ⅓ cup molasses

Combine flours. In large bowl stir 2 cups flour mixture, salt, caraway seeds, and undissolved yeast. Add margarine. Gradually add water and molasses to dry mixture. Beat 2 minutes at medium speed of electric mixer, scraping bowl occasionally. Stir in enough additional flour to make stiff dough. If using dough hook, continue kneading 5 minutes. If not, turn mixture onto floured board; knead for 10 minutes or until dough is smooth and elastic. Shape into 2 round loaves; * place on greased cookie sheet. Cover lightly; allow to rise until doubled in bulk. Bake at 350°F for 35 minutes. To freeze: At indicated point (*) place loaves in freezer on ungreased cookie sheet; when frozen transfer to plastic bags. When needed remove from freezer; allow to thaw at room temperature (approximately 2 hours). Let rise additional 2 hours or until doubled in bulk. Bake as directed. **Variation: Rye Rolls or Rye Sandwich Buns -** Shape dough appropriately. Allow to rise and bake as directed, removing from oven when lightly browned.

Betty Dvorak
Valdosta, Georgia

Oatmeal Bread

Preparation: Average
Cooking Time: 45-50 Minutes
Oven Temperature: 350°F

Yield: 4 (9 x 5-inch) Loaves
Must Do Ahead

    2 cups rolled oats
    4 cups scalded milk
    2 packages dry yeast
    1 cup warm water
    1 cup molasses
    4 teaspoons salt
    ½ teaspoon ground ginger
    4½ cups white flour
    4½ cups whole wheat flour

Place oats and milk in large mixing bowl. Stir; let stand until lukewarm. Add yeast to water; let stand until foam forms on top. When yeast mixture has cooled, add to oats. Mix in molasses, salt, and ginger. Mix flours thoroughly. Stir 4½ cups mixed flour into liquid mixture. Mix with electric mixer at low speed. Gradually add remaining flour. If using heavy duty mixer with dough hooks, all mixing and kneading can be done by machine. If not, add final flour and mix by hand. Knead with dough hooks or by hand until dough is smooth and elastic. Place in greased bowl; let rise until doubled in bulk. Turn onto floured surface; punch down. Shape into 4 loaves. Place in well-greased (not oiled) 9 x 5-inch loaf pans. Let rise one hour or until almost doubled. Bake at 350°F for 45-50 minutes. If not serving immediately, turn onto wire rack to cool.

Kaye Fairweather Mixon

Irish Soda Bread

A delicious combination of flavors!

Preparation: Average
Cooking Time: 30 Minutes
Oven Temperature: 350°F

Yield: 1 (8-inch) Round Loaf
Must Do Ahead

- 2¼ - 2¾ **cups unsifted flour, divided**
- 3 **tablespoons sugar**
- 1 **tablespoon caraway seed**
- ½ **teaspoon salt**
- ½ **teaspoon baking soda**
- 1 **package dry yeast**
- 1 **cup buttermilk**
- 2 **tablespoons margarine**
- ¾ **cup dark seedless raisins**

In small mixing bowl thoroughly mix 1 cup flour, sugar, caraway seed, salt, baking soda, and undissolved yeast. Combine buttermilk and margarine in saucepan; heat until very warm, not boiling. Gradually add to dry ingredients. Beat with electric mixer 2 minutes at medium speed. Add ¼ cup flour; beat at high speed 2 minutes. Stir in raisins and enough additional flour to make soft dough. Cover bowl; let rise in warm place until doubled in bulk, about 1 hour. Punch down. Turn onto lightly floured board. Knead 20 times, forming smooth round ball. Place on greased baking sheet. Press dough to flatten into 8-inch circle. Cover; let rise in warm draft-free place until doubled in bulk, about 1 hour. Sprinkle dough lightly with flour; cut shallow cross in top of dough. Bake at 350°F about 30 minutes or until done. Cool on wire rack.

Kitty Carter Lane

One-Rise Whole Wheat Bread

A loaf of whole wheat bread, a bottle of wine, and Monterey Jack cheese make a special gift or an even more special picnic! Don't be afraid to tackle yeast breads. Here is an easy recipe with delicious results!

Preparation: Average
Cooking Time: 25 Minutes
Oven Temperature: 375°F

Yield: 2 (9 x 5-inch) Loaves
Must Do Ahead

- 2 **packages dry yeast**
- ½ **cup + 1 teaspoon sugar, divided**
- ¼ **cup warm water**
- 2 **cups milk**
- 2 **tablespoons shortening**
- 2½ **teaspoons salt**
- 5-6 **cups whole wheat flour**
- 2 **eggs, slightly beaten**

Dissolve yeast and 1 teaspoon sugar in water. Scald milk (very hot - steaming but not boiling). Place ½ cup sugar, shortening, and salt in large bowl of electric mixer. Pour hot milk over shortening mixture; beat at medium speed until dissolved. Cool to lukewarm. Add small amount of flour; beat at medium speed until blended. Add eggs; continue beating. Blend in yeast mixture. Add remaining flour, continuing to beat. If dough becomes too heavy for mixer, continue to blend by hand. Dough will be soft. Cover; allow dough to rise in warm place away from drafts. When doubled in bulk (about 2 hours), grease hands and punch dough down. Place in well-greased loaf pans. (A wet, rubber spatula smoothes the tops nicely.) Bake immediately at 375°F for 25 minutes. Buttering the top of the loaf upon removal from oven makes it slice easily. Turn out at once onto towel. Cover lightly; cool.

Jane Eve Fair Wilheit

Light Pumpernickel Bread

A native German's answer to "the real thing."

Preparation: Average
Cooking Time: 35 Minutes
Oven Temperature: 425°F

Yield: 2 Loaves
Must Do Ahead

　3　packages dry yeast
1½　cups warm water
　2　tablespoons caraway seeds
　4　teaspoons salt
½　cup molasses
　2　tablespoons margarine,
　　　softened
2¾　cups sifted rye flour
3¾　cups sifted white bread
　　　flour, divided
　　Corn meal
　　Melted margarine

Combine yeast and water in large mixing bowl; stir to dissolve. Add caraway, salt, molasses, and margarine; blend well. In separate bowl mix rye flour and 3½ cups white flour. Add flour mixture, ½ cup at a time, to liquids; mix well after each addition, until all flour mixture is incorporated. Sprinkle remaining ¼ cup white flour onto bread board. Turn out dough onto flour; knead until smooth and elastic (dough may remain slightly sticky). Place in large, well-greased bowl; cover with wet cloth. Set in warm place to rise until doubled in bulk, about 2 hours. Grease 1 large or 2 average baking sheets; sprinkle with corn meal. Punch dough down; divide in half. Form each half into smooth ball. Place on prepared baking sheet (s). Cover with damp cloth. Let rise in warm place 40 minutes. Brush tops of loaves with melted margarine. Bake at 425°F for 10 minutes. Reduce heat to 350°F; continue baking for 25 minutes longer. Transfer loaves to wire racks to cool. Brush with additional melted margarine if desired.

Doris Porter Jones

Beer Cheese Bread

Preparation: Average
Cooking Time: 35 Minutes
Oven Temperature: 350°F

Yield: 1 Loaf
Must Do Ahead

　4　ounces pasteurized,
　　　processed Swiss or
　　　American cheese, diced
　1　tablespoon butter
　1　tablespoon sugar
1½　teaspoons salt
¾　cup light beer
¼　cup water
　1　package dry yeast
2½　cups flour, divided

Combine cheese, butter, sugar, salt, beer, and water in saucepan; heat until warm. (Cheese does not need to melt completely.) Combine yeast and 1 cup flour in large mixing bowl. Add cheese mixture; beat with electric mixer at low speed until blended. Beat 3 minutes at medium speed. With wooden spoon stir in enough remaining flour to make firm dough. Turn out onto floured board; knead 3 minutes. Place dough in greased bowl; turn once. Cover with plastic wrap; let rise 45 minutes or until doubled in bulk. Punch dough down; roll into 14 x 7-inch rectangle. Cut into 3 long strips. Braid and shape strips to fit 1½-quart greased casserole. Let rise 30 minutes. Bake at 350°F for 35 minutes.

Jane Reynolds Hemmer

Lemon Tea Bread

Preparation: Easy
Cooking Time: 1 Hour 20 Minutes
Oven Temperature: 325°F

Yield: 1 (9 x 5-inch) Loaf

¾ cup margarine
1 cup sugar
3 eggs
2¼ cups flour
¼ teaspoon salt
¼ teaspoon baking soda
¾ cup buttermilk
   Grated rind of 1 lemon
¾ cup pecans
   Juice of 2 lemons
¾ cup confectioners' sugar

Cream margarine and sugar. Beat in eggs, one at a time. Combine dry ingredients; add to creamed mixture alternately with buttermilk. Mix well. Stir in lemon rind and pecans. Spoon into greased and floured 9 x 5 x 3-inch loaf pan. Bake at 325°F for 1 hour and 20 minutes or until cake tester inserted in center comes out clean. Cool 15 minutes in pan. Blend lemon juice and confectioners' sugar until sugar is dissolved. Remove loaf from pan; place on wire rack. Pierce top several times with toothpick. Spoon lemon glaze over warm loaf.

Marian Martin Hosch

Herb Bread

Great with any Italian meal.

Preparation: Easy
Cooking Time: 20 Minutes
Oven Temperature: 350°F

Yield: 1 (14-ounce) Loaf

½ cup butter or margarine,
   softened
2 teaspoons Parmesan cheese
1 teaspoon parsley flakes
½ teaspoon onion or
   garlic salt
½ teaspoon Italian seasoning
¼ teaspoon oregano
¼ teaspoon dill weed
¼ teaspoon celery seed
1 (14-ounce) loaf French
   or Italian bread

Combine butter and seasonings. Place bread on aluminum foil; slice crosswise into ½-inch slices. Spread herb-butter mix lightly on each slice. Spread remaining mix on top of loaf. Close foil; bake at 350°F for 20 minutes.

Bette Ferguson Edwards
Lincolnton, Georgia

Fresh Apple-Orange Bread

Preparation: Easy
Cooking Time: 1 Hour 15 Minutes
Oven Temperature: 350°F

Yield: 1 (9 x 5-inch) Loaf

  3   cups sifted flour
1½   teaspoons baking powder
  1   teaspoon baking soda
  1   teaspoon salt
  ½   cup orange juice
  2   eggs
  ½   cup shortening
1⅓   cups sugar
1½   unpeeled apples,
          cored and sliced
  ¼   unpeeled orange, seeded
  1   cup raisins
  ½   cup nuts

Sift together flour, baking powder, soda, and salt. Place orange juice, eggs, shortening, and sugar in blender; process until well blended. Add apples and orange; process until finely chopped. Add raisins and nuts; process 15 seconds. Stir into dry ingredients. Turn into greased and floured 9 x 5-inch pan. Bake at 350°F for 1 hour and 15 minutes.

Cynthia Sims Syfan

Berry Patch Bread

For a light lunch, bake in miniature muffin pans and serve with a fruit salad.

Preparation: Easy
Cooking Time: 35 Minutes
Oven Temperature: 350°F

Yield: 1 (13 x 9) pan or 3-4 Dozen Miniature Muffins

  1   (8-ounce) package cream
          cheese, softened
  1   cup sugar
  ½   cup margarine
  2   eggs
  2   cups sifted cake flour
  1   teaspoon baking powder
  ½   teaspoon baking soda
  ¼   teaspoon salt
  ¼   cup milk
  ½   teaspoon vanilla extract
  ½   cup raspberry preserves
          (can use strawberry jam)
  ½   cup chopped pecans
          (optional)

Combine cream cheese, sugar, and margarine. Beat with mixer until well blended. Add eggs, beating well after each. Sift dry ingredients; add alternately with milk, mixing well after each addition. Stir in vanilla. Pour into greased and floured 13 x 9-inch pan. Dot with preserves. Cut through batter with knife several times for marbled effect. Bake at 350°F for 35 minutes. For miniature muffins, bake at 400°F for 15-20 minutes.

Judy Evans Harrison

Georgia Peach Bread

Georgia cooks are constantly coming up with new ways to show off our delicious peaches. Freeze a loaf to remind you of the joys of summer.

Preparation: Average
Cooking Time: 1 Hour
Oven Temperature: 325°F

Yield: 2 (9 x 5-inch) Loaves

3 cups sliced fresh peaches
1¾ cups + 2 tablespoons
     sugar, divided
2 cups flour
1 teaspoon baking powder
1 teaspoon baking soda
1 teaspoon ground cinnamon
¼ teaspoon salt
½ cup shortening
2 eggs
1 cup finely chopped pecans
1 teaspoon vanilla extract

Purée peaches and 6 tablespoons of sugar in food processor or blender. (Mixture should yield 2¼ cups.) Combine dry ingredients; set aside. Combine remaining sugar and shortening; cream well. Add eggs; mix well. Blend in peach purée, then dry ingredients. Stir in nuts and vanilla. Spoon batter into 2 well-greased and floured 9 x 5 x 3-inch loaf pans. Bake at 325°F for 55 minutes or until done. Cool 10 minutes in pan; turn out on rack and cool completely.

Doris Porter Jones

Rich Banana Bread

Preparation: Easy
Cooking Time: 1 Hour
Oven Temperature: 350°F

Yield: 1 (9 x 5-inch) Loaf

½ cup butter
1 cup sugar
2 eggs
1 teaspoon vanilla extract
1 cup mashed bananas
    (2-3 fully ripe bananas)
½ cup chopped nuts
½ cup sour cream
1½ cups flour
1 teaspoon baking soda
½ teaspoon salt

Combine ingredients in order listed, mixing after each addition. Beat 1 minute. Bake in greased and floured 9 x 5-inch loaf pan or 2 prepared 7 x 3⅝-inch loaf pans, at 350°F for 1 hour. If spread is desired, see (page 294).

Cindy Collins Randolph

Light-as-a-Feather Refrigerator Rolls

Preparation: Average
Cooking Time: 10-15 Minutes
Oven Temperature: 450°F

Yield: 4 Dozen Rolls
Must Partially Do Ahead

1 cup shortening
1 cup sugar
1½ teaspoons salt
1 cup boiling water
2 eggs, lightly beaten
2 packages yeast
1 cup lukewarm water
6 cups flour
   (approximately)
¼ cup margarine or
   butter, melted

Place shortening, sugar, and salt in large mixing bowl. Add boiling water. Beat with electric mixer until shortening is melted and mixture has cooled slightly. Add eggs; continue beating. Dissolve yeast in lukewarm water. Add to shortening mixture, beating well. Add flour gradually, continuing to beat until soft dough forms. If dough becomes too stiff for electric mixer to handle, add remaining flour by hand. Cover; store in refrigerator up to 10 days. Remove desired portion to floured surface. Roll out to less than ¼-inch thickness. Cut with biscuit cutter. Brush surface with butter; fold over, pinching edges together slightly. Place on lightly greased baking sheet. Cover; let rise until doubled in bulk, 1½-2 hours. Bake at 450°F for 10-15 minutes. Brush tops with butter. (To always have hot rolls on hand; make out rolls and place in foil pans. Rolls should completely fill pan. Bake at 450°F until rolls are set but not brown. Remove from oven; butter tops. When cool, place pan of rolls in plastic bag; freeze. To serve, brown at 450°F for 10 minutes.)

Jane Eve Fair Wilheit

Cottage Cheese Rolls

Preparation: Average
Cooking Time: 20 Minutes
Oven Temperature: 350°F

Yield: 2 Dozen Rolls
Must Partially Do Ahead

2 packages dry yeast
½ cup very warm water
2 cups cottage cheese
¼ cup sugar
2 teaspoons salt
½ teaspoon baking soda
2 eggs, beaten
5 cups flour, approximately
   (all white or ½ white
   and ½ whole wheat)

Dissolve yeast in water. Heat cottage cheese in small saucepan over low heat until warm, but not hot (110°F if using temperature probe in microwave); remove from heat. Combine cottage cheese, yeast mixture, sugar, salt, soda, eggs, and 1 cup flour in large bowl; beat at medium speed of electric mixer 2 minutes. Gradually mix in remaining flour until soft dough forms. Place dough in greased bowl, turning to grease all sides. Cover, let rise in warm, draft-free place until doubled in bulk, about 1½ hours. Turn dough onto floured board. Divide into 24 equal pieces; shape each into a ball. Place balls into 2 greased 9-inch round pans. Cover; let rise 30 minutes. Bake at 350°F for 20 minutes.

Jean Bennett Oliver

Too little heat means pale wan doughy rolls, and too much means rolls of charcoal. When properly done, the rolls are light as feathers, done to great flakiness, hazel-nut brown, and of a flavor achieved under no other circumstances.

Croissants

A less-sweet version. These freeze beautifully, so make up a batch on a quiet day and keep in the freezer to turn any day into a special occasion. They may also be filled. (A cheese or meat filling is nice.)

Preparation: Complex
Cooking Time: 25 Minutes
Oven Temperature: 350°F

Yield: 36 Croissants
Must Partially Do Ahead

1 **package dry yeast**
¼ **cup warm water**
2½ **cups flour**
1 **tablespoon sugar**
1 **teaspoon salt**
1½ **cups + 3 tablespoons butter, divided**
1 **cup milk**
   Melted butter

Dissolve yeast in warm water. In mixing bowl or food processor mix flour, sugar, and salt; cut in 3 tablespoons butter. Combine dissolved yeast and milk; add to flour mixture. Blend to form soft dough. Turn onto heavily floured board or pastry cloth; knead 5 minutes, until dough is smooth and elastic. Place dough in greased bowl, turning to coat; let rise 1½-2 hours. Cream remaining 1½ cups butter. Punch dough down; turn onto floured board or pastry cloth. Roll into large rectangle, approximately ¼-inch thick. Spread ⅓ butter over ⅔ of rectangle. Fold unbuttered third to center of rectangle. Fold opposite side toward center to form 3 layers. Roll dough again into large rectangle. Spread with half remaining butter. Fold sides into center as before; roll again. Repeat process again with remaining butter. Refrigerate folded dough 2-3 hours. Divide into fourths. Roll each piece into a circle ¼-inch thick. Cut each circle into 9 wedges. Roll up each wedge beginning at long side. **Place, tips down,** on greased baking sheet; let rise 2 hours. If desired, brush with melted butter. Bake at 350°F for 25 minutes.

Connie Kemp Goldfarb

Tips for successful croissants:

1. *Temperature in your kitchen should be cool to keep buttery dough from becoming greasy; refrigerate dough at once if you see it becoming soft and shiny.*

2. *Try not to handle dough too much.*

3. *Be sure to let croissants rise maximum time before baking.*

Croissants with Walnut-Cream Cheese Filling

Croissants, especially the filled variety, have become the latest rage. Use the suggested filling or come up with your own.

Preparation: Complex
Cooking Time: 15-20 Minutes
Oven Temperature: 425°F

Yield: 8 Croissants
Must Do Ahead

1 package dry yeast
¼ cup warm water
⅓ cup milk, scalded
    and cooled
3 tablespoons sugar
1 tablespoon cooking oil
1 large egg, beaten
½ teaspoon salt
¼ teaspoon mace
2½ cups sifted flour,
    divided
½ cup butter, softened
1 egg white
1 tablespoon cold water
    Walnut-Cream Cheese
    Filling
3 tablespoons finely
    chopped walnuts

In large mixing bowl sprinkle yeast over water. Let stand 5 minutes. Add lukewarm milk, sugar, oil, egg, salt, and mace; blend well. Gradually blend in 2¼ cups flour. Turn out onto floured surface; knead slightly, until dough is smooth. Return to bowl, cover, and let rise in warm place until doubled in bulk (about 1 hour). Cream butter with remaining ¼ cup flour; set aside. Slightly beat egg white with cold water; set aside. Prepare Walnut-Cream Cheese filling; set aside. Turn risen dough back onto floured surface; punch down. Roll to 15 x 12-inch rectangle. Spread ⅓ of butter mixture evenly over ⅔ length of the dough, leaving ½-inch margins at sides and one end. Fold dough in thirds, turning end without butter inward first. Let stand 5 minutes; give dough half turn. Repeat roll-spread-fold-stand process 2 more times. Roll dough into 14-inch circle. Let stand 5 minutes. Cut into 8-16 wedges. Divide filling among wedges placing on broad end. Roll up; place with points down on greased baking sheets, curving ends. Let rise 15 minutes. Brush with egg white; sprinkle with walnuts. Bake at 425°F for 5 minutes, until lightly brown. Reduce heat to 350°F. Bake 15 minutes more, until nicely browned. Cool on rack. Serve hot or cold.

Walnut-Cream Cheese Filling

3 ounces cream cheese,
    softened
2 tablespoons sugar
¼ teaspoon grated orange rind
½ cup medium chopped
    walnuts

Combine all ingredients; blend well.

Jane Hix Oliver

Brioche

Preparation: Average
Cooking Time: 15 Minutes
Oven Temperature: 375°F

  1¼ **cups milk, scalded**
   ¼ **cup solid shortening**
   ¼ **cup sugar**
   2 **teaspoons salt**
   1 **package dry yeast**
   2 **eggs**
3½-4 **cups flour**
  4½ **teaspoons butter**
   1 **egg white, slightly**
         beaten

Yield: 18 Rolls
Must Partially Do Ahead
Must Serve Immediately

In large bowl combine milk, shortening, sugar, and salt, stirring until all is dissolved; cool to lukewarm. Add yeast; mix well. Blend in eggs. Gradually add flour. Refrigerate at least 2 hours or overnight. From ¼ of the dough, shape 18 small balls (approximately ¾-inch in diameter); set aside. Shape remaining dough into 18 muffin-like discs. Place in 18 greased muffin cups. With thumb make identation in each; fill with ¼ teaspoon butter. Top each with one small ball of dough. Brush tops with egg white. Let rise in warm place until doubled in bulk, approximately 1-1½ hours. Bake at 375°F for 15 minutes.

Joan Price Sites

Quick and Easy Spoon Rolls

Preparation: Easy
Cooking Time: 15-20 Minutes
Oven Temperature: 425°F

  1 **package dry yeast**
  2 **cups warm water**
  1 **egg, beaten**
 ¾ **cup margarine, melted**
 ¼ **cup sugar**
  4 **cups self-rising flour**

Yield: 24 Large or 48 Miniature Rolls

Dissolve yeast in warm water; let stand 10 minutes. Add egg, margarine, and sugar to yeast mixture, stirring well. Gradually add flour; mix well. Spoon into greased muffin pans. (For small rolls use an iced tea spoon and miniature muffin pans.) Bake 15-20 minutes, depending on size of muffin. Dough can be kept in refrigerator for 2 days. Do not stir before spooning into pans. Rolls can also be baked until almost done, cooled, and frozen. To serve; thaw, bake at 425°F for 5 minutes or until browned.

Patricia Horkan Smith

Popovers

Preparation: Easy
Cooking Time: 50 Minutes
Oven Temperature: 375°F

  2 **eggs, beaten**
  1 **cup milk**
  1 **cup sifted flour**
 ¼ **teaspoon salt**
  1 **teaspoon melted butter**

Yield: 8 Popovers
Must Serve Immediately

Combine eggs, milk, flour, and salt; blend until smooth. Stir in butter. Pour into 8 well-greased popover pans or small, deep custard cups, filling each cup half full. Place cups several inches apart in large, shallow pan. Bake at 375°F for 50 minutes or until puffed and golden. Remove popovers from cups to wire rack. Serve hot!

Elaine Caras Waller

Buttermilk Biscuits

Be prepared to make more than one dozen; these have a way of disappearing - especially when there are hungry men present!

Preparation: Easy
Cooking Time: 15-17 Minutes
Oven Temperature: 450°F

Yield: 12 Biscuits

       2 **cups self-rising flour**
     ¼ **teaspoon baking soda**
       4 **tablespoons shortening**
    ¾-1 **cup buttermilk**

Mix flour and soda. Cut shortening into flour until mixture resembles cornmeal. Add buttermilk; mix to form soft dough. (May be done to this point in food processor, using steel blade.) Turn onto floured board; knead lightly several times until dough is smooth. Roll to desired thickness. Cut with floured biscuit cutter. Place on lightly greased baking sheet. Bake at 450°F for 15 minutes or until golden brown. **Variation: Whole-Wheat Biscuits -** Substitute 1 cup whole wheat flour for half white flour. Add 2 teaspoons sugar. Proceed as above.

Theretha Neel McLemore

My father never forgot the taste of those biscuits, the big, crusty tender kind made with buttermilk and soda, with melted butter and honey, every blessed Sunday that came. "They almost made a Christian of me," he said.

Katherine Anne Porter, *Collected Essays & Occasional Writings of Katherine Anne Porter*
Delacorte Press/Seymour Lawrence, Copyright 1983. Used with permission.

Fluffy Baking Powder Biscuits

Have fun making these tasty biscuits with a "secret ingredient."

Preparation: Average
Cooking Time: 10 Minutes
Oven Temperature: 450°F

Yield: 12 Biscuits
Must Serve Immediately

       2 **cups sifted flour**
       4 **teaspoons baking powder**
       1 **teaspoon salt**
     ½ **cup solid shortening**
     ¾ **cup cold 7-Up beverage**
          Melted butter
             (optional)

Sift flour, baking powder, and salt into bowl. Cut in shortening, blending until mixture is like coarse cornmeal. Add **cold** 7-Up all at once. Stir with fork only until ingredients are evenly moistened. Turn onto lightly floured surface. Knead quickly 8-10 times. Roll to ¾-inch thickness. Allow dough to rest 5 minutes. Cut with floured biscuit cutter. Place on ungreased baking sheet; brush with melted butter if desired. Bake at 450°F for 10 minutes or until golden brown. Serve immediately.

Nancy Lawson Clark

Quick Butter Biscuits

Just right for the new bride - or any cook who wants homemade bread without spending a lot of time in the kitchen.

Preparation: Easy
Cooking Time: 10 Minutes
Oven Temperature: 425°F

Yield: 14-18 Biscuits

½ cup margarine or
   butter
3 cups self-rising flour
1¼ cups milk

Melt margarine in 2-quart oblong baking dish. Combine flour and milk to form soft dough. Turn on floured board; knead several times. Roll into 14 x 7-inch rectangle. Cut in half lengthwise, then crosswise into ½-inch wide strips. Turn each strip in melted margarine; place close together in baking dish. Bake at 425°F for 10 minutes or until brown.

Patsy Lothridge Hicks

...we should consider ourselves deficient in hospitality if we served a company meal without hot biscuits...biscuits that would have melted the heart of Sherman.

Marjorie Kinnan Rawlings, from *Cross Creek.*
Charles Scribner's Sons, Copyright 1942. Reprinted with permission of Charles Scribner's Sons.

Scones

An authentic touch of the British Isles. This recipe came from an historic English inn.

Preparation: Easy
Cooking Time: 15-20 Minutes

Serves: 8

1 cup flour
1 tablespoon baking powder
½ teaspoon salt
4 tablespoons margarine
¼ cup sugar
⅓ cup warm milk or water
¼ cup raisins (optional)
¼ cup chopped pecans
   (optional)
Milk
Honey-Butter Spread
   (optional)
Jam and cream
   (optional)

Sift flour, baking powder, and salt; cut in margarine until mixture is of sandy texture. Make well in center. Dissolve sugar in milk; add to well. Add raisins and nuts if desired. Mix lightly. Turn onto floured board; divide into 2 pieces. Roll each piece to ½-inch thickness. Use as 2 large scones or cut into small scones with biscuit cutter. Place on greased cookie sheet. With knife cut shallow cross halfway through rounds. Brush scones with milk; bake at 350°F for 15-20 minutes. Accompany with Honey-Butter Spread (page 294) or serve them the British way, with jam and fresh cream.

Kathryn Hamilton Millikan

Herbed Dinner Triangles

Preparation: Easy
Cooking Time: 10 Minutes
Oven Temperature: 375°F

Yield: 16 Triangles
Must Serve Immediately

6 tablespoons grated
   Parmesan cheese
½ teaspoon thyme leaves
½ teaspoon dill weed
   (optional)
½ teaspoon basil (optional)
1 egg white
1 tablespoon water
2 (8-ounce) packages
   refrigerated crescent
   dinner rolls
   Poppy seeds

In small bowl combine cheese and thyme, mixing well. (For a delicately-flavored roll, use only thyme; for heartier flavor, add dill and basil.) Set aside. In separate bowl lightly beat egg white and water; set aside. Separate dough into 8 rectangles. Press perforations together. Lightly brush each rectangle with egg white mixture. Sprinkle 6 rectangles with cheese mixture. Stack 3 cheese-topped rectangles; top with plain rectangle. Repeat. Cut each stack in half lengthwise and crosswise. Cut each quarter into 2 triangles. Sprinkle with poppy seeds. Place on ungreased baking sheet. Bake at 375°F for 10 minutes or until golden. Serve hot.

Cookbook Committee

Perhaps no bread in the world is quite so good as Southern cornbread, and perhaps no bread in the world is quite so bad as the Northern imitation of it.

Mark Twain

Crispy Cornsticks

Would it be the South without cornsticks? Serve as cornbread or split for creamed chicken or turkey open-face sandwiches.

Preparation: Easy
Cooking Time: 15 Minutes
Oven Temperature: 450°F

Yield: 14 Cornsticks

1 cup cornmeal
½ cup flour
2½ teaspoons baking powder
1 teaspoon sugar
½ teaspoon salt
⅛ teaspoon baking soda
2 eggs
1 cup buttermilk
2 tablespoons oil

Heavily grease cornstick pans. Place in oven to heat. Combine dry ingredients. Beat eggs with buttermilk and oil. Add to dry ingredients. Mix until smooth. Pour into hot cornstick pans. Bake at 450°F for 15 minutes or until brown. Works equally well baked in 9-inch square pan for 25 minutes.

Frances Jolley Syfan

Cracklin' Cornbread

Real connoisseurs of cracklin' bread insist it be crumbled into a bowl, topped with chopped onion (preferably Vidalia), sprinkled with salt and pepper, covered with fresh buttermilk, and eaten with a spoon!

Preparation: Easy
Cooking Time: 25 Minutes
Oven Temperature: 450°F

Serves: 8-10

¼ cup bacon drippings
2 cups plain or
    self-rising cornmeal
2 teaspoons baking soda
1 teaspoon salt
2 eggs, beaten
2 cups buttermilk
¾ cup cracklings
    (bits of skin and fat
    from rendered pork)

Place bacon drippings in 10 or 12-inch iron skillet. Place in oven which is preheating to 450°F. Combine cornmeal, soda, and salt. Stir in eggs and buttermilk. Fold in cracklings. When bacon drippings are very hot, remove from oven. Carefully swirl around skillet to coat. Pour drippings into batter; stir until well blended. Pour batter into hot skillet. Bake at 450°F for 25 minutes, until golden brown. (Diced fried bacon may be substituted for cracklings, but it's not nearly as good!)

Patsy Spiers Mercer

The way things were cooked was perhaps the main splendor--particularly a certain few of the dishes. For instance, the corn bread, the hot biscuits and wheat bread, and the fried chicken. These things have never been properly cooked in the North--in fact, no one there is able to learn the art, so far as my experience goes. The North thinks it knows how to make corn bread, but this is mere superstition.

Mark Twain

Corn Lightbread

Preparation: Easy
Cooking Time: 1 Hour
Oven Temperature: 350°F

Serves: 12-15

3 cups cornmeal
1 cup flour
¾ cup sugar
2 teaspoons baking powder
1 teaspoon salt
3 cups buttermilk
½ cup shortening, melted
2 eggs, slightly beaten

Combine all ingredients, mixing well. Spoon into well-greased 10-inch tube pan; let stand 10 minutes. Bake at 350°F for 1 hour or until done. Cool 5 minutes before removing from pan. (Recipe halves nicely. Bake in 9-inch square pan or 1½-quart round casserole.)

Jean Bennett Oliver

Hush Puppies

Hush puppies are no longer just a regional delicacy, but we Southerners still think we do them best. There is no better accompaniment to fried fish or seafood of any type.

Preparation: Easy
Cooking Time: 10 Minutes

Serves: 6
Must Serve Immediately

- 2 cups cornmeal
- 1 tablespoon flour
- 1 teaspoon baking powder
- 1 teaspoon salt
- ½ teaspoon baking soda
- 3 tablespoons finely chopped onion
- 1 cup buttermilk
- 1 large egg, beaten

Combine dry ingredients. Stir in onion and buttermilk. Blend in egg last. Drop by spoonfuls into hot oil in skillet of frying fish or immediately after removing fish. Hush puppies will float when done. Drain well on absorbent toweling. Serve piping hot.

Mary Hart Keys Wilheit

I do not know where, among the cornbreads, to place hush-puppies ... any huntsman would not exchange them for a plate of crepe suzettes ... Hush-puppies have a background, which is more than many fancy breads can claim.

Marjorie Kinnan Rawlings, from *Cross Creek*.
Charles Scribner's Sons, Copyright 1942. Reprinted with permission of Charles Scribner's Sons.

Appalachian Spoon Bread

Preparation: Easy
Cooking Time: 1 Hour
Oven Temperature: 350°F

Serves: 6
Must Serve Immediately

- 2½ cups water
- ½ cup uncooked grits
- 1½ teaspoons salt, divided
- 1 tablespoon butter
- 3 eggs, separated
- ½ cup cornmeal
- 2 teaspoons baking powder
  Butter
  Brown Sugar

Bring water to boil in medium saucepan. Stir in grits and 1 teaspoon salt. Cover; cook over low heat 30 minutes. Place 2 cups hot grits in mixing bowl. Stir in butter. Beat egg yolks until thick and lemon-colored. Gradually whisk into grits. Sift together cornmeal, ½ teaspoon salt, and baking powder. Stir into grits batter. Beat egg whites until stiff. Gently fold into batter. Pour into buttered souffle dish. Bake at 350°F for 1 hour. Serve hot. Top each serving with pat of butter and sprinkle of brown sugar.

Archer D. Smith
Atlanta, Georgia

Pecan Muffins

Especially good served with a fresh fruit salad.

Preparation: Easy
Cooking Time: 20-25 Minutes
Oven Temperature: 400°F

Yield: 10 Muffins

1½ cups flour
½ cup sugar
½ cup chopped pecans
2 teaspoons baking powder
½ teaspoon salt
1 egg, beaten
½ cup milk
¼ cup vegetable oil

Combine flour, sugar, chopped pecans, baking powder, and salt in a large bowl; stir well. Combine egg, milk, and oil. Make well in center of dry ingredients; pour in liquid ingredients and stir just until moistened. Fill greased muffin pans ⅔ full. (If using dozen-size pan, fill two remaining muffin cups with cold water to same level as muffin batter.) Bake at 400°F for 20-25 minutes. Remove from pan immediately.

Sandra Gilmer Souther

Banana Muffins

Preparation: Easy
Cooking Time: 15 Minutes
Oven Temperature: 300°F

Yield: 6 Dozen Miniature

½ cup margarine, softened
1 cup sugar
2 eggs
2 cups flour
1 teaspoon baking soda
⅛ teaspoon salt
½ cup raisins, chopped
½ cup pecans, chopped
3 ripe bananas, mashed
1 teaspoon vanilla extract

Cream margarine and sugar. Add eggs, one at a time, beating well after each. Combine flour, soda, and salt; add to creamed mixture. Fold in remaining ingredients. Pour into small muffin pans that have been greased or lined with paper baking cups. Bake at 300°F for 15 minutes.

Carolyn Elliott Smith

Variations: Surprise Muffins - Omit raisins and nuts. Spoon batter into greased regular muffin pans, filling ⅓ full. Spoon 1 teaspoon strawberry preserves into center of each muffin; spoon remaining batter over preserves, filling each cup ⅔ full.

Carolyn Cathey Brinson

Banana Picnic Cupcakes - Bake as directed. Cool. Ice with Cream Cheese Icing (page 362) or Easy Peanut Butter Icing (page 326).

Debbie Holder Kelly

Blueberry Muffins

Preparation: Easy
Cooking Time: 20 Minutes
Oven Temperature: 425°F

Yield: 12 Muffins

    1 egg
    ½ cug sugar
    ½ cup melted butter,
        margarine or oil
    2 cups sifted flour
    2 teaspoons baking powder
    ⅛ teaspoon salt
    ¾ cup milk
    1 cup blueberries
        (well-floured)

Combine egg, sugar, and shortening. Blend well. Sift dry ingredients together. Add to egg mixture. Add milk and blueberries. Mix with wooden spoon **only** until flour is moistened. Pour into muffin pans which have been greased or lined with paper baking cups. Bake at 425°F for approximately 20 minutes. (Time varies according to size pans used.)

Frances Rozier Birdsong
Sparta, Georgia

Molasses Muffins

Preparation: Easy
Cooking Time: 15 Minutes
Oven Temperature: 400°F

Yield: 42 Muffins

    1¼ cups margarine, softened
    1 cup sugar
    4 eggs
    ½ cup molasses
    2 teaspoons baking soda
    1 cup buttermilk
    4 cups self-rising flour
    ½ teaspoon cinnamon
    ¼ teaspoon ginger
    1 cup raisins

In large bowl of electric mixer cream margarine and sugar. Add eggs, one at a time, beating well after each. Add molasses. Combine soda with buttermilk; add to mixture, blending well. Sift flour and spices; add to molasses mixture. Blend well. Stir in raisins. Fill greased muffin pans ⅔ full. Bake at 400°F for 15 minutes. Batter will keep in refrigerator tightly covered for 2 weeks.

Sandra Gilmer Souther

Wheat Germ Muffins

Kids of all ages will love these muffins, and they're nutritious too!

Preparation: Easy
Cooking Time: 20 Minutes
Oven Temperature: 375°F

Yield: 6 Muffins

    ⅔ cup packaged biscuit mix
    ⅓ cup wheat germ
    ¼ cup sugar
    1 egg, slightly beaten
    ⅓ cup water
    2 tablespoons peanut butter
    ½ teaspoon vanilla extract
        Butter curls (optional)

In mixing bowl combine biscuit mix, wheat germ, and sugar. In separate small bowl combine egg, water, peanut butter, and vanilla; beat until smooth with rotary beater. Add egg mixture to dry ingredients, stirring only until dry ingredients are moistened. (Do not over-mix.) Spoon batter into greased 2½-inch muffin pans, filling cups ⅔ full. Bake at 375°F for 20 minutes or until golden brown. Serve with butter curls if desired.

Gail Adams Thomas

Orange Sour Cream Muffins

Preparation: Easy
Cooking Time: 12 Minutes
Oven Temperature: 375°F

Yield: 16-18 Muffins

- 6 tablespoons butter, softened
- 1 cup sugar
- 1 egg
- ½ cup sour cream
- 2 tablespoons + 2 teaspoons orange juice
- 2 tablespoons grated orange rind
- ½ teaspoon orange extract
- 1¼ cups flour
- ½ teaspoon baking soda
- ½ teaspoon salt
- ½ cup chopped pecans
  Honey-Butter Spread (optional)

Cream butter and sugar. Beat in egg. Fold in sour cream, orange juice, rind, and extract. Sift dry ingredients; add to orange mixture, blending well. Stir in pecans. Fill greased muffin pans ½-¾ full. Bake at 375°F for 12 minutes. Serve with Honey-Butter Spread (page 294).

Suzanne Gardner Sullivan
Valdosta, Georgia

French Toast

Serve with a broiled ham slice and broiled peach half which has been filled with a mixture of butter, brown sugar, and cinnamon.

Preparation: Easy
Cooking Time: About 8 Minutes for Each Batch

Serves: 4
Must Partially Do Ahead

- 8 slices French bread, ¾-inch thick
- 4 eggs
- 1 cup milk
- 2 tablespoons Grand Marnier or other orange-flavored liqueur
- 1 tablespoon sugar
- ½ teaspoon vanilla extract
- ¼ teaspoon salt
- 2 tablespoons butter or margarine
  Confectioners' sugar

Arrange bread in single layer in 12 x 8 x 2-inch baking dish. Combine eggs, milk, Grand Marnier, sugar, vanilla, and salt in medium bowl; beat until well blended. Pour over bread; turn slices to coat evenly. Cover; refrigerate overnight. Melt butter in skillet; sauté bread in butter until golden, about 4 minutes on each side. Sprinkle with confectioners' sugar.
Variations: Cinnamon French Toast - Add ½ teaspoon cinnamon to egg mixture with or without liqueur.

Nell Cromer Freeman
Stillwater, Oklahoma

Amaretto French Toast - Substitute 1 tablespoon Amaretto for orange liqueur; proceed as directed above. Top with apricot preserves, whipped cream, and chopped nuts.

Judy Ferguson Field

Apple Pancakes with Cinnamon Cream Syrup

These fabulous pancakes with syrup are a snap to make. We think you'll agree they are among the best you have ever eaten.

Preparation: Easy
Cooking Time: 10 Minutes

Yield: 15-20 Pancakes
Must Serve Immediately

Apple Pancakes

    1 egg
    1 tablespoon sugar
    1 tablespoon butter,
       softened
    1 medium apple, peeled,
       cored, and quartered
    1 cup evaporated milk
    1 cup packaged pancake mix
       Cinnamon Cream Syrup

Place egg, sugar, butter, apple, and evaporated milk in blender. Cover; process at low speed several seconds or until apple is chopped. Add pancake mix. Cover; process at high speed several seconds, until blended. Pour by ¼ cupfuls onto preheated (400°F) griddle or electric skillet. Cook until bubbles appear on top of cakes and under side is browned. Turn; brown on second side. (May transfer to electric hot tray for buffet service.) Serve hot with Cinnamon Cream Syrup.

Cinnamon Cream Syrup

    1 cup light corn syrup
    2 cups sugar
    ½ cup water
    2 teaspoons ground
       cinnamon
    1 cup evaporated milk

In medium saucepan combine corn syrup, sugar, water, and cinnamon. Bring to full boil over medium heat, stirring constantly. Boil 2 minutes, stirring constantly. Cool 5 minutes. Stir in evaporated milk. Serve warm over Apple Pancakes.

Micronote: Place ingredients in large mixing bowl. Bring to boil on HIGH (5 minutes). Reduce power to MEDIUM; cook 2 minutes, stirring several times.

Cynthia Sims Syfan

Quick and Easy Buttermilk Pancakes

These pancakes are as easy as a mix, but so much better. Be creative; add blueberries, shredded apples or pears, chopped nuts, crumbled bacon, grated orange rind, or your favorite flavorings.

Preparation: Easy
Cooking Time: 2-3 minutes

Yield: 8-10 Pancakes

    1 cup fresh buttermilk
       (not powdered)
    1 egg
    1 tablespoon sugar
    1 tablespoon oil
    1 teaspoon baking soda
    ½ teaspoon salt
    1 cup flour

Combine ingredients in order listed in 1-quart measuring cup. Blend with wire whisk until large lumps disappear. Pour cakes from measuring cup onto hot griddle; cook until golden brown, turning only once. (Extra pancakes freeze well; warm in microwave.)

Sally Butts Darden

Sour Cream Pancakes

Preparation: Easy
Cooking Time: Approximately 5 Minutes

Serves: 3
Must Serve Immediately

1 scant cup flour
½ teaspoon baking soda
½ teaspoon salt
¼ teaspoon sugar
1 cup sour cream
1 egg, well beaten

Sift dry ingredients together. Fold sour cream into egg. Make well in flour mixture; pour in sour cream mixture. Stir quickly, but do **not** beat. (Mixture will be thicker than regular pancake batter.) Cook on greased, hot griddle or skillet. If first pancake appears too thick, add 1 teaspoon milk to batter.

Jane Beckett Sims

Buttermilk Waffles

Preparation: Easy
Cooking Time: Approximately 5 Minutes Each

Serves: 2-4
Must Serve Immediately

¾ cup buttermilk
¼ teaspoon baking soda
¾ cup self-rising flour
2 eggs, well beaten
4 tablespoons oil

Dissolve soda in buttermilk. Add small portion of flour to eggs. Add buttermilk mixture and remaining flour to eggs alternately, 3 times, to form thin batter. Blend in oil. Cook immediately in preheated waffle iron. A special morning treat with Umma's Maple Syrup (page 289).

Patsy Lothridge Hicks

Austria Twists

Preparation: Average
Cooking Time: 18-20 Minutes
Oven Temperature: 350°F

Yield: 64 Twists
Must Partially Do Ahead

1 package dry yeast
3 cups flour
1 cup butter, softened
3 egg yolks
1 (8-ounce) package cream cheese, softened
1 cup sugar
1 cup finely chopped nuts
1 teaspoon ground cinnamon
Glaze

Combine yeast, flour, and butter; mix well. Blend in egg yolks and cream cheese. Divide into 4 balls. Wrap each in waxed paper; refrigerate overnight. Roll each ball into circle, ¼-inch thick. Mix together sugar, nuts, and cinnamon; divide into fourths. Spread ¼ cinnamon-sugar mixture over each circle. Cut each circle into 16 equal wedges. Beginning at wide side, roll each wedge toward small end. Place on greased baking sheet, point side down; bake at 350°F for 18-20 minutes. Spoon glaze over twists while warm.

Glaze

2 cups confectioners' sugar, sifted
2 tablespoons cream
1 teaspoon vanilla extract

Combine all ingredients; mix until smooth.

Jane Elizabeth Carter

Bagels

With cream cheese, butter, jam, or plain, these are delicious!

Preparation: Complex
Cooking Time: 50 Minutes
Oven Temperature: 375°F

Yield: 1 Dozen Bagels

4¼ - 4½ **cups flour,**
    divided
2 **packages dry yeast**
1½ **cups warm water**
3 **tablespoons sugar**
1 **tablespoon salt**
1 **gallon water + 1**
    tablespoon sugar

In large mixing bowl combine 1½ cups flour and yeast. Stir together water, sugar, and salt; add to dry ingredients. Beat with electric mixer at low speed for 30 seconds, scraping bowl. Beat 3 minutes at high speed. By hand, stir in enough remaining flour to make moderately stiff dough. Turn onto lightly floured surface; knead until smooth and elastic, 8-10 minutes. Cover; let rest 15 minutes. Divide into 12 parts; shape each into smooth ball. Punch hole in center of each ball with floured finger. Pull to enlarge hole, working each bagel into uniform shape. Place on greased baking sheet. Cover; let rise 20 minutes. Broil 5 inches from heat for 1½-2 minutes each side. In large kettle bring sugar-water to boil. Reduce to simmer. Place 4 bagels into water. Cook 7 minutes, turning once. Drain. Place on greased baking sheet. Repeat with remaining bagels. Bake at 375°F for 25 minutes. Serve immediately or transfer to wire rack to cool.

Variations: Whole Wheat Bagels - Prepare as for basic bagels except use 2¾-3 cups all-purpose flour and 1¼ cups whole wheat flour mixed together with yeast.

Herb Bagels - Prepare as for basic bagels or whole-wheat bagels adding 2 teaspoons dried marjoram or 1 teaspoon dried dillweed to flour-yeast mixture.

Onion Bagels - Prepare as for basic bagels. While bagels are baking, sauté ½ cup finely chopped onion in 3 tablespoons butter or margarine until just tender. Brush onion-butter mixture over tops of bagels after first 15 minutes of baking. Return to oven.

Cookbook Committee

Scrumptious Breakfast Rolls

Give your houseguests a breakfast to remember. Also nice for a family gathering or a gift for a special friend.

Preparation: Complex
Cooking Time: 12 Minutes
Oven Temperature: 375°F

Yield: 2-3 Dozen Rolls or 4 Braids
Must Do Ahead

1	cup sour cream, scalded
½	cup butter or margarine, melted
½	cup sugar
1	teaspoon salt
2	packages dry yeast
½	cup warm water
2	eggs, beaten
4	cups flour
	Cheese Filling
	Glaze

Combine sour cream, margarine, sugar, and salt. Mix well; cool to lukewarm. In large mixing bowl, dissolve yeast in warm water. Add sour cream mixture; blend well. Blend in eggs. Gradually stir in flour to form soft dough. Cover tightly. Chill overnight. Divide dough into 4 equal portions; knead several times on lightly floured surface. Roll each portion into 12 x 8-inch rectangle. Spread with ¼ of Cheese Filling to within ½ inch of edges. Beginning with long side, roll up; firmly pinch edge and ends to seal. Repeat with each portion of dough. Cut each roll into 1½-inch thick slices, placing slices flat on greased baking sheets. Cover; let rise in warm place until doubled in bulk. Bake at 375°F for 12 minutes or until golden brown. Drizzle glaze over each roll. (May be baked for 6-8 minutes or until set, stored, then reheated for remaining cooking time and glazed.) For a braided loaf, divide dough into 4 equal portions. Fill and roll up as above. When filled dough has been rolled and sealed, place each long roll seam-side down on greased baking sheets. Slit each roll at 2-inch intervals about ⅔ way through to resemble braid. Let rise as above. Bake at 375°F for 12 minutes or until browned. Glaze as directed.

Cheese Filling

2	(8-ounce) packages cream cheese, softened
¾	cup sugar
1	egg
2	teaspoons vanilla extract
½	teaspoon salt

Combine all ingredients. Process with food processor or mixer until blended.

Glaze

2	cups sifted confectioners' sugar
¼	cup milk
2	teaspoons vanilla extract

Combine all ingredients; blend well.

Jane Hix Oliver

Sticky Buns

Serve them with ambrosia for Christmas or Thanksgiving.

Preparation: Complex
Cooking Time: 45 Minutes
Oven Temperature: 350°F

Yield: 18 Buns
Must Do Ahead

4-5 cups flour, divided
½ cup sugar
½ teaspoon salt
1 package dry yeast
¾ cup milk
¼ cup water
1 cup + 2 tablespoons butter, divided
1 egg
3 tablespoons dark corn syrup
1 cup light brown sugar, divided
1 cup coarsely chopped pecans
2 teaspoons ground cinnamon

In large bowl combine 1 cup flour, sugar, salt, and yeast. In medium saucepan over low heat, heat milk, water, and ½ cup butter until very warm (120°F-130°F). (Butter does not need to melt.) With electric mixer at low speed, gradually pour warm liquids into dry ingredients. Increase speed to medium; beat 2 minutes, occasionally scraping bowl with rubber spatula. Beat in egg and 1 more cup flour; continue beating 2 minutes. With spoon, stir in enough additional flour (about 2¼ cups) to make soft dough. Turn dough onto lightly floured surface; knead until smooth and elastic, 8-10 minutes. Shape dough into ball; place in large greased bowl, turning once to coat. Cover with towel; let rise in warm draft-free place (80°F-85°F) until doubled in bulk, 1-1½ hours. Punch dough down. Turn onto lightly floured surface; cover with towel. Let rest 15 minutes. In 13 x 9-inch baking pan, over low heat, melt ½ cup butter; stir in corn syrup and ¾ cup brown sugar. Sprinkle with pecans; set aside. In small bowl, combine cinnamon and remaining ¼ cup brown sugar; set aside. On lightly floured surface, with lightly floured rolling pin, roll dough into 18 x 12-inch rectangle. Melt remaining 2 tablespoons butter; brush over rolled dough. Sprinkle with cinnamon mixture. Starting with 18-inch side, tightly roll dough, jelly roll fashion; pinch seam to seal. Place roll, seam side down, on lightly floured surface. With sharp knife, cut roll into 18 slices; place in prepared baking pan, cut sides down. Cover with towel. Let rise in warm place until doubled, 45 minutes - 1 hour. Bake at 350°F for 30 minutes or until browned. Immediately invert pan onto platter. Let pan remain over buns 1 minute to allow syrup to drip onto buns; remove pan. Serve warm.

Dee Lawson Morris

Cinnamon Buns

Preparation: Complex
Cooking Time: 30 Minutes
Oven Temperature: 350°F

Yield: 2 Dozen Buns
Must Do Ahead

2 rounded tablespoons sugar
½ cup oil
½ cup boiling water
1 package dry yeast
½ cup warm water
  (105-115°F)
1 egg
3 cups slightly
  packed flour
1 teaspoon salt
4 tablespoons margarine,
  melted, divided
¼ cup sugar
1¼ teaspoons ground
  cinnamon
1 cup chopped nuts
1 cup seedless raisins
1 cup confectioners' sugar
¼ teaspoon vanilla extract
2 tablespoons water

Combine sugar, oil, and water in large mixing bowl; stir until sugar is dissolved. Combine yeast and warm water; stir until dissolved. Beat egg into oil mixture. Stir in yeast. Sift flour with salt; add to above mixture. Beat with wooden spoon until smooth. Cover with waxed paper; refrigerate at least 12 hours or overnight. To make buns, place half of dough on floured surface. Knead lightly. Roll or pat into 15 x 10-inch rectangle. Brush with 2 tablespoons margarine. Mix sugar and cinnamon; sprinkle half over dough. Top with half of nuts and raisins, leaving small margin on one long side. Start with other long side and roll dough as for a jelly roll, leaving seam side down. Cut into ½-inch slices, using long, doubled piece of sewing thread, keeping thread well-floured. Place rolls in greased 15½ x 10½-inch pan or in paper baking cups. Repeat with remaining dough and filling. Let rise in warm place 30 minutes. Bake at 350°F for 30 minutes. Blend confectioners' sugar, vanilla, and water. Drizzle over warm buns. Place on racks to cool.

Frances Rozier Birdsong
Sparta, Georgia

In the morning they rose in a house pungent with breakfast cookery . . .
Thomas Wolfe, from *Look Homeward, Angel*

Diana's Almond Morning Cake

Preparation: Easy
Cooking Time: 30 Minutes
Oven Temperature: 350°F

Yield: 20 (1½-inch) Squares

1 cup butter, softened
¾ cup sugar
1 egg, separated
½ cup almond paste
1 teaspoon almond extract
2 cups sifted flour
¼ cup sliced almonds

In large bowl of electric mixer, beat butter and sugar at medium speed until light and fluffy. Beat egg yolk into butter mixture. Beat in almond paste and almond extract until smooth. At low speed, beat in flour just until well-blended. Press into ungreased 8-inch square pan. Beat egg white until frothy; brush over surface of dough. Cover with almonds. Bake at 350°F for 30 minutes or until tests done. Cool completely on wire rack. Cut into 1½-inch squares.

Carolyn Hartford Mahar

English Tea Cake

These make delicious Christmas gifts. Bake several ahead and freeze them in round foil pans for last-minute gift-giving.

Preparation: Average
Cooking Time: 20 Minutes
Oven Temperature: 350°F

Yield: 3 (8-inch) Round Cakes
Must Do Ahead

2 eggs, beaten
½ cup sugar
½ cup butter, melted
2 packages dry yeast
1 cup warm water
1 cup warm milk
1 cup currants
2 tablespoons citron
2 tablespoons candied
   orange peel
2 teaspoons ground nutmeg
2 teaspoons salt
6 plus cups flour
   Butter-Cream Filling

Blend eggs, sugar, and butter. Dissolve yeast in water. Add yeast to egg mixture; beat well. Add milk; mix thoroughly. Add currants, citron, candied orange peel, nutmeg, salt, and flour; blend well. (Mixture should resemble biscuit dough; can be kneaded lightly.) Turn into greased bowl; let rise until double in bulk, one hour. Grease and flour 3 (8-inch) round layer pans. Punch dough down; divide into thirds. Press into pans, mashing down middle to make sides higher. Let rise again until doubled, 1 hour. Bake at 350°F for 20 minutes. Cool in pans; turn out. Split each cake in half; fill with ¼-inch thickness of Butter-Cream Filling. Reassemble cakes; wrap well in foil. (May be frozen at this point.) To serve: Thaw if frozen; heat slowly at 325°F for 30-45 minutes.

Butter-Cream Filling

1½ cups butter, softened
1 pound confectioners'
   sugar

Combine butter and sugar; cream thoroughly.

Cathy McLanahan Nix

Basically Blintzes

These rolls take a little time but are not difficult. Keep a bag in your freezer for a special treat or a last-minute occasion.

Preparation: Average
Cooking Time: 10-15 Minutes
Oven Temperature: 350°F

Yield: 80-100 Rolls
Must Do Ahead

2 (1¼-pound) loaves
   soft bread
2 (8-ounce) packages cream
   cheese, softened
2 egg yolks
½ cup sugar
1 teaspoon lemon juice
2 cups light brown sugar
2 teaspoons cinnamon
¼ cup butter or margarine,
   melted

Trim crusts from bread; flatten with rolling pin. Mix cream cheese, egg yolks, sugar, and lemon juice. Spread 1 teaspoon cheese mixture on each piece of flattened bread. Mix brown sugar and cinnamon. Roll up bread slices; dip each piece into butter, then roll in cinnamon-sugar mixture. Cut each roll in half; freeze at least 3 hours on cookie sheet. Store in plastic bags. When ready to use, remove from freezer; bake at 350°F for 10-15 minutes.

Carol Dean Greene

Pumpkin Roll

Nice for a morning coffee. It freezes nicely, so it is a great do-ahead idea.

Preparation: Average
Cooking Time: 15 Minutes
Oven Temperature: 375°F

Yield: 1 Large Roll
Must Partially Do Ahead

- 3 eggs
- 1 cup sugar
- ⅔ cup canned pumpkin
- 1 teaspoon lemon juice
- ¾ cup flour
- 2 teaspoons ground cinnamon
- 1 teaspoon baking powder
- 1 teaspoon ground ginger
- ½ teaspoon ground nutmeg
- ½ teaspoon salt
- 1 cup finely chopped nuts
  Confectioners' sugar
  Cream Cheese Filling

Beat eggs with electric mixer for 5 minutes. Gradually add sugar while continuing to beat. Stir in pumpkin and lemon juice. Sift together dry ingredients; fold into egg mixture. Pour batter into greased and floured jelly roll pan; sprinkle with nuts. Bake at 375°F for 15 minutes. Sift confectioners' sugar onto cloth towel; turn warm cake out onto cloth. Starting at narrow end, roll up cake and towel together. (This keeps cake from breaking.) Place in refrigerator 1 hour to cool. Unroll carefully; spread with Cream Cheese Filling. Roll filled cake again in jelly roll fashion. Cover; refrigerate. To serve, return to room temperature or heat slightly.

Cream Cheese Filling

- 2 (3-ounce) packages cream cheese, softened
- 1 cup confectioners' sugar
- 4 tablespoons butter, softened
- ½ teaspoon vanilla extract

Combine all ingredients; mix until smooth.

Angela Avant Brown

Crescent Nut Rolls

Preparation: Easy
Cooking Time: 8-10 Minutes
Oven Temperature: 375°F

Yield: 16 Rolls

- 1 (8-ounce) can refrigerated crescent dinner rolls
- 4-6 tablespoons butter or margarine, softened
- 4 tablespoons cinnamon sugar
- 4-6 tablespoons chopped nuts
  Sugar Glaze

Completely separate rolls. Cut each triangle in half lengthwise. Butter each with ¼ tablespoon butter. Sprinkle with cinnamon sugar and nuts. Roll up each triangle beginning with wide side; place on ungreased baking sheet, point side down. Bake at 375°F for 7-8 minutes. Spoon Sugar Glaze over each roll. Return to oven for 2 additional minutes or until glaze sets.

Sugar Glaze

- 1 cup confectioners' sugar
- 1½ tablespoons milk or cream
- ½ teaspoon vanilla extract

Combine all ingredients; blend well.

Nell Whelchel Wiegand

Cranberry Coffee Cake

Create a holiday tradition served with hot cider or spiced punch.

Preparation: Easy
Cooking Time: 1 Hour
Oven Temperature: 350°F

Yield: 1 (10-inch) Cake

- ½ cup butter or margarine
- 1 cup sugar
- 2 eggs
- 2 cups flour
- 1 teaspoon baking powder
- 1 teaspoon baking soda
- ½ teaspoon salt
- 1 cup sour cream
- 1 teaspoon almond extract
- 1 (16-ounce) can whole-berry cranberry sauce
- ½ cup chopped pecans
  Almond Glaze

Cream butter and sugar with electric mixer until light and fluffy. Add eggs; beat well. Sift together dry ingredients. Add to creamed mixture alternately with sour cream, beating well after each addition. Stir in almond extract. Spoon ⅓ of batter into greased and floured 10-inch tube pan. Spread ⅓ cranberry sauce over batter. Repeat layers twice more, ending with cranberry sauce. Sprinkle pecans over top. Bake at 350°F for 1 hour or until cake tests done. Cool on rack 10 minutes. Remove from pan. Drizzle Almond Glaze over top.

Almond Glaze

- ¾ cup powdered sugar
- 1 tablespoon water
- ½ teaspoon almond extract

Combine all ingredients, mixing well.

Sally Butts Darden

Mincemeat Coffee Cake

Festive for a holiday brunch or breakfast.

Preparation: Easy
Cooking Time: 20-25 Minutes
Oven Temperature: 400°F

Serves: 8-10

- ¾-1 cup prepared mincemeat
- ½ cup milk
- 1 egg
- 2 tablespoons butter, melted
- 2 cups buttermilk baking mix
- ¼ cup sugar
  Orange Icing

Combine mincemeat, milk, egg, and butter. Stir in buttermilk baking mix and sugar with fork. Beat vigorously for ½ minute. Pour into greased 6-cup metal ring mold. Bake 20 minutes or until brown. Cool in mold on rack 5 minutes. Invert onto rack; cool 10 minutes. Drizzle Orange Icing evenly over cake. Cool to room temperature before serving.

Orange Icing

- 1½ cups confectioners' sugar, sifted
- 2 tablespoons orange juice
- ½ teaspoon grated orange rind
- ½ cup chopped nuts (optional)

Blend confectioners' sugar, orange juice, and orange rind. Stir in nuts.

Cathy McLanahan Nix

Coconut Croissant Coffee Cake

Preparation: Average
Cooking Time: 25 Minutes
Oven Temperature: 350°F

Yield: 2 (9-inch) Round Cakes
Must Do Ahead

1 package dry yeast
¼ cup warm water
2 eggs, beaten
1 cup sugar, divided
½ cup sour cream
½ cup butter, melted and divided
1 teaspoon salt
2¾-3¼ cups flour, divided
1 cup flaked coconut, divided
2 teaspoons grated orange rind
Orange Glaze

Dissolve yeast in water. Whisk in eggs, ¼ cup sugar, sour cream, 6 tablespoons butter, and salt. Stir in 2¾ cups flour. Place remaining ½ cup flour on flat surface. Turn dough onto flour; knead in enough flour to make moderately soft dough which is smooth and elastic, 3 to 5 minutes. Place in greased bowl; turn once. Cover; let rise until double, 1½ hours. Punch down; turn onto floured surface. Divide dough in half, shaping each half into ball. Cover; let rest 10 minutes. Roll each ball to 12-inch circle; brush with remaining butter. Combine ¾ cup sugar, ¾ cup coconut, and orange rind; sprinkle over circles. Cut each circle into 12 wedges. Roll up wedges, beginning at wide end. Arrange rolls, points down, pinwheel style, in 2 greased 9-inch round pans. Cover; let rise until doubled, 30 minutes. Bake at 350°F for 25 minutes, until lightly browned. Turn immediately from pans onto wire racks over waxed paper. Top with Orange Glaze; sprinkle with remaining ¼ cup coconut.

Orange Glaze

½ cup sugar
½ cup sour cream
¼ cup orange juice
¼ cup butter

Combine all ingredients. Cook and stir over medium heat until sugar dissolves and mixture boils. Boil 3 minutes, stirring constantly.
Micronote: Combine all ingredients in 4-cup glass measure. Cook on HIGH until mixture boils. Stir to dissolve sugar. Cook on HIGH 4 more minutes.

Cookbook Committee

German Stollen (Kuchen)

An old German pastry recipe is converted for our use. Since one recipe makes several stollen, some can be given as gifts or frozen for the family to enjoy later. Because of its versatility, it is sure to be a favorite. Use your imagination for fillings and shapes.

Preparation: Complex
Cooking Time: 15 Minutes per Stollen
Oven Temperature: 350°F

Yield: 4-5 Stollen
Must Do Ahead

1 cup sugar
1 cup vegetable shortening
2 eggs
1 teaspoon salt
¼ teaspoon vanilla extract
¼ teaspoon lemon juice (optional)
4 packages dry yeast
1 cup warm milk
1 cup warm water
4-5 cups flour (cake flour is preferred)
Filling of choice

Cream sugar, shortening, eggs, salt, vanilla, and lemon juice. Dissolve yeast in milk and water; add to creamed mixture. Stir in enough flour to knead; dough will be sticky. Knead until dough begins to loosen from sides of bowl, approximately 5 minutes. Cover; let rise in warm place until doubled in bulk, 1 hour. Punch down, folding sides of dough into center. Cover; let rest 5 minutes. Turn out onto well-floured board or pastry cloth; divide into 4 or 5 equal portions. Roll each portion into rectangle ½-inch thick. Dampen top with water so filling will stick. Spread with desired filling. Beginning with long side, roll jelly-roll fashion. Place on lightly greased baking pan. Cover with towel; let rise until light, 45 minutes to 1 hour.
Kuchen: Leave dough rolled long as described above or bring ends together to form circle. Cut through kuchen at 1-inch intervals and pull cuts slightly apart.
Sweet Rolls: Cut filled and rolled dough into slices. Place slices side by side or overlapping in circle or line. Bake at 350°F for 15 minutes or until golden brown. Cool on wire rack; frost when slightly cool. Serve warm with butter.

Fillings:

Butter Cream

½ cup butter, softened
1½ cups confectioners' sugar
½ teaspoon vanilla extract
Warm water
Ground cinnamon (optional)
Chopped pecans (optional)

Blend butter, sugar and vanilla until smooth. Add warm water if needed to make creamy. If desired sprinkle spread filling with cinnamon and pecans before rolling up.

Cherry-Almond Filling

1 (8-ounce) package cream cheese, softened
¼ cup sugar
1½ teaspoons rum flavoring
¼ cup chopped blanched almonds
¼ cup chopped maraschino cherries, drained

Beat cream cheese and sugar until fluffy. Stir in remaining ingredients.

Apricot Filling
1 (6-ounce) package dried
    apricots, finely chopped
1 cup water
3 tablespoons brown sugar
2 teaspoons orange juice
¼ cup coarsely chopped nuts

Cook apricots and water over medium heat, stirring occasionally, until water is absorbed and apricots are soft, 20 minutes. Add brown sugar, orange juice, and nuts; cool.

Prune Filling
2 cups cooked chopped
    prunes
3 tablespoons sugar
2 tablespoons lemon juice

In medium saucepan combine prunes, sugar, and lemon juice; bring to a boil. Boil 1 minute, stirring occasionally; cool.

Poppy Seed Filling
¾ cup poppy seeds
½ cup sugar
¾ cup milk
½ teaspoon vanilla extract
½ teaspoon almond extract
1 egg white, slightly beaten

Grind poppy seeds in blender at medium speed for 1 minute, scraping sides once. In medium saucepan combine poppy seeds, sugar, and milk. Cover; cook over medium heat 20 minutes or until milk is absorbed. Cool to lukewarm; stir in vanilla, almond extract, and egg white.

Prepared Almond Filling

Spread rolled dough with desired amount of filling.

Chocolate or Butterscotch Chips

Sprinkle desired number of chips over rolled dough.

Assorted Jams or Preserves

Spread rolled dough with desired amount of jam.

Frosting for One Kuchen
½ cup confectioners' sugar
2-3 teaspoons water

Mix sugar and water until well blended.

Marty Brauch Owens

Glazed Pineapple Coffee Ring

Allow full rising time for the dough. It will not double, but don't worry, results are delicious.

Preparation: Average
Cooking Time: 35-40 Minutes
Oven Temperature: 375°F

Serves: 8-10
Must Do Ahead

1 (13¼-ounce) can crushed
   pineapple
1 package dry yeast
½ cup sour cream
4 tablespoons melted butter
   or margarine, divided
¼ cup sugar
1 teaspoon salt
½ teaspoon grated lemon
   rind
2½ cups sifted flour
¼ cup firmly packed light
   brown sugar
4 teaspoons cornstarch
⅛ teaspoon ground ginger
   Pineapple Glaze

Drain pineapple, reserving syrup. Heat 3 tablespoons pineapple syrup to lukewarm. Add yeast; stir to dissolve. To yeast add sour cream, 2 tablespoons melted butter, sugar, salt, and lemon rind. Blend well. Stir in half flour; beat until smooth. Gradually blend in remaining flour to make soft dough. Cover; let rise 2 hours. Meanwhile, place drained pineapple and ¼ cup reserved syrup in small saucepan. Stir in brown sugar, cornstarch, and ginger. Cook, stirring constantly, until mixture is clear and thick. Remove from heat; cool. Turn dough onto floured board; punch down. Roll to form 10 x 14-inch rectangle. Brush with 1 tablespoon melted butter. Spread pineapple filling over dough. Roll up from long side, jelly-roll fashion. Lift into well-greased 9-inch round cake pan, shaping into ring and joining ends. With kitchen shears, make cuts about 1 inch apart from top to bottom, part-way through ring. Twist slice slightly so cut side is up. Let rise for 1 hour. Bake at 375°F for 35 minutes, until baked through and richly browned. Remove from oven; brush with remaining butter. Turn out onto rack to cool; drizzle with Pineapple Glaze while warm.

Pineapple Glaze

¾ cup sifted confectioners'
   sugar
1 tablespoon pineapple
   syrup
1 tablespoon flaked
   coconut (optional)

Mix confectioners' sugar with pineapple syrup until smooth. Stir in coconut.

Phyllis Wade Anderson

Cheese and Pear Danish

Perfect with coffee for a breakfast, brunch, or for an anytime sweet treat.

Preparation: Easy
Cooking Time: 20 Minutes
Oven Temperature: 375°F

Serves: 8

1 (3-ounce) package cream
cheese, softened
½ cup cottage cheese
⅓ cup confectioners' sugar
½ teaspoon lemon extract
1 egg, separated
1 (8-ounce) package
refrigerated crescent
dinner rolls
1 small ripe pear,
peeled and diced
1 tablespoon water

In small bowl of electric mixer, beat cream cheese, cottage cheese, sugar, extract, and egg yolk at medium speed until well blended. Set aside. Unroll dough into 2 (10 x 3½-inch) rectangles. Overlap long sides to form 10 x 6½-inch rectangle; press perforations together. Place on ungreased cookie sheet and roll lightly into 13 x 8-inch rectangle. Spoon 2-inch-wide strip of cheese mixture lengthwise down center of dough; top with pear. Cut dough on both sides of filling crosswise into ¾-inch strips. Wrap each strip at slight angle across filling, alternating sides. Slightly beat egg white with water; brush over pastry top. Bake at 375°F for 20 minutes. Serve hot, or cool on rack.

Cookbook Committee

Batter for Frying

Excellent for veal, fish, or pork chops. The trick here seems to be pressing the flour and crumbs into the meat.

Preparation: Easy

2 eggs
½ cup milk
Salt and pepper to taste
Flour
Bread crumbs, cracker
meal, or cracker
crumbs
Oil

Beat eggs, milk, salt, and pepper together. Dip meat into egg mixture, then into flour, patting flour into meat. Dip back into egg mixture, then back into crumbs, pressing crumbs into meat. Fry in hot oil until golden brown. (Doing this process a little ahead of time and refrigerating will guarantee that batter won't fall off meat during frying.)

Margaret McGowan Peacock

Basic Entrée Crêpes

You don't have to be Julia Child to turn our fancy crêpes. They are deceivingly simple and infinitely versatile. Make a large batch and freeze them for those times when last-minute masterpieces are in order.

Preparation: Easy
Cooking Time: 2 Minutes Per Crêpe

1½ **cups milk or buttermilk**
2 **tablespoons oil**
3 **eggs**
1½ **cups flour**
½ **teaspoon salt**
½ **teaspoon sugar**

Yield: 12 Crêpes
Must Partially Do Ahead

Place all ingredients in blender in order listed. Cover; process at high speed until smooth. Refrigerate 1 hour. Use crêpe pan, according to manufacturer's instructions, to make 12 crêpes. Crêpes may be prepared ahead, stacked between layers of waxed paper, and refrigerated or frozen until ready to use.

Variation: Crêpe Cups - Cook crêpes as above. Generously grease one 10-ounce custard cup per crêpe; place on baking sheet. Fit one crêpe into each cup (edges will be ruffled.) Bake at 400°F for 8 minutes, until edges are light golden brown and crisp. Let cool 1-2 minutes. Carefully remove from cups. Fill with desired crêpe, egg, or salad filling.

Doris Duke Sosebee

Suggested Crêpe Fillings:
Spinach Cheese Filling For Crêpes (page 268)
Chicken Curry Crêpes (page 171)
Crêpes d'Or (page 238)

Whole Wheat Crêpes

Preparation: Easy
Cooking Time: 2 Minutes per Crêpe

1 **cup whole wheat flour**
¼ **teaspoon salt**
2 **eggs**
½ **cup milk**
½ **cup water**
2 **tablespoons melted margarine**

Yield: 6-10 Crêpes
Must Partially Do Ahead

Combine all ingredients in electric blender. Blend 30 seconds; scrape down sides; blend 30 seconds more. Refrigerate batter 1-1½ hours. Cook with a crêpe pan according to manufacturer's instructions. (Stack extras between layers of waxed paper. Refrigerate or freeze for later use.)

Cookbook Committee

Cornbread Dressing

Serve with any poultry.

Preparation: Average
Cooking Time: 30-45 Minutes
Oven Temperature: 350°F

Serves: 6

1 pan cornbread (page 140) or 1 bag cornbread stuffing mix, prepared according to package directions
1 cup finely chopped celery
1 large onion, minced
½ cup finely chopped Irish potato, cooked
2 slices bread, cubed
3 biscuits (day-old is fine), crumbled
1 teaspoon poultry seasoning
½ teaspoon salt (or to taste)
¼ teaspoon pepper (or to taste)
Drippings from turkey or hen
1 (10¾-ounce) can chicken broth
¼ cup butter, melted
1 apple, finely chopped (optional)
Sliced water chestnuts, to taste (optional)

Crumble cornbread until fine. Add remaining ingredients; blend well. Turn into greased 15 x 9 x 2-inch baking dish. Bake at 350°F for 30-45 minutes or until nicely browned and slightly firm.

Ruth Puckett Martin

Naturally, my family ate cornbread, day in, day out, for years. Finally Hard Times eased up a little, and they had hot biscuits, nearly all they could eat, once a week for Sunday breakfast.

Katherine Anne Porter, *Collected Essays & Occasional Writings of Katherine Anne Porter*
Delacorte Press/Seymour Lawrence, Copyright 1973. Used with permission.

Oyster Dressing

Preparation: Average
Cooking Time: 40 Minutes
Oven Temperature: 400°F

Yield: 3-4 Quarts
Must Partially Do Ahead

1	recipe Buttermilk Cornbread, cooked 1 day ahead and crumbled
1	cup finely chopped celery
1	small onion, chopped
6	slices hard-toasted bread, crumbled
6	eggs, beaten
2	cups (approximately) turkey or chicken stock
1	pint oysters, undrained

Combine cornbread, celery, onion, and toast crumbs. Add eggs and stock. Stir until well blended. Stir in oysters. Pour into 2 (1½-quart) casseroles. Bake at 400°F for 40 minutes or until browned on top and knife inserted in center comes out clean.

Buttermilk Cornbread

1	cup cornmeal
2	teaspoons baking powder
1	teaspoon sugar
½	teaspoon salt
¼	teaspoon baking soda
1	egg
1½	cups buttermilk
¼	cup oil

Thoroughly grease 9-inch round cake pan; place in oven to heat. Stir dry ingredients in mixing bowl. Add remaining ingredients in order listed, beating well after each addition. Pour mixture into hot pan. Place in lower half of 450°F oven. When cornbread rises, move pan to upper half of oven; continue baking until top is lightly browned, 20-30 minutes. (Take care not to over-cook.)

Allie Wimberly Wofford
Cochran, Georgia

Scottish Dressing

Serve with turkey and the trimmings. The ground cornflakes approximate a coarse meal used in Scotland. Canned chicken stock or bouillon cubes may be used, but drippings are preferred.

Preparation: Average
Cooking Time: 1 Hour
Oven Temperature: 350°F

Serves: 6-8

1	(18-ounce) package cornflakes
2	pounds sausage (1 pound hot - 1 pound medium)
3½	teaspoons poultry seasoning
1½	cups celery, diced
1	small onion, diced
2	or more cups of liquid made from boiling giblets or turkey drippings

Place cornflakes in food processor or blender; process until a fine meal consistency. Mix flakes with sausage by hand. Add poultry seasoning, celery, and onion. Pour in liquid; blend well. Turn into greased 12 x 8-inch pan. Cover; bake at 350°F for 1 hour. (May be cooked in skillet over medium heat; but be careful, it sticks easily to bottom.)

Charlotte Morrow Dunlap

Poultry

Lady's Slipper

Lady's Slipper (Cypripedium calceolus)

The lady's slipper is a treasure of our rich Southern woodlands where it blooms in late spring. Its powdered roots, mixed with sugar, were once used as a sedative by the Cherokee Indians. Although it is classified as an herb, today this orchid is rare and finding it in bloom is a treat to be admired only visually.

On Poultry

- An imaginative use of herbs and spices allows the creation of an endless variety of chicken dishes using very simple cooking methods. The following herbs and spices are particularly compatible with chicken and yield exciting results. The approximate amounts are for 3 pounds of chicken.
  - CELERY SALT - Use 1¼ teaspoons; reduce salt in recipe.
  - DILL WEED - Use ½ teaspoon. Delicate flavor.
  - FENNEL SEED - Use ¼ teaspoon. Faint licorice flavor.
  - GARLIC - Use 1 average clove fresh garlic, minced, ¼ teaspoon garlic powder, or ½ teaspoon garlic salt.
  - MARJORAM - Use ¼ teaspoon. Pleasant aromatic mint with bitter undertone.
  - MUSTARD - Use ½ teaspoon dry ground mustard.
  - OREGANO - Use ¼ teaspoon ground, ½ teaspoon dried leaves. Strong aromatic flavor.
  - PAPRIKA - Amounts may vary considerably. Use ½ teaspoon to 2 tablespoons. Mild, slightly sweet flavor.
  - POULTRY SEASONING - Blend of herbs created primarily for stuffings. Use ¼-¾ teaspoon for frying; use ½ teaspoon per 4 cups creamed chicken; use ½-2 teaspoons per 4 cups bread for stuffing.
  - ROSEMARY - Use ¼ teaspoon. Sweet, pine woods flavor.
  - SAFFRON - Use ⅛ teaspoon crushed. Dried stigmas of crocus with pleasantly bitter flavor.
  - SAGE - Use ½ teaspoon per 4 cups bread cubes for stuffing or mix with ⅓ cup flour for dredging.
  - SAVORY - Use ¼-½ teaspoon over chicken, use ¼ teaspoon per 3 cups bread cubes for stuffing. Aromatic and piquant; blends well with other herbs.
  - SESAME SEED - Use ⅓ cup toasted per 3 cups stuffing or as garnish. Rich, nut-like flavor.
  - TARRAGON - Use ¼ teaspoon ground, ½ teaspoon dried leaves. Slightly astringent flavor.
  - THYME - Use ¼ teaspoon ground, ½ teaspoon dried leaves. Mix with ⅓ cup flour for dredging or sprinkle over chicken. Warm, aromatic flavor.
- Chicken may be seasoned before, during, or after cooking.
- Herbs may be used alone, combined, or mixed with salt and pepper; rub them into chicken or sprinkle over before baking or broiling.
- Add herbs and spices to melted butter to create simple marinades, basting sauces, or topping sauces.
- When precooked chicken is needed in a recipe, microwave chicken, covered, on HIGH for 6 minutes per pound. Omit salt until end of cooking time.
- A whole broiler-fryer is 50% edible cooked meat. A 3-pound bird yields approximately 3 cups edible meat.
- If a stuffing is not desired in turkey, place a mixture of vegetables and herbs in the cavity for flavor.

Gainesville is "Poultry Capital of the World" and proud of it! We are happy to wear this label, distinguishing Gainesville as the focal point for Georgia's gigantic poultry industry. The industry with its many allied business and scientific fields, attracts visitors and residents from all over the world. Georgia may be known as The Peach State but, in fact, the annual poultry farm income from Gainesville and Hall County alone amounts to over two-and-a-half times the statewide income from peaches. Chicken and eggs from our area are shipped to every state in the United States and to many other countries. Chances are excellent that, wherever you live, your Thanksgiving turkey, fried chicken, and scrambled eggs all originated right here. We invite you to share our favorite poultry recipes and hope you will think of us as you enjoy them.

"In the heart of this city, where it is against the law to use anything but fingers to eat fried chicken, stands a symbol. It is a bronze statue of a rooster raised on a 25-foot marble monument above a grassy triangle called the Georgia Poultry Park.

"The ordinance on eating chicken in this city of about 20,000 people was adopted in an interlude of humor 22 years ago, but the statue was raised in serious and proud tribute to the area's major industry. It stands at the center of what a plaque describes as the poultry capital of the world."

Copyright © 1983 by The New York Times Company.
Reprinted by permission.

Simply Delicious Southern Fried Chicken

The Southern specialty! Mrs. Smith, wife of a past Chairman of the National Broiler Council Board, has perfected this recipe after many years of close association with poultry and the poultry industry.

Preparation: Average
Cooking Time: 30-40 Minutes

Serves: 6

6 **chicken breast halves or 3½ pounds assorted chicken pieces or 1 pound chicken livers, halved**
  Salt
1 **cup buttermilk**
2 **cups self-rising flour**
1 **teaspoon lemon-pepper seasoning**
  Oil

Lightly salt chicken to taste. Place buttermilk in shallow dish and flour onto waxed paper. Dip each piece of chicken into buttermilk; sprinkle with lemon-pepper. Roll in flour, coating well; shake off any excess flour. Heat 2-inch depth of oil in large skillet to 350°F. Place chicken, a few pieces at a time, in hot oil. (Take care to add extra chicken pieces slowly enough that oil temperature does not drop below 325°F.) Cook until chicken is crisp and richly browned, turning once. Drain well on absorbent toweling. To keep hot, hold in warm oven.

Menu Suggestion: Collard Green Soup (page 62), Southern Caviar (page 81), Beaumont Inn Corn Pudding (page 275), Cracklin' Cornbread (page 119), Buttermilk Pie (page 338).

Beverage Suggestion: Iced Tea.

Ellorie Smith
Cumming, Georgia

The North seldom tries to fry chicken, and this is well; the art cannot be learned north of the line of Mason and Dixon, nor anywhere in Europe.

Mark Twain

Oven-Fried Chicken

A wonderful substitute for "real" fried chicken. It's just possible you may like it better.

Preparation: Easy
Cooking Time: 50 Minutes
Oven Temperature: 425°F

Serves: 4

½ cup butter or margarine
4 chicken breast halves,
    skinned, or assorted
    chicken pieces
  Flour
  Paprika
  Lemon-pepper
  Garlic salt

Melt butter in shallow baking dish. Dredge chicken pieces in flour; place skin-side down in butter. Sprinkle liberally with paprika, lemon-pepper, and garlic salt. Bake, uncovered, at 425°F for 30 minutes. Turn chicken pieces; sprinkle again with seasonings. Bake 20 additional minutes.

Menu Suggestion: Banana-Pineapple Cloud (page 91), Macaroni and Cheese Deluxe (page 288), Nanny's Southern Green Beans (page 265), Granny's Date Nut Cake (page 320).

Wine Suggestion: A zestful white such as a Riesling.

Ginny Wiegand Crumley

Chicken with Orange Sauce

Preparation: Easy
Cooking Time: 1 Hour

Serves: 6

1 broiler-fryer or selected
    chicken pieces, salted
4 tablespoons butter, melted
2 tablespoons flour
¼ teaspoon salt
⅛ teaspoon ground cinnamon
⅛ teaspoon ground cloves
1½ cups orange juice
¼ teaspoon Tabasco
½ cup slivered almonds
½ cup golden raisins
1 orange, peeled and
    sectioned
  Cooked yellow rice

In large skillet sauté chicken in butter until browned. Remove chicken pieces; set aside. To drippings add flour, salt, cinnamon, and cloves; stir to a smooth paste. Add orange juice and Tabasco; cook, stirring constantly, until mixture thickens and comes to boil. Add chicken, almonds, and raisins. Simmer, covered, approximately 45 minutes. Stir occasionally; add water if necessary. Add orange sections last 5 minutes of cooking time. Serve over yellow rice.

Micronote: Preheat browning skillet 4½ minutes on HIGH; sauté chicken. Cook on HIGH 6 minutes, turning dish twice. Remove chicken. Add to drippings flour, salt, cinnamon, cloves, orange juice, and Tabasco; stir until smooth. Cook 3 minutes on HIGH, stirring every 30-45 seconds. Add chicken, almonds, and raisins. Cook on HIGH 10-12 minutes in covered browning dish. Add orange sections; cook on HIGH 1 minute.

Menu Suggestion: Cranberry Salad Ring (page 88), Asparagus of Renown (page 258), Sour Cream Mini Biscuits (page 380).

Wine Suggestion: A spicy white such as a California Gewürtztraminer.

Sally Butts Darden

Cognac Chicken Flambé

Dazzle your guests by igniting this at the table in an attractive pan or chafing dish.

Preparation: Average
Cooking Time: 30 Minutes

Serves: 4
Must Serve Immediately

4 **boneless skinless chicken breast halves**
¼ **cup flour**
1 **teaspoon salt**
½ **teaspoon rosemary**
¼ **teaspoon pepper**
3 **tablespoons margarine, melted**
½ **cup chicken broth**
2 **tablespoons lemon juice**
1 **tablespoon Dijon mustard**
⅓ **cup cognac**

Place chicken between sheets of waxed paper; pound thin. Combine flour, salt, rosemary, and pepper; dredge chicken in seasoned flour. Sauté chicken breasts in margarine over medium-high heat for 10-15 minutes, turning frequently. Remove from skillet. Add broth, lemon juice, and mustard to pan drippings, stirring to loosen any browned bits. Return chicken to skillet; simmer 15 minutes, turning once. Heat cognac in small long-handled saucepan. Remove from heat, ignite, and pour over chicken. Stir to blend into sauce. Place chicken on serving platter, covering with any remaining sauce.
Menu Suggestion: Green Bean Casserole (page 265), Pecan Pilaf (page 285), Cheesecake Receipt (page 323).
Wine Suggestion: A light red French Bordeaux.

Dee Lawson Morris

Chicken with Oyster Sauce

Preparation: Easy
Cooking Time: 25 Minutes

Serves: 4
Must Serve Immediately

6 **tablespoons butter or margarine, divided**
2 **cups sliced mushrooms**
4-6 **shallots, chopped**
4 **boneless skinless chicken breast halves, cut into ¼-inch slices**
8 **fresh or canned oysters (reserve liquor)**
1 **cup sour cream**
½ **teaspoon dried dill weed**
Salt and freshly ground black pepper
Toasted sourdough muffins, cooked rice, or cooked pasta

Melt 4 tablespoons butter in large skillet over medium-high heat. Add mushrooms and shallots; sauté until tender, about 8 minutes. Transfer to platter; set aside. Melt remaining 2 tablespoons butter in same skillet. Add chicken; sauté, turning frequently, until just cooked, about 4 minutes. Add to mushrooms and shallots. Pour oyster liquor into skillet, scraping up any browned bits. Cook until reduced by ¼. Add oysters and sour cream; whisk until well blended. Simmer 3-5 minutes. Stir in dill weed, salt, and pepper. Return chicken, shallots, and mushrooms to skillet; cook until heated through, about 2 minutes but **do not boil**. Spoon over muffins, rice, or pasta.
Micronote: Sauté mushrooms and shallots in butter on HIGH 2 minutes. Preheat browning skillet 4½ minutes. Sauté chicken. Cook on HIGH 6-8 minutes, stirring once, until chicken is done. Pour only half of oyster liquor into skillet. Stir in sour cream and dill. Cook on HIGH 3 minutes. Season with salt and pepper.
Menu Suggestion: Spinach Soup (page 61), Mandarin Carrots (page 274), Pecan Pie (page 335).
Wine Suggestion: A dry white French Muscadet will complement the oysters.

Dana Blum Barclay

Chicken Kiev with Mushroom Sauce

Preparation: Average
Cooking Time: 20 Minutes

Serves: 6
Must Partially Do Ahead
Must Serve Immediately

8 **large boneless skinless chicken breast halves**
Salt to taste
1 **tablespoon chopped green onion**
1 **tablespoon chopped parsley**
½ **cup butter**
Flour
1 **egg, beaten**
1 **tablespoon water**
½ **cup fine dry bread crumbs**
Oil
Mushroom Sauce
Lemon wedges (optional)

Place each breast, boned side up, between 2 pieces of clear plastic wrap. Working from center, pound with meat mallet to make ¼-inch thick cutlets. Peel off wrap. Sprinkle with salt, onion, and parsley. Divide butter into 8 equal oblong pieces. Place 1 piece at end of each cutlet and roll as for jelly roll, tucking in sides and sealing end. Place flour in shallow dish. Blend egg and water in separate dish. Coat each roll with flour; dip in egg mixture; coat with crumbs. Chill 1-24 hours. Deep-fry rolls in hot (365°F) fat 5 minutes or until golden brown. Ladle Mushroom Sauce over each roll; garnish with lemon wedges.

Mushroom Sauce

½ **pound fresh mushrooms, sliced**
3 **tablespoons butter or magarine, melted**
1 **tablespoon flour**
1 **teaspoon soy sauce**
¾ **cup light cream**
Salt and pepper to taste

Combine mushrooms and butter in saucepan. Sprinkle with flour; toss. Cook over medium heat, stirring occasionally, 8 minutes or until tender. Add soy sauce. Gradually stir in cream. Cook, stirring, until mixture bubbles and thickens. Season with salt and pepper.
Micronote: Combine mushrooms, butter, and flour. Cook on HIGH 3 minutes. Add remaining ingredients; cook on HIGH 1-2 minutes, stirring often.
Menu Suggestion: Apricot Mousse Salad (page 90), Broccoli Ring (page 260).
Wine Suggestion: A fuller white such as a white French Rhône.

Cheryl Gibbons McElveen

We are not just now in a condition to sacrifice much to fancy or ornament....The days for romance have passed....A crisis is upon us which demands the development of the will and energy of Southern character....As woman has been queen in the parlor, so, if need be, she will be queen in the kitchen.

Mrs. Hill's Cookbook, circa 1890.

Chicken Surprise

Preparation: Easy
Cooking Time: 30 Minutes

Serves: 4

4 boneless chicken breast
    halves
Salt and pepper to taste
2 tablespoons olive oil
1 leek, chopped
1 small onion, sliced
    Fresh mushrooms (optional)
    Green peppers, sliced
    (optional)
    Zucchini, sliced (optional)
3 tomatoes, peeled and
    chopped
½ teaspoon tarragon
1 cup dry vermouth

Sprinkle chicken with salt and pepper. Sauté in olive oil until golden. Remove chicken from pan. Sauté vegetables. Sprinkle with tarragon, additional salt, and pepper. Add vermouth; cook 1 minute. Return chicken to pan; cover with vegetables. Simmer, covered, until tender.

Menu Suggestion: Delicious Summer Fruit Salad (page 92), Potato Fresh (page 75).

Wine Suggestion: A dry white such as a white Spanish Rioja.

Ann Couch Alexander

Chicken à la Francaise

The perfect combination for busy lives, an elegant effect for minimum effort and time.

Preparation: Easy
Cooking Time: 35 Minutes

Serves: 6
Must Partially Do Ahead

1½ pounds boneless chicken
    breasts, cut into
    thin strips
1½ teaspoons salt
¼ teaspoon pepper
2 tablespoons butter, melted
1 pound fresh mushrooms,
    sliced
1 cup sliced green onions
1 cup fresh or frozen green
    peas
1¼ cups chicken broth,
    divided
½ cup dry sherry
1 tablespoon lemon juice
¾ teaspoon chopped fresh
    basil or ¼ teaspoon
    dried basil
3 fresh tomatoes, peeled
    and cut into eighths
2 tablespoons cornstarch
3 cups hot cooked rice

Season chicken with salt and pepper; sauté in butter until browned. Add mushrooms and onions; sauté 2 minutes longer. Stir in peas, 1 cup broth, sherry, lemon juice, and basil. Simmer, covered, 20 minutes. Add tomatoes. Dissolve cornstarch in remaining broth; stir into chicken mixture. Cook, stirring frequently, 5 minutes longer. Serve over bed of rice.

Micronote: Preheat browning skillet 4½ minutes. Sauté chicken in butter until browned. Cook on HIGH 6-8 minutes, stirring twice. Add mushrooms and onions; cook on HIGH 1-2 minutes. Add peas, 1 cup broth, sherry, lemon juice, and basil. Cook, covered, on HIGH 8-10 minutes or until peas are tender. Add tomatoes; cook on HIGH 2-3 minutes, stirring every 30-45 seconds. Dissolve cornstarch in remaining broth. Cook on HIGH until thickened or until mixture comes to boil; stir into chicken. Add salt and pepper. Cook on HIGH 2-3 minutes or until heated through.

Menu Suggestion: Heavenly Lime Salad (page 90), Blueberry Muffins (page 122), Boiled Custard Banana Pudding (page 346).

Wine Suggestion: A light French Côte de Beaune.

Jean Bennett Oliver

Chicken Piccata

Preparation: Average
Cooking Time: 30 Minutes

Serves: 8
Must Partially Do Ahead

8 boneless skinless chicken breast halves
2 tablespoons lemon juice
1 cup + 2 tablespoons water, divided
1½ teaspoons salt, divided
¼ teaspoon pepper
⅓ cup flour
⅓ cup olive oil
2 tablespoons butter
½ cup dry white wine
1 chicken-flavored bouillon cube
2 lemons
Parsley sprigs
Fettucine (page 286)

Marinate chicken breasts in lemon juice and 2 tablespoons water for 30 minutes. Place between layers of waxed paper; pound with meat mallet to ⅛-inch thickness. Sprinkle with 1 teaspoon salt and pepper; coat with flour. Heat oil and butter in 12-inch skillet over medium heat. Sauté chicken breasts, a few at a time, until lightly browned on both sides, adding more oil if necessary. Remove chicken from skillet. Reduce heat to low. Stir remaining 1 cup water, wine, bouillon cube, and ½ teaspoon salt into drippings to deglaze; stir to loosen browned bits. Return chicken to skillet; simmer, covered, 15 minutes or until tender. Remove to warm platter. Squeeze juice of 1 lemon into liquid in skillet; stir and heat to boiling. Pour over chicken. Thinly slice remaining lemon; arrange with parsley sprigs over chicken. Serve with Fettucine.

Menu Suggestion: Tomato Aspic (page 85), Sesame Broccoli (page 261).

Wine Suggestion: A full, dry white such as Spanish Rioja.

Dee Lawson Morris

Chicken Cacciatore

Preparation: Easy
Cooking Time: 1 Hour 15 Minutes

Serves: 6

1 (2½-pound) broiler-fryer, cut into parts
¼ cup olive oil
2 medium onions, cut into ¼-inch slices
2 medium cloves of garlic, minced
2 (16-ounce) cans whole tomatoes
1 (15-ounce) can herb tomato sauce
1 teaspoon salt
1 teaspoon dried oregano
½ teaspoon celery seed
¼ teaspoon pepper
1-2 bay leaves
½ cup Sauterne
Hot cooked spaghetti
Grated Parmesan cheese

Sauté chicken in olive oil in large skillet; remove chicken and set aside. Add onion and garlic to pan drippings; sauté until tender. Combine tomatoes, tomato sauce, salt, oregano, celery seed, pepper, and bay leaves; blend well. Return chicken to skillet; add sauce. Simmer, covered, 45 minutes. Stir in wine; simmer, uncovered, 15 minutes turning chicken occasionally. Skim off any excess fat. Place chicken and sauce over spaghetti; sprinkle with grated cheese.

Micronote: Preheat browning skillet 4½ minutes. Rub chicken with olive oil; brown chicken. Place thinner pieces in center of skillet and thicker ones on outside. Cook on HIGH 6-10 minutes, turning dish once. Combine tomatoes, tomato sauce, seasonings, and wine; pour over chicken. Cook on HIGH until mixture boils; reduce power to MEDIUM; cook 12-15 minutes.

Menu Suggestion: West Coast Salad (page 80), Herbed Dinner Triangles (page 118), Top Hat Brownies (page 359).

Wine Suggestion: A light red Italian such as Bardolino or serve a wine similar to that used in recipe.

Kitty Carter Lane

Lemony Chicken

A real gem. It enables you to create a first-rate entrée out of common ingredients kept on hand in most any kitchen.

Preparation: Average
Cooking Time: 45 Minutes

Serves: 4
Must Serve Immediately

4 large chicken breast
    halves
2 lemons
¼ cup flour
½ teaspoon paprika
2 tablespoons oil
2 tablespoons light brown
    sugar
1½ teaspoons salt
½ cup chicken broth

Remove skin from chicken; pat dry. Grate rind from 1 lemon; set aside. Squeeze juice from this lemon over chicken. Combine flour and paprika in shallow dish. Turn each breast in flour to coat. In skillet sauté chicken in hot oil until brown on all sides, approximately 10 minutes. Mix reserved lemon rind, brown sugar, and salt; sprinkle over chicken. Add broth to skillet. Cook, covered, over low heat 25 minutes. Thinly slice second lemon; arrange over chicken. Cook, covered, additional 10 minutes or until fork-tender.

Micronote: Preheat browning skillet 4½ minutes. Squeeze juice of 1 lemon over chicken. Coat with flour-paprika mixture. Brown chicken in oil in skillet. Sprinkle with lemon rind and brown sugar; add broth. Cook on High 10-12 minutes, allowing 6-7 minutes cooking time per pound of chicken. Add second lemon, thinly sliced; cook on HIGH 2-3 minutes longer. Add salt.

Menu Suggestion: Pecan Pilaf (page 285), Hot Sherried Fruit (page 283).

Wine Suggestion: A simple, dry white such as French Mâcon Blanc.

Cindy Collins Randolph

International Date-Line Chicken

Preparation: Average
Cooking Time: 1 Hour

Serves: 6
Must Serve Immediately

6 chicken breast halves
    or 1½ pounds boneless
    chicken breast chunks
¼ cup butter or margarine,
    melted
1 (10¾-ounce) can chicken
    broth
1 tablespoon minced onion
1 teaspoon salt
½ teaspoon curry powder
½ teaspoon pepper
1 (11-ounce) can mandarin
    orange sections
2 tablespoons cornstarch
1 teaspoon lemon juice
1 cup thinly sliced green
    pepper
1 cup pitted dates, halved
    Cashews (optional)
    Shredded coconut (optional)

Remove skin from chicken; pat dry. In large skillet sauté chicken slowly in butter until deep golden brown. Combine broth, onion, salt, curry powder, and pepper. Pour over chicken. Simmer, covered, 45 minutes or until chicken is fork-tender. Drain oranges, reserving syrup. Combine syrup, cornstarch, and lemon juice. Transfer chicken to warm serving platter; keep warm. Stir cornstarch mixture into pan juices in skillet. Cook, stirring constantly, until thickened and clear. Add green pepper and dates; simmer 3-4 minutes. Gently stir in orange sections. Pour sauce over chicken. Sprinkle with cashews and/or coconut to garnish.

Micronote: Preheat browning skillet 4½ minutes. Sauté chicken in skillet. Cook on HIGH 6-8 minutes or until tender. Combine broth, onion, salt, curry, and pepper; pour over chicken. Cook on HIGH until mixture boils. (Reduce power if mixture boils over.) Cook 2-3 minutes longer. Remove chicken. Combine syrup, cornstarch, and lemon juice; add to pan juices. Cook on HIGH 2-3 minutes, stirring several times. Add peppers and dates; cook on HIGH 1-2 minutes. Stir in orange sections. Proceed as above.

Menu Suggestion: Cream Soup Base with Broccoli (page 64), Popovers (page 115), Dessert Fondue (page 358).

Wine Suggestion: A fruity white generic such as California Rhine.

Patricia Franklin Rauch

Breast of Chicken in Wine

Preparation: Easy
Cooking Time: 30 Minutes
Oven Temperature: 350°F

Serves: 6
Must Partially Do Ahead

6 large boneless skinless
   chicken breast halves
Salt and pepper to taste
½ cup dry white wine or
   dry vermouth
¾ teaspoon dried tarragon
1 large garlic clove, halved
3-4 tablespoons grated Parmesan
   cheese
Paprika
Parsley

Season both sides of chicken breasts with salt and pepper. Place in greased 10 x 6 x 2-inch baking dish. Combine wine, tarragon, and garlic; pour over chicken. Marinate at room temperature for 1 hour, turning occasionally. (Chicken may be covered and marinated overnight. Return to room temperature before baking.) Sprinkle chicken with Parmesan cheese and very lightly with paprika. Bake uncovered at 350°F for 30 minutes or until done. Garnish with fresh parsley.

Micronote: Prepare as directed but do not salt until end of cooking time. Cook on HIGH 6 minutes per pound of chicken (10-15 minutes total). Cover dish with waxed paper to prevent splattering.

Menu Suggestion: Vegetable Aspic (page 84), Barley Casserole (page 284), Orange Charlotte (page 349).

Wine Suggestion: A full, dry white such as a French Pouilly-Fuissé.

Sherrie Nathan Schrage

Rolled Breast of Chicken

Individual servings make this ideal for a buffet dinner party.

Preparation: Average
Cooking Time: 1 Hour 15 Minutes
Oven Temperature: 350°F

Serves: 6

6 large boneless skinless
   chicken breast halves
Salt
6 thin slices boiled ham
6 ounces natural Swiss cheese,
   cut in 6 sticks
¼ cup + 2 tablespoons flour,
   divided
2 tablespoons butter or
   margarine, melted
1 cup water, divided
1 chicken bouillon cube
1 (3-ounce) can sliced
   mushrooms, drained
⅓ cup Sauterne
Toasted slivered almonds

Place chicken breasts between layers of plastic wrap; pound to flatten into cutlets ¼-inch thick. Sprinkle with salt. Arrange ham slice and cheese stick on each cutlet. Roll up as for jelly roll; tie securely with string. Roll in ¼ cup flour to coat. Brown in butter in skillet over medium heat, turning until golden on all sides. Transfer rolls to 11 x 7 x 1½-inch baking dish. Add ½ cup water, bouillon cube, mushrooms, and Sauterne to skillet. Heat, stirring in any crusty bits from skillet. Pour mixture over chicken. Bake covered, at 350°F for 1 hour or until tender. Arrange chicken on heated platter; remove strings. In small saucepan blend remaining 2 tablespoons flour with remaining ½ cup water; add pan drippings. Cook and stir until thickened. Pour small amount of gravy over chicken; garnish with almonds. Pass remaining gravy.

Menu Suggestion: Tomato Aspic (page 85), Green Bean Casserole (page 265), Strawberries à la Colony (page 354).

Wine Suggestion: A crisp, fruity wine such as California Chenin Blanc.

Dee Lawson Morris

Baked Chicken with Peanuts

Created at The Island Packet, Second Course Cooking School, Hilton Head Island, S.C.

Preparation: Easy
Cooking Time: 25 Minutes
Oven Temperature: 400°F

Serves: 4
Must Serve Immediately

4 boneless skinless chicken
    breast halves
Salt and pepper
1 cup finely diced Mozzarella
    cheese
½ cup **finely** chopped
    unsalted peanuts
½ cup bread crumbs, from
    French or Italian bread
½ cup mayonnaise
4 tablespoons unsalted butter,
    melted
4 tablespoons chopped parsley

Cut large pocket in each breast. Season pocket with salt and pepper and stuff with as much cheese as possible. Combine peanuts and bread crumbs in shallow dish. Coat each piece of chicken with mayonnaise, top and bottom, then roll in peanut mixture. Bake on rack in 400°F oven for 25 minutes. Serve on warm plate, dressed with melted butter and parsley. (It is important that peanuts be very finely chopped; use food processor or blender.)
Menu Suggestion: Sunshine Salad (page 91), Broccoli with Olive Sauce (page 259).
Wine Suggestion: A dry white such as a flavorful California Sauvignon Blanc.

Gus Wavpotich
Hilton Head Island, South Carolina

Paella

Preparation: Average
Cooking Time: 2 Hours
Oven Temperature: 350°F

Serves: 4-6

1 medium onion, chopped
¼ cup olive oil
8 assorted chicken pieces
1 (10-ounce) package long grain
    yellow (saffron) rice mix
1½ (10¾-ounce) cans chicken
    consommé
1 clove garlic, minced
1 bay leaf
1 small green pepper, chopped
2 (¼-inch thick) slices Genoa
    salami, slivered
½ cup white cooking wine
1 (6½-ounce) can minced clams,
    drained
8 raw jumbo shrimp, shelled
½ (10-ounce) package frozen
    green peas
1 (3-ounce) jar sliced
    pimiento
¼ cup freshly shredded
    Parmesan cheese

In large heavy oven-proof skillet sauté onions in olive oil until golden. Remove onions to holding dish. Brown chicken in oil approximately 5 minutes; remove to holding dish. Add rice to oil (adding slightly more oil if needed); cook, stirring, until golden. In separate saucepan heat consommé, garlic, bay leaf, and green pepper; **do not boil**. Return chicken and onions to rice. Add consommé mixture, salami, and wine. Bake, covered, at 350°F until rice is tender, approximately 1-1½ hours. Remove from oven; let cool slightly. Carefully stir in minced clams. Push shrimp down into rice. Sprinkle frozen peas over top. (May be prepared ahead to this point and refrigerated; return to room temperature before continuing.) Bake, covered, at 350°F for additional 30 minutes. Garnish with pimiento; sprinkle with cheese.
Menu Suggestion: Delicious Summer Fruit Salad (page 92), Quick and Easy Spoon Rolls (page 115), Crème Reversée au Caramel (page 345).
Wine Suggestion: A dry white such as Rioja.

Elaine Caras Waller

Mexicali Chicken

Preparation: Easy
Cooking Time: 20 Minutes
Oven Temperature: Broil

Serves: 4

2 whole boneless skinless
   chicken breasts, halved
1 tablespoon butter or
   margarine, melted
½ teaspoon salt
⅓ cup sour cream
1 canned green chili, drained
   and finely chopped
½ cup shredded Monterey Jack
   cheese
   Avocado slices

Place chicken breasts between 2 sheets of waxed paper. Pound to ¼ or ½-inch thickness. In large skillet sauté chicken in butter over medium-high heat 3-4 minutes on each side. Transfer chicken to foil-lined broiler tray. Sprinkle with salt. In small bowl blend sour cream, chili, and cheese; spread 1 rounded tablespoon on each chicken piece. Broil 6 inches from heat for 5 minutes. Garnish with avocado slices.
Menu Suggestion: Sour Cream Enchiladas (page 252), Fresh Fruit Tart (page 330).
Wine Suggestion: Sangria (page 11) or a generic dry white such as California Chablis.

Cookbook Committee

Chicken and Spinach Roll-Ups

Preparation: Average
Cooking Time: 1 Hour 15 Minutes
Oven Temperature: 350°F

Serves: 8-12

1 (10-ounce) package frozen
   chopped spinach, thawed
   and drained
1 cup herb-seasoned stuffing
1 medium onion, finely
   chopped
3 eggs, beaten
¼ cup grated Parmesan cheese
¼ cup butter, melted
½ teaspoon whole thyme
   leaves
½ teaspoon garlic powder
½ teaspoon pepper
12 boneless skinless chicken
   breast halves
1 (2½-ounce) jar sliced dried
   beef
12 slices bacon
1 (10¾-ounce) can cream of
   celery soup
1 cup sour cream
¼ cup white wine

Combine spinach, stuffing, onion, eggs, cheese, butter, thyme, garlic powder, and pepper; mix well. Shape into 12 balls; set aside. Use meat mallet to flatten breast halves to ¼-inch between layers of waxed paper. Place 1 slice dried beef and 1 spinach ball on each chicken piece. Roll up; secure with wooden pick. Cook bacon until soft but not crisp. Wrap 1 slice around each roll. Place rolls in greased 12 x 9 x 2-inch baking dish. Blend soup, sour cream, and wine; spoon over rolls. Bake, covered, at 350°F for 45 minutes. Remove cover; bake 30 minutes more. (May prepare and refrigerate overnight before baking. May freeze before baking; thaw in refrigerator. Bake as directed, or place directly in oven from freezer, adding 30 minutes to baking time.)

Marilyn Woodberry McCarver

Variation: Omit spinach balls. Sprinkle each breast with lemon-pepper seasoning. Place 1 whole mushroom on boned side of each breast. Roll breast over mushroom; wrap with one strip of bacon and secure with wooden pick. Line baking dish with dried beef. Place rolls atop beef. Proceed as above.
Menu Suggestion: Hot Sherried Fruit (page 283), Brioche (page 115), Cranberry Chiffon Pie (page 332).
Wine Suggestion: A light red wine such as Beaujolais.

Kathy Reeves Mathis

Capitol Chicken Casserole

A $10,000 winner in the 1980 National Poultry Cooking Contest sponsored by the National Broiler Council.

Preparation: Average
Cooking Time: 1 Hour 30 Minutes
Oven Temperature: 350°F

Serves: 4

4 tablespoons butter
1 tablespoon oil
1 broiler-fryer chicken, cut into parts
8 ounces fresh mushrooms, sliced
1 tablespoon flour
1 (10¾-ounce) can cream of chicken soup
1 cup dry white wine
1 cup water
½ cup whipping cream
1 teaspoon salt
¼ teaspoon tarragon leaves
¼ teaspoon pepper
1 (15-ounce) can artichoke hearts, drained
6 green onions, chopped (tops included)
2 tablespoons chopped parsley

Place butter and oil in large skillet; heat over medium heat until butter melts. Add chicken; sauté 10 minutes or until browned on all sides. Transfer chicken to baking pan or casserole. In same skillet sauté mushrooms 5 minutes or until tender. Stir in flour. Add soup, wine, and water. Simmer, stirring, 10 minutes or until sauce thickens. Stir in cream, salt, tarragon, and pepper; pour over chicken. Bake, uncovered, at 350°F for 1 hour. Mix in artichoke hearts, green onions, and parsley. Bake 5 additional minutes or until chicken is fork-tender.

Micronote: Preheat browning skillet 4½ minutes. Add oil, then chicken; brown. Place thicker pieces around outside. Cook on HIGH 6 minutes per pound of chicken, approximately 15-20 minutes. Transfer to baking dish or casserole. In skillet sauté mushrooms 3 minutes. Add flour, soup, wine, and water; cook on HIGH 6-8 minutes. Stir in cream, salt, tarragon, and pepper; pour over chicken. Cook on HIGH 10 minutes. Mix in artichoke hearts, green onions, and parsley. Cook on HIGH 2 minutes longer. Rotate dish several times during cooking.

Menu Suggestion: Amelia's Cranberry Pears (page 93), Sour Cream Mini Biscuits (page 380), Pecan Chiffon Pie (page 336).

Wine Suggestion: A full, dry white such as Chardonnay.

Cathy Brown Wilson

Chicken Breast in Foil

Want a different chicken for a box lunch or tailgate picnic? This one is a winner!

Preparation: Easy
Cooking Time: 30 Minutes
Oven Temperature: 350°F

Serves: 4

4 **chicken breast halves or 1-1½ pounds boneless chicken breast chunks**
1 **tablespoon chopped green onion**
2 **tablespoons butter, melted**
8 **fresh mushrooms**
2 **tablespoons chopped fresh parsley**
½ **cup dry white wine**
¼ **teaspoon garlic salt**
⅛ **teaspoon tarragon**

Lightly oil one side of 4 (12 x 12-inch) pieces foil; set aside. Sauté chicken and onions in butter until chicken is lightly browned; remove from heat. Lift chicken and onions from skillet with slotted spoon, dividing evenly among pieces of foil. Place 2 mushrooms atop each. Sprinkle parsley over each. Return skillet to heat. Add wine, stirring well to loosen any pan drippings. Add garlic salt and tarragon. Cook 3-5 minutes. Fold edges of each piece of foil upward to contain sauce. Spoon wine sauce over chicken, dividing evenly. Fold edges tightly to seal individual packets. (May be prepared ahead to this point and refrigerated.) Bake at 350°F for 30 minutes. Place sealed packets on dinner plates or in picnic boxes.

Micronote: Omit foil. Preheat browning skillet 4½ minutes. Brown chicken and onion in margarine. Cook on HIGH 6-8 minutes, turning twice. With slotted spoon remove chicken and onions to small "browning" bags. Place mushrooms over chicken; sprinkle with parsley. Add wine, garlic salt, and tarragon to drippings; cook sauce on HIGH 1 minute or until boiling. Spoon sauce over chicken. Tuck under ends of browning bag, but do not seal. Cook 2-3 minutes until hot.

Menu Suggestion: Broccoli and Cauliflower Salad (page 83), Oatmeal Bread (page 106), Chocolate Pound Cake (page 315).

Wine Suggestion: A dry white varietal from California such as a Sauvignon Blanc.

Joanne Portman McDonald

Gingered Pear Chicken and Walnuts

Chicken at its best! This dish has a nice Oriental flair when prepared using the boneless chicken option.

Preparation: Easy
Cooking Time: 40 Minutes
Oven Temperature: 350°F

Serves: 4

2 whole broiler-fryer chicken breasts, halved and skinned or 1½ pounds boneless chicken breast chunks
3 tablespoons margarine, melted
¼ teaspoon salt
1 (16-ounce) can pear halves
¾ cup ginger ale
¼ cup light brown sugar
3 tablespoons soy sauce
2 teaspoons cornstarch
¼ cup water
¼ teaspoon powdered ginger
¼ cup walnuts, coarsely broken

Sauté chicken in margarine over medium heat until brown on both sides, about 10 minutes. Sprinkle with salt. Drain pear juice into measuring cup; add water, if necessary, to make ¾ cup liquid. Mix together pear liquid, ginger ale, brown sugar, and soy sauce; pour over chicken. Cook, covered, over medium heat, turning occasionally, until fork-tender, about 25 minutes. Use slotted spoon to transfer chicken from skillet to large shallow baking dish. Cut each pear half into 2 wedges. Place pear wedges around chicken. In small bowl stir cornstarch into water until smooth. Stir in ginger. Pour cornstarch mixture into pan juices; cook, stirring, 5 minutes or until thick. Pour thickened mixture over chicken and pears. Sprinkle walnuts on top. (Casserole may be refrigerated at this point for up to 24 hours.) Bake, uncovered, at 350°F for 10 minutes or until very hot.

Micronote: Preheat browning skillet 4½ minutes. Sauté chicken in margarine. Place thinner pieces of chicken in center of skillet. Cook on HIGH 8-10 minutes. Mix pear juice, ginger ale, brown sugar, and soy sauce; pour over chicken. Cook, covered, 3-5 minutes or until chicken is tender. Remove chicken to shallow baking dish. Place pear wedges around chicken. Mix cornstarch with water; add ginger; stir. Cook on HIGH 3 minutes, stirring several times. Pour over chicken. Cover with waxed paper; cook on HIGH 5 minutes or until heated through.

Menu Suggestion: Herbed Pastry with Spinach Filling (page 268), Mandarin Carrots (page 274), Frozen Mocha Meringue Pie (page 334).

Wine Suggestion: A spicy white wine such as Alsatian Gewürztraminer.

National Chicken Cooking Contest
National Broiler Council.
Second Place, 1979, $4,000 Award.

My Favorite Easy Chicken Casserole

Preparation: Easy
Cooking Time: 45 Minutes
Oven Temperature: 350°F

Serves: 8

2 cups boneless cooked
    chicken breast chunks
1 cup diced celery
1 cup cooked rice
1 (10¾-ounce) can cream of
    mushroom soup
¾ cup mayonnaise
1 cup sliced water chestnuts
½ cup sliced almonds, toasted
1 (2-ounce) jar diced pimiento
1 tablespoon chopped onion
½ teaspoon salt
¼ teaspoon black pepper
¼ teaspoon cayenne
⅔ cup shredded Cheddar
    cheese (optional)
    Paprika (optional)

Mix all ingredients except cheese and paprika until well blended. Place in 2-quart casserole. Bake, uncovered, at 350°F for 45 minutes. Garnish with cheese and/or paprika during last 10 minutes baking time.

Micronote: Assemble as directed. Cook 10-12 minutes on HIGH, turning dish halfway through cooking period. Garnish.

Menu Suggestion: Mincemeat Salad (page 91), Broccoli Sunburst (page 260).

Wine Suggestion: A fuller white such as a German Rheingau.

Frances Miller Mathis

Simon and Garfunkel Chicken

A catchy name for a prizewinning recipe.

Preparation: Average
Cooking Time: 50 Minutes
Oven Temperature: 350°F

Serves: 4-6

6 boneless chicken breast
    halves
½ cup butter, divided
    Salt and pepper to taste
6 slices Mozzarella cheese
    Flour
1 egg, beaten
    Fresh bread crumbs
2 tablespoons chopped fresh
    parsley
¼ teaspoon sage
¼ teaspoon rosemary
¼ teaspoon thyme
½ cup dry white wine

Flatten chicken breasts between sheets of waxed paper. Use ¼ cup butter to spread on one side of each breast. Season with salt and pepper. Roll up each piece of chicken; wrap each with 1 slice of Mozzarella. Coat lightly with flour. Dip in egg. Roll in bread crumbs. Secure with wooden picks. Arrange in shallow baking dish. Melt remaining ¼ cup butter; add herbs. Baste chicken rolls with herbed butter. Bake, covered, at 350°F for 30 minutes, basting again during cooking. Pour wine over chicken. Bake, uncovered, 20 minutes more, continuing to baste frequently with herbed butter.

Menu Suggestion: Heavenly Lime Salad (page 90), Company Carrots (page 274), Frozen Mocha Meringue Pie (page 334).

Wine Suggestion: A dry white such as a California "classic white" (use same in recipe).

Cathy Brown Wilson
Rita Rhinehart
Oakwood, Georgia
First Place Winner, 1974, **The Times** Cooking Contest

Chicken Lafayette

Preparation: Easy
Cooking Time: 45 Minutes
Oven Temperature: 375°F

Serves: 6-8

8 boneless skinless chicken
    breast halves
Seasoned salt
½ cup butter or margarine,
    divided
2 (9-ounce) packages frozen
    artichoke hearts, thawed
    and halved
½ pound mushrooms, sliced
3 tablespoons flour
1½ cups chicken broth
⅓ cup sherry

Sprinkle chicken with salt. Brown in ¼ cup melted butter. Arrange chicken in shallow baking dish. Add artichokes; set aside. Sauté mushrooms in ¼ cup melted butter until tender. Sprinkle flour over mushrooms, stirring until blended. Gradually add chicken broth and sherry, stirring constantly; simmer 5 minutes. Pour over chicken. Bake, covered, at 375°F for 45 minutes.

Micronote: Preheat browning skillet 4½ minutes. Sauté chicken in ¼ cup butter; cook on HIGH 6 minutes. Add artichokes. In small glass dish sauté mushrooms in ¼ cup butter on HIGH 2-3 minutes. Add flour, broth, and sherry. Cook on HIGH 3-4 minutes, stirring several times. Pour over chicken. Cook on MEDIUM 10-12 minutes. Salt to taste.

Menu Suggestion: Bridal Salad (page 89), Pecan Pilaf (page 285), Fresh Apple-Orange Bread (page 110).

Wine Suggestion: A full white such as California Chardonnay.

Gail Adams Thomas

Chicken au Champagne

A beautiful dish enhanced by the flavor of champagne and liqueur.

Preparation: Average
Cooking Time: 45 Minutes
Oven Temperature: 350°F

Serves: 6-8

4 boneless skinless chicken
    breast halves
8 boneless skinless chicken
    thighs
6 tablespoons flour
Salt
5 tablespoons butter, divided
3 tablespoons oil
¾ cup champagne
4 tablespoons Curaçao
1 cup chicken broth
1 cup fresh mushrooms
½ cup whipping cream
Orange sections
Grapes
Parsleyed rice

Dredge chicken in flour and salt. Heat 3 tablespoons butter with oil in skillet. Add chicken; sauté until brown on all sides. Transfer chicken to shallow baking dish. Bake, uncovered, at 350°F for 20 minutes. Meanwhile, pour fat from skillet; add champagne, Curaçao, and broth. Simmer until hot. Pour over chicken; cook 20 additional minutes. Melt remaining 2 tablespoons butter in skillet. Add mushrooms; sauté lightly. Remove from heat; stir in cream. Pour over chicken; bake just long enough to heat through. Place in serving dish; garnish with orange sections and grapes. Serve over parsleyed rice.

Menu Suggestion: Ambrosia Mold (page 89), Broccoli Elegant (page 261), Charlotte Russe (page 349).

Wine Suggestion: A Brut champagne from Spain.

Jane Elizabeth Carter

Ritzy Chicken

Preparation: Easy
Cooking Time: 1 Hour
Oven Temperature: 350°F

Serves: 8

- 2 cups **Ritz cracker crumbs**
- ¾ cup **grated Parmesan cheese**
- ¼ cup **chopped fresh parsley**
- 2 teaspoons **salt**
- ⅛ teaspoon **pepper**
- ⅛ teaspoon **minced garlic**
- 1 cup **butter, melted**
- ⅓ cup **sherry**
- 8-10 **boneless chicken breast halves**

With steel blade of food processor, or by hand, blend crumbs, cheese, parsley, salt, pepper, and garlic. Place in shallow dish. Mix butter and sherry in second shallow dish. Dip each chicken piece in butter mixture, then roll in crumb mixture. Arrange in shallow foil-lined pan. Drizzle remaining butter mixture over chicken. Bake, uncovered, at 350°F for 1 hour. (Do not turn.)

Micronote: Prepare chicken as above. Arrange in circle on microwave-safe rack. Sprinkle with paprika, if desired. Cover with plastic wrap. Cook on HIGH 15-20 minutes, depending on thickness of breasts. Uncover; let stand 5 minutes.

Menu Suggestion: Green Bean Casserole (page 265), Molly's Butterscotch Pie (page 336).

Wine Suggestion: A light red such as California Gamay.

Carrie McClain Hatfield

Chicken-Artichoke Casserole

A luncheon specialty with great do-ahead potential.

Preparation: Easy
Cooking Time: 25 Minutes
Oven Temperature: 350°F

Serves: 8-10

- 2 (14-ounce) cans **artichoke hearts, drained and quartered**
- 3 cups **cooked diced chicken**
- 2 (10¾-ounce) cans **cream of chicken soup**
- 1 cup **mayonnaise**
- 1 teaspoon **lemon juice**
- ¼ teaspoon **curry powder**
- 1-1½ cups **grated sharp Cheddar cheese**
- 1¼ cups **bread cubes or crumbs**
- 2 tablespoons **butter, melted**
- ⅓ cup **white wine (optional)**

Arrange artichokes over bottom of greased 12 x 9 x 2-inch baking dish. Layer chicken over artichokes. Blend soup, mayonnaise, lemon juice, curry powder, and wine; pour over chicken. Sprinkle with cheese. Toss bread cubes with butter; arrange over cheese. (May be covered at this point and refrigerated for later use. Allow to return to room temperature before baking.) Bake at 350°F for 25 minutes.

Micronote: Assemble as directed. Cook on HIGH 10-12 minutes, turning dish twice during cooking.

Variation: Chicken-Broccoli-Rice - Instead of artichokes layer casserole with 2 boxes, slightly cooked chopped broccoli, then 3 cups cooked rice and cooked chicken. Cover with sauce and proceed as directed.

Menu Suggestion: Delicious Summer Fruit Salad (page 92), Spinach-Stuffed Tomatoes (page 270), Chocolate-Amaretto Mousse Pie (page 335).

Wine Suggestion: A white Zinfandel.

Carrie McClain Hatfield

Avocado Chicken

Preparation: Easy
Cooking Time: 5-10 Minutes
Oven Temperature: 350°F

Serves: 4
Must Serve Immediately

4 **(8-ounce) whole boneless skinless chicken breasts**
Salt
Pepper
Flour
2 **eggs, beaten**
2 **tablespoons milk**
4 **tablespoons butter, melted**
4 **thick slices avocado**
Bernaise Sauce (page 292)

Flatten chicken breasts with rolling pin. Season to taste with salt and pepper; dust with flour. Combine eggs and milk. Dip chicken breasts into egg mixture. Sauté chicken in butter until lightly browned on both sides (about 3 minutes per side). Transfer to baking dish; bake at 350°F for 5 minutes. Top each chicken breast with avocado slice and Bernaise Sauce.

Menu Suggestion: Gazpacho (page 65), Spinach-Stuffed Squash (page 270), Brioche (page 115), Coeur à la Crème (page 347).

Wine Suggestion: A full, rich, dry white such as Chardonnay.

Cookbook Committee

Chicken Alouette with Dill Butter Sauce

Definitely "haute cuisine" - and it's not even hard! (Conceal this fact from your guests and preserve your reputation.)

Preparation: Average
Cooking Time: 20 Minutes
Oven Temperature: 400°F

Serves: 4
Must Partially Do Ahead

4 **(6-ounce) whole boneless skinless chicken breasts**
8 **ounces herb-garlic cheese**
3 **eggs**
¼ **cup milk**
Flour
2 **cups dry bread crumbs**
Oil

Lightly flatten chicken breasts between layers of waxed paper to ½-inch thickness. Quarter cheese; spread evenly on each breast. Fold breasts in half, tucking ends under. Cover; chill 1 hour. Beat eggs and milk. Dredge stuffed breasts in flour, dip into egg mixture, then coat with bread crumbs. Heat oil in large skillet; brown breasts evenly on all sides. Transfer from skillet to baking sheet. Bake at 400°F for 8-10 minutes. Serve with Dill Butter Sauce.

Dill Butter Sauce

2 **tablespoons minced shallots**
½ **cup dry white wine**
1½ **tablespoons fresh lemon juice**
¾ **cup whipping cream**
1 **tablespoon dill weed**
1 **teaspoon salt**
½ **teaspoon hot pepper sauce**
1 **cup unsalted butter, cut into pieces**

Combine shallots, white wine, and lemon juice in a small saucepan. Simmer over moderate heat until liquid is reduced to 2 tablespoons. Add cream; reduce again until liquid is ½ cup. Stir in dill weed, salt, and hot pepper sauce. Just before serving heat sauce slowly, whisking constantly. Slowly whip in pieces of butter. Do not allow sauce to boil. (Also delicious over seafood and fresh vegetables.)

Menu Suggestion: Cauliflower Cream Soup (page 62), Spinach-Stuffed Squash (page 270), Black Bottom Pie (page 337).

Wine Suggestion: A quality full white such as a French Chablis.

Dana Blum Barclay

Durkee's Chicken

We predict that this will become a mainstay of your busy-day repertoire. Incredibly easy, with a delicious, zesty flavor.

Preparation: Easy
Cooking Time: 1 Hour
Oven Temperature: 350°F

Serves: 4-6

6 **chicken breast halves**
½ **cup butter, melted, or**
  ½ **cup oil**
½ **cup Durkee's Famous Sauce**
3 **cups cooked rice**

Place chicken breasts in single layer in shallow baking dish. Blend butter and Durkee's; pour over chicken. Bake, covered, at 350°F for 45 minutes. Uncover; bake 15 minutes more or until brown. Serve chicken atop bed of rice; pour drippings over all.

Micronote: Blend butter and Durkee's; pour over chicken in shallow glass dish. Cover with waxed paper. Cook on HIGH 6 minutes per pound of chicken, turning dish several times.

Menu Suggestion: Gazpacho Salad (page 65), French Fried Mushrooms (page 258).

Wine Suggestion: A dry white generic such as California "classic white."

Lucy Fokes Link

Mushroom Chicken en Phyllo

Preparation: Average
Cooking Time: 20 Minutes
Oven Temperature: 375°F

Serves: 8

4 **ounces mushrooms, thinly**
  sliced
¼ **cup finely chopped onion**
4 **tablespoons butter, melted**
  and divided
4 **cups diced cooked chicken**
1½ **cups shredded Swiss cheese**
2 **eggs, beaten**
¼ **cup chopped parsley**
1 **teaspoon salt**
½ **teaspoon tarragon**
16 **sheets phyllo pastry**
  Sour cream

Sauté mushrooms and onions in 1 tablespoon butter until limp. Remove from heat. Stir in chicken, cheese, eggs, parsley, salt, and tarragon until well blended. [See "On Phyllo," (page 399).] Spread 1 sheet of phyllo on smooth-working surface. Brush lightly with some of remaining butter. Cover with second sheet of phyllo; brush with butter. Spoon ribbon of chicken filling (approximately ⅔ cup) along narrow end of phyllo. Fold in sides of phyllo and roll loosely. Place seam-side down on greased baking sheet; brush with butter. Repeat with remaining ingredients to make 8 rolls. Bake at 375°F for 20 minutes or until lightly browned. Top each with dollop of sour cream when serving.

Menu Suggestion: Spinach-Stuffed Tomatoes (page 270), Red Devil's Food Cake (page 307).

Wine Suggestion: A crisp dry white such as California Chenin Blanc.

Lou Bowen Powers
Wilmington, North Carolina

Chicken Veron
é

Preparation: Easy
Cooking Time: 1 Hour 15 Minutes
Oven Temperature: 325°F

Serves: 6

2½-3   **pounds chicken breasts, skinned**
3   **tablespoons oil**
3   **tablespoons butter or margarine**
1   **tablespoon snipped chives**
¼   **cup dry white wine**
1   **cup sour cream**
1   **teaspoon salt**
¼   **teaspoon ground white pepper**
1⅓   **cups seedless green grapes**

Pat chicken dry. Heat oil and butter in skillet. Add chicken; sauté until brown. Simmer, covered, 30 minutes. Transfer chicken to shallow baking dish; set aside. Pour off grease from skillet. Add chives and wine to pan drippings. Heat to boiling, stirring to loosen browned bits. Remove from heat. Stir in sour cream, salt, and pepper. Pour sauce over chicken. Bake, covered, at 325°F for 30 minutes. Remove cover; stir in grapes. Bake 10 minutes longer.
Menu Suggestion: Apricot Mousse Salad (page 90), Carrot and Zucchini Julienne (page 273), Japanese Fruit Pie (page 331).
Wine Suggestion: A flavorful white such as French Alsatian.

Judy Mynatt Bush

Chicken Roquemore

Preparation: Complex
Cooking Time: 30 Minutes
Oven Temperature: 350°F

Serves: 4
Must Partially Do Ahead

4   **(6-ounce) whole boneless skinless chicken breasts**
   Oregano
   Salt
   White pepper
4   **tablespoons shredded Swiss cheese**
4   **tablespoons shredded Mozzarella cheese**
4   **tablespoons shredded Gouda cheese**
4   **tablespoons cream cheese, softened**
   Butter
   Fresh bread crumbs
4   **eggs, beaten**
4   **tablespoons milk**
   Flour
4   **tablespoons butter, melted**
4   **tablespoons oil**
   Chopped parsley
16   **fresh asparagus tips, cooked**
   Large mushroom caps
   Blender Hollandaise Sauce (page 290)

Season chicken with oregano, salt, and pepper to taste. Pound with mallet to ½-inch thickness. Combine cheeses; place equal amounts on one side of each breast. Add 2 thin slices of butter to each; sprinkle with bread crumbs. Fold over; place in freezer until firm. Blend eggs and milk. Assemble crumbs and flour in separate dishes. Remove chicken from freezer. Roll each in bread crumbs; dust with flour; submerge in egg mixture; remove and roll in crumbs again. Heat butter and oil in skillet; sauté chicken until lightly brown. Transfer to baking dish. Bake at 350°F for 15-20 minutes. Remove from oven. Separate along folded edges; press open. Slightly press 4 asparagus tips into open edge of each breast. Sprinkle with parsley. Top each with mushroom cap and Hollandaise Sauce.
Menu Suggestion: Cream of Artichoke Soup (page 60), Gourmet Rice-Stuffed Tomatoes (page 277), Croissants (page 113), Crème Courvoisier (page 352).
Wine Suggestion: A full, flavorful dry white such as a quality California Chardonnay.

Cookbook Committee

Elegant Chicken Divan

A favorite for dinner parties. There are many easier chicken divans, but none can beat this classic version.

Preparation: Average
Cooking Time: 1 Hour
Oven Temperature: Broil

Serves: 6

6 **whole chicken breasts**
1 **cup water**
3 **tablespoons sherry**
3 **celery tops**
1 **teaspoon salt**
½ **teaspoon pepper**
2 **bunches fresh broccoli, cooked, or 4 (10-ounce) packages frozen broccoli spears, cooked**
1 **recipe Divan Sauce**
  Parmesan cheese, grated

Combine chicken, water, sherry, celery, salt, and pepper. Bring to boil; simmer or steam until chicken is cooked and tender. Remove chicken from stock; cool and slice. Strain stock, reserving 1 cup for Divan Sauce. Line large shallow baking dish with well-drained broccoli, turning tops to outside. Arrange chicken slices over broccoli. Spoon sauce over all. Sprinkle with Parmesan. Place under broiler until lightly browned (approximately 10 minutes).

Divan Sauce

½ **cup butter or margarine**
½ **cup flour**
1 **cup milk**
1 **cup chicken stock**
½ **teaspoon salt**
½ **teaspoon pepper**
2 **tablespoons grated Parmesan cheese**
½ **teaspoon Worcestershire**
¼ **cup sherry**
½ **cup Blender Hollandaise Sauce (page 290)**
1 **cup whipping cream, whipped**

Melt butter in medium saucepan; stir in flour. Add milk, stock, salt, and pepper. Cook, stirring, over medium heat until thickened. Add cheese, Worcestershire, and sherry; blend well. Fold in Hollandaise and whipped cream.
Menu Suggestion: Cranberry Salad Ring (page 88), Light-as-a-Feather Refrigerator Rolls (page 112), Red Velvet Cake (page 311).
Wine Suggestion: A full, dry white such as a French Chablis from Burgundy.

Susan Henson Frost

There is real enjoyment in a well-cooked meal.
Mrs. Hill's New Cookbook circa 1890.

Chicken and Vegetables Chablis

An especially attractive dish which can be kept ready in the freezer to whisk out for company.

Preparation: Easy
Cooking Time: 1 Hour 30 Minutes
Oven Temperature: 325°F

Serves: 6

6-8 **boneless skinless chicken breast halves**
   Salt and pepper to taste
¼ **cup flour**
   Oil
1 **pound fresh mushrooms, sliced**
2 **(8-ounce) cans pearl onions, drained**
2 **cups Chablis**
½ **teaspoon dried thyme**
1 **(16-ounce) can whole baby carrots, drained**
   Cooked wild rice

Sprinkle chicken breasts with salt and pepper; dredge lightly in flour. Sauté in small amount of oil over medium-high heat until browned. Transfer from skillet to greased 13 x 9-inch baking dish. In same skillet lightly sauté mushrooms, adding additional oil if necessary. Stir in onions. Spoon mushrooms and onions over chicken. Add wine to skillet; stir well to deglaze. Pour over chicken and vegetables. (May be frozen at this point if desired.) Sprinkle with thyme. Bake, covered, at 325°F for 1 hour. Add carrots; bake, uncovered, additional 15 minutes. Serve over wild rice.

Micronote: Do not salt until end of cooking time. Preheat browning skillet on HIGH 4½ minutes. Add oil; brown floured chicken. Cook chicken 6 minutes per pound, turning dish during cooking. Remove chicken. Add mushrooms; cook 2-3 minutes on HIGH, stirring several times. Add chicken, onions, and other ingredients. Cook, covered, on MEDIUM 12-15 minutes.

Menu Suggestion: Heavenly Lime Salad (page 90), Cottage Cheese Rolls (page 112), Classic Pound Cake (page 314) with Almond-Honey Ice Cream Sauce (page 357).

Wine Suggestion: A dry white similar to that used in recipe.

Patricia Franklin Rauch

Cookery is my one vanity and I am a slave to any guest who praises my culinary art.
Marjorie Kinnan Rawlings, from *Cross Creek*.
Charles Scribner's Sons. Copyright 1942. Reprinted with permission of Charles Scribner's Sons.

Sweet and Sour Grilled Chicken

Preparation: Easy
Cooking Time: 50 Minutes

Serves: 4-6

1 broiler-fryer chicken,
  cut into parts
¼ cup prepared yellow mustard
¼ cup orange marmalade
2 tablespoons soy sauce

Grill chicken pieces 4 inches above hot coals for 20 minutes, turning occasionally. Combine mustard, marmalade, and soy sauce; blend well. Brush over chicken. Grill additional 20-30 minutes, turning frequently and brushing with glaze. **Micronote:** While coals are heating, cook chicken in shallow dish, covered, at MEDIUM for 20 minutes; turn once after 10 minutes. Remove to grill, brush with glaze, and continue as above for last 20-30 minutes of grilling time. **Menu Suggestion:** Green Salad with Mama's French Dressing (page 100), Duo-Squash Casserole (page 272), Herbed Dinner Triangles (page 118), Fresh and Crunchy Peach Pie (page 333). **Wine Suggestion:** A dry white such as Italian Soave.

Cindy Collins Randolph

Lemon-Garlic Grilled Chicken

Preparation: Easy
Cooking Time: 1 Hour 30 Minutes (Grill)
              40 Minutes (Oven)

Serves: 4-8
Must Partially Do Ahead

1 cup butter or margarine,
  melted
1 cup lemon juice
2 (.7-ounce) packages garlic
  salad dressing mix
2 broiler-fryer chickens,
  halved or 8 chicken breast
  halves

Blend butter, lemon juice, and dressing mix. Refrigerate overnight. Place chicken on grill, skin-side up, 6 inches above grayed coals. Grill 1 hour, turning every 15 minutes. Meanwhile, heat sauce just until warm. Brush chicken generously with sauce; grill 30 minutes longer, brushing with sauce and turning every 2-3 minutes. To oven-broil, brush chicken with warmed sauce on all sides. Place skin-side down on broiler rack; set 7-8 inches from heat. Broil 15 minutes; turn. Brush with sauce; broil 15 additional minutes, brushing 1-2 times more, until richly browned. Test for doneness by making slit near hip joint; if juices are pink, broil additional 5 minutes or until juices run clear. **Menu Suggestion:** Fresh Asparagus with Blender Hollandaise Sauce (page 290), Casserole of Sweet Vidalias (page 255), Beech Island Bread (page 103), Brown Sugar Pound Cake (page 316). **Wine Suggestion:** A dry white such as Italian Soave.

Ellorie Smith
Cumming, Georgia

Grilled Coriander Chicken

Preparation: Easy
Cooking Time: 30 Minutes

Serves: 4
Must Partially Do Ahead

4 tablespoons soy sauce
2 teaspoons ground coriander
1 teaspoon brown sugar
8 peppercorns, crushed
2 cloves garlic, minced
8 chicken thighs or 4
    breast halves

In shallow bowl combine soy sauce, coriander, brown sugar, peppercorns, and garlic; blend well. Add chicken, turning to coat. Cover; marinate at room temperature 30 minutes, basting occasionally. Reserve marinade. Place chicken on grill over hot coals about 8 inches from heat. Cook on one side for 10 minutes. Turn chicken, basting with reserved marinade; cook 20 minutes longer or until fork-tender.

Menu Suggestion: Artichoke-Rice Salad (page 80), Zesty Squash (page 271), Frozen Peach Cream Pie (page 334).

Wine Suggestion: A light red such as Italian Bardolino.

Diane Derrick Blalock

Glazed Chicken en Brochette

Chicken kabobs with a deliciously different flavor. They can be grilled, broiled, or microwaved with equal success.

Preparation: Easy
Cooking Time: 20 Minutes

Serves: 4

2 whole boneless skinless
    chicken breasts, halved
¼ pound medium mushrooms
3 green onions, cut in
    2-inch pieces
½ cup orange marmalade
¼ cup soy sauce
2 tablespoons honey
½ teaspoon ground ginger
½ teaspoon salt
1 clove garlic, minced
1 (8-ounce) package bacon

Cut each breast half into 5 pieces; place in bowl. Add all remaining ingredients except bacon; stir to coat well. Cook bacon just until limp; drain. Cut each bacon piece in half. Wrap each chicken chunk with 1 piece of bacon. Thread onto skewers in following order: chicken, mushrooms, and onions. Repeat to fill skewers. Pour remaining marinade into saucepan. Bring to boil over high heat; boil gently 6-8 minutes until slightly thickened and reduced by half. Place skewers on grill rack over medium coals (may also be done under broiler). Grill 15 minutes or until chicken is fork-tender, brushing occasionally with sauce and turning.

Micronote: Prepare chicken, vegetables, and sauce as directed. Cook bacon on HIGH 1 minute. Fill wooden skewers as directed. Pour marinade into large glass measure; cook on HIGH 3 minutes. Place skewers on microwave rack or across shallow glass baking dish. Cover loosely with waxed paper. Cook on HIGH 10-14 minutes, until bacon is crisp and chicken tests done; turn skewers and brush with sauce every 2-3 minutes. Rearrange skewers after 6 minutes.

Menu Suggestion: Creamy Asparagus Salad (page 85), Quick Butter Biscuits (page 117), Pecan Chiffon Pie (page 336).

Wine Suggestion: A California Riesling.

Cynthia Sims Syfan

Marinated Grilled Chicken

Preparation: Easy

Serves: 8-10
Must Partially Do Ahead

1¼ cups butter, melted
1¼ cups white wine
1 cup soy sauce
4 teaspoons tarragon
4 teaspoons prepared
    mustard
1 teaspoon monosodium
    glutamate
12-16 chicken pieces

Combine all ingredients except chicken; blend well. Pour over chicken. Marinate 3-4 hours. Cook chicken over low charcoal fire until tender and juicy, basting often with marinade.
Menu Suggestion: Marinated Vegetable Medley (page 82), Cheesy Vidalia Onion Casserole (page 255), Helen Johnson's Caramel-Vanilla Ice Cream (page 354).
Wine Suggestion: A dry white such as California Chablis (use same in marinade).

Patsy Lothridge Hicks

Oriental Grilled Chicken

Preparation: Easy
Cooking Time: 20-40 Minutes

Serves: 4
Must Partially Do Ahead

½ cup pineapple juice
½ cup oil
¼ cup soy sauce
1 tablespoon brown sugar
2 teaspoons ground ginger
1 teaspoon dry mustard
1 teaspoon garlic salt
1 pound boneless chicken
    breasts

Combine juice, oil, soy sauce, brown sugar, ginger, mustard, and garlic salt in small saucepan. Simmer 5 minutes; **do not boil.** Let cool. Place chicken in shallow baking dish; pour marinade over chicken. Cover; refrigerate 2-3 hours or overnight. Grill over hot coals, basting occasionally, until chicken is tender. (May be oven-broiled on rack or in marinade.)
Menu Suggestion: Honeydew Lime Bisque (page 67), Chutney-Rice Salad (page 78), Chocolate Pound Cake (page 315).
Wine Suggestion: Try a fruitier type such as a French Alsatian white.

Helen Johnson Morris

Sherried Almond Chicken

Preparation: Easy
Cooking Time: 15 Minutes

Serves: 4

1½ pounds boneless skinless chicken breasts
2 tablespoons cornstarch
4 teaspoons light brown sugar
2 teaspoons ground ginger
⅔ cup sherry
6 tablespoons soy sauce
6 tablespoons water
¼ cup oil
1 cup whole almonds
2 (6-ounce) packages frozen pea pods, thawed

Cut chicken into 1-inch cubes; set aside. Combine cornstarch, brown sugar, ginger, sherry, soy sauce, and water. Mix well; set aside. Drain pea pods and blot dry with absorbent toweling; set aside. Heat oil in skillet or wok over medium heat. Add almonds; stir-fry 3 minutes. Add chicken; stir-fry just until chicken turns white. Add sherry mixture; cook 3 minutes, until sauce thickens. Add pea pods; stir-fry 4 minutes, until hot and glazed.

Menu Suggestion: Sunshine Salad (page 91), Shrimp Fried Rice (page 286).

Wine Suggestion: A white wine such as Italian Frascati.

Joanne Portman McDonald

Cashew Chicken

Preparation: Average

Serves: 6
Must Partially Do Ahead
Must Serve Immediately

2 teaspoons fresh minced ginger or ½ teaspoon powdered ginger
¼ cup soy sauce, divided
2 teaspoons monosodium glutamate, divided
1 tablespoon rice wine
1 pound boneless skinless chicken breasts, cubed
1 cup cubed bamboo shoots, drained
1 cup green pepper squares (1-inch)
½ cup quartered mushrooms
1 clove garlic, minced
1 tablespoon sugar
½ teaspoon salt
2 tablespoons cornstarch, divided
½ cup water or chicken broth
1 egg white
¾ cup oil
1½ cups cashews

Combine ginger, 3 tablespoons soy sauce, 1 teaspoon monosodium glutamate, and wine. Pour over chicken; marinate one hour or overnight. Combine bamboo shoots, green pepper, mushrooms, garlic, sugar, salt, 1 tablespoon soy sauce, and 1 teaspoon monosodium glutamate; marinate 30 minutes or overnight. Blend 1 tablespoon cornstarch and water; set aside. Beat egg white until stiff; beat in 1 tablespoon cornstarch. Heat oil in wok to 360°F. Place cashews in metal strainer; immerse in hot oil just until golden. Remove; set aside. Drop chicken into egg white batter to coat; fry in hot oil until slightly brown. Remove; set aside. Drain all but ¼ cup oil from wok. Stir-fry vegetable mixture in remaining hot oil until tender-crisp. Return chicken and nuts to wok; stir. Add water-cornstarch mixture. Stir until all ingredients are well coated with sauce. (In a pinch, this dish may be held in 150°F oven for 1 hour.)

Menu Suggestion: Sesame Broccoli (page 261), Frozen Peach Cream Pie (page 334).

Wine Suggestion: A dry white French vin ordinaire.

Mimi Luebbers Gerding

Sugar Snap Chow Guy Kew

This may sound difficult because of the variety of ingredients, but do not be intimidated. The secret is to have all ingredients ready on the counter. Stir-fry cooking is quick, easy, and usually low-calorie.

Preparation: Average
Cooking Time: 15 Minutes

Serves: 6

2 teaspoons soy sauce, divided
1 teaspoon dry white wine
1 teaspoon finely shredded
   ginger
½ cup + 1 tablespoon water,
   divided
1 tablespoon cornstarch
1 teaspoon sugar
   Pinch white pepper
1 tablespoon oil
1 teaspoon salt
1 clove garlic, minced
1 pound white chicken meat,
   thinly sliced
¼ pound lean fresh pork,
   thinly sliced
1 cup canned bamboo shoots,
   drained
½ cup thinly sliced
   mushrooms
1 cup thinly sliced celery
¼ cup canned sliced water
   chestnuts, drained
½ cup sliced onions
¼ pound sugar snaps or
   snow peas
1 cup chicken broth
½ teaspoon Mei Yen
   seasoning
½ teaspoon Beau Monde
   seasoning

In small container combine 1 teaspoon soy sauce, wine, ginger, and 1 tablespoon water; set aside. In separate container combine 1 teaspoon soy sauce, ½ cup water, cornstarch, sugar, and pepper; set aside. In wok or heavy skillet heat oil. Add salt and garlic; stir. Add chicken and pork; stir-fry until meat rolls up like little balls. Add first soy sauce mixture; stir-fry 1 minute. Add bamboo shoots, mushrooms, celery, water chestnuts, and onions; stir-fry 5 minutes. Add sugar snaps and chicken broth; cover and cook 2 minutes. Uncover, stir in second soy sauce mixture, Mei Yen seasoning, and Beau Monde seasoning; cook until gravy thickens and is smooth.

Micronote: In large microwave-proof casserole heat oil on HIGH 1 minute. Add salt, garlic, chicken, and pork; cover and cook on HIGH 2 minutes. Add first soy sauce mixture; cover and cook on HIGH 1 minute. Add bamboo shoots, mushrooms, celery, water chestnuts, and sliced onions; cover and cook on HIGH 3-4 minutes, until vegetables are slightly cooked. Add sugar snaps and chicken broth; cover and cook on HIGH 1 minute. Stir in second soy sauce mixture, Mei Yen seasoning, and Beau Monde seasoning; cover and cook on HIGH 2 minutes, stirring once.

Menu Suggestion: Shrimp Fried Rice (page 286), Egg Rolls (page 30), Lemon Meringue Nests (page 343).

Wine Suggestion: Try warm Saki.

Carol Cratin Ferrell

Oriental Sesame Chicken Dinner

Preparation: Easy
Cooking Time: 10 Minutes

Serves: 4

6 **boneless skinless chicken breast halves**
3 **tablespoons soy sauce**
3 **tablespoons oil**
2 **tablespoons sesame seeds**
1 **tablespoon lemon juice**
¼-½ **teaspoon garlic powder**
1 **(8-ounce) package chicken-flavored rice, cooked**
1 **bunch fresh broccoli, cooked or 2 (10-ounce) packages frozen broccoli spears, cooked**
Lemon wedges

Cut each chicken breast half into 3 lengthwise strips. Toss with soy sauce and oil; set aside. Toast sesame seeds in large skillet or wok over medium heat, stirring constantly. Turn seeds out; set aside. Add chicken mixture to skillet or wok; stir-fry until browned and tender, about 7 minutes. Stir in lemon juice; sprinkle with garlic. Mound rice onto serving platter. Surround with broccoli and lemon wedges. Arrange chicken over rice. Sprinkle sesame seeds over all.

Menu Suggestion: Gourmet Fruit Salad (page 87), Buttermilk Pound Cake (page 316) with Mother's Caramel Icing (page 326).

Wine Suggestion: A dry white such as California Sauvignon Blanc.

Ann Ash Hartness

Szechuan Chicken

A good stir-fry dish for those who like spicy foods.

Preparation: Average
Cooking Time: 15-20 Minutes

Serves: 4
Must Serve Immediately

3 **tablespoons oil, divided**
½ **cup slivered almonds**
2 **whole boneless skinless chicken breasts**
2 **tablespoons cornstarch**
2 **cloves garlic, minced and divided**
2-3 **teaspoons freshly grated ginger root or ½-1 teaspoon ground ginger, divided**
1 **red or green sweet pepper**
½ **cup sliced green onions**
⅛-¼ **teaspoon ground red pepper**
3 **tablespoons soy sauce**
1 **tablespoon sherry**
1 **teaspoon vinegar**

In large skillet or wok heat 1 teaspoon oil over medium-high heat. Add almonds; toast until golden brown, stirring occasionally. Remove almonds; set aside. Cut chicken into ¾-inch cubes; toss with cornstarch until well-coated. Heat 2 tablespoons oil in skillet or wok over medium-high heat. Cook chicken with half the garlic and ginger about 3-5 minutes, stirring occasionally. Remove chicken; set aside. Heat 2 teaspoons oil in skillet or wok. Cut sweet pepper into ½-inch pieces. Add remaining garlic and ginger, sweet pepper, green onions, and red pepper. Stir-fry 3-4 minutes. Add remaining ingredients; return chicken to skillet. Cook 1 minute. Stir in toasted almonds.

Menu Suggestion: Stir-Fry Pea Pods (page 267), Egg Foo Yong (page 248), Pineapple Sherbet (page 356).

Wine Suggestion. A California vin ordinaire, white or red; or beer.

Cookbook Committee

Walnut Chicken - Chinese Style

Preparation: Average
Cooking Time: 20-25 Minutes

Serves: 4
Must Serve Immediately

3 boneless skinless chicken
   breast halves
2½ tablespoons soy sauce,
   divided
¾ cup condensed chicken
   broth
2 teaspoons cornstarch
3 tablespoons oil, divided
1½ cups snow peas
1½ cups sliced fresh
   mushrooms
1 cup sliced celery
1 cup onion wedges
¼ cup green pepper strips
½ cup large walnut pieces
   Cooked rice
   Chinese noodles (optional)

Slice chicken into thin strips. Toss with 1½ teaspoons soy sauce; marinate while preparing vegetables. Blend broth, cornstarch, and remaining soy sauce; set aside. Heat 1 tablespoon oil in wok or large skillet. Stir-fry chicken strips until browned and cooked through. Remove chicken from wok. Heat remaining 2 tablespoons oil in wok. Stir-fry snow peas, mushrooms, celery, onion, and green pepper over medium heat 5 minutes. Add broth mixture; bring to boil, stirring. Return chicken to wok; add walnuts and heat 1 minute. Serve over hot rice; top with noodles.
Menu Suggestion: Banana-Pineapple Cloud (page 91), Crunchy Pound Cake (page 315).
Wine Suggestion: A dry white French vin ordinaire.

Coraleen Edmondson Davidson

Chicken Curry Crêpes

Preparation: Average
Cooking Time: 10-15 Minutes
Oven Temperature: 375°F

Serves: 12

1 cup diced celery
½ cup chopped onion
¼ cup butter, melted
2 tablespoons flour
1 teaspoon salt
½ teaspoon curry powder
1 chicken bouillon cube
¼ cup hot water
1½ cups milk
2 cups diced cooked chicken
¼ cup chopped black olives
   (optional)
12 Basic Entrée Crêpes
   (page 138)
   Parmesan cheese

Sauté celery and onion in butter until tender-crisp. Sprinkle flour, salt, and curry powder over vegetables. Dissolve bouillon cube in water. Add to vegetables; stir until well blended. Gradually stir in milk; cook, stirring until thickened. Fold in chicken and olives; heat through. Place ⅓ cup filling mixture in center of each crêpe. Fold two sides over filling. Place in lightly buttered shallow baking dish. Sprinkle with Parmesan. Bake at 375°F for 10-15 minutes.
Micronote: Sauté celery and onion in butter on HIGH 2-3 minutes, stirring several times. Add flour, salt, curry, and bouillon cube dissolved in water. Cook on HIGH 3-4 minutes, stirring every 30 seconds. Fold in chicken and olives. Fill crêpes as above. Cook on HIGH 5 minutes or until crêpes are heated.
Menu Suggestion: Spinach-Cheese Crêpes (page 269), Mandarin Carrots (page 274), Coconut Mousse (page 348).
Wine Suggestion: A light red California vin ordinaire.

Doris Duke Sosebee

Chicken Livers in Sour Cream

Preparation: Easy
Cooking Time: 25 Minutes

Serves: 2-4

½ cup butter or margarine, melted
⅓ pound fresh mushrooms, sliced
1 large onion, chopped
½ teaspoon salt
½ teaspoon pepper
½ teaspoon tarragon
1 pound chicken livers, drained
¼ cup white wine or ⅓ cup sherry
1 tablespoon soy sauce
1 cup sour cream
Cooked rice, patty shells, or toast points

In medium skillet combine butter, mushrooms, and onions; sauté until onions are limp. Add salt, pepper, tarragon, and livers; sauté 1 minute more. Cook, covered, over low heat 15 minutes, stirring often. Add wine and soy sauce. Stir in sour cream; heat well but **do not boil**. Serve over rice, patty shells, or toast points.

Micronote: In small dish sauté mushrooms and onions in ¼ cup margarine on HIGH 2-3 minutes. Preheat browning skillet 4½ minutes. Prick livers with fork; sauté in ¼ cup margarine. Cook, covered, on HIGH 5 minutes. Add mushrooms, onions, salt, pepper, and tarragon. Cook on MEDIUM 10 minutes or until livers are done, stirring often. Add wine, soy sauce, and sour cream. Cook on HIGH 1-2 minutes.

Variation: Shrimp may be substituted for chicken livers; reduce 15-minute cooking time to 8 minutes.

Menu Suggestion: Broiled Sherried Tomatoes (page 277), Chocolotta Cake (page 317).

Wine Suggestion: A medium-full red such as a California Cabernet.

Marilyn Murphy Doveton

Melt-in-your-Mouth Quick Chicken Pie

Preparation: Easy
Cooking Time: 1 Hour
Oven Temperature: 350°F

Serves: 6

3-4 cups cubed, cooked chicken
1 (10¾-ounce) can cream of chicken soup
1 (10¾-ounce) can chicken broth
½ teaspoon tarragon (optional)
2 boiled eggs, sliced (optional)
1½ cups self-rising flour
1½ cups buttermilk
½ cup butter, melted

Place chicken in lightly greased 12 x 9-inch baking dish. Blend soup with broth and tarragon. Pour over chicken. Arrange egg slices over chicken. Combine flour, buttermilk, and butter; mix well. Pour evenly over chicken mixture. Bake, uncovered, at 350°F for 1 hour or until crust rises to top and is golden brown.

Menu Suggestion: Ambrosia Mold (page 89), Spinach Soufflé (page 270).

Wine Suggestion: A crisp dry white such as Italian Orvieto.

Mary Lou Greer Melvin

Cold Pasta with Chicken - European Style

A specialty of the Memphis Golf Club, this dish has Italian and French roots.

Preparation: Average
Cooking Time: 30 Minutes

Serves: 6-8
Must Do Ahead

½ **pound pasta, preferably vermicelli**
   French Garlic Dressing
1 **(3-pound) chicken**
¾ **cup fresh mayonnaise (page 98)**
   Leaf lettuce
   Assorted seasonal vegetables (mushrooms, tomatoes, avocados, artichoke hearts, beets, etc.)
   Scallions (optional)
   Parsley (optional)
   Fresh herbs (optional)
   Bacon bits (optional)

Cook pasta in boiling, salted water 3 minutes; drain well. Toss with ⅓ cup French Garlic Dressing. Refrigerate overnight. Boil chicken in seasoned broth 30 minutes. Cool and debone; cut into bite-sized pieces. Just before serving, combine pasta, chicken, and mayonnaise; toss gently. Mound over leaf lettuce. Toss raw vegetables in remaining dressing. Arrange around pasta. Garnish with scallions, parsley, fresh herbs, and/or bacon bits.

French Garlic Dressing

1 **cup olive oil**
¼ **cup wine vinegar**
2 **teaspoons Dijon mustard**
2 **teaspoons finely chopped garlic**
1 **teaspoon paprika**
   Salt and pepper to taste

Combine all ingredients in covered jar; shake to blend.
Menu Suggestion: Honeydew Lime Bisque (page 67), Popovers (page 115), Dark Chocolate Mousse (page 350).
Wine Suggestion: A simple but full white such as Italian Soave.

Suzanne Roberts Greene

Jesse Jewell sells everything about a chicken but its cackle.

P. C. King, Jr., *The Chattahoochee River*
Used with permission.

Hunter's Stew

Preparation: Average
Cooking Time: 2 Hours

Yield: 2-3 Gallons

2 (3-pound) chickens
  Water
½ cup margarine
2 cups chopped onion
2 cups chopped celery
4-6 cups smoked ham, diced
3 (10-ounce) packages frozen
  whole-kernel corn
2 (10-ounce) packages frozen
  cut okra
2 (28-ounce) cans tomatoes,
  chopped
¼ cup sugar
2-3 bay leaves
4 tablespoons chopped parsley
2-3 tablespoons salt
1 teaspoon rosemary
1 teaspoon black pepper
¼ teaspoon Tabasco
4 cups diced potatoes
2 (10-ounce) packages frozen
  baby limas

Cook chickens in salted water to cover. When tender, remove meat from bones, reserving stock. Cut meat into chunks. In large kettle melt margarine; sauté onions and celery. Add remaining ingredients except potatoes and limas; add stock. Cook 45 minutes to 1 hour. Add potatoes and limas; cook 20-30 minutes or until vegetables are tender. (If broth needs to be thickened, blend 4 tablespoons flour into ½ cup cold water; stir into stew.) Flavor improves after a day in refrigerator.
Menu Suggestion: Crispy Cornsticks (page 118), Apple Cake Pie (page 328).
Wine Suggestion: A medium red such as California Zinfandel.

Connie Harris Callahan

Chicken à la King Deluxe

Preparation: Easy
Cooking Time: 15-20 Minutes

Serves: 4

1 tablespoon butter, melted
1¼ tablespoons flour
1 cup milk
4 chicken breast halves,
  cooked and cubed
8 ounces small fresh
  mushrooms
½ cup shredded Swiss cheese
1 (2-ounce) jar diced
  pimiento
3 tablespoons chopped green
  pepper
1 teaspoon minced onion
¼ teaspoon salt
⅛ teaspoon pepper
3 tablespoons white wine
1 teaspoon soy sauce

In medium saucepan blend butter and flour. Gradually stir in milk; cook until thickened. Add remaining ingredients. Cook over low heat until cheese is melted and mixture is thoroughly heated. Serve over puff pastry or patty shells, toasted English muffins, or cornbread wedges.
Micronote: Melt margarine in glass container; add flour. Stir in milk gradually. Cook on HIGH 3 minutes, stirring every 30 seconds. Add remaining ingredients. Cook on MEDIUM 10 minutes, stirring several times.
Menu Suggestion: Sour Cherry Salad (page 88), Corn Lightbread (page 119), Harvest Sweet Potato Pie (page 330).
Wine Suggestion: A dry white such as an Italian Soave.

Connie Kemp Goldfarb

Riley Red Chicken Stew

Prepare this a day ahead to allow flavors to blend. A sure winner with men.

Preparation: Average
Cooking Time: 1½-2 Hours

Serves: 8

1 (4½ to 5-pound) hen
3½ cups water, divided
4 slices bacon, cut
    into fourths
6 onions, sliced
1 (16-ounce) bottle catsup
½ cup butter
4 tablespoons Worcestershire
1 teaspoon salt
1 teaspoon black pepper
¼ teaspoon cayenne
½ cup flour
4 hard-cooked eggs, sliced
    Cooked rice

Steam chicken in 3 cups water until tender. Remove chicken; reserve stock. Debone chicken; cut into bite-sized pieces (including giblets). Set aside. Fry bacon in large Dutch oven until crisp. Add onions; steam until tender but not brown. Add reserved stock, catsup, butter, Worcestershire, salt, pepper, and cayenne. Combine flour and remaining ½ cup water to form paste. Add to stock mixture; cook, stirring, until smooth and creamy. Add chicken and eggs. (Freezes well at this point.) Let stand over low heat until ready to serve. Ladle into bowls over rice.

Micronote: Prepare hen conventionally. Cook bacon in large glass container on HIGH for 4 minutes. Add onion; cook on HIGH 4-5 minutes. Add stock, catsup, butter, Worcestershire, salt, and peppers. Combine flour and ½ cup water to form paste. Stir into stock mixture. Cook on HIGH 8-10 minutes or until smooth and creamy, stirring several times. (Exact cooking time will vary according to beginning temperature of stock.) Continue as above, using LOW power to hold or reheat.

Menu Suggestion: Bavarian Sweet and Sour Salad (page 77), Hush Puppies (page 120), Pecan Pie (page 335).

Wine Suggestion: A generic California red, or to match the region, a Cabernet from South Carolina's Truluck vineyards.

Robert E. Lee
Hilton Head Island, South Carolina

Chicken n' Dumplings

A real "old timey" favorite that's just as good today. Rich and filling - guaranteed to satisfy your heartiest eater!

Preparation: Average
Cooking Time: 1 Hour 20 Minutes

Serves: 4-6

1 (2 to 3-pound) broiler-fryer,
   cut into parts
3 quarts water
1 carrot
1 onion
1 tablespoon salt
½ teaspoon pepper
¼ cup butter or margarine
¼ teaspoon garlic powder
   Drop Dumplings or
     Rolled Dumplings
1-2 cups milk

Combine chicken, water, carrot, onion, salt, and pepper in large kettle. Boil, covered, 50 minutes or until chicken is tender. Remove chicken; strain broth. Debone chicken, discarding skin and bones; cut meat into bite-sized pieces. Set aside. Return broth to boiling. Add butter and garlic powder. Add additional salt and pepper if needed. Lower heat to maintain just a gentle boil. Gradually add dumplings. Simmer, covered, 15 minutes. Stir in milk and reserved chicken. Turn off heat. Cover; let stand 5 minutes. Ladle into bowls to serve.

Drop Dumplings

½ cup shortening
3 cups self-rising flour
1-1⅓ cups ice water

Cut shortening into flour until crumbly. Stir in just enough water to make soft dough. Drop by rounded teaspoonfuls into boiling broth, spacing as evenly as possible.

Ellorie Smith
Cumming, Georgia

Rolled Dumplings

½ cup vegetable shortening
4 cups self-rising flour,
   divided
1 cup buttermilk

Cut shortening into 3 cups flour until crumbly. Stir in buttermilk until stiff dough is formed, gradually adding remaining flour if needed. Turn dough onto well-floured surface; knead until smooth. Divide dough into thirds. Roll each third on floured surface until very thin. Cut into 1 x 3-inch strips. Drop strips, a few at a time, into boiling broth. Stir gently once or twice. (Broth needs to boil slightly harder for these dumplings.)
Menu Suggestion: Green Salad with Kumback Dressing (page 99), Simple Summer Cobbler (page 333).
Beverage Suggestion: Iced Tea

Ruby Allen Hix
Winder, Georgia

Hollis came to the big house every day for dinner. This was long before lunch was invented....

Ferrol Sams, *Run With the Horsemen*
Peachtree Publications, Ltd., Copyright 1982. Used with permission.

Aunt Lou's Chicken Pie

Old-fashioned chicken and dumplings in pie form.

Preparation: Average
Cooking Time: 2½ Hours
Oven Temperature: 400°F

Serves: 10

1 (3-pound) broiler-fryer
6 cups water
1½ teaspoons salt, divided
1½ cups flour
3 tablespoons butter, divided
   Lukewarm water
   Pastry

Combine chicken, water, and 1 teaspoon salt in Dutch oven. Cook, covered, until chicken is tender. Remove chicken; strain and reserve stock. Debone chicken; set aside. Make dumplings by combining flour, 1 teaspoon butter, and ½ teaspoon salt. Add just enough lukewarm water to make stiff dough. Turn out onto floured surface. Roll as thin as possible. Cut into 1 x 3-inch strips. Return chicken stock to boiling. Gradually drop pastry strips into boiling stock. Add chicken. Simmer, covered, 45 minutes. Season with additional salt and pepper, if desired. Simmer 15 minutes more, adding additional water if needed to prevent sticking. Pour into 13 x 9 x 2-inch baking pan. Dot with remaining butter. Cover with pastry. Bake at 400°F until pastry is golden brown.

Pastry

2 cups sifted flour
½ teaspoon salt
½ cup vegetable shortening
2-3 tablespoons cold water

Combine flour and salt. Cut in shortening until mixture is consistency of coarse cornmeal. Sprinkle with water, 1 tablespoon at a time, tossing mixture lightly and stirring with fork just until dough is moist enough to hold together (not sticky). Turn onto floured surface. Roll into 13 x 9-inch rectangle.

Menu Suggestion: Southern Squash Boats (page 272), Nanny's Southern Green Beans (page 265), Nona's Egg Custard Pie (page 337).
Wine Suggestion: A dry white French vin ordinaire.

Peggy Sheridan Cathey

Kentucky Hot Brown

This recipe originated at the Brown Hotel in Louisville, Kentucky. More than just a sandwich - it's substantial enough for lunch or dinner.

Preparation: Average
Cooking Time: 5-10 Minutes
Oven Temperature: 425°F

Serves: 4

2 tablespoons butter or
   margarine
¼ cup flour
2 cups milk
¼ teaspoon salt
½ teaspoon Worcestershire
¼ cup Cheddar cheese, grated
¾ cup Parmesan cheese,
   grated and divided
1 pound sliced turkey
   or chicken
8 slices trimmed toast
8 slices tomato
8 slices cooked bacon

Melt butter in saucepan. Add flour; stir well. Add milk, salt, Worcestershire, Cheddar, and ¼ cup Parmesan. Cook, stirring constantly, until thick. Arrange turkey on toast on an ovenproof platter. Cover with cheese sauce. Top with tomato slices and bacon. Sprinkle with remaining Parmesan. Bake at 425°F until bubbly.

Micronote: Melt butter in glass bowl, 30-45 seconds. Add flour and milk. Cook on HIGH 5 minutes, stirring every 45 seconds until thick. Add Cheddar, ¼ cup Parmesan, salt, and Worcestershire. Arrange sandwich as directed. Cook on HIGH 6-8 minutes, rotating dish once or twice.

Menu Suggestion: Cold Strawberry Soup (page 67), Broccoli and Cauliflower Salad (page 83), Brownie Baked Alaska (page 350).

Wine Suggestion: A light dry red such as Beaujolais.

Madge Farra Burch

Drumettes in Caper Sauce

An excellent and unusual flavor combination. Messy to eat, but well worth the sticky fingers. (Don't use your prized table linens! Paper suggested!)

Preparation: Average
Cooking Time: 50 Minutes

Serves: 6
Must Serve Immediately

24 - 32 chicken drumettes
1 teaspoon salt
½ teaspoon pepper
   Flour
3-6 tablespoons olive oil
1 cup minced onions
½ cup tomato purée
1 tablespoon tomato paste
½ cup dry white wine
½ cup chicken broth
2 tablespoons lemon juice
3 tablespoons minced parsley
2 large cloves garlic,
   minced
2 tablespoons drained capers
4 anchovy fillets, minced

Sprinkle drumettes with salt and pepper; dredge with flour, shaking off excess. Heat 3 tablespoons oil in large skillet. Sauté drumettes until nicely browned on both sides, taking care not to overcrowd skillet; add oil as needed. Remove from skillet; reserve. Add onions to skillet; cook until lightly browned, stirring occasionally. Add tomato purée, tomato paste, wine, and broth; bring to boil. Return drumettes to skillet; simmer, covered, 30 minutes. Combine lemon juice, parsley, garlic, capers, and anchovies in small bowl. Use slotted spoon to transfer drumettes to deep serving platter. Raise heat; reduce skillet juices slightly, if needed, to make thick sauce. Add lemon juice mixture; heat through. Pour sauce over drumettes to serve.

Menu Suggestion: Layered Walnut-Herb Salad (page 77), Best-Ever Lemon Pie (page 331).

Wine Suggestion: A light red French vin ordinaire.

Cookbook Committee

Stuffed Cornish Hens with Mushroom Wine Sauce

Preparation: Average
Cooking Time: 1½ - 1¾ Hours
Oven Temperature: 375°F

Serves: 6

1 (6-ounce) package long grain and wild rice mix
2½ cups chicken broth
⅔ cup sliced water chestnuts
½ cup diced celery
½ cup sliced green onion
1 (3-ounce) can chopped mushrooms, drained
6 tablespoons margarine, melted
2 tablespoons soy sauce
6 Cornish hens
Salt
Melted butter
Mushroom Wine Sauce

Prepare rice mix according to package instructions, substituting chicken broth for water; cool. Add water chestnuts, celery, green onion, mushrooms, margarine, and soy sauce. Stir lightly. Sprinkle inside of hens with salt; stuff lightly with rice mixture; truss hens. Place breast side up in shallow roasting pan. Bake at 375°F for 1 hour or until juice runs clean when thigh is pierced with fork; baste frequently with melted butter during baking. Ladle Mushroom Wine Sauce over hens.

Micronote: Prepare hens as directed. Cook 2 hens at a time. Cover with waxed paper. Cook 6-8 minutes; turn dish half-way through cooking.

Mushroom Wine Sauce

½ pound fresh mushrooms, sliced
¼ cup margarine, melted
Pan drippings from hens
3 tablespoons dry white wine
2 tablespoons sliced green onion

Sauté mushrooms in margarine; set aside. Combine pan drippings, wine, and green onions in small saucepan. Cook over high heat 10 minutes. Remove from heat; stir in mushrooms and butter.

Micronote: Sauté mushrooms in margarine in preheated browning skillet. Cook on HIGH 2-3 minutes. Add remaining ingredients; cook on HIGH 1 minute longer.

Menu Suggestion: Cold Apple Soup (page 66), Spinach-Stuffed Squash (page 270), English Trifle (page 345).

Wine Suggestion: A quality red California Cabernet Sauvignon.

Connie Wallis Dixon

Rock Cornish Hens with Port Sauce

Cornish hens have long been considered a delicacy. Here is a treatment worthy of them. Very rich and an excellent alternative to rice stuffing.

Preparation: Average
Cooking Time: 50 Minutes
Oven Temperature: 400°F

Serves: 6

½ **pound bulk sausage**
6 **Cornish hen livers, chopped**
1 **cup toasted bread crumbs
   or herb stuffing**
2 **tablespoons butter**
1 **tablespoon chopped parsley**
⅛ **teaspoon thyme**
⅛ **teaspoon freshly ground
   black pepper**
6 **Cornish hens**
6 **slices bacon**
½ **cup chicken stock**
½ **cup port wine**
1 **teaspoon flour**
1 **teaspoon butter**
½ **cup hot whipping cream**

Crumble sausage into skillet. Sauté until lightly browned; drain well. Add livers, bread crumbs, butter, parsley, thyme, and pepper; mix well. Stuff hens with sausage mixture. Sprinkle with additional salt and pepper, if desired. Place in roasting pan; cover breasts with bacon. Add stock and port. Bake at 400°F for 35-45 minutes, basting several times with pan juices. Remove hens; discard bacon. Skim excess fat from pan juices. Combine flour and butter; add to pan juices. Stir in cream. Spoon sauce over hens. Pass additional sauce.

Menu Suggestion: Spinach Salad with Hot Bacon Dressing (page 100), Carrot and Zucchini Julienne (page 273), Snowballs with Sauce (page 353).

Wine Suggestion: A lighter French Bordeaux such as a Médoc.

Cathy Cox Miller

Baked Hen Supreme

An elegant golden-brown bird with its own rich, creamy gravy.

Preparation: Easy
Cooking Time: 1 Hour 45 Minutes
Oven Temperature: 425°F

Serves: 6-8

1 **(5-pound) baking hen**
   Salt and pepper
1 **orange, quartered**
1 **pint half-and-half,
   divided**
1 **pound fresh mushrooms**
   Parsley (optional)

Wipe hen with damp cloth. Rub inside and out with salt and pepper. Place orange quarters in cavity. Place in baking dish slightly larger than hen. Bake at 425°F for 20 minutes. Reduce heat to 350°F. Pour 1 cup half-and-half over hen. Bake at 350°F for 10 minutes. Pour remaining half-and-half over hen. Bake at 350°F for 1 hour. Place mushrooms around hen; stir to coat with juices. Place tent of foil over hen; bake 15 minutes more. Garnish with parsley to serve. (Same method can be used for turkey breast or whole broiler-fryer, increasing or decreasing baking time according to size of fowl.)

Menu Suggestion: Cranberry Salad Ring (page 88), Sweet Potato Dream (page 280), Green Bean Casserole (page 265), Oyster Dressing (page 140), Confetti Christmas Cake (page 320).

Wine Suggestion: A quality full white such as a French Chablis.

Laura Fair Smyth
Denver, Colorado

Hickory Smoked Turkey

Get a good book, sit back, and tend the turkey.

Preparation: Easy
Cooking Time: 5-7 Hours

Serves: Variable

Hickory chips or twigs
1 turkey breast
Oil or margarine
Salt

Soak hickory in water 1-2 hours. In one side of covered grill build fire of 20-25 charcoal briquets. Place pan to catch drippings under rack on other side of grill. Open vents **under** fire and **over** drip pan. Rub turkey with oil and salt. Insert meat thermometer in thickest part; place over pan. Place several hickory pieces over charcoal; close lid and cook slowly 5-7 hours. Baste with additional oil several times each hour. Add several briquets and more hickory each hour as needed. Take care that smoke continues to blow across charcoal, then turkey. Turkey is done when temperature reaches 195°F. (If whole turkey is desired increase cooking time to 9-10 hours.)

Menu Suggestion: Amelia's Cranberry Pears (page 93), Yam Baskets Louisianne (page 279), Broccoli Ring (page 260), Harvard Beets (page 279), Cornbread Dressing (page 139), Holiday Coconut Cake (page 308).

Wine Suggestion: A more substantial red such as California Zinfandel.

J. Randall Frost

For the Thanksgiving and Christmas feasts four heavy turkeys were brought and fattened for weeks...the whole energy of the family focused upon the great ritual of the feast. A day or two before, the auxiliary dainties arrived in piled grocer's boxes--the magic of strange foods and fruits was added to familiar fare.

Thomas Wolfe, from *Look Homeward, Angel*

Wild Duck in Orange Sauce

A great surprise for those who like game fowl; the best introduction for newcomers!

Preparation: Average
Cooking Time: 3-5 Hours

Serves: 6

4 large or 8 small wild
    ducks
Celery, chopped
Onion, chopped
Apple slices
Salt and pepper
Bacon
Orange Sauce

Clean and prep ducks. Stuff with equal amounts of celery, onion, and apple. Wrap each duck with bacon strips. Place in heavy Dutch oven. Cover with water; sprinkle with salt and pepper. Simmer, covered, until meat is falling away from bones; add water as needed to keep moist. (May be cooked in pressure cooker 1 hour.) Lift ducks from liquid with slotted spoon; remove meat from bones. Pour hot Orange Sauce over duck meat.

Orange Sauce

2 cups orange juice
⅔ cup brown sugar
⅔ cup sugar
2 tablespoons flour
⅛ teaspoon salt
Grated rind of 1 orange

Combine all ingredients. Simmer until thickened.
Menu Suggestion: Fettucine (page 286), Broccoli Elegant (page 261).
Wine Suggestion: A substantial red such as a French Côte de Nuits (from the Burgundy region).

Lucy Fokes Link

There is no more delicious food than quail or dove, the one white meat, the other dark....They must be picked, never skinned.

Marjorie Kinnan Rawlings, from *Cross Creek*.
Copyright 1942. Charles Scribner's Sons. Reprinted with permission of Charles Scribner's Sons.

Smothered Doves

Preparation: Easy
Cooking Time: 2 Hours
Oven Temperature: 350°F

Serves: 6

2 tablespoons flour
½ cup butter, melted
2 cups water
1 tablespoon Worcestershire
Juice of ½ lemon or
    1 tablespoon vinegar
Salt and pepper to taste
6 doves

Cook flour in butter until brown. Stir in water, Worcestershire, lemon juice, salt, and pepper. Arrange doves in 2-quart baking dish; cover with sauce. Bake, covered, at 350°F for 2 hours, basting occasionally (add water if necessary to cover doves).
Menu Suggestion: Honeyed Citrus Nut Salad (page 79), Gruyere Cheese Grits (page 287), Cottage Cheese Rolls (page 112).
Wine Suggestion: A full dry white such as Chardonnay.

Dale Gladstone Duggan

Meat

Bee Balm

Bee Balm (Monarda didyma)

Bee balm, a member of the mint family, was used by the Cherokee Indians and early settlers as medicine. This late summer bloomer is a healthful drink, as it does not contain caffeine and can be used as a tea substitute. One or two of the smaller-sized leaves can be used as an herb; add them whole to a fruit cup or cut for a gelatin mold.

On Meat

- After removing a roast from the oven, let it rest at least 15 minutes before carving.
- To oven-fry bacon: Place strips side by side on the broiler rack of an unheated broiler pan. Bake at 400°F for 12-15 minutes. No need to turn!
- If meat is seared before seasoning, more juices will be retained.
- Accent the flavor of meat by rubbing with garlic, onion, herbs, or spices 30 minutes before cooking. Slivers of garlic or onion may be inserted into roasts near the bone or scattered over the cut surface.

- Always handle ground meat lightly to avoid a dense finished texture.
- A quick glaze for baked ham: pour cola beverage or ginger ale over ham at 30 minute intervals during baking.
- Lemon juice is a natural tenderizer for beef.
- Meat broils best when it goes into the broiler at room temperature.
- When broiling place meat on a cold rack to keep it from sticking or grease a hot rack.

Broiling or Grilling Timetable									
	Thick-ness (in.)	Approximate Total Cooking Time				Thick-ness (in.)	Approximate Total Cooking Time		
		rare	medium	well done			rare	medium	well done
BEEF Delmonico Rib	1½ 2	10-15 15-20	15-20 20-25	20-25 25-30	SHISH KABOB (Beef or Lamb)	(1" cubes)	6-8	8-10	12-15
Hamburger	1	6-10	15	20	LAMB CHOPS	1 1½ 2	6-8 9-12 13-15	12 15 16-18	15 16-18 20-22
Porterhouse	1	6-8	10-12	15-18					
T-bone	1	10-12	15-18	20-25	VEAL CHOPS	½ 1			15-16 18-20
Sirloin	2	12-15	18-20	25-30	PORK CHOPS	½ 1			15-20 20-25
Tenderloin Filet Mignon	(4-8 oz)	8-10	15	15-20	HAM STEAKS	1			30

Stuffed Eye of Round Roast

Preparation: Average
Cooking Time: 3 Hours
Oven Temperature: 325°F

Serves: 8

1 (3 to 4-pound) eye of round
   roast
1 chorizo sausage, chopped
1 medium slice cured ham,
   chopped
1 clove garlic, minced
1 medium Spanish onion,
   chopped
½ green pepper, chopped
   Salt
   Pepper
   Paprika
3 tablespoons bacon drippings
¾ cup hot water
1 long strip suet
1 bay leaf
4 whole cloves

Have a butcher cut lengthwise pocket in center of beef, leaving one end closed. Mix sausage, ham, garlic, onion, and green pepper. Use to stuff pocket of beef, packing well but not too tightly. Cover hole in end with aluminum foil; secure with picks. Sprinkle beef with salt, pepper, and paprika to moderately coat outside. Heat bacon drippings in Dutch oven of sufficient size to hold beef. Brown beef well in drippings over medium heat. Add hot water, scraping pan well. Lay suet on top of meat; add bay leaf and cloves to liquid. Cover; bake at 325°F, basting occasionally, for about 3 hours. Let stand 15-30 minutes before slicing. (If chorizo sausage is unavailable, substitute Italian sausage.)

Menu Suggestion: Cream of Artichoke Soup (page 60), West Coast Salad (page 80), Pecan Pilaf (page 285), Cheesecake Receipt (page 323).

Wine Suggestion: A red Spanish Rioja Reserve.

Sally Wilson Sites

The thoughtful host put the first stain on the dinner tablecloth himself.

Anonymous

Dill Roast with Carrot Gravy

This does wonderful things to common pot roast!

Preparation: Easy
Cooking Time: 3 Hours

Serves: 6-8

1 (3 to 4-pound) pot roast
6 tablespoons flour, divided
3 teaspoons salt
½ teaspoon pepper
3 tablespoons shortening
1 medium onion, sliced
1 tablespoon dill seed
2 tablespoons vinegar
1 cup water, divided
1 cup grated carrots

Dredge roast in combined 4 tablespoons flour, salt, and pepper. Heat shortening in large Dutch oven; add roast and brown on all sides. Pour off drippings. Add onion, dill seed, vinegar, and ½ cup water. Cover tightly; cook over low heat 2 hours. Add carrots; cook 1 hour more. Remove meat to platter. Mix remaining 2 tablespoons flour and remaining ½ cup water. Add to liquid in pan; cook, stirring constantly, until thickened.

Menu Suggestion: Potato-Onion Piquante (page 280), Nanny's Southern Green Beans (page 265), Fluffy Baking Powder Biscuits (page 116).

Wine Suggestion: A dry red French vin ordinaire.

Linda Graves Sigler

Lazy Man's Roast

A wonderful dish for entertaining - no one is in the kitchen!

Preparation: Easy
Cooking Time: 1½-2 Hours
Oven Temperature: Highest Possible

Serves: 8-10

1 (3½ to 8-pound) eye of round
    roast beef or tenderloin
Salt, pepper and
    lemon-pepper seasoning,
    to taste

Preheat oven to highest possible setting. Sprinkle roast with salt, pepper, and lemon-pepper. Place on rack in shallow roasting pan. Bake only **four minutes per pound.** Turn off oven; **do not open door.** Leave roast in oven for 1½-2 hours. If desired warm, reheat in moderate oven, but careful not to overcook. (The roast will be pink on the inside.)

Menu Suggestion: Bernaise Sauce (page 292), Green Salad Unique (page 75), Beech Island Bread (page 103).

Wine Suggestion: A quality dry red such as French Chambertin (Burgundy).

Cathy McLanahan Nix

Marinated Tenderloin

Preparation: Average
Cooking Time: 1½ Hours
Oven Temperature: 375°-400°F

Serves: 8-10
Must Partially Do Ahead

1⅓ cups wine vinegar
 1 cup catsup
 ½ cup oil
 ½ cup soy sauce
 ¼ cup Worcestershire
 4 teaspoons prepared mustard
 4 teaspoons monosodium
     glutamate
 4 teaspoons salt
2-4 teaspoons garlic powder
 3 teaspoons onion powder
 1 teaspoon pepper
 1 (7 to 9-pound) beef tenderloin
6-8 strips bacon

Combine all ingredients except beef and bacon. Set aside. Strip fat from tenderloin; place in heavy duty gallon plastic bag. Add marinade; seal; gently squeeze bag to coat well. Marinate 48 hours in refrigerator, squeezing and turning twice per day. Remove from marinade; wrap with bacon. Place in shallow pan; insert meat thermometer.

To Grill: Use covered grill. Place coals in one end of grill. When coals are ready, place pan containing meat on rack on opposite side of grill from coals. Cover; cook by indirect method to temperature indicated for "rare" (about 1½ hours). Baste occasionally with marinade.

To Oven Cook: Bake at 375°-400°F until meat thermometer indicates "rare" (about 1½ hours). Baste occasionally with marinade. Slice and serve with additional warmed marinade.

Menu Suggestion: Iced Cucumber Soup (page 65), Puttin' on the Ritz Salad (page 76), Gourmet Rice-Stuffed Tomatoes (page 277), Croissants (page 113), Cappucino Ice Cream (page 354).

Wine Suggestion: A dry red such as California Cabernet Sauvignon.

John D. Spivey

Marinated Roast for Grill

Your family or guests will think they're eating choice steak.

Preparation: Easy
Cooking Time: 45 Minutes

Serves: 6-8
Must Partially Do Ahead

1 (3 to 5-pound) chuck roast, English cut, or shoulder roast (2-inch thickness) or 8-10 boneless chuck steaks (1-inch thickness)
Meat tenderizer
1 large onion, chopped
½ cup strongly brewed coffee
½ cup soy sauce
1 tablespoon Worcestershire
1 tablespoon vinegar
1 tablespoon sesame seeds, browned in butter

Sprinkle roast with tenderizer. Combine remaining ingredients for marinade. Pour over roast; marinate 6 hours at room temperature. Lift meat from marinade; reserve marinade. Charcoal broil 45 minutes for medium doneness. Slice into thin strips. (Reduce cooking time for steaks.) Simmer marinade while roast is grilling; pass as sauce.
Menu Suggestion: Marinated Vegetable Medley (page 82), Potato Fresh (page 75), Caramel Bars (page 361).
Wine Suggestion: A full red such as Italian Barolo.

Louise Hendrix Forrester

Standing Rib Roast

Preparation: Easy
Cooking Time: See Below
Oven Temperature: 325°F

Serves: 8-10

1 (4 to 6-pound) rib roast
Salt
Pepper
1 cup water (optional)
Worcestershire (optional)

Salt and pepper roast. Place meat on trivet in open pan with fat side up. Bake at 325°F:
    25 minutes per pound for rare roast
    30 minutes per pound for medium roast
    35 minutes per pound for well-done roast
Remove to platter; slice. If gravy is desired, pour off some grease from roasting pan. Add water, Worcestershire, salt, and pepper to taste to remaining drippings. Heat through. Pass with roast.
Menu Suggestion: Super Simple Crab Bisque (page 55), Company Carrots (page 274), Herbed Pastry with Spinach Filling (page 268), Pumpkin Cheesecake (page 324).
Wine Suggestion: A French Burgundy from the Côte de Nuits.

Johnnie Bowie Swetenburg

Corned Beef

Preparation: Easy
Cooking Time: 4 Hours
Oven Temperature: 300°F

Serves: 8-10

1 (4 to 6-pound) corned beef round
1 orange, peeled and sliced
1 onion, cut in wedges
1 stalk celery, cut in several pieces
1 carrot, cut in several pieces
2-3 cloves
2-3 peppercorns
1 small bay leaf
½ cup water
Pepper
Sprinkling of brown sugar

Combine all ingredients on aluminum foil; wrap securely twice. Bake at 300°F for 4 hours. Slice thinly to serve.
Menu Suggestion: Frozen Pineapple Salad (page 86), Company Cabbage (page 264), Honey Whole Wheat Bread (page 104).
Wine Suggestion: A light red such as a Beaujolais.

Lynda Dickens Askew

Sussex Stewed Steak

Originating in Sussex County, England, this dish dates back to the time of King Henry VIII. It is traditionally served with mashed potatoes and field mushrooms.

Preparation: Easy
Cooking Time: 3 Hours
Oven Temperature: 275°F

Serves: 6

2-2½ pounds sliced top rump or chuck steak
Salt
Pepper
Flour
1 large onion, sliced
3 ounces stout
3 ounces port
3 tablespoons catsup or wine vinegar

Season meat with salt and pepper; rub with flour on all sides. Place in shallow, ovenproof dish in which meat can lie flat. Place even layer of onions over meat. Pour stout, port, and catsup over all. Cover tightly with foil; bake at 275°F for 3 hours. (Any wine or dark beer may be used, but stout and port are preferable.)
Menu Suggestion: Mandarin Carrots (page 274), Party Potatoes (page 281).
Wine Suggestion: A red French vin ordinaire, or try English stout or ale.

Kim McElhenny Humphrey

Flank Steak with Wine Sauce

Preparation: Easy
Cooking Time: 10-20 Minutes

Serves: 4
Must Partially Do Ahead

1 (1½ to 2-pound) flank steak
1 teaspoon salt
1 teaspoon pepper
1 teaspoon thyme
  Soy sauce
  Wine sauce

Lightly score steak; rub in salt, pepper, and thyme. Brush on soy sauce with pastry brush until lightly coated on one side. Allow to stand at room temperature 30-45 minutes. Cook steak on grill to desired doneness. Slice in thin diagonal strips. Arrange on platter; pass with Wine Sauce.

Wine Sauce

1 cup chopped shallots or
  ¾ cup chopped green onions
1¼ cups red wine
½ cup butter or margarine
2 tablespoons chopped parsley

Mix shallots and wine in saucepan. Bring to boil; add butter and parsley. Heat until butter is melted.

Micronote: Combine all ingredients. Cook at HIGH until mixture boils and butter is melted.

Menu Suggestion: Cossack's Delight (page 257), Broccoli Elegant (page 261), Light-as-a-Feather Refrigerator Rolls (page 112), Spoom (page 353).

Wine Suggestion: A quality California Zinfandel. (Use same or similar wine in recipe.)

Dana Blum Barclay

French Beef Rolls

An elegant, inexpensive, and delicious entrée. What more could you ask!

Preparation: Average
Cooking Time: 1 Hour

Serves: 8

8 thinly sliced pieces of
  beef steak
¾ pound bulk sausage
1 cup raisins
½ cup chopped parsley
½ cup chopped green onions
¼ cup chopped chives
2 cloves garlic, minced
¾ teaspoon salt
¼ teaspoon pepper
1 cup flour
3 tablespoons olive oil
1 (1-ounce) package Natural
  Gravy au Jus Mix
3 cups Burgundy
2 tablespoons tomato paste
1 (8-ounce) can mushroom stems
  and pieces, drained
1 cup stuffed olives, chopped

Have butcher cut 8 thin slices of sirloin tip beef or other roast cut. Mix sausage, raisins, parsley, green onions, chives, garlic, salt, and pepper to form a paste. Spread ⅛ mixture on each slice of steak. Roll steaks; tie with cord at each end of roll. Flour each roll well. Heat olive oil in heavy skillet until it covers bottom well; add rolls and brown on all sides. Prepare Gravy au Jus Mix according to package directions. Add wine and tomato paste. Simmer, covered, 45 minutes. Add mushrooms and olives; simmer, uncovered, 15 minutes more or until reduced enough to slightly thicken. (If preferred, water can be substituted for Burgundy.) Ladle over each roll as served.

Menu Suggestion: French Onion Soup (page 59), Bridal Salad (page 89), Broccoli Sunburst (page 260), Picanchagne (page 329).

Wine Suggestion: A dry full red from the Burgundy region. (Use similar or same in recipe.)

Carol Cratin Ferrell

Sukiyaki

Preparation: Easy
Cooking Time: 15 Minutes

Serves: 4
Must Serve Immediately

2 tablespoons butter
1 pound lean round steak
   or sirloin, thinly sliced
½ pound fresh mushrooms
1 bunch green onions, sliced
1 cup celery sticks
1 cup sliced onions
1 cup bamboo shoots
2 tablespoons sugar
⅓ cup soy sauce
1 beef bouillon cube
¼ cup hot water
3 cups wet spinach leaves
   Cooked rice

Heat butter in large skillet. Add meat; brown very quickly on both sides. Add remaining ingredients except spinach. Simmer, uncovered, stirring occasionally, for 3 minutes or until vegetables are tender-crisp. Add spinach; cover and cook 3 minutes longer. Serve over hot, fluffy rice.

Menu Suggestion: Gourmet Fruit Salad (page 87), Lemon Soufflé (page 341).

Wine Suggestion: A generic California red.

Lynda Truluck Stewart

London Broil

Preparation: Easy
Cooking Time: Variable

Serves: 4
Must Partially Do Ahead

1½ pounds round steak
   Unseasoned meat tenderizer
3 tablespoons soy sauce
2 tablespoons oil
2 tablespoons catsup
1 teaspoon black pepper
2 cloves garlic, quartered
   (optional)

Sprinkle steak with tenderizer. In small mixing bowl whisk together remaining ingredients. Using fingers, rub marinade into steak on each side. Place steak and remaining marinade in baking dish or other suitable container; cover and marinate in refrigerator for 8-9 hours. Grill (covered grill preferred) over charcoal to desired doneness using chart below. Slice thinly to serve.

THICKNESS	RARE		MEDIUM		WELL	
	1st side	2nd side	1st side	2nd side	1st side	2nd side
1 inch	2 min.	3 min.	4 min.	4 min.	5 min.	6 min.
1½ inch	5 min.	6 min.	7 min.	8 min.	9 min.	10 min.
2 inch	7 min.	8 min.	9 min.	9 min.	10 min.	11 min.

Menu Suggestion: Bernaise Sauce (page 292), Casserole of Sweet Vidalias (page 255), Spinach-Stuffed Squash (page 270), Croissants (page 113), Orange Charlotte (page 349).

Wine Suggestion: A Pomerol from the St-Emilion region of Bordeaux.

J. David Burroughs

Korean Flank Steak

Preparation: Easy
Cooking Time: 15 Minutes

    1 flank steak
    ½ cup sugar
    ½ cup soy sauce
    1 clove garlic, minced, or
          1 tablespoon garlic salt
       Flour
    2 eggs, well beaten
    2 green onions, chopped
    4 tablespoons olive or
          vegetable oil
       Cooked rice

Serves: 4
Must Partially Do Ahead

Have butcher run steak through tenderizer one time. Marinate steak in sugar, soy sauce, and garlic at least 30 minutes or overnight if possible. Drain. Coat meat with flour; dip into mixture of egg and green onion. Fry in hot oil approximately 7 minutes on each side. (Be careful; egg coating scorches easily.) Serve with white fluffy rice or fried rice.

Menu Suggestion: Dilly Brussels Sprouts (page 262), Southern Squash Boats (page 272).

Wine Suggestion: A full red such as a French Hermitage (Rhône region).

Judy Ferguson Field

Pepper Steak

For those who "like it hot," use full amount of pepper as indicated.

Preparation: Easy
Cooking Time: 45 Minutes

    1 medium onion, coarsely
          chopped
    2 cloves garlic, minced
    1 tablespoon oil
    1½ pounds tender lean beef
          cut into 1-inch cubes
    1½ cups sliced fresh mushrooms
    1½ cups sliced green pepper
    ¾-1½ teaspoons coarsely
          ground black pepper
    1 teaspoon salt
    1 (6-ounce) can tomato paste
    1 (10½-ounce) can beef bouillon
          + water to equal 2 cups
    ½ cup Burgundy
    1 tablespoon cornstarch
          (optional)
    ¼ cup water (optional)
       Cooked rice

Serves: 6

Sauté onion and garlic in oil in skillet. Add beef; brown on all sides. Add mushrooms, green pepper, black pepper, salt, tomato paste, and bouillon; blend well. Bring to boil. Reduce heat to simmer; cook, covered, for 45 minutes or until beef is tender. Add Burgundy; heat through. If desired thicken with cornstarch dissolved in water. Serve over hot fluffy rice.

Menu Suggestion: Creamy Asparagus Salad (page 85), Best-Ever Lemon Pie (page 331).

Wine Suggestion: A California Pinot Noir. (May also be used in recipe.)

Sally Butts Darden

Simply Elegant Steak

This is one of those great dishes that gives you good results with minimal effort. Nice for your family, but just as good for quick company fare. Try it also in a puff pastry shell or over toast points.

Preparation: Average
Cooking Time: 1 Hour
Oven Temperature: 350°F

Serves: 6

1½ **pounds boneless round steak**
1½ **tablespoons oil**
2 **medium onions, cut in ½-inch slices and separated into rings**
1 **(4-ounce) can sliced mushrooms**
1 **(10¾-ounce) can condensed cream of celery soup**
½ **cup dry sherry**
1½ **teaspoons garlic salt**
3 **cups hot cooked rice**

Cut steak into thin (¼-inch) strips. In large skillet brown meat in oil over high heat. Add onions. Sauté until tender. Drain mushrooms, reserving liquid. Blend soup, sherry, mushroom liquid, and garlic salt in bowl; pour over steak. Add mushrooms. Reduce heat to simmer; cook 1 hour or until steak is tender, stirring occasionally. (Can be baked, covered, at 350°F for 1 hour.) Serve over bed of fluffy rice.
Menu Suggestion: Zesty Broccoli Spears (page 262), Quick and Easy Spoon Rolls (page 115).
Wine Suggestion: A red French Côte de Beaune.

Doris Duke Sosebee

Beef Stroganoff

Preparation: Easy
Cooking Time: 1 Hour 45 Minutes

Serves: 4-6

1¼ **pounds top round beef, cut in 2-inch squares or narrow strips**
⅓ **cup + 2 tablespoons oil, divided**
1 **medium onion, thinly sliced**
⅓ **cup flour**
2 **beef bouillon cubes**
2½ **cups boiling water**
1 **tablespoon tomato paste**
1½ **teaspoons Worcestershire**
1½ **teaspoons salt**
¼ **teaspoon black pepper**
1 **(4-ounce) can sliced mushrooms, drained**
2 **tablespoons sherry**
⅔ **cup sour cream**
1 **(8-ounce) package egg noodles, cooked**

In large skillet or Dutch oven brown beef in 2 tablespoons oil; add onions. Mix flour with remaining ⅓ cup oil to form roux. Add to beef and onions, mixing well. Dissolve bouillon cubes in boiling water; blend into beef mixture. Add tomato paste, Worcestershire, salt, and pepper, mixing thoroughly. Simmer, covered, 1 - 1½ hours; stir occasionally to prevent sticking. Stir in mushrooms and sherry; simmer for 5 minutes. Blend in sour cream; heat through, but **do not boil.** Serve over egg noodles (or cooked rice).
Micronote: Preheat browning skillet 4½ minutes. Add beef and 2 tablespoons oil; cook on HIGH 6-8 minutes to brown. Add remaining ingredients except sour cream. Cook, covered, on MEDIUM 20-25 minutes, stirring occasionally. Blend in sour cream. Cook on MEDIUM until just heated through, approximately 2 minutes; **do not boil.**
Menu Suggestion: Heavenly Lime Salad (page 90), Broiled Sherried Tomatoes (page 277), Crème Courvoisier (page 352).
Wine Suggestion: A light dry red from Bordeaux such as Pomerol.

Alice Ann Edwards Mundy

Beef Bourguignonne

This is good for family and company. For a more economical version substitute stew beef for the sirloin.

Preparation: Average
Cooking Time: 1½ Hours

Serves: 16

12 slices bacon
8 pounds lean sirloin or
    round, cut into thin strips
4 cloves garlic, minced, or
    ⅛ teaspoon garlic powder
2 (4-ounce) cans sliced
    mushrooms, undrained
4 bay leaves, crushed
4 tablespoons chopped parsley
    or 2 tablespoons dehydrated
    parsley flakes
2 teaspoons thyme
1 teaspoon salt
½ teaspoon pepper
1 cup flour
5 (10½-ounce) cans beef
    consommé, divided
1 cup red wine or water
    Cooked rice or pasta

Fry bacon until crisp; drain, crumble, and set aside. Brown beef in bacon drippings. Add garlic, mushrooms, bay leaves, parsley, thyme, salt, pepper, and bacon. Blend 1 can consommé and flour, whisking until all lumps are dissolved. Add flour mixture to meat, stirring until well blended. Add remaining consommé. Cook, stirring, until slightly thickened. Add wine or water. Simmer, covered, 1½ hours, stirring occasionally. Serve over rice or noodles.

Menu Suggestion: Layered Walnut-Herb Salad (page 77), Communion Bread (page 103), Cheesy Apple Pie (page 328).
Wine Suggestion: A California Pinot Noir.

Margaret Stout Ellett

Poor Boy Fillets

A nice change from the usual grilled burger. Arrange on casual platter using parsley and cherry tomatoes for color.

Preparation: Easy
Cooking Time: Approximately 20 Minutes

Serves: 4-6
Must Partially Do Ahead

1 pound ground beef
1 (4-ounce) can chopped
    mushrooms, drained
3 tablespoons finely chopped
    pimiento-stuffed olives
2 tablespoons finely chopped
    green pepper
2 tablespoons finely chopped
    onion
¼ cup grated Parmesan cheese
½ teaspoon salt
½ teaspoon lemon-pepper
    seasoning
6 slices bacon

Shape ground beef into 12 x 7½-inch rectangle on sheet of waxed paper. Sprinkle remaining ingredients except bacon evenly over beef. Beginning at short end, roll up jelly roll fashion, lifting waxed paper to help support ground beef. Slide roll onto baking sheet, seam-side down; smooth and shape roll. Refrigerate 2-3 hours. Cook bacon until transparent (not crisp); drain. Cut beef roll into 1½-inch thick slices. Wrap 1 slice of bacon around edges of each fillet; secure with wooden pick. Grill fillets 4-5 inches from hot coals, 8 minutes on each side, or until desired doneness.

Menu Suggestion: Onion Rings (page 256), Spinach-Stuffed Tomatoes (page 270).
Wine Suggestion: A dry red such as Italian Chianti.

Kaye Cooper Rigdon

Pastichio with Crema Sauce

Haven't you searched for a good ground beef casserole which is a bit unusual? This one is rich, tasty, and serves a crowd.

Preparation: Average
Cooking Time: 30 Minutes
Oven Temperature: 350°F

Serves: 12

1 **pound macaroni (long, if available), cooked al dente**
½ **cup butter, melted and divided**
¼-½ **cup bread crumbs**
1 **cup freshly grated Parmesan cheese, divided**
Meat Sauce
Crema Sauce

Rinse pasta in cold water; drain well. Grease 14 x 11 x 2-inch baking dish with some of butter. Sprinkle bread crumbs, then ½ cup Parmesan evenly over bottom of dish. Layer half of pasta in dish; sprinkle with Parmesan, then half remaining butter. Layer Meat Sauce evenly over macaroni. Cover with remaining pasta, cheese, and butter. Pour Crema Sauce over all. Sprinkle with additional grated Parmesan to garnish. Bake at 350°F for 30 minutes or until lightly browned and firm. Let stand a few minutes before serving.

Meat Sauce

2 **pounds ground beef**
1 **medium onion, chopped**
2 **teaspoons salt**
¼ **teaspoon pepper**
1 **(8-ounce) can tomato sauce**
½ **cup water**
4 **tablespoons chopped fresh parsley**
4 **tablespoons butter**
⅛ **teaspoon cinnamon**

Sauté beef, onion, salt, and pepper in heavy deep skillet until meat is browned and juices are absorbed. Add tomato sauce, water, parsley, butter, and cinnamon; simmer 20 minutes or until mixture thickens.

Crema Sauce

½ **cup butter**
8 **tablespoons flour**
4 **cups milk**
6 **egg yolks, beaten**
Salt and pepper to taste

Melt butter in saucepan over low heat. Gradually add flour, stirring constantly, until smooth. Remove from heat; gradually add milk. Return to low heat; stir constantly until mixture thickens slightly. Gradually add very small portion of hot mixture to egg yolks, stirring briskly to prevent curdling. Add egg yolk mixture to creamed mixture; cook over very low heat, stirring constantly, until thickened. Season with salt and pepper.
Menu Suggestion: Layered Walnut-Herb Salad (page 77), Southern Squash Boats (page 272), Pear Pie (page 329).
Wine Suggestion: A dry red such as Chianti or a Greek white Domestica.

Ethel Martin Caras

Moussaka

Preparation: Average
Cooking Time: 35-40 Minutes
Oven Temperature: 350°F

Serves: 6-8

2 large eggplant
  Salt
½ cup butter, melted
½ cup grated Parmesan cheese,
  divided
½ cup grated Cheddar cheese,
  divided
  Meat Sauce
  Cream Sauce

Halve unpared eggplant lengthwise; slice crosswise (½-inch thickness). Place in broiler pan. Sprinkle with salt. Brush with butter. Broil until golden. On bottom of shallow 2-quart baking dish layer half of eggplant, slightly overlapping slices. Sprinkle with 2 tablespoons each Parmesan and Cheddar. Spoon Meat Sauce over eggplant. Sprinkle with 2 more tablespoons each Parmesan and Cheddar. Layer remaining eggplant slices over cheese. Pour Cream Sauce over all. Sprinkle with remaining cheese. Bake at 350°F 35 minutes or until golden brown. Cool slightly. Cut into squares to serve.

Meat Sauce

1½ pounds ground chuck
  or lamb
1 cup chopped onion
1 clove garlic, minced
2 tablespoons butter, melted
1 teaspoon basil
1 teaspoon salt
½ teaspoon oregano
½ teaspoon cinnamon
⅛ teaspoon pepper
2 (8-ounce) cans tomato
  sauce
2 tablespoons dry bread
  crumbs

In 3½-quart Dutch oven sauté meat, onion, and garlic in butter until brown. Add herbs, spices, and tomato sauce; bring to boil. Reduce heat; simmer, uncovered, 30 minutes. Stir in bread crumbs.
Micronote: Preheat browning skillet 4½ minutes. Add all ingredients except bread crumbs. Cook on HIGH until mixture boils. Reduce power to MEDIUM; cook 20-25 minutes.

Cream Sauce

2 tablespoons butter, melted
2 tablespoons flour
½ teaspoon salt
⅛ teaspoon pepper
2 cups milk
2 eggs, beaten
½ cup grated Parmesan cheese
½ cup grated Cheddar cheese

In medium saucepan blend butter, flour, salt, and pepper. Gradually stir in milk. Bring to boil, stirring until mixture is thick. Remove from heat. Stir some of hot mixture into eggs. Return all to saucepan; mix well.
Micronote: Place butter, flour, salt, pepper, and milk into blender; process until smooth. Pour into glass measure. Cook on HIGH 5 minutes, stirring every 30-45 seconds. Process eggs in blender until well mixed. Stir small amount of hot sauce into eggs; return all to sauce. Cook on HIGH 1½ minutes, stirring several times.
Menu Suggestion: West Coast Salad (page 80), Light Pumpernickel Bread (page 108), Baklava (page 344).
Wine Suggestion: A dry red such as Spanish Rioja or Greek white wine.

Ann Branch Smith

Spinach Lasagna

A unique version of an ever-popular recipe. Highly recommended.

Preparation: Easy
Cooking Time: 40 Minutes
Oven Temperature: 375°F

Serves: 8

1 **pound ground beef**
1 **clove garlic, minced**
1 **(4-ounce) can mushroom stems and pieces**
2 **stalks celery, diced**
1 **(32-ounce) jar Ragu Spaghetti Sauce with Mushrooms**
½ **teaspoon Worcestershire**
½ **teaspoon anise seed**
¼ **teaspoon oregano**
¼ **teaspoon thyme**
1 **(10-ounce) package frozen chopped spinach, thawed**
1 **(8-ounce) carton cottage or Ricotta cheese**
4 **ounces grated Parmesan cheese, divided**
1 **(6-ounce) package long sliced Mozzarella cheese**
9-12 **Lasagna noodles, cooked according to package directions**

In skillet brown ground beef. Stir in garlic, mushrooms, and celery. Add Ragu Sauce and all seasonings; mix well. Simmer 1 hour. Drain spinach; squeeze out excess liquid. Mix with cottage cheese and 2 ounces Parmesan cheese. In long 2-quart casserole, spread ⅓ meat sauce. Arrange half of noodles, lengthwise, over sauce. Cover with another ⅓ meat sauce, then spinach-cottage cheese mixture. Sprinkle with half remaining Parmesan. Add remaining half of noodles; top with remaining ⅓ meat sauce. Cover with Mozzarella cheese; sprinkle with remaining Parmesan. Bake at 375°F for 45 minutes, until lightly browned; let stand 15 minutes before serving.

Micronote: Cook beef 6 minutes on HIGH; stir twice during cooking to break up beef. Add garlic, mushrooms, celery, sauce, and seasonings. Cook on MEDIUM for 12-15 minutes. Assemble as above, using **two** smaller dishes. Cook each casserole for 10 minutes on MEDIUM.

Menu Suggestion: Honeyed Citrus Nut Salad (page 79), Herb Bread (page 109), Best-Ever Lemon Pie (page 331).

Wine Suggestion: A light red such as Italian Barbera.

Carol Ann Alexander Armstrong

There is a very great deal of difference between originality and novelty.
James Dickey, *Sorties*
Doubleday, Copyright 1971. Used with permission.

Peking Hamburgers

Looking for a different, quick, and tasty way to fix hamburger? This is it! Guaranteed to become a family favorite!

Preparation: Easy
Cooking Time: 10 Minutes

Serves: 2

½ **pound ground beef**
1 **(8½-ounce) can sliced pineapple**
3 **tablespoons brown sugar**
1 **teaspoon cornstarch**
1½ **tablespoons red wine vinegar**
1½ **teaspoons soy sauce**
1½ **teaspoons Worcestershire**

Shape ground beef into 2 patties. Brown over medium heat 3 minutes on each side. Drain pineapple, reserving 2 tablespoons syrup. Combine remaining ingredients, including reserved syrup. Heat with pineapple slices in separate saucepan, stirring occasionally until sauce thickens. Place pineapple slices on burgers; spoon sauce over.
Menu Suggestion: Parmesan Potato Fingers (page 281), Spinach Soufflé (page 270).
Wine Suggestion: A red California vin ordinaire.

Gail Adams Thomas

Herbed Beef en Phyllo

Preparation: Average
Cooking Time: 20 Minutes
Oven Temperature: 400°F

Serves: 8-10
Must Partially Do Ahead

1 **small onion, finely chopped**
4 **tablespoons butter, divided and melted**
2 **pounds lean ground beef**
¼ **pound mushrooms, chopped**
1½ **teaspoons salt**
½ **teaspoon crumbled oregano**
¼ **teaspoon pepper**
¼ **teaspoon garlic powder**
3 **eggs, beaten**
1½ **cups shredded Swiss cheese**
½ **cup chopped walnuts**
¼ **cup dry bread crumbs**
¼ **cup minced parsley**
12 **sheets phyllo pastry**
1 **cup sour cream**
2 **teaspoons dill weed**

Sauté onion in 2 tablespoons melted butter until transparent. Add beef and mushrooms; sauté until meat loses pink color. Drain off any excess fat. Turn meat mixture into large bowl. Add salt, oregano, pepper, and garlic; cool slightly. Add eggs, beating lightly. Stir in cheese, nuts, crumbs, and parsley. Chill well. [See "On Phyllo" (page 399).] Spread 1 phyllo sheet on smooth-working surface. Brush lightly with some of remaining butter. Cover with second sheet of phyllo; brush with butter. Divide into 3 equal strips, each 5½ x 12 inches. At narrow end of each strip place ⅓ cup meat mixture. Fold over flag-style into triangular shape, following diagrams on page 399. Place on greased baking sheet. Brush tops with butter. Repeat with remaining phyllo and filling to form 18 pastries. (May be frozen at this point.) Bake at 400°F for 20 minutes, until lightly browned. Combine sour cream and dill; stir well. Top each pastry with 1 tablespoon sour cream-dill mixture.
Menu Suggestion: Tomato Aspic (page 85), Zucchini Julienne (page 273), Oranges Côte d'Azur (page 352).
Wine Suggestion: A Greek white wine or a light red vin ordinaire.

Lou Bowen Powers
Wilmington, North Carolina

Unique Spaghetti Sauce

This recipe can easily be halved for the family or doubled for a crowd.

Preparation: Average
Cooking Time: 3 Hours

Yield: 5-6 Quarts

6	tablespoons olive oil
⅓-½	cup butter or margarine
1½-2	onions, chopped finely
3	cloves garlic, minced
1	cup grated carrot
1	cup chopped celery
3	cups fresh sliced mushrooms
2	(28-ounce) cans Italian (plum) tomatoes
2	(28-ounce) cans stewed tomatoes
1	(12-ounce) can tomato paste
2	tablespoons oregano
2	teaspoons basil
2	bay leaves
5	teaspoons sugar
	Freshly ground black pepper
4	teaspoons parsley
1	teaspoon salt
1	cup dry red wine
2	pounds ground beef
1	pound sweet Italian sausage (bulk)

In large pot (8-10 quart) heat olive oil and butter. Sauté onions and garlic in oil; add carrot, celery, and mushrooms. Cut up or mash tomatoes; add with juice. Add tomato paste, spices, and wine. In skillet brown ground beef and sausage; add to sauce mixture. Cook, uncovered, 2-3 hours over low heat, stirring occasionally.

Menu Suggestion: Majestic Layered Spinach Salad (page 79), Onion Bread (page 104).

Wine Suggestion: An Italian red such as Barbera or Bardolino.

Beth Hitchcock Sullivan
Valdosta, Georgia

Beef Pie

Preparation: Easy
Cooking Time: 35-45 Minutes
Oven Temperature: 375°F

Yield: 1 (9-inch) Pie

¾ **pound ground beef**
2 **teaspoons Worcestershire**
¾ **teaspoon salt**
⅛ **teaspoon allspice**
⅛ **teaspoon pepper**
⅛ **teaspoon garlic powder**
⅓ **cup chopped onion**
⅓ **cup chopped green pepper**
1 **tablespoon oil**
½ **cup mayonnaise**
½ **cup milk**
2 **eggs, beaten**
1 **tablespoon cornstarch**
1½ **cups shredded Cheddar or Swiss cheese, divided**
1 **(9-inch) pastry shell precooked at 400°F for 5-7 minutes**

Brown ground beef in skillet; drain well. Add Worcestershire, salt, allspice, pepper, and garlic powder to beef; set aside. Sauté onion and green pepper in oil; add to meat mixture. Combine mayonnaise, milk, eggs, and cornstarch; mix thoroughly. Add custard to meat mixture. Stir in half of cheese. Pour into pastry shell; sprinkle with remaining cheese. Bake at 375°F for 35-45 minutes or until firm in center.

Micronote: Preheat browning skillet 4½ minutes. Add beef; stir. Cook on HIGH 6 minutes, stirring several times. Add seasonings; set aside. Sauté vegetables 2-3 minutes or until tender. Add to meat. Combine mayonnaise, milk, eggs, and cornstarch; add to meat mixture. Add fillings to cooked pastry (must be in glass plate). Cook on MEDIUM 8-10 minutes, turning dish several times.

Variation: Prebake crust and prepare beef filling as directed. Sprinkle 2 tablespoons dry bread crumbs evenly over crust. Slice 2 medium tomatoes into ¼-inch slices; cut each slice in half. Arrange half of tomato slices over crumbs. Add beef mixture and bake 30 minutes. Arrange remaining tomato slices over top in an overlapping pattern. Bake until custard sets.

Menu Suggestion: Frozen Fruit Salad (page 87), Broccoli with Olive Sauce (page 259), Fig Preserve Cake (page 321).

Wine Suggestion: A hearty red varietal such as California Zinfandel.

Jean Bennett Oliver

Savory Meat Loaf Roll

Guaranteed to please husbands and children alike - the best meat loaf you've ever eaten!

Preparation: Easy
Cooking Time: 1 Hour
Oven Temperature: 350°F

Serves: 6-8

1½ pounds ground chuck
1 cup soft bread crumbs
1 egg, beaten
2 teaspoons prepared mustard
1½ teaspoons salt
1 teaspoon prepared
    horseradish
1 teaspoon Worcestershire
½ teaspoon thyme leaves
¼-½ teaspoon rosemary leaves,
    crushed
⅛ teaspoon pepper
1 (8-ounce) can tomato sauce
1½ cups (about ⅓ pound)
    shredded Cheddar cheese
Barbecue Sauce (optional)

Combine all ingredients except cheese and Barbecue Sauce. Shape into 14 x 10-inch rectangle on sheet of waxed paper. Sprinkle meat mixture with cheese. Beginning at short end of rectangle, roll in jelly roll fashion. (Lift waxed paper to aid in rolling.) Press together ends and edges to seal. Place roll, seam-side down, in shallow baking dish. Bake at 350°F for 45 minutes. If desired, top with Barbecue Sauce or additional ½ cup tomato sauce; bake 15 minutes more. Let stand 10 minutes before serving.

Micronote: Prepare roll as indicated. Place roll seam-side down on a meat rack in shallow casserole. Spread desired sauce over top. Cook on HIGH 12 minutes. Let stand 10 minutes before serving.

Barbecue Sauce

1 clove garlic
1 tablespoon oil
1 teaspoon salt
1 teaspoon pepper
⅛ teaspoon oregano
½ cup tomato sauce
1-2 tablespoons honey

Brown garlic clove in oil; discard garlic. Add other ingredients to oil; simmer 10 minutes or until bubbly. Pour over loaf.

Menu Suggestion: Onion Pie (page 256), Nanny's Southern Green Beans (page 265), Quick Butter Biscuits (page 117).

Wine Suggestion: A California vin ordinaire.

Ocie Rich Pope

Cheesy Ground Beef Casserole

A great do-ahead to refrigerate and bake at the last minute.

Preparation: Easy
Cooking Time: 25 Minutes
Oven Temperature: 350°F

Serves: 6

1 (5-ounce) package medium noodles
½ cup chopped green onion, divided
2 tablespoons butter or margarine
1½ pounds ground beef
2 (8-ounce) cans tomato sauce
1 teaspoon salt
¼ teaspoon oregano
¼ teaspoon basil
⅛ teaspoon pepper
1 cup small curd cottage cheese
1 cup sour cream
¾ cup grated sharp Cheddar cheese

Cook noodles according to package directions; drain, rinse well, and set aside. Sauté ¼ cup onion in butter in large skillet until tender. Add beef and brown lightly; drain well. Stir in tomato sauce and seasonings; simmer 20 minutes. Blend cottage cheese, sour cream, and remaining green onion; set aside. Place noodles in lightly greased 2½-quart casserole; spoon cottage cheese mixture over noodles. Spoon meat mixture over cheese mixture, sprinkle with Cheddar. Bake at 350°F for 25 minutes.

Micronote: Place onion and butter in 2-quart casserole. Cook on HIGH 2 minutes or until onion is tender. Add beef; cook on HIGH 4 minutes or until beef is no longer pink. Stir halfway through cooking time; drain. Add tomato sauce and seasonings; blend well. Cook, covered, on HIGH 5 minutes; stir halfway through cooking time. Proceed as indicated above.

Menu Suggestion: Party Pea Salad (page 82), Herbed Dinner Triangles (page 118).

Wine Suggestion: A light, dry red such as Italian Lambrusco.

Martha Ann Davis Crenshaw

Brunswick Stew

A real Southern crowd-pleaser. We couldn't observe the Fourth of July or Labor Day without it!

Preparation: Average
Cooking Time: Approximately 5 Hours

Yield: 2 Gallons

4 **pounds beef roast**
2 **pounds pork roast**
1 **(5 to 6-pound) hen**
3 **quarts water**
2 **(16-ounce) cans tomatoes**
4 **medium onions**
½ **cup vinegar**
½ **cup margarine**
  Salt, black pepper, and
    red pepper to taste
1 **(16-ounce) can cream style**
    corn
  Juice and rind of 2 lemons
4 **slices bread, toasted**
1 **cup catsup**

With water to almost cover, boil beef and pork together, until tender; cool. Separately boil hen until tender in 3 quarts water. Reserve chicken stock. Remove all meats from bones; grind or chop finely in food processor, using steel blade. Grind or process tomatoes and onions. Place ground foods, vinegar, margarine, salt, and pepper in reserved chicken stock. Cook **slowly** 2 hours, stirring often. Add corn, lemon juice, and rinds. Crush toast to fine crumbs. Stir crumbs and catsup into stew. Cook **slowly** 1 hour. Remove lemon rinds before serving.

Micronote: Combine as above. Cook on HIGH until thoroughly heated. Cook on LOW for times indicated above. (There is no substantial time saved by microwaving. However, Brunswick Stew scorches **VERY** easily when cooking conventionally; this will not happen in microwave.)

Menu Suggestion: Marinated Vegetable Medley (page 82), Fan-Style Bread (page 105), Nona's Egg Custard Pie (page 337).

Beverage Suggestion: Beer or Iced Tea

Lynn Newman McCranie

In the good old patriarchal times most every family of wealth kept what was called 'open house' and all who came were welcome. There was no need to send word you were coming, for food and shelter were always available.

Bill Arp

Savory Chili with Beans

Preparation: Easy
Cooking Time: 1-1½ Hours

Serves: 10-12

2 pounds ground chuck
1 large onion, chopped
3 green onions, chopped
1 tablespoon chopped parsley
4 ribs celery (with leaves), chopped
1 teaspoon garlic
1 (6-ounce) can tomato paste
1 (15-ounce) can tomato sauce
5-6 cups water
1 (1½-ounce) can chili powder
1¼ teaspoons salt
⅛ teaspoon red pepper
1 cup cooked red beans
1 cup cooked pinto beans
Shredded lettuce
Shredded Cheddar cheese
Diced onion
Tortilla chips

Brown meat with onions in Dutch oven. Add parsley, celery, and garlic to meat. Stir in tomato paste, tomato sauce, water, chili powder, salt, and pepper. Bring to boil; reduce heat and simmer 1 hour. Add beans after 45 minutes. Serve lettuce, cheese, onion, and chips as condiments. (Can be served over rice, omitting condiments.)

Menu Suggestion: One-Bowl Wheat Germ Casserole Bread (page 105), Pineapple Upside Down Cake (page 322).

Beverage Suggestion: Mexican Beer

Evanda Gravitte Moore

Stir-Fry Liver with Onions

Preparation: Easy
Cooking Time: 13 Minutes

Serves: 2
Must Serve Immediately

½ pound calf liver, cut into ¼-inch strips
2 tablespoons flour
⅛ teaspoon pepper
2 tablespoons hot oil
1 large onion, sliced into strips
2 tablespoons soy sauce

Coat liver with combined flour and pepper. Heat 2 tablespoons oil in wok or skillet. Add liver; stir-fry 3 minutes. Reduce heat; add onions and stir. Cover; simmer 10 minutes. Add soy sauce; stir.

Menu Suggestion: Frozen Pineapple Salad (page 86), Heavenly Vegetable Casserole (page 275), Quick Butter Biscuits (page 117).

Wine Suggestion: A white or red vin ordinaire.

Melba Clark Jacobs

Braised Veal

Preparation: Easy
Cooking Time: 30 Minutes

2 pounds veal cutlets
2 tablespoons oil
2 medium onions, cut into rings
1 garlic clove (optional)
½ cup water or white wine
2 tablespoons lemon juice
1 teaspoon salt
½ teaspoon oregano
2 tablespoons chopped parsley

Serves: 4-6
Must Serve Immediately

Cut veal into serving pieces. Heat oil in large skillet; add veal and sauté until brown. Remove to holding dish. Add onions and garlic; cook over low heat until onions are tender. **Remove** garlic clove. Return veal; add water, lemon juice, salt, and oregano. Cover; simmer 30 minutes, adding more water if necessary. Sprinkle with parsley; serve immediately.

Menu Suggestion: Artichoke-Tomato Casserole (page 278), Fettucine (page 286), Creole Fudge Cake (page 305).

Wine Suggestion: A quality dry light red from Bordeaux such as a Médoc.

Beth Sullivan Copeland

Veal in Port Sauce

A gourmet delight! This recipe works equally well with boneless chicken breasts if veal is unavailable or too expensive.

Preparation: Average
Cooking Time: 20-30 Minutes

8 (3-ounce) veal medallions (cut from loin)
Salt to taste
White pepper to taste
2 tablespoons flour
⅓ cup butter, melted
2 cups sliced mushrooms
1½ ounces prosciutto, diced
½ teaspoon shallots, chopped
1 cup port wine
1 cup whipping cream
1 teaspoon fresh parsley, chopped
1 teaspoon lime juice
Tomato roses (optional)
Lime slices (optional)

Serves: 4

Season veal slices with salt and pepper. Dust lightly with flour. Sauté veal in butter until tender and done. Remove from pan; drain. In same skillet sauté mushrooms until tender. Add prosciutto, shallots, and wine; cook to reduce liquid by half. Add cream; continue to reduce until sauce reaches medium-thick consistency. Add parsley and lime juice. Return veal to pan; heat through. Garnish with tomato roses and lime slices.

Menu Suggestion: Green Salad Unique (page 75), Frosted Cauliflower (page 260), Coeur à la Crème (page 347).

Wine Suggestion: Deserves a quality Bordeaux such as a Château Margaux.

David S. Flanary
Houston, Texas

Veal Amelio

Preparation: Easy
Cooking Time: 30 Minutes

Serves: 8

2 pounds veal fillets, cut into
    serving-sized portions
Flour
Salt
Pepper
2 tablespoons olive oil
1 cup butter, divided
6 tablespoons dry white wine
1 tablespoon lemon juice
1 pound fresh mushrooms,
    sliced

Pound veal gently with wooden mallet. Sprinkle lightly with flour, salt, and pepper to taste. Heat olive oil and 2 table-spoons butter. Add veal; sauté on both sides without browning. Remove veal; set aside, keeping warm. Add wine to pan; heat slightly. Add remaining butter and lemon juice. Add mushrooms; sauté briefly. Place several veal slices on each plate. Top with mushrooms and sauce.

Menu Suggestion: Spinach Soup (page 61), Asparagus with Cashew Sauce (page 258), Chocolate Cheesecake (page 325).

Wine Suggestion: A quality red from Bordeaux such as St-Julien.

Susie White Gignilliat

Veal Parmigiana

Preparation: Average
Cooking Time: 15-20 Minutes
Oven Temperature: 350°F

Serves: 6

1 cup packaged bread crumbs
¾ cup grated Parmesan cheese,
    divided
12 thinly sliced veal scallops
2 eggs, slightly beaten
1 cup chopped onion
1 clove garlic, minced
4 tablespoons olive oil,
    divided
1 (16-ounce) can tomatoes
2 (8-ounce) cans tomato sauce
1½ teaspoons leaf basil,
    crumbled
1½ teaspoons leaf thyme,
    crumbled
½ teaspoon salt
½ teaspoon onion salt
¼ teaspoon pepper
2 tablespoons butter
1 (8-ounce) package Mozzarella
    cheese

Mix bread crumbs and ¼ cup Parmesan cheese. Dip veal into beaten eggs; coat well with crumb mixture. Let stand to dry on rack while preparing sauce. In skillet sauté onion and garlic in 2 tablespoons oil. Add tomatoes, tomato sauce, basil, thyme, salts, and pepper. Cover; simmer 15 minutes. Heat 2 tablespoons oil and butter in separate skillet until mixture foams. Add veal scallops, a few at a time, browning on both sides. Layer veal, sliced Mozzarella cheese, and sauce in shallow baking dish. Sprinkle ½ cup Parmesan cheese on top. Bake at 350°F for 15 minutes or until sauce bubbles and cheese melts.

Micronote (Sauce): Sauté onion and garlic in oil on HIGH 3-4 minutes, until tender. Add tomatoes, tomato sauce, basil, thyme, salts, and pepper. Cook on HIGH 10 minutes. Continue as directed above.

Menu Suggestion: Majestic Layered Spinach Salad (page 79), Fettucine (page 286), Zabaglione (page 347).

Wine Suggestion: A quality red Italian such as Barolo.

Jacqueline Mabry Frankum

Veal Cordon Bleu

Preparation: Average
Cooking Time: 15-20 Minutes

Serves: 6
Must Serve Immediately

12 veal scallops (3 to 4-ounces each), preferably cut from leg
Salt and pepper to taste
6 very thin slices ham
6 thin slices Swiss cheese
2 eggs, slightly beaten
1 teaspoon water
Flour
1½ cups plain bread crumbs
½-¾ cup butter
Fresh parsley

Flatten each veal scallop with mallet or bottom of heavy skillet until thin. Sprinkle each with salt and pepper. Place one slice ham in center of each of 6 scallops; place slice of cheese on top of ham. Blend eggs and water. Brush outside edge of veal scallops with egg mixture; top with remaining scallops, sealing edges so that ham and cheese are completely enclosed. Dredge lightly and carefully in flour. Dip in remaining egg mixture then in crumbs until well coated. Pat pieces lightly with heavy knife so crumbs will stick. Place on wire rack; refrigerate for 2-3 hours. Heat butter in large skillet (do not brown); add scallops and sauté until golden on both sides. (Add a little more butter if needed.) Place on warm platter; garnish with parsley sprigs. Serve immediately.

Menu Suggestion: Broiled Sherried Tomatoes (page 277), Zucchini Julienne (page 273), Sour Cream Mini Biscuits (page 380), Strawberry Champagne Sherbert (page 357).
Wine Suggestion: A dry medium-full red such as Cabernet Sauvignon.

Elaine Caras Waller

Wiener Schnitzel

Preparation: Easy
Cooking Time: 8 Minutes

Serves: 4-8

4-8 veal cutlets (approximately 1½-pounds)
¼ cup flour
¼ teaspoon salt
⅛ teaspoon pepper
1 egg, beaten
1 teaspoon oil
Dry bread crumbs
6 tablespoons clarified butter
Lemon wedges (optional)

Pound cutlets with flat mallet; pat dry. Mix flour, salt, and pepper. Coat cutlets with seasoned flour, patting thoroughly. Blend egg and oil; brush onto cutlets. (Egg may be seasoned with basil, garlic, or oregano if desired.) Cover cutlets with bread crumbs, pressing to coat. If desired, place cutlets on wire rack; let stand in refrigerator 1 hour for coating to better adhere. Heat butter in large skillet. Add veal; sauté over medium heat 3-4 minutes on each side, until tender and golden brown. For crisp coating do not let cutlets touch in pan, and do not move them for first 2-3 minutes cooking time. Remove veal from pan; drain thoroughly on absorbent toweling. Garnish with lemon wedges.

Menu Suggestion: Bavarian Cheese Soup (page 63), Cucumbers in Sour Cream Dressing (page 81), Broccoli with Carnival Sauce (page 259), Pecan Chiffon Pie (page 336).
Wine Suggestion: A German Schloss Vollrads (dry white).

Charlotte Morrow Dunlap

Pork Tenderloin with Mustard Sauce

A special company dish.

Preparation: Average
Cooking Time: 2 Hours
Oven Temperature: 300°F

Serves: 4-6
Must Partially Do Ahead

1 (2½ to 3-pound) pork tenderloin
¼ cup soy sauce
¼ cup bourbon
2 tablespoons brown sugar
Mustard Sauce

Place tenderloin in glass dish. Combine soy sauce, bourbon, and brown sugar. Pour over pork; refrigerate several hours. Return meat to room temperature; place on rack in shallow pan. Bake at 300°F for 2 hours, basting frequently with marinade. Slice. Serve with Mustard Sauce.

Mustard Sauce

⅓ cup sour cream
⅓ cup mayonnaise
1 tablespoon dry mustard
1 tablespoon finely chopped scallions
1½ teaspoons wine vinegar
Salt and pepper to taste

Combine all ingredients; blend well.
Menu Suggestion: Congealed Asparagus Salad (page 85), Lemony Apple Bake (page 282), Yam Baskets Louisianne (page 279), Chocolate-Amaretto Mousse Pie (page 348).
Wine Suggestion: A dry California Rosé.

Cathy McLanahan Nix

Pork Loin Braised in Milk

A traditional Bolognese dish, the milk makes the meat tender and juicy with a delicate rich flavor.

Preparation: Easy
Cooking Time: 2 Hours
Oven Temperature: 350°F

Serves: 4-6

2 tablespoons butter
2 tablespoons oil
1 (2-pound) pork loin roast
1 teaspoon salt
Freshly ground pepper to taste
2½ cups milk
Carrots (optional)

Heat butter and oil in casserole large enough to just contain roast. Brown loin thoroughly on all sides. Add salt, pepper, and milk. When milk comes to boil, lower heat to medium. Cook with lid partly askew either on top of range (medium) or in oven (350°F) for 1½-2 hours. When meat is cooked, milk should have reduced into small nut-brown clusters. Baste occasionally while cooking. After removing roast for carving, skim away fat (2-3 tablespoons) from residue. Add small amount of warm water. Over high heat, scrape and loosen all milk clusters. Spoon over sliced pork. (Carrots may be cooked in pot during last 30 minutes of cooking time.)
Menu Suggestion: Sour Cherry Salad (page 88), Fettucine (page 286), Apple Dumplings (page 341).
Wine Suggestion: A rich white such as Alsatian.

William W. Greene

Bacon-Wrapped Pork Chops

Preparation: Easy
Cooking Time: 1-1½ Hours
Oven Temperature: 325°F

Serves: 4

      4 **pork chops (thick cut)**
      4 **slices bacon**
      ½ **cup soy sauce**
      2 **tablespoons grated onion**
      1 **tablespoon vinegar**
      ½ **teaspoon sugar**
      ⅛ **teaspoon cayenne**
      1 **clove garlic, crushed**

Wrap each chop with 1 slice of bacon, securing with toothpick. Place chops in 2-quart shallow casserole in single layer. Combine remaining ingredients; pour over chops. Cover. Bake at 325°F for 1-1½ hours; turn once and remove cover after 40 minutes.
Micronote: Prepare as above. Cook, covered, on HIGH for 15 minutes or on MEDIUM for 30 minutes.
Menu Suggestion: Cheesy Apples (page 282), Sesame Broccoli (page 261), Molasses Muffins (page 122).
Wine Suggestion: A flavorful dry wine such as California Zinfandel.

Paddy McClendon Estes
Atlanta, Georgia

Glazed Pork Roast

Preparation: Average
Cooking Time: 1 Hour
Oven Temperature: 350°F

Serves: 6

         Dijon mustard
         Brown sugar
      1 **(4 to 5-pound) rolled**
         pork loin
      ½ **cup bourbon, cognac,**
         or brandy
      ½ **cup beef bouillon**

Blend equal amounts of mustard and brown sugar sufficient to coat roast. Rub mustard-sugar mixture on all surfaces of roast. Sear roast on all sides in very hot skillet. Place in roasting pan; pour liquor over roast. Ignite carefully; fire will burn only about 30 seconds or until liquor is gone. Add bouillon to pan juices. Roast at 350°F for 1 hour or until roast is done. Use meat thermometer to assure doneness.
Micronote: Prepare roast as above. Use preheated browning skillet for searing and cooking. Calculate cooking time according to weight of roast, allowing 10-12 minutes per pound. If oven has temperature probe, follow manufacturer's instructions, cooking to 160°F. Allow to stand until temperature reaches 170°F. If probe is unavailable, cover meat with heavy plastic wrap or place in browning bag. Punch several holes in plastic. Cook first half of calculated time on HIGH; cook last half on MEDIUM. Meat may be turned once or twice during cooking.
Menu Suggestion: Carrot and Zucchini Julienne (page 273), Barley Casserole (page 284), Harvest Sweet Potato Pie (page 330).
Wine Suggestion: A full red such as California Cabernet Sauvignon.

Ann Couch Alexander

Pozole

Preparation: Average
Cooking Time: 1 Hour

Serves: 12

6 tablespoons olive oil
4 pounds lean pork, cut in
    thin strips
4 cups chopped onions
6 tablespoons sweet Mexican
    chili powder
3 tablespoons flour
4 teaspoons salt
1 teaspoon oregano
2 bay leaves
4 (16-ounce) cans tomatoes,
    undrained
4 tablespoons Jalapeño relish
2 (16-ounce) cans white hominy,
    drained
Mexican Rice (page 285)
Condiments:
    Thinly sliced green onions
    Chopped ripe avocado
    Shredded lettuce
    Grated Monterey Jack
        cheese
    Chopped radishes
    Toasted, slivered almonds
    Sliced black olives
    Jalapeño relish
    Sour cream
    Corn chips

Heat oil. Add pork, a little at a time; brown and remove. Sauté onions in same pan. Return pork to pan. Mix chili powder and flour; add to pork and onions. Cook, stirring, 1-2 minutes. Add salt, oregano, bay leaves, tomatoes, and relish. Bring to boil. Reduce heat; simmer, covered, 1 hour or until pork is tender. (May make ahead and refrigerate or freeze at this point.) Add hominy; heat through. Serve in bowls over Mexican Rice. Top with condiments.

Menu Suggestion: Green Salad with Creamy Garlic Dressing (page 100), Fresh Fruit Tart (page 330).
Wine Suggestion: Sangria (page 11).

Nell Cromer Freeman
Stillwater, Oklahoma

Honey Glazed Ham

Preparation: Easy
Cooking Time: 45 Minutes
Oven Temperature: 350°F

Yield: Variable

<pre>
    1 fully cooked boneless ham
10-12 whole cloves
    2 tablespoons brown mustard
    2 teaspoons lemon juice
    1 teaspoon ground cloves
    1 teaspoon orange juice
   ¼ cup dark brown sugar
   ¼ cup honey
</pre>

Make several criss-cross cuts on top side of ham. Stud with whole cloves. Blend mustard, lemon juice, ground cloves, and orange juice. Stir in brown sugar and honey. Brush ⅓ of glaze over ham. Bake at 350°F for 20 minutes. Baste with another ⅓ of glaze. Return to oven; bake additional 25 minutes, basting once more with remaining glaze. If thick crusty glaze is desired, combine 1-2 tablespoons brown sugar and 1-2 tablespoons honey; pack over ham during last 15 minutes of cooking time.
Menu Suggestion: Mincemeat Salad (page 91), Beaumont Inn Corn Pudding (page 275), Green Bean Casserole (page 265), Tennessee Jam Cake (page 312).
Wine Suggestion: German Liebfraumilch.

Marjorie Gay Gunter
Atlanta, Georgia

The long table in the dining room was more than lavishly laid and replenished. The air was so thick with the odor of ham, spareribs, and whiskey that it seemed one might almost eat it with a spoon....The sideboard was perhaps the gayest spot....

From *Reflection in a Golden Eye*, Carson McCullers
Copyright 1941 by Carson McCullers. Copyright renewed 1968 by Floria V. Lansky, as Executrix of the Estate of Carson Smith McCullers.
Reprinted by permission of Houghton Mifflin Company.

Marinated Barbecued Pork Chops

Preparation: Easy
Cooking Time: 30-45 Minutes

Serves: 6-8
Must Partially Do Ahead

<pre>
  ½ cup oil
  ¼ cup olive oil
  ¼ cup lemon juice
   3 cloves garlic, minced
   1 tablespoon salt
   1 teaspoon paprika
  ½ teaspoon pepper
   6 bay leaves, halved
 6-8 (1-inch thick) loin or
         rib pork chops
</pre>

Mix all ingredients except chops in shallow baking dish. Add chops, turning to coat. Cover; marinate overnight in refrigerator. Remove chops from marinade; grill over slow to medium coals, 4-5 inches from heat, for 30 minutes or until chops are no longer pink. Turn and baste occasionally with marinade.
Menu Suggestion: Herbed Roasting Ears (page 276), Orange Sour Cream Muffins (page 123), Chocolate Lover's Ice Cream (page 356).
Wine Suggestion: A flavorful generic such as California Rhine.

Lynda Dickens Askew

Golden Grilled Ham

Preparation: Easy
Cooking Time: 30 Minutes

Serves: 4
Must Partially Do Ahead

   1 (1½-pound) pre-cooked ham
      steak (1-inch thick)
   1 cup ginger ale
   1 cup orange juice
   ½ cup brown sugar, firmly
      packed
   3 tablespoons oil
   1 tablespoon wine vinegar
   2 teaspoons dry mustard
   ¾ teaspoon ground ginger
   ½ teaspoon ground cloves

Score fat edge of ham; place in shallow baking dish. Combine remaining ingredients; pour over ham. Refrigerate overnight or let stand one hour at room temperature, occasionally spooning marinade over ham. Place ham on grill over low coals; grill 15 minutes on each side, brushing frequently with marinade. Heat remaining marinade as sauce for ham.

Menu Suggestion: Glazed Acorn Squash with Onions (page 271), Down South Beans (page 266), Sour Cream Banana Pudding (page 340).

Wine Suggestion: A Rosé or dry Lambrusco.

Bonnie Wood Fellers

A pitcher of clear, cold water is indispensable.
Mrs. E. R. Tennent
Housekeeping in the Sunny South, 1885

Pork Chops Paprikash

The gravy is plentiful and scrumptious over almost any type of rice.

Preparation: Easy
Cooking Time: 1 Hour

Serves: 4

   4 loin pork chops (¾-inch
      thickness)
   1½ tablespoons oil
   1 large onion, thinly sliced
   ½ teaspoon caraway seed
   ½ teaspoon salt
   ½ teaspoon paprika
   ¼ teaspoon dill weed
   ¼ teaspoon garlic powder
   ⅓ cup water
   ⅔ cup sour cream

Trim fat from chops. Brown chops in oil in large skillet; drain excess fat. Combine remaining ingredients except sour cream; add to skillet. Simmer, covered, 1 hour or until tender. Remove chops to warm platter. Stir sour cream into meat drippings in skillet. Heat, but **do not boil**. Spoon sauce over chops.

Micronote: Preheat browning skillet 4½ minutes. Add oil, then chops; brown. Cover; cook on MEDIUM for 5 minutes. Turn chops. Cook on MEDIUM 15 minutes more. Remove chops to warm platter; continue as directed above. (Browning dish may be sprayed with vegetable coating instead of using oil.)

Menu Suggestion: Broccoli Ring (page 260) with Harvard Beets (page 279), Buttermilk Biscuits (page 116).

Wine Suggestion: A light dry red such as Beaujolais.

Flo Criss Smith

California Pork Chops

A great dish for a busy day!

Preparation: Easy
Cooking Time: 30 Minutes

Serves: 4

    4 pork chops
    ½ cup catsup
    4 tablespoons water
    2 tablespoons brown sugar
    4 lemon slices

Brown chops on both sides in skillet. Pour off grease. Mix catsup, brown sugar, and water. Place 1 lemon slice on each chop; pour catsup mixture over chops. Simmer, covered, 30 minutes or until tender.

Micronote: Preheat browning skillet 4½ minutes. Add chops; brown on both sides. Pour off grease. Mix catsup, sugar, and water. Place lemon slice on each chop. Pour catsup mixture over chops. Cover; cook on HIGH 15-20 minutes depending on thickness of chops.

Menu Suggestion: Country Fried Okra (page 264), Macaroni and Cheese Deluxe (page 288).

Wine Suggestion: A fruity white such as German Liebfraumilch.

Violet Lee Nicholson

Ham-Asparagus Crêpes

Preparation: Average
Cooking Time: 25 Minutes
Oven Temperature: 350°F

Serves: 8

    1 (10-ounce) package frozen
         asparagus spears
    2 tablespoons diced onions
    3 tablespoons butter or
         margarine, melted
    3 tablespoons flour
    ½ teaspoon salt
    ⅛ teaspoon cayenne
    ¾ cup milk
    1 cup whipping cream, divided
    1½ cups finely diced cooked
         ham
    ½ cup mayonnaise
       Paprika
    8 crêpes (page 138)

Cook asparagus according to package directions; drain. Sauté onion in butter for 2 minutes. Stir in flour, salt, and cayenne; cook, stirring constantly, until bubbly. Stir in milk and ¾ cup cream; continue cooking and stirring until sauce thickens and bubbles for 1 minute. Reserve ¼ cup sauce for topping. Stir ham into remaining sauce. To fill crêpes, place 2-3 asparagus spears on each crêpe. Add approximately ¼ cup ham filling; roll up and place, seam-side down, in buttered 13 x 9 x 2-inch baking dish. Whip remaining ¼ cup cream. Stir in reserved cream sauce and mayonnaise. Spoon over crêpes; sprinkle with paprika. Bake at 350°F for 25 minutes.

Micronote: Cook asparagus 7 minutes; set aside. Melt margarine 45 seconds; add onion; cook 1 minute. Add flour, salt, pepper, milk, and ¾ cup cream. Cook on HIGH 5 minutes, stirring every 45 seconds. Proceed as directed above.

Menu Suggestion: Heavenly Lime Salad (page 90), Brioche (page 115), Oranges Côte d'Azur (page 352).

Wine Suggestion: A fresh, flavorful German white such as Moselle.

Marty Brauch Owens

Grilled Chops Oriental

Served at the Georgia Governor's Mansion.

Preparation: Easy
Cooking Time: 1 Hour
Oven Temperature: 350°F

Serves: 8
Must Partially Do Ahead

8 pork chops (thick cut)
½ cup soy sauce
½ cup lemon juice
2 tablespoons ground ginger
or 4 tablespoons grated
fresh ginger
½ teaspoon garlic salt

Place chops in shallow pan in single layer. Mix remaining ingredients; pour over chops. Marinate, covered, in refrigerator overnight; turn once or twice. Cook on hot charcoal grill until done. Baste occasionally with marinade. Chops may be baked in marinade in 350°F oven for 1-1¼ hours.
Micronote: Preheat browning skillet 4½ minutes on HIGH. Drain chops. Place in skillet to sear on both sides. Cook on HIGH for 5 minutes. Reduce power to MEDIUM; cook 10-12 minutes. Turn dish several times during cooking.
Variation: Marinated Pork Loin Roast - Marinate roast as above. Bake on rack at 350°F timed according to weight.
Menu Suggestion: Chutney-Rice Salad (page 78), Stir-Fry Pea Pods (page 267), Lemon Meringue Nests (page 343).
Wine Suggestion: A dry light red such as California Gamay.

Janette McGarity Barber
Commerce, Georgia
Sarah Nichols Dunlap

Barbecued Ribs with Uncle Phil's Sauce

Preparation: Average
Cooking Time: 1 Hour 30 Minutes

Serves: 6-8
Must Partially Do Ahead

6-8 **pounds pork ribs**
1 **medium onion, whole**
1 **cup vinegar**
1 **tablespoon salt**
Water
Basting Sauce
Uncle Phil's Sauce

Cut ribs into serving pieces; place in large covered pot. Add onion, vinegar, salt, and enough water to cover ribs. Boil 1 hour. Cool and drain. Pour Basting Sauce over ribs. Refrigerate 2-48 hours. Place ribs in single layer on grill over charcoal fire. Cook until between brown and charred, about 15-30 minutes, basting often with excess sauce. Pass Uncle Phil's Sauce with ribs when serving for all who like really hot, tangy ribs. Ribs may be cooked under broiler instead of on grill (only if it rains!) but will not have quite as much flavor.

Basting Sauce

¾ **cup catsup**
¾ **cup water**
⅓ **cup lemon juice**
3 **tablespoons sugar**
3 **tablespoons Worcestershire**
2 **tablespoons prepared mustard**
3 **teaspoons salt**
½ **teaspoon Tabasco**
¾ **cup finely chopped onion**

Combine all ingredients; simmer 15 minutes.
Micronote: Cook on HIGH for 2 minutes. Stir. Cook on MEDIUM until very hot.

Uncle Phil's Sauce

1 **cup oil**
1 **cup cider vinegar**
Black pepper (lots)

Combine all ingredients in covered jar; shake well.
Menu Suggestion: Brunswick Stew (page 202), Southern Caviar (page 81), Corn-in-the-Shuck (page 276), Southern-Style Fried Pies (page 327).
Beverage Suggestion: Beer

Edward H. Shannon

I was a Sanders 'fore I married, an' when I come 'way from Pa's house hit was jes like turnin' my back on a barbecue.

Joel Chandler Harris

Sausage and More

Perfect for an autumn evening or any time of the year! A wonderful blend of flavors.

Preparation: Easy
Cooking Time: 45 Minutes
Oven Temperature: 375°F

Serves: 4

½ **pound sausage**
2 **medium sweet potatoes,
    peeled and sliced**
3 **medium apples, peeled
    and sliced**
2 **tablespoons sugar**
1 **tablespoon flour**
½ **teaspoon salt**
½ **cup cold water**
1 **tablespoon sausage
    drippings**

Cut sausage into ½-inch pieces or form bulk sausage into small balls. Fry until well done; drain, reserving 1 tablespoon drippings. Arrange layers of potatoes, apples, and sausage in buttered 1½-quart casserole. Combine sugar, flour, and salt; blend with water. Pour mixture over layers. Drizzle drippings over all. Cover; bake at 375°F for 45 minutes or until apples and potatoes are tender.

Menu Suggestion: Appalachian Spoon Bread (page 120), Molly's Butterscotch Pie (page 336).

Wine Suggestion: A California hearty Burgundy.

Susan Bible Jessup

Red Peppers and Sausage

Preparation: Average
Cooking Time: 30 Minutes

Serves: 2-3
Must Serve Immediately

3 **large fresh red peppers**
3 **tablespoons finely chopped
    onion**
5 **tablespoons olive oil,
    divided**
  Salt and pepper
4 **fresh ripe tomatoes, peeled,
    seeded, and chopped (or to
    equal 2 cups)**
1½ **cups mild bulk sausage**
⅓ **pound fettucine (tomato
    or egg), cooked al dente**
⅓ **cup red wine**
2 **tablespoons butter**
⅓ **cup freshly grated
    Parmesan cheese**

Halve peppers; remove seeds and ribs; cut into 1-inch squares. In large skillet over medium heat sauté onions in 3 tablespoons olive oil for 2 minutes. Add peppers; cook over medium-high heat for 8 minutes. Season with salt and pepper; set aside. In small skillet heat 2 tablespoons olive oil. Add tomatoes; cook over medium heat 10 minutes or until slightly reduced. Add tomato mixture to peppers. (Mixture freezes well at this point.) Shape sausage into 1-inch balls. In separate skillet cook sausage in red wine over medium heat until wine is evaporated and sausage browns in its own fat. Add sausage to pepper mixture; stir and heat. Drain fettucine; top with butter. Dress pasta with peppers and sausage, then Parmesan cheese. Serve immediately. Pass additional Parmesan if desired.

Menu Suggestion: Sautéed Cauliflowerets (page 262), Grandmamma's Gingerbread (page 322) with Lemon Fondue Sauce (page 358).

Wine Suggestion: A flavorful California Zinfandel.

Paula Eubanks Smith

Sausage and Cabbage Stir-Fry

A good one-dish meal. Each serving has approximately 385 calories.

Preparation: Easy
Cooking Time: 25-30 Minutes

Serves: 4
Must Serve Immediately

1 cup egg noodles, cooked
¾ pound Polish sausage, sliced
8 cups coarsely chopped cabbage
1 small onion, chopped
1 apple, cored and grated
½ teaspoon caraway seed
1 tablespoon brown sugar
½ teaspoon salt
2 tablespoons cider vinegar

Rinse noodles with hot water; drain and set aside. In large skillet over medium heat cook sausage until brown, about 10 minutes. Remove with slotted spoon; set aside. Add cabbage, onion, apple, and caraway seed to skillet. Increase heat to medium-high. Cook, stirring, until cabbage is tender, 7-10 minutes. Add brown sugar, salt, and vinegar. Cover; cook over low heat 5 minutes. Return sausage to skillet. Add noodles and toss.

Menu Suggestion: Sunshine Salad (page 91), Honey Bars (page 362).

Beverage Suggestion: Full-bodied German beer.

Debbie Jacobs Springle

Sausage and Wild Rice Casserole

Preparation: Average
Cooking Time: 25-30 Minutes

Serves: 8

1 pound well-seasoned bulk sausage
1 pound fresh mushrooms, sliced or 1 (8-ounce) can sliced mushrooms, drained
1 medium onion, chopped
4 tablespoons butter, melted
¼ cup flour
½ cup cream
2½ cups chicken broth
⅛ teaspoon oregano
⅛ teaspoon thyme
⅛ teaspoon marjoram
Monosodium glutamate
Salt
Freshly ground pepper
Hot pepper sauce (optional)
1 (6-ounce) box white and wild rice, cooked
½ cup toasted almonds

Crumble and cook sausage in skillet; drain. Sauté mushrooms and onions in butter until limp but not brown. Blend flour with cream until smooth. Add broth; cook until thickened. Combine sausage, mushrooms, onions, and sauce. Season with oregano, thyme, marjoram, monosodium glutamate, salt, and pepper. Add hot pepper sauce as desired. Stir in rice. Pour into 2-quart casserole. Bake at 350°F for 25-30 minutes. Sprinkle with toasted almonds before serving.

Micronote: Preheat browning skillet 4½ minutes. Add sausage; stir to brown. Cook 6-8 minutes on HIGH; drain. In same skillet sauté mushrooms and onions in butter 3-5 minutes. Mix flour and cream in glass dish; add broth. Cook on HIGH 6-8 minutes, stirring often. Combine ingredients as directed above. Cook on HIGH for 10 minutes, turning dish several times during cooking time.

Variation: For wild rice side dish, omit sausage; proceed as above.

Menu Suggestion: Cold Apple Soup (page 66), Yam Baskets Louisianne (page 279), Japanese Fruit Pie (page 331).

Wine Suggestion: A red French vin ordinaire.

Joyce Jackson Rabb

Sausage Lasagna

A spicy lasagna which may be "toned down" by using all mild sausage. Bulk sausage can also be substituted for Italian.

Preparation: Average
Cooking Time: 45 Minutes
Oven Temperature: 350°F

Serves: 8
Must Do Ahead

1 pound hot Italian sausage
1 pound mild Italian sausage
¾ cup chopped onion
2 cloves garlic, minced
2 tablespoons olive or
  vegetable oil, divided
1 (28-ounce) can whole
  tomatoes
1 (8-ounce) can tomato
  sauce
1 (6-ounce) can tomato
  paste
4 tablespoons snipped
  parsley, divided
1 tablespoon dried basil
  leaves
4 teaspoons salt, divided
1 teaspoon sugar
½ teaspoon pepper, divided
4 quarts boiling water
1 (8-ounce) box Lasagna
  noodles
1 pound Ricotta cheese
  or cottage cheese
2 egg yolks, slightly
  beaten
¾ pound Mozzarella cheese,
  sliced
½ cup grated Romano cheese

Remove casing from Italian sausage. Cook and stir sausage in skillet over medium heat until brown; drain. Sauté onion and garlic in 1 tablespoon oil in Dutch oven over high heat for 3 minutes. Stir in sausage, tomatoes, tomato sauce, tomato paste, 2 tablespoons parsley, basil, 1 teaspoon salt, sugar, and ¼ teaspoon pepper. Heat to boiling. Reduce heat; simmer, uncovered, until mixture is consistency of spaghetti sauce (about 1 hour). Combine remaining oil, 2 teaspoons salt, and boiling water; add noodles. Boil gently until noodles are tender, 10-12 minutes. Drain; rinse with cold water. Mix Ricotta cheese, egg yolks, remaining parsley, 1 teaspoon salt, and ¼ teaspoon pepper. Cover bottom of 13 x 9 x 2-inch baking dish with small amount of meat sauce. Cover with half of noodles then layer in order half the remaining meat sauce, Ricotta cheese mixture, and Mozzarella cheese. Repeat layers with remaining ingredients. Sprinkle with Romano cheese. Bake, uncovered, at 350°F for 45 minutes. Let stand 15 minutes before cutting. (May be refrigerated, covered, up to 24 hours before baking; allow 10-15 minutes extra baking time.)

Menu Suggestion: Layered Walnut-Herb Salad (page 77), Herb Bread (page 109), Crème Reversée au Caramel (page 345).

Wine Suggestion: A red Italian Brolio.

Carol Lynn Dobson Waggoner

The tapping of the bell ... was rung loud and long for dinner. The local students went home for this but those who walked two and three and four miles took their tin buckets and went out under the shade of trees and exchanged smoke ham, sausage, yam potatoes, "bo'ly-hole biscuits," and red apples.

A school boy's composition-circa 1885. Elizabeth Wiley Smith, *The History of Hancock County.*
Wilkes Publishing Co., Inc., Copyright 1974. Used with permission.

Roast Lamb

A magnificent leg of lamb. It's sure to get rave reviews.

Preparation: Average
Cooking Time: 2 - 2½ Hours
Oven Temperature: 350°F

Serves: 6-8

1	**(4 to 5-pound) leg of lamb**
	Salt
	Pepper
	Flour
⅛	**teaspoon ginger**
2	**tablespoons shortening**
1	**small onion, chopped**
1	**tablespoon Worcestershire**
1	**tablespoon catsup**
⅛	**teaspoon sugar**
	Sliced tomatoes (optional)
2	**cups boiling water**

Wash roast thoroughly in cold water; dry with absorbent toweling. Dredge with salt, pepper, flour, and ginger. Melt shortening in roasting pan. Add onion; sauté until brown. Remove onion; discard. Place lamb in pan. Pour Worcestershire and catsup over lamb; sprinkle with sugar. Cover with sliced tomatoes. Pour boiling water around lamb; stir. Cook, covered, at 350°F for 2 - 2½ hours or until tender, basting frequently with pan drippings. Remove cover to brown during last 30 minutes of baking time.

Menu Suggestion: Apricot Mousse Salad (page 90), Spanokopita (page 269), Blue Ribbon Carrot Cake (page 312).

Wine Suggestion: A full, flavorful red such as Mouton-Cadet from Bordeaux.

Katherine Hobbie Griffin

Real Shish Kebob

Preparation: Easy

Serves: 4-6
Must Partially Do Ahead

1	**cup Burgundy or any dry red wine**
1	**cup oil**
2	**tablespoons lemon juice**
2	**tablespoons sugar**
1	**tablespoon catsup**
2	**medium garlic cloves, minced**
1	**teaspoon salt**
¼	**teaspoon coarsely ground black pepper**
⅛	**teaspoon basil**
⅛	**teaspoon parsley**
⅛	**teaspoon rosemary**
⅛	**teaspoon thyme**
1	**leg of lamb, boned and cut into 2-inch cubes**
	Mushrooms
	Cherry tomatoes
	Sliced squash
	Green pepper squares
	Onion quarters

Combine wine, oil, lemon juice, sugar, catsup, garlic, salt, pepper, and herbs. Pour over lamb and mushrooms; marinate 4 hours. Drain, reserving marinade. Place on skewers, alternating with vegetables. Cook on grill (or broil in oven), basting frequently with marinade, until lamb is medium (center should be pink).

Menu Suggestion: Gourmet Artichoke-Mushroom Salad (page 84), Barley Casserole (page 284), Cottage Cheese Rolls (page 112), Summer's Fresh Fruit Torte (page 344).

Wine Suggestion: A full red such as a French Châteuneuf-du-Pape (Rhône region).

Vee Vee Smith Blackshear

Rolled Lamb

Preparation: Easy
Cooking Time: 1 Hour 15 Minutes
Oven Temperature: 350°F

Serves: 6-8
Must Partially Do Ahead

  1 cup Dijon mustard
  2 tablespoons soy sauce
  2 tablespoons oil
  1 tablespoon rosemary
  ¼ teaspoon ginger
  1 (6-pound) leg of lamb,
      boned and rolled

Mix mustard, soy sauce, oil, rosemary, and ginger. Brush on lamb with pastry brush. Let stand in refrigerator 10-12 hours. Roast on rack at 350°F for 1¼ hours. Meat should be medium rare.

Menu Suggestion: Sunshine Salad (page 91), Minted Peas (page 267), Party Potatoes (page 281).

Wine Suggestion: A quality California Cabernet Sauvignon.

Kathryn Hamilton Millikan

Eight Boy Curry

Serving this dish is part of its charm. Traditionally, each condiment was served by a different serving boy. The more boys used, the more lavish the meal. Today we may not have the servers, but many condiments, or "boys," add to the flavor of the curry.

Preparation: Average
Cooking Time: 1 Hour

Serves: 4

  4 tablespoons butter or
      margarine
  4 tablespoons flour
  2 cups chicken stock
  2 tablespoons lemon juice
  2 teaspoons curry powder
  ½ teaspoon ground ginger
  ½ teaspoon salt
  ⅛ teaspoon black pepper
  2 cups chopped lean-cooked
      lamb (see Roast Lamb,
      page 218)
  3 cups hot cooked rice
    Condiments or "Boys"
    ½-1 cup each:
      Chutney
      Crumbled crisp bacon
      Grated coconut
      Toasted slivered almonds
      Chopped onion
      Sweet pickle relish,
        drained
      Hard- cooked eggs, sieved
      Chopped green peppers

In top of double boiler melt butter over low heat. Slowly add flour, stirring until blended. Gradually add stock, stirring until thickened. Stir in lemon juice and seasonings. Add lamb; heat thoroughly over simmering water 35-45 minutes. If sauce is too thick, add more stock. (Lamb curry may be cooled, refrigerated overnight, or frozen for future use.) Place layer of rice on each plate. Ladle sauce over rice. Pass "Boys" for individual garnish.

Micronote: Melt butter in glass bowl on HIGH 1 minute. Stir in flour, then stock. Cook on HIGH 4-5 minutes, stirring often, until thickened. Add seasonings and lamb; cook on HIGH 4-5 minutes or until heated.

Menu Suggestion: Gourmet Fruit Salad (page 87), Oranges Côte d'Azur (page 352).

Wine Suggestion: A full generic red such as California Burgundy.

Elizabeth Platt Johnson

Bill's Barbecued Venison

If there is a hunter in your family, you will enjoy this excellent way to prepare venison.

Preparation: Easy
Cooking Time: 10-12 Hours

Serves: 8-10

1 large venison roast, tenderloin, whole leg or other portion
Water
2 tablespoons vinegar
1 (18-ounce) bottle hickory-flavored barbecue sauce
½-¾ cup cream sherry
¼-⅓ cup packed light brown sugar
½ cup butter
Salt and pepper to taste

Place roast, water, and vinegar in crock pot. Cover; cook at low setting for 12 hours or until meat falls off bones. Remove all bones; pour off fat and juices. Shred meat; return to crock pot. Pour remaining ingredients over meat. Cover; continue cooking 2 hours, stirring occasionally, until butter has melted.

Micronote: Combine roast, 1 cup water, and vinegar in large covered dish. Cook on medium until roast is very tender (falling apart). Turn several times during cooking. Remove meat from bones. Continue as above. Combine sauce in glass measure. Bring to boil. Pour over meat; cook at low until heated throughout.

Variation: For Barbecued Pork substitute 1 (3 to 5-pound) pork roast for venison. Proceed as above.

Menu Suggestion: Southern Caviar (page 81), Corn-in-the-Shuck (page 276), Appalachian Spoon Bread (page 120), Cream Cheese Brownies (page 360).

Wine Suggestion: A full California Zinfandel.

Judy Mynatt Bush

Fish

Spiderwort

Spiderwort (Tradescantia virginiana)

Once thought to cure spider bites, this early bloomer has varied uses in the kitchen. Its stems and leaves can be used raw in salads or cooked as a green vegetable. Its delicate blue flowers are lovely candied for use in decorating cakes.

On Fish

- Servings of fresh fish are usually based on ⅓ to ½ pound portions of fillet per person.
- Lemon-pepper seasoning makes an interesting addition to broiled and baked fish dishes and shrimp.
- Take care not to overcook fish. Fish is done when the internal temperature reaches 140°F. At 150°F its tissues begin to break down, allowing both juices and flavors to escape. Lacking a thermometer, doneness of fish is determined when the thickest part flakes readily with a toothpick.
- When fish or onion odors linger on your hands, rub hands with a little lemon juice, vinegar, or parsley. Then wash in soapy water.
- The flavor of canned shrimp is improved if shrimp are soaked in ice water for 1 hour prior to use.
- One pound raw shrimp yields about 2 cups cooked and peeled shrimp. Two to 2½ pounds shrimp in shells yield about 1 pound cooked shrimp.
- To season seafood with wine, allow for every 6 servings: 2 tablespoons dry sherry, 4 tablespoons white wine, or 1 tablespoon cognac.
- Three-fourths pound of crabmeat yields 1½ cups.
- For 6 persons allow 3 dozen oysters in shell or 1 quart shucked oysters.
- Recipes for mussels, oysters, and clams are usually interchangeable.
- Fish has more flavor and retains its juices if it is cooked with the head intact.
- To prevent fish from sticking, rub pan with salad oil, olive oil, or bacon fat. Never use butter or margarine.
- For best results bake fish in a **preheated** 400°F oven. Fish will not bake, but steam, if placed in a cold oven.
- Baked fish will be tasty and moist if basted every 5 to 10 minutes. Try:
  — ½ water and ½ butter, hot
  — ½ water and ½ white wine, hot
  — ½ cup water and juice of ½ lemon, cold
  — Apple or tomato juice, hot
  — Dry white wine, cold
  — Sour cream or heavy cream, cold
  — French dressing, cold

Salmon Mousse with Dill Sauce

A winner any time of the day. Delicious for brunch, lunch, or for a delightfully cool summer supper-on-the-deck.

Preparation: Average

Serves: 6-8
Must Do Ahead

2 envelopes unflavored
   gelatin
½ cup cold water
½ cup boiling water
½ cup mayonnaise
1 tablespoon fresh lemon
   juice
1 tablespoon grated onion
1 teaspoon salt
½ teaspoon Tabasco
¼ teaspoon paprika
1 (16-ounce) can salmon,
   drained and finely chopped
1 tablespoon chopped capers
   (optional)
1 cup whipping cream,
   whipped
   Lemon wedges
   Parsley
   Capers
   Dill Sauce

In mixing bowl soften gelatin in cold water. Add boiling water; stir until gelatin is dissolved. Cool. Add mayonnaise, lemon juice, onion, salt, Tabasco, and paprika; mix well. Chill until slightly thickened. Add salmon and capers; beat well. Fold in whipped cream. Pour into well-oiled 1-1½-quart fish mold, ring mold, or individual molds. Chill until firm. Unmold; garnish with lemon wedges, capers, and parsley; serve with Dill Sauce.

Dill Sauce

1 egg
4 teaspoons fresh lemon
   juice
2 tablespoons fresh dill,
   finely cut (or dill weed)
1 teaspoon salt
1 teaspoon grated onion
⅛ teaspoon sugar
   Freshly ground black pepper
   to taste
1½ cups sour cream

In mixing bowl beat egg until fluffy and light yellow in color. Blend in remaining ingredients in order listed.
Menu Suggestion: Broccoli and Cauliflower Salad (page 83), Croissants (page 113), Fresh Lemon Ice Cream (page 356).
Wine Suggestion: A crisp, dry, light wine such as German Schloss Vollrads.

Sherrie Nathan Schrage

- - - *Oysters, salmon, cold fowl, and champagne - - - heaven on the half shell.*

Mark Twain

Salmon Croquettes

Preparation: Easy
Cooking Time: 15 Minutes

Serves: 4-6

1 **(16-ounce) can red or pink salmon, drained**
½ **cup cornmeal**
¼ **cup chopped fresh parsley**
1 **medium onion, grated**
1 **egg, beaten**
Juice of 1 lemon
1½ **teaspoons baking powder**
¼ **teaspoon salt**
¼ **teaspoon pepper**
Oil

Remove bones and skin from salmon; crumble fish into mixing bowl. Add cornmeal, parsley, onion, egg, lemon juice, baking powder, salt, and pepper; stir until well blended. Shape into 6 patties or 12 (2-inch long) rolls. Deep fry in hot oil until browned; drain on absorbent toweling. Serve hot, alone, or with Mustard Sauce.

Becky Smith Dadisman

Mustard Sauce

½ **cup mayonnaise**
½ **cup sour cream**
2 **tablespoons sweet pickle relish, drained**
1 **tablespoon prepared mustard**
Juice of ½-1 lemon
½ **teaspoon sugar**
½ **teaspoon salt**
½ **teaspoon cayenne**

Combine all ingredients; mix well. Serve hot or cold (if heating, **do not boil**).
Menu Suggestion: Sunshine Salad (page 91), Barley Casserole (page 284), Corn Lightbread (page 119).
Wine Suggestion: A dry, white California generic.

Helen Odom Rice

Smoked Trout or Salmon

A real showpiece for a buffet dinner; or use as an appetizer with unsalted crackers.

Preparation: Easy
Cooking Time: 4 Hours
Oven Temperature: 200°F

Serves: 8
Must Do Ahead

4 **large or 8 small trout or 1 large salmon**
½ **cup rock salt**
1 **gallon cold water**
8 **teaspoons liquid smoke**
Parsley or lettuce (optional)
Lemon wedges

Rinse fish. Combine salt, water, and liquid smoke in heavy plastic bag or other non-metallic container. Add fish. Soak fish, refrigerated, for 24 hours; drain. Place fish on greased cookie sheet. Bake at 200°F for 4 hours. Open door once after 2 hours to turn fish. Chill. (Freezes well. Wrap securely; thaw as needed.) Remove skin just before serving. Place on bed of parsley or other greens. Squeeze lemon juice over fish; garnish with additional lemon wedges.
Menu Suggestion: Herbed Tomatoes (page 83), Broccoli with Shrimp Sauce (page 259).
Wine Suggestion: A quality California Chardonnay.

Jane Eve Fair Wilheit

Salmon Steaks Poached in Wine

A superb entrée for a small dinner party - no one will guess how little time was involved.

Preparation: Easy
Cooking Time: 8-15 Minutes

Serves: 4
Must Serve Immediately

4 fresh salmon steaks,
    each ½-inch thick
¼ cup margarine, melted
½ cup chopped green onions
3 tablespoons fresh parsley
    or 1 tablespoon dry
1 tablespoon fresh dill
    or 1 teaspoon dry
1 teaspoon salt
¼ teaspoon pepper
¼ cup white wine
2 teaspoons capers
    Lemon wedges
    Parsley (optional)
    Dill (optional)

In covered skillet sauté onions in margarine until tender. Add parsley, dill, salt, pepper, and wine. Reduce heat to medium-low. Add salmon; cook, covered, just until salmon flakes (about 5-8 minutes). Carefully transfer salmon to warm serving dish. Sprinkle with capers. Carefully ladle sauce over salmon. Garnish with lemon wedges or squeeze juice over before serving. May garnish with sprigs of fresh parsley and/or dill, when available.

Micronote: Place salmon in single layer in 13 x 8 x 2-inch glass dish. Combine margarine, onions, parsley, dill, salt, and pepper in glass measure; cook on HIGH 4 minutes. Stir in wine. Pour over salmon. Sprinkle with capers. Cover with waxed paper. Cook on HIGH 4 minutes. Continue as above.

Menu Suggestion: West Coast Salad (page 80), Spinach-Stuffed Squash (page 270), Black Bottom Pie (page 337).

Wine Suggestion: A rich, dry white such as Chardonnay.

W. Jackson Thompson

Trout Italiano

Preparation: Easy
Cooking Time: 1 Hour
Oven Temperature: 350°F

Serves: 4

1 medium onion, chopped
1 medium green pepper, chopped
1 medium potato, peeled
    and chopped
¼ teaspoon dried basil
¼ teaspoon dried oregano
    Salt and pepper to taste
2 (1½-pound) trout, cleaned
    and dressed, or 4 large
    trout fillets
    Butter
    Lemon slices

Combine onion, green pepper, potato, basil, oregano, salt, and pepper. Stuff into each trout cavity (or place half mixture between 2 fillets); repeat. Place fish on sheet of lightly greased, heavy-duty foil. Dot with butter. Sprinkle any extra stuffing over fish; fold foil over fish; seal tightly. Bake at 350°F for 1 hour or until fish flakes easily with fork. Squeeze lemon over fish before serving.

Menu Suggestion: Heavenly Lime Salad (page 90), Eggplant Italiano (page 279).

Wine Suggestion: A dry medium-full white such as Italian Verdicchio.

Rita G. Dorsey
Dalton, Georgia

Gourmet Trout

Preparation: Easy
Cooking Time: 10 Minutes

  12 **small trout**
      Dijon mustard
      Salt and lemon-pepper
        to taste
  ½ **cup butter (no substitution)**
      Lemon wedges

Serves: 6
Must Serve Immediately

Rub inside of trout with mustard; sprinkle inside with salt and lemon-pepper. Heat skillet to medium. Add butter to melt. Fry trout in butter 4 minutes on each side. Flake with fork to test for doneness; do not overcook. Serve with lemon wedges.

Frances Jolly Syfan

To Bake: Line shallow baking pan with aluminum foil. Prepare trout as above. Place in pan in single layer. Add milk to ¼-inch depth around trout. Bake at 350°F for 20 minutes, until fish flakes easily.
Micronote: Rub inside of trout with mustard; do not salt until end of cooking period. Cover with plastic wrap; vent. Cook on HIGH 6-8 minutes or until fish flakes easily; turn dish several times while cooking.
Menu Suggestion: Artichoke-Tomato Casserole (page 278), Potato-Onion Piquante (page 280), Pear Pie (page 329).
Wine Suggestion: A quality medium-full dry white such as French Fumé Blanc.

Karen Turner Syfan

Trout Amandine

Preparation: Average
Cooking Time: 20 Minutes

  ½ **cup slivered blanched**
      almonds
  ¼ **cup butter or margarine,**
      melted
  12 **large trout (or bass)**
      fillets
      Salt and pepper to taste
      Thyme leaves to taste
      Milk
      Flour
  ½ **cup oil**
  2 **teaspoons chopped parsley**
      Lemon wedges

Serves: 6-8
Must Serve Immediately

Sauté almonds in butter until golden brown; set aside. Sprinkle fillets with salt, pepper, and thyme; dip in milk; dredge in flour. Fry fillets in hot oil over medium heat until golden brown, turning once. Drain on absorbent toweling. Transfer to warm serving dish; sprinkle with almonds and parsley. Garnish with lemon wedges.
Menu Suggestion: Tomato Aspic (page 85), Savory Eggplant and Clams (page 278), Fresh and Crunchy Peach Pie (page 333).
Wine Suggestion: An austere dry white such as a Graves from Bordeaux.

Patsy Spiers Mercer

Grilled Fish

Preparation: Easy
Cooking Time: 25 Minutes

6 tablespoons salt
1 quart water
6 medium fresh water fish
   (trout or bass)
10 hickory chips
   Lemon wedges

Serves: 6
Must Partially Do Ahead

Combine salt and water. Place fish in covered plastic container or heavy plastic bag. Cover with salt water. Soak several hours. (Brine water soaking is the key; do not cheat on this step.) Cover hickory chips with plain water; soak while fish are soaking. Cover grill rack with aluminum foil; spray with non-stick vegetable coating. Punch holes in foil with knife tip or fork. Drain hickory chips; place over hot coals. Arrange fish on prepared rack. Cover, if possible; cook 25 minutes or until fish flakes easily with fork. Garnish with lemon wedges. Serve hot as an entrée or chill and serve with crackers as an appetizer.
Menu Suggestion: Sanford House Cucumber Mousse (page 86), Zucchini and Tomato Bake (page 273).
Wine Suggestion: A crisp white such as French Beaujolais.

Mary Hart Keys Wilheit

Cracker Fish

When you must resort to frozen fish, don't despair! This recipe makes it tastier than you ever thought possible.

Preparation: Easy
Cooking Time: 30 Minutes
Oven Temperature: 375°F

1 (16-ounce) package frozen
   haddock, sole, or perch
1 (10¾-ounce) can cream of
   shrimp soup
¼ cup butter or margarine,
   melted
1 tablespoon chopped onion
1½ teaspoons Worcestershire
¼ teaspoon garlic salt
30 crushed Ritz crackers
   (approximately 1½ cups)

Serves: 4
Must Serve Immediately

Place slightly thawed fish in lightly-greased shallow baking dish. Spread soup over fish. Bake, covered, at 375°F for 20 minutes. Meanwhile, mix remaining ingredients; sprinkle over fish. Bake, uncovered, 10 additional minutes.
Micronote: Place slightly thawed fish in greased baking dish. Spread soup over fish. Cook, covered, on HIGH 4-5 minutes or until fish flakes easily; turn dish half turn after 2½ minutes. Add remaining ingredients. Cook 2 minutes longer.
Menu Suggestion: Spinach Soufflé (page 270), Parmesan Potato Fingers (page 281).
Wine Suggestion: A crisp white such as Johannisberg Riesling.

Adelaide Gregory Norton

Casserole of Baked Fish Leicester

A traditional English dish. It works equally well for a family dinner or as a fish accompaniment for a meat entrée or a large party buffet.

Preparation: Average
Cooking Time: 30-45 Minutes
Oven Temperature: 325°F

Serves: 6

10 tablespoons butter or margarine, divided
1 small onion, chopped
2 cups fresh mushrooms
¼ cup coarse bread crumbs
1½-2 pounds filleted fat fish
6 slices Canadian bacon or 6 strips smoked bacon, fried
½ cup flour
1 cup milk
1 cup grated Leicester cheese or sharp Cheddar
Salt and pepper to taste
2 medium tomatoes, peeled and sliced
½ teaspoon oregano
Fresh parsley sprigs (optional)

Melt 4 tablespoons butter in small skillet. Sauté onion, mushrooms, and bread crumbs in butter. Turn into shallow casserole; spread evenly over bottom. Place fillets atop vegetable mixture. Arrange bacon over fish. In medium saucepan melt 4 tablespoons butter; blend in flour. Gradually whisk in milk and cheese. Cook and whisk over low heat until cheese melts and sauce thickens. Add salt and pepper to taste. Pour over casserole. Arrange tomatoes on top. Dot with remaining 2 tablespoons butter; sprinkle with salt, pepper, and oregano. Bake, uncovered, at 325°F for 30-45 minutes. Garnish with parsley.

Micronote: Melt 4 tablespoons margarine in shallow glass dish 1-2 minutes on HIGH. Sauté vegetables and bread crumbs on HIGH 3-4 minutes or until tender. Place fillets over vegetables, then bacon over fillets. Melt remaining margarine in glass dish; add flour and milk. Cook on HIGH 2½ minutes, stirring every 30 seconds. Add cheese; cook on HIGH 30-45 seconds or until cheese melts. Add salt and pepper. Pour over casserole. Arrange tomatoes over; dot with 2 tablespoons butter; sprinkle with salt, pepper, and oregano. Cook 8-10 minutes on HIGH or until fish flakes easily.

Menu Suggestion: Delicious Summer Fruit Salad (page 92), Sesame Broccoli (page 261), Brownie Baked Alaska (page 350).

Wine Suggestion: A dry white such as a Graves from Bordeaux.

Agnes Broadnax Parker

To dream of fish is a sign of motherhood.

A Treasury of Georgia Folklore by Ronald G. Killion and Charles T. Walker
(Atlanta: Cherokee Publishing Company, 1983). Used by permission.

Fried Catfish

It may not be fancy, but Southerners are rather partial to catfish. Whether a fish fry for two hundred or a family supper for two, it's a perennial favorite.

Preparation: Easy
Cooking Time: 8-10 Minutes

Serves: 4
Must Serve Immediately

6 small catfish, cleaned and dressed
1 teaspoon salt
¼ teaspoon pepper
2 cups self-rising cornmeal
Oil

Sprinkle catfish with salt and pepper. Place cornmeal in paper bag. Drop catfish in bag, one at a time; shake until coated. Fry in deep hot oil (375°F) until golden brown; drain well.

Menu Suggestion: Onion Rings (page 256), Herbed Roasting Ears (page 276), Hush Puppies (page 120), Best-Ever Lemon Pie (page 331).

Beverage Suggestion: A dry California white or beer.

Patsy Spiers Mercer

Shrimp Myrez

Preparation: Easy
Cooking Time: 25 Minutes
Oven Temperature: 450°F

Serves: 6-8
Must Partially Do Ahead

6 pounds whole shrimp
1 pound butter
½ cup olive oil
Juice of 2 lemons
2 tablespoons black pepper
4 teaspoons finely chopped garlic
1 teaspoon paprika
½ teaspoon oregano
½ teaspoon basil
½ teaspoon rosemary
½ teaspoon salt
French bread

Wash shrimp; let drain 1 hour. Spread shrimp over bottom of 13 x 9 x 2-inch baking dish. Combine remaining ingredients in saucepan; bring to boil. Pour over shrimp. Bake, uncovered, at 450°F for 20 minutes. Ladle shrimp into bowls; cover generously with sauce. Peel shrimp at table. Dip French bread into sauce. (Also good with half headless shrimp, half sea scallops. Add 1 tablespoon fresh dill to sauce.)

Micronote: Place prepared shrimp in shallow casserole. Melt margarine on MEDIUM 3 minutes. Add other ingredients; pour over shrimp. Cook on HIGH 15 minutes turning dish during cooking; or divide shrimp in 2 dishes; cook 7 minutes each.

Menu Suggestion: Majestic Layered Spinach Salad (page 79), Gourmet Rice-Stuffed Tomatoes (page 277), Fresh Fruit Tart (page 330).

Wine Suggestion: A dry medium-full white such as Italian Soave.

Robin Talley Myers

Shrimp Bayou

Very appealing on a bed of lettuce garnished with lemon wedges.

Preparation: Easy

Serves: 6
Must Do Ahead

2 pounds shrimp, boiled and
   peeled
⅔ cup chopped celery
¼ cup chopped onions
2 tablespoons chopped chives
   (optional)
1 cup oil
½ cup chili sauce
3 tablespoons lemon juice
2 tablespoons horseradish
1 tablespoon prepared mustard
½ teaspoon paprika
½ teaspoon salt
⅛ teaspoon hot sauce

Place shrimp, celery, onion, and chives in large covered container. Combine remaining ingredients in tightly capped jar; shake to blend well. Pour over shrimp mixture; stir gently. Cover securely; refrigerate 12 hours before serving, stirring 2-3 times.

Menu Suggestion: Iced Cucumber Soup (page 65), Puttin' on the Ritz (page 76), Beech Island Bread (page 103).

Wine Suggestion: A generic California white.

Suzanne Johnson Ingle

Shrimp Egg Roll Crêpes

East meets West - and the result will be enjoyed by all.

Preparation: Average
Cooking Time: 30 Minutes

Serves: 6

1 cup finely chopped celery
1 green onion with top,
   sliced
2 tablespoons margarine,
   melted
2 cups fresh bean sprouts,
   chopped or 1 (14-ounce)
   can bean sprouts, drained
1 (6-ounce) package frozen
   shrimp, cooked, drained,
   and chopped
2 tablespoons soy sauce
1 tablespoon sherry
1 tablespoon cornstarch
3 tablespoons water, divided
2 eggs, divided
12 Basic Entrée Crêpes
   (page 138)
   Oil

Sauté celery and onion in margarine until tender. Add bean sprouts, shrimp, soy sauce, and sherry. Combine cornstarch, 2 tablespoons water, and 1 egg; beat well. Stir into shrimp mixture; cook until thickened. Beat remaining egg with remaining 1 tablespoon water. Place ¼ cup filling in center of each crêpe. Fold envelope-style, brushing last fold with egg-water mixture; roll between palms to seal and shape. Preheat oil for deep frying to 375°F. Brown 2-3 egg rolls at a time in oil; drain on absorbent toweling. Keep warm in low oven until ready to serve. Serve with Chinese hot mustard sauce or sweet and sour sauce.

Menu Suggestion: Delicious Summer Fruit Salad (page 92), Stir-Fry Pea Pods (page 267).

Wine Suggestion: A dry, medium-full white such as Spanish Rioja.

Doris Duke Sosebee

Shrimp and Wild Rice

Preparation: Easy
Cooking Time: 30 Minutes
Oven Temperature: 325°F

Serves: 8

- ½ cup thinly sliced onion
- ½ cup sliced mushrooms
- ¼ cup diced green pepper
- ¼ cup butter or margarine
- 1 pound shrimp, cooked and cleaned
- 1 tablespoon Worcestershire
- 4 drops Tabasco
- 2 cups cooked long grain and wild rice
- 2 cups Cream Sauce
  Paprika (optional)
  Fresh parsley (optional)

Sauté onion, mushrooms, and green pepper in butter until tender. Toss shrimp with Worcestershire and Tabasco. Combine rice and sautéed vegetables. Spread in lightly buttered baking dish. Arrange shrimp over rice. Pour Cream Sauce over all. Sprinkle with paprika. Bake at 325°F for 15 minutes. Garnish with sprigs of parsley.

Micronote: Sauté vegetables in butter on HIGH 3-5 minutes. Combine ingredients and assemble as directed. Cook on HIGH 8 minutes. Garnish.

Cream Sauce

- ½ cup flour
- ½ cup butter, melted
- 1½ cups chicken broth
- ½ cup white wine

Blend flour into butter. Gradually stir in broth and wine. Cook over low heat until thickened.

Micronote: Melt butter 1-2 minutes on HIGH. Add flour; blend. Add broth and wine. Cook on HIGH 6 minutes, stirring every 30-45 seconds.

Menu Suggestion: Sour Cherry Salad (page 88), Broccoli Sunburst (page 260), Lemon Cheese Cake (page 306).

Wine Suggestion: A full white such as Chardonnay.

Jane Byerly Allgood

Lemon-Garlic Broiled Shrimp

Preparation: Easy
Cooking Time: 5-8 Minutes

Serves: 4-6
Must Serve Immediately

- 2 pounds medium shrimp, peeled and deveined
- 2 cloves garlic, halved
- ¼ cup butter, melted
- 3 tablespoons lemon juice
- 1 tablespoon Worcestershire
- ½ teaspoon salt
  Coarsely ground black pepper
- 3 tablespoons chopped fresh parsley

Place shrimp in single layer in 15 x 10 x 1-inch jelly roll pan; set aside. Sauté garlic in butter until brown; remove and discard garlic. Add lemon juice, Worcestershire, salt, and pepper; stir well. Pour mixture over shrimp. Broil shrimp 4 inches from heat 5-8 minutes, basting once. Sprinkle with parsley; serve immediately.

Menu Suggestion: Gourmet Artichoke-Mushroom Salad (page 84), Pecan Pilaf (page 285), Cauliflower in Sour Cream (page 263), Key Lime Pie (page 332).

Wine Suggestion: A crisp, flavorful white Beaujolais.

Jean Bennett Oliver

Low Country Shrimp

A traditional recipe from the coastal South Carolina "Low Country."

Preparation: Average
Cooking Time: 20-30 Minutes

Serves: 6

4 slices bacon
1 cup raw rice
2 cups water
2 cups cleaned raw shrimp
1 teaspoon Worcestershire
2-3 tablespoons flour
7 tablespoons butter or
    margarine, divided
½ cup finely chopped celery
2 tablespoons finely chopped
    bell pepper
2 teaspoons salt
¼ teaspoon pepper
    Tabasco (optional)

Fry bacon until crisp; reserve grease. Crumble bacon; set aside. Combine rice, water, and reserved bacon grease in medium saucepan. Boil until water is absorbed and rice is tender. Meanwhile spread shrimp in plate or shallow pan. Sprinkle with Worcestershire; let stand 20 minutes. Drain shrimp well; blot with absorbent toweling. Dredge with sufficient flour to coat well. In medium-large skillet melt 3 tablespoons butter. Add celery and bell pepper; sauté 5 minutes, stirring often. Add shrimp; sauté until flour is browned, stirring often. Combine hot rice, shrimp mixture, remaining butter, salt, pepper, and Tabasco. Toss well. Adjust seasonings; add extra Worcestershire to taste, if desired. Turn into serving bowl; sprinkle with crumbled bacon.

Menu Suggestion: Green Salad Unique (page 75), Carrot Julienne (page 273).

Wine Suggestion: A dry white such as white Spanish Rioja.

Evelyn Atwater Langston

Shrimp de Jonghe

Preparation: Easy
Cooking Time: 20 Minutes
Oven Temperature: 350°F

Serves: 4

⅔ cup butter, melted
2 tablespoons dried chives
½ teaspoon garlic powder
⅛ teaspoon pepper
1 pound shrimp, shelled
1½ cups crushed thin
    bacon-flavored crackers

Combine butter, chives, garlic powder, and pepper; stir to blend. Dip each shrimp into butter mixture, then roll in crumbs to coat. Layer shrimp in 8-inch square baking dish. Stir remaining crumbs into remaining butter mixture; sprinkle over shrimp. Bake at 350°F for 20 minutes or until shrimp are tender.

Micronote: Melt butter on HIGH 2 minutes. Prepare shrimp as directed. Cook on HIGH 6-8 minutes, rotating dish twice.

Menu Suggestion: Broccoli and Cauliflower Salad (page 83), Corn-in-the-Shuck (page 276).

Wine Suggestion: A dry white such as Spanish Rioja.

Ann Branch Smith

Shrimp-Asparagus-Artichoke Casserole

With all these good things, how can it go wrong? Want to economize, yet remain elegant? Substitute boneless, cooked chicken chunks for shrimp!

Preparation: Average
Cooking Time: 20 Minutes
Oven Temperature: 375°F

Serves: 6

1 pound fresh asparagus, steamed or 2 (10½-ounce) cans asparagus tips, drained
1 (14-ounce) can artichoke hearts, drained and quartered
1½ pounds shrimp, cooked and cleaned
¼ pound fresh mushrooms or 1 (4-ounce) can button mushrooms, drained
6½ tablespoons butter, divided
4½ tablespoons flour
¾ cup whipping cream
¾ cup milk
¾ teaspoon salt
¼ teaspoon pepper
⅛ teaspoon cayenne
¼ cup dry sherry
1 tablespoon Worcestershire
¼ cup grated Parmesan cheese Paprika

Arrange asparagus, artichokes, and shrimp in 2-quart casserole in order stated. Lightly sauté mushrooms in 2 tablespoons butter. Arrange over shrimp. Melt remaining 4½ tablespoons butter in saucepan. Stir in flour; cook 2 minutes. Add cream and milk, stirring constantly. When thick and smooth, season with salt and peppers. Stir in sherry and Worcestershire. Pour over casserole. Sprinkle with cheese and paprika. (May do ahead and refrigerate at this point. Let stand at room temperature 30 minutes before continuing.) Bake at 375°F for 20 minutes.

Micronote: Cook fresh asparagus in covered dish with ¼ cup water 8-10 minutes on HIGH. Layer asparagus, artichokes, and shrimp as above. Melt 2 tablespoons butter; add mushrooms; cook on HIGH 2 minutes, stirring twice. Layer over shrimp. Melt remaining butter. Stir in flour; cook 2 minutes on HIGH, stirring every 30 seconds. Add cream, milk, salt, peppers, sherry, and Worcestershire. Cook on HIGH until thick and smooth; stir every 30 seconds. Pour over casserole; sprinkle with cheese and paprika. Cook 10-12 minutes on MEDIUM.

Menu Suggestion: Cranberry Salad Ring (page 88), Light-as-a-Feather Refrigerator Rolls (page 112), Chocolate-Amaretto Mousse (page 348).

Wine Suggestion: A full white such as French Puligny-Montrachet.

Sally Butts Darden

Shrimp in Beer

Spread the newspapers and bring on the shrimp! Makes a great "peel your own" picnic feast.

Preparation: Easy
Cooking Time: 5 Minutes

Serves: 4-6

48 ounces beer
16 ounces water
1 tablespoon salt
8-10 peppercorns
1 tablespoon celery seeds
2 bay leaves
3 pounds fresh shrimp

Combine all ingredients except shrimp. Bring to rapid boil. Drop shrimp into boiling liquid. Simmer, covered, 2-5 minutes until shrimp turn pink. Drain. Serve hot or cold.

Menu Suggestion: Spicy Red Cocktail Sauce (page 292), Coleslaw Divine (page 81), Corn-in-the-Shuck (page 276).

Beverage Suggestion: Proceed with beer!

Mary Beth Wiegand Wood

Shrimp Jambalaya

Preparation: Easy
Cooking Time: 20 Minutes

Serves: 4

½ cup chopped onion
½ cup chopped green pepper
1 clove garlic, minced
4 tablespoons margarine, melted
1 (16-ounce) can tomatoes
1 teaspoon dried chopped parsley
½ teaspoon salt
¼ teaspoon chili powder
¼ teaspoon thyme
¼ teaspoon curry powder
1 (12-ounce) bottle Extra Dry Sparkling Champale
1 pound medium shrimp, peeled and cleaned
4 tablespoons chutney
Champale Rice

In large saucepan sauté onion, green pepper, and garlic in margarine until tender. Add tomatoes, parsley, salt, chili powder, thyme, and curry powder. Cook over medium heat 10 minutes, stirring often. Add Champale. Bring to full boil; reduce heat to simmer. (If Champale is unavailable, use 1½ cups dry sherry.) Add shrimp and chutney; cook, stirring, 3-5 minutes. (May be prepared ahead, reheating and adding shrimp and chutney just before serving.) If jambalaya needs thickening, add mixture of 1 tablespoon cornstarch plus ¼ cup water to final cooking or use Creole filé to thicken if available. (If using filé, be sure to add last and **do not boil**.) Serve over bed of Champale Rice.

Micronote: Sauté onion, green pepper, and garlic in margarine on HIGH 1½-2 minutes. Add tomatoes and seasonings. Cook on MEDIUM 5-6 minutes, stirring several times. Add Champale. Bring to boil on HIGH, 3 minutes. Add shrimp and chutney. Cook on HIGH 3-5 minutes; if mixture boils over, reduce power to MEDIUM.

Champale Rice

¾ cup long grain rice
1 (12-ounce) bottle Extra Dry Sparkling Champale

Combine rice and Champale in covered saucepan. Bring to boil. Reduce heat; simmer until all liquid is absorbed and rice is tender.

Menu Suggestion: Honeyed Citrus Nut Salad (page 79).
Beverage Suggestion: Continue with Sparkling Champale.

Connie Wallis Dixon

Fried Shrimp

Preparation: Easy
Cooking Time: 10 Minutes

Serves: 4
Must Serve Immediately

1 egg
½ cup milk
1 cup flour
2 cups bread crumbs
1 pound shrimp, shelled
Oil

Combine egg and milk; beat well. Arrange successive containers of flour, milk-egg mixture, and bread crumbs. Dip each shrimp into flour, then into liquid mixture, then roll in bread crumbs. Deep fry in hot oil just until lightly browned. Drain on absorbent toweling.

Menu Suggestion: Bavarian Sweet and Sour Salad (page 77), Hushpuppies (page 120).
Wine Suggestion: A crisp, dry white such as Italian Orvieto.

Ann Branch Smith

Baba's Shrimp Creole

A favorite of three generations - it has stood the test of time! Sauce, without shrimp, freezes well; add shrimp when reheating.

Preparation: Average
Cooking Time: 1 Hour

Serves: 8

1½-2 cups chopped celery
1 large onion, chopped
1 large green pepper, chopped
4 tablespoons bacon drippings
1 bay leaf
2 (16-ounce) cans stewed
    tomatoes
3 tablespoons tomato paste
1 tablespoon sugar
    Salt to taste
    Pepper to taste
⅛ teaspoon curry powder
    (optional)
    Louisiana Creole Seasoned
    Salt (optional)
2½-3 pounds shrimp, boiled
    and peeled
    Cooked rice

Slowly cook celery, onion, and green pepper in bacon drippings until light brown, about 15-20 minutes. Add bay leaf, tomatoes, tomato paste, and sugar; mix well. Add salt, pepper, curry powder, and a generous sprinkle of Louisiana Creole Seasoned Salt. Cook very slowly for 30-45 minutes. Add shrimp; heat through. Serve over rice.

Micronote: Sauté celery, onion, and green pepper in drippings on HIGH 2 minutes. (Browning skillet may be used.) Add other ingredients except shrimp and rice. Cook in covered casserole or crockery container on MEDIUM 15-20 minutes. If mixture boils too rapidly, lower power. Add cooked shrimp. Cook on HIGH until mixture boils. Serve.

Menu Suggestion: Congealed Asparagus Salad (page 85), Quick and Easy Spoon Rolls (page 115), Best-Ever Lemon Pie (page 331).

Wine Suggestion: A full white such as a French white Rhône wine.

Nelson Hilty Carter

Sumptuous Grilled Shrimp and Scallops

If you have never had grilled seafood you're in for a treat. These kabobs are nothing short of heavenly.

Preparation: Average
Cooking Time: 25 Minutes

Serves: 6
Must Partially Do Ahead

1 (16-ounce) bottle Catalina
    French Dressing
2 tablespoons Worcestershire
2 teaspoons garlic powder
2 teaspoons black pepper
2-3 drops Tabasco
1 pound large shrimp,
    shelled and cleaned
1 pound large scallops
1 large onion, cut in
    medium pieces

Combine dressing, Worcestershire, garlic powder, pepper, and Tabasco. Place shrimp, scallops, and onion in large container; pour marinade over all, covering completely. Refrigerate overnight, if possible, or at least one hour. Thread shrimp, scallops, and onions onto skewers. Cover grill rack with foil; punch several holes in foil with fork. Place over gray coals. Place skewers on foil. Cook with cover on grill (if possible) until shrimp and scallops are cooked through, about 25 minutes. Turn occasionally, brushing with marinade.

Menu Suggestion: Zesty Broccoli Spears (page 262), Fresh Peach Meringue Cake (page 321).

Wine Suggestion: A fruity white such as a generic California Rhine wine.

Mary Hart Keys Wilheit

Bacon-Wrapped Scallops

Good as an entrée or as an appetizer.

Preparation: Average
Cooking Time: 20-25 Minutes
Oven Temperature: 400°F

Serves: 6

½ **cup flour**
1½ **teaspoons salt**
1½ **teaspoons paprika**
½ **teaspoon ground white pepper**
½ **teaspoon garlic powder**
1 **egg**
1 **cup milk**
24 **sea scallops**
1 **cup unseasoned bread crumbs**
8 **bacon strips, cut into thirds**

Combine flour, salt, paprika, pepper, and garlic powder in shallow dish. Beat egg with milk. Roll each scallop in seasoned flour, shaking off excess; dip in egg mixture; coat with bread crumbs, covering completely. Wrap each breaded scallop in bacon; secure with toothpick. Place on lightly greased baking sheet. Bake at 400°F until bacon is crisp and scallops are cooked through, about 20-25 minutes.

Menu Suggestion: World's Best Tartar Sauce (page 293) or Spicy Red Cocktail Sauce (page 290), Apricot Mousse Salad (page 90), Broccoli Elegant (page 261), Frozen Mocha Meringue Pie (page 334).

Wine Suggestion: A quality full white such as French Pouilly-Fuissé.

Suzanne Richard Cannon

New Orleans Oysters Bienville

Preparation: Average
Cooking Time: 45 Minutes
Oven Temperature: 350°F

Serves: 6-8

4 **tablespoons butter, melted**
4 **tablespoons flour**
½ **cup liquid (juice from mushrooms and oysters)**
1 **clove garlic, minced**
1 **tablespoon onion juice**
1½ **teaspoons Worcestershire**
2 **dozen shrimp, cooked and finely chopped**
1 **(4-ounce) can mushrooms, drained**
1 **tablespoon sherry**
1 **quart shucked oysters, drained**
Parmesan cheese

Combine butter and flour in saucepan. Cook over medium heat until browned. Add liquid, garlic, onion juice, and Worcestershire. Cook, stirring, until smooth and thickened. Add shrimp, mushrooms, and sherry. Broil oysters until edges just curl; drain. Place oysters in small ramekins. Cover with sauce; sprinkle liberally with Parmesan. Bake at 350°F for 15 minutes or until bubbly.

Micronote (Sauce): Melt margarine on HIGH 1 minute. Add flour, liquid, garlic, onion juice, and Worcestershire. Cook on HIGH 2½ minutes, stirring every 30 seconds. Continue as directed.

Menu Suggestion: Creamy Asparagus Salad (page 85), One-Rise Whole Wheat Bread (page 107).

Wine Suggestion: A crisp dry white French Muscadet.

Jane Adams Lindsay

Oyster Roast on the Grill

Great fun for a party and easy on the hostess.

Preparation: Easy

Serves: 6-8

1 bushel unshucked oysters
Lemons
Melted butter
Saltine crackers

Fire charcoal in grill until coals reach white-ash stage. Place oysters in single layer on grill. Cover with wet burlap sack. Cook until shells pop open. Remove to spread newspapers. Have each person squeeze lemon juice into cups with melted butter. Complete opening shells with oyster knives. Scoop oysters into lemon-butter. Pass saltines.

Micronote: A "mock oyster roast" can be done in microwave. Place 6-8 oysters at a time in shallow baking dish. Cook on HIGH for 1-2 minutes or until shells begin to open. Repeat with remaining oysters. Proceed as above.

Menu Suggestion: Artichoke-Rice Salad (page 80).

Wine Suggestion: French Muscadet, a flavorful dry white wine, an established complement to oysters.

Katherine Hobbie Griffin

Baked Herbed Seafood

Very versatile; great for a backyard party or picnic; guests peel their own!

Preparation: Easy
Cooking Time: 45 Minutes
Oven Temperature: 350°F

Serves: 6

5 pounds shrimp, in shells,
   or 3 pounds fish fillets,
   or 3-4 pounds whole fish,
   or 5 pounds raw oysters
1 (16-ounce) bottle Italian
   dressing
2 cups butter or margarine,
   melted
2 scant tablespoons black
   pepper
4 lemons, halved

Place shrimp in large roasting pan. Combine dressing, butter, and pepper; pour over shrimp. Squeeze lemons over all; place squeezed halves in pan. Bake covered at 350°F for 35 minutes. Remove cover; bake additional 5-10 minutes. Remove shrimp with slotted spoon to serve.

Menu Suggestion: German Potato Salad (page 76), Herbed Tomatoes (page 83), Frozen Peach Cream Pie (page 334).

Wine Suggestion: A dry white California generic.

Mary Frances Ferguson Leigh

Crêpes d'Or

If you have the gourmet spirit, here is your chance to soar. This ravishing dish could make you famous!

Preparation: Average
Cooking Time: 45 Minutes
Oven Temperature: 350°F

Serves: 6
Must Partially Do Ahead

- 36 **fresh mushrooms, quartered**
- ¼ **cup butter**
- 3 **king crab legs**
- ⅛ **teaspoon dill**
- 1 **(.5-ounce) can truffles, drained**
- 3 **whole chicken breasts, skinned, boned, and cubed**
- ½ **cup cognac**
- ¼ **teaspoon salt, divided**
- ¼ **teaspoon white pepper, divided**
- ⅛ **teaspoon ground marjoram**
- 6 **tablespoons clarified butter**
- ⅓ **cup sherry**
- 1½ **cups whipping cream**
- 3 **egg yolks**
- ⅛ **teaspoon nutmeg**
- 1¾ **cups grated Swiss cheese, divided**
- 12 **Basic Entrée Crêpes (page 138)**

Sauté mushrooms in butter 5-10 minutes; set aside. Boil crab legs in salted water to which dill has been added. Cook just until done; rinse with cold water. Pick crab; refrigerate until used. Combine truffles and chicken; add cognac. Marinate 20 minutes; drain and separate. Rub chicken with ⅛ teaspoon each salt, white pepper, and marjoram. Heat clarified butter in skillet until foamy. Add chicken; sauté over low heat until golden brown and tender. Remove chicken with slotted spoon; keep warm. Add sherry to skillet; cook, stirring, until wine is almost evaporated. Beat cream, egg yolks, nutmeg, and remaining salt and white pepper together. Gradually add to skillet. Cook, stirring constantly, 3 minutes or until thick. Set aside 12 tablespoons each of sauce and cheese. Add remaining cheese to sauce in skillet; stir until melted. Stir in chicken, crab, mushrooms, and truffles. Fill each crêpe with 1/12 of chicken-crab mixture. Roll up; place seam-side down in lightly buttered shallow baking dish. Spoon 1 tablespoon each reserved sauce and cheese on top of each crêpe. Bake at 350°F for 15 minutes, until sauce is bubbly and slightly brown. (For added elegance, top each crêpe with a crabmeat-filled mushroom cap before adding final sauce and cheese.)

Menu Suggestion: Mincemeat Salad (page 91), Carrot and Zucchini Julienne (page 273), Crème Courvoisier (page 352).

Wine Suggestion: A flavorful white such as California Chenin Blanc.

Carol Cowart Highsmith
Brunswick, Georgia

By then my grandmother, her brocaded wedding gown cut up and made over to the last scrap for a dozen later brides in the connection, had become such a famous cook that it was mentioned in her funeral eulogies.

Katherine Anne Porter, *Collected Essays & Occasional Writings of Katherine Anne Porter*

Seafood Gumbo

Preparation: Average
Cooking Time: 1½ Hours

Serves: 6-8
Must Partially Do Ahead

  1   **pound fish fillets, thawed**
6-8 **strips bacon, fried**
       or ¼ cup margarine,
       melted
  1   **cup chopped onion**
  1   **cup chopped celery**
  1   **cup sliced fresh mushrooms**
  ¾   **cup chopped green pepper**
  1   **tablespoon flour**
  1   **(16-ounce) can tomato**
       wedges, undrained
  1   **(8-ounce) can tomato sauce**
  ½   **cup water**
1½   **tablespoons Worcestershire**
       (optional)
  1   **tablespoon parsley flakes**
  1   **tablespoon minced garlic**
  1   **teaspoon paprika**
  ½   **teaspoon chili powder**
  ⅛   **teaspoon cayenne**
  1   **(10-ounce) package frozen**
       cut okra, thawed
  8   **ounces shelled fresh or**
       frozen shrimp
  1   **(8-ounce) can oysters**
       (optional)
       Tabasco (optional)
       Cooked rice

Poach fillets in small amount of water, just until done. Drain, cube, and set aside. Crumble bacon; set aside. In large covered soup kettle sauté onion, celery, mushrooms, and green pepper in bacon drippings. Stir in flour. Add tomatoes, tomato sauce, water, Worcestershire, parsley, garlic, paprika, chili powder, and cayenne. Bring to boil; lower heat; simmer 30 minutes. Add okra; simmer 15 more minutes. Add shrimp, oysters, and fish; cook just until shrimp are done. Remove from heat; let stand 1-2 hours to blend flavors. Reheat to serving temperature. If spicier flavor is desired, add Tabasco to taste. Spoon into bowls over hot rice. Sprinkle with crumbled bacon.

Micronote: Cook fish fillets, covered, on HIGH 4 minutes; drain, cube, and set aside. Crumble bacon; set aside. In large crock sauté onion, celery, mushrooms, and green pepper in bacon drippings on HIGH 6 minutes. Stir in flour. Add water and spices. Cook on MEDIUM 10 minutes. Add tomatoes and tomato sauce. Cook on MEDIUM 20 minutes; stir twice. Add fish, shrimp, oysters, and okra. Cook on LOW 20 minutes; stir once. Let stand 1-2 hours. Reheat on HIGH to serving temperature. Proceed as directed.

Menu Suggestion: West Coast Salad (page 80), Crispy Cornsticks (page 118), Lemon Soufflé (page 341).

Wine Suggestion: A dry white such as Italian Soave.

W. Jackson Thompson

Bouillabaisse

The traditional French seafood stew. It's a natural anytime the luscious ingredients are available.

Preparation: Average
Cooking Time: 30 Minutes

Serves: 4
Must Serve Immediately

1 onion, minced
1 green pepper, minced
2 garlic cloves, minced
¼ cup oil
3 cups tomato juice
2 cups dry white wine
1 cup chicken stock or canned chicken broth
2 large tomatoes, peeled, seeded, and chopped
¾ teaspoon salt
¼ teaspoon thyme
¼ teaspoon cayenne
¼ teaspoon pepper
2 bay leaves
4 clams in shell, scrubbed
½ pound red snapper fillets, cut in 1-inch cubes
½ pound lobster or crab, cut in 1-inch cubes
1 pound shrimp, shelled
¼ cup chopped fresh parsley

Sauté onion, green pepper, and garlic in oil over moderate heat, stirring, for 10 minutes or until softened. Add tomato juice, wine, chicken stock, tomatoes, salt, thyme, cayenne, pepper, and bay leaves. Bring mixture to boil; simmer 10 minutes. Add clams; simmer until shells open. Add snapper, lobster, and shrimp; simmer just until shrimp are firm and snapper flakes when tested with fork. Garnish with parsley.
Micronote: Prepare in large casserole or crockery cooker. Sauté vegetables on HIGH 3-5 minutes until just tender. Add tomato juice, wine, stock, tomatoes, and seasonings. Cook on HIGH 12-15 minutes or until mixture boils. Add clams; cook on HIGH until shells open. Add other ingredients except parsley. Cook 6 minutes or until snapper flakes. Garnish with parsley.
Menu Suggestion: Green Salad Unique (page 75), Communion Bread (page 103).
Wine Suggestion: A light red French vin ordinaire.

Ann Branch Smith

We do not desecrate the dish by serving any other, neither salad or dessert. We just eat crab Newburg. I sit alone and weep for the misery of a world that does not have blue crabs and a Jersey cow.

Eggs & Cheese

Catesby's Trillium

Catesby's Trillium (Trillium catesbaei)

Catesby's trillium, a member of the lily family, was once abundant. The underground stem was chewed by the Cherokee Indians as a cure for snakebites and was used to ease the pain of childbirth. Its young leaves are delicious used in salads, but become bitter when the flower appears. Today these plants are rare in many locations, so pick only where abundant.

On Eggs and Cheese

- Shell color of eggs is determined by the breed of hen; neither cooking performance nor nutritive value of the egg is affected by the color of its shell.
- The chalaza - a thick, white coil next to the yolk - is a natural component of the egg and anchors the yolk to the white. There is no reason to remove it before cooking. Its presence indicates fresh, high-quality eggs.
- For a different taste try poaching an egg in tomato juice.
- Remove scrambled eggs and omelets from pan when thickened throughout but still moist. The heat retained in the egg will complete the cooking.
- To hard-cook eggs, never boil. Place in saucepan; cover with water to 1-inch above eggs. Rapidly bring to boil. Remove from heat; let stand in hot water 15 minutes for large eggs, adjusting 3 minutes up or down according to egg size.
- For easy peeling of hard-cooked eggs: Submerge cooked eggs in iced water for 1 minute. Transfer to boiling water for 10-20 seconds. Remove from water; peel when cool.
- Curry is an especially compatible spice with most egg dishes.
- If a recipe calls for ½ egg, beat egg lightly and halve the amount. An average egg measures about 3-4 tablespoons when lightly beaten.
- Separate eggs directly from the refrigerator. They will break cleanly and the yolks are less likely to shatter than ones at room temperature.
- When a recipe calls for only egg yolks, freeze each white in an ice cube tray; transfer to a freezer bag. Thaw desired number of frozen whites overnight in refrigerator or place container under cold running water. Use thawed whites just as you would fresh ones.
- Egg whites that have been refrigerated up to 2 weeks produce a better meringue than do fresh ones.
- When making meringues add sugar slowly to insure a full, fluffy volume. A rule of thumb is to use 1 tablespoon sugar per egg white and a little cream of tartar. Beat in deep glass or metal bowl. Bake at 250°F for 15 minutes.
- For best results with meringue shells, make on a cool, dry day. They should be crisp but tender and the palest shade of beige. They will keep in a metal box in a cool, dry place for 3 weeks, but do not refrigerate.
- Warm cheese before serving; it is more flavorful at room temperature. In microwave 1 ounce will take about 15 seconds on HIGH. Allow to stand 1 minute. Serve with fresh fruit.
- One pound firm cheese yields 4 cups grated cheese.
- Freeze soft cheese 15 minutes to make shredding easier.
- Brushing grater with a small amount of oil before shredding cheese will make cleaning easier.

Eggs à la Henry

We don't know Henry personally but he deserves a vote of thanks for this original concoction. Hearty enough for supper, it's a special occasion dish which is deceivingly simple.

Preparation: Average
Cooking Time: Approximately 15 Minutes

Serves: 6-8
Must Serve Immediately

½	cup butter
1	large onion, chopped
1	(6-ounce) can sliced mushrooms
2-3	(10¾-ounce) cans mushroom soup
½-¾	cup sherry
¼	teaspoon Worcestershire
⅛	teaspoon garlic salt
⅛	teaspoon onion salt
⅛	teaspoon coarsely ground black pepper
⅛	teaspoon oregano
⅓	cup grated Cheddar cheese Eggs
6-8	slices ham or Canadian bacon
6-8	toasted English muffin halves

Melt butter in 10-12 inch skillet. Add onions and mushrooms; sauté until tender. Add soup, sherry, seasonings, and cheese, blending well. Simmer over very low heat 5-10 minutes. Poach 1-2 eggs per serving by dropping gently into sauce. Cover; cook until eggs are firm. Remove eggs from sauce. Place one ham slice atop each English muffin; carefully lift eggs from sauce onto ham. Spoon sauce over all.
Menu Suggestion: Hot Sherried Fruit (page 283).
Wine Suggestion: A German Moselle.

Helen Odom Rice

Sausage Strata

For a special breakfast or brunch. Serve with a muffin and fresh fruit.

Preparation: Average
Cooking Time: 30 Minutes
Oven Temperature: 350°F

Serves: 4-6
Must Serve Immediately

6	slices bread (white and whole wheat)
1	pound bulk pork sausage (mild)
1	teaspoon prepared mustard
1	cup grated processed Swiss cheese
3	eggs, slightly beaten
1¼	cups milk
¾	cup half-and-half
1	teaspoon Worcestershire
½	teaspoon salt
½	teaspoon pepper
	Dash nutmeg

Trim crusts from bread. Place in greased 10 x 6 x 1½-inch baking dish. Brown sausage; drain well. Stir mustard into sausage. Spoon evenly over bread. Sprinkle cheese over top. (May freeze or refrigerate at this point.) Combine eggs, milk, half-and-half, Worcestershire, salt, pepper, and nutmeg; beat with wire whisk or egg beater until frothy. Pour over cheese. Bake at 350°F for 30 minutes or until puffed and set. (If frozen, remove from freezer night before it is to be served; refrigerate until morning. Add remaining ingredients and bake.)

Mary Anderson Casper

Sausage-Grits Soufflé

A wonderful do-ahead dish! It will keep 2 to 3 days in the refrigerator before baking or in the freezer for a month.

Preparation: Easy
Cooking Time: 1-1½ Hours
Oven Temperature: 350°F

Serves: 10-12

1	pound hot sausage
1	cup quick grits
6-8	eggs, well beaten
1½	cups milk
	Salt and pepper to taste
¼	cup margarine
2	cups grated sharp Cheddar cheese, divided

Stir-fry sausage until cooked and brown. Drain well; set aside. Cook grits in large Dutch oven according to package instructions. Combine eggs, milk, salt, and pepper; slowly stir into grits. Add margarine and 1½ cups cheese, stirring until cheese melts. Add sausage; mix well. Bake in 3-quart round casserole at 350°F for 1 - 1½ hours. Sprinkle remaining ½ cup cheese on top; return to oven just until cheese melts.

Micronote: Preheat browning skillet 4½ minutes. Cook sausage 6-8 minutes on HIGH, stirring several times; drain. Place grits, eggs, milk, salt, and pepper in large casserole. Cook on HIGH 2½ minutes, stirring several times. Stir in margarine and 1½ cups cheese. Cook on MEDIUM 8-10 minutes, stirring often. Add sausage; sprinkle with remaining cheese. Let stand until cheese melts.

Menu Suggestion: Lemony Apple Bake (page 282), Cinnamon Buns (page 129).

Beverage Suggestion: Orange Blush (page 3).

Joanne Moore Frierson

Never-Fail Cheese Soufflé

Preparation: Easy
Cooking Time: 1 Hour
Oven Temperature: 350°F

Serves: 6
Must Partially Do Ahead

3	eggs, beaten
2	cups milk
½	teaspoon Worcestershire
½	teaspoon dry mustard
¼	teaspoon salt
⅛	teaspoon cayenne
7	slices white bread
½	cup butter, melted
8	ounces sharp Cheddar cheese, grated

Blend eggs, milk, and seasonings. Trim bread and cut into cubes. Pour butter over bread cubes, stirring gently; let stand until butter is absorbed. Layer half of bread cubes in lightly buttered soufflé dish; top with half of cheese. Repeat layers. Pour egg mixture over all. Refrigerate several hours or overnight. Remove from refrigerator 1 hour before baking. Bake at 350°F for 1 hour or until firm.

Micronote: Assemble as above. Cook on MEDIUM 10-12 minutes or until firm. Rotate dish twice during cooking.

Menu Suggestion: Delicious Summer Fruit Salad (page 92), Blueberry Muffins (page 122).

Wine Suggestion: A full-flavored white such as a California Chardonnay.

Idalu Haugabook Slack

Texas Brunch

A hearty taste treat. Try this on men who are turned off by egg-casseroles - we'll bet it's a hit.

Preparation: Average
Cooking Time: 45 Minutes
Oven Temperature: 400°F

Serves: 8

3 tablespoons butter or
  margarine, melted
3 tablespoons flour
2 cups milk
6 hard-cooked eggs, chopped
½ cup salad dressing or
  mayonnaise
1 tablespoon lemon juice
1 tablespoon dry mustard
¼ teaspoon salt
⅛ teaspoon freshly ground
  black pepper
  Buttermilk Cornbread Squares
  Shredded Cheddar cheese
  Chopped green onion
  Crumbled cooked bacon

Blend butter and flour in heavy saucepan until smooth. Cook 1 minute, stirring constantly. Gradually add milk; cook until thick, stirring constantly. Add remaining ingredients. Cook, stirring, until thoroughly heated. Slice each cornbread square in half horizontally; top with egg sauce. Sprinkle with cheese, onion, and bacon.
Micronote: Melt butter on HIGH 45 seconds. Stir in flour, then milk. Cook on HIGH 3½ minutes, stirring every 30 seconds. Add remaining sauce ingredients. Proceed as directed above.

Buttermilk Cornbread Squares

1 cup yellow cornmeal
⅓ cup flour
1 teaspoon baking powder
½ teaspoon salt
¼ teaspoon baking soda
1 egg, beaten
1 cup buttermilk

Combine dry ingredients; add egg and buttermilk, mixing well. Pour batter into well-greased 8-inch square pan. Bake at 400°F for 20 minutes or until lightly browned. Cut into squares.
Menu Suggestion: Cheesy Apples (page 282).
Beverage Suggestion: "Marinated" Bloody Marys (page 8).

Kaye Cooper Rigdon

I have always been a discriminating but light eater, and never sit down to breakfast. Being also by habit a late riser, I await the joys of "brunch."

William Styron, *Sophie's Choice*
Random House, Inc., Copyright 1979. Used with permission.

Brunch Casserole

Preparation: Easy
Cooking Time: 1 Hour
Oven Temperature: 350°F

Serves: 6-8
Must Partially Do Ahead

16 slices white bread,
    crusts removed
8 or more slices Canadian
    bacon
8 or more slices sharp
    Cheddar cheese
6 eggs, beaten
3 cups milk
¼ cup minced onion
¼ cup finely chopped
    green pepper
2 teaspoons Worcestershire
½ teaspoon salt
½ teaspoon freshly ground
    black pepper
½-1 teaspoon dry mustard
⅛ teaspoon cayenne
½ cup butter, melted
1 cup crushed cracker
    crumbs

Place 8 bread slices in buttered 13 x 9-inch baking dish. Cover with Canadian bacon, then cheese. Top with remaining bread slices. Combine eggs, milk, onion, green pepper, Worcestershire, salt, pepper, mustard, and cayenne. Pour butter over top; cover with cracker crumbs. Bake at 350°F for 1 hour.

Menu Suggestion: Hot Sherried Fruit (page 283), Austria Twists (page 125).
Beverage Suggestion: White Sangria (page 11).

Helen Odom Rice

Baked Eggs in Ramekins

Preparation: Easy
Cooking Time: 10 Minutes
Oven Temperature: 375°F

Serves: 6

6 chicken livers
2 tablespoons butter, melted
½ teaspoon dried mustard
⅛ teaspoon cayenne
6 tablespoons cream or
    half-and-half
6 eggs
Salt to taste
½ teaspoon ground pepper
1 slice bacon, cooked
    and drained

Sauté liver in butter until brown, 5 minutes. Mix mustard, cayenne, and cream. Place one liver in each of 6 buttered ramekins or custard cups. Top each with 1 tablespoon cream. Add 1 egg to each. Sprinkle with salt and pepper. Break bacon into 6 pieces; place 1 piece atop each dish. Bake, covered, at 375°F for 10 minutes.

Menu Suggestion: Baked Cheese Grits (page 287), Fresh Apple-Orange Bread (page 110).
Beverage Suggestion: Orange Julius (page 3).

Marie Dover Carter

Chili-Ham Ramekins

A spicy eye-opener. Nice in that it can be prepared the night before and baked in the morning.

Preparation: Easy
Cooking Time: 40-45 Minutes
Oven Temperature: 350°F

Serves: 4
Must Partially Do Ahead

1 (4-ounce) can whole green chilies
1 cup cooked ham, finely chopped
2 cups shredded Monterey Jack or Cheddar cheese, divided
8 slices firm white bread
6 eggs, beaten
2 cups milk
½ teaspoon chili powder
½ teaspoon dry mustard

Drain chilies; pat dry. Chop chilies; mix with ham and 1 cup cheese. Divide mixture into fourths; spread over 4 bread slices. Top with remaining 4 bread slices. Place each sandwich in well-buttered shallow ramekin or 9-inch square pan. Combine remaining ingredients; pour over sandwiches. Chill at least 2 hours or overnight. Sprinkle with remaining 1 cup cheese. Bake, uncovered, at 350°F for 40-45 minutes. Let stand 5 minutes before serving.

Lynn Newman McCranie

Nothing helps scenery like ham and eggs.

Mark Twain

Brunch Eggs

Scrambled eggs in their Sunday best.

Preparation: Average
Cooking Time: 10 Minutes

Serves: 4
Must Serve Immediately

6 slices thick-cut bacon
6 tablespoons butter, divided
1 medium onion, diced
1 tablespoon flour
1 cup whipping cream
Salt
Pepper
8 eggs
3 tablespoons chopped fresh parsley
4 English muffin halves, toasted
Parsley sprigs

Fry bacon until crisp; drain, crumble, and set aside. Melt 2 tablespoons butter in skillet over medium heat. Add onions; sauté until tender, approximately 5 minutes. Stir in flour, blending well. Pour in cream; mix thoroughly. Increase heat and bring to boil, stirring constantly. Reduce heat and simmer until thickened, 2-3 minutes. Season with salt and pepper to taste. Keep warm. Mix eggs and 2 tablespoons butter in food processor or blender until smooth. Melt remaining 2 tablespoons butter in large skillet over medium heat. Add eggs; scramble until creamy, but **not** set. Stir bacon and chopped parsley into sauce. Arrange muffins on serving plates. Divide eggs evenly over muffins; spoon sauce over eggs. Garnish with sprigs of parsley.

Cookbook Committee

Omelet Deluxe

With an omelet you are only limited by your imagination. You will be surprised how many foods go well with the basic egg!

Preparation: Easy
Cooking Time: 5 Minutes

Serves: 2
Must Serve Immediately

- 4 eggs
- 2 teaspoons margarine
  Freshly ground black pepper
  Monosodium glutamate
  Garlic or seasoned salt
- ½ small onion, minced
- ½ medium tomato, diced
- ½ green pepper, chopped
- 2 slices American cheese
  Sliced ham (optional)
- 3-4 slices cooked bacon (optional)
  Parsley for garnish

Break eggs into electric blender jar; process until well blended. Melt margarine in non-stick medium skillet over medium heat. Pour eggs into skillet. Sprinkle with pepper, monosodium glutamate, and garlic salt. Sprinkle onions, tomatoes, green pepper, and cheese over half of egg surface. Top with meat if desired. When eggs begin to bubble around the edge and cheese begins to melt, fold plain side over toppings with spatula. Slide omelet from pan onto plate. Halve to serve. Garnish with parsley.

Janice Fant Boetz

Egg Foo Yong

Here is one Chinese food so easy that you need never get "take-out" again.

Preparation: Easy
Cooking Time: 15 Minutes

Serves: 4

- 8 eggs
- 1¼ teaspoons salt
- ⅛ teaspoon freshly ground pepper
- 1 (14-ounce) can bean sprouts, drained
- ¼ pound mushrooms, sliced
- 2 green onions, thinly sliced
- ½ cup cooked chopped pork, shrimp, crab, or chicken (optional)
  Oil
  Brown Sauce

In large bowl beat eggs, salt, and pepper; stir in bean sprouts, mushrooms, and green onions. Add optional ingredient of choice if desired. In large skillet heat ⅛-inch oil; drop in egg mixture ¼ cup at a time. Cook until golden brown on both sides. Serve with Brown Sauce.

Brown Sauce

- 1 cup chicken or vegetable broth
- 2 tablespoons soy sauce
- 1 tablespoon cornstarch
- 2 teaspoons vinegar
- 2 teaspoons sugar

In small saucepan blend all ingredients. Bring to boil; cook, stirring, 1 minute.
Micronote: Blend ingredients; cook on HIGH 3½ minutes, stirring several times.

Ann Branch Smith

Jeanette's Pink Pickled Eggs

A wonderful way to dispose of all those leftover Easter eggs! Use as garnish for a salad, to complement a dinner plate, or quartered with onions and crackers as an appetizer.

Preparation: Easy

Yield: 10
Must Do Ahead

10 eggs
⅔ cup vinegar
½ cup beet juice (or water)
2 tablespoons sugar
1 teaspoon salt

Boil eggs 5-7 minutes only; cool and remove shells. Mix remaining ingredients in quart jar. (Add more beet juice for extra zest.) Add eggs; refrigerate overnight. Will keep several weeks in refrigerator. (As eggs disappear, sliced cucumbers and onions can be added to the marinade.)

Janice Fant Boetz

Cooking was a matter of born sense, ordinary good judgment, enough experience, materials worth the bothering about, and tasting.

Eudora Welty, *The Eye of the Story: Selected Essays and Reviews.*
Random House, Inc., Copyright 1978. Used with permission.

Zucchini-Mushroom Quiche

Preparation: Average
Cooking Time: 30 Minutes
Oven Temperature: 375°F

Yield: 1 (10-inch) Quiche

¼ pound fresh mushrooms, sliced
1 small onion, sliced
2 tablespoons butter, melted
1 cup grated Swiss cheese, divided
1 cup milk
1 cup zucchini slices, cooked and well-drained
3 eggs, beaten
½ teaspoon salt
¼ teaspoon pepper
1 (10-inch) pastry crust
   or 2 (9-inch) prepared crusts

Sauté mushrooms and onions in butter until tender. Remove from pan with slotted spoon. Combine sautéed vegetables, ½ cup cheese, and remaining ingredients except pastry in large bowl. Mix well. Pour into crust. Top with remaining ½ cup cheese. Bake at 375°F for 30 minutes or until set.

Micronote: Melt margarine 30-45 seconds on HIGH. Add vegetables; cook 5 minutes or until tender. Place pastry in glass plate; cook on HIGH 2 minutes, turning dish once. Combine ingredients and assemble as above. Cook on MEDIUM 8-10 minutes, rotating dish several times.

Menu Suggestion: Frozen Fruit Salad (page 87), Ritzy Chicken (page 159), Pecan Muffins (page 121).

Wine Suggestion: A light, flavorful wine such as a German Riesling.

Ann Ash Hartness

Cheese Crust Crabmeat Quiche

Preparation: Average
Cooking Time: 30-40 Minutes
Oven Temperature: 350°F

Yield: 1 (9 or 10-inch) Quiche
Serves: 6-8

Cheese Pastry

    1 packaged pie crust stick
    ½ cup grated Cheddar cheese
  2-3 tablespoons cold water

Crumble pie crust stick in 9 or 10-inch pie or quiche pan. Stir in cheese. Sprinkle water over top. Mix with fingers or fork until dough is blended and forms ball. With floured hands press pastry out to edge of pan; flute if desired. Prick bottom and sides lightly with fork. Bake at 350°F until lightly browned, about 10 minutes. (Also good with other quiche fillings or fruit pies.)

Crab Filling

    ½ pound Swiss cheese, cut
        into ¼-inch cubes
    1 (6-ounce) package frozen
        crabmeat, thawed and
        drained
    ⅓ cup chopped green onion
    ½ cup mayonnaise
    2 tablespoons flour
    2 eggs, beaten
    ½ cup milk
      Parsley

In baked shell layer half cheese, crabmeat, onions, and remaining half of Swiss cheese. In separate bowl thoroughly blend mayonnaise, flour, eggs, and milk. Pour over cheese. Sprinkle parsley over top. Bake at 350°F 30-40 minutes or until knife inserted in center comes out clean.

Micronote: Prepare crust as above in 9 or 10-inch microwave-safe pie dish. Cover with paper towel, slightly pressed to dough. Cook on HIGH 3-4 minutes. Remove paper towel. Proceed with filling as above. Cook on MEDIUM 11-13 minutes or until knife inserted in center comes out clean. Rotate dish ½ turn once during cooking. Sprinkle top with parsley and paprika.

Menu Suggestion: Delicious Summer Fruit Salad (page 92), Sour Cream Mini Biscuits (page 380).

Wine Suggestion: A crisp dry white such French Chablis.

Jane Hix Oliver

Spinach Quiche

Using prepared spinach makes it a snap. Substitute bulk sausage and add oregano or Italian seasoning if Italian sausage is unavailable.

Preparation: Easy
Cooking Time: 25-30 Minutes
Oven Temperature: 400°F

Yield: 1 (9-inch) Quiche

- 1 (12-ounce) package spinach soufflé, thawed
- 2 eggs, beaten
- 3 tablespoons milk
- 2 teaspoons chopped onion
- ½ cup sliced mushrooms
- ¾ cup cooked, crumbled Italian sausage
- ¾ cup grated Swiss cheese
- 1 (9-inch) unbaked pie crust

Mix all ingredients except pastry. Pour into pie crust. Bake at 400°F for 25-30 minutes.
Micronote: Cook crust 2 minutes on HIGH, rotating dish halfway through cooking. Mix ingredients; pour into crust. Cook on MEDIUM 8 minutes or until firm.
Menu Suggestion: Frozen Pineapple Salad (page 86), Remelle's Oatmeal Cookies (page 370).
Wine Suggestion: A light, flavorful wine such as a German Mozelle

Suzanne Richard Cannon

Sausage 'n Cheese Tarts

Preparation: Easy
Cooking Time: 25 Minutes
Oven Temperature: 375°F

Yield: 12 Large Tarts

- ½ pound bulk pork sausage
- 1¼ cups buttermilk biscuit mix
- ¼ cup margarine or butter, softened
- 2 tablespoons boiling water
- ½ cup half-and-half
- 1 egg
- 2 tablespoons thinly sliced green onions
- ¼ teaspoon salt
- ½ cup shredded Swiss or Cheddar cheese

Generously grease 12 muffin cups, 2½ x 1¼-inches. In skillet cook and stir sausage until brown; drain. In bowl blend biscuit mix and butter. Add water, stirring vigorously until soft dough forms. Press 1 level tablespoonful dough on bottom and up side of each cup. Divide sausage evenly among cups. Beat half-and-half and egg; stir in onions and salt. Spoon about 1 tablespoon custard mixture into each cup; sprinkle cheese over tops. Bake until edges are golden brown and centers are set, about 25 minutes. (May also prepare in mini-muffin pans as appetizer. Refrigerate or freeze any extra tarts.)
Menu Suggestion: Lemony Apple Bake (page 282), Gruyère Cheese Grits (page 287).
Beverage Suggestion: Orange Blush (page 3).

Jean Bennett Oliver

Sour Cream Enchiladas

Preparation: Easy
Cooking Time: 15-20 Minutes
Oven Temperature: 350°F

Serves: 4-8

    1 **cup sour cream**
    2 **cups shredded Monterey Jack cheese**
    1 **medium onion, chopped**
    1 **(3½-ounce) can ripe olives, drained and chopped**
   ¾ **cup oil**
 8-10 **corn tortillas**
    1 **(14-ounce) can enchilada sauce**
   ½ **cup shredded Cheddar cheese**

Combine sour cream, Monterey Jack cheese, onion, and olives. Mix well; set aside. Heat oil in medium skillet. Fry each tortilla in oil just until limp; drain well. Coat tortillas with enchilada sauce. Place 2 tablespoons sour cream mixture on each tortilla; roll up and place (seam-side down) in 13 x 9-inch baking dish. Spoon remaining enchilada sauce over all. Sprinkle with Cheddar. Bake at 350°F for 15-20 minutes.
Variation: For an entrée enchilada add 1 cup cooked, chopped chicken to sour cream mixture.

Jane Hix Oliver

A well-cooked meal has lots of delicate flavors.
Tennessee Williams, *A Glass Menagerie*
Random House, Inc., Copyright 1966. Used with permission.

Swiss Cheese Fondue

Serving fondue almost guarantees a good time. Experiment with different dippers according to your taste.

Preparation: Average
Cooking Time: 10 Minutes

Serves: 6

    1 **clove garlic, halved**
    1 **pound natural Swiss cheese, cubed**
    2 **cups dry white wine, divided**
   ⅛ **teaspoon cayenne**
    2 **tablespoons cornstarch**
   ¼ **cup kirsch or brandy**
      Dippers: (optional)
      Broccoli flowerets, lightly steamed
      Cherry tomatoes
      Mushrooms
      Smoked sausage links, sautéed
      Baked ham cubes
      Boiled shrimp
      Apple or pear wedges
      French bread cubes

Rub cut garlic clove over inside of fondue pot; discard garlic. Place cheese, 1 cup wine, and cayenne into pot. Cook over medium heat, stirring constantly, just until cheese melts. Remove from heat. Stir cornstarch into remaining cup of wine until dissolved; whisk into cheese mixture. Return to medium heat. Cook, stirring constantly, until creamy (2-3 minutes). Stir in kirsch. Set in fondue stand over warmer. Pass selection of dippers.
Menu Suggestion: West Coast Salad (page 80), Pecan Chiffon Pie (page 336).
Wine Suggestion: A crisp, dry California Chenin Blanc.

Linda Wilson Cornett

Accompaniments

Jerusalem Artichoke

Jerusalem Artichoke (Helianthus tuberosus)

The Jerusalem artichoke, a perennial, is a member of the sunflower family. Its tubers are among the most widely favored wild edibles in the United States. Gathered after the first frost, they can be eaten raw and are similar in taste, crunch, and use to water chestnuts. The knotty tubers are nutritious and, when boiled, can be eaten like potatoes with butter, salt, and pepper. Jerusalem artichokes make a delicious pickle or relish as an accompaniment for meat or poultry.

On Accompaniments

- For quick additions to enhance simple vegetables: add chopped pimiento to cauliflower, grated lemon rind to buttered bread crumbs for casserole toppings, chopped mint over peas and carrots, rum to baked carrots, sesame seeds to buttered squash.
- To remove silks from corn on the cob, dampen a clean toothbrush and brush downward on the cob to remove all strands.
- Blend small amount of maple syrup and/or grated orange rind into softened butter or margarine to accompany baked sweet potatoes.
- A lemon or orange that has been submerged in hot water for 15 minutes before squeezing will yield more juice.
- For easy peeling of peaches and tomatoes: insert a fork into the end of the fruit, submerge in a saucepan of boiling water for 20-30 seconds, remove, and peel from top to bottom with fruit still on fork.
- Aroma is a major factor in determining the ripeness of a honeydew or cantalope.
- To ripen an avocado place in a brown paper bag in a warm place. The top of the refrigerator works well.
- Add a few salad greens when cooking canned vegetables to give a fresh taste. Discard greens before serving.

- For crème fraîche combine 1 tablespoon buttermilk and 1 cup whipping cream. Heat to lukewarm and pour into glass jar. Cover loosely and allow to stand at room temperature overnight. Stir, cover tightly, and chill.
- If you need only 1-2 tablespoons of hollandaise for a sauce or glaze, you can substitute a good quality mayonnaise.
- Eight ounces of pasta will serve 3-4 people.
- To make rice white and fluffy, add 1 teaspoon lemon juice to each quart of cooking water.
- To reheat cooked pasta or rice, place in strainer over a pan of boiling water. Cover and steam 10-15 minutes.
- Use jelly glasses for jelly only. For jam and other products containing pieces of fruit, use standard canning jars with lids for proper processing.
- A boiling water bath may be made by using any large, deep pan which will cover jars with boiling water. (A 4-quart pressure cooker is a good size.)
- Never double or triple a pickle recipe because the ratio of ingredients to vinegar may be altered, thus affecting flavor and texture and possibly causing spoilage.
- Store pickles 4-6 weeks before serving to allow flavors to blend and peak.

Casserole of Sweet Vidalias

Another way to glorify those prized Vidalia onions (or any sweet onion). This dish travels well, as it is still tasty when served at room temperature.

Preparation: Easy
Cooking Time: 1 Hour
Oven Temperature: 325°F

Serves: 8

¼ cup unsalted butter
7 medium Vidalia onions, sliced
½ cup uncooked rice
5 cups boiling water
1 teaspoon salt
1 cup slivered Jarlesberg cheese
    or Swiss cheese
⅔ cup half-and-half or
    evaporated milk

Melt butter in heavy skillet. Sauté onions in butter until soft and transparent, stirring frequently. Cook rice in boiling salted water 5 minutes. Drain well. Blend rice with onions, cheese, and half-and-half. Put into greased shallow baking dish. Bake at 325°F for 1 hour.

Micronote: In large microwave container melt butter; add onions. Cook on HIGH until onions are soft and transparent, about 9 minutes; stir every 3 minutes. In separate container bring water and salt to boiling. Add rice; cook on HIGH for 5 minutes. Drain rice. Combine all ingredients; spread into shallow 13 x 8-inch casserole. Cook 15-18 minutes at MEDIUM, rotating dish after 7 minutes. (Half-and-half should appear to be somewhat "set" and no longer liquid. May want to sprinkle a little paprika over the top before or after final cooking.)

Jane Eve Fair Wilheit

Cheesy Vidalia Onion Casserole

Preparation: Average
Cooking Time: 30 Minutes
Oven Temperature: 350°F

Serves: 6

5-6 Vidalia onions, sliced
½ cup butter or margarine,
    melted
    Parmesan cheese
¾ cup Ritz cracker crumbs,
    divided
¾ cup cheese cracker
    crumbs, divided
    Salt and pepper to taste
1 (10¾-ounce) can condensed
    cream of mushroom soup,
    undiluted
1 cup grated Cheddar cheese
    Paprika

Sauté onions in butter. Layer half onions in 1½-quart casserole. Top with Parmesan, half Ritz crumbs, half cheese cracker crumbs, salt, and pepper. Repeat layers, beginning with remaining onions. Spread with mushroom soup; sprinkle with Cheddar cheese, then more Parmesan. Garnish with paprika. Bake at 350°F for 30 minutes.

Micronote: Sauté onions in butter on HIGH 5-8 minutes. Layer as directed above. Cook on HIGH 6-8 minutes, turning casserole once or twice.

Nelson Hilty Carter

Onion Pie

Serve with beef - a welcome change from potatoes.

Preparation: Easy
Cooking Time: 30 Minutes
Oven Temperature: 350°F

Yield: 1 (9-inch) Pie

 1 cup crushed saltines
 6 tablespoons margarine, melted and divided
 2 large onions, thinly sliced (approximately 2-3 cups)
 2 eggs, beaten
 1 (8-ounce) carton sour cream or 1 cup Ricotta cheese or ½ cup each
1-2 tablespoons fresh dill (optional)
 ¾ teaspoon salt
 ¾ teaspoon pepper
 ½ teaspoon Worcestershire
 ½ cup grated Cheddar cheese
 4 slices bacon, fried, drained, and crumbled

Combine saltines and 4 tablespoons margarine. Press into 9-inch pie plate. Sauté onions in remaining butter; place in pie shell. Combine eggs, sour cream, dill, salt, pepper, and Worcestershire. Pour mixture over onions. Sprinkle with cheese; garnish with bacon. Bake at 350°F for 30 minutes.

Evanda Gravitte Moore

They ruin us early in the South. Our mothers do it. Heaping plates of country-fried steak, smothered in gravy, and the like. And when they cook vegetables, they cook them in conjunction with something known as "fatback," which is something left over from a pig, and the resulting taste defies description.

Lewis Grizzard, *Kathy Sue Loudermilk, I Love You.*
Peachtree Publications, Ltd., Copyright 1979. Used with permission.

Onion Rings

Once again, we recommend sweet Vidalias, but any onion will do.

Preparation: Easy

Serves: 6-8
Must Serve Immediately

 3 large onions, sliced and separated into rings
 Buttermilk (optional)
 2 cups packaged extra-light pancake mix
1-1½ cups club soda
 Oil

Soak onions in buttermilk for 30 minutes if desired. Blend pancake mix with club soda according to preference (less soda for thickly battered rings). Dip rings into batter. Fry in hot oil until golden. Drain on absorbent toweling; serve at once. (Leftover onion rings may be frozen in single layer on cookie sheet. When frozen, place in plastic bag. Reheat in oven on cookie sheet.)

Glenda Lee Scroggs

Cossack's Delight

Preparation: Average

Serves: 4
Must Serve Immediately

1 pound small mushrooms
2 tablespoons butter
2 tablespoons olive oil
1 large clove garlic, minced
1 small onion, grated
½ teaspoon - 1 tablespoon
    soy sauce, to taste
½ teaspoon Worcestershire
⅛ teaspoon ground mustard
⅛ teaspoon paprika
⅛ teaspoon seasoned salt
    Salt and pepper to taste
1 tablespoon flour
1 cup sour cream

Wash mushrooms, separating stems and caps; reserve stems for later use. Heat butter and oil in medium saucepan. Add mushroom caps, garlic, onion, soy sauce, Worcestershire, mustard, paprika, salt, and pepper. Cook, stirring, 1-2 minutes over high heat. Cover; reduce heat and simmer 5 minutes, stirring occasionally. Meanwhile, blend flour and sour cream until smooth; add to mushroom mixture. (If mushrooms have released a great deal of liquid, some liquid should be poured off before adding sour cream.) Heat thoroughly; **do not boil**. (For a different presentation, use to fill 4-6 baked patty shells; or use as chafing dish appetizer with crackers.)

Debbie Jacobs Springle

Broiled Marinated Mushrooms

Preparation: Easy
Cooking Time: 5-8 Minutes
Oven Temperature: Broil

Serves: 6-8
Must Partially Do Ahead

1 pound fresh mushrooms,
    thinly sliced
½ cup olive oil
3 tablespoons tarragon
    vinegar
1 tablespoon grated onion
1 tablespoon chopped green
    onion
1 tablespoon chopped chives
1 tablespoon snipped parsley
¾ teaspoon salt
⅛ teaspoon thyme
⅛ teaspoon freshly ground
    black pepper
1 clove garlic
    Toasted bread crumbs

Place mushrooms in shallow dish. Combine remaining ingredients except bread crumbs. Pour over mushrooms; marinate at least 2 hours. Remove garlic; top with bread crumbs. Place under broiler until evenly brown, 5-8 minutes.

Anne Warren Thomas

French Fried Mushrooms

This batter may be used for frying other vegetables, too. Try cauliflower, okra, broccoli, eggplant, etc. A great idea for children who otherwise might not eat any of the above.

Preparation: Easy
Cooking Time: 10 Minutes

Serves: 4-6
Must Serve Immediately

1 pound fresh medium
    mushrooms
¼ cup flour
1 teaspoon salt
⅛ teaspoon pepper
2 eggs, beaten
¾ cup fine dry Italian-
    style bread crumbs
    Shortening or oil for
    frying

Wash mushrooms, leaving stems attached; drain well. Combine flour, salt, and pepper. Coat each mushroom with seasoned flour, dip in eggs, and roll in bread crumbs. Fry in deep, hot oil (365°F) until golden. Drain on absorbent toweling.

Brenda Jones Adams

Asparagus with Cashew Sauce

This has been one family's "special occasion" vegetable for twenty years.

Preparation: Easy
Cooking Time: 15 Minutes

Serves: 6-8
Must Serve Immediately

1 pound fresh asparagus or
    2 (10-ounce) packages
    frozen asparagus spears
½ cup butter, melted
½ cup salted cashews, halved
    lengthwise
4 teaspoons lemon juice
½ teaspoon dried marjoram
    leaves, crushed

Cook asparagus with stems in boiling water until tender-crisp. (Prepare frozen asparagus according to package instructions; drain.) Arrange asparagus spears on heated serving platter. Combine butter, cashews, lemon juice, and marjoram; simmer, stirring, over low heat 5 minutes. Pour over asparagus. Serve hot. (Cashew-butter sauce is also good over other green vegetables.)

Nell Cromer Freeman
Stillwater, Oklahoma

Asparagus of Renown

Preparation: Easy
Cooking Time: 5-8 Minutes
Oven Temperature: Broil

Serves: 4

½ cup cracker crumbs
½ cup grated Parmesan cheese
½ cup finely chopped unsalted
    peanuts
½ cup chopped fresh mushrooms
1 (2-ounce) jar diced pimiento,
    drained
½ cup butter or margarine,
    melted
1 pound fresh asparagus,
    cooked

Combine cracker crumbs, cheese, peanuts, mushrooms, and pimiento. Add butter; toss to coat. Place hot asparagus in shallow casserole; sprinkle with desired amount of crumb topping mixture. Broil until golden brown. Refrigerate excess topping in airtight container. (Topping is also excellent over cauliflower or broccoli.)

Gail Adams Thomas

Broccoli with Sauces

A trio of simple sauces to pep up "plain old" broccoli.

Preparation: Easy   **Serves:** 6

Broccoli

2 pounds fresh broccoli

Wash and remove tough ends of broccoli. Make lengthwise slits in thick stalks. Arrange broccoli in steaming rack with stalks to center of rack. Cover; steam over small amount of water 10-15 minutes. Arrange in serving dish. Pour desired sauce over broccoli.

Carnival Sauce

½ cup sliced green onion
2 tablespoons butter, melted
2 tablespoons chopped pimiento
2 tablespoons lemon juice
1 tablespoon grated lemon rind
1 teaspoon salt
⅛ teaspoon pepper

Sauté onion in butter until tender. Remove from heat; stir in remaining ingredients.

Linda Portman Spencer
Cumming, Georgia

Olive Sauce

¾ cup butter, melted
2 cloves garlic, minced,
      or 1 teaspoon garlic salt
      or ½ teaspoon garlic powder
¼ cup lemon juice
12 pimiento-stuffed olives,
      chopped

Combine all ingredients. Heat thoroughly, but **do not boil**.

Louise Hendrix Forrester

Shrimp Sauce

1 (3-ounce) package cream
      cheese, softened
1 tablespoon chopped chives
¼ cup milk
1 (10¾-ounce) can cream
      of shrimp soup
2 tablespoons lemon juice
2 tablespoons slivered almonds,
      toasted

In saucepan blend cream cheese, chives, and milk. Add soup; heat until hot, stirring constantly. Stir in lemon juice. Pour over broccoli. Sprinkle with almonds.

Sally Butts Darden

Broccoli Sunburst

The flavor of elaborate-looking foods often does not equal their appearance. Not so in this case-it tastes as good as it looks!

Preparation: Average
Cooking Time: 20 Minutes
Oven Temperature: 350°F

Serves: 12

3 (10-ounce) packages frozen broccoli flowerets or 1 head cauliflower
2 tablespoons butter, melted
Juice of ½ lemon
4 egg whites
⅔ cup mayonnaise
3-4 tablespoons Parmesan cheese
Paprika to garnish

Prepare broccoli according to package directions, only partially cooking; drain. Arrange in deep round plate with flowerets on edge, stems in center. Combine butter with lemon juice and pour over flowerets. Beat egg whites until stiff. Mix mayonnaise with cheese; fold into egg whites. Frost center stems with mixture; sprinkle with paprika. Bake at 350°F for 20 minutes or until lightly brown.

Variation: Frosted Cauliflower - Cook whole cauliflower 10 minutes in boiling, salted water; drain. Proceed as above, leaving cauliflower whole and frosting to completely cover.

Jane Elizabeth Carter
Dana Blum Barclay

Broccoli Ring

Preparation: Average
Cooking Time: 50 Minutes
Oven Temperature: 350°F

Serves: 8

2 (10-ounce) packages frozen chopped broccoli
3 tablespoons butter, melted
3 tablespoons flour
¼ cup chicken broth
1 cup sour cream
⅓ cup minced green onions
3 eggs, lightly beaten
¾ cup grated Cheddar or Swiss cheese
½ cup slivered almonds
1 teaspoon salt
½ teaspoon pepper
½-1 teaspoon nutmeg (optional)

Prepare broccoli according to package instructions, cooking until barely tender; drain thoroughly. Chop finely, but do not use food processor or blender. Set aside. Combine butter and flour in large saucepan; stir until blended. Gradually blend in chicken broth, sour cream, and onion. Cook and stir over low heat until thick. Add eggs; cook, stirring constantly, for 1 minute. Add cheese; stir until melted. Stir in remaining ingredients, including reserved broccoli. Spoon into oiled 1-quart ring mold. Place mold in pan of hot water; bake at 350°F for 50 minutes or until knife inserted in center comes out clean. (May be frozen before baking; add 30 minutes to baking time.) For a special effect fill ring with Broiled Marinated Mushrooms (page 257) or Harvard Beets (page 279).

Micronote: Cook broccoli on HIGH 7-8 minutes; drain thoroughly; chop finely. Melt margarine 30 seconds on HIGH; add flour; blend. Add broth, sour cream, onions. Cook on HIGH 1 minute; stir well. Continue cooking 2-3 minutes longer, stirring every 30 seconds. Add eggs. Cook 1 minute longer, stirring once. Add cheese and continue as directed above.

Carol Dean Greene

Broccoli Elegant

Preparation: Average
Cooking Time: 35 Minutes
Oven Temperature: 350°F

Serves: 8

1½ cups water
6 tablespoons butter, divided
1 (6-ounce) package cornbread stuffing mix with seasoning
2 (10-ounce) packages frozen broccoli spears, thawed
2 tablespoons flour
1 teaspoon chicken bouillon granules
¾ cup milk
1 (3-ounce) package cream cheese, softened
¼ teaspoon salt
4 green onions, sliced
1 cup shredded Cheddar cheese
Paprika

Combine water, 4 tablespoons butter, and seasoning packet from stuffing; bring to boil. Remove from heat. Stir in stuffing crumbs; let stand 5 minutes. Spoon stuffing around inside edge of lightly buttered 13 x 9 x 2-inch baking dish, leaving well in center. Place broccoli in well; set aside. Melt remaining 2 tablespoons butter in heavy saucepan over low heat; add flour, stirring until smooth. Cook for 1 minute, stirring constantly. Stir in bouillon. Gradually add milk; cook over medium heat, stirring constantly, until thickened and bubbly. Add cream cheese and salt, stirring until smooth. Stir in onion. Spoon mixture over center of broccoli, sprinkle with Cheddar and paprika. Cover with foil. Bake at 350°F for 35 minutes; remove foil and bake 10 minutes longer.

Micronote: In glass container combine water, seasoning mix, and butter; cook on HIGH 3 minutes or until mixture boils. Proceed with stuffing and assemble as directed above. Melt remaining margarine on HIGH for 45 seconds. Add flour; cook 30 seconds. Add bouillon and milk; cook on HIGH 3 minutes or until thick, stirring every 30-45 seconds. Stir in cream cheese, salt, and onion. Spoon over broccoli; sprinkle with cheese and paprika. Cover with waxed paper. Cook on MEDIUM 8-10 minutes, rotating container several times.

Carol Lynn Dobson Waggoner

Sesame Broccoli

Preparation: Average
Cooking Time: 15 Minutes

Serves: 4-6
Must Serve Immediately

1 bunch fresh broccoli
2 tablespoons sesame seed
3 tablespoons oil
2 teaspoons minced garlic
½ cup sliced water chestnuts
3 tablespoons white wine
3 tablespoons soy sauce
½ teaspoon sugar
½ teaspoon salt (optional)

Remove large leaves and tough ends of broccoli stalks. Cut away flowerets; set aside. Cut stems into ¼-inch slices; set aside. Toast sesame seed in wok or skillet; remove and set aside. Heat oil in wok or skillet at 325°F for 3 minutes. Add garlic; stir-fry briefly. Add broccoli stalks; stir-fry 5 minutes. Add water chestnuts, wine, soy sauce, sugar, salt, and flowerets; mix well. Cover; cook 5 minutes. Transfer to serving dish; garnish with toasted sesame seed.

Carolyn Hartford Mahar

Zesty Broccoli Spears

Preparation: Easy
Cooking Time: 5-10 Minutes

Serves: 6
Must Do Ahead

1 pound fresh broccoli,
   cut into small flowerets
3 tablespoons safflower oil
3 tablespoons fresh lemon
   juice
1 medium clove garlic,
   thinly sliced
¼ teaspoon salt
⅛ teaspoon pepper

Steam or cook broccoli until tender-crisp, about 10 minutes. Drain and chill thoroughly. Combine remaining ingredients; mix thoroughly. Pour over broccoli; chill 12 hours or overnight. Drain before serving.

Micronote: Microwave broccoli in 1 tablespoon water, covered, on HIGH for 7-9 minutes; turn once after 4 minutes.

Sherrie Nathan Schrage

Dilly Brussels Sprouts

Preparation: Easy
Cooking Time: 6 Minutes

Serves: 4-6
Must Do Ahead

1 (10-ounce) package frozen
   Brussels sprouts
1 tablespoon chopped green
   onion
½ teaspoon dill weed
½ cup Italian salad dressing
   Cherry tomatoes (optional)
   Mushrooms (optional)

Cook Brussels sprouts in small amount of boiling water 5-6 minutes, until tender-crisp; drain. Combine onion, dill weed, and salad dressing. Pour over sprouts. Add tomatoes and mushrooms if desired. Marinate in refrigerator overnight. (May be served as a vegetable accompaniment, a salad, or an appetizer.)

Jean Davis Brown

Sautéed Cauliflowerets

Preparation: Easy
Cooking Time: 15-20 Minutes

Serves: 6

1 large head cauliflower
1 teaspoon salt
2 eggs, beaten
1 cup seasoned bread
   crumbs
½ cup oil
   Catsup (optional)

Remove outside leaves and part of core from cauliflower. Place whole cauliflower and salt in small amount of water; parboil 8-10 minutes. Drain and cool. Separate flowerets. Dip each into eggs, then into bread crumbs. Sauté slowly in hot oil until golden brown on all sides. Drain on absorbent toweling. If desired, serve with catsup or Mustard Sauce (page 289).

Seasoned Bread Crumbs

Day old bread
¼ cup grated Romano cheese
½ teaspoon garlic powder
½ teaspoon salt
⅛ teaspoon black pepper

Process bread to form fine crumbs. To each 1 cup crumbs add remaining ingredients, mixing well.

Mary Ferrara Seitz
Reading, Pennsylvania

Cauliflower in Sour Cream

Preparation: Easy
Cooking Time: 7-8 Minutes

Serves: 6-8

1 head cauliflower
  Salted water
1 cup mayonnaise
1 cup sour cream
1 teaspoon Worcestershire
½ teaspoon salt
  Pepper to taste
½ cup grated Cheddar cheese
½ cup chopped green onion

Trim and separate cauliflower into flowerets. Cook in boiling salted water 7-8 minutes or until tender-crisp. Drain; set aside. In small bowl combine mayonnaise, sour cream, Worcestershire, salt, and pepper; set aside. Add cheese and onion to cauliflower; toss. Add sauce; toss again.

Pamela K. Spivey

Cauliflower is nothing but cabbage with a college education.
Mark Twain

Baked Swiss Cauliflower

Preparation: Easy
Cooking Time: 15-20 Minutes
Oven Temperature: 350°F

Serves: 6

1 large head cauliflower
  or 2 (10-ounce) packages
  frozen cauliflower
2¾ cups shredded Swiss cheese
1½ cups half-and-half
3 egg yolks, beaten
½ teaspoon salt
¼ teaspoon pepper
¼ teaspoon ground nutmeg
½ cup bread crumbs
¼ cup margarine, melted

Wash cauliflower; discard leaves and break into flowerets. Cook, covered, 10 minutes in small amount of boiling water; drain. (Prepare frozen cauliflower according to package directions.) Place cauliflower in greased 1½-quart shallow baking dish. Combine cheese, half-and-half, egg yolks, salt, pepper, and nutmeg; pour over cauliflower. Combine crumbs and margarine; sprinkle over top. Bake at 350°F for 15-20 minutes.
Micronote: Place cauliflower in glass baking dish. Add 2 tablespoons water. Cook, covered, on HIGH for 8-10 minutes. Drain well. Prepare cheese-egg mixture as above; pour over cauliflower. Drizzle half margarine over all. Cook on HIGH for 3 minutes. Turn dish. Cook on MEDIUM 5 minutes. Toast bread crumbs; mix with remaining margarine. Sprinkle crumbs atop casserole at end of cooking time.

Carolyn Cathey Brinson

Country Fried Vegetables

Not the dieter's way to eat vegetables, but some things are just too good to be low in calories!

Preparation: Easy

Serves: 4-6

Green tomatoes, okra,
    squash, or eggplant
Salt to taste
Pepper to taste
½ cup cornmeal
½ cup flour
½ cup buttermilk
1 cup oil

Slice tomatoes to ¼-inch thickness. Salt and pepper. Combine cornmeal and flour in dish. Dip vegetables in buttermilk, then coat with meal mixture. Fry in moderately hot oil, turning once, until brown.

Nancy Martin Brewer

Okra is a Cinderella among vegetables....To bring it to its glamorous fulfillment, only the very small tender young pods must be used.

Marjorie Kinnan Rawlings, from Cross Creek.
Charles Scribner's Sons. Copyright 1942.
Reprinted with permission of Charles Scribner's Sons.

Company Cabbage

Preparation: Average
Cooking Time: 10-15 Minutes

Serves: 6-8

5 cups shredded cabbage
1 cup shredded carrots
½ cup chopped green
    onion, including tops
½ teaspoon salt
⅛ teaspoon freshly
    ground pepper
1 beef bouillon cube
¼ cup hot water
⅓ cup chopped pecans
¼ cup butter, melted
2-3 tablespoons prepared mustard
Paprika

In large saucepan combine cabbage, carrots, green onion, salt, and pepper. Dissolve bouillon in hot water; add to vegetables. Toss with fork to blend. Cover tightly; cook over low heat 5 minutes, stirring once during cooking. Drain excess liquid. Turn into warm serving dish. Combine pecans, butter, and mustard; heat thoroughly. Pour over vegetables. Sprinkle with paprika.

Ann Harris Gignilliat

Nanny's Southern Green Beans

In the South we grow up eating these tender, slow-cooked green beans. There is nothing more typical of our part of the country than this time-honored recipe.

Preparation: Easy
Cooking Time: Several Hours

Serves: 6-8

    3 **pounds fresh white half-runner beans, washed**
        Salt
    1 **(2-3 inch) square of streak o' lean cooking meat**

White half-runner beans are string beans. To remove the string, break off the blossom end and pull the string toward the stem end. Break into pieces, place in large pot and fill with water 1-inch over top of beans. Add cooking meat and salt. Bring to a boil; cover and cook **slowly** until all water is absorbed.

Carole Ann Carter Daniel

If you want to get good string beans, you must go to a Methodist dinner on the ground. The Methodists are far and away the best string-bean cooks on the face of the earth.

Ludlow Porch, *A View from the Porch.*
Peachtree Publications Ltd., Copyright 1981. Used with permission.

Green Bean Casserole

Preparation: Average
Cooking Time: 30 Minutes
Oven Temperature: 350°F

Serves: 12

    3 **(10-ounce) packages frozen French-style green beans**
    1 **(16-ounce) can mushrooms, drained**
    1 **large onion, chopped**
   ½ **cup butter, melted**
   ¼ **cup flour**
    1 **cup milk**
    1 **cup whipping cream**
   ¾ **pound sharp Cheddar cheese, grated**
    2 **teaspoons soy sauce**
    1 **teaspoon monosodium glutamate**
   ½ **teaspoon Worcestershire**
   ½ **teaspoon pepper**
   ⅛ **teaspoon Tabasco**
    1 **(8-ounce) can water chestnuts, drained and chopped**
        Butter-flavored crackers, crushed
        Butter

Prepare beans according to package directions; drain and set aside. Sauté mushrooms and onions in butter. Add flour, milk, and cream. Stir in cheese, soy sauce, monosodium glutamate, Worcestershire, pepper, and Tabasco. Combine sauce with beans and water chestnuts. Turn into 2-quart casserole. Sprinkle with cracker crumbs; dot with butter. Bake at 350°F for 30 minutes.

Carol Cato Mendenhall

Cuban Black Beans

A great dish to serve a football game-watching crowd!

Preparation: Easy
Cooking Time: 2 Hours

Serves: 8
Must Do Ahead

2 quarts water
1 (16 or 24-ounce) package
    black beans
1 meaty ham hock
2 medium onions, chopped
1 large bell pepper, chopped
1 bay leaf
1 garlic clove, minced
1 teaspoon salt or
    to taste
½ teaspoon freshly ground
    black pepper
2 tablespoons vinegar
1 package yellow rice, cooked

Put water and beans in 3-quart Dutch oven; bring to boil. Boil 10 minutes. Remove from heat; cover; allow to stand 1 hour. Add onions, pepper, bay leaf, garlic, salt, pepper, and vinegar to beans. Cook, covered, on low heat for 2 hours. May be thickened by removing lid last 30 minutes of cooking. Serve beans over yellow rice with Honeyed Citrus Nut Salad (page 79) for a complete meal.

Jean Davis Brown

Down South Beans

A longtime staple of Southern eating. These spicy beans make an excellent meat substitute. Also good for picnics.

Preparation: Average
Cooking Time: 8 Hours

Serves: 6

1 (16-ounce) package dried
    pinto beans
1 tablespoon salt
1 tablespoon chili powder
¼ teaspoon cayenne
¼ teaspoon black pepper
2 garlic cloves, minced
2 small (or 1 large) meaty
    ham hocks (approximately
    ½ pound)
  Chopped sweet onions or
    sliced green onions
    (optional)

Do not soak beans. Wash beans twice, discarding any bad ones. Place beans in large, heavy kettle or Dutch oven; cover with 3-4 inches of water. Add seasonings and ham hocks; bring to boil. Reduce to lowest heat; simmer 8 hours, stirring occasionally to keep beans from sticking. Add additional water as needed. When beans are cooked, remove ham fat and bone, leaving lean meat. Garnish with onions, if desired. Serve in bowls with Crispy Cornsticks (page 118) or Corn Lightbread (page 119).

Sarah Grimes Butts
Sparta, Georgia

South Louisiana Red Beans and Rice

Preparation: Average
Cooking Time: 6-8 Hours (Crock Pot)

1 pound dried red
    kidney beans
1 pound sliced pepperoni
2 tablespoons flour
2 tablespoons shortening, melted
1 large onion, chopped
    Meaty ham bone
1 bay leaf
⅛ teaspoon cayenne
    Water
    Cooked white rice

Serves: 6-8
Must Partially Do Ahead

Wash beans; soak overnight in water to cover; drain. Sauté pepperoni in its own fat; drain. Make roux by browning flour in shortening. In crock pot combine all ingredients except rice; cover with water. Cook, covered, 6-8 hours on low heat. Serve over rice. (May be cooked **very slowly** in large heavy pot on range.)

Lynda Truluck Stewart

Minted Peas

Sometimes it takes inspiration rather than effort to create a new taste. Try this inspired creation with lamb.

Preparation: Easy
Cooking Time: 5-10 Minutes

2 pounds fresh, frozen,
    or canned small English
    peas, cooked
1 (6-ounce) jar mint jelly

Serves: 6-8
Must Do Ahead

Drain peas; rinse with cold water. Melt mint jelly over low heat or in microwave; combine with peas. Cool in refrigerator, stirring occasionally.

W. C. Wyatt, Jr.
Fort Valley, Georgia

Stir-Fry Pea Pods

Preparation: Easy
Cooking Time: 5 Minutes

2 tablespoons peanut oil
2 cloves garlic, chopped
½ pound mushrooms, sliced
1 (8-ounce) can water
    chestnuts, sliced
½ pound snow pea pods,
    strung and cleaned
2 teaspoons sesame seed oil
3 tablespoons soy sauce
2 teaspoons sesame seeds
    (optional)
1 teaspoon sugar
½ teaspoon salt

Serves: 4
Must Serve Immediately

Heat peanut oil in wok or large heavy skillet until very hot, almost smoking. Sauté garlic. Add mushrooms, water chestnuts, and pea pods. Stir-fry 2 minutes (vegetables should be crisp). Add sesame seed oil; stir well. Remove from heat. Combine soy sauce, sesame seeds, sugar, and salt. Add to pea pods; toss to coat.

Susie White Gignilliat

Herb Pastry with Spinach Filling

An impressive offering - well worth every minute spent in preparation. Filling and dough may be done a day ahead, assemble several hours ahead. Only baking need be done immediately before serving.

Preparation: Average
Cooking Time: 35 Minutes
Oven Temperature: 375°F

Serves: 10
Must Partially Do Ahead

Herb Pastry
Spinach Filling
1 egg, beaten

Roll pastry into 15-inch circle. Roll up on rolling pin; transfer to large greased baking sheet. Spread filling over half of circle, stopping ½-inch from edge. Brush margin of filled half with egg. Fold unfilled pastry over filling to form half-circle shape. Trim edges evenly; crimp with fork tines to seal. Brush top with beaten egg. Use pastry scraps to make decorations; place on top. Chill at least 30 minutes. Brush again with egg. Bake at 375°F for 30 minutes or until brown.

Herb Pastry
2 cups flour
½ teaspoon dried tarragon
½ teaspoon dried oregano
½ teaspoon dried basil
½ teaspoon dried chives
¼ teaspoon salt
¾ cup very cold, unsalted butter
1 egg
2-3 tablespoons ice water

Combine flour, herbs, and salt in mixing bowl or food processor bowl; mix well. Cut butter into chunks; cut into flour until mixture resembles coarse meal. Add egg and 1 tablespoon water. Mix, gradually adding more water as needed, until dough forms ball. Turn onto lightly floured waxed paper. Flatten into disc; wrap in paper; refrigerate at least 1 hour.

Spinach Filling
1½ cups chopped onion
2 tablespoons butter, melted
¼ pound mushrooms, sliced
1 (10-ounce) package frozen chopped spinach, cooked and squeezed
1 (8½-ounce) can artichoke hearts, drained and chopped
2 ounces cream cheese
¼ cup whipping cream
1 clove garlic, minced
1½ teaspoons lemon juice
1 teaspoon salt
½ teaspoon fresh chives
¼ teaspoon dried tarragon
¼ teaspoon pepper
¼ teaspoon nutmeg
3 tablespoons Parmesan cheese

Sauté onions in butter until tender. Add mushrooms; sauté 2-3 minutes. Combine spinach, artichokes, cream cheese, cream, and garlic. Add to onion mixture; stir until cheese melts. Remove from heat. Stir in lemon juice, salt, chives, tarragon, pepper, and nutmeg; cool. Stir in Parmesan cheese.

Jane Hix Oliver

Spanokopita (Greek Spinach Pie)

An elegant international dish which can be done ahead. A nice accompaniment to lamb.

Preparation: Complex
Cooking Time: 45 Minutes
Oven Temperature: 325°F

Yield: (9 or 10-inch) Pie
Must Serve Immediately

- 1 (10-ounce) package frozen chopped spinach
- 16 ounces small-curd cottage cheese
- 8 ounces Feta cheese
- ½ cup grated Parmesan cheese
- 4 eggs, beaten
- 1 cup sour cream
- 2 tablespoons flour
- ¾ cup chopped fresh parsley
- ½ cup chopped green onions, with tops
- ½ teaspoon dill weed
- ½ teaspoon salt
- ¼ teaspoon pepper
- 1¼ cups butter, melted
- 20 sheets phyllo dough

Prepare spinach according to package instructions. Drain and squeeze all water from spinach. Blend spinach with cottage cheese, Feta cheese, Parmesan cheese, eggs, sour cream, flour, parsley, onions, dill weed, salt, and pepper. Set aside. Read "On Phyllo" (page 399). Clear large working area; assemble cloth-covered phyllo, butter, pastry brush, and 9 or 10-inch round serving dish. Brushing top of each sheet completely with butter as you go, layer overlapping phyllo in clockwise direction, extending half of each sheet beyond edges of pan. Continue until all 20 sheets are used. Pour filling into "bed" of phyllo. Individually fold each extended sheet of phyllo over filling, buttering other side of each, moving counter-clockwise until filling is totally encased. Bake at 325°F for 45 minutes or until golden. (May be frozen before baking. Allow to thaw overnight in refrigerator. Bake as directed. May be prepared day before and baked 30 minutes. Refrigerate. Before serving, allow to stand at room temperature 30-45 minutes; finish baking until crust is golden.)

Cookbook Committee

Spinach-Cheese Crêpes

Preparation: Average
Cooking Time: 30 Minutes
Oven Temperature: 350°F

Yield: 8 Crêpes

- 1 (10-ounce) box frozen chopped spinach
- 1 medium onion, chopped
- 1 clove garlic, minced
- 1 tablespoon margarine, melted
- 1 cup Ricotta cheese
- ½ cup crumbled Feta cheese
- ¼ cup Parmesan cheese
- 2 eggs, beaten
- 1 tablespoon lemon juice
- ¼ teaspoon salt
- ¼ teaspoon nutmeg
- ⅛ teaspoon pepper
  Paprika
- 8 Basic Entrée Crêpes (page 138)

Prepare spinach according to package directions. Drain, squeezing out all possible liquid. Sauté onion and garlic in margarine until onion is tender. Combine all ingredients except paprika in mixing bowl. (May refrigerate until ready to use.) Divide filling evenly among 8 crêpes. Roll up and place seam-side down in well-greased shallow rectangular baking dish. Sprinkle paprika over top. Bake at 350°F for 30 minutes.
Micronote: Punch several holes in spinach box and cook on HIGH 7 minutes. In glass bowl sauté onion and garlic in margarine on HIGH 2 minutes. Combine all ingredients and proceed as above.

Jane Hix Oliver

Spinach-Stuffed Squash

Preparation: Easy
Cooking Time: 18 Minutes
Oven Temperature: 350°F

Serves: 4-6

4 **medium yellow squash**
 Spinach Stuffing
¼ **cup dry bread crumbs**
2 **tablespoons Parmesan cheese**
 Paprika

Rinse squash. Place whole squash in saucepan with water to cover. Boil until just tender. Rinse in cold water until cool enough to handle. Split each squash lengthwise. Scoop out and discard seeds and pulp. Place cut-side up in shallow baking dish. Fill each squash cavity with Spinach Stuffing. Top with bread crumbs and Parmesan cheese. Sprinkle with paprika. (May do ahead to this point and refrigerate.) Bake at 350°F just until hot throughout, 15-20 minutes.
Micronote: Split squash lengthwise. Place with "tails" to the center in 10-inch round dish with 2 tablespoons water. Cover; cook on HIGH 4 minutes. Prepare shells as above. Cook on HIGH 4-5 minutes.

Spinach Stuffing

1 **(10-ounce) package**
 frozen chopped spinach
1 **small onion, chopped**
1 **tablespoon vinegar**
1 **(3-ounce) package cream**
 cheese
1 **teaspoon salt**
¼ **teaspoon pepper**
¼ **teaspoon nutmeg**

Cook spinach according to package directions, adding onion and vinegar to saucepan also; drain well. Place all ingredients in blender or food processor; process until well blended.
Micronote: Open spinach box. Place onion and vinegar over frozen spinach. Partially close lid. Cook on HIGH 7 minutes. Continue as directed above.
Variations: Creamed Spinach - Place Spinach Stuffing mixture in casserole after processing; heat through in oven or microwave.
Spinach Soufflé - Add 1 or 2 eggs to Spinach Stuffing mixture while processing. Turn into casserole. Bake at 350°F or in microwave until hot and puffed.
Spinach-Stuffed Tomatoes - Scoop pulp from 4 medium tomatoes. Brush insides lightly with prepared mustard; sprinkle with crumbled bacon. Fill with Spinach Stuffing mixture. Sprinkle with bread crumbs and Parmesan. Bake at 350°F for 20 minutes.

Emily Warfield Thompson

Glazed Acorn Squash with Onions

A lovely, tasty dish for autumn.

Preparation: Average
Cooking Time: 45 Minutes
Oven Temperature: 350°F

Serves: 6

3 medium acorn squash
⅔ cup water
2 cups canned small onions
½ cup chopped California walnuts
¼ teaspoon ground cinnamon
½ cup dark corn syrup
6 tablespoons margarine, melted

Halve squash lengthwise; remove seeds. Pour water into large shallow baking dish. Place squash, cut-side down, in water. Bake at 350°F until tender, 20-25 minutes. Remove squash; discard liquid. Return squash, cut-side up to baking dish. Divide onions and nuts evenly to fill each squash cavity. Mix cinnamon, corn syrup, and margarine. Spoon evenly over filling. Return to oven. Bake at 350°F for 15 minutes or until bubbly.

Micronote: Prepare squash as directed above using half the amount of water. Punch a few holes in outer covering of squash. Cook until tender on HIGH, 12-15 minutes. Remove squash to baking dish. Fill cavity with onions and nuts; spoon syrup-margarine mixture over each. Cook on HIGH 8-10 minutes, turning dish twice during cooking.

Melba Clark Jacobs

Zesty Squash

A microwave delight. It can be prepared in no time and makes a perfect accompaniment to a summer supper.

Preparation: Easy
Cooking Time: 10-12 Minutes

Serves: 4

¼ cup butter or margarine
1 clove garlic, minced
1 tablespoon fresh oregano or
    1 teaspoon dried oregano
1½ teaspoons fresh basil or
    ½ teaspoon dried basil
½ teaspoon salt
⅛ teaspoon pepper
2 medium zucchini, thinly
    sliced
1 medium yellow squash,
    thinly sliced
1 large tomato, cut into
    8 wedges

Place butter and garlic in 2-quart casserole. Cook in microwave on HIGH for 45 seconds or until butter melts. Add remaining ingredients except tomato; toss. Cook on HIGH until tender, 8-10 minutes. Stir in tomato wedges; cover and let stand 2 minutes before serving.

Sandra Adams McAlister

Southern Squash Boats

Two cheeses and brown sugar make this one special.

Preparation: Easy
Cooking Time: 15 Minutes
Oven Temperature: Broil

Serves: 6-8

12 **summer squash**
½ cup **brown sugar**
¼ cup **grated Cheddar cheese**
1 tablespoon **Parmesan cheese**
½ cup **crushed Ritz crackers**
   (plain or cheese)
¼ cup **butter, melted**

Boil whole squash 15 minutes or until tender. Slice each squash in half lengthwise. Place on foil-lined baking sheet. Mix brown sugar, cheeses, and cracker crumbs. Brush butter over each squash half. Mound sugar-cheese mixture onto each. Broil until cheese melts.
Micronote: Punch holes in squash. Place in covered casserole with ¼ cup water. Cook on HIGH 8-10 minutes (longer if squash are large). Continue as directed.

Betty Garrett Mansfield

Duo-Squash Casserole

Preparation: Average
Cooking Time: 30 Minutes
Oven Temperature: 350°F

Serves: 6

1 **pound yellow squash, cut**
   into ½-inch slices
1 **pound zucchini squash, cut**
   into ½-inch slices
1 **medium onion, chopped**
2 tablespoons **bacon drippings**
1 **(8-ounce) can tomato sauce**
1 **(4-ounce) can green chilies**
½ teaspoon **salt**
1 cup **shredded sharp Cheddar**
   cheese
   Seasoned bread crumbs

Cook yellow squash and zucchini separately in small amount of boiling salted water for 5 minutes. Drain well. Sauté onion in bacon drippings until tender. Combine tomato sauce, chilies, and salt. Layer yellow squash in 1½-quart deep casserole dish; add onion, spreading evenly. Pour half tomato mixture over onion. Add zucchini layer. Pour remaining tomato mixture over top. Sprinkle with cheese; top with bread crumbs. Bake at 350°F for 30 minutes.
Micronote: Place squash in separate covered containers with ¼ cup water. Cook each on HIGH 6-8 minutes or until tender. Sauté onion in drippings 2 minutes. Assemble as directed. Return casserole to microwave; cook on MEDIUM, uncovered, 10-12 minutes.

Carol Dean Greene

Zucchini and Tomato Bake

Preparation: Easy
Cooking Time: 40 Minutes
Oven Temperature: 350°F

Serves: 8

   4 **medium zucchini, sliced**
   ½ **teaspoon soy sauce, divided**
   ¼ **teaspoon salt, divided**
   ¼ **teaspoon garlic salt, divided**
   ¼ **teaspoon pepper, divided**
   ⅛ **teaspoon basil, divided**
   ⅛ **teaspoon oregano, divided**
   2 **medium tomatoes, cut
       in thin wedges**
   1 **medium onion, thinly sliced**
   3 **tablespoons grated Parmesan
       cheese**
1½ **cups (6 ounces) shredded
       Cheddar cheese**
   3 **tablespoons butter
       or margarine**

Place zucchini in 2½-quart casserole. Sprinkle with half of each seasoning. Layer tomatoes and onions over zucchini; sprinkle with remaining seasonings. Top with Parmesan and Cheddar cheeses. Dot with butter. Bake, covered, at 350°F for 40 minutes.

Micronote: Assemble casserole as directed except for cheeses. Cook on HIGH 10-12 minutes, turning dish several times. Sprinkle with cheeses; cook on MEDIUM 1-2 minutes to melt.

Jean Bennett Oliver

Carrot and Zucchini Julienne

Preparation: Average
Cooking Time: 10 Minutes

Serves: 4

Carrot

   6 **carrots, peeled**
   2 **tablespoons butter, melted**
   2 **teaspoons sugar**
     Salt and pepper to taste
   ⅓ **cup water**

Cut carrots into long julienne strips. In saucepan blanch carrots in boiling salted water to cover for 1½ minutes. Drain; refresh under cold running water. Pat carrots dry with absorbent toweling. In skillet toss carrots with butter, sugar, salt, and pepper, until well coated. Add water; cook over moderately high heat, tossing until water evaporates (very short time).

Zucchini

   6 **(6-inch) zucchini**
   1 **teaspoon salt**
   2 **tablespoons butter, melted**
     Salt and pepper to taste
   ⅓ **cup water**
     Parsley (garnish)

Scrub and trim zucchini. Cut into long julienne strips. Sprinkle with salt; drain for 30 minutes. Press out moisture; pat dry with absorbent toweling. In skillet toss zucchini with butter, salt, and pepper. Add water; cook over moderately high heat, tossing until water evaporates (very short time).

Cathy McLanahan Nix

Company Carrots

A real change-of-pace carrot dish. It goes especially well with ham.

Preparation: Easy
Cooking Time: 20 Minutes
Oven Temperature: 375°F

Serves: 6-8

- 2½ **pounds carrots, peeled**
- ½ **cup mayonnaise**
- 1 **tablespoon onion, chopped**
- 1 **tablespoon horseradish**
   **Salt and freshly ground
      black pepper to taste**
- ¼ **cup crushed saltine
      crackers**
- 2 **tablespoons butter
   Parsley
   Paprika**

Cook carrots in enough water to cover until tender-crisp. Drain, reserving ½ cup liquid. Cut carrots into strips. Place in 2-quart baking dish. Combine reserved liquid, mayonnaise, onion, horseradish, salt, and pepper. Pour over carrots. Sprinkle crackers on top. Dot with butter; sprinkle with parsley and paprika. Bake at 375°F for 20 minutes or until thoroughly heated.

Micronote: Place carrots in covered casserole with ½ cup water. Cook on HIGH until tender, approximately 15 minutes. Assemble casserole as above. Cook on HIGH for 6 minutes.

Mary Ross Ward Carter

Mandarin Carrots

Preparation: Easy
Cooking Time: 15 Minutes
Oven Temperature: 350°F

Serves: 8
Must Partially Do Ahead

- 2 **(11-ounce) cans mandarin
      oranges, drained**
- 2 **(16-ounce) cans cut carrots,
      drained**
- 1½ **cups sugar**
- 1 **(6-ounce) can frozen
      orange juice concentrate,
      thawed**
- ½ **cup butter**

Mix carrots and oranges in large bowl. In saucepan combine sugar, orange juice, and butter; simmer 20 minutes, stirring constantly. Pour hot juice mixture over carrots and oranges. Cover tightly; let stand overnight in refrigerator. To serve turn into 1½-quart casserole; heat at 350°F for 15 minutes or until heated thoroughly.

Micronote: In large glass bowl combine sugar, orange juice, and butter. Heat on HIGH 2 more minutes. Add butter and sugar. Cook on HIGH until mixture boils; stir once or twice. Reduce power to MEDIUM; cook 10-15 minutes. Continue as directed above. To serve heat on HIGH 4-5 minutes or until warm throughout; stir several times.

*Willie Warren Grimes
Perry, Georgia*

Heavenly Vegetable Casserole

Very rich and creamy. It should be served with a plain meat, steak, or roast.

Preparation: Average
Cooking Time: 40-50 Minutes
Oven Temperature: 325°F

Serves: 12

1 (10-ounce) package frozen French-style green beans
1 (10-ounce) package frozen baby lima beans
1 (10-ounce) package frozen small English peas
3 green peppers, seeded and cut into narrow strips
1½ cups whipping cream, whipped
1½ cups mayonnaise
¾ cup grated Parmesan or Cheddar cheese
   Freshly ground pepper to taste
   Salt to taste

Place beans, peas, and peppers in just enough boiling, salted water to avoid sticking. Cook only until thawed; separate with fork. Drain and cool. Pour into buttered 2½ or 3-quart casserole. Fold together remaining ingredients; pour over vegetables. (May do ahead to this point and refrigerate.) Bake, uncovered, at 350°F for 40 minutes or until top is brown and puffy.

Cheryl Gibbons McElveen

Corn: As poets should,/ Thou hast built up thy hardihood/ With universal food,/ Drawn into select proportion fair/ From honest mould and vagabond air.
Sidney Lanier, "Corn."

Beaumont Inn Corn Pudding

Served for 75 years in Harrodsburg, Kentucky, at the Beaumont Inn.

Preparation: Easy
Cooking Time: 45 Minutes
Oven Temperature: 375°F

Serves: 10

4 eggs
½ cup flour
4 teaspoons sugar (or to taste)
1 teaspoon salt
4 cups milk (3½ cups if using frozen corn)
4 tablespoons butter, melted
3 cups fresh or frozen whole kernel corn

Beat eggs with mixer. Combine flour, sugar, and salt; add to eggs. Mix in milk and butter. Stir in corn. Pour into 3-quart greased oblong or round casserole. Bake on lower rack of 375°F oven for 10-15 minutes; stir. Bake 5-10 minutes more; stir again. Move to top rack. Bake until knife inserted in center comes out clean and top is slightly brown, approximately 20-30 minutes longer.

Madge Farra Burch

Herbed Roasting Ears

Fresh corn-on-the-cob is one of the highlights of summer. Here is an interesting new twist to an old favorite.

Preparation: Easy
Cooking Time: 20-25 Minutes
Oven Temperature: 450°F

Serves: 6
Must Serve Immediately

¼ **cup butter or margarine, softened**
1 **teaspoon dried rosemary or 1 tablespoon fresh rosemary**
½ **teaspoon dried marjoram or 1½ teaspoons fresh marjoram**
½ **teaspoon salt (optional)**
6 **ears sweet corn, shucked**
1 **small head romaine lettuce, well rinsed**

Combine butter, rosemary, marjoram, and salt. Spread butter mixture on each ear of corn. Wrap each ear in 2-3 leaves of romaine. Place in shallow baking dish. Cover tightly with foil. Bake at 450°F for 20-25 minutes.
Micronote: Prepare corn as above. Place wrapped ears on glass tray or baking dish. Cook on HIGH for 2 minutes per ear (for 6 ears, 12 minutes).

Sherrie Nathan Schrage

Next day, Mr. Rabbit an' Mrs. Rabbit got up soon 'fo day, en raided on a garden like Miss Sally's out dar, en got some cabbiges, en some roas'n years, en some sparrar-grass, en dey fix up a smashin' dinner.

Joel Chandler Harris

Corn-in-the-Shuck

This method eliminates the bother of shucking and cleaning the corn before boiling. Fresh corn can also be frozen in the shuck and then cooked.

Preparation: Easy
Cooking Time: 15 Minutes

Yield: Variable

Fresh ears of corn-in-the-shuck
Pot of water
Butter, melted
Salt

Cut off top of corn shuck, removing exposed tassel. Place corn-in-the-shuck in large pot of water. Bring to boil; boil 15 minutes. Remove from water. Fold shuck back; shake lightly to allow tassels to fall away. Brush with butter; salt lightly. For a picnic by the lake, cook corn in black wash pot. Using folded shucks as handle, dip corn in pot of butter. Salt lightly. You'll never taste better!
Micronote: Prepare as above. Place on glass tray or baking dish. Cook on HIGH for 2-3 minutes per ear, according to size. Continue as directed.

Mary Lou Greer Melvin

Broiled Sherried Tomatoes

Preparation: Easy
Cooking Time: 5-9 Minutes
Oven Temperature: Broil

Serves: 2

Medium tomato
Sherry
Garlic salt
Mayonnaise
Grated Parmesan cheese

Wash tomato, but do not peel. Cut in half crosswise. Holding tomato half in palm of hand, gently squeeze out juice. Sprinkle tomato with sherry. Season with garlic salt. Broil until heated through, 5-7 minutes. Place spoonful of mayonnaise on each tomato half; sprinkle with cheese. Return to broiler and brown lightly. Serve in separate side dish to contain juices.

Nell Cromer Freeman
Stillwater, Oklahoma

I should buy cooking sherry with my last dollar.
Marjorie Kinnan Rawlings, from *Cross Creek.*
Charles Scribner's Sons. Copyright 1942.
Reprinted with permission of Charles Scribner's Sons.

Gourmet Rice-Stuffed Tomatoes

Preparation: Average
Cooking Time: 1 Hour
Oven Temperature: 350°F

Serves: 6

6 medium ripe tomatoes
1 medium onion, chopped
3 tablespoons butter, melted
1½ cups water
½ cup rice
½ cup raisins
½ cup pignolia nuts
  (pine nuts)
3 tablespoons chopped fresh
  parsley
Salt and pepper to taste

Cut tops off tomatoes; scoop out pulp into bowl. Set shells aside. Sauté onions and pulp in butter. Simmer slowly until mixture cooks down and becomes thick. Add 1½ cups water; bring to boil. Add rice; cover and cook over medium heat 10 minutes. Add raisins, pignolia nuts, chopped parsley, salt, and pepper. Lightly salt tomato shells. Stuff with rice mixture. Place in baking dish; cover lightly with foil. Bake at 350°F until tomatoes are heated through, but shells are still firm, approximately 30 minutes.

Ethel Martin Caras

Artichoke-Tomato Casserole

Preparation: Easy
Cooking Time: 10-15 Minutes
Oven Temperature: 325°F

Serves: 6-8

8 tablespoons butter, melted
1 large onion, sliced
2 (8½-ounce) cans quartered
   artichoke hearts
2 (16-ounce) cans tomato
   wedges, drained
2 tablespoons sugar
2 tablespoons chopped parsley
   Salt to taste
   Pepper to taste
½ cup Italian bread crumbs
½ cup Parmesan cheese

Sauté onion in butter. Add artichokes, tomatoes, sugar, and parsley. Heat 2-3 minutes. Season with salt and pepper. Place in 1-quart baking dish. Top with bread crumbs and cheese. Bake at 325°F for 10-15 minutes.

Micronote: In 1-quart casserole sauté onion in butter on HIGH 2-2½ minutes. Add artichokes, tomatoes, sugar, parsley, salt, and pepper. Top with bread crumbs and cheese. Cook on HIGH 8-10 minutes.

Mary Ross Ward Carter

Savory Eggplant and Clams

An unlikely combination? Maybe, but the blend is delicious.

Preparation: Average
Cooking Time: 30 Minutes
Oven Temperature: 350°F

Serves: 8-10

1 large eggplant, peeled
   and cubed
1 teaspoon salt, divided
¼ cup + 2 tablespoons butter
   or margarine, divided
¼ cup finely chopped
   onions
¼ cup chopped celery
¼ cup flour
½ cup milk
1 (7-ounce) can minced
   clams, undrained
1 egg, well-beaten
½ cup grated Cheddar cheese
2 tablespoons Parmesan cheese
1 cup soft bread crumbs

Place eggplant in saucepan with ½ teaspoon salt and just enough water to cover; bring to boil. Lower temperature; cook over moderate heat until tender. Drain eggplant; place in lightly greased 1½-quart shallow casserole. While eggplant is cooking, melt ¼ cup butter in heavy saucepan or skillet. Add onions and celery; sauté until soft. Stir in flour and ½ teaspoon salt. Gradually add milk, stirring constantly. Add clams; continue to cook and stir until mixture thickens. Add small amount of hot mixture to egg, stirring constantly; return to remaining sauce, mixing well. Pour clam sauce over eggplant. Dot top with remaining 2 tablespoons butter. Sprinkle with cheeses; cover with bread crumbs. Bake at 350°F for 30 minutes.

Micronote: Place eggplant in glass dish with ¼ cup water. Cook on HIGH 7-8 minutes; drain and place in glass casserole. Melt ¼ cup butter on HIGH 1 minute; add onion and celery. Cook on HIGH 1½-2 minutes; add flour, salt, milk, and clams. Cook on HIGH 2 minutes, stirring several times. Stir small amount of sauce into egg; return to hot mixture. Continue as directed above.

Charlotte Morrow Dunlap

Eggplant Italiano

Preparation: Average
Cooking Time: 45 Minutes
Oven Temperature: 350°F

Serves: 6

> 2 pounds eggplant
>   (approximately 2 medium)
> 3 (8-ounce) cans tomato sauce
> ½ cup finely chopped onion
> 1½ teaspoons Italian seasoning
> ½ teaspoon garlic salt
> ¼ teaspoon salt
> ⅛ teaspoon pepper
> 1 cup Ricotta cheese
> 2 cups grated Parmesan
>   cheese
> ½ cup Ritz cracker crumbs
>   or dry bread crumbs

Cut eggplant into ½-inch cubes. Parboil in salted boiling water until tender, about 8-10 minutes; drain well. Combine tomato sauce, onion, Italian seasoning, garlic salt, salt, and pepper. Spread thin layer of sauce mixture in bottom of 3-quart dish. Layer in order: eggplant, Ricotta cheese, remaining sauce, and Parmesan cheese. Sprinkle crumbs on top. Bake at 350°F for 45 minutes.
Micronote: Place cubed eggplant and ¼ cup water in glass casserole; cook, covered, on HIGH 8-10 minutes. Drain. Prepare casserole as directed above. Cook 8-10 minutes on HIGH, turning casserole several times.

Jean Thompson Brannon

Harvard Beets

Preparation: Easy
Cooking Time: 20-25 Minutes

Serves: 6

> ½ cup sugar
> 2 tablespoons flour
> ½ teaspoon salt
> 1 (8-ounce) can tiny beets
>   (whole or sliced)
> ½ cup vinegar
> 2 tablespoons butter
>   Grated rind of 1 orange

Mix sugar, flour, and salt in medium saucepan. Drain beets, reserving juice. Add vinegar and ¼ cup beet juice to saucepan. Heat to boiling, stirring constantly. Reduce heat; add beets. Simmer 15 minutes. Add butter and orange rind.
Micronote: Combine sauce mixture in large, glass casserole. Bring to boil on HIGH for 1½ minutes. Add beets; cook 6-8 minutes. Add butter and orange rind.

Johnnie Bowie Swetenburg

Yam Baskets Louisianne

Preparation: Easy
Cooking Time: 15 Minutes
Oven Temperature: 325°F

Serves: 4

> 4 medium yams, baked
> 1 (4-ounce) package whipped
>   cream cheese with chives
> ¾ teaspoon freeze-dried
>   chives
> 2 tablespoons margarine
> ¼ teaspoon salt
> ⅛ teaspoon pepper
> ¼ cup milk

Cut horizontal slice off top of each yam. Carefully scoop out and reserve pulp, leaving ¼-inch yam shell. In electric mixer bowl combine reserved yams and remaining ingredients. Beat at medium speed until mixture is light and fluffy. Spoon into shells. Bake at 325°F 15 minutes or until hot. (For a sweeter variation add 1 egg, 1 teaspoon vanilla extract, 2 tablespoons sugar.)

Melba Clark Jacobs

Sweet Potato Dream

Sweet potatoes at their most sophisticated. Unsurpassed.

Preparation: Average
Cooking Time: 20 Minutes
Oven Temperature: 350°F

Serves: 8-10

    5 large sweet potatoes,
          cooked
    ½ cup butter, melted
    1 (20-ounce) can crushed
          pineapple, including juice
    ¾ cup light brown sugar
    1 (5.33 ounce) can evaporated
          milk
    ½ cup raisins
    2 eggs, beaten
    ½ cup Grand Marnier
    ¼ cup orange liqueur
    2 tablespoons grated orange
          rind
    1 cup miniature marshmallows
    ½ cup chopped pecans

Purée sweet potatoes and butter in food processor. Combine with pineapple and juice, sugar, milk, raisins, and eggs. Mix well. Add Grand Marnier, orange liqueur, and orange rind. Pour into buttered casserole. Sprinkle marshmallows and pecans on top. Bake at 350°F for 20 minutes.

Connie Kemp Goldfarb

Potato-Onion Piquante

Preparation: Easy
Cooking Time: 1 Hour 15 Minutes
Oven Temperature: 450°F

Serves: 8

    6 medium potatoes
    2 medium onions, thinly
          sliced
    2 tablespoons margarine
    1 (4-ounce) package
          buttermilk ranch-style
          dressing
    1 cup mayonnaise
    1 cup buttermilk

Make several crosswise slices in each potato, not cutting quite all the way through bottom peel (each slice to be approximately ½-inch thickness). Gently open cuts and place one onion slice in each. Place in shallow dish. Cover and bake at 450°F 1 hour or until potatoes are done. Dot with margarine. Combine dressing mix, mayonnaise, and buttermilk, beating well. Pour over potatoes. Lower oven temperature to 350°F; bake, uncovered, approximately 15 minutes or just until entire dish is well heated.
Micronote: Assemble potatoes and onions as above. Cover with plastic wrap. Cook on HIGH 10-12 minutes or until potatoes are done. Dot with margarine. Prepare dressing as above. Pour over potatoes. Cover; cook on MEDIUM 5 minutes or until well heated.

W. Jackson Thompson

Party Potatoes

Pretty to serve and so good. Your guests will be suitably impressed!

Preparation: Average
Cooking Time: 20 Minutes
Oven Temperature: 350°F

Serves: 8-10

> 1 (5-pound) bag white potatoes, peeled and boiled
> 1 (8-ounce) package cream cheese, softened
> ½ cup butter, melted
> 1 (8-ounce) carton sour cream
> 1 small onion, grated
> ¼ cup chopped chives (optional)
>   Salt and pepper to taste
> ½ pint whipping cream, whipped
> 6 ounces Cheddar cheese, grated
> ½ pound bacon, fried, drained, and crumbled (optional)

Drain potatoes; cream. Mix with cream cheese, butter, sour cream, onion, chives, salt, and pepper. Spread in greased 13 x 9-inch casserole dish. Ice with whipped cream. Sprinkle with cheese and bacon. Bake at 350°F for 20 minutes. If not brown, place under broiler.

Susie White Gignilliat

Parmesan Potato Fingers

Children love this - and adults find it a nice change from French fries!

Preparation: Easy
Cooking Time: 1 Hour
Oven Temperature: 375°F

Serves: 8-10
Must Serve Immediately

> ¼ cup flour
> ¼ cup grated Parmesan cheese
> 2 tablespoons parsley flakes
> ¾ teaspoon salt
> ⅛ teaspoon pepper
> ⅓ cup margarine
> 6 medium potatoes, cut in eighths lengthwise, peel or not as desired

In plastic bag combine flour, cheese, parsley, salt, and pepper. Melt margarine in large shallow baking pan. Drop potatoes, a few at a time, into flour mixture; shake to coat. Place potatoes in single layer in margarine. Bake, uncovered, at 375°F for 1 hour; turn potatoes once after 30 minutes.

Jane Hix Oliver

Cheesy Apples

A guaranteed family favorite. It goes anywhere - picnic, ball game, covered dish supper - as it doesn't have to be served piping hot.

Preparation: Easy
Cooking Time: 30-40 Minutes
Oven Temperature: 350°F

Serves: 6-8

    1 (16-ounce) can Comstock
          sliced apples, undrained
    ½ cup butter or margarine,
          melted
    ½-1 cup sugar
    ¾ cup flour
    8 ounces Velveeta cheese,
          cubed
    ¼ cup milk

Place apples in greased 1½-quart casserole. Combine remaining ingredients in saucepan. Cook and stir over medium heat until cheese melts and ingredients are well blended. Spread over apples. Bake uncovered at 350°F for 30-40 minutes, until top is lightly browned. (May be served as a dessert, using the larger amount of sugar.)

Micronote: Place apples in casserole. Melt margarine in glass bowl or large glass measuring cup 3 minutes on HIGH. Add flour, sugar; mix well. Add milk and a few cubes of cheese. Return to microwave 1 minute on HIGH. Stir and add a few cheese cubes every 45 seconds, continuing until cheese melts and ingredients are blended. Spread over apples. Return to microwave for 10 minutes on MEDIUM; turn container halfway through cooking time. (If a "browned" color is desired, sprinkle cinnamon into cheese mixture before cooking.)

Bonnie Stanley Martin

In the autumn, they barrelled huge frosty apples in the cellar. Smoked bacons hung in the pantry, the great bins were full of flour, the dark recessed shelves groaned with preserved cherries, peaches, apples, pears.

Thomas Wolfe, from *Look Homeward, Angel*
Copyright 1929 Charles Scribner's Sons; copyright renewed 1957 Edward C. Aswell, Administrator, C.T.A. and/or Fred W. Wolfe.
Reprinted with the permission of Charles Scribner's Sons.

Lemony Apple Bake

Preparation: Easy
Cooking Time: 30-45 Minutes
Oven Temperature: 350°F

Serves: 4-6

    8 cups apples, peeled,
          cored, and quartered
    ⅓-½ cup brown sugar
    ½ teaspoon cinnamon
    ¼ teaspoon nutmeg
    ⅓ cup butter or margarine
       Juice of 1 lemon

Place apples in lightly buttered 2-quart casserole. Sprinkle with sugar, cinnamon, and nutmeg. Dot with butter. Squeeze lemon juice over all. Bake, covered, at 350°F for 30-45 minutes, until apples are just tender.

Micronote: Assemble as above. Cook, covered, on HIGH for 5 minutes. Stir well. Cover; cook on HIGH 3-5 more minutes, until apples are just tender. Stir once before serving.

W. Jackson Thompson

Hot Sherried Fruit

Preparation: Easy
Cooking Time: 30 Minutes
Oven Temperature: 350°F

Serves: 8

1 (16-ounce) can pineapple
   chunks, drained
1 (16-ounce) can pears,
   drained
1 (16-ounce) can peaches,
   drained
1 (16-ounce) can apricots,
   drained
½ cup margarine
½ cup sugar
2 tablespoons flour or
   cornstarch
1 cup sherry
   Maraschino cherries (optional)
   Raisins (optional)

Arrange fruit attractively in glass casserole. Melt margarine in saucepan. Stir in sugar, flour, and sherry. Heat until thickened. Pour over fruit. Bake at 350°F for 30 minutes. **Micronote:** Arrange fruit as above. Melt margarine in glass bowl 1-2 minutes. Stir in sugar, flour, and sherry. Microwave on HIGH 1½-2 minutes, stirring every 30 seconds. Pour over fruit. Cook 12-15 minutes on MEDIUM.

Irene Baker Davenport

Homemade Yogurt

Recommended for those who eat a lot of yogurt. A mild flavor and very economical.

Preparation: Easy
Standing Time: 8-10 Hours
Oven Temperature: 275°F

Yield: 2 Quarts
Must Do Ahead

1 teaspoon unflavored gelatin
¼ cup cold water
¾ cup boiling water
1-2 tablespoons sugar
3 cups instant powdered
   milk
5 cups tepid water, divided
1 (8-ounce) can evaporated
   milk
3 tablespoons plain yogurt
   Fresh fruit (optional)
   Honey (optional)
   Extract of choice
      (optional)
   Chopped nuts (optional)
   Granola (optional)

Soften gelatin in cold water. Add boiling water; stir until dissolved. Stir in sugar; let cool to lukewarm. In large heat-proof bowl mix powdered milk with 3 cups tepid water. Stir in evaporated milk, remaining tepid water, gelatin mixture, and 3 tablespoons prepared yogurt. (Prepared yogurt acts as "starter"; may be commercial or from earlier homemade batch.) Blend thoroughly, cover, and place in 275°F oven. Turn heat OFF. Leave 8-10 hours or overnight. Stir in one or more optional ingredients if desired. Store in refrigerator. (May be used plain as substitute for sour cream.)

Flo Criss Smith

Joy!

A boon to senior citizens and expectant mothers. Of greatly reputed medicinal value.

Preparation: Average

> 1 (6-ounce) box dried prunes
> 1 (8-ounce) box dried apricots
> 1 (15-ounce) box raisins
> ½-1 (1-ounce) box senna leaves (available at pharmacy)

Yield: 1 Roll
Must Do Ahead

Grind all ingredients together by hand, or chop small amounts at a time in food processor using steel blade. Form into one inch thick roll. Chill. Slice a piece and eat every night.

Marilyn Woodberry McCarver

Prunes Deluxe

Good also as a light dessert.

Preparation: Easy

> 1 pound prunes
> 2½ cups apple cider or apple juice
> ⅓ cup sugar
> 2 cinnamon sticks

Yield: 1 Quart
Must Do Ahead

Soak prunes overnight in cider. Bring to boil; add sugar and cinnamon sticks. Cover and cook slowly for 20 minutes. Cool and store in refrigerator. Serve cold.
Micronote: Soak prunes as directed. Cover with waxed paper to prevent splatter. Cook on HIGH 6 minutes or until boiling; add other ingredients. Cook on MEDIUM 7-10 minutes. (Use 1-quart measuring cup for both measuring juice and cooking.)

Betty Garrett Mansfield

Barley Casserole

Unusual and nutritious.

Preparation: Easy
Cooking Time: 1 Hour
Oven Temperature: 350°F

> ½ cup butter
> 1 cup medium pearl barley
> 1 medium onion, chopped
> ½ cup slivered almonds
> 1 (1.37-ounce) package onion soup mix
> 2 cups chicken broth
> 1 (4-ounce) can sliced mushrooms, undrained
> 1 (8-ounce) can water chestnuts, drained and sliced

Serves: 6

In heavy skillet heat butter; add barley and onion, browning lightly. Add remaining ingredients; stir well. Turn into 2-quart casserole. Bake covered at 350°F for 1 hour, adding more liquid if necessary. (May be prepared ahead and refrigerated until baking time.)

Ann Branch Smith

Pecan Pilaf

Excellent with any meat; a complete meal with a baked fruit dish.

Preparation: Easy
Cooking Time: 18-20 Minutes

Serves: 8

8 tablespoons butter or
    margarine, divided
1 cup chopped pecans
½ cup chopped onion
2 cups long grain rice,
    uncooked
4 cups chicken broth
1 teaspoon salt
¼ teaspoon thyme
⅛ teaspoon pepper
2 tablespoons chopped parsley

In large skillet melt 3 tablespoons butter. Add pecans; sauté 10 minutes or until lightly browned. Remove pecans; cover and set aside. In same skillet melt remaining butter. Add onion; sauté until tender. Add rice; stir to thoroughly coat grains. Add broth, salt, thyme, and pepper. Cover; simmer 18 minutes or until rice is tender and all liquid is absorbed. Remove from heat; stir in nuts and parsley. (To prepare ahead: Before adding nuts and parsley, cover and refrigerate up to 24 hours. To heat, add extra ¾ cup water to cooked rice in skillet. Cover; heat 5-8 minutes until hot. Stir in nuts and parsley.)

Suzanne Richard Cannon

Vegetable Rice

Preparation: Easy
Cooking Time: 45 Minutes
Oven Temperature: 350°F

Serves: 8-12

2 large onions, minced
4 ribs celery, minced
2 cups mushrooms
¼ cup green pepper, chopped
½ cup butter, melted
2 chicken bouillon cubes
½ cup boiling water
4 cups cooked rice
2 cups processed cheese,
    cubed
¾ cup toasted slivered
    almonds

Sauté vegetables in butter until tender. Add bouillon cubes to boiling water. Mix all ingredients except almonds in 2-quart casserole. Bake at 350°F for 45 minutes. Stir in almonds just before serving.

Anne Warren Thomas

Mexican Rice

Preparation: Easy
Cooking Time: 40 Minutes

Serves: 12

3 cups long grain
    rice, uncooked
1 cup finely chopped onion
4 tablespoons olive oil
3 cups water
3 (8-ounce) cans tomato
    sauce
1 tablespoon salt

Sauté rice and onion in oil until lightly browned. Add water, tomato sauce, and salt; bring to boil. Cover; lower heat and cook until tender, approximately 40 minutes.

Nell Cromer Freeman
Stillwater, Oklahoma

Shrimp Fried Rice

Preparation: Average
Cooking Time: 10 Minutes

Serves: 6-8

6 ounces fresh or frozen shrimp, shelled and deveined
4 tablespoons vegetable oil, divided
1-2 eggs, beaten (optional)
1 cup uncooked rice, prepared according to package directions (day-old rice is preferred)
¼ cup frozen green peas
¼ cup chopped green onions
1 tablespoon soy sauce
1 tablespoon oyster sauce (if unavailable, substitute 1 additional tablespoon soy sauce)

In wok sauté shrimp in 2 tablespoons oil until they begin to curl. Remove; drain on absorbent toweling. Wipe wok with toweling. Scramble eggs in wok in remaining 2 tablespoons oil. Remove; set aside. Wipe wok with toweling. Oil wok lightly with toweling. Add cooked rice, stirring to keep from sticking. Move rice to side of wok; add remaining ingredients, stirring briefly. Return eggs and shrimp to wok. Turn off heat; let stand 1 minute. (Best done in wok; however, can easily be prepared in large skillet. May substitute chicken or pork for shrimp.)

Nelson Hilty Carter

Fettucine

Preparation: Average
Cooking Time: 20-25 Minutes

Serves: 6-8
Must Serve Immediately

1 pound fettucine
1 tablespoon olive oil
Salt
½ cup butter
2 shallots, chopped
½-¾ cup chicken broth
½ cup whipping cream
¾ cup freshly grated Parmesan cheese
1 egg, beaten (optional)
1 cup sour cream
2 tablespoons chopped chives
Salt
Freshly ground black pepper

Cook noodles 8-10 minutes, or according to package directions, in boiling, salted water to which olive oil has been added. Drain well. Sauté shallots in butter. Stir in chicken broth; boil 2-3 minutes. Remove from heat. Gradually add cream, Parmesan cheese, and egg; stir until thickened. Add sour cream, chives, and salt and pepper to taste. Add pasta; toss lightly until noodles are coated. Serve at once on warm plates.

Variation: Sliced assorted vegetables (mushrooms, zucchini, broccoli, etc.) may be sautéed in small amount of butter until tender-crisp and tossed with pasta.

Nelson Hilty Carter

Gruyère Cheese Grits

Always appropriate for brunch - or any meal.

Preparation: Easy
Cooking Time: 30 Minutes
Oven Temperature: 400°F

Serves: 8

1 quart milk
½ cup margarine, divided
1½ cups shredded Gruyère cheese
1 cup uncooked regular grits
1 teaspoon salt
½ teaspoon garlic powder
¼ teaspoon freshly ground pepper
⅓ cup grated Parmesan cheese

Bring milk to boil in large, heavy saucepan. Add ¼ cup margarine and Gruyère cheese; stir until cheese melts. Slowly add grits. Boil until thick, stirring occasionally. Stir in seasonings. Over low heat beat mixture at low speed of electric mixer for 5 minutes. Pour into lightly greased 8-inch square pan. Mix Parmesan cheese with ¼ cup melted margarine. Spread over top of grits mixture. Bake at 400°F for 30 minutes.

Micronote: In large mixing bowl or glass casserole combine milk, ¼ cup margarine, and Gruyère cheese. Cook on HIGH, stirring often, until mixture boils, approximately 10 minutes. Add grits. Boil 1 minute on HIGH. Reduce power to MEDIUM; cover and cook for recommended time on grits package. If mixture boils over, lower power. Stir often. Beat as directed. Top with Parmesan and remaining margarine. Return to microwave on LOW for 10 minutes.

Pamela K. Spivey

Baked Cheese Grits

Preparation: Easy
Cooking Time: 1 Hour 40 Minutes
Oven Temperature: 350°F

Serves: 8-10

1 cup grits
2 teaspoons salt
4 cups boiling water
½ cup butter
1 cup grated sharp Cheddar cheese, divided
1 cup milk
4 eggs, beaten
1 teaspoon Worcestershire Freshly ground black pepper to taste
½ teaspoon garlic powder (optional)

Add grits to boiling, salted water and cook until **very** thick, at least 40 minutes. Cool. Add remaining ingredients, reserving half cheese to sprinkle over top. Pour into buttered baking dish; sprinkle with reserved cheese. Bake at 350°F for 1 hour.

Micronote: In large bowl boil water on HIGH 8-10 minutes; add grits. Cover. Reduce power to MEDIUM; cook 15-20 minutes, stirring often. If grits boil over, reduce power to low. Add remaining ingredients as directed; sprinkle with cheese. Cook on MEDIUM 12-15 minutes.

Judy Mynatt Bush

Macaroni and Cheese Deluxe

Preparation: Easy
Cooking Time: 45 Minutes
Oven Temperature: 350°F

Serves: 6-8

1 (8-ounce) package elbow
    macaroni, cooked
2 cups cream-style cottage
    cheese
1 (8-ounce) carton sour
    cream
1 egg, slightly beaten
¾ teaspoon salt
2 cups shredded sharp
    Cheddar cheese
    Paprika

Drain and rinse macaroni; set aside. Blend cottage cheese, sour cream, egg, salt, and Cheddar. Fold in macaroni. Spoon into lightly greased 2-quart casserole. Sprinkle with paprika. Bake at 350°F for 45 minutes.

Micronote: Prepare as above in glass casserole. Cook on MEDIUM for 12-15 minutes; turn dish several times.

Jean Bennett Oliver

Pasta Primavera

Preparation: Average
Cooking Time: 6 Minutes

Serves: 8-10

1 pound fresh asparagus
6 ounces cauliflower or
    broccoli
1-2 tender carrots
1 medium zucchini
½ pound fresh mushrooms
1 cup fresh peas (sugar
    snaps preferred)
¼ cup unsalted butter
    or margarine
1 medium onion, finely
    diced
1 clove garlic, minced
1 cup whipping cream
    or evaporated milk
½ cup chicken stock
2 tablespoons chopped basil
2 ounces chopped prosciutto
    or ham
5 green onions or
    2 green shallots, chopped
    Salt and pepper to taste
1 pound fettucine, cooked
    al dente and thoroughly
    drained
1 cup freshly grated
    Parmesan cheese

Clean all vegetables and cut into bite-sized pieces. Blanch asparagus, cauliflower, and carrots until tender-crisp. Heat wok or deep skillet over medium-high heat. Melt butter; sauté onions and garlic until onions are translucent, about 2 minutes. Add vegetables; toss thoroughly and frequently. Increase heat to high; add cream, stock, and basil; boil about 3 minutes, until slightly reduced. Stir in ham and green onions; cook 1 minute. Season with salt and pepper. Toss vegetables with pasta and cheese. Serve immediately.

Variations: One pound shelled, cooked shrimp may be added with ham. For fewer calories, substitute milk for cream and thicken with 1 tablespoon arrowroot dissolved in cold water; add with ham.

Paula Eubanks Smith

Palmour Sauce

The aroma of this old family recipe will drive you wild!

Preparation: Easy
Cooking Time: 30 Minutes

Serves: 6-8

- 2 cups canned tomatoes
- 3 large onions, chopped
- 2 cups cider vinegar
- 1 cup sugar
- 1 teaspoon ground cloves
- 1 teaspoon ground cinnamon
- ⅛ teaspoon salt
  Cayenne to taste (some like it hot)

Combine all ingredients and simmer in saucepan until thick. Stir frequently, being careful that mixture does not stick. Pour into jars and store in refrigerator. Serve hot or cold with greens, dried beans, peas, or meats.

Mary Palmour Castle
Mary Foote Simmons Paris

Umma's Maple Syrup

Preparation: Easy

Yield: 5 Cups
Must Do Ahead

- 4 cups sugar
- ½ cup firmly packed brown sugar
- 2 cups water
- 1 teaspoon maple extract
- 1 teaspoon vanilla extract

Combine sugars and water in saucepan. Bring to boil. Boil very slowly 15-20 minutes. Remove from heat; cool slightly. Stir in maple and vanilla extracts. Let stand until completely cool. Pour into covered container. Refrigerate.
Micronote: Combine as directed. Bring to boil on HIGH, 5 minutes. Reduce to MEDIUM; cook 10 minutes; add flavorings; cool.

Ethel Martin Caras

Salvation had never challenged him . . . eating hot graham biscuits with plenty of butter and ribbon cane syrup. . . it never occurred to him that he did not already dwell in some superior state of salvation.

Ferrol Sams, *Run With the Horsemen.*
Peachtree Publications, Ltd., Copyright 1982. Used with permission.

Jezebel Sauce

Spoon over cream cheese and use as spread on crackers. Great as a dip for fried chicken or served as an accompaniment for roast pork, ham, or chicken.

Preparation: Easy

Yield: 4 Cups

- 3 ounces horseradish
- 1 (1⅜-ounce) can dry mustard
- 1 (18-ounce) jar pineapple preserves
- 1 (18-ounce) jar apple jelly
- 1 tablespoon coarsely ground black pepper (more if you prefer really spicy)

Blend horseradish and mustard. Add remaining ingredients, stirring until thoroughly blended. Refrigerate; keeps well for months.

Joyce Hagen Hornor

Spicy Red Cocktail Sauce

This is not for the timid of palate! Ideal for a cocktail buffet at Christmas or anytime. Spear shrimp with toothpicks; stick into foil-covered styrofoam cone; fill in with parsley.

Preparation: Easy

Serves: 4
Must Do Ahead

½ cup catsup or chili sauce
2 tablespoons lemon juice
2 tablespoons prepared horseradish (or more to taste)
1 tablespoon Worcestershire
Few drops Tabasco

Combine all ingredients in a bowl. Stir until well blended. Chill. Serve cold with boiled shrimp.

Connie Wallace Murphy

"Pig Out" Barbecue Sauce

A great sauce for a crowd. Always a hit when served with fresh hams cooked over a slow fire - Southern style!

Preparation: Easy

Yield: 1¼ Gallons

½ gallon pure cider vinegar
½ gallon tomato catsup
1½ pints molasses
1 cup oil
3 tablespoons crushed red pepper
2 teaspoons dry mustard
1½ teaspoons salt

Mix all ingredients thoroughly. The red pepper may be adjusted to taste. May be used with beef, pork, or chicken.

Patsy Lothridge Hicks

John Graham's Barbecue Sauce

A different barbecue sauce. Try it on grilled chicken or ribs. Baste meat constantly for best results.

Preparation: Easy
Cooking Time: 5-10 Minutes

Yield: 1½ Cups

8 tablespoons butter
1 cup vinegar
1 tablespoon Worcestershire
4 round slices lemon
1 teaspoon brown sugar
1 teaspoon horseradish
⅛ teaspoon salt
Pepper (as much as your conscience will allow - just keep shaking until you think you've ruined it!)

Combine all ingredients; mix thoroughly. Heat slowly until butter melts, stirring constantly. Keep warm until ready to use.
Micronote: Cook all ingredients on HIGH for 2 minutes; stir. Continue cooking on MEDIUM until butter melts and sauce is heated through; stir occasionally.

Cathy Turner Cleveland

Food Processor Pesto Sauce

Preparation: Average

2 tablespoons pine nuts
1-2 cloves garlic, chopped
2 cups gently packed
   FRESH basil leaves
⅛ teaspoon freshly ground
   black pepper
½ cup freshly ground
   Parmesan cheese
¾ cup fine olive oil

Serves: 6

Grind pine nuts in food processor; with motor running add garlic, basil leaves, salt, and pepper. Slowly add cheese through feed tube. When mixture becomes a creamy thick paste, add olive oil, a few drops at a time, until mixture resembles thickness of mayonnaise. Pour into jar; cover with thin layer of olive oil. Keeps 7-10 days in refrigerator; freezes well. (Fresh spinach plus 2 tablespoons dried basil may substitute for fresh basil; walnuts may substitute for pine nuts.)

Serving Suggestions:
1. Mix with sautéed scallops and herbs.
2. Serve as sauce with fish.
3. Mix with mayonnaise for chicken salad.
4. Serve with pasta. Blend Pesto Sauce with 2 tablespoons hot pasta water. Toss with cooked pasta.

Dana Blum Barclay

The most homely fare may be made relishing, and the most excellent and independent improved by a well-made sauce.

Mrs. Hill's New Cookbook, circa 1890.

World's Best Tartar Sauce

Preparation: Easy

2 tablespoons tarragon
   vinegar
1 teaspoon dry mustard
½ teaspoon salt
⅛ teaspoon cayenne
¼ cup finely chopped
   dill pickles
2 tablespoons finely chopped
   onions
1 tablespoon finely chopped
   chives
1 tablespoon finely chopped
   parsley
1 teaspoon finely chopped
   capers
1 cup mayonnaise

Yield: 1½ Cups

Combine vinegar, mustard, salt, and cayenne; beat with wire whisk. Stir in pickles, onions, chives, parsley, and capers. Blend in mayonnaise. Cover and refrigerate.

Ellen Bowers Wittel

Blender Hollandaise Sauce

Enhance the flavor of vegetables, fish, and other dishes with this gourmet sauce. A classic, yet so easy. Try the Bernaise variation on steak or any beef.

Preparation: Easy

Yield: ¾ Cup
Do Not Double

8 tablespoons butter
3 egg yolks
2 tablespoons lemon juice
½ teaspoon salt
⅛ teaspoon cayenne

Heat butter just until foamy; do not brown. Place egg yolks, lemon juice, salt, and cayenne into blender. Turn blender on; as blades reach full speed, slowly add melted butter in thin stream. (Sauce thickens as you pour.) May be kept warm over warm water; may be refrigerated then reheated over warm, not hot, water. Additional melted butter may be whisked into sauce, if desired.

Micronote: Melt butter on HIGH. Combine egg yolks, lemon juice, salt, and cayenne in glass bowl; whisk until smooth. Slowly whisk in butter. Cook on MEDIUM 1½-2 minutes, stirring every 30 seconds during first minute and every 15 seconds during second minute, until sauce is thick and smooth. Reheats well on LOW for 30 second intervals.

Jane Eve Fair Wilheit

Variation:

Bernaise Sauce

2 tablespoons white wine
1 tablespoon tarragon vinegar
1 teaspoon dried tarragon
2 teaspoons minced onion
¼ teaspoon ground pepper
Blender Hollandaise Sauce

Combine wine, vinegar, tarragon, onion, and pepper in saucepan. Bring to boil; cook until most of liquid has evaporated. Place Blender Hollandaise Sauce in blender jar. Add reduced herb mixture; process 10 seconds.

Helen Helms Stewart

The Hollandaise must be perfect; just holding its shape; velvety in texture; properly acid....The only other place I have eaten Hollandaise as good as mine is at the Ritz-Carlton, and even theirs does not have quite enough lemon juice to suit me.

Marjorie Kinnan Rawlings, from *Cross Creek*.
Copyright 1942. Charles Scribner's Sons. Reprinted with permission of Charles Scribner's Sons.

Salt-Free Seasoning

Preparation: Easy

Yield: ¼ Cup

2½ teaspoons marjoram
2½ teaspoons savory
2 teaspoons thyme
2 teaspoons rosemary
1½ teaspoons sage

Combine all ingredients. Store in shaker bottle. Shake on meats, vegetables, or casseroles.

Cookbook Committee

All Seasons Salt

Preparation: Easy

¾ cup salt
2 teaspoons garlic powder
2 teaspoons dry mustard
1 teaspoon onion powder
1 teaspoon dried oregano
1 teaspoon dried thyme
½ teaspoon celery seed
½ teaspoon dried dill weed

Yield: 1 Cup

Combine all ingredients in covered container; shake until well mixed. Store in airtight container. Use as flavor enhancer for vegetables and meats.

Mary Hart Keys Wilheit

Mighty Mustard

Serve like any other mustard, but beware, it is hot!

Preparation: Easy
Cooking Time: 5 Minutes

1 cup dry mustard
1 cup white vinegar
2 eggs, well-beaten
1 cup sugar or equivalent
    amount sugar substitute
¼ teaspoon salt

Yield: 3 Cups
Must Do Ahead

Mix mustard and vinegar; refrigerate overnight. Blend remaining ingredients. Add vinegar-mustard mixture; bring to boil. Cook until mixture thickens, approximately 5 minutes. Cool, then refrigerate.
Micronote: Mix as above. Place mixture in glass container; cook in microwave on HIGH 3-4 minutes, stirring every 30 seconds.

Mary Hart Keys Wilheit

Mustard Mold Classique

Good with baked ham, roast leg of lamb, or crown pork roast.

Preparation: Average

1 envelope unflavored
    gelatin
½ cup cold water
1 cup mayonnaise
½ cup prepared mustard
¼ teaspoon salt
¼ teaspoon paprika
½ cup whipping cream,
    whipped
Lettuce

Serves: 8
Must Do Ahead

Soften gelatin in cold water; stir over low heat until dissolved. Cool. Combine mayonnaise, mustard, salt, and paprika. Gradually stir in gelatin. Chill until slightly thickened; fold in whipped cream. Pour into lightly oiled 1-quart mold. Chill until set. Unmold onto lettuce.

Beth Davies Davidson

Creamy Spreads

Choose one or more to use with gingersnaps or fruit breads.

Preparation: Easy   **Yield:** ¾ Cup

Ginger Cream Spread

1 (3-ounce) package cream
    cheese, softened
1 teaspoon milk
2 tablespoons finely chopped
    crystallized ginger
2 tablespoons finely chopped
    almonds

Blend cream cheese with milk. Mix in ginger and almonds.

Honey Cream Spread

1 (3-ounce) package cream
    cheese, softened
1 tablespoon honey
1 teaspoon lemon juice

Whip cream cheese. Blend in honey and lemon juice.

Cookbook Committee

Butter Spreads

Choose one or more to accompany hot muffins.

Preparation: Easy   **Yield:** ½ Cup

Orange Butter Spread

½ cup butter, softened
1 tablespoon orange juice
1 tablespoon grated orange
    rind

Blend all ingredients thoroughly.

Almond Butter Spread

½ cup butter, softened
1 tablespoon finely chopped
    almonds
½ teaspoon almond extract

Blend all ingredients thoroughly.

Honey Butter Spread

¼ cup butter, softened
¼ cup honey
⅛ teaspoon ground cinnamon
⅛ teaspoon ground nutmeg

Blend all ingredients thoroughly.

Cookbook Committee

Mama's Ketchup

If your mama never made it you can start the tradition!

Preparation: Average
Cooking Time: 2½-3½ Hours

Yield: 5 Pints
Must Do Ahead

25 pounds tomatoes (enough
   to equal 6 quarts of liquid
   and pulp after using sieve)
1 large onion, diced
1 large green or red
   pepper, chopped
2 cups sugar
1 cup white vinegar
¼ cup salt
1 tablespoon ground black
   pepper
1 tablespoon ground cinnamon
1 tablespoon celery seed
1 teaspoon ground cloves
1 teaspoon ground dry
   mustard

Due to acidity use only enameled ware, glass, stainless steel, or stoneware when preparing ketchup. Wash tomatoes, remove core, and cut into quarters. Place in large pot; add onion and pepper. Simmer, stirring often, approximately 30 minutes or until soft. Press contents through sieve. Discard skin, seeds, and waste. There should be 6 quarts of juice and pulp. Return juice and pulp to large pot. Add sugar, vinegar, salt, pepper, cinnamon, celery seed, cloves, and mustard. Cook down for 2-3 hours, until reduced by half or to desired thickness. Fill hot sterile jars to within ⅛-inch from top; seal.

Al Owens
Chester, Virginia

Watermelon Rind Pickles

Preparation: Average
Cooking Time: 1 Hour 30 Minutes

Yield: 5 Pints
Must Do Ahead

1 large watermelon
   rind, peeled
¼ cup salt
10 cups water, divided
2 quarts cider vinegar
9 cups sugar
1 lemon, thinly sliced
2 tablespoons whole cloves
2 tablespoons allspice
2 tablespoons cracked
   cinnamon
1 piece ginger root

Cut rind into ½ x 2-inch strips. Combine rind, salt, and 8 cups water; let stand overnight. Drain. Cover with fresh cold water; simmer until tender. Drain. Prepare syrup by combining vinegar, 2 cups water, sugar, and lemon. Place spices in cheese cloth bag; tie securely. Add spice bag to syrup. Bring to boil; simmer 5 minutes. Pour syrup over rind; bring to boil. Simmer 1 hour or until clear. (Add 1-2 drops food coloring, if color is desired.) Pack in hot sterile jars, cover with hot syrup, and seal. Process 5 minutes in boiling water bath.
Micronote: Prepare and tenderize rind as directed. Bring vinegar, 2 cups water, sugar, lemon, and spice bag to boil on HIGH. Reduce power to LOW; cook 5 minutes. Pour over rind. Bring to boil on HIGH, then cook on MEDIUM until clear, stirring every 10 minutes. Pack in hot sterile jars; cover with boiling syrup and seal.

Jane Hix Oliver

It (the watermelon) is the chief of this world's luxuries....When one has tasted it, he knows what angels eat. It was not a Southern watermelon that Eve took, we know it because she repented.

Mark Twain

Bread and Butter Pickles

Preparation: Easy
Cooking Time: 4-5 Minutes

Yield: 7 Pints
Must Do Ahead

1 gallon small cucumbers
8 small onions
½ cup salt
Ice
5 cups vinegar
5 cups sugar
2 tablespoons mustard seed
1½ teaspoons turmeric
1 teaspoon celery seed
½ teaspoon ground cloves

Wash, but do not peel cucumbers. Slice cucumbers and onions paper thin. Place in large container; mix with salt. Bury pieces of cracked ice in mixture. Cover tightly; let stand 3 hours. Drain thoroughly. Combine remaining ingredients in large saucepan. Heat mixture over low heat to very hot, but not boiling; stir occasionally. Combine hot syrup with drained cucumbers. Pack into hot sterile jars; seal. Process 5 minutes in boiling water bath.

Mimi Luebbers Gerding

Squash Pickles

Preparation: Easy
Cooking Time: 15 Minutes

Yield: 6-8 Pints
Must Do Ahead

1 gallon tender yellow
    squash, sliced
1-2 cups sliced onions
⅓ cup salt
3 cloves garlic (optional)
    Ice water
5 cups sugar
3 cups vinegar
2 teaspoons mustard seed
1½ teaspoons celery seed
1½ teaspoons turmeric

Place squash and onions in bowl; sprinkle with salt. Add garlic. Cover with ice water; let soak 3 hours. Drain well. Mix remaining ingredients; pour over squash. Bring to boil; cook 8-10 minutes. Pack in hot sterile jars; seal. Process 5 minutes in boiling water bath.

Lynn Zellner Martin

Pickled Okra

A good accompaniment to outdoor cooking and picnics.

Preparation: Easy
Cooking Time: 15 Minutes

Yield: 5 Pints
Must Do Ahead

5 hot red peppers
5 cloves garlic
3½ pounds small okra
    pods
5 teaspoons dill seed
    or dill weed
1 pint white vinegar
4 cups water
⅓ cup salt

Place one pepper and one garlic clove in 5 hot sterile pint jars. Remove part of stem from each okra pod. Pack okra tightly into jars. Add 1 teaspoon dill to each jar. Combine vinegar, water, and salt in saucepan; bring to boil, simmering 5 minutes. Pour over okra. Adjust lids; process in boiling water bath at simmering temperature (180°F to 200°F) for 10 minutes. Let pickles stand in cool, dark place for several weeks before opening.

Carolyn Hartford Mahar

Green Tomato or Cucumber Crisp

Makes a nice gift; a delicious addition to any meal.

Preparation: Average
Cooking Time: 1 Hour 15 Minutes

Yield: 8-10 Pints
Must Do Ahead

        2 gallons water
        3 cups pickling lime
        7 pounds green tomatoes
            or cucumbers, sliced
        4 pounds sugar
        2 quarts cider vinegar
        1 teaspoon each of cloves,
            ginger, cinnamon, allspice,
            celery seed, mace, and salt
           Green food coloring
            (optional)

Day 1: In large plastic or enameled dishpan mix water and lime, stirring well. Add cucumbers or green tomatoes. Soak 24 hours at room temperature.

Day 2: Drain vegetables, rinse well. Soak 4 hours in fresh, cold water, changing water once each hour; drain. Prepare syrup in separate container by combining sugar, vinegar, and spices. Bring syrup to boil; simmer 5 minutes. Pour hot syrup over vegetables. Let stand overnight at room temperature.

Day 3: Boil vegetables in syrup for 1 hour. Stir in food coloring if desired. Pack in hot sterile jars; cover with hot syrup and seal. Process 5 minutes in boiling water bath.

Betty Gail Parker Gunter

Tina's Spiced Brandied Peaches

Preparation: Average
Cooking Time: 45 Minutes-1 Hour

Yield: Approximately 4 Pints
Must Do Ahead

        7 pounds (approximately 8
            cups) peeled peaches
        1 teaspoon whole cloves
        1 teaspoon whole allspice
        3 sticks cinnamon
      3½ pounds sugar
        ½ pint vinegar
           Brandy

Day 1: Halve most of peaches; leave stones in remainder. Place peaches in large container. Tie spices in spice bag or cheese cloth. Combine sugar, vinegar, and spice bag; bring to boil. Pour over peaches; let stand overnight.

Day 2: Drain fruit; bring syrup to boil. Pour over fruit; let stand overnight.

Days 3 and 4: Repeat process for Day 2.

Day 5: Remove fruit. Add ⅓ cup brandy for each cup of syrup. Return fruit to syrup. Cook until peaches are tender and syrup thickens. Place in hot sterile jars; seal in boiling water bath.

Cindy Collins Randolph

Pickled Beets

Preparation: Easy
Cooking Time: 45 Minutes

Yield: 6 Pints
Must Do Ahead

        3 quarts peeled small
            beets
        2 cups sugar
        2 sticks cinnamon
        1 tablespoon allspice
      1½ teaspoons salt
      3½ cups white vinegar
      1½ cups water

Wash and drain beets. (Leave 1 inch of stem and taproot to prevent bleeding.) Cover with boiling water; cook until tender. Combine remaining ingredients in separate saucepan; simmer 15 minutes. Pack beets into jars leaving ½-inch head space. Remove cinnamon from liquids; return to boil. Pour boiling hot liquid over beets, still leaving ½ inch of head space. Adjust lids. Process 30 minutes in boiling water.

Eleanor McGarity
Fort Valley, Georgia

Cranberry Chutney

A colorful condiment for the holidays. It also makes a nice gift.

Preparation: Easy
Cooking Time: 30 Minutes

Yield: 4 Pints
Must Do Ahead

4 cups (1 pound) cranberries
1 cup raisins
1½ cups honey
1 tablespoon ground cinnamon
1½ teaspoons ground ginger
¼ teaspoon ground cloves
¾ cup water
¼ cup vinegar
½ cup chopped almonds
½ cup chopped onion
1 medium apple, pared, cored, and chopped
½ cup thinly sliced celery

Combine berries, raisins, honey, cinnamon, ginger, cloves, water, and vinegar in large saucepan. Simmer 15 minutes. Stir in almonds, onion, apple, and celery. Simmer 15 minutes. Cool. Pour into jars. Chill. Keeps indefinitely in refrigerator.

Micronote: Place first 8 ingredients in large bowl. Cook on HIGH until mixture boils, 6 minutes. Reduce power to MEDIUM; cook 8-10 minutes. Add remaining ingredients; cook on HIGH 7-10 minutes. Continue as above.

Variation: Chutney Peaches - Place canned peach halves in baking dish. Fill with Cranberry Chutney. Dot with butter. Broil or microwave on HIGH until heated thoroughly.

Betty Davis Davis

Artichoke Relish

Preparation: Average
Cooking Time: 30-40 Minutes

Yield: 12-13 Pints
Must Do Ahead

6 pounds Jerusalem artichokes
3 pounds coarsely diced cabbage
4 cups coarsely diced onions
6 coarsely diced green sweet peppers
½ cup salt
Water
1 quart white vinegar, divided
1 (9-ounce) jar mustard
¾ cup flour
6 cups sugar
3 tablespoons mustard seed
1 tablespoon turmeric
1 tablespoon black pepper

Day 1: Scrub artichokes with wire brush until clean. Slice thinly into large, non-metal container. Add cabbage, onions, and peppers. Sprinkle with salt. Add water to cover. Stir until well mixed. Let stand overnight. Whisk together ½ cup vinegar, mustard, and flour to form smooth paste; refrigerate overnight.

Day 2: Drain vegetables well. Combine remaining vinegar, sugar, mustard seed, turmeric, and black pepper in large pot. Heat until sugar is dissolved and mixture is almost boiling. Add vegetables. Bring to boil; boil 10 minutes, stirring occasionally. Add mustard paste. Boil 5 more minutes, stirring to prevent sticking. Remove from heat. Pack into hot sterile jars; seal.

Margaret McGowan Peacock

Pepper Jelly

Preparation: Easy
Cooking Time: 10 Minutes

- ¼ cup finely chopped red or green hot peppers
- 1½ cups finely chopped sweet green peppers
- 6½ cups sugar
- 1½ cups vinegar
- 1 bottle liquid pectin
  Green or red food coloring (optional)

Yield: 3 Pints
Must Do Ahead

Mix peppers, sugar, and vinegar. Bring to boil; boil 3 minutes. Stir in pectin; boil 1 minute more. Remove from heat; let stand 5 minutes. Add food coloring if desired. Pour into hot sterile jars and seal.

Micronote: In large glass mixing bowl combine peppers, sugar, and vinegar. Cook on HIGH until mixture boils, approximately 5 minutes. Reduce power to MEDIUM; cook 3 minutes. Add pectin. Cook on HIGH 1 minute. Remove from oven; let stand 5 minutes. Continue as directed above.

Susan Henson Frost

Jalapeño Jelly

Preparation: Easy
Cooking Time: 5-10 Minutes

- ⅔ cup cider vinegar
- 1 small onion, cubed
- ½ medium green pepper, seeded and cut into squares
- 2-3 jalapeño peppers, seeded and quartered (Wear gloves when handling.)
- 2 cups sugar
- 1 (3-ounce) pouch liquid pectin

Yield: 1-2 Cups
Must Do Ahead

In blender combine vinegar, onion, and peppers. Blend at high speed for 25 seconds or until smooth. In medium saucepan heat pepper mix with sugar to boiling. Remove from heat; spoon off foam. Stir in pectin. Return to boiling; boil 1 minute. Pour into hot sterile jars. Cool to room temperature. Cover; refrigerate up to 2 months.

Micronote: Prepare ingredients as directed; place in large glass bowl. Bring to boil on HIGH, 2½ minutes. Spoon off foam; stir in pectin. Return to boil on HIGH; boil 1 minute. Pour into hot sterile jars.

B. Sanford Butts
Sparta, Georgia

Pepper Relish

Preparation: Average
Cooking Time: 20-25 Minutes

- 1 gallon bell peppers (half red, half green)
- 6 medium onions, peeled
- 4-6 pods hot pepper, washed and seeded
- 1 tablespoon flour
- 3 cups vinegar
- 2⅓ cups sugar
- 1 tablespoon salt
- ½ box mixed pickling spices, tied loosely in cloth

Yield: 5 Pints
Must Do Ahead

Wash and seed peppers. Quarter peppers and onions; grind all peppers and onions in food grinder or processor. Drain off liquid. Add flour to vegetables. In heavy aluminum 5 to 6-quart container combine vinegar, sugar, salt, and spice bag. Bring to boil. Add vegetables; return to boil over medium heat. Boil 15-20 minutes. Pack hot relish into hot sterile jars, leaving ½-inch head space. Adjust lids. Process 5 minutes in boiling water bath.

Dot Coleman Alfriend
Sparta, Georgia

Gourmet Hot Dog Relish

Transforms ordinary fare into an extraordinary treat.

Preparation: Average
Cooking Time: 20-30 Minutes

Yield: 8-9 Pints

1 gallon Jerusalem artichokes,
  washed and scrubbed
4 onions
4 sweet red peppers
3 cups sugar
2½ tablespoons salt
2 tablespoons celery salt
2 tablespoons mustard seed
1 tablespoon turmeric
½ teaspoon red pepper
3 pints vinegar

Grind artichokes, onions, and red peppers in food grinder or food processor. Combine with remaining ingredients. Bring to boil; cook 20-30 minutes. Pack in hot sterile jars; seal. Process 5 minutes in boiling water bath. (Pimiento may be substituted for red peppers, if they are not in season.)

Sally Butts Darden

Apple Butter

One of the specialties of the North Georgia area.

Preparation: Easy
Cooking Time: 45 Minutes

Yield: 3 Pints
Must Do Ahead

4 quarts sweet apple cider
2½ quarts peeled, quartered
   tart apples
2 cups sugar (white, brown,
   or mixed)
  Spices (cinnamon, cloves,
   or ginger to taste)

Boil cider to reduce to 2 quarts. Add apples; cook until very tender. Mash through colander or put through food mill. Add sugar and spices. Return to heat; cook until thick, stirring frequently. Pour into hot sterile jars; seal. Process 5 minutes in boiling water bath.

Cookbook Committee

Blackberry-Apple Jam

Preparation: Average
Cooking Time: 35 Minutes

Yield: 4-6 Pints
Must Do Ahead

5 cups peeled, chopped
   tart apples
2 teaspoons lemon juice
7 cups sugar, divided
6 cups blackberries

In large bowl mix apples with lemon juice and 3 cups sugar. Let stand about 2 hours. Combine blackberries and remaining sugar in large, heavy Dutch oven or kettle. Add apples; bring to boil over medium-high temperature. Lower heat to simmer; cook, stirring occasionally, until jellying point is reached (8°F above the boiling point of water if you use a candy thermometer or until syrup "sheets" off a metal spoon). As mixture thickens, stir frequently to prevent sticking. Pour boiling hot jam into hot sterile jars. When cool, seal with melted paraffin.

Addie DeLong Wright

Blackberry Jelly

Wild or cultivated cherry leaves add extra flavor, but if they are not available, this jelly is still delicious without them. For a taste treat just this side of heaven, bake a pan of biscuits or rolls; add butter and a generous helping of blackberry jelly. Wonderful!

Preparation: Average
Cooking Time: Approximately 1 Hour

Yield: 3 Pints
Must Do Ahead

1 gallon blackberries
   (1-1½ cups must be green berries)
   Water
4 handfuls cherry leaves,
   if available
   Sugar
   Juice of 1 lemon

Wash berries. Place in large kettle with barely enough water to cover; add cherry leaves. Boil until berries are tender. Strain juice through cheesecloth and measure. Place up to 5 cups juice into large, heavy kettle. (Do not cook more than 5 cups of juice at one time.) Add 1 cup sugar for each cup of juice; add lemon juice. Bring to rolling boil. Continue cooking until 2 drops fall as 1 from spoon (approximately 30 minutes). Pour into hot sterile jars. When cool, seal with melted paraffin.

Dot Coleman Alfriend
Sparta, Georgia

Rosé Wine Jelly

Preparation: Easy
Cooking Time: 10-15 Minutes

Yield: 5 Cups
Must Do Ahead

3 cups sugar
2 cups Rosé wine
6 ounces liquid fruit pectin

Combine sugar and wine in large saucepan. Bring to boil; cook until temperature of 214°F is reached and sugar is well dissolved. Stir occasionally. Add pectin; stir until mixed. Remove from heat. Pour into hot sterile jars. Seal with paraffin or refrigerate. (For gifts pour jelly into inexpensive wine glasses; seal with paraffin. Before paraffin completely hardens, slightly press holly sprig into surface. Add holiday bow to glass stem.)
Micronote: Combine sugar and wine in 5-quart casserole. Cook on HIGH for 2 minutes. Continue cooking until sugar dissolves (214°F on candy thermometer); stir occasionally. Add pectin; stir until mixed. Pour into jars. Seal with paraffin or refrigerate.

Cookbook Committee

Peach Preserves

Reserve extra syrup after filling jars - it's great over pancakes!

Preparation: Easy
Cooking Time: 20 Minutes
Oven Temperature: 300°F

Yield: 2 Pints
Must Do Ahead
Do Not Double

5 cups sliced or coarsely
   chopped peaches
3 cups sugar

Place peaches in large saucepan. Place sugar in shallow baking dish. Simultaneously: (1) warm peaches over medium heat and (2) heat sugar in 300°F oven for 5 minutes. Pour warm sugar over peaches. Stir and cook 12-15 minutes over medium-high heat, until syrup is clear and thickened. While peaches are cooking, invert 2 pint jars, 2 rings, and 2 lids in 3-4 inches of water in separate saucepan. Bring to boil. Carefully remove sterilized jars. Fill hot jars with peach preserves. Wipe jar tops well. Add a hot lid and ring to each jar. Screw tight. These will seal as they cool.

Jody Bacon Mulkey
Chattanooga, Tennessee

Peach and Pear Marmalade

A flavorful, unusual marmalade - another use for good Georgia peaches.

Preparation: Average
Cooking Time: 30 Minutes

Yield: 2 Pints
Must Do Ahead

3 large firm, ripe pears,
   peeled
3 large freestone peaches,
   peeled
1 orange
1 cup water
3 cups sugar
   Juice of 1 lime

Finely chop pears and peaches. Sliver orange rind; cut orange pulp finely, removing membrane and discarding seeds. In large kettle combine orange rind, pulp, and water; bring to boil. Cook until rind is tender and water is reduced by half. Add fruit, sugar, and lime juice; cook rapidly until marmalade is thick. Spoon into hot sterile jars; seal. Process 5 minutes in boiling water bath.

Paula Eubanks Smith

Blueberry Jam

Preparation: Average
Cooking Time: 15 Minutes

Yield: 4-5 Pints
Must Do Ahead

6 cups fresh blueberries,
   stemmed and washed
7 cups sugar
¼ cup lemon juice
1 (1-inch) stick cinnamon
2 (3-ounce) packages
   liquid fruit pectin

Place blueberries in Dutch oven. Using a wooden spoon crush approximately half the berries. Add sugar, lemon juice, and cinnamon. Bring mixture to boil, stirring often, until sugar dissolves. Cook at rolling boil for 2 minutes, stirring frequently; remove from heat. Discard cinnamon stick. Add pectin to blueberry mixture; stir 5 minutes. Skim off foam with metal spoon. Quickly pour jam into hot sterile jars, leaving ⅛-inch head space; cover at once with metal lids and bands. Process 5 minutes in boiling water bath.

Doris Porter Jones

Sweets

Blackberry

Blackberry (Rubus frondosus)

Valued as an important wildlife food and ground cover, the blackberry has long been appreciated for the taste of its ripe fruit and for its medicinal properties. In addition to the pleasure of eating freshly gathered blackberries with cream and sugar, many a Southern housewife surprises her family with a traditional summer favorite - a mouth-watering blackberry pie. This common summer fruit, well-guarded by thorns, makes a most delicious jam, flavored vinegar, or wine.

On Sweets

- Creaming shortening and sugar generally takes 7 minutes. Adding a little hot milk will aid the creaming process.
- To make whipped cream hold up under refrigeration, as in icing for a cake: Soften 2 teaspoons unflavored gelatin in 2 tablespoons cold water for every 2 cups whipping cream. Heat gelatin over hot water to dissolve. Cool. As cream is whipped, blend in dissolved gelatin.
- Waxed paper method for layering dough: Spread one layer of cookie dough over another; spoon second layer atop first layer. Gently press with waxed paper until evenly spread. Peel away paper.
- On a hot, humid day cook candy 2°F higher than would be called for in cold, dry weather.
- Sixteen to 18 graham crackers yield 1⅓ cups crumbs. Mix with ⅓ cup brown sugar, ½ teaspoon cinnamon, and ⅓ cup melted butter for 1 (9-inch) pie shell.
- Put dates or other sticky fruits in freezer for 1-2 hours before cutting up.
- To tint shredded or flaked coconut: place in a screw-top jar, add a few drops of food coloring, screw on top, and shake.
- Using too much flour when rolling pastry results in a tough crust. To reduce excess flour use a stockinette rolling pin cover.
- To prevent splitting, cracking, and breaking up of pastries - refrigerate dough an hour before rolling.
- Never knead pastry dough; handle as little as possible.
- To prevent soggy crusts in custard-type pies: brush the unbaked pie crust with egg white; bake at 425°F for 5-10 minutes before adding filling.
- To transfer rolled pastry to a pie plate: fold into quarters, place on pan, and unfold; or roll up over rolling pin and unroll over pie plate.
- For a fast topping on cakes: Place a paper doily on top and dust with confectioners' sugar. Gently remove doily.
- Make your own super-fine sugar by whirling granulated sugar in the blender or food processor.
- For quick and efficient flouring of baking pans, keep flour in a large shaker.
- For a fast icing on cupcakes, place a marshmallow on each shortly before removing from oven.
- Eight ounces pitted dates yield 1½ cups chopped dates.
- Partially freeze cheesecake before cutting for prettier slices.
- For miniature cheesecakes spoon desired cheesecake filling into 2-inch diameter petits four foil holders. Cook just until firm.
- To have pastry crust mix on hand: Blend 3 cups flour, 2 teaspoons sugar, and 1 teaspoon salt. Cut in 1 cup shortening. Store in covered container and refrigerate. Measure out amount needed and mix with just enough iced water to hold together. For a single 9-inch crust use 1-1¼ cups mix; for a double crust use 2-2¼ cups mix. This yields 4 cups mix; may be doubled or tripled.

Creole Fudge Cake

Preparation: Average
Cooking Time: 25-30 Minutes
Oven Temperature: 350°F

Yield: 1 (8-inch) 3-layer Cake
Must Partially Do Ahead

- 4 squares unsweetened chocolate
- 1 cup firmly packed light brown sugar
- ½ cup water
- 1 tablespoon instant coffee granules
- 1 cup sugar
- ½ cup butter or margarine, softened
- 3 eggs
- 2½ cups sifted cake flour
- 2 teaspoons baking powder
- ½ teaspoon baking soda
- ¼ teaspoon salt
- 1 cup mik
- Cocoa
- Coffee Buttercream Icing
- Chocolate shavings

Combine chocolate, brown sugar, water, and coffee in top of double boiler. Heat over simmering water until chocolate is melted; cool. Add sugar slowly to butter, beating at medium speed until blended. Add eggs, one at a time, beating well after each addition; continue beating until mixture is light and fluffy. Beat in cooled chocolate mixture. Sift together dry ingredients; add alternately with milk to creamed mixture. Divide batter among 3 (8-inch) round cake pans that have been greased and dusted with cocoa. Stagger pans in oven; bake at 350°F for 25-30 minutes. Cool 10 minutes in pans. Turn onto racks; refrigerate until cold. Frost between layers, on sides, and top with Coffee Buttercream Icing. Sprinkle with chocolate shavings. (For a smaller cake use 2 eggs and halve all other ingredients. Bake in a 9 x 9 x 2-inch pan.)

Coffee Buttercream Icing
- 2 tablespoons instant coffee granules
- ¼ cup hot water
- 1 cup butter or margarine, softened
- 2 egg yolks
- 6 cups sifted confectioners' sugar

Dissolve coffee in hot water. Cool. Blend butter and egg yolks at medium speed of electric mixer. Add confectioners' sugar alternately with coffee mixture; blend until smooth.

Jane Byerly Allgood

It is best to begin cake-making as early after breakfast as is convenient.
Mrs. Hill's New Cookbook circa 1890.

Lemon Cheese Cake with Divinity Icing

An elegant and delicious cake; takes some time to prepare, but just the thing for a special occasion.

Preparation: Complex
Cooking Time: 35-40 Minutes
Oven Temperature: 350°F

Yield: 1 (9-inch) 3-layer Cake
Must Do Ahead

1¾ cups sugar
¾ cup shortening
1 teaspoon vanilla extract
⅛ teaspoon salt
1 cup ice water
3 cups sifted flour, divided
1 tablespoon baking powder
6 egg whites
Lemon Filling
Divinity Icing

Cream sugar, shortening, vanilla, and salt until light and fluffy. Add water and 2 cups flour. Mix baking powder with remaining flour; add to creamed mixture alternately with egg whites, using 2 whites at a time. Do not overbeat. Grease, flour, and line with waxed paper 3 (9-inch) round layer pans. Pour batter into pans. Bake at 350°F for 35-40 minutes. Turn onto racks to completely cool. Spread Lemon Filling between layers. Frost with Divinity Icing.

Lemon Filling

¼ cup butter
¾ cup sugar
Grated rind and juice
of 2 large lemons
⅛ teaspoon salt
6 egg yolks, slightly beaten

In double boiler, melt butter over boiling water. Add sugar, lemon rind, juice, and salt. Slowly stir in egg yolks; cook, stirring constantly, until thick.
Micronote: Combine butter, sugar, lemon rind, juice, and salt. Cook on HIGH until sugar dissolves; stir once. Stir in egg yolks. Cook on MEDIUM until thick; stir occasionally.

Divinity Icing

3 cups sugar
½ cup water
¼ cup light corn syrup
⅛ teaspoon salt
3 egg whites, stiffly beaten
1 teaspoon vanilla extract

Combine sugar, water, corn syrup, and salt. Cook over moderate heat, using a candy thermometer, until temperature reaches 240°F or until mixture spins a good thread. Pour slowly over egg whites, beating constantly. Add vanilla. Continue beating until mixture reaches spreading consistency. (If frosting is too thin, add confectioners' sugar. If it is too thick, add hot water.)
Micronote: Cook sugar, water, syrup, and salt on HIGH to temperature of 240°F. Continue as directed above.

Louise Hendrix Forrester

Red Devil's Food Cake

Draw raves from your guests or just treat your family. A chocolate delight!

Preparation: Average
Cooking Time: 25-30 Minutes
Oven Temperature: 350°F

Yield: 1 (8-inch) 2-layer Cake
Must Do Ahead

1½ cups sugar
½ cup margarine, softened
2 eggs
¼ cup cocoa
¼ cup hot coffee
2 teaspoons red food coloring
2 cups flour
1 teaspoon salt
1 teaspoon baking soda
1 cup buttermilk

Cream sugar and margarine at medium speed of electric mixer. Beat in eggs. Make paste of cocoa, coffee, and food coloring. Stir into creamed mixture, blending well. Sift together dry ingredients; add alternately with buttermilk to creamed mixture. Pour batter into 2 greased and floured 8-inch cake pans. Bake for 25-30 minutes. Remove from pan onto wire racks; cool thoroughly. Spread Chocolate Filling between layers. Frost sides and top of cake with Fluffy White Icing.

Chocolate Filling

1½ cups confectioners' sugar
¼ teaspoon salt
¼ cup shortening
1 egg
1½ squares unsweetened
     chocolate, melted

Combine all ingredients in mixing bowl. Beat with electric mixer until light and fluffy.

Fluffy White Icing

1 cup sugar
⅓ cup water
⅓ teaspoon cream of tartar
2 egg whites, room
     temperature
1½ teaspoons vanilla extract

Combine sugar, water, and cream of tartar in a heavy saucepan. Cook over medium heat, without stirring, until mixture reaches 240°F on candy thermometer (thread stage). Meanwhile, beat egg whites until soft peaks form; continue to beat, slowly adding syrup mixture. Add vanilla; beat until icing reaches spreading consistency.
Micronote: Cook sugar, water, and cream of tartar on HIGH to temperature of 240°F. Continue as above.

Betty Gail Parker Gunter

Holiday Coconut Cake

The ultimate coconut cake - with a variation for every taste.

Preparation: Complex
Cooking Time: 45 Minutes
Oven Temperature: 350°F

Yield: 1 (8-inch) 3-layer Cake
Must Do Ahead

⅓ cup butter or
    margarine, softened
⅓ cup shortening
1¾ cups sugar
3 cups cake flour
3½ teaspoons baking powder
¾ teaspoon salt
1⅓ cups milk or
    fresh coconut juice
    plus milk to equal
    1⅓ cups
2 teaspoons vanilla extract
4 egg whites, stiffly beaten

Cream butter and shortening at medium speed of electric mixer. Add sugar **very** slowly, creaming until light and fluffy. Sift together flour, baking powder, and salt. Reduce speed to low. Add dry ingredients to creamed mixture alternately with milk, beating well after each addition. Stir in vanilla. Fold egg whites into batter. Pour into 3 greased and floured 8-inch cake pans. Bake at 350°F for 20-30 minutes. Turn out onto wire racks; cool completely. Fill and frost with Variation I or Variation II below.

Variation I:
Lemon Filling
1 cup + 2 tablespoons sugar
¼ cup cornstarch
1 cup + 2 tablespoons water
2 egg yolks, slightly beaten
2 tablespoons margarine
3 tablespoons lemon juice
1 tablespoon grated lemon
    rind
1 cup shredded coconut
    (optional)

Combine sugar and cornstarch in saucepan; gradually stir in water. Cook over medium heat, stirring constantly, until mixture boils and thickens; boil 1 minute. Slowly stir small amount of hot mixture into egg yolks; gradually add egg yolks to hot mixture in saucepan. Boil 1 minute longer, stirring constantly. Remove from heat; continue stirring until smooth. Stir in margarine, lemon juice, and rind. Cool. (Add 1-2 drops yellow food coloring for rich, yellow color, if desired.) Stir in coconut. Spread between cooled layers.
Micronote: Combine sugar, cornstarch, and water in large glass bowl; cook on HIGH 2½ minutes or until mixture boils; stir every 30-45 seconds. Boil 1 minute longer. Stir small amount of hot mixture into egg yolks; gradually add egg yolks to hot mixture. Cook 1 minute on HIGH. Stir in margarine, lemon juice, and rind. Cool. Continue as above.

Seven-Minute White Icing
1½ cups sugar
2 egg whites
5 tablespoons cold water
¼ teaspoon cream of tartar
1 teaspoon vanilla extract
1 cup finely grated
    fresh coconut

In top of double boiler place sugar, egg whites, water, and cream of tartar; beat until thoroughly blended. Place over rapidly boiling water; beat with electric hand mixer for seven minutes. Remove from heat; add vanilla. Continue beating until icing is of spreading consistency. Frost top and sides of cake. Sprinkle with fresh coconut. Refrigerate. (If coarser coconut texture and more taste is desired, use 1½ cups shredded fresh coconut in frosting and sprinkle another ½ cup coconut over frosted cake.)

Connie Wallis Dixon

Variation II:
Sour Cream Filling
   1¾ cups confectioners' sugar
   1½ cups grated fresh
         or frozen coconut
   ½ cup sour cream
   1 teaspoon vanilla extract
   ¼ teaspoon coconut extract

Combine all ingredients, mixing well. Spread between cake layers.

Coconut Divinity Icing
   ½ cup sugar
   ¼ cup light corn syrup
   2 tablespoons water
   2 egg whites, room
         temperature
   1 teaspoon vanilla extract
   4½ cups fresh or frozen
         grated coconut

Combine sugar, corn syrup, and water in heavy saucepan. Cover; bring to boil. Uncover; continue cooking over medium-high heat until mixture reaches 248°F on candy thermometer. Meanwhile, beat egg whites until stiff peaks form. Slowly pour hot syrup over egg whites, beating constantly until mixture has cooled and reached spreading consistency. Stir in vanilla. Frost top and sides of cake. Cover with coconut. Refrigerate.

Micronote: Combine sugar, corn syrup, and water in 4-cup glass measure. Cook on HIGH for 2 minutes. Stir once to dissolve sugar. Cook on HIGH until mixture reaches 248°F on candy thermometer (or spins a thread), approximately 4-6 minutes. Proceed as above.

Mary Conner Martin
Brenau College Tea Room

Best Birthday Cake

Preparation: Average
Cooking Time: 1 Hour
Oven Temperature: 325°F

Serves: 12-14
Must Do Ahead

   1 cup butter, softened
   ½ cup shortening
   3 cups sugar
   5 eggs
   3 cups unsifted flour
   ½ teaspoon baking powder
   ¼ teaspoon salt
   1 cup milk
   1 teaspoon vanilla extract
   1 teaspoon lemon or
         almond extract
      Decorator Icing (see
         following page)

Beat the butter and shortening at medium speed of electric mixer until fluffy. Add sugar; beat well. Add eggs, one at a time, beating well after each. Sift together flour, baking powder, and salt; add alternately with milk, beginning and ending with flour. Add extracts. Grease and flour desired pans. Bake at 325°F according to chart below.

Pan Size	Baking Time
1 (13 x 9-inch) sheet pan	1 hour
2 (8-inch) square pans	45-50 minutes
3 (8-inch) round pans	35-40 minutes

Remove from the oven; let stand in pan for 10 minutes. Remove from pan; cool completely. Frost with Decorator Icing.

Decorator Icing

½ cup butter or margarine,
    cold and firm
½ cup shortening
4 cups sifted confectioners'
    sugar
1 teaspoon vanilla extract
2 tablespoons milk

Cream butter and shortening in small bowl until fluffy. Add sugar, ½ cup at a time, beating until smooth. Add vanilla and milk. Beat well. (To thin, add more milk.)

Carolyn Cathey Brinson

German Chocolate Cake with Pineapple Filling

Preparation: Average
Cooking Time: 30 Minutes
Oven Temperature: 350°F

Yield: 1 (9-inch) 2-layer Cake
Must Partially Do Ahead

1 (4-ounce) package
    German sweet chocolate
¼ cup hot water
2 cups sugar
1 cup shortening
4 eggs, separated
1 cup buttermilk
1 teaspoon baking soda
2½ cups sifted flour
1 teaspoon salt
½ teaspoon vanilla extract
    Pineapple Filling

Melt chocolate in water; set aside. In large bowl beat sugar, shortening, and egg yolks until creamy. Mix buttermilk and soda; add alternately with flour to creamed mixture. Blend in chocolate, salt, and vanilla. Beat egg whites separately until stiff; fold into batter. Pour into 2 greased and floured 9-inch round cake pans. Bake at 350°F for 30 minutes. Turn onto wire racks to cool. Spread Pineapple Filling between layers and on top of cake.

Pineapple Filling

1 cup sugar
1 cup whipping cream
½ cup margarine
3 egg yolks
1 (20-ounce) can crushed
    pineapple, drained
1 (3½-ounce) can flaked
    coconut
1 cup chopped pecans
½ teaspoon vanilla extract

Combine sugar, cream, margarine, and egg yolks in heavy saucepan; cook and stir until thickened. Add pineapple, coconut, pecans, and vanilla; mix well.

Estelle Wimberly Thompson
Cochran, Georgia

Red Velvet Cake

This cake is what we would all like to be — rich and good-looking!

Preparation: Average
Cooking Time: 25-30 Minutes
Oven Temperature: 375°F

Yield: 1 (9-inch) 2-layer Cake
Must Partially Do Ahead

2 (1-ounce) bottles red
    food coloring
3 tablespoons sifted cocoa
1½ cups sugar
½ cup shortening
2 eggs
2¼ cups cake flour, unsifted
½ teaspoon salt
1 cup buttermilk
1 teaspoon vanilla extract
1 teaspoon almond extract
1 tablespoon vinegar
1 teaspoon baking soda
    Cream Cheese Nut Icing
    or Creamy Icing

Mix food coloring and cocoa to form paste. Add sugar, shortening, and eggs; cream thoroughly at medium speed of electric mixer. Sift together flour and salt; and add alternately, at low speed, to creamed mixture with buttermilk and extracts. Mix vinegar and soda; blend into batter. Pour into 2 greased and floured 9-inch layer pans. Bake at 375°F for 25-30 minutes. Turn onto wire racks to completely cool. Frost with Cream Cheese-Nut Icing or Creamy Icing.

Cream Cheese-Nut Icing

1 (8-ounce) package cream
    cheese, softened
½ cup margarine, softened
1 (16-ounce) box confectioners'
    sugar, sifted
2 teaspoons vanilla extract
⅓ cup chopped pecans
    (optional)

Combine cheese and margarine; cream well. Add sugar gradually, beating until smooth. Blend in vanilla. Spread on layers. Sprinkle top of cake with chopped nuts.

Debbie Holder Kelly

Creamy Icing

1 cup milk
3 tablespoons flour
1 cup butter or margarine
1 cup sugar
1 teaspoon vanilla extract

In a heavy saucepan add milk gradually to flour, stirring constantly. Cook and stir over low heat until very thick; cool. Cream butter, sugar, and vanilla until fluffy. Add to cooled flour mixture. Whip with electric mixer at high speed until mixture resembles whipped cream. Spread on cake. Cake should be refrigerated.

Diane Derrick Blalock

Blue Ribbon Carrot Cake with Cream Cheese Icing

Preparation: Average
Cooking Time: 35-40 Minutes
Oven Temperature: 350°F

Yield: 1 (9-inch) 3-layer Cake
Must Partially Do Ahead

2 cups flour
2 teaspoons baking powder
2 teaspoons ground cinnamon
1½ teaspoons baking soda
1½ teaspoons salt
2 cups sugar
1½ cups oil
4 eggs
2 cups finely grated carrots
1 (8½-ounce) can crushed pineapple, drained
½ cup chopped nuts
1 (3½-ounce) can flaked coconut (optional)
Cream Cheese Icing

Sift together flour, baking powder, cinnamon, baking soda, and salt into large mixing bowl. Add sugar, oil, and eggs; mix well. Add carrots, pineapple, nuts, and coconut. Blend thoroughly until moist. Grease 3 (9-inch) round cake pans; line with waxed paper. Divide batter equally among pans. Bake at 350°F for 35-40 minutes. Cool 10-15 minutes in pans. Turn onto wire racks; cool completely. Fill and frost layers with Cream Cheese Icing. Cake will keep covered in refrigerator for two weeks.

Cream Cheese Icing

½ cup butter, softened
1 (8-ounce) package cream cheese, softened
1 teaspoon vanilla extract
1 (16-ounce) box confectioners' sugar, sifted

Combine butter, cream cheese, and vanilla in small bowl. Cream well. Add sugar gradually, beating until smooth. If mixture is too thick, add small amount of milk to thin.

Jacqueline Mabry Frankum

Tennessee Jam Cake with Hermitage Icing

Preparation: Average
Cooking Time: 30 Minutes
Oven Temperature: 350°F

Yield: 1 (9-inch) 3-layer Cake
Must Do Ahead

1½ cups sugar
1 cup margarine, softened
1 cup seedless blackberry jam
4 large eggs
2½ cups flour
1 teaspoon baking soda
1 teaspoon ground nutmeg
1 teaspoon ground cinnamon
1 teaspoon ground cloves
¼ teaspoon salt
1 cup buttermilk
1½ cups chopped pecans
Hermitage Icing (see following page)

Cream sugar and margarine at medium speed of electric mixer. Add jam and eggs; mix well. Sift together flour, soda, spices, and salt. Reduce speed to low. Add dry ingredients alternately with buttermilk, mixing well after each addition. Fold in nuts. Pour into 3 greased and floured 9-inch layer pans. Stagger pans on oven racks. Bake at 350°F for 30-35 minutes, testing each layer separately to insure doneness. Cool in pans 10 minutes. Turn onto racks to cool completely. Fill and frost with Hermitage Icing. Prepare cake 4 to 5 days ahead; it becomes more moist with keeping.

Hermitage Icing

2 cups firmly packed
    light brown sugar
1 cup margarine
½ cup milk
6 cups sifted confectioners'
    sugar

Combine brown sugar, margarine, and milk in saucepan; bring to boil, stirring constantly (or microwave on HIGH until mixture boils). Cool 10 minutes. Gradually add confectioners' sugar, beating until smooth. If frosting stiffens before spreading is completed, add a few drops of milk.

Jean Osborn Sawyer

George Washington's Birthday Cake

Celebrate George's (or anyone else's) birthday with this tasty and colorful cake.

Preparation: Average
Cooking Time: 20-25 Minutes
Oven Temperature: 375°F

Yield: 1 (8-inch) 2-layer Cake
Must Partially Do Ahead

2½ cups sifted flour
1½ cups sugar
3½ teaspoons baking powder
1 teaspoon salt
½ cup shortening
¾ cup milk
¼ cup maraschino cherry
    juice
1 teaspoon vanilla extract
2 teaspoons almond extract
4 egg whites
¾ cup chopped nuts
18 maraschino cherries,
    drained and chopped
    Mt. Vernon Icing

Sift flour, sugar, baking powder, and salt together into mixing bowl. Cut in shortening. Combine milk and cherry juice. Gradually add liquid mixture and flavorings to dry ingredients. Beat 2 minutes. Beat in egg whites. Fold in nuts and cherries. Pour batter into 2 greased and floured 8 or 9-inch pans. Bake at 375°F for 20-25 minutes. Turn onto racks to cool completely. Fill and frost with Mt. Vernon Icing.

Mt. Vernon Icing

2 tablespoons shortening
2 tablespoons butter, softened
1 teaspoon almond extract
1 teaspoon vanilla extract
½ teaspoon salt
4 cups confectioners' sugar,
    sifted
9 tablespoons scalded cream
    Red food coloring

Combine shortening, butter, flavorings, and salt; blend well. Add sugar and cream alternately, mixing until icing is of spreading consistency. Add coloring by drops, mixing well after each addition, until desired pinkness is attained.

Cathy McLanahan Nix

Classic Pound Cake

Everyone needs a tried and true pound cake recipe; this is our favorite.

Preparation: Average
Cooking Time: 1 Hour
Oven Temperature: 350°F

Yield: 1 (10-inch) Cake
Must Do Ahead

2 cups sugar
1 cup butter, softened
4 eggs
3 cups twice-sifted flour
2 teaspoons baking powder
1 scant cup milk
1 teaspoon vanilla extract
½ teaspoon almond extract
1 teaspoon rum extract
(optional)
1 teaspoon lemon extract
(optional)

Cream sugar and butter thoroughly, until light and fluffy. Add eggs, one at a time, beating well after each addition. Combine flour and baking powder. Add dry ingredients alternately with milk, blending well. Blend in flavorings. Pour into greased and floured tube or Bundt pan. Bake at 350°F for 50 minutes - 1 hour. Cool in pan 10 minutes. Turn onto rack or plate to cool completely.

Jean Thompson Brannon

Six Flavor Pound Cake

A large, moist cake with a delicious blend of flavors.

Preparation: Average
Cooking Time: 1 Hour 45 Minutes
Oven Temperature: 300°F

Yield: 1 (10-inch) Cake
Must Do Ahead

3 cups sugar
1 cup butter, softened
½ cup shortening
5 large eggs
1 teaspoon vanilla extract
1 teaspoon coconut extract
1 teaspoon almond extract
1 teaspoon lemon extract
1 teaspoon rum extract
1 teaspoon vanilla butter
and nut extract
3 cups sifted flour
½ teaspoon baking powder
1 cup evaporated milk
Six Flavor Glaze

Cream sugar, butter, and shortening at medium speed of electric mixer. Add eggs, one at a time, beating well after each. Add extracts, one at a time, mixing thoroughly after each addition. Combine flour and baking powder; add alternately with milk, blending well at low speed. Pour into greased and floured 10-inch tube pan. Bake at 300°F for 1 hour 45 minutes. Pierce top of cake with toothpick. Pour cooled glaze over warm cake before removing from pan. Let stand 15-20 minutes. Turn onto plate. Cool completely.

Six Flavor Glaze

1 cup sugar
½ cup water
½ teaspoon of each
extract used in cake

Combine all ingredients in saucepan; cook over low heat, stirring constantly, until sugar melts. Cool.
Micronote: Cook all ingredients on HIGH until sugar melts; stir once.

Polly Cross Moore

Crunchy Pound Cake

Delicious served with ice cream and warm butterscotch sauce.

Preparation: Average
Cooking Time: 1 Hour 25 Minutes
Oven Temperature: 300°F

Yield: 1 (10-inch)Cake
Must Do Ahead

½ cup butter, softened
½ cup shortening
1 (8-ounce) package cream
    cheese, softened
2½ cups sugar
6 eggs
3 cups sifted flour, divided
1 teaspoon vanilla extract
1 (12-ounce) package
    butterscotch morsels
1 cup chopped nuts

Cream butter, shortening, cream cheese, and sugar at medium speed of electric mixer, beating until light and fluffy. Add eggs, one at a time, beating well after each addition. Fold in 2½ cups flour; stir in vanilla. Mix remaining ½ cup flour with butterscotch morsels and nuts; fold into batter. Pour into greased and floured 10-inch tube pan. Bake at 300°F for 1 hour 25 minutes. Cool in pan 15 minutes. Remove from pan to cool completely.

Pamela K. Spivey

Chocolate Pound Cake

Preparation: Average
Cooking Time: 1 Hour 20 Minutes
Oven Temperature: 300°F

Yield: 1 (10-inch) Cake
Must Do Ahead

3 cups sugar
1 cup butter, softened
½ cup shortening
5 eggs
3 cups flour
½ cup cocoa
½ teaspoon baking powder
¼ teaspoon salt
1 cup milk
1 teaspoon vanilla extract
    Fudge Icing

Cream sugar, butter, and shortening at medium speed of electric mixer. Add eggs, one at a time, beating well after each addition. Sift together flour, cocoa, baking powder, and salt. Combine milk and vanilla. Reduce mixer speed to low. Add dry ingredients and milk alternately to creamed mixture, beating well after each addition. Pour into greased and floured 10-inch tube pan. Bake at 300°F for 1 hour 20 minutes. Cool 10 minutes in pan. Turn onto rack or plate to cool completely. Frost with Fudge Icing. Let stand until icing is thoroughly cooked and set.

Fudge Icing

2 cups sugar
⅔ cup milk
½ cup butter
¼ cup cocoa
¼ teaspoon salt
1 teaspoon vanilla extract

Combine all ingredients except vanilla in heavy saucepan. Bring to boil; boil 2 minutes, stirring constantly. Remove from heat; add vanilla. Beat by hand or with electric mixer until creamy.
Micronote: Combine all ingredients except vanilla in glass bowl. Cook on HIGH 4-5 minutes, until mixture boils, stirring twice. Boil on HIGH 2 minutes. Add vanilla. Beat until creamy.

Kayanne Shoffner Massey

Buttermilk Pound Cake

A good all purpose pound cake which may also be made in layers.

Preparation: Average
Cooking Time: 1 Hour 30 Minutes
Oven Temperature: 300°F

Yield: 1 (10-inch) cake

2½ cups sugar
1 cup shortening
½ cup margarine, softened
4 eggs
½ teaspoon baking soda
1 tablespoon water
1 cup buttermilk
1 tablespoon vanilla extract
1 tablespoon bourbon
3½ cups sifted flour
½ teaspoon salt

Cream sugar, shortening, and margarine at medium speed of electric mixer until thoroughly blended. Add eggs one at a time, beating well after each addition. Dissolve soda in water. Add to creamed mixture along with buttermilk, vanilla, and bourbon; blend well. Add flour and salt. Beat until fluffy. Turn into greased and floured tube pan (or layer pans). Bake at 300°F for 1 hour 30 minutes or until cake tests done. (Bake layers approximately 30 minutes.)

Patsy Lothridge Hicks

Brown Sugar Pound Cake with Caramel Icing

Preparation: Average
Cooking Time: 1-1½ Hours
Oven Temperature: 325°F

Yield: 1 (10-inch) Cake
Must Partially Do Ahead

1 (16-ounce) box light
    brown sugar
1 cup granulated sugar
1½ cups butter or margarine
5 large eggs
3 cups sifted flour
1 cup milk
1 cup chopped pecans
1 teaspoon vanilla extract
½ teaspoon baking powder
    Caramel Icing

Cream sugars and butter at medium speed of electric mixer. Add eggs, one at a time, beating well after each addition. Reduce speed to low. Add flour and milk alternately. Add pecans, vanilla, and baking powder. Line tube pan with waxed paper; grease and flour. Pour batter into pan. Bake at 325°F for 1-1½ hours, until cake tests done. Cool 10 minutes in pan. Turn onto rack or plate to cool completely. Frost with Caramel Icing.

Caramel Icing

1 cup firmly packed light
    brown sugar
½ cup margarine
⅓ cup evaporated milk
2 cups confectioners' sugar
¼ cup chopped pecans
    (optional)

In small saucepan heat brown sugar and margarine over medium heat to boiling. Add evaporated milk. Boil and stir 2 minutes. Remove from heat; cool. Place cooled mixture in small mixing bowl. Gradually beat in confectioners' sugar until smooth. (Add more confectioners' sugar if icing is too thin.) Garnish frosted cake with pecans.

Micronote: Combine sugar, margarine, and milk. Cook on HIGH until mixture boils. Stir to dissolve sugar and completely melt margarine. Cook on HIGH 4 more minutes. Continue as above.

Karen Turner Syfan

Chocolotta Cake

Preparation: Average
Cooking Time: 1 Hour
Oven Temperature: 350°F

Yield: 1 (10-inch) Cake

2 cups sugar
1 cup butter
4 eggs
1 cup chocolate syrup
2¼ cups flour
½ teaspoon salt
1 cup buttermilk
¼ teaspoon baking soda
7 (1.45-ounce) Hershey
    chocolate bars or
    1 (8-ounce) Hershey
    chocolate bar

Cream sugar and butter at medium speed of electric mixer. Add eggs, one at a time, beating well after each addition. Blend in syrup. Sift together flour and salt. Combine buttermilk and soda. Reduce speed to low. Add dry ingredients to chocolate mixture alternately with buttermilk. Melt chocolate bars in double boiler over hot water. Blend into batter. Pour batter into greased and floured 10-inch tube pan or Bundt pan. Bake at 350°F for 1 hour 15 minutes or until cake tests done. Cool in pan 10 minutes. Turn onto rack or plate.

Mimi Jackson Fox

French Crunch Cake

Delicious served with fresh strawberries and Coffee Mocha Punch (page 4).

Preparation: Average
Cooking Time: 55 Minutes-1 Hour
Oven Temperature: 350°F

Yield: 1 (10-inch) Cake
Must Partially Do Ahead

Crunch

⅓ cup butter, melted
    (no substitute)
⅓ cup sugar
⅓ cup fine bread crumbs,
    toasted
⅔ cup finely chopped pecans

Combine melted butter, sugar, and crumbs. Mix until crumbly; stir in pecans. Grease 10-inch tube pan; line with waxed paper. Press mixture firmly onto bottom and halfway up sides of pan; set aside.

Cake

½ cup butter, softened
1 cup sugar
2 eggs
2 tablespoons rum or
    rum extract
2 cups sifted flour
2 teaspoons baking powder
⅔ cup milk
    Rum Glaze

Cream butter at medium speed of electric mixer until light. Add sugar, creaming well. Beat in eggs, one at a time. Add rum. Sift together flour and baking powder. Reduce mixer speed to low. Fold in dry ingredients alternately with milk. Carefully spoon batter into crumb-lined pan. Bake at 350°F for 55 minutes-1 hour. Remove from oven. Cool in pan for 2 minutes; turn onto rack to cool completely. Cover with Rum Glaze.

Rum Glaze

2 cups confectioners' sugar
2 tablespoons melted butter
1½ tablespoons rum or
    rum extract
1 tablespoon boiling water

Combine all ingredients, blending until smooth.

Virginia Parks Souther

Lemon-Pecan Cake

An excellent holiday alternative to fruitcake. Store in a tightly covered container with sliced apple or sprinkle with rum, wine, or bourbon to keep it moist. It also freezes well.

Preparation: Average
Cooking Time: 2-2½ Hours
Oven Temperature: 250°F

Yield: 1 (10-inch) Cake
Must Do Ahead

2¼ cups sugar
2 cups butter, softened
6 eggs
4 cups flour
1 (2-ounce) bottle lemon extract
3½ cups pecan halves (1 pound)
2¾ cups white raisins (1 pound)

Cream sugar and butter at medium speed of electric mixer until light and fluffy. Add eggs, one at a time, beating well after each addition. Reduce speed to low. Add flour, blending well. Stir in extract, pecans, and raisins. Spoon batter into well-greased and floured 10-inch tube pan. Bake at 250°F for 2-2½ hours. Remove from pan; cool completely. Store in tightly covered container in refrigerator or other cool place. Let stand at least 1 day before slicing.

Margaret Stout Ellett

Thirty-one cakes, dampened with whiskey, bask on window sills and shelves. Who are they for? Friends. Not necessarily neighbor friends: indeed, the larger share are intended for persons we've met maybe once, perhaps not at all. People who've struck our fancy.

Truman Capote, *Selected Writings of Truman Capote*
Random House, Inc., Copyright 1966. Used with permission.

Amazin' Raisin Cake

Preparation: Average
Cooking Time: 45 Minutes
Oven Temperature: 350°F

Yield: 1 (9-inch) 2-layer Cake
Must Partially Do Ahead

3 cups unsifted flour
2 cups sugar
2 teaspoons baking soda
1½ teaspoons ground cinnamon
½ teaspoon ground nutmeg
½ teaspoon salt
¼ teaspoon ground cloves
1 cup mayonnaise
⅓ cup milk
2 eggs, slightly beaten
3 cups peeled chopped apples
1 cup raisins
½ cup coarsely chopped walnuts
2 cups whipped cream (optional)

Combine dry ingredients in large mixing bowl. In separate bowl mix mayonnaise, milk, and eggs, blending well. Add to dry ingredients. Beat with electric mixer for 2 minutes. Stir in apples, raisins, and walnuts. Pour into 2 greased and floured 9-inch round cake pans. Bake at 350°F for 45 minutes. Cool in pans 10 minutes. Remove from pans to cool completely. Better when layers are prepared 1-2 days ahead. Just before serving, fill and frost with whipped cream. [Also good with Mother's Caramel Icing (page 326) or Burnt Caramel Icing (page 326).]

Barbara Eberhart Griffin

Mom's Fruitcake

Great Christmas gift for a special friend; it can be made in October for use at Thanksgiving and Christmas. A very special version of a holiday tradition.

Preparation: Complex
Cooking Time: 3-4 Hours
Oven Temperature: 275°F

Yield: 3 (9-inch) Cakes
Must Do Ahead

1 pound Brazil nuts
1 pound dark raisins
1 pound light raisins
2 cups port wine, divided
4 cups sugar
2 cups margarine, softened
8 eggs
2 cups honey or light
    corn syrup
1 cup milk
5 cups flour
2 tablespoons baking powder
1 tablespoon baking soda
2 teaspoons ground cloves
2 teaspoons ground cinnamon
1 teaspoon salt
1 pound candied cherries,
    chopped
1 pound candied pineapple,
    chopped
1 pound candied mixed
    fruit
2 quarts chopped pecans
1 pint fig preserves,
    undrained (optional)
1 pint watermelon preserves
    (optional)

Day before: Freeze Brazil nuts overnight for easy removal from shells. Soak dark and light raisins overnight in ½ cup port wine.
Baking day: Shell and chop Brazil nuts; set aside. Cream sugar and margarine at medium speed of electric mixer until light and fluffy. Add eggs, honey, milk, flour, baking powder, soda, cloves, cinnamon, and salt. Mix well. Drain raisins, reserving port. Lightly coat raisins, Brazil nuts, candied fruits, and pecans with extra flour. Fold fruits (including figs and preserves) and nuts into batter. Divide batter between three greased and floured 9-inch tube pans. Bake at 275°F for 3-4 hours. Remove from oven; pour about ½ cup port wine over each cake. Remove from pans. When cool wrap each cake well. Will keep in cool place for several months. (Recipe can be reduced to a third to make one 9-inch cake. Bake at 275°F for 1 hour 20 minutes.)

Joan Driskell Hopkins

Simon brought in pies of three kinds, and a small, deadly plum pudding, and a cake baked cunningly with whiskey and nuts and fruits and ravishing as odors of heaven...; and, at last, with an air sibylline and solemnly profound, a bottle of port.

William Faulkner, *Sartoris*

Granny's Date Nut Cake

Preparation: Average
Cooking Time: 1 Hour
Oven Temperature: 350°F

Yield: 1 (10-inch) Cake
Must Do Ahead

1 (8-ounce) package dates,
   cut in thirds
1 cup chopped nuts
1 cup buttermilk
1 teaspoon baking soda
1 cup sugar
¾ cup butter
2 well beaten egg yolks
2½ cups sifted flour
1 teaspoon baking powder
2 stiffly beaten egg whites
   Citrus Glaze

Soak dates and nuts in buttermilk and soda. Cream sugar and butter at medium speed of electric mixer. Beat in egg yolks. Stir in date mixture. Sift together flour and baking powder; gradually blend into creamed mixture. Fold in egg whites. Pour into greased and floured 10-inch tube pan. Bake at 350°F for 1 hour. Cool slightly. Turn onto plate. Pour Citrus Glaze over warm cake. Let stand until cool.

Citrus Glaze

2 scant cups sugar
   Grated rind and juice of
    2 oranges

Combine sugar, juice, and rind; stir to dissolve sugar.

Louise Hendrix Forrester

Confetti Christmas Cake

A gorgeous and delicious holiday dessert. Nice for a buffet or a large family dinner. Light enough to follow a big meal perfectly.

Preparation: Average

Serves: 12-16
Must Do Ahead

1½ cups golden raisins
   Boiling water
2 envelopes unflavored gelatin
½ cup cold water
1 cup hot water
1 cup sugar
½ teaspoon salt
1 cup orange juice concentrate
2 cups whipping cream, whipped
⅔ cup candied fruit
   (mixture of red and
   green cherries and
   pineapple)
½ cup chopped pecans
1-2 packages split ladyfingers

Cover raisins with boiling water. Let stand 10 minutes; drain. Soften gelatin in cold water; add hot water, stirring to dissolve. Stir in sugar, salt, and orange juice concentrate; blend thoroughly. Chill until thick. Fold whipped cream into orange mixture along with raisins, candied fruit, and pecans. Line bottom and sides of a 10-inch springform pan with ladyfingers. (Ladyfingers may need to be trimmed to fit pan.) Carefully spoon fruit mixture over ladyfinger lining. Refrigerate until congealed. Keeps well for several days.

Sally Butts Darden

Fig Preserve Cake

Preparation: Easy
Cooking Time: 40 Minutes
Oven Temperature: 350°F

Yield: 1 (13 x 9-inch) Cake
Must Do Ahead

2 cups flour
1½ cups sugar
1 cup oil or melted margarine
1 cup buttermilk
1 cup fig preserves, mashed
1 cup chopped nuts
(optional)
3 eggs
1 teaspoon baking soda
1 teaspoon ground cinnamon
1 teaspoon ground cloves
1 teaspoon vanilla extract
Buttermilk Glaze
Whipped cream (optional)
Ground nutmeg (optional)

Combine all ingredients. Blend well. Pour into greased and floured 13 x 9-inch pan. Bake at 350°F for 40 minutes or until cake tests done. (May also be made in round layers.) Pour Buttermilk Glaze slowly over hot cake. Cool. Cut into squares; garnish each square with a dollop of whipped cream and sprinkle with nutmeg.

Variation: Prune Cake - Substitute 1 cup cooked, chopped prunes for fig preserves.

Buttermilk Glaze

1 cup sugar
½ cup margarine
½ cup buttermilk
½ teaspoon baking soda
½ teaspoon vanilla extract

Combine all ingredients in medium saucepan. Bring to boil; boil 4 minutes.
Micronote: Cook all ingredients on HIGH until mixture boils; stir. Boil on HIGH 4 minutes. Proceed as above.

Cheryl Clark Brown

Fresh Peach Meringue Cake

A Phi Mu favorite at the University of Georgia; from the recipes of Mrs. Haney, a Phi Mu House Mother who had a special gift for preparing and serving food.

Preparation: Average
Cooking Time: 30 Minutes
Oven Temperature: 325°F

Yield: 2 (9-inch) Cakes
Must Partially Do Ahead

1 box white cake mix
4 egg whites
1¼ cups sugar
¾ cups chopped nuts (pecans, walnuts, or almonds)
Vanilla ice cream
Sliced fresh peaches

Prepare cake mix according to package instructions. Spread in 2 greased and floured 8-inch round cake pans or springform pans. Beat egg whites until stiff. Gradually add sugar, beating thoroughly. Spread meringue over cake batter. Sprinkle with chopped nuts. Bake at 325°F for 30 minutes, or until center tests done. Cool. Cut into pie-shaped wedges. Top each wedge with a scoop of vanilla ice cream and sliced fresh peaches. (If fresh peaches are not available, other fresh fruit or berries may be substituted.)

Cathy McLanahan Nix

Pineapple Upside Down Cake

An old favorite that's sure to please.

Preparation: Average
Cooking Time: 45 Minutes
Oven Temperature: 325°F

Yield: 1 (13 x 9 x 2-inch) Cake

1¼ cups margarine or butter,
    divided
1¼ cups light brown sugar
1 (10-ounce) jar maraschino
    cherries, drained and
    halved
1 (20-ounce) can crushed
    pineapple, drained
    (reserve juice)
1½ cups sugar
3 medium eggs
2 cups sifted flour
1 teaspoon baking powder
    Reserved pineapple juice
    plus milk to equal 1
    cup liquid
1 teaspoon vanilla extract
    Vanilla ice cream
    (optional)

Melt ½ cup margarine in bottom of 12-inch cast iron skillet or 13 x 9 x 2-inch pan. (May be done as oven preheats.) Sprinkle brown sugar over margarine, dot with cherries, and evenly spread with pineapple. Set aside. Cream remaining ¾ cup margarine and sugar at medium speed of electric mixer. Beat in eggs. Sift flour together with baking powder. Reduce speed to low. Add dry ingredients alternately with milk-juice liquid; blend thoroughly. Add vanilla. Pour batter over sugar-fruit mixture in pan. Bake 45 minutes or until done. Remove from oven; let stand 10 minutes. Loosen edges with knife; turn out onto serving platter. Let cool completely or serve warm with ice cream.

Dorothy Dudley McLanahan
Elberton, Georgia

Grandmamma's Gingerbread

Preparation: Average
Cooking Time: 30-40 Minutes
Oven Temperature: 350°F

Serves: 12

½ cup margarine
½ cup sugar
1 egg
1 cup molasses
2½ cups sifted flour
1 teaspoon ground cinnamon
1 teaspoon ground ginger
1 teaspoon ground cloves
½ teaspoon salt
1½ teaspoons baking soda
1 cup hot water
    Whipped cream (optional)
    Lemon Fondue Sauce (page 358)
    (optional)

Cream margarine and sugar with electric mixer. Add egg and molasses; blend well. Sift together dry ingredients; add to batter. Add hot water; beat until smooth. Turn into greased 13 x 9-inch pan. Bake at 350°F for 30-40 minutes. Top with whipped cream or serve warm with Lemon Fondue Sauce (page 358).

Sandra Gilmer Souther

Cheesecake Receipt

Loosen your belt; throw away the calorie-counter! This is it...the richest, creamiest cheesecake ever. Serve with a fruit topping or whipped cream.

Preparation: Average
Cooking Time: 2 Hours 10 Minutes
Oven Temperature: Crust: 350°F
                                    Cake: 450°F

Serves: 12
Must Do Ahead

Crust

  2½ **cups crushed vanilla wafers**
  ½ **cup sugar**
  ½ **cup chopped pecans**
     (optional)
  ½ **cup margarine, melted**

Combine crumbs, sugar, and pecans. Stir in margarine. Press onto bottom and sides of 9-inch springform pan. Bake at 350°F for 10 minutes. Cool.

Filling

  5 **(8-ounce) packages cream**
     cheese, softened
  1¾ **cups sugar**
  3 **tablespoons flour**
  ¼ **teaspoon vanilla extract**
  5 **eggs + 2 egg yolks**
  ½ **cup whipping cream**
     Strawberry or Blueberry
     Glaze (optional)

Blend cheese, sugar, flour, and vanilla at high speed of electric mixer. Add eggs and yolks, one at a time; beat until smooth, occasionally scraping bowl with spatula. Beat in cream. Pour into crust. Bake at 450°F for 10 minutes. Reduce temperature to 250°F; bake 2 hours more. Cool completely; refrigerate. To serve remove sides of pan. Top with Strawberry or Blueberry Glaze, if desired.

Strawberry Glaze

  ⅔ **cup frozen strawberries,**
     thawed
  1 **tablespoon cornstarch**

Combine strawberries and cornstarch in small saucepan. Bring to boil; cook 3 minutes, stirring constantly. Cool completely. Pour on top of cake; let drizzle down sides. (If fresh berries are available, arrange, sliced or whole, atop cake. Pour glaze over all.)

Blueberry Glaze

  1 **cup fresh blueberries**
  6 **tablespoons water, divided**
  ¼ **cup sugar**
  2 **teaspoons unflavored gelatin**
  ½-1 **teaspoon lemon juice**
  ¼ **teaspoon ground cinnamon**

Place berries and 2 tablespoons water in small saucepan. Cook until berries burst, about 3 minutes. Press through sieve into ⅓ cup measure; set aside. In same saucepan combine remaining water, sugar, and gelatin. Let stand 1 minute. Add strained berries. Cook and stir over medium heat until gelatin is dissolved. Stir in lemon juice and cinnamon. Chill until consistency of unbeaten egg whites, 5-10 minutes.

Frances Jolley Syfan
Brenda Barr
Tennessee State Department of Education

Pumpkin Cheesecake

Don't be fooled into passing this one by. A very special dessert that's not "for pumpkin lovers only." Trust us! This is truly extraordinary.

Preparation: Average
Cooking Time: 55 Minutes
Oven Temperature: Crust: 425°F
                Cake: 325°F
                Topping: 425°F

Serves: 12-15
Must Do Ahead

Crust

1½ **cups graham cracker crumbs**
⅓ **cup ground almonds**
½ **teaspoon ground ginger**
½ **teaspoon ground cinnamon**
⅓ **cup butter, melted**

Mix crumbs, almonds, ginger, and cinnamon. Stir in butter. Press onto bottom of 10-inch springform pan. Bake at 425°F for 10 minutes. Remove pan from oven; reduce temperature to 325°F.

Filling

4 **(8-ounce) packages cream cheese, softened**
1¼ **cups sugar**
3 **tablespoons maple syrup**
3 **tablespoons cognac or brandy**
1 **teaspoon ground ginger**
1 **teaspoon ground cinnamon**
½ **teaspoon ground nutmeg**
4 **eggs, room temperature**
1 **cup cooked pumpkin**
¼ **cup whipping cream**

Beat cream cheese at high speed of electric mixer until smooth. Gradually add sugar, beating until fluffy and light. Add syrup, cognac, ginger, cinnamon, and nutmeg; blend well. Add eggs, one at a time, beating well after each addition. Add pumpkin and cream; mix well. Pour into prepared crust. Bake at 325°F for 45 minutes. Turn off oven. Do not open oven door during baking or for 1 hour thereafter. Remove cake after 1 hour. Return oven to 425°F.

Topping

2 **cups sour cream**
¼ **cup sugar**
1 **tablespoon maple syrup**
1 **tablespoon cognac or brandy**
¼ **cup almonds, sautéed in butter**

Blend sour cream, sugar, syrup, and cognac. Spread over cake. Bake at 425°F for 10 minutes. Allow to cool to room temperature for 1 hour. Arrange almonds around top edges of cake. Chill at least 3 hours before removing form.

David Flanary
Houston, Texas

Chocolate Cheesecake

Can be made up to one week in advance; it improves with age.

Preparation: Average
Cooking Time: 1 Hour 40 Minutes
Oven Temperature: Crust 400°F
                       Cake: 475°F

Serves: 18
Must Do Ahead

Crust

- 1¼ cups flour
- ¼ cup sugar
- ¾ cup butter or margarine, softened
- 1 egg yolk

Combine flour and sugar. Cut in butter until small crumbs form. Add egg yolk. Process until smooth. Press ⅓ of dough onto bottom of 10-inch springform pan. Wrap remaining dough in plastic; refrigerate. Bake crust at 400°F for 8 minutes; cool. Press remaining dough around sides of pan to within 1 inch of top; do not bake.

Filling

- 5 (8-ounce) packages cream cheese, softened
- 1¾ cups sugar
- 2 egg yolks
- 3 tablespoons flour
- 5 eggs
- 1 (6-ounce) package semi-sweet chocolate bits, melted
- ¼ cup milk
- 2 tablespoons Amaretto or 1 teaspoon almond extract (optional)
- ¼ teaspoon salt
  Whipped cream (optional)
  Semi-sweet chocolate curls (optional)

In large electric mixer bowl beat cream cheese at medium speed until smooth. Reduce speed to low; beat in sugar, egg yolks, and flour. Add remaining ingredients; blend well. Increase speed to medium; beat 5 minutes, scraping sides of bowl occasionally. Pour into prepared pan. Bake at 475°F for 12 minutes. Lower oven temperature to 300°F; bake 50 minutes more. Turn oven off; let cheesecake remain in oven for 30 minutes. Remove to rack. Cool 30 minutes. Cover and refrigerate. To serve remove sides of pan; loosen cake and slide onto serving plate. Garnish with whipped cream and semi-sweet chocolate curls as desired.

Marquita Croft Nix

Fudge Cupcake Supreme

Preparation: Average
Cooking Time: 30 Minutes
Oven Temperature: 325°F

Yield: 24 Cupcakes
Must Partially Do Ahead

- 4 (1-ounce) squares semi-sweet chocolate
- 1 cup margarine
- 1½ cups chopped pecans
- 1¾ cups sugar
- 1 cup flour
- 4 eggs, beaten
- 1 teaspoon vanilla extract

Melt chocolate and margarine in heavy saucepan over low heat. Stir in pecans. Set aside to cool. Combine sugar and flour. Add eggs and vanilla, blending well. Stir in chocolate, mixing well. Pour into muffin pans lined with cupcake papers. Bake at 325°F for 30 minutes. Cool on wire racks. If icing is desired try Fudge Icing (page 315), Easy Peanut Butter Icing (page 326), or Decorator Icing (page 310).

Joyce Jackson Rabb

Mother's Caramel Icing

Recipe demands care in achieving exactly the right consistency; but when you taste it, we think you will agree it's worth the effort.

Preparation: Average
Cooking Time: 20-30 Minutes

Yield: Frosts 1 (2-layer) Cake

3 cups sugar
1 (13-ounce) can evaporated milk
½ cup margarine
⅛ teaspoon salt
1 teaspoon vanilla extract

Combine all ingredients except vanilla in deep saucepan; cook and stir over medium-high heat until mixture boils. Reduce heat to very low; cook, stirring occasionally, until mixture reaches 235°F on candy thermometer (soft-ball stage). Remove from heat. Add vanilla. Beat with electric mixer until of creamy spreading consistency, 10-15 minutes. **Micronote:** Cook on HIGH, covered, for 5 minutes, stirring once. Continue to cook on HIGH, uncovered, until 235°F (soft-ball stage) is reached, about 10 additional minutes. Beat with electric mixer as above.

Cheryl Gibbons McElveen

Burnt Caramel Icing

An old Southern recipe. It still can't be beat.

Preparation: Average
Cooking Time: 20-25 Minutes

Yield: Frosting for 3-Layer Cake

3 cups sugar, divided
1 cup milk
½ cup butter
⅛ teaspoon baking soda

Place 2½ cups sugar in heavy saucepan; add milk, butter, and soda. Bring to boil over medium heat, stirring well. Place remaining ½ cup sugar in iron skillet; cook over medium heat, stirring constantly, until sugar is browned and melted. Add to first mixture, stirring constantly. Cook over medium heat until mixture reaches 240°F on candy thermometer. Remove from heat; beat with large spoon until cooled and thickened. Use to fill and frost 3-layer cake.

Patsy Spiers Mercer

Easy Peanut Butter Icing

Try this quick icing on banana bread cupcakes.

Preparation: Easy

Yield: Frosts 2 Dozen Cupcakes

2 cups confectioners' sugar
⅔ cup chunk style peanut butter
⅓ cup evaporated milk
¼ cup margarine, softened
Few grains salt

Combine all ingredients in large mixing bowl; beat at low speed until well blended. Reduce speed to medium. Beat until fluffy and light.

Elaine Matthews Ralston

Southern-Style Fried Pies

There is nothing more typical of a North Georgia autumn than sweet, crisp fried pies filled with the fruits of the summer's harvest. They are sold on every corner at the many fairs and festivals of the season. Enjoy, and think of the heritage of the hills.

Preparation: Average
Cooking Time: 2-3 Minutes
Oven Temperature: 350°F

Yield: 1 Dozen Pies

Filling

- 2 cups cooked, drained, and mashed dried fruit (apples, peaches, etc.)
- ¼ cup butter or margarine
- ⅓ cup sugar

Combine all ingredients. Stir well to melt butter and sugar. Set aside to cool.

Pastry

- 3 cups flour
- ¼ cup sugar
- 1 teaspoon salt
- ¾ cup shortening
- 1 egg, beaten
- ¼ cup cold water
- 1 teaspoon vinegar
- Butter (optional)
- Sugar (optional)

Mix flour, sugar, and salt. Using pastry blender or food processor, cut in shortening until mixture resembles cornmeal. Combine egg, water, and vinegar. Sprinkle over flour mixture or add to food processor with motor running. Process until mixture clings together and forms ball. Divide dough in half. Roll each half very thin. Cut into circles, 5 inches in diameter. Combine pastry scraps and repeat until all dough is used. Place 2 tablespoons cooled fruit mixture on each circle. Fold pastry in half to encase fruit. Crimp edges with fork. Prick top twice with fork for ventilation. To fry: Heat ¼-inch depth of oil in skillet at 375°F. Gently place pies, a few at a time, in hot oil. Cook until brown on both sides, turning once. Drain on absorbent toweling. For extra richness brush each side with melted butter and sprinkle lightly with granulated sugar. Serve hot or cold. To bake: Melt ½ cup butter or margarine. Generously brush both sides of each pie with melted butter. Place on lightly greased baking sheet. Bake at 350°F for 30 minutes or until golden brown. Cool on wire rack.

Jane Hix Oliver

When you are served a piece of pie, cut the point off and save it for the last bite; make a wish and it will come true.

A Treasury of Georgia Folklore, by Ronald G. Killion and Charles T. Walker
(Atlanta; Cherokee Publishing Company), 1983. Used with permission.

Cheesy Apple Pie

The cheese pastry gives it that extra zest.

Preparation: Average
Cooking Time: 1 Hour
Oven Temperature: 400°F

Yield: 1 (9-inch) Pie
Must Partially Do Ahead

Cheese Pastry

      2 **cups flour**
    ½-l **cup grated sharp cheese**
      ½ **teaspoon salt**
     ⅔ **cup cold butter**
    4-5 **tablespoons ice water**

In food processor or by hand, mix flour, cheese, and salt. Cut in butter. Add ice water slowly with processor running, or mix lightly with fork. Wrap and chill. Flour board **very** well. Roll half of dough for bottom crust. Carefully transfer to 9-inch pie pan. Roll remaining half of dough for top crust; set aside.

Filling

    6-7 **tart apples**
     ¾ **cup sugar**
      2 **tablespoons flour**
    ½-1 **teaspoon ground cinnamon**
     ⅛ **teaspoon ground nutmeg**
     ⅛ **teaspoon salt**
      4 **tablespoons butter or**
        margarine
        Vanilla ice cream
        (optional)

Pare and slice apples to ¼-inch thickness (approximately 6 cups). Combine sugar, flour, spices, and salt; mix with apples. Spoon apple mixture into bottom pastry crust. Dot with butter. Place reserved pastry top over apples. Pinch edges together and flute. Bake at 400°F for 1 hour or until apples are done. If fluted edges begin to brown too much, cover with foil. Serve plain or with vanilla ice cream.

Susan Bible Jessup

Apple Cake Pie

Another way to use delicious North Georgia apples. Tastes a lot like apple cake, but much easier.

Preparation: Easy
Cooking Time: 45 Minutes
Oven Temperature: 350°F

Serves: 6-8

     ¼ **cup shortening or 2**
        tablespoons butter,softened
        + 2 tablespoons oil
      1 **cup sugar**
      1 **egg**
     ¼ **teaspoon salt**
      1 **teaspoon ground cinnamon**
      1 **teaspoon ground nutmeg**
      1 **teaspoon baking soda**
      1 **cup flour**
     ½ **cup chopped pecans**
    2½ **cups thinly sliced apples**
      2 **tablespoons hot water**
      1 **teaspoon vanilla extract**
        Vanilla ice cream (optional)
        Whipped cream (optional)

Mix ingredients in order given. Pour into greased 9-inch pie plate. Bake 45 minutes at 350°F. Serve warm with ice cream or whipped cream.

Judy Mynatt Bush

Pear Pie

Make it extra special by serving warm, with a dollop of slightly sweetened whipped cream, to which a small amount of ground ginger has been added.

Preparation: Average
Cooking Time: 1 Hour
Oven Temperature: 425°F

Yield: 1 (10-inch) Deep-Dish Pie

Cheese Pastry (page 328)

Prepare Cheese Pastry, reserving 1 cup flour mixture **before** adding water. Add water; roll dough for single 10-inch crust. Place in deep-dish 10-inch pie plate.

Filling

```
5-7   firm ripe pears, peeled
        and sliced (approximately
        4½ cups)
  2   tablespoons lemon juice
  ½   cup sugar
  ¼   cup flour
  ¼   teaspoon salt
        Margarine
```

Sprinkle pears with lemon juice. Toss with sugar, flour, and salt. Spoon into crust; dot with margarine.

Topping

```
  1   cup reserved pastry mixture
  ½   cup light brown sugar
  1   teaspoon ground cinnamon
  ¼   teaspoon ground nutmeg
  ¼   teaspoon ground cloves
```

Mix reserved pastry mixture with brown sugar and spices. Sprinkle over filling. Bake at 425°F for 40 minutes. Cover loosely with foil; continue baking for 20 minutes.

Jane Hix Oliver

Picanchagne (Pear Pie)

Not too sweet; very continental. A change-of-pace dessert.

Preparation: Easy
Cooking Time: 45 Minutes
Oven Temperature: 325°F

Yield: 1 (9-inch) Pie
Must Do Ahead

```
 12   ounces sour cream
  4   tablespoons sugar
  2   eggs, slightly beaten
  ⅛   teaspoon pepper
1½   pounds ripe pears, peeled
        and thinly sliced
  1   double pie crust, unbaked
        Whipped cream (optional)
```

Combine sour cream, sugar, eggs, and pepper. Add pears, mixing gently. Pour filling into prepared pie crust. Place top crust over filling; prick top to allow steam to escape. Bake at 325°F for approximately 45 minutes. Cool sufficiently for pie to set up before serving. Serve with a dollop of whipped cream.

Marlynne Ramey
San Luis Obispo, California

Fresh Fruit Tart

Strawberries, pineapple, and bananas make an interesting combination, but use your imagination and pick your own favorites.

Preparation: Average
Cooking Time: 8 Minutes
Oven Temperature: 400°F

Yield: 1 (9-inch) Tart
Must Do Ahead

Cookie Crust

- ¼ cup margarine
- ¼ cup sugar
- 1 egg yolk
- 1 cup flour

Cream margarine and sugar at medium speed of electric mixer. Add egg yolk, then flour. Beat until mixture makes fine crumbs. Press into bottom and up sides of 9-inch pie or tart pan. Bake at 400°F for 8 minutes or until edges brown. Cool completely.

Filling

- ½ cup sugar
- 3 tablespoons cornstarch
- 1½ cups orange juice
- ¼ cup lemon juice
- 1 teaspoon grated lemon rind
- 6 cups sliced, drained, assorted fresh fruit

Mix sugar and cornstarch in saucepan. Gradually add orange juice, stirring until smooth. Bring to boil over medium heat, stirring constantly; boil 1 minute. Remove from heat; stir in lemon juice and rind. Cool completely. Fold in fruit. Turn into baked crust. Chill 4 hours.
Micronote: Mix sugar and cornstarch in glass bowl; add orange juice. Cook on HIGH 2½ minutes or until mixture boils. Boil 1 minute. Stir in lemon juice and rind. Cool completely; proceed as directed.

Judy Stover Tritt

Harvest Sweet Potato Pie

Preparation: Average
Cooking Time: 40 Minutes
Oven Temperature: 400°F

Yield: 1 (10-inch) Pie

- 2 cups cooked mashed sweet potatoes
- ½ cup butter or margarine, softened
- 2 eggs, separated
- 1 cup firmly packed light brown sugar
- ½ teaspoon ground ginger
- ½ teaspoon ground cinnamon
- ½ teaspoon ground nutmeg
- ¼ teaspoon salt
- ½ cup milk or 2 tablespoons milk and 2 tablespoons bourbon
- ¼ cup sugar
- 1 unbaked (10-inch) pie crust or 1 frozen (deep-dish) pie crust
- Whipped cream (optional)

Combine sweet potatoes, butter, egg yolks, brown sugar, spices, and salt; mix well. Add milk, blending until smooth. Beat egg whites until foamy; gradually add ¼ cup sugar, beating until stiff. Fold into sweet potato mixture. Pour filling into crust; sprinkle with additional spices, if desired. Bake at 400°F for 10 minutes. Reduce heat to 350°F; bake 30 additional minutes. When cool, garnish with whipped cream.
Hint: Canned sweet potatoes may be substituted for fresh; reduce amount of sugar indicated according to taste.

Jean Bennett Oliver

Best-Ever Lemon Pie

Preparation: Average
Cooking Time: 45 Minutes
Oven Temperature: 350°F

Yield: 1 (9-inch) Pie
Must Do Ahead

Pie

1¼ cups sugar
6 tablespoons cornstarch
2 cups water
⅓ cup lemon juice
1½ teaspoons lemon extract
3 egg yolks, beaten
2 tablespoons butter
2 teaspoons vinegar
1 (9-inch) pie crust, baked
Meringue

Mix sugar and cornstarch in top of double boiler. Stir in water. Cook over medium heat 25 minutes, stirring occasionally with wire whisk. Add lemon juice, lemon extract, egg yolks, butter, and vinegar. Cook until thick, stirring constantly, approximately 10 minutes. Pour into cooled pie crust. Top with meringue. Bake at 350°F for 10 minutes or until golden brown. Cool before serving.

Micronote: Mix sugar, cornstarch, and water in glass bowl. Cook 4-5 minutes on HIGH, whisking every 45 seconds. Add remaining ingredients; cook 6 minutes, whisking frequently. Pour into pie crust; top with meringue. Pie may be cooked in microwave, but meringue will not have browned appearance. Cook 3 minutes on HIGH, turning pie a quarter turn every 30 seconds.

Meringue

3 egg whites
6 tablespoons sugar
½ teaspoon cream of tartar

Beat egg whites until foamy. Gradually add sugar and cream of tartar, beating until stiff peaks form.

Carole Ann Carter Daniel

Japanese Fruit Pie

Preparation: Easy
Cooking Time: 30 Minutes
Oven Temperature: 325°F

Yield: 1 (9-inch) Pie

½ cup butter or margarine, melted
1 cup sugar
2 eggs, well-beaten
½ cup raisins
½ cup shredded coconut
1 teaspoon vanilla extract
1 (9-inch) pie crust, unbaked
Vanilla ice cream (optional)
Whipped cream (optional)

Combine margarine and sugar; beat well. Beat in eggs. Stir in remaining ingredients. Pour in crust. Bake at 325°F for 30 minutes. Top each serving with ice cream or sweetened whipped cream.

Betty Nichols Livingston

Key Lime Pie

Tart and delicious!

Preparation: Easy

Yield: 1 (9-inch) Pie
Must Do Ahead

Crust

1 (5½-ounce) package chocolate-covered graham crackers
3 tablespoons butter, softened

Roll crackers between layers of waxed paper to make 1½ cups fine crumbs. Combine with butter. Press into 9-inch pie pan.

Filling

2 eggs, separated
1 (15-ounce) can sweetened condensed milk
⅔ cup lime juice (5-6 limes)
1 tablespoon grated fresh lime rind
Few drops green food coloring
⅓ cup sugar
Sweetened whipped cream
Shaved chocolate

Beat egg yolks until thick; stir in condensed milk. Stir in lime juice and rind. Tint pale green with food coloring. Beat egg whites until stiff, but not dry. Add sugar gradually, continuing to beat until very stiff. Fold egg whites into lime mixture; turn into crust. Freeze until firm, approximately 6 hours. To serve garnish with whipped cream and shaved chocolate.

Sally Looker Beurke
Tampa, Florida

Cranberry Chiffon Pie

Tart flavor, nice after a heavy meal.

Preparation: Average
Cooking Time: 10-15 Minutes

Yield: 1 (9 or 10-inch) Pie
Must Do Ahead

2 cups cranberries
½ cup + 2 tablespoons water, divided
1 cup sugar, divided
⅛ teaspoon salt
1 envelope unflavored gelatin
2 tablespoons lemon juice
2 egg whites
½ cup whipping cream, whipped
1 (9 or 10-inch) pie crust, baked

Cook cranberries in ½ cup water until skins pop. Stir in ½ cup sugar; cook 5 minutes more. Add salt. Remove from heat. Soften gelatin in remaining tablespoons water. Add to cranberries with lemon juice. Chill until mixture begins to gel. Beat egg whites until stiff. Gradually beat in remaining ½ cup sugar. Fold beaten egg whites and whipped cream into cranberry mixture. Turn into pie crust. Chill until set.

Martha Rand Jacobs

Fresh and Crunchy Peach Pie

The crunchy shell is really special!

Preparation: Average
Cooking Time: 10-12 Minutes
Oven Temperature: 375°F

Yield: 1 (9-inch) Pie
Must Do Ahead

Shell

  1 **cup crushed almonds**
  1 **cup coconut**
 ¼ **cup sugar**
 ¼ **cup butter, softened**

Spray 9-inch pie plate with vegetable coating. Mix all ingredients; pat into prepared pan. Bake at 375°F for 10-12 minutes. Cool completely.

Filling

  1 **cup sour cream**
  6 **tablespoons sifted confectioners' sugar, divided**
  1 **teaspoon orange juice**
  1 **teaspoon grated orange rind**
  1 **teaspoon vanilla extract**
 ⅛ **teaspoon salt**
  3 **cups sliced peaches, lightly sprinkled with lemon or orange juice**
  1 **cup whipping cream**

Beat sour cream with 4 tablespoons confectioners' sugar, orange juice, orange rind, vanilla, and salt. Spread over pie shell. Cover with peaches. Whip cream with remaining 2 tablespoons sugar. Spoon over peaches. Chill at least 1 hour before serving. Best when served same day of preparation.

Cindy Collins Randolph

Simple Summer Cobbler

The name says it all. Make the most of summer's bounty without spending a long time in the kitchen.

Preparation: Easy
Cooking Time: 30 Minutes
Oven Temperature: 350°F

Serves: 6-8

 ¾ **cup margarine**
1½ **cups sugar, divided**
 ¾ **cup flour**
1½ **teaspoons baking powder**
  1 **teaspoon salt**
 ¾ **cup milk**
  1 **tablespoon lemon juice**
  3 **cups fruit (blueberries, peaches, apples, etc.)**
   Vanilla ice cream (optional)

Melt margarine in 11 x 9-inch pan in preheating oven. In separate bowl mix ¾ cup sugar, flour, baking powder, and salt. Stir in milk, blending well. Add remaining ¾ cup sugar and lemon juice to fruit. Place fruit in pan over margarine; pour batter over all. Do not stir. Bake at 350°F for 30 minutes. Top each serving with a scoop of ice cream.

Debbie Jacobs Springle

Frozen Peach Cream Pie with Gingersnap Shell

An easy way to have homemade peach ice cream. No ice cream freezer necessary.

Preparation: Easy
Cooking Time: 6 Minutes
Oven Temperature: 375° F

Yield: 1 (9-inch) Pie
Must Do Ahead

2	cups fresh or frozen peaches
¼	cup lemon juice
½	cup sugar
1	(7-ounce) jar marshmallow creme
1²⁄₃	cups evaporated milk
	Gingersnap Shell
	Peach slices

Purée peaches in food processor. Blend in lemon juice, sugar and marshmallow creme. Let stand 25 minutes, stirring occasionally. Chill milk in tray in freezer until soft ice crystals form (approximately 25-30 minutes). Turn into electric mixer bowl; whip until soft peaks form. Fold peach mixture into whipped milk. Spoon into 13 x 9-inch pan. Freeze 2 hours, stirring occasionally to break up ice crystals. When ice cream is firm, spoon into Gingersnap Shell; return to freezer until ready to serve. Garnish with slices of fresh peach.

Gingersnap Shell

1	cup crushed gingersnaps (15 cookies)
2	tablespoons butter, melted

Combine crushed cookies with butter. Press into 9-inch pie pan to form shell. Bake at 375°F for 6 minutes. Cool completely.

Beth Davies Davidson

Frozen Mocha Meringue Pie

Preparation: Average
Cooking Time: 30 Minutes
Oven Temperature: 350°F

Serves: 8
Must Do Ahead

3	egg whites
½	teaspoon baking powder
¾	cup sugar
⅛	teaspoon salt
1	cup chocolate wafer crumbs
½	cup chopped pecans
1	teaspoon vanilla extract
1	quart coffee ice cream, softened
1	cup whipping cream, whipped
½	cup confectioners' sugar
	Chocolate curls (sweet chocolate)
½-⅔	cup Kahlúa or other coffee-flavored liqueur

Beat egg whites at room temperature until frothy; add baking powder, beating slightly. Gradually add sugar and salt, beating until very stiff and glossy. Fold in chocolate wafer crumbs, pecans, and vanilla. Spoon meringue into buttered 9-inch pie pan; use spoon to shape meringue into pie shell, swirling sides high. Bake at 350°F for 30 minutes. Cool. Spread ice cream evenly over meringue shell. Cover. Freeze overnight. Combine whipped cream and sugar, beating until light. Spread on pie. Garnish with chocolate curls; freeze until firm. Let stand 10 minutes to slice. Pour one tablespoon Kahlúa over each serving.

Cathy Cox Miller

Pecan Pie

What is more Southern or more delicious than pecan pie? Plain or à la mode, we think this one will stand the test of time.

Preparation: Easy
Cooking Time: 50 Minutes
Oven Temperature: 350°F

Yield: 1 (9-inch) Pie
Must Do Ahead

- ¾ cup sugar
- 2 tablespoons flour
- 1 teaspoon salt
- 1 cup dark corn syrup
- 2 eggs
- ½ cup evaporated milk
- 1½ teaspoons maple extract or vanilla extract
- 1 cup pecans
- 2 (9-inch) unbaked pie crusts, or 1 (deep-dish) unbaked crust

In 1½-quart bowl mix sugar, flour, and salt. Stir in syrup. Beat in eggs, one at a time. Blend in milk and flavoring. Stir in pecans. Pour into crusts. Bake at 350°F for 50 minutes, or until firm. Cool before serving.

Brenda Jones Adams

Chocolate - Amaretto Mousse Pie

Your guests will never suspect how easy this is to prepare.

Preparation: Easy

Yield: 1 (9-inch) Pie
Must Do Ahead

- 2 (1.5-ounce) envelopes whipped topping mix
- 1½ cups milk
- 2 (4 ⅛-ounce) packages chocolate instant pudding and pie filling mix
- ⅓ cup Amaretto
- 1 (9-inch) deep-dish pie crust, baked and cooled
- 1 (8-ounce) container frozen whipped topping, thawed
  Chocolate candy bar, shaved

Prepare topping mix according to package instructions. Add milk, pudding mix, and Amaretto; beat with electric mixer 2 minutes at high speed. Spoon mixture into pastry. Top with whipped topping. Chill 4 hours. When ready to serve, shave candy bar over topping.

Willia Beth Buquet Banks

Pecan Chiffon Pie

A truly delicious way to enjoy Georgia pecans.

Preparation: Average
Cooking Time: 8 Minutes

Yield: 1 (9-inch) Pie
Must Do Ahead

1 envelope unflavored gelatin
¾ cup milk
3 eggs, separated
1½ cups sugar, divided
½ cup Praline Liqueur or
  Crème de Cacao
½ teaspoon cream of tartar
1 cup whipping cream, whipped
1 cup chopped pecans, divided
1 (9-inch) baked pie crust
  or 1 (deep-dish) prepared
  crust, baked

In saucepan sprinkle gelatin over milk. Add slightly beaten egg yolks and 1 cup sugar. Place over low heat; stir constantly until gelatin dissolves and mixture thickens slightly, about 8 minutes. Remove saucepan from heat; add liqueur. Chill until mixture is consistency of egg whites. Beat egg whites with cream of tartar until soft peaks form. Gradually add remaining ½ cup sugar, beating to stiff peaks. Fold meringue into gelatin mixture. Fold in whipped cream and ¾ cup pecans. Pour into crust; refrigerate until set. Garnish with remaining pecans.

W. C. Wyatt, Jr.
Fort Valley, Georgia

Molly's Butterscotch Pie

Preparation: Average
Cooking Time: 30 Minutes
Oven Temperature: 325°F

Yield: 1 (9-inch) Pie

1 cup firmly packed light
  brown sugar
3 rounded tablespoons flour
¼ teaspoon salt
1½ cups milk
6½ tablespoons butter
3 egg yolks
1 teaspoon vanilla extract
  Partially baked (9-inch)
    pie crust or Brown Sugar
    No-Roll Crust (page 339)
  Meringue

In top of double boiler mix brown sugar, flour, and salt. Gradually stir in milk; add butter. Heat over boiling water until butter melts, stirring occasionally. Beat egg yolks slightly and stir quickly into hot mixture. Continue cooking and occasionally stirring until butterscotch is of thick pudding consistency. Blend in vanilla and pour into crust. Spread meringue over filling, sealing to crust. Bake at 325°F for 30 minutes or until meringue is golden. Cool slightly before serving or serve chilled.

Micronote: Mix brown sugar, flour, and salt in large glass bowl. Cook on HIGH, stirring several times, for 3½ minutes or until mixture almost boils. Add butter; return to microwave for 30 seconds or until butter melts. Add beaten egg yolks; cook 3 minutes on MEDIUM or until mixture thickens, stirring often. Blend in vanilla; pour into shell. Continue as directed.

Meringue

1 tablespoon cornstarch
½ cup water
3 egg whites
6-8 tablespoons sugar

Combine cornstarch and water in small saucepan. Bring to boil, stirring until transparent. Set aside to cool. Beat egg whites with electric mixer until stiff, but not dry. Gradually beat in 6-8 tablespoons sugar. Add cornstarch mixture; blend thoroughly.

Jean Davis Brown

Black Bottom Pie

Sinfully rich but worth the calories!

Preparation: Complex
Cooking Time: 20-30 Minutes

1 envelope unflavored gelatin
1¾ cups milk, divided
1 cup sugar, divided
½ teaspoon salt
4 teaspoons cornstarch
4 eggs, separated
1½ ounces unsweetened
   chocolate, melted
1 teaspoon vanilla extract
1 (9-inch) graham cracker,
   vanilla wafer, or chocolate
   wafer pie shell
1 tablespoon rum or bourbon
1 cup whipping cream
2 tablespoons confectioners'
   sugar
½ cup chopped pecans
   Shaved chocolate

Yield: 1 (9-inch) Pie
Must Do Ahead

Soften gelatin in ¼ cup milk. Scald remaining milk in double boiler. Mix ½ cup sugar, salt, and cornstarch. Add egg yolks; beat until thick and lemon-colored. Slowly add to hot milk, stirring constantly. Cook, stirring constantly, until custard is thick and coats metal spoon. Remove from heat; strain, if necessary, to remove any lumps. Remove 5 tablespoons custard; set aside. Add softened gelatin to remaining custard; stir until gelatin is dissolved. Chill until mixture begins to thicken. Stir together chocolate, reserved custard, and vanilla. Beat with rotary beater. When cool, spread chocolate mixture over crust. Beat egg whites until soft peaks form; gradually add remaining sugar, continuing to beat until stiff, but not dry. Fold rum and beaten egg whites into chilled custard. Pour over chocolate layer in pie shell; chill until firm. Whip cream with confectioners' sugar. Spread over pie. Sprinkle with pecans and shaved chocolate. Refrigerate until ready to serve.

Micronote: To scald milk, cook on HIGH 3 minutes in large glass measuring cup; stir several times. Mix ½ cup sugar, salt, cornstarch; add egg yolks; beat well. Add hot milk, stirring constantly. Return to microwave; cook on HIGH 2½ - 3 minutes, stirring every 30 seconds. Proceed with recipe as directed. Chocolate may also be melted in microwave, 30 seconds to 1 minute on HIGH.

Malissa Norton Tubbs

Nona's Egg Custard Pie

Just like grandma used to make!

Preparation: Easy
Cooking Time: 35 Minutes
Oven Temperature: 400°F

1 (9-inch) unbaked pie crust
1 tablespoon butter or
   margarine, melted
¼ cup sugar
2 tablespoons butter or
   margarine, softened
1 rounded tablespoon flour
1 cup warm milk
3 eggs, beaten
1 teaspoon vanilla extract

Yield: 1 (9-inch) Pie

Brush pie crust with melted butter; prebake at 400°F for 5 minutes. Remove from oven; set aside. Reduce oven to 325°F. Cream sugar and margarine. Add remaining ingredients, mixing well. Pour into pie crust. Bake at 325°F for 30 minutes or until custard is set.

Nancy Martin Brewer

Coconut Cream Pie

Preparation: Average
Cooking Time: 30 Minutes
Oven Temperature: 350°F

Yield: 1 (9-inch) Pie
Must Do Ahead

⅔ cup sugar
⅓ cup sifted flour or
⠀⠀¼ cup cornstarch
¼ teaspoon salt
2 cups scalded milk
3 slightly beaten egg yolks
1 cup shredded coconut
2 tablespoons butter
½ teaspoon vanilla extract or
⠀⠀1 teaspoon coconut extract
⠀⠀Baked 9-inch pie crust

Sift sugar, flour, and salt together. Place flour mixture in top of double boiler. Gradually stir in milk. Place over boiling water. Cook over medium heat, stirring constantly, until mixture thickens and boils. Cook 2 minutes more. Remove from heat. Add small amount of hot mixture to egg yolks, blending well. Stir egg yolks into remaining hot mixture. Return to heat; cook 1 minute, stirring constantly. Remove from heat. Stir in coconut, butter, and vanilla. Cool slightly. Pour into pie crust.

Micronote: In 2-quart covered bowl mix sugar, flour, and salt. Add milk; stir well. Cook 5 minutes on HIGH until very thick, stirring after 3 minutes, then 2 minutes. Cook 3 minutes on MEDIUM, stirring after 2 minutes then 1 minute. Stir small amount of hot mixture into egg yolks; blend well. Stir yolks into remaining hot mixture. Cook on MEDIUM for 2 minutes; stir in butter, vanilla, and coconut. Pour into pie crust.

Meringue

3 egg whites
¼ teaspoon cream of tartar
6 tablespoons sugar
½ teaspoon coconut extract
⠀⠀(optional)
½ cup shredded coconut

Beat egg whites with cream of tartar until foamy. Gradually add sugar and extract, beating until stiff peaks form. Spread over filling. Sprinkle coconut over meringue. Bake at 350°F for 12 minutes or until meringue browns. Chill before serving.

Variations: Banana Cream - Substitute 3 bananas, sliced, in custard instead of coconut.

Butterscotch Cream - Substitute 1 cup light brown sugar for ⅔ cup sugar; increase butter to 3 tablespoons.

Kathy Reeves Mathis

Buttermilk Pie

Preparation: Easy
Cooking Time: 50 Minutes
Oven Temperature: 350°F

Yield: 1 (10-inch) Pie
Must Do Ahead

2 cups sugar
½ cup butter or margarine,
⠀⠀softened
4 eggs
¼ cup self-rising flour
1 cup buttermilk
1 tablespoon lemon juice
⅛ teaspoon ground nutmeg
1 unbaked (10-inch) pie crust
⠀⠀Sweetened whipped cream
⠀⠀(optional)

Cream sugar and butter with electric mixer until light and fluffy. Add eggs and flour; beat at least 2 minutes. Fold in buttermilk, lemon juice, and nutmeg. Pour into pie crust. Bake at 350°F for 50 minutes or until knife inserted in center comes out clean. Cool. Serve plain or topped with sweetened whipped cream.

Cookbook Committee

Food Processor Pastry for Pies

Let your processor do the work for you and enjoy homemade pastry any time.

Preparation: Easy

1⅓ cups flour
½ cup cold margarine or butter,
    cut into 6 or 7 pieces
1 teaspoon salt
2-4 tablespoons ice water

Yield: 1 (9-inch) Crust

Using steel knife blade, place all ingredients except water in work bowl. Process 5-10 seconds or until mixture resembles coarse meal. With machine running, pour ice water, 1 tablespoon at a time, slowly through feed tube. Stop processing as soon as dough forms ball. Dough may be rolled to be used immediately, wrapped and chilled until ready to use, or bagged and frozen for future use.

Doris Porter Jones

Pastry

Preparation: Average
Cooking Time: 12-15 Minutes
Oven Temperature: 425°F

3 cups flour
½ teaspoon salt
½ cup shortening
½ cup butter, cut into
    small pieces
8-10 tablespoons iced water

Yield: 3 (9-inch) Pie Crusts or
        2 Dozen Large Tart Shells

Mix flour and salt. Cut shortening and butter into flour with pastry blender until mixture is consistency of coarse cornmeal. Add iced water, 2 tablespoons at a time, stirring with fork until mixture clings together and forms ball. Chill, if desired, for 15 minutes (no longer). Divide according to need; roll out on floured board. Carefully line pie pan. For recipes needing baked crust, prick shell with fork. Bake at 425°F for 12-15 minutes. Cool; fill as desired. Unused pastry may be refrigerated or frozen for later use.

Lynda Dickens Askew

Brown Sugar No-Roll Pie Crust

Preparation: Easy
Cooking Time: 15 Minutes
Oven Temperature: 400°F

1¼ cups flour
½ cup margarine, sliced
½ cup firmly packed light
    brown sugar
⅓ cup coconut and/or nuts

Yield: 1 (9-inch) Pie Shell
Must Do Ahead

Place all ingredients into 9-inch pie pan. Place in 400°F oven. Stir every 5 minutes until all ingredients are well mixed and brown (approximately 15 minutes). Remove from oven; press into pan to form crust. Cool completely; fill as desired. [Try Butterscotch Filling (page 346).]

Doris Duke Sosebee

Strawberry-Apricot Pastry Strip

Pastry lover's delight. A rich and beautiful change from coffee cake for a morning refreshment.

Preparation: Average
Cooking Time: 25 Minutes
Oven Temperature: 375°F

Serves: 8
Must Partially Do Ahead

 2 pints small strawberries,
    hulled and washed
⅓ cup + ¼ cup sugar, divided
 2 cups sifted flour
½ teaspoon salt
¾ cup butter (no
    substitutions here!)
1-4 tablespoons cold water
 1 egg, beaten
½ teaspoon arrowroot
 1 teaspoon vanilla extract
½ cup apricot preserves

Toss strawberries with ⅓ cup sugar. Let stand 30 minutes. Sift together flour, ¼ cup sugar, and salt. Cut in butter with pastry blender or food processor until mixture resembles cornmeal. Gradually sprinkle cold water over flour mixture, blending with fork or food processor, until flour is moistened and pastry clings together. Handle as little as possible. Roll pastry on lightly floured board to 7 x 14-inch rectangle. If necessary, lightly flour underneath pastry to keep it free-moving. Trim edges evenly. Fold strip in half lengthwise and lift onto cookie sheet with spatula. Unfold. Cut ½-inch wide strip from each long side of pastry. Moisten along edges of remaining rectangle with water. Place cut strips atop moist edges. Score strips with criss-cross design, using back of knife blade. Brush with egg. Bake at 375°F for 25 minutes. Cool. Drain strawberries, reserving juice; add water, if necessary, to make ⅓ cup liquid. Mix juice with arrowroot and vanilla. Bring to boil, stirring constantly. Simmer 1 minute. Remove from heat; cool. Spread apricot preserves over bottom of pastry strip. Arrange strawberries over preserves. Pour thickened juice mixture over all. Store at room temperature. Slice crosswise into small slices to serve. (Can be done a day early and assembled easily at the last minute. Large strawberries should be halved.)

Cookbook Committee

Sour Cream Banana Pudding

A breeze to prepare - no cooking involved. The sour cream gives it a special flavor.

Preparation: Easy

Serves: 12-16
Must Do Ahead

 3 cups milk
 1 (5⅝-ounce) box vanilla
    instant pudding or
    pie filling
 1 cup sour cream
 1 (12-ounce) container
    frozen whipped topping
 1 (10-ounce) box vanilla
    wafers
 4 large bananas

Combine milk and pudding mix in large bowl of electric mixer. Beat at low speed until thickened. Add sour cream; beat 2 minutes more. Fold in whipped topping. Line bottom of 3-quart container with vanilla wafers. Cover with layer of 2 sliced bananas. Add half pudding mixture. Repeat layers. Crumble a few wafers over top and/or place whole wafers around edges of container as garnish. Refrigerate several hours or overnight.

Grace Hooten Moore

Apple Dumplings with Nutmeg Sauce

A dish with Williamsburg, Virginia, origins which tastes ever so good on a cold winter evening. Try it with pears, too.

Preparation: Average
Cooking Time: 50 Minutes
Oven Temperature: 450°F

Serves: 6
Must Partially Do Ahead
Must Serve Immediately

    2 cups flour
    ¾ teaspoon salt
    ⅔ cup + 2 tablespoons solid
       shortening
  6-8 tablespoons cold water
    6 whole, medium-large apples,
       peeled and cored
  1½ cups sugar
    ¾ teaspoon ground cinnamon
    6 tablespoons margarine,
       divided

Combine flour and salt. Cut in shortening with pastry blender or food processor until mixture resembles peas. Add just enough cold water to make dough hold together. Roll pastry on a lightly floured surface to ⅛-inch thickness. Cut into six 7-inch squares. Center 1 apple on each square. Combine sugar and cinnamon. Divide equally to fill centers of apples. Top each apple with 1 tablespoon margarine. Moisten edges of pastry with water; fold up around apples, pressing edges together firmly to seal. Prick each pastry in several places. Place apple dumplings in 12 x 9-inch baking dish. Chill 1 hour. Bake at 450°F for 10 minutes. Reduce heat to 350°F; bake additional 40 minutes. Place dumplings in individual serving dishes; top with hot Nutmeg Sauce. Serve warm.

Nutmeg Sauce

    1 cup sugar
    1 tablespoon cornstarch
    1 cup boiling water
    1 tablespoon butter
       or margarine
    1 teaspoon ground nutmeg

Mix sugar and cornstarch. Stir in boiling water. Cook, stirring constantly, until sauce bubbles and thickens slightly. Add margarine; simmer gently 5 minutes. Remove from heat; stir in nutmeg.
Micronote: Mix sugar and cornstarch; stir in boiling water. Add butter. Cook on HIGH 2½ minutes, stirring every 30 seconds. Stir in nutmeg.

Sandra Gilmer Souther

Lemon Soufflé

Looking for a different lemon dessert? Good served hot or cold.

Preparation: Average
Cooking Time: 50 Minutes
Oven Temperature: 325°F

Serves: 10
Must Do Ahead

  2¼ cups sugar
    5 tablespoons flour
    ¼ teaspoon salt
    5 tablespoons butter, softened
    6 eggs, separated
    2 cups milk
    ¾ cup lemon juice
       Grated rind of 3 lemons
    1 cup chopped dates
    ¾ cup chopped pecans or
       walnuts

Into large bowl of electric mixer sift together sugar, flour, and salt. Add butter; cream until blended. In separate bowl beat egg yolks until light. Beat milk into egg yolks. Add to creamed mixture, blending well. Blend in lemon juice and rind. In separate bowl beat egg whites until stiff. Fold into lemon mixture. Fold in dates and nuts. Pour into lightly buttered 2-quart soufflé dish. Place dish in shallow pan of hot water. Bake at 325°F for 50 minutes. Allow to cool, then refrigerate. Soufflé does not rise above dish rim. Top should have fluffy cake-like consistency and bottom should be a lemon-date-nut sauce.

Lynda Dickens Askew

Amelia's Fruit Supreme

Absolutely scrumptious buffet dessert. Encourage guests or family to create their own "sundae."

Preparation: Average
Cooking Time: 10-12 Minutes
Oven Temperature: 300°F

Serves: 8
Must Partially Do Ahead

1 large pineapple, peeled,
   cored, and slivered
   Sugar
2 quarts strawberries, hulled
4-6 bananas, peeled and sliced
   Lemon juice
1 cup slivered almonds
   Supreme Sauce
2 quarts vanilla ice cream
   or lemon sherbert

Sprinkle pineapple lightly with sugar. Place in serving bowl. Place strawberries in separate bowl. Sprinkle bananas with lemon juice; place in separate bowl. Toast almonds at 300°F for 8-10 minutes or until lightly browned; place in separate serving bowl. Place warm Supreme Sauce in separate serving bowl. Scoop ice cream or sherbet into large bowl. Place on tray surrounded by fruits, sauce, and nuts. Layer ice cream or sherbet, fruit, sauce, and nuts in individual dishes.

Supreme Sauce

½ cup butter
3 cups firmly packed light
   brown sugar
⅔ cup pineapple juice
1 cup orange juice, divided
¼ cup light rum or rum
   extract to taste

Melt butter in skillet. Add brown sugar. Cook over moderate heat 2-3 minutes, watching carefully not to burn. Add pineapple juice and ⅔ cup orange juice. Cook until sugar dissolves and sauce is consistency of syrup. Add remaining ⅓ cup orange juice and rum. Serve warm or refrigerate to use later, reheated. (Keeps well indefinitely.)

Micronote: Melt butter in glass dish on HIGH for 45-60 seconds. Stir in sugar. Cook on MEDIUM for 1 minute. Add pineapple juice and ⅔ cup orange juice. Cook 3½-4 minutes on HIGH. Add ⅓ cup orange juice and rum.

Sally Butts Darden

Christmas Ambrosia

To make this traditional holiday treat extra-special, place a spoonful of orange sherbet in each serving dish and ladle ambrosia over the top.

Preparation: Easy

Serves: 6-8
Must Do Ahead

9-12 oranges
2 (20-ounce) cans crushed
   pineapple, drained
1 cup flaked coconut
1 cup honey
¼ cup Cointreau, Triple Sec,
   or apricot brandy (optional)
2 teaspoons almond extract

Peel oranges by cutting through rind and white membrane in circular motion beginning at top of orange and going around orange to bottom. Run knife blade down one side of each section and up the other; sections will pop out leaving no membrane attached. Combine orange sections and any rendered juice with all remaining ingredients. Refrigerate overnight.

Cindy Collins Randolph
Kitty Carter Lane

Lemon Meringue Nests

Preparation: Average
Cooking Time: 45-55 Minutes
Oven Temperature: 300°F

Serves: 6
Must Do Ahead

Meringue Nests

½ **cup egg whites**
⅛ **teaspoon salt**
¾ **cup sugar**
½ **teaspoon vanilla extract**
   Lemon Filling

Combine egg whites and salt; beat with electric mixer at high speed until stiff. Add sugar, 1 tablespoon at a time, beating well after each addition. Stir in vanilla. Grease cookie sheet or line with heavy brown paper. Spoon meringue onto cookie sheet in six equal mounds. Make deep well in center of each mound, building up sides with back of spoon to form nests. Bake at 300°F until meringues are delicate golden color, 12-15 minutes. Lower heat to 250°F; continue baking until dry and light brown in color, 30-40 minutes. Turn off heat; leave shells in oven with door closed 1-2 hours. Remove from oven to cool completely. When completely cooled, fill with Lemon Filling. Refrigerate uncovered at least 2 hours. (Shells may be frozen before or after filling. Store in airtight container. Return unfilled shells to oven to crisp lightly before filling.) Garnish with whipped cream reserved from filling preparation.

Lemon Filling

3 **eggs yolks, beaten**
⅔ **cup sugar**
¼ **cup lemon juice**
   Grated rind of 1 lemon
2 **cups whipping cream,**
   whipped

Combine egg yolks, sugar, lemon juice, and rind in top of double boiler. Stir well. Cook over boiling water until thick. Cool. Remove ½ cup whipped cream; set aside for garnish. Fold remaining whipped cream into cooled lemon mixture. **Micronote:** Combine egg yolks, sugar, lemon juice, and rind. Cook 2½ minutes on HIGH, stirring every 30 seconds. Cool. Proceed as directed above.

Emily Warfield Thompson

Summer's Fresh Fruit Torte

Pretty and colorful. A delicious way to use the fruits of the season.

Preparation: Average
Cooking Time: 15 Minutes
Oven Temperature: 375°F

Serves: 8-12
Must Do Ahead

Crust

1½ cups packaged biscuit mix
¼ cup sugar
¼ cup butter, softened

Combine ingredients. Process with pastry blender or food processor until mixture resembles coarse crumbs. Press into false-bottom 10-inch quiche pan, pizza pan, or springform pan. Bake at 375°F for 15 minutes. Cool completely.

Filling

6 ounces cream cheese, softened
½ cup whipping cream
⅓ cup sugar
1 teaspoon vanilla extract
1 pint strawberries, hulled
4-6 peaches, peeled and sliced or halved
1 cup blueberries
½ cup apple jelly

Combine cream cheese, cream, sugar, and vanilla. Blend with electric mixer or food processor until smooth. Spread on cooled crust. Refrigerate until cheese mixture is set. Arrange fruits in the following manner, beginning at outer edges of torte; one circle of strawberries, one circle of peach halves or slices, blueberries mounded in center. Heat apple jelly just until melted (lukewarm). Spoon over fruit. Refrigerate overnight.

Connie Kemp Goldfarb

Baklava

This Greek delicacy will bring you raves! The process is time-consuming but not difficult; well worth the effort.

Preparation: Average
Cooking Time: 50 Minutes
Oven Temperature: 300°F

Yield: 7-8 Dozen Pieces
Must Partially Do Ahead

2½ pounds shelled pecans, coarsely ground
1 tablespoon ground cinnamon
½ teaspoon ground nutmeg
⅛ teaspoon ground allspice
⅛ teaspoon ground cloves
1 pound butter, melted
1 pound phyllo pastry
3 cups sugar
1½ cups water
½ cup honey
Juice of 1 lemon

In a bowl mix pecans, cinnamon, nutmeg, allspice, and cloves; set aside. Grease large 16 x 11-inch jelly roll pan with melted butter. Layer 6 phyllo sheets in the pan, brushing each sheet lightly with butter before adding the next. Sprinkle layer of nut mixture over sheets. Layer 3 more sheets of phyllo, again brushing each lightly with butter. Top with another layer of nut mixture. Continue process until all nut mixture is used. Finish with 4 phyllo sheets on top, brushing each one with butter. Partially cut phyllo into small squares or diamonds with sharp-pointed knife to aid baking. Bake at 300°F for 50 minutes or until lightly browned. (May require up to 1 hour 30 minutes.) Cool completely. Combine sugar, water, honey, and lemon juice in saucepan. Cook over medium heat until mixture reaches medium syrup consistency. Pour warm syrup over cooled pastry. Carefully cut squares completely apart.

Elaine Caras Waller

English Trifle

A long-time holiday favorite. This one requires no gourmet cooking skills, but definitely yields a gourmet dessert.

Preparation: Average

Serves: 10-12
Must Do Ahead

1 quart Boiled Custard
    (page 346)
2 dozen ladyfingers
    or slices of pound cake
    Raspberry or cherry
    preserves
2 dozen almond macaroons,
    crushed
⅓ cup cream sherry
    or Cherry Herring
1 cup whipping cream
1 tablespoon confectioners'
    sugar
¼ cup blanched slivered
    almonds

Prepare Boiled Custard, using 2½ tablespoons flour. Spread part or all of the ladyfingers with preserves. Line bottom and sides of trifle dish or glass bowl with some of ladyfingers; sprinkle with ⅓ macaroon crumbs and ⅓ sherry. Cover with ⅓ custard. Repeat layers 2 more times, beginning with ladyfingers. Cover; chill 6-24 hours. Whip cream with confectioners' sugar. Cover trifle with whipped cream; decorate with almonds inserted at angles.

Cindy Collins Randolph

...a feeling of good fellowship passed around the circle like a mystic cord, holding and binding these people together with jest and laughter.

Kate Chopin, *The Awakening*

Crème Reversée au Caramel

A classic French dessert, but quick and easy to make. Very light and smooth following a heavy meal.

Preparation: Easy
Cooking Time: 45 Minutes
Oven Temperature: 350°F

Serves: 4-6
Must Do Ahead

⅓ cup + ¼ cup sugar
2 cups milk
3 eggs
½ teaspoon vanilla extract
⅛ teaspoon water

Combine ⅓ cup sugar, milk, eggs, and vanilla; beat with electric mixer until thoroughly blended. Skim off any foam. Set aside. Combine ¼ cup sugar and water in small saucepan. Cook, stirring constantly, over high heat until mixture boils and turns deep caramel color. Pour over bottom of round soufflé dish; immediately top with egg mixture. Place dish in pan containing 1-inch depth of hot water. Bake at 350°F for 45 minutes or until custard is firm. Refrigerate until completely cooled. When ready to serve, dip dish into hot water a few seconds to loosen bottom. Invert onto serving plate.

Kim McElhenney Humphrey

Boiled Custard

Part of the cooking tradition of the South. When done in the microwave, this versatile custard is so easy grandmother would never believe it!

Preparation: Easy
Cooking Time: 20 Minutes

Yield: 5-6 Cups
Must Do Ahead

1 cup sugar
1 tablespoon flour
3-4 eggs, beaten
1 quart milk
1 teaspoon vanilla extract
½ teaspoon almond extract
   (optional)
Nutmeg (optional)

In medium saucepan combine sugar and flour. Beat in eggs. Gradually stir in milk. Cook over medium-high heat, stirring constantly, until thickened sufficiently to coat metal spoon well. **Never let boil.** Remove from heat. Stir in extracts. Cool. Refrigerate. Sprinkle each serving with nutmeg.

Micronote: In covered 2 to 2½-quart round casserole mix sugar and flour. Add eggs; beat well. Gradually stir in milk. Cover; cook on HIGH for 4 minutes; stir. Cook on HIGH for 3 minutes; stir. Cook on MEDIUM for 3 minutes; stir. Cook on MEDIUM for 2 minutes. **Never let boil.** Stir in flavorings. Cool; refrigerate.

Variations: Vanilla Pudding - Increase flour to 4 tablespoons. Proceed as above.

Chocolate Custard or Pudding - Add 1 cup semi-sweet chocolate chips with milk. Proceed as above.

Butterscotch Custard or Pudding - Add 1 cup butterscotch chips with milk. Proceed as above.

Banana Pudding - Line serving dish with vanilla wafers. Alternate layers of bananas and additional wafers to fill dish. Cover layers with custard. If topping is desired, spread with whipped topping and a sprinkle of nutmeg. Refrigerate. If baked pudding is desired, spread with sweetened meringue and bake at 350°F until brown. [Meringue, see Molly's Butterscotch Pie (page 336).] Pineapple, peaches, or berries are also good substitutes for bananas.

Mary Chandler Oliver
Commerce, Georgia
Becky Telford Broxton

Syllabub

Delicious served with holiday meals. Another Southern tradition.

Preparation: Easy

Serves: 8
Must Partially Do Ahead
Must Serve Immediately

1 quart whipping cream,
   24 hours old
1 cup fresh milk
1 cup sugar
½ cup grape juice
¼ cup orange juice
¼ cup dry sherry
1 teaspoon vanilla extract

Mix all ingredients. Chill thoroughly. Mix on low speed in electric mixer until frothy. Serve immediately in chilled wine glasses.

Marilyn Woodberry McCarver

Zabaglione

A light and elegant dessert to follow an Italian dinner.

Preparation: Average
Cooking Time: 12-15 Minutes

Serves: 6-8

1 **pound fresh bing cherries, halved and pitted, or 1 (16-ounce) can pitted bing cherries, drained**
½ **cup cognac or apricot brandy**
10 **egg yolks**
1 **cup sugar**
1 **cup Marsala wine**

Soak cherries in cognac; set aside. Place egg yolks in electric mixer bowl. Beat at high speed while slowly adding sugar; beat until light lemon in color. Beat in Marsala wine. Pour into top of double boiler; place over rapidly boiling water. (Do not let water touch the upper boiler.) Beat continuously until mixture has doubled in bulk and is quite thick, about 12 minutes. Serve hot at once or pour into serving dish and refrigerate until very cold. Garnish with cherries at serving time.

Frances Jolley Syfan

Coeur à la Crème

A perfect alternative to mousse or cheesecake.

Preparation: Easy

Serves: 12
Must Do Ahead

1 **envelope unflavored gelatin**
½ **cup cold water**
1 **cup half-and-half, scalded**
8 **ounces cream cheese, softened**
2 **cups whipping cream**
1¼ **cups sugar**
½ **cup sweet or creme sherry**
   Fresh strawberries, washed and hulled, or Cherry Sauce

Soften gelatin in water. Add gelatin to half-and-half; stir until dissolved. Cool. Blend cream cheese with whipping cream. Stir in sugar and sherry. Fold gelatin mixture into cream cheese mixture. Pour into oiled 8-cup mold. Chill at least 3 hours. Unmold; serve with strawberries, other fresh fruit, or Cherry Sauce.

W. C. Wyatt, Jr.
Fort Valley, Georgia

Cherry Sauce

1 **(16-ounce) can sour pitted cherries**
½ **cup sugar**
1½ **tablespoons cornstarch**
   Dash of salt
1 **tablespoon butter**
⅛ **teaspoon almond extract**

Drain cherries, reserving juice. Set cherries aside. Add water to juice, if necessary, to make 1¼ cups liquid. Place liquid in saucepan; bring to boil. Mix sugar, cornstarch, and salt; add to hot juice. Cook, stirring constantly, until sauce boils. Remove from heat; cool slightly. Add butter, almond extract, and cherries.
Micronote: Pour cherry juice and water into bowl or large glass measure. Cook on HIGH 2-3 minutes, until boiling. Mix dry ingredients; add to hot juice, stirring until dissolved. Cook on HIGH 2 minutes, or until thickened. Mix well with whisk; cool slightly. Add butter, cherries, and almond extract.

Lynda Dickens Askew

Coconut Mousse

Preparation: Easy
Cooking Time: 5 Minutes

Serves: 10
Must Do Ahead

3 tablespoons unflavored
    gelatin
⅓ cup water
2 cups half-and-half
1 cup sugar
2 cups grated coconut
3 cups whipping cream, whipped
1 teaspoon almond extract

Soften gelatin in water. In saucepan heat half-and-half to boiling. Add gelatin mixture and sugar; stir to dissolve. Cool. Add coconut. Stir almond extract into whipped cream. Fold into coconut mixture. Pour into lightly oiled 8-cup mold or serving bowl. Chill until firm.

Rebecca Gail Jackson
Winder, Georgia

The black stove, stoked with coal and firewood, glows like a lighted pumpkin. Eggbeaters whirl, spoons spin round in bowls of butter and sugar, vanilla sweetens the air, ginger spices it; melting, nosetingling odors saturate the kitchen, suffuse the house, drift out to the world on puffs of chimney smoke.

Truman Capote, *Selected Writings of Truman Capote.*
Random House, Inc., Copyright 1966. Used with permission.

Chocolate-Amaretto Mousse

A firmer-textured mousse which can be decorated and sliced. For both appearance and taste, you can't go wrong here.

Preparation: Complex
Cooking Time: 20 Minutes

Serves: 10-12
Must Do Ahead

18 whole blanched almonds
6 ounces semi-sweet chocolate
    morsels, melted
½ cup Amaretto
2 envelopes unflavored gelatin
¼ cup water
4 eggs, separated
⅓ cup sugar
2 cups milk
2 cups whipping cream, whipped
2 (3-ounce) packages split
    ladyfingers

Dip bottom half of almonds into melted chocolate; place on waxed paper; chill. Gradually stir Amaretto into remaining chocolate. Soften gelatin in water. Mix egg yolks, sugar, and milk; cook, stirring until custard coats spoon. Add gelatin to hot custard; stir until dissolved. Remove from heat. Stir in chocolate mixture. Cool until mixture mounds. Beat egg whites until stiff; fold into custard. Reserve 1 cup whipped cream; refrigerate. Fold remaining cream into chocolate mixture. Chill until cold, but not set. Line bottom and sides of springform pan with split ladyfingers; fill with chocolate mixture. Chill until firm. Remove sides of pan; decorate outer edge of mousse with reserved whipped cream and almonds.

Micronote: Melt chocolate 1 minute on HIGH. Dip bottom half of almonds into melted chocolate; chill. Add Amaretto to remaining chocolate. Mix egg yolks, sugar, and milk; cook on HIGH 3-3½ minutes, stirring every 30 seconds. Add softened gelatin; stir until dissolved. Stir in chocolate mixture. Chill. Proceed as directed above.

Carol Ann Alexander Armstrong

Charlotte Russe

Preparation: Average
Cooking Time: 20 Minutes

Serves: 12
Must Do Ahead

1 envelope + 1 teaspoon
    unflavored gelatin
1 cup sugar, divided
¼ teaspoon salt
3 eggs, separated
¼ cup bourbon
2 cups milk
1 cup whipping cream, whipped
16 ladyfingers, split

Combine gelatin, ½ cup sugar, and salt in medium saucepan. In separate bowl beat egg yolks until pale yellow. Gradually beat bourbon into yolks. Stir in milk until well blended. Gradually stir egg mixture into gelatin mixture. Cook over low heat, stirring constantly, until custard consistency. Pour into bowl; refrigerate until almost set. Beat egg whites until soft peaks form. Gradually beat in remaining ½ cup sugar; beat until stiff. Fold into custard. Fold in whipped cream. Line large serving dish with ladyfingers. Pour Charlotte over ladyfingers. Cover with plastic wrap. Chill until set (keeps well 3-4 days).

Micronote: In blender or food processor blend gelatin, ½ cup sugar, salt, egg yolks, bourbon, and milk. Pour into glass bowl. Cook on HIGH 5 minutes or until thick, stirring every 45 seconds. Chill until almost set; proceed as directed above.

Betty Gail Parker Gunter

Orange Charlotte

A delicious, light dessert that is only slightly sweet.

Preparation: Average
Cooking Time: 15-20 Minutes

Serves: 6-8
Must Do Ahead

1 tablespoon unflavored gelatin
¼ cup cold water
2 eggs, separated
½ cup sugar
¼ teaspoon salt
1½ cups orange juice, divided
2 tablespoons lemon juice
1 cup whipping cream, whipped
    Whipped cream (optional)
    Orange slices (optional)

Sprinkle gelatin over water to soften; set aside. In top of double boiler, thoroughly beat egg yolks. Add sugar and salt, beating well. Stir in ¾ cup orange juice. Cook over boiling water until mixture thickens sufficiently to coat metal spoon. Add gelatin; stir until completely dissolved. Stir in remaining orange juice and lemon juice. Pour into mixing bowl; refrigerate until mixture begins to thicken. Beat with rotary beater or wire whisk until light. With electric mixer, beat egg whites until very stiff. Fold into orange mixture along with whipped cream. Turn into 1-quart serving bowl or individual compotes. Refrigerate until firm. Garnish each serving with additional whipped cream and/or a thinly sliced twist of fresh orange.

Micronote: Add sugar and salt to well-beaten egg yolks; stir in ¾ cup orange juice. Cook on HIGH 2½ minutes, stirring every 30 seconds. Stir in softened gelatin, then remaining orange juice and lemon juice. Chill and proceed as directed above.

Sarah Grimes Butts
Sparta, Georgia

Dark Chocolate Mousse

Preparation: Average
Cooking Time: 5 Minutes

Serves: 8-10
Must Do Ahead

- ¾ **pound dark sweet chocolate**
- ⅓ **cup light rum**
- 2 **tablespoons water**
- ¾ **cup unsalted butter, softened**
- ¾ **cup confectioners' sugar, divided**
- 3 **eggs, separated**
- 1 **teaspoon vanilla extract**
- 2 **cups whipping cream**

Melt chocolate in heavy saucepan over low heat with rum and water, stirring constantly. Cool to lukewarm. Cream butter; gradually add ½ cup confectioners' sugar, beating well. Add egg yolks, one at a time, mixing after each. Blend in chocolate mixture and vanilla. Whip cream; gradually blending in remaining ¼ cup confectioners' sugar; continue whipping until cream holds shape well. Fold half of whipped cream into chocolate mixture; refrigerate remaining whipped cream. Beat egg whites to soft peaks. Fold into chocolate mixture. Pour mousse into serving dish. Cover with plastic wrap. Freeze 2 hours or refrigerate 8-10 hours. At serving time decorate with reserved whipped cream. (If mousse is to be chilled for several hours, or overnight, whip cream in two amounts.)

Louise Hendrix Forrester

Brownie Baked Alaska

Preparation: Average
Cooking Time: 35 Minutes
Oven Temperature: 350°F and 500°F

Serves: 10-12
Must Partially Do Ahead
Must Serve Immediately

- 1 **quart vanilla ice cream, softened (or flavor of choice)**
- ½ **cup margarine, softened**
- 2 **cups sugar, divided**
- 2 **eggs**
- 1 **cup flour**
- 2 **tablespoons cocoa**
- ½ **teaspoon baking powder**
- ¼ **teaspoon salt**
- 1 **teaspoon vanilla extract**
- 5 **egg whites**

Line 1-quart mixing bowl (about 7-inch diameter) with waxed paper, leaving an overhang around edges. Pack ice cream into bowl; freeze until very firm. Cream margarine and 1 cup sugar until light and fluffy. Add eggs, one at a time, beating well after each addition. Combine flour, cocoa, baking powder, and salt. Add to creamed mixture, mixing well. Stir in vanilla. Spoon batter into greased and floured 8-inch round cake pan. Bake at 350°F for 25-30 minutes. Let cool in pan for 10 minutes. Turn onto wire rack; cool completely. Place cake on ovenproof wooden board or serving dish. Invert bowl of ice cream onto brownie, leaving waxed paper intact. Remove bowl; place ice cream-topped cake in freezer. Beat egg whites until frothy; gradually add 1 cup sugar, continuing to beat until stiff. Remove cake from freezer; peel off paper. Quickly spread meringue over entire surface, making sure edges are sealed with meringue. (May return to freezer at this point for 1 week.) Bake at 500°F or until meringue is browned. Serve immediately. **Note:** Packaged brownie mix may be substituted for scratch. For variety add 3 tablespoons Kahlúa, crème de menthe, or Amaretto to ice cream before molding.

Carolyn Hartford Mahar

Chocolate Intemperance

Indecently rich! A chocolate lover's idea of heaven.

Preparation: Average
Cooking Time: 10-12 Minutes
Oven Temperature: 350°F

Serves: 12-16
Must Do Ahead

Mousse Filling

 1½ pounds semi-sweet chocolate
 ½ cup brewed coffee
 3 eggs, separated
 ½ cup Tia Maria
 2 tablespoons sugar
 1 cup whipping cream, whipped

Combine chocolate and coffee in top of double boiler. Heat over boiling water until chocolate is completely melted; remove from heat. Beat egg yolks with electric mixer until pale yellow. Blend into chocolate. Gradually stir in Tia Maria. Set aside until cooled completely. (Prepare cake at this point; see instructions below.) Beat egg whites with electric mixer until soft peaks form. Gradually add sugar, continuing to beat until stiff. Gently fold whipped cream into cooled chocolate mixture. Fold in beaten egg whites.

Cake

 1 (23-ounce) package
 brownie mix
 3 eggs
 2 tablespoons water

Combine all ingredients; beat at medium speed of electric mixer until smooth. Grease 15 x 11-inch jelly roll pan; line with waxed paper. Grease and flour paper. Spread butter evenly on paper. Bake 10 minutes or until cake tests done. Turn cake onto rack; peel off paper.

Glaze

 ½ pound semi-sweet chocolate
 ⅓ cup water

Combine chocolate and water. Heat and stir until chocolate is melted and mixture is smooth. Lightly oil 8-inch spring-form pan (or 2-quart charlotte mold). Cut 2 circles from cake: one 7 inches in diameter; one 8 inches in diameter. Place 7-inch layer on bottom of pan. Cut remaining cake in strips to fit around sides of pan (may need to piece). Spoon filling into center. Fit 8-inch layer on top. Chill 3-4 hours. Spread glaze over top and drizzle down sides; chill.

Carmela Addessi Hargraves

Oranges Côte d'Azur

Preparation: Average
Cooking Time: 15 Minutes
Oven Temperature: 400°F

Serves: 8
Must Partially Do Ahead
Must Serve Immediately

8 medium navel oranges
1½ cups sugar
½ cup butter, melted
⅓ cup fresh lemon juice
Grated rind of 1 lemon
¼ teaspoon salt
3 eggs, separated
1 cup heavy cream, whipped
1 teaspoon cream of tartar

Slice thin piece from top of each orange. Remove pulp from oranges, leaving shell; discard pulp. Set shells aside to drain on absorbent toweling. In top of double boiler over hot water combine sugar, butter, juice, rind, and salt. Beat egg yolks; add to lemon mixture. Cook, stirring until thick and shiny. Set aside to cool. Fold whipped cream into lemon mixture. Place in large bowl; freeze 3-4 hours. Beat egg whites with cream of tartar until stiff. Fill orange shells with frozen lemon filling; top with meringue. Brown at 400°F for 5 minutes or until meringue is brown.

Micronote: In glass bowl heat lemon juice to boiling, 1 minute on HIGH. Add sugar, butter, juice, rind, salt, and beaten egg yolks. Cook on MEDIUM 4-5 minutes or until thick and shiny, stirring several times. Cool. Proceed as directed above.

Georgia Eubanks Griffin
Atlanta, Georgia

Crème Courvoisier

A heavenly treat originating with Arno B. Schmidt, executive chef of New York's Waldorf Astoria.

Preparation: Average
Cooking Time: 7-10 Minutes

Serves: 6-8
Must Do Ahead

1 cup sugar
¾ cup water
8 egg yolks
⅓ cup Courvoisier
1 cup whipping cream
Nutmeg

In 1½-quart saucepan over high heat, stir sugar and water to dissolve. Boil without stirring for 5 minutes. Meanwhile, in large bowl of electric mixer beat egg yolks at high speed. Continuing to beat at high speed, very gradually add hot syrup. Continue beating until thick and completely cool. Gradually fold in Courvoisier. In chilled bowl with chilled beaters, whip cream only until it holds soft shape, not stiff. Lightly fold about half egg yolk mixture into cream; then fold cream into remaining egg yolk mixture. Leave in bowl or pour into stemmed glasses. Cover; freeze until firm, 8 hours or more. Sprinkle with nutmeg; accompany with pirouettes or other wafer-thin cookies.

Suzanne Richard Cannon

Spoom

A delightful ending for a summer dinner party. Light and pretty to serve.

Preparation: Easy
Cooking Time: 10 Minutes

Serves: 6
Must Do Ahead

½ cup sugar
¼ cup water
2 egg whites, stiffly beaten
1 pint lemon sherbet, softened
  Champagne (inexpensive)
  Strawberries

Combine sugar and water; cook over high heat until mixture reaches soft ball stage (238°F). Pour hot syrup into egg whites while continuing to beat as for divinity. Fold into sherbet. Fill stemmed sherbet glasses ½-¾ full. Freeze (will keep in freezer for 1 week). When ready to serve, lace each serving with champagne and a strawberry. (Lime sherbet may be substituted for lemon; Christian Brothers Château La Salle wine for champagne.)

Micronote: Combine sugar and water. Cook on HIGH for 2 minutes; stir to dissolve sugar. Continue cooking on HIGH to 238°F (approximately 3-4 minutes). Continue as above.

W. C. Wyatt, Jr.
Fort Valley, Georgia

Snowballs with Brandied Date and Walnut Sauce

For a special touch, ignite sauce with an extra ¼ cup brandy.

Preparation: Average

Serves: 16
Must Do Ahead

1 quart orange sherbet
½ gallon vanilla ice cream
3-4 cups grated fresh coconut
  or frozen coconut, thawed
  Brandied Date and Walnut
  Sauce

Divide and form sherbet into 16 equal balls. Slice ice cream into 16 equal pieces. Wrap each slice of ice cream around one sherbet ball. Roll in coconut. Place on cookie sheet; freeze. When firm wrap in waxed paper, place in large plastic bag, and freeze until served. Remove from freezer a few minutes before serving to soften. Place in individual compotes. Ladle Brandied Date and Walnut Sauce over top.

Brandied Date and Walnut Sauce

Yield: 3½ Cups

2 cups light brown sugar,
  packed
1 cup water
1 package pitted chopped
  dates
¼ cup brandy
1 cup chopped English
  walnut pieces

Combine sugar and water in medium saucepan. Cook 20 minutes over medium heat, stirring often. Remove from heat. Add dates, brandy, and nuts; stir. Pour into covered container; refrigerate. To serve warm over low heat. May also be served over vanilla or coffee ice cream.

Micronote: In glass bowl boil water and sugar for 2½-3 minutes. Reduce power to MEDIUM; cook 12-15 minutes, stirring often. Add remaining ingredients; refrigerate.

Debbie Jacobs Springle

Strawberries à la Colony

It looks fancy, tastes great, and fools everyone into thinking you went to a lot of trouble. A terrific way to "dress-up" fresh strawberries.

Preparation: Easy

Serves: 6-8
Must Partially Do Ahead
Must Serve Immediately

2 pints strawberries,
    washed and hulled
½ cup sugar
⅓ cup Cointreau or
    Grand Marnier
½ cup whipping cream, whipped
¼ teaspoon almond extract
½ pint vanilla ice cream,
    softened

Leave berries whole or slice in half as desired. Sprinkle berries with sugar and Cointreau. Chill 1-3 hours. Fold almond extract into whipped cream. Gently fold whipped cream into ice cream. Drain berries. Fold into ice cream mixture. Serve at once in glass bowl.

Karen Durisch Helme
Jacksonville, Florida

Cappuccino Ice Cream

A wonderfully rich touch of Italy. Serve in demitasse cups with a small dollop of whipped cream and/or shaved semi-sweet chocolate on top.

Preparation: Easy

Yield: 2 Quarts
Must Do Ahead

1¼ cups very strong
    hot coffee
¾ cup sugar
½ cup dark corn syrup
3 tablespoons dark rum
½ teaspoon ground cinnamon
2 cups whipping cream

Combine coffee, sugar, corn syrup, rum, and cinnamon. Stir until sugar dissolves. Stir in cream. Pour mixture into 2-quart ice cream freezer can. Freeze according to manufacturer's instructions. Pack in extra ice; let "ripen" at least 1 hour.

Nell Whelchel Wiegand

Helen Johnson's Caramel-Vanilla Ice Cream

Perfect just as it is, but sliced fresh fruit or berries make an extra-good topping.

Preparation: Easy
Cooking Time: 2 Hours

Yield: 1 Gallon
Must Do Ahead

2 (14-ounce) cans sweetened
    condensed milk
4 eggs
2 cups sugar
1 quart half-and-half
1 quart milk
2 cups whipping cream

Cover unopened cans of condensed milk with water in heavy boiler. Boil gently for 2 hours, taking care to keep cans covered with water. Turn cans after 1 hour. (This caramelizes the condensed milk.) **Cool.** Beat eggs with sugar until thick. Add cooled condensed milk, half-and-half, milk, and cream. Mix well. Pour into 1-gallon freezer can; freeze according to manufacturer's instructions. Let ice cream "ripen" in churn one hour or more before serving.

Sally Butts Darden

Basic Vanilla Ice Cream

This is ice cream as you remember it from your childhood! That's where the taste is from - only the no-cook method is thoroughly modern!

Preparation: Easy

Yield: 1 Gallon
Must Do Ahead

5 eggs
1 (14-ounce) can sweetened
    condensed milk
1 cup sugar
1-3 tablespoons vanilla extract
1 (13-ounce) can evaporated
    milk, very cold
1 cup whipping cream
    (optional)
    Whole milk (approximately
    1½ quarts)

In small bowl beat eggs with electric mixer until very foamy, about 5 minutes. Add condensed milk, sugar, and vanilla, beating until well blended. In large bowl beat evaporated milk at high speed until very thick, resembling whipped cream. By hand fold in egg mixture. Pour into 1-gallon freezer can. Add cream and whole milk to fill-line on freezer can; stir well. (May refrigerate at this point for several hours.) Freeze according to manufacturer's instructions. Pack well in extra ice; let "ripen" for 1 hour before serving.

Variations: Fruit and Cream - Mash or purée in electric blender or food processor, 2 cups fruit of your choice (peaches, strawberries, blueberries, bananas, cherries, etc.). Add ½ cup sugar to fruit if needed, depending upon ripeness of fruit. Stir into contents of freezer can just before adding whole milk. Proceed as above.

Chocolate Chip Ice Cream - Finely chop 1 (6-ounce) package chocolate chips in electric blender or food processor. Stir into contents of freezer can just before adding whole milk. Proceed as above.

Peppermint Ice Cream - Omit vanilla extract. Coarsely break up 1 pound peppermint candy. Place candy and 2 cups whole milk in electric blender container; process until candy is thoroughly crushed. Stir into contents of freezer can just before adding remainder of whole milk. Proceed as above.

Substitute other flavorings for all or part of the vanilla. Suggested possibilities: lemon, almond, coconut, rum, brandy.

Becky Smith Dadisman
Ann Ash Hartness
Carol Cato Mendenhall
Beth Davies Davidson

Fresh Lemon Ice Cream

More suitable as an elegant dessert than as a make-in-the-backyard variety.

Preparation: Easy

Yield: 1 Gallon
Must Do Ahead

1 **quart whipping cream**
1 **quart whole milk**
4 **cups sugar**
  Juice of 6 lemons
  Grated rind of 2 lemons
  Lemon slices (optional)

Pour all ingredients into 1-gallon ice cream freezer can. Stir until thoroughly blended. Freeze according to manufacturer's instructions. Serve immediately, or pack and store for later use. (Maintains nice creamy texture for several weeks.) Scoop into compotes, topping with thinly sliced lemon twists or fresh blueberry sauce.

Helen Odom Rice

The ice-cream was passed around with cake -- gold and silver cake arranged on platters in alternate slices....It was pronounced a great success....

Kate Chopin, *The Awakening*

Chocolate Lover's Ice Cream

Preparation: Easy

Yield: 1 Gallon
Must Do Ahead

3 **eggs**
1 **cup sugar**
1 **quart half-and-half**
1 **pint whipping cream**
1 **cup chocolate syrup**
1 **tablespoon vanilla extract**
  Approximately 3 cups milk

Beat eggs with electric mixer at medium speed until frothy. Gradually add sugar, beating until thick. Add half-and-half, cream, syrup, and vanilla; mix well. Pour into 1-gallon freezer can. Add enough milk to fill can ¾ full. Freeze according to manufacturer's instructions. Pack with extra ice. Let "ripen" in freezer at least one hour.

Brenda Jones Adams

Pineapple Sherbet

Sherbet is often overlooked as a homemade ice cream. This one is good and creamy, but still very light. Use unsweetened canned pineapple to reduce the calories.

Preparation: Easy

Yield: 1 Gallon
Must Do Ahead

3 **cups sugar**
6 **cups whole milk**
3 **(7½-ounce) cans**
  crushed pineapple
3 **lemons, juice and**
  grated rind

Combine sugar and milk; stir until sugar is dissolved. Stir in pineapple and juice. Add lemon juice and rind. Pour into 1-gallon freezer can; freeze according to manufacturer's instructions. Pack well with additional ice; let "ripen" in churn for 1 hour before serving.

Susan Bible Jessup

Strawberry-Champagne Sherbet

Preparation: Easy

Yield: 1¼ Quarts
Must Do Ahead

1 cup whipping cream
¾ cup sugar, divided
1½ cups champagne
1 (10-ounce) package
    frozen strawberries or
    peaches, thawed
2 egg whites
¼ teaspoon cream of tartar
    Red food coloring
    (optional)
    Whole strawberries
    (optional)

In small saucepan combine cream and ½ cup sugar. Cook and stir over medium heat until sugar is dissolved. Let cool. Stir in champagne and undrained berries. Pour into 8 x 8 x 2-inch pan. Cover; freeze until firm. Using electric mixer, beat egg whites and cream of tartar until soft peaks form. Slowly add remaining ¼ cup sugar, beating until stiff peaks form. Remove champagne mixture from freezer; break into chunks. Turn into large chilled mixer bowl. Beat with electric mixer until smooth. By hand fold in beaten egg whites. Tint with food coloring, if desired. Cover; freeze again until firm. Serve in champagne glasses; garnish with whole berry on the rim.

Connie Kemp Goldfarb

Lemon Ice Cream Sauce

Preparation: Easy
Cooking Time: 5 Minutes

Serves: 4

½ cup sugar
3 tablespoons butter
1 beaten egg
2 tablespoons fresh lemon
    juice
    Grated rind of ½ lemon

Combine all ingredients in saucepan. Cook over low heat until mixture coats metal spoon. Serve warm or cold over vanilla ice cream.
Micronote: Combine ingredients. Cook on HIGH 1-1½ minutes, stirring every 30 seconds.

Flo Criss Smith

Almond-Honey Ice Cream Sauce

Great to have on hand for a busy day or unexpected guests. Keeps well refrigerated in a covered jar; when ready to serve, reheat just until warm.

Preparation: Easy
Cooking Time: 10 Minutes

Yield: 1 Cup

3 tablespoons butter, melted
2 tablespoons cornstarch
⅔ cup honey
½ cup sliced or slivered
    almonds
2 tablespoons brandy
½-1 teaspoon lemon juice

Mix butter and cornstarch until smooth. Add honey. Cook over low heat for 5 minutes, stirring constantly. Add almonds, brandy, and lemon juice. Stir until well blended. Serve warm sauce over individual servings of vanilla, coconut, or coffee ice cream.
Micronote: Mix melted butter, cornstarch, and honey. Cook on HIGH 1½-2 minutes, stirring several times. Add remaining ingredients; stir to blend.

Patricia Franklin Rauch

Dessert Fondues

Serve dessert fondue with fruit (pineapple chunks, dates, strawberries, orange sections, banana chunks) or with dippers of pound or angel food cake. For a crowd fix all three sauces and let them experiment. Simple to prepare and fun for everyone.

Preparation: Easy
Cooking Time: 10 Minutes

Lemon Fondue Sauce

2¼ cups water
1½ cups confectioners' sugar
6 tablespoons cornstarch
12 inches lemon rind,
      ½ inch wide
¾ cup butter
1 (6-ounce) can lemonade
      concentrate

Yield: 3½ Cups

Combine water, sugar, cornstarch, and lemon rind in electric blender jar. Cover and process until rind is finely grated. Pour into saucepan. Add butter. Cook over medium heat, stirring constantly, until butter is melted and mixture is thick and shiny. Stir in lemonade concentrate. Delicious served warm over pound cake or gingerbread.

Micronote: Combine all ingredients except lemonade concentrate. Place in glass bowl; cook on HIGH 6-7 minutes or until thick, stirring often. Add lemonade concentrate.

Cynthia Sims Syfan

Fruit Blush

1 (10-ounce) package frozen
      strawberries or other
      fruit, thawed
¼ cup whipping cream
1 teaspoon cornstarch
½ teaspoon lemon juice

Yield: 1½ Cups

Combine all ingredients in electric blender container; blend well. Pour into saucepan or fondue pot. Heat over medium heat. Reduce temperature to warm for serving.

Micronote: Combine ingredients in blender; blend well. Heat in microwave on MEDIUM for 5 minutes. (Time may vary due to temperature of fruit.)

Cynthia Sims Syfan

Brandied Chocolate Sauce

1 cup semi-sweet chocolate
      pieces
½ cup evaporated milk,
      scalded
2 tablespoons brandy or 1
      teaspoon brandy extract
   Dash salt

Yield: 1 Cup

Combine chocolate and scalded milk, stirring until chocolate melts and mixture is smooth. Stir in brandy and salt. Serve in fondue pot or chafing dish.

Micronote: Scald milk in microwave 2 minutes on MEDIUM. Add chocolate, stirring to melt. Stir in brandy and salt.

Gail Adams Thomas

Famous Chocolate Fudge Sauce

Delicious over peppermint ice cream!

Preparation: Easy
Cooking Time: 30 Minutes

Yield: 4 Cups

    7 ounces unsweetened chocolate
    1¾ cups sugar
    1 tablespoon butter or margarine
    ¼ teaspoon salt
    1 (12-ounce) can evaporated
        milk
    1 teaspoon vanilla extract

In double boiler melt chocolate; add sugar, butter, and salt, stirring until well blended. Add evaporated milk; cook until thick. Remove from heat; stir in vanilla. Serve warm.
Micronote: Place all ingredients in large glass bowl. Cook on HIGH 3½-4 minutes, or until thick, stirring every minute.

Frances Jolley Syfan

Top Hat Brownies

Dark, rich, and elegant - with or without the icing.

Preparation: Average
Cooking Time: 40-45 Minutes
Oven Temperature: 325°F

Yield: 2 Dozen
Must Do Ahead

    4 eggs
    2 cups sugar
    1½ cups sifted flour
    1 teaspoon baking powder
    ½ teaspoon salt
    ⅔ cup oil
    2-3 tablespoons cocoa
    2 teaspoons vanilla extract
    1 cup chopped pecans
        Fudge Icing

Beat eggs well. Gradually add sugar while continuing to beat. Add flour, baking powder, and salt. Mix until thoroughly blended. In separate bowl blend oil and cocoa; add to egg mixture. Stir in vanilla and pecans. Turn into greased 13 x 9-inch pan. Bake at 325°F for 40-45 minutes. Spread Fudge Icing over warm brownies. Cool completely before cutting.

Fudge Icing

    ½ cup margarine
    2-3 tablespoons cocoa
    ¼ cup milk
    1 (16-ounce) box
        confectioners' sugar
    1 teaspoon vanilla extract

Melt margarine in large saucepan. Add cocoa and milk; bring to boil. Immediately add confectioners' sugar and beat with wire whisk until smooth. Stir in vanilla.
Micronote: Place margarine in large glass measure. Cook on HIGH for 45 seconds. Add cocoa and milk; cook on HIGH until mixture boils. Proceed as above.

Jody Bacon Mulkey
Chattanooga, Tennessee

Cheesecake Bars

Preparation: Average
Cooking Time: 20-25 Minutes
Oven Temperature: 350°F

Yield: 3 Dozen
Must Do Ahead

¾ cup finely crushed graham crackers, divided
½ cup flour
½ cup chopped nuts
¼ cup sugar
½ cup butter or margarine, melted
2 (8-ounce) packages cream cheese, softened
⅔ cup sugar
2 eggs
2 tablespoons lemon juice
1 teaspoon grated lemon rind

Stir together ⅔ cup crumbs, flour, nuts, and sugar. Add butter; mix until crumbly. Pat into ungreased 13 x 9 x 2-inch baking pan. Bake at 350°F for 12 minutes. Beat cream cheese and sugar until light. Add eggs, lemon juice, and rind; mix well. Pour over baked layer. Bake at 350°F for 20-25 minutes. Sprinkle with remaining crumbs. Cool; cut into bars. Chill at least 4 hours before serving. Store in refrigerator. Each bar can be topped with fresh or canned fruit or with preserves.

Carol Lynn Dobson Waggoner

Cream Cheese Brownies

Preparation: Average
Cooking Time: 35-40 Minutes
Oven Temperature: 350°F

Yield: 16-20
Must Do Ahead

1 (4-ounce) package German Sweet Chocolate
5 tablespoons butter or margarine, divided
1 (3-ounce) package cream cheese, softened
1 cup sugar, divided
3 eggs
½ cup + 1 tablespoon flour
1½ teaspoons vanilla extract, divided
½ teaspoon baking powder
¼ teaspoon salt
½ cup chopped nuts
¼ teaspoon almond extract

Over low heat melt chocolate with 3 tablespoons butter, stirring constantly; cool. Cream remaining 2 tablespoons butter with cream cheese. Gradually add ¼ cup sugar, creaming well. Blend in 1 egg, 1 tablespoon flour, and ½ teaspoon vanilla; set aside. Beat 2 eggs until thick and light in color. Gradually add ¾ cup sugar, beating until thickened. Add baking powder, salt, and ½ cup flour. Blend in chocolate mixture, nuts, 1 teaspoon vanilla, and almond extract. Spread half of mixture in greased 9-inch square pan. Spread cheese mixture over top; spoon on remaining chocolate batter. [Use waxed paper method (page 304) to spread layers.] Zig-zag through batters with spatula to marble. Bake at 350°F for 35-40 minutes. Cool completely before cutting. Store in refrigerator.

Mardy Miller Fulenwider

Praline Brownies

Extra moist and chewy. We defy anyone to guess that these scrumptious brownies come from a mix.

Preparation: Easy
Cooking Time: 25-30 Minutes
Oven Temperature: 350°F

Yield: 2 Dozen
Must Do Ahead

1 (22½-ounce) package
    brownie mix
¾ cup firmly packed
    light brown sugar
¾ cup chopped pecans
3 tablespoons margarine,
    melted

Prepare brownie mix according to package directions. (Do not add nuts.) Place in greased 13 x 9 x 2-inch pan. In small mixing bowl combine remaining ingredients. Sprinkle over brownie batter. Bake 25-30 minutes. Cut when thoroughly cooled. These freeze well or can be stored in a tin.

Sherrie Nathan Schrage

Toffee Squares

Preparation: Average
Cooking Time: 20 Minutes
Oven Temperature: 350°F

Yield: 5-6 Dozen

1 cup butter or ½ cup
    butter and ½ cup
    margarine, softened
1 cup firmly packed
    light brown sugar
1 egg yolk
1 teaspoon vanilla extract
2 cups self-rising flour
¼ teaspoon salt
3-4 (⅞-ounce) milk
    chocolate candy bars
½ cup chopped nuts

Cream butter, sugar, egg yolk, and vanilla. Thoroughly blend in flour and salt. Spread dough in greased 15½ x 10½-inch jelly roll pan. Bake at 350°F for 20 minutes or until nicely browned. (Cookies will be soft to touch.) Remove from oven. Immediately place separated squares of chocolate on top. Let stand until chocolate is soft, then spread evenly over entire surface. Sprinkle with nuts. Cut into small squares while warm.

Coraleen Edmondson Davidson

Caramel Bars

Preparation: Easy
Cooking Time: 50 Minutes-1 Hour
Oven Temperature: 300°F

Yield: 2 Dozen
Must Do Ahead

1 cup butter, melted
1 (16-ounce) package light
    brown sugar
½ cup sugar
4 eggs, separated
2 cups sifted flour
1 teaspoon baking powder
2 teaspoons vanilla extract
1 cup toasted chopped nuts
    Confectioners' sugar

Cream butter and sugars. Beat in egg yolks. Sift together flour and baking powder. Add to creamed mixture, beating well. Stir in vanilla. In separate bowl beat egg whites until stiff. Fold nuts and beaten egg whites into batter. Pour into well-greased 13 x 9-inch pan. Bake at 300°F for 50 minutes to 1 hour. Let cool in pan. Cut into squares; dust tops with confectioners' sugar.

Paddy McLendon Estes
Atlanta, Georgia

Pumpkin Bars

Great for a fall picnic.

Preparation: Average
Cooking Time: 25-30 Minutes
Oven Temperature: 350°F

Yield: 2 Dozen

4 eggs
1⅔ cups sugar
1 cup oil
1 (16-ounce) can pumpkin
2 cups flour
2 teaspoons baking powder
2 teaspoons ground cinnamon
1 teaspoon salt
1 teaspoon baking soda
Cream Cheese Icing

Beat eggs, sugar, oil, and pumpkin until light and fluffy. Mix flour, baking powder, cinnamon, salt, and soda. Add to pumpkin mixture, blending thoroughly. Spread batter in ungreased 15 x 10 x 1-inch baking pan. Bake at 350°F for 25-30 minutes. When cool frost with Cream Cheese Icing. Cut into bars to serve.

Cream Cheese Icing

1 (3-ounce) package cream cheese, softened
½ cup butter or margarine, softened
1 teaspoon vanilla extract
2 cups sifted confectioners' sugar

Combine cream cheese and butter; cream well. Stir in vanilla. Add confectioners' sugar, beating until mixture is smooth.

Judy Mynatt Bush

Honey Bars

Preparation: Easy
Cooking Time: 12-15 Minutes
Oven Temperature: 325°F

Yield: 36

2 cups flour
1 scant teaspoon baking soda
1½ teaspoons ground cinnamon
¼ teaspoon salt
1 cup sugar
¾ cup oil
¼ cup honey
1 egg
¼ cup chopped pecans (optional)
Topping

Combine flour, soda, cinnamon, and salt. Mix well; set aside. Combine remaining ingredients. Mix with dry ingredients. (This is a sticky dough not suitable for mixer.) Press onto ungreased 12 x 9-inch cookie sheet. Bake at 325°F for 12-15 minutes. Cool only slightly before spreading with topping. Cut into bars.

Topping

1 cup confectioners' sugar
3 tablespoons mayonnaise
1½ tablespoons water
1 teaspoon vanilla extract

Mix all ingredients; spread over warm cookies.

Kaye Cooper Rigdon

Chess Squares

A marvelous recipe with which to experiment. Try plain vanilla bars or lemon; add coconut, nuts, or both. You can't go wrong!

Preparation: Easy
Cooking Time: 35-45 Minutes
Oven Temperature: 350°F

Yield: 2 Dozen
Must Do Ahead

1 box yellow cake mix or 1 box lemon supreme cake mix
4 eggs, divided
½ cup margarine, softened
1 (8-ounce) package cream cheese
1 (16-ounce) box confectioners' sugar
1 cup finely chopped coconut (optional)
1 cup chopped nuts (optional)

Thoroughly blend cake mix, 1 egg, and margarine. Spread in greased 13 x 9 x 2-inch pan; smooth with spatula. Blend 3 eggs, cream cheese, and sugar. Stir in coconut and/or nuts, if desired. Pour over cake mixture. Bake at 350°F for 35-45 minutes. Cool before cutting.

Lois Tanner Wallis

Crème de Menthe Squares

A cookie version of the popular candy. Now you can make your own! Nice served with after-dinner coffee. Also makes a good gift.

Preparation: Average

Yield: 8 Dozen
Must Do Ahead

1¼ cups butter or margarine, divided
½ cup cocoa
3½ cups sifted confectioners' sugar, divided
1 beaten egg
1 teaspoon vanilla extract
2 cups graham cracker crumbs
⅓ cup green crème de menthe
1½ cups semi-sweet chocolate pieces

Bottom layer: In saucepan combine ½ cup butter and cocoa. Heat and stir until well blended. Remove from heat; add ½ cup confectioners' sugar, egg, and vanilla. Stir in cracker crumbs. Mix well. Press into bottom of ungreased 13 x 9 x 2-inch baking pan. Middle layer: Melt another ½ cup butter. In small mixer bowl combine melted butter and crème de menthe. At low speed of electric mixer beat in remaining 3 cups of confectioners' sugar until smooth. Use waxed paper method (page 304) to spread over chocolate layer. Chill 1 hour. Top layer: In small saucepan combine remaining ¼ cup butter and chocolate pieces. Cook and stir over low heat until melted. Spread over mint layer. Chill 1-2 hours. Set out at room temperature a few minutes before cutting. Cut into small squares. Store in refrigerator.

Lylla Crum Bowen

Orange Morsels

Great for a party; but be prepared - they disappear fast!

Preparation: Easy

Yield: 7-8 Dozen Balls

2¾ cups fine vanilla wafer
    crumbs
1 cup confectioners' sugar
1 cup chopped pecans
⅓ cup butter, melted
¼ cup undiluted orange
    juice concentrate
Butter Icing
1 (3½-ounce) can coconut

Combine all ingredients; shape into bite-sized balls. Dip each ball into Butter Icing; roll in coconut.

Butter Icing

1 cup confectioners' sugar
2 tablespoons melted butter
Orange juice or milk
    to make a thin icing
    (approximately 3
    tablespoons)

Mix all ingredients until smooth.

Peggy Sheridan Cathey

Susie Hutchens' Marmalade Tarts

One of our greatest "tasting party" hits.

Preparation: Average
Cooking Time: 12-15 Minutes
Oven Temperature: 400°F

Yield: 20
Must Partially Do Ahead

1 cup grated Cheddar cheese
½ cup butter, softened
1 cup sifted flour
Orange marmalade

Cream butter and cheese. Add flour; mix thoroughly. Wrap in waxed paper; refrigerate overnight. Roll dough on lightly floured surface to thin pastry. Cut with 3 to 4-inch round biscuit cutter. Place ½ teaspoon orange marmalade on each round. Fold over; press edges with fork to seal. Bake at 400°F for 12-15 minutes. (Substitute apricot or strawberry preserves for a different taste treat.)

Sue Hutchens Henson
Monroe, Georgia

Gingerbread Boys

Decorate with confectioners' sugar icing or prepared decorator icing for Christmas or Halloween. Try placing a lollypop stick in each cookie before baking; insert into an apple for an attractive decoration.

Preparation: Average
Cooking Time: 6 Minutes
Oven Temperature: 375°F

Yield: 6-7 Dozen
Must Partially Do Ahead

    1 cup sugar
    1 cup shortening
    ½ teaspoon salt
    1 cup molasses
    1 egg
    2 tablespoons vinegar
    5 cups sifted flour
    1 tablespoon ground ginger
    1½ teaspoons baking soda
    1 teaspoon ground cinnamon
    1 teaspoon ground cloves
       Red hot candies

Thoroughly cream shortening, sugar, and salt. Stir in molasses, egg, and vinegar; beat well. Sift together dry ingredients; stir into molasses mixture. Chill at least 3 hours or overnight. On lightly floured surface, roll to ⅛-inch thickness. Cut with gingerbread boy cookie cutter. Place 1 inch apart on greased cookie sheet. Use red hots for faces and buttons. Bake at 375°F about 6 minutes. Cool slightly; remove from cookie sheet to cooling racks.

Frances Rozier Birdsong
Sparta, Georgia

Cut-Out Cookies

A wonderful cut-out cookie for any season of the year!

Preparation: Average
Cooking Time: 8-10 Minutes
Oven Temperature: 375°F

Yield: 3 Dozen
Must Partially Do Ahead

    1   cup sugar
    1   cup firmly packed
          light brown sugar
    ½   cup margarine
    ½   cup shortening
    2   eggs
    3½ cups flour
    ½   teaspoon salt
    ¼   teaspoon baking powder
    ¼   teaspoon baking soda
    ½-1 teaspoon each of vanilla,
          lemon, and almond extract
          (or equivalent flavoring of
          your choice)

Cream sugars, margarine, and shortening. Add eggs and beat well. Sift together dry ingredients. Blend sifted ingredients into creamed mixture; knead. Divide into 3 parts; add choice of extracts. (If making only 1 or 2 flavors, adjust amount of extracts accordingly.) Chill dough for 2 hours in refrigerator. Roll to desired thinness; cut out with cookie cutters. Bake on greased cookie sheets at 375°F for 8-10 minutes. Remove to racks to cool.

Mary Kelly Rogers

Swedish Almond Cookies

Preparation: Average
Cooking Time: 12 Minutes
Oven Temperature: 375°F

Yield: 6 Dozen

½ cup shortening
½ cup butter or margarine,
    softened
1 cup sifted confectioners'
    sugar
½ teaspoon salt
2 cups flour
1 tablespoon water
2 teaspoons almond extract
1 cup ground almonds
    Confectioners' sugar

Cream shortening and butter until light and fluffy. Add confectioners' sugar and salt; mix well. Stir in flour. Add water, almond extract, and almonds, stirring to blend. Shape dough into 1-inch balls; place on ungreased cookie sheets. Flatten slightly with bottom of floured glass. Bake at 375°F for 12 minutes or until done. Dredge cookies in confectioners' sugar while still warm.

Diane Derrick Blalock

Pecan Fingers

Preparation: Average
Cooking Time: 15-20 Minutes
Oven Temperature: 300°F

Yield: 2½ Dozen

1 cup butter or margarine,
    softened
4 heaping tablespoons
    confectioners' sugar
¼ teaspoon salt
2 teaspoons vanilla extract
1 teaspoon water
2 cups sifted flour
1 cup finely chopped pecans

Using hands mix butter with remaining ingredients in order listed to make stiff dough. Pinch off small pieces of dough; form into 1-inch long rolls. Place on ungreased cookie sheet. Bake on top shelf of oven at 300°F until light brown, 15-20 minutes. Roll in confectioners' sugar while still warm. Store in covered tin.

Susan Lynch Gilliam

Almond Madeleines

A variation on the classic French tea cake immortalized by Marcel Proust. Try them as an attractive substitute for sweet bread or muffins.

Preparation: Average
Cooking Time: 12 Minutes
Oven Temperature: 400°F

Yield: 2 Dozen

2 eggs, separated
⅔ cup sugar
½ cup butter, softened
1 cup sifted flour
1 teaspoon baking powder
¼ cup ground toasted almonds
1 teaspoon almond extract
    Confectioners' sugar
    (optional)

Butter and flour madeleine molds. Combine egg yolks and sugar; blend in butter. Mix flour and baking powder; stir into egg-sugar mixture. Beat egg whites until stiff; fold into batter. Fold in almonds and almond extract. Fill each mold half full of batter. Bake at 400°F for 12 minutes or until golden. Sprinkle with confectioners' sugar; serve warm. (Best when served the day they are baked, but can be kept overnight and reheated.)

Flo Criss Smith

Brown Sugar Icebox Cookies

Keep a roll or two of these in your freezer for those times when your family wants home-baked cookies and you want to be out of the kitchen.

Preparation: Easy
Cooking Time: 10-15 Minutes
Oven Temperature: 400°F

Yield: 6 Dozen
Must Partially Do Ahead

2 **cups light brown sugar**
1 **cup butter or shortening**
2 **eggs**
3 **cups sifted flour**
1 **teaspoon baking soda**
1 **teaspoon salt**
1 **teaspoon cream of tartar**
1 **teaspoon ground cinnamon (optional)**
1 **teaspoon vanilla extract**
1 **cup chopped nuts**

Cream sugar and butter; add eggs, beating well. Sift together flour, soda, salt, cream of tartar, and cinnamon. Add to creamed mixture, blending well. Add vanilla and nuts. Form into rolls; wrap in waxed paper. Refrigerate overnight or until well chilled (may also be frozen). Dough will keep up to four weeks in refrigerator. To bake slice very thin. Place on ungreased baking sheet. Bake at 400°F for 10-15 minutes.

Violet Lee Nicholson

Cream Cheese Cookies

Decorate and flavor according to the season. Icing or dough can be tinted any color or left plain. Omit vanilla from icing and add a few drops of peppermint, wintergreen, orange, or other flavors. Dough can be refrigerated if necessary.

Preparation: Average
Cooking Time: 10-12 Minutes
Oven Temperature: 400°F

Yield: 5 Dozen
Must Partially Do Ahead

½ **cup shortening**
1 **(3-ounce) package cream cheese, softened**
⅓ **cup sugar**
1 **egg yolk**
1½ **teaspoons orange extract**
1½ **cups flour**
½ **teaspoon salt**
Creamy Icing

Cream shortening and cheese. Add sugar gradually, creaming until light and fluffy. Add egg yolk and orange extract; beat well. Sift together flour and salt; add to creamed mixture by thirds, beating well after each addition. Chill dough 15 minutes or more. Pack into cookie press; make into desired shapes. (Set cookie dial between thin and medium to make 5 dozen.) Bake at 400°F for 10-12 minutes. Cool on wire racks. Frost with Creamy Icing using decorating gun or spread over tops.

Creamy Icing

2 **cups confectioners' sugar**
¼ **cup margarine**
1 **teaspoon vanilla extract**
1 **tablespoon cream**

Combine all ingredients; blend until smooth. Flavor and color as desired. Beat until fluffy.

Melba Clark Jacobs

Mincemeat Cookies

Start a Christmas tradition with these crisp, delicious cookies.

Preparation: Easy
Cooking Time: 10 Minutes
Oven Temperature: 350°F

Yield: 12 Dozen
Must Partially Do Ahead

4 cups sifted flour
1 teaspoon baking powder
1 teaspoon ground nutmeg
½ teaspoon salt
⅛ teaspoon ground ginger
1 cup butter, softened
2 cups sugar
3 eggs
1 cup mincemeat with
    brandy-rum
½ cup chopped pecans

Sift together dry ingredients. Cream butter and sugar; add eggs, beating well. Fold in dry ingredients, mincemeat, and pecans. Refrigerate dough until slightly chilled. Drop from teaspoon onto lightly greased cookie sheet. Bake at 350°F for 10 minutes or until golden brown. Remove onto wire rack to cool. Store in tin to preserve crispness.

Jean Thompson Brannon

Apricot Cookies

It's nice to find a cookie that is both different and good. You'll enjoy serving these.

Preparation: Average
Cooking Time: 10-14 Minutes
Oven Temperature: 350°F

Yield: 2½ Dozen

½ cup butter or margarine,
    softened
1 (3-ounce) package cream
    cheese, softened
1¼ cups flour
¼ cup sugar
1 teaspoon baking powder
½ cup apricot preserves
½ cup chopped pecans
    Apricot Icing

Combine butter and cream cheese, beating until smooth. In separate bowl combine dry ingredients; stir into creamed mixture. Add preserves and nuts; mix well. Use tablespoon to drop dough onto greased cookie sheet. Bake at 350°F for 10-14 minutes. Cool slightly. While still warm, frost with Apricot Icing.

Apricot Icing

1 cup sifted confectioners'
    sugar
¼ cup apricot preserves
1 tablespoon butter or
    margarine, softened

Combine all ingredients, beat until smooth.

Patricia Franklin Rauch

Christmas Fruit Cookies

Preparation: Average
Cooking Time: 20-30 Minutes
Oven Temperature: 300°F

Yield: 6-8 Dozen

1 cup butter
1 cup firmly packed light
    brown sugar
3 eggs
3 cups flour
1 teaspoon ground cinnamon
1 teaspoon baking soda
½ cup bourbon or milk
2 cups chopped candied
    cherries
2 cups chopped dates
6 slices crystallized
    pineapple, chopped
7 cups chopped pecans

Cream butter and sugar. Add eggs, one at a time, beating well after each addition. Sift together dry ingredients. Add flour mixture alternately with bourbon, blending well. Add fruits and nuts to batter. (Dough can be refrigerated at this point if necessary.) Drop from teaspoon onto greased cookie sheet. Bake at 300°F for 20-30 minutes.

Sarah Grimes Butts
Sparta, Georgia

There were glossed sticky dates, cold rich figs, cramped belly to belly in small boxes.

Thomas Wolfe, from *Look Homeward, Angel.*
Charles Scribner's Sons, Copyright 1929.
Copyright renewed 1957 Edward C. Aswell, Administrator, C.T.A. and/or Fred W. Wolfe.
Reprinted with the permission of Charles Scribner's Sons.

Morning Delights

Try these instead of bread for breakfast or brunch; they are truly a morning delight!

Preparation: Average
Cooking Time: 12 Minutes
Oven Temperature: 350°F

Yield: 4 Dozen Cookies
Must Serve Immediately

1 cup flour
¾ cup sugar
¼ teaspoon baking soda
12-15 slices bacon, cooked, drained
    and broken into bits
½ cup margarine, softened
1 egg
2 cups raisin bran cereal
½ teaspoon vanilla extract

Mix flour, sugar, and soda in bowl. Add bacon, margarine, and egg. Mix until all ingredients are well blended. Stir in cereal and vanilla. Drop by spoonfuls onto greased baking sheet. (They spread, so don't place too close together.) Bake at 350°F for 12 minutes until lightly browned. (They burn easily, so watch cooking time!) Better if eaten right away.

Nell Whelchel Wiegand

Gingersnaps

Homemade are always better than "store-bought." Bet you didn't know they were so easy.

Preparation: Easy
Cooking Time: 8-10 Minutes
Oven Temperature: 350°F

Yield: 3 Dozen

    2 **cups sugar, divided**
    ¾ **cup shortening**
    1 **egg**
    ¼ **cup molasses**
    2 **cups flour**
 1½ **teaspoons baking soda**
    1 **teaspoon ground cloves**
    1 **teaspoon ground cinnamon**
    1 **teaspoon ground ginger**

Cream 1 cup sugar and shortening. Add egg and molasses, beating well. Combine dry ingredients; add to creamed mixture. Drop heaping teaspoonfuls of dough into remaining 1 cup sugar. Remove and shape into balls. Place on lightly greased cookie sheet. Bake at 350°F for 8-10 minutes.

Nancy Martin Brewer

Remelle's Oatmeal Cookies

Oatmeal cookies as good as those you remember from your childhood. Use the basic recipe or try the optional ingredients.

Preparation: Easy
Cooking Time: 10 Minutes
Oven Temperature: 375°F

Yield: 5 Dozen

  ½ **cup firmly packed light brown sugar**
  ½ **cup sugar**
  ½ **cup shortening**
  1 **egg**
  1 **tablespoon water**
  2 **teaspoons vanilla extract**
  1 **cup flour**
  ½ **teaspoon salt**
  ½ **teaspoon baking powder**
  ½ **teaspoon baking soda**
  ¼ **teaspoon cinnamon (optional)**
  ¼ **teaspoon nutmeg (optional)**
 1½ **cups rolled oats**
  ½ **cup chopped nuts (optional)**
  ½ **cup raisins (optional)**
  ½ **cup shredded coconut (optional)**

Cream sugars and shortening. Add egg, water, and vanilla; blend well. Combine flour, salt, baking powder, soda, and desired spices. Gradually blend into creamed mixture. Fold in oats and any remaining optional ingredients. (Mixes well in food processor.) Drop by teaspoonfuls onto greased baking sheets. Bake at 375°F for 10 minutes.

Jane Hix Oliver

Fruit Jewels

The chocolate makes an interesting flavor combination with the candied fruit. Different from the usual fruitcake cookie and very good.

Preparation: Average
Cooking Time: 12 Minutes
Oven Temperature: 375°F

Yield: 3 Dozen Cookies

  1 cup flour
  1 teaspoon baking powder
  1 teaspoon salt
  2 teaspoons ground cinnamon
  ¼ teaspoon ground nutmeg
  ¼ teaspoon ground cloves
  ¼ cup butter or margarine
  ½ cup firmly packed light
       brown sugar
  ½ cup evaporated milk
  2 cups chopped mixed
       candied fruit
  1 cup walnuts
  1 (6-ounce) package semi-sweet
       chocolate morsels
  1 cup raisins

Sift together dry ingredients. Cream butter and sugar. Add milk. Stir dry ingredients into creamed mixture. Add remaining ingredients, mixing well. Drop by heaping table-spoonfuls onto greased cookie sheet. Bake at 375°F for 12 minutes.

Nancy Martin Brewer

100 Cookies

The name only tells you how many - not how yummy they are.

Preparation: Easy
Cooking Time: 10-12 Minutes
Oven Temperature: 350°F

Yield: 100

  1 cup sugar
  1 cup firmly packed light
       brown sugar
  1 cup margarine, softened
  1 cup oil
  1 cup Rice Krispies
  1 cup flaked coconut
  1 cup quick oats
  1 egg
  1 teaspoon vanilla extract
  3½ cups unsifted flour
  1 teaspoon baking soda
  1 teaspoon cream of tartar
  ¾ teaspoon salt
  1 (6-ounce) package
       Bits of Brickle

In large bowl mix sugars, margarine, oil, cereal, coconut, oats, egg, and vanilla. Mix well. Sift together flour, soda, cream of tartar, and salt; add to sugar mixture. Mix well. Fold in Bits of Brickle. Drop by teaspoonfuls onto greased cookie sheet. Bake at 350°F for 10-12 minutes. (May use chocolate chips in place of Brickle, if desired.)

Joyce Jackson Rabb

Sugar Cookies

It sounds basic, but if you have searched for just the right recipe for this ever-popular cookie, you will appreciate this one.

Preparation: Easy
Cooking Time: 7 Minutes
Oven Temperature: 350°F

Yield: 6 Dozen
Must Do Ahead

- 1 cup margarine, softened
- 1 cup oil, less 1 tablespoon
- 1 cup sugar
- 1 cup confectioners' sugar
- 2 eggs
- 1 teaspoon vanilla extract
- ½ teaspoon other extract of choice (optional)
- 4 cups sifted flour
- 1 teaspoon cream of tartar
- ½ teaspoon salt
- ½ teaspoon baking soda
  Sugar

Cream margarine, oil, and sugars. Add eggs and flavorings mixing well. Add flour, cream of tartar, and soda, blending well. Chill dough overnight. (Dough may be kept covered in refrigerator up to 1 month.) To make cookies, roll 1 teaspoon of dough into ball; roll ball in sugar. Place on ungreased cookie sheet; flatten crisscross with fork. Bake at 350°F for 7 minutes or until very lightly browned. Store in a tin.

Becky Smith Dadisman

Microwave Toffee

Good and crunchy.

Preparation: Average
Cooking Time: 8-12 Minutes

Yield: 1 (15 x 10 x 1-inch) Pan
Must Do Ahead

- 2 cups sugar or 2¼ cups firmly packed light brown sugar
- ⅔ cup margarine or ⅓ cup margarine and ⅓ cup butter
- 2 tablespoons water
- 1 tablespoon light corn syrup
- 1 teaspoon vanilla extract
- 1 (6-ounce) package semi-sweet chocolate morsels
- ¾ cup chopped pecans

Combine sugar, margarine, water, and corn syrup in deep 3-quart casserole. Microwave on HIGH for 8-12 minutes until mixture reaches hard-crack stage (300-325°F), stirring once halfway through cooking time. Stir in vanilla. Pour onto greased 15 x 10 x 1-inch jelly roll pan, quickly spreading to edges of pan. Sprinkle chocolate morsels over toffee; let stand 1 minute or until chocolate begins to melt. Spread chocolate over entire candy layer. Press pecans lightly into chocolate. Let stand until set. Break into pieces. Store refrigerated in covered container.

Jacqueline Mabry Frankum

Candied Orange Pecans

Our members begged for this recipe when it was served at a tasting brunch. It also makes a good gift. Wrap in colored cellophane and tie with ribbon.

Preparation: Average
Cooking Time: 20 Minutes

Yield: 1 Pound
Must Do Ahead

        2 **cups sugar**
        ¾ **cup fresh orange juice**
        1 **tablespoon grated**
            orange rind
        3 **cups pecan halves**

Mix sugar and orange juice in 2-quart saucepan. Bring to boil over medium heat. Reduce heat to low; cook to soft-ball stage, 235°F on candy thermometer (approximately 15-20 minutes). Check frequently to be sure not to overcook. Remove from heat; add rind and pecans. Stir until mixture turns cream color, 7-10 minutes. Pour onto waxed paper. When cool, break apart; store in airtight container.
Micronote: Mix orange juice and sugar in large glass bowl. Cook on HIGH 2 minutes or until mixture boils. Reduce power to MEDIUM; cook to soft-ball stage. (Check temperature with candy thermometer, as time may vary.) Remove from microwave; add rind and pecans. Continue as directed above.

Sandra Gilmer Souther

It is unlucky to eat twin nuts from one shell. Give one to somebody else.

A Treasury of Georgia Folklore, by Ronald G. Killion and Charles T. Walker
Atlanta: Cherokee Publishing Company, 1983. Used by permission.

Buttermilk Fudge

Yes, you read it right! But don't dismiss this unusual candy until you have tried it. Rich and good.

Preparation: Average
Cooking Time: 20-25 Minutes

Yield: 1 Dozen Pieces
Must Do Ahead

        2 **cups sugar**
        1 **cup buttermilk**
        1 **teaspoon baking soda**
        3 **tablespoons butter**
        1 **cup chopped pecans**

Combine sugar and buttermilk in saucepan. Bring to rolling boil. Add baking soda and butter; cook to medium-ball stage (245°F). Remove from heat; add pecans. Beat until slightly cool.(Be careful not to overbeat; this will harden fast.) Drop by spoonfuls onto a greased cookie sheet. Cool completely.
Micronote: Combine sugar and buttermilk in large glass bowl. Cook on HIGH until mixture boils, 2½-3 minutes. Add baking soda and butter. Cook on MEDIUM until medium-ball stage (245°F) is reached, 18-20 minutes. Remove from microwave; check temperature with candy thermometer. Proceed as directed above.

Elizabeth Martin Jennings

Classic Chocolate Fudge

This is the traditional rich chocolate fudge. We think it's still the best.

Preparation: Average
Cooking Time: 20 Minutes

Yield: 3-4 Dozen Pieces
Must Do Ahead

- 2 **cups sugar**
- ½ **cup milk**
- ½ **cup butter or margarine**
- ¼ **cup light corn syrup**
- 2 **squares (2 ounces) unsweetened baking chocolate**
- ¼ **teaspoon salt**
- 1 **teaspoon vanilla extract**
- ½-1 **cup chopped pecans**

In heavy saucepan combine sugar, milk, butter, corn syrup, chocolate, and salt. Stir over low heat until chocolate and butter melt, approximately 15 minutes. Gradually turn up heat to medium-high, stirring mixture constantly. Bring to rolling boil; boil 1 minute. Remove from heat; beat with wooden spoon until lukewarm. Stir in vanilla. Continue beating until mixture resembles spreading consistency of frosting, approximately 12-14 minutes. Stir in nuts. Pour into buttered platter or 12 x 8-inch pan. When set, cut into squares.

Micronote: In large bowl combine all ingredients except vanilla and pecans. Cook on HIGH, stirring frequently, for 2½-3 minutes or until mixture boils. Boil 1 minute longer. Remove from microwave; beat with wooden spoon until lukewarm. Proceed as directed above.

Marian Martin Hosch

New Orleans-Style Pralines

Our New Orleans native stands by this recipe as "the real thing." Good, smooth texture.

Preparation: Average
Cooking Time: 15-20 Minutes

Yield: 2-3 Dozen
Must Do Ahead

- 2 **cups sugar**
- 1 **cup firmly packed light brown sugar**
- 1 **cup evaporated milk**
- ½ **cup butter**
- 1 **teaspoon salt**
- 2 **teaspoons vanilla extract**
- 1-2 **cups whole or chopped pecans**

Combine sugars, milk, butter, and salt. Cook gently, stirring constantly, to 235°F on candy thermometer, soft-ball stage. Remove from heat; cool to lukewarm (110°F). Stir in vanilla and nuts. Beat with long-handled, wooden spoon until mixture begins to thicken. Quickly drop onto waxed paper (with newspaper under it) to form patties about 4 inches in diameter. When firm, wrap individually in waxed paper.

Micronote: Combine sugars, milk, melted butter, and salt. Cook 1½ minutes on HIGH, stirring every 30 seconds until mixture begins to boil. Reduce power to MEDIUM; cook to soft-ball stage, 235°F. (Syrup will form soft ball when dropped in cold water; ball will flatten when removed.) To assure accuracy, remove from microwave and check temperature with candy thermometer unless microwave is equipped with a temperature probe. Cool mixture to 110°F and proceed as directed above.

Willia Beth Buquet Banks

Chocolate-Dipped Candies

Choose any version of these chocolate balls that strikes your fancy. You won't be disappointed. They are all delicious. Nice for holiday gifts.

Preparation: Average

Yield: 60 (1-inch) Balls
Must Do Ahead

Chocolate Dip

1 (12-ounce) package semi-
    sweet chocolate chips
¼ pound paraffin

After preparing candy balls (see below) and chilling several hours, melt paraffin and chocolate chips in top of double boiler. Using toothpicks, dip each ball into chocolate mixture. Drop onto waxed paper to cool. Store in airtight container in refrigerator.

Chocolate-Covered Peanut Butter Balls

6 ounces crunchy peanut
    butter
½ cup margarine
1 cup graham cracker crumbs
½ (16-ounce) box
    confectioners' sugar
1 teaspoon vanilla extract
¾ cup finely chopped peanuts

Combine all ingredients until well blended. (Can be done in food processor.) Shape into small balls. Place on waxed paper-lined baking sheet. Refrigerate several hours or overnight. Dip as above.

Mary Kelly Rogers

Bourbon Balls

1 (16-ounce) box confectioners'
    sugar
8 tablespoons butter, softened
¾-1 cup finely chopped nuts
¼ cup bourbon
⅛ teaspoon salt

Cream sugar and butter. Blend in nuts, bourbon, and salt. Refrigerate mixture 30 minutes; shape into small balls. Place on waxed paper-lined baking sheet. Refrigerate several hours or overnight. Dip as above.

Louise Hendrix Forrester

Coconut Balls

2 (16-ounce) boxes
    confectioners' sugar
2-3 cups finely chopped nuts
1 (14-ounce) can condensed
    milk
8 tablespoons butter, melted
1 (7-ounce) can or package
    flaked coconut

Combine all ingredients in large bowl. Chill. Shape into small balls. Place on waxed paper-lined cookie sheet. Refrigerate several hours or overnight. Dip as above.

Sidney Moring Frost
Baxley, Georgia

Party Mints

A very creamy mint. These can also be pressed into a candy mold to make attractive shapes for special occasions.

Preparation: Easy

Yield: 3 Dozen

1 (16-ounce) box confectioners' sugar
4 ounces cream cheese, softened
4 drops oil of peppermint
Food coloring

Using hands, thoroughly combine sugar, cream cheese, and peppermint. Add food coloring to desired shade. Shape into small balls; place on waxed paper. Flatten balls with fork. Mints should be refrigerated until ready to use. Can be made ahead and frozen.

Mary Ann Leathers Morrison

Chocolate Peanut Squares

Better than Reeses!

Preparation: Easy

Yield: 50
Must Do Ahead

3 cups confectioners' sugar
1½ cups graham cracker crumbs
1 cup butter, melted
1 cup peanut butter
1 (12-ounce) package chocolate chips, melted

Combine sugar, crumbs, butter, and peanut butter. Press mixture into rectangular 3-quart casserole. Refrigerate to cool. Spread chips evenly on top of peanut butter mixture. Refrigerate until firm. Cut into squares; store in airtight container. (May also be made in individual mini-foil candy cups.)

Valerie McLanahan Goetz
Atlanta, Georgia

Pecan Clusters

You will not find a candy more delicious or easier than this one.

Preparation: Easy
Cooking Time: 10 Minutes

Yield: 12 Dozen
Must Do Ahead

1½ pounds milk chocolate
1 (7-ounce) jar marshmallow creme
5 cups sugar
1 (13-ounce) can evaporated milk
½ cup butter
6 cups pecan halves

Place chocolate and marshmallow creme in large bowl; set aside. Combine sugar, milk, and butter in saucepan. Bring mixture to boil; cook 8 minutes. Pour over creme and chocolate mixture, stirring until well blended. Mix in pecans. Drop by teaspoonfuls onto waxed paper. Cool until set.

Micronote: Place marshmallow creme and chocolate in large glass bowl. Combine sugar, milk, and butter in another glass bowl. Cook milk mixture on HIGH for 5 minutes or until boiling, stirring often. Reduce power to MEDIUM; cook 6-8 minutes, stirring often. Continue as directed above.

Brenda Jones Adams

children

Dandelion

Dandelion (Taraxacum officinale)

The dandelion is an all-too-familiar lawn weed. All parts of this wildflower are edible: the flowers can be buttered and fried and are a good source of vitamin A; the young leaves can be gathered in spring and served as salad greens or cooked and eaten like spinach; the roots may be dried and ground, then steeped for a hot drink.

The dandelion has traditionally been a favorite with children of the South, who enjoy blowing the feathery, tufted seeds. A Cherokee Indian legend recounts how the South Wind saw in a distant meadow a beautiful golden-haired maiden. He was captivated by her beauty and longed to woo her. The South Wind was extremely lazy and somehow never did so. Much later he thought he saw her again, but her hair had turned white. He immediately suspected that his brother the North Wind had stolen her away. Angrily, the South Wind blew into the air with all his might. Lightly as snowflakes, the fluffy seeds (her white hair) scattered; she was gone. The South Wind mourned for the maiden, yet to this day he does not know that it was the dandelion.

On Children's Treats

- To dye Easter eggs: combine ⅓ - ½ cup warm tap water, 2 tablespoons vinegar, ¼ teaspoon food coloring with a plastic spoon. Spoon color over hard-cooked egg while turning.
- Place miniature marshmallows on graham crackers. Top with a maraschino cherry and bake 7 minutes at 325°F for a quick treat.
- Place a maraschino cherry in each section of an ice tray; add water and freeze. Prepare lemonade concentrate; add cherry ice cubes for an easy punch.
- For a real breakfast treat make homemade doughnuts: Punch holes in refrigerator biscuits. Fry in hot oil until lightly browned. Drain and sprinkle with cinnamon-sugar mixture.
- For quick gingerbread cookies: Mix 1 package gingerbread mix with ⅓ cup lukewarm water. Chill dough overnight. Knead slightly, roll out, cut, then bake 8-10 minutes at 375°F.
- Make breakfast more interesting. Cut a 2-inch round from a slice of buttered bread. Fry an egg in the hole.
- For supper in a hurry: top baked potatoes with an assortment of cheeses, chopped ham, hamburger, mushrooms, sautéed peppers and onions, chopped broccoli, or chili. A Super Spud!
- For a nutritious treat serve corn on the cob spread with softened peanut butter.
- When it snows add milk, sugar, and vanilla to fresh snow to make snow ice cream.
- Make a wintertime treat for the birds. Mix pan drippings with bits of leftover cornmeal, grits, seeds, or crumbs. Let solidify in desired form.
- To make butter: Pour whipping cream into small baby food jars and close lid tightly. Shake 5 minutes and pour off liquid. Shake 2-3 more minutes until butter is creamy. Salt to taste.
- Make your own ice cream sandwiches. Slice block ice cream into ½-inch thick slices; cut into quarters. Place each quarter between 2 big oatmeal cookies. Eat or freeze.
- Thread chunks of fruit, cheese, and lunch meat on skewers for a quick lunch or snack.

Mother's Day Lunch

**Fruit Mountain Salad
with Honey Nut Dressing**

Potato Chip Chicken

Cranberry Carrots

Minted Peas (page 267)

Sour Cream Mini Biscuits

Chocolate Mousse Parfaits

Fruit Mountain Salad with Honey Nut Dressing

Preparation: Easy

Serves: 4
Must Partially Do Ahead

Honey Nut Dressing
½ cup mayonnaise
1 tablespoon peanut butter
1 tablespoon honey

1. Combine all ingredients and blend thoroughly.
2. Refrigerate until ready to use.

Salad
4 lettuce leaves
4 slices canned pineapple
2 bananas, sliced
4 maraschino cherries
Honey Nut Dressing

1. Place 1 lettuce leaf on each of 4 salad plates.
2. Top each with 1 pineapple slice, next a mound of banana slices, and last a cherry.
3. Drizzle dressing over each salad. Serve.

Gail Adams Thomas

Cranberry Carrots

Preparation: Easy
Cooking Time: 15 Minutes

Serves: 4-6

¼ cup margarine
¼ cup jellied cranberry sauce
2 tablespoons sugar
½ teaspoon salt
2 (16-ounce) cans sliced
   carrots, drained

1. Combine margarine, cranberry sauce, sugar, and salt in medium saucepan.
2. Simmer on low heat until cranberry sauce melts; stir often.
3. Add carrots to cranberry mixture; stir well.
4. Lower heat to simmer; cook 10 minutes or until carrots are hot.

Micronote:
1. Combine margarine, cranberry sauce, sugar, and salt in 1½-quart covered casserole.
2. Cook on HIGH 2 minutes or until cranberry sauce melts; stir once.
3. Add carrots; stir well.
4. Cover; cook on HIGH 4 minutes or until carrots are hot.

Judy Evans Harrison

Potato Chip Chicken

Preparation: Easy
Cooking Time: 1 Hour
Oven Temperature: 350°F

Serves: 4
Must Serve Immediately

1 broiler-fryer, cut up,
    or assorted chicken pieces
1 (16-ounce) bag potato chips
½ cup butter or margarine, melted

1. Preheat oven to 350°F.
2. Remove skin from chicken pieces if desired.
3. Remove half of potato chips from bag. (Save to eat later.)
4. Holding top of bag closed, crush remaining chips until they are in small crumbs.
5. Dip one piece of chicken in butter and drop into bag of crumbs. Shake until crumbs stick to chicken.
6. Place on rack of broiler pan. Repeat for each piece of chicken.
7. Drizzle remaining butter over chicken pieces.
8. Bake at 350°F.

Judy Evans Harrison

And one more thing, an ingredient most important. The last woman to cook biscuits for me in the mornings was a lady I lived with for seventeen years. I can remember asking her, "What makes these biscuits so good?" "Love, son," she would say, "I put in lots of love." Homemade biscuits for breakfast, ladies? At least once? And soon? He'll taste the love. I promise.

Lewis Grizzard, *Kathy Sue Loudermilk, I Love You.*
Peachtree Publications, Ltd., Copyright 1979. Used with permission.

Sour Cream Mini Biscuits

Preparation: Easy
Cooking Time: 20 Minutes
Oven Temperature: 350°F

Yield: 36

¾ cup butter, softened
1 cup sour cream
2 cups sifted self-rising flour

1. Preheat oven to 350°F.
2. Combine all ingredients in large electric mixer bowl.
3. Beat with electric mixer until just blended.
4. Spoon into ungreased miniature muffin pans.
5. Bake at 350°F for 20 minutes or until golden brown.
6. Batter may be made ahead and kept in refrigerator for about 1 week. After cooking, these may be placed in plastic bag and frozen.

Meredith Melvin

Chocolate Mousse Parfait

For chocolate lovers, this can't be beat!

Preparation: Easy

Serves: 6
Must Do Ahead

6 ounces semi-sweet chocolate
   bits
2 teaspoons hot water
½ cup whipping cream
2 tablespoons confectioners' sugar
4 eggs, separated
2 teaspoons vanilla extract

1. Combine chocolate bits and water in small saucepan.
2. Cook over low heat until melted.
3. Place melted chocolate, cream, sugar, and egg yolks in blender container.
4. Cover; blend at medium speed for 3 minutes.
5. Add egg whites and vanilla.
6. Cover; blend at medium speed for 3 more minutes.
7. Pour into 6 small parfait glasses or demitasse cups.
8. Refrigerate for 2 hours or until set.
9. For a very grown-up dessert, substitute 2 teaspoons strong coffee for water and 1 tablespoon brandy for vanilla.

Linda Wilson Edmonds

Father's Day Dinner

Super Simple Crab Bisque (page 55)

Green Salad

Spaghetti Bravissimo

Sesame Breadsticks

Fudge Pie

Spaghetti Bravissimo

Preparation: Easy
Cooking Time: 30 Minutes

Serves: 4-6

1 (1.37-ounce) envelope dry
   onion soup mix
1 (8-ounce) package spaghetti
   noodles
1½ quarts boiling water
1 pound ground beef
1 (8-ounce) can tomato sauce
1 (7-ounce) can tomato paste
1 teaspoon parsley flakes
1 teaspoon basil
1 teaspoon oregano

1. Add soup mix and spaghetti to water; simmer 20 minutes (do not drain).
2. Meanwhile, crumble ground beef into skillet; cook over medium heat until browned. Drain.
3. Add beef and remaining ingredients to spaghetti mixture.
4. Simmer just until hot.

Violet Lee Nicholson

Sesame Breadsticks

Preparation: Easy
Cooking Time: 10 Minutes
Oven Temperature: 400°F

Serves: 6-8
Must Serve Immediately

1 (10-count) package refrigerated
    biscuits
¼ cup butter, melted
    Sesame seeds

1. Preheat oven to 400°F.
2. Shape each biscuit into 6 to 8-inch long stick.
3. Pour half the butter into 12 x 9-inch baking pan.
4. Place sticks in butter.
5. Pour remaining butter over sticks.
6. Sprinkle with sesame seeds.
7. Bake at 400°F for 10 minutes.

Dana Leigh Askew

How Many Times

Four of us times all the years
She stirred batter in the crockery bowl,
Making crusty cakes to warm small hands
For winter years to come.

Bettie M. Sellers, *Westward from Bald Mountain.*
Copyright, 1974. Used with permission.

Fudge Pie

Preparation: Easy
Cooking Time: 25-30 Minutes
Oven Temperature: 375°F

Yield: 1 (9-inch) Pie

1 cup butter or margarine, melted
1 cup sugar
¼ cup cocoa
¼ cup flour
2 eggs, beaten
1 teaspoon vanilla
¼ cup chopped nuts (optional)
1 (9-inch) prepared pie
    crust, thawed (if
    frozen) and unbaked
Vanilla ice cream or
    whipped cream (optional)

1. Preheat oven to 375°F.
2. Combine butter, sugar, cocoa, and flour. Stir well.
3. Add eggs, vanilla, and nuts (if using).
4. Stir until all ingredients are well blended.
5. Pour into pie crust.
6. Bake at 375°F for 25-30 minutes. (Be careful not to overcook. Pie will not be firm in center; it should shake slightly, like a custard.)
7. Serve warm with a scoop of vanilla ice cream or whipped cream, or let cool and reheat when ready to serve. (Slices may be warmed by microwaving on HIGH 5-10 seconds.)

Flo Criss Smith

Pizza Party

A-B-C-D Fondue

Green Salad

Mini Pizzas

Chocolate Chip Pizza

Great Tasting Grape Juice

A - B - C - D Fondue

A fun appetizer when children or teens have company for dinner.

Preparation: Easy

Yield: 1 Pint
Must Serve Immediately

1 (15½-ounce) jar spaghetti sauce
1 (8-ounce) package shredded
    Mozzarella cheese
¼ cup Parmesan cheese
2 teaspoons oregano
1 teaspoon minced onion
¼ teaspoon garlic salt
    Corn chips or French
      bread cubes for dipping

A. Mix all ingredients together in fondue pot or saucepan.
B. Cook over low heat until cheese melts; place fondue pot on its stand over low burner.
C. Dip corn chips into sauce by hand or spear French bread cubes on fondue forks and dip.
D. Enjoy!

Anne Bailey Catherine Durisch

Great Tasting Grape Juice

Preparation: Easy

Serves: 4-5

1 (6-ounce) can frozen grape
    juice concentrate, thawed
2 cups water
1 (12-ounce) can ginger
    ale, chilled
    Lemon slices (optional)

1. Combine grape juice and water; stir well.
2. Add ginger ale just before serving.
3. Pour over ice; garnish with lemon slices.

Cookbook Committee

Mini Pizzas

Preparation: Easy
Cooking Time: 12 Minutes
Oven Temperature: 375°F

Yield: 4
Must Serve Immediately

2 English muffins, split
    Pizza-Quick Sauce or Thick and
      Zesty Ragu Spaghetti Sauce
    Pepperoni slices (optional)
    Ground beef, browned,
      crumbled, and well-drained
      (optional)
    Mozzarella cheese, shredded
    Parmesan cheese, grated

1. Preheat oven to 375°F.
2. Spoon pizza sauce on each English muffin half.
3. Add pepperoni or ground beef, if desired.
4. Top with shredded Mozzarella cheese.
5. Sprinkle a little Parmesan over all.
6. Bake in 375°F oven for 12 minutes or until bubbly.

Katy Darden

Chocolate Chip Pizza

Preparation: Easy
Cooking Time: 15 Minutes
Oven Temperature: 375°F

Serves: 15-20
Must Do Ahead

½ cup sugar
½ cup firmly packed
   brown sugar
½ cup margarine, softened
½ cup peanut butter
½ teaspoon vanilla extract
1 egg
1½ cups flour
2 cups miniature marshmallows
6 ounces semi-sweet
   chocolate chips
½ cup pecan halves (optional)

1. Preheat oven to 375°F.
2. In large bowl combine sugar, brown sugar, margarine, peanut butter, vanilla, and egg. Blend well.
3. Add flour and stir until soft dough forms.
4. Press dough evenly over bottom of 12 to 14-inch pizza pan, forming rim along edge.
5. Bake at 375°F for 10 minutes.
6. Remove from oven. Sprinkle with marshmallows, chocolate chips, and pecans.
7. Continue baking for 5 minutes or until marshmallows are puffy and lightly browned.
8. Cool and cut into wedges. (May store in tightly covered container.)

Susan Leanne Oliver

Halloween Party

Witches' Brew

Haystacks

Popcorn Balls

Halloween Pumpkin Cake

Witches' Brew

For Halloween serve in a black pot. Stud 3 or 4 small oranges with whole cloves and float in the brew. If using a hot drink is not convenient, this is also good cold.

Preparation: Easy
Cooking Time: 20 Minutes

Yield: 8 (5½-ounce) Servings

1 quart apple juice
1½ cups canned unsweetened
   pineapple juice
2 tablespoons honey
2 tablespoons fresh lemon juice
3 cinnamon sticks

1. Combine all ingredients in medium saucepan.
2. Heat over low heat until ready to serve, about 20 minutes.
3. Remove cinnamon sticks.
4. Ladle brew into serving container or individual cups.

Sonya Wood Hancock

Haystacks

Adults like these too!

Preparation: Easy

Yield: 30
Must Do Ahead

1 (6-ounce) package butterscotch
   morsels
1 (5-ounce) can chow mein
   noodles
1 (6½-ounce) can peanuts

1. Melt butterscotch morsels in top of double boiler or in microwave.
2. Reduce heat to low; stir in noodles and peanuts until well coated.
3. Remove from heat.
4. Drop by teaspoonfuls onto a sheet of waxed paper.
5. Let cool. Peel from paper and store in airtight container. (May be placed in plastic bags and frozen.)

Carolyn Cathey Brinson

Popcorn Balls

Peanut Butter Popcorn Balls

Preparation: Easy
Cooking Time: 15 Minutes

Yield: 4 Balls

½ **cup unpopped popcorn**
2 **tablespoons butter, melted**
   Salt to taste
⅓ **cup white corn syrup**
½ **cup brown sugar, packed**
½ **cup peanut butter**

1. Pop corn; season with butter and salt.
2. Place in large buttered bowl.
3. Combine syrup and sugar in small saucepan.
4. Stir over medium heat until hot and bubbly.
5. Add peanut butter; cook over low heat until well blended.
6. Pour syrup evenly over popcorn; mix well.
7. With well-buttered hands, form quickly into balls.

Ashley and Ron Wilson

Colored Popcorn Balls

Preparation: Easy
Cooking Time: 5 Minutes

Yield: 12 Balls

3 **cups miniature marshmallows**
6 **tablespoons margarine, melted**
3 **tablespoons dry strawberry**
   gelatin
12 **cups unsalted popped**
   popcorn

1. Combine marshmallows and margarine in saucepan.
2. Stir over medium-low heat until melted.
3. Remove from heat; stir in gelatin. (Any flavor gelatin may be used to suit the season: lime and strawberry for Christmas, orange for Halloween, etc.)
4. Pour over popcorn; stir to coat.
5. Using buttered hands, form into balls.
6. Store in individual plastic bags.

Bette Ferguson Edwards
Lincolnton, Georgia

Halloween Pumpkin Cake

Preparation: Easy
Cooking Time: 1 Hour
Oven Temperature: 300°F

Yield: 1 (10-inch) Cake

1 box Lemon Supreme
    Cake Mix
½ cup cooking oil
4 eggs
¾ cup apricot nectar
    Decorator Icing (page 310)
    Green, yellow, and red
    food coloring
1 banana

1. Preheat oven to 300°F.
2. Grease and flour Bundt pan.
3. Empty cake mix into mixer bowl; add remaining ingredients.
4. Beat 2 minutes on medium speed.
5. Pour into prepared pan.
6. Bake at 300°F for 1 hour.
7. Cool cake 3 minutes, then remove from pan. Cool on rack.
8. Prepare Decorator Icing as directed.
9. Remove ½ cup frosting; tint green. To remaining frosting add a few drops yellow food coloring, then 1 or 2 drops red coloring to make orange.
10. Place cake on a plate; stand a peeled banana in center to form pumpkin stem.
11. Ice stem with green frosting and cake with orange frosting.

Your Halloween pumpkin is complete!

Martha Ann Davis Crenshaw

A Birthday Party for "Little Mothers" - Ages Four to Eight

Invitation: Dainty luncheon invitations or notepaper with a doll on it can be used. State on the invitations to dress like your mother and bring your favorite "baby."

Entertainment: When the guests have been greeted and the "babies" assembled, the "mothers" may want to model their attire. Music can be played. As each "mother" is modeling, her picture is taken and given to her as a favor. Have each guest ice and decorate cupcakes to be used for dessert or to take home. Have assembled: baked cupcakes, chocolate and vanilla canned icing, assorted sprinkles, prepared decorator icing in assorted colors, and aprons or smocks.

Luncheon Menu

Raggedy Ann Salad

Tray of party sandwiches
(peanut butter and jelly, cut into various shapes)

"Coffee"
(pour cola from a coffee pot into demitasse cups)

Cupcakes or Doll Cake

Recipes begin on page 387

Raggedy Ann Salad

Body: Peach half
Arms and Legs: Celery sticks
Head: Half a hard-boiled egg
Eyes, Nose, Buttons, Shoes: Raisins
Mouth: Slice of cherry
Hair: Grated cheese
Skirt: Leaf lettuce

Doll Cake

1 (12-inch) plastic doll
Bundt pound cake
Decorator Icing (page 310)

Place a 12-inch plastic doll in the center of a pound cake baked in a bundt pan. With decorator icing decorate cake and doll to look like doll is wearing a formal gown.

Conclusion:

As the party draws to a close, prizes may be awarded to "mothers" and "babies" in several categories. Present each "mother" with paper dolls, since **all** are winners!

Possible Categories:

Mother wearing the most striking outfit.
Baby wearing the daintiest dress.
Mother with the most elaborate jewelry.
Most well-behaved baby.
Mother with the prettiest make-up.

Nancy Johnson Bailey

Take Me Out to the Ball Game - Ages Five to Ten

Invitation: Make tickets out of construction paper with the details of the party included. Each child should wear his uniform and bring his glove, ball and bat.

Entertainment: Have this party at a neighborhood park with a ball field, or just use the back yard. Set up teams, get dad to umpire, and "play ball."

Seventh Inning Stretch

Nona's Snackin' Jacks

Easy-Cheesy Pronto Pups

Peanut Butter Ice Cream

**Fudge Cupcake Supreme (page 325)
with Easy Peanut Butter Icing (page 326)**

Ice Cold Colas

Recipes begin on page 388

Conclusion: Give bubble gum with baseball cards as favors.

Nona's Snackin' Jacks

So much better than the packaged variety - for a fraction of the cost!

Preparation: Easy
Cooking Time: 30 Minutes
Oven Temperature: 300°F

Yield: 2½ Quarts
Must Do Ahead

½ cup butter or margarine, melted
1 cup packed brown sugar
¼ cup corn syrup
½ teaspoon salt
½ teaspoon vanilla extract
¼ teaspoon baking soda
3 quarts popped popcorn (about ½ cup uncooked kernels)
1 cup peanuts (optional)

1. In 1½-quart saucepan combine butter, brown sugar, corn syrup, and salt.
2. Bring mixture to boiling, stirring constantly.
3. Boil over medium heat without stirring for 5 minutes.
4. Remove from heat; stir in vanilla and baking soda.
5. In a large bowl gradually pour hot syrup over popcorn, mixing well to coat the corn.
6. Turn popcorn into greased 17 x 12 x 2-inch roasting pan.
7. Bake, uncovered, at 300°F for 30 minutes, stirring the popcorn after 15 minutes.
8. Remove from oven; cool completely in pan.
9. Loosen popcorn with spatula.
10. Break into pieces.
11. Stir in peanuts.
12. Store in tightly covered container.

Matthew Mahar

Easy-Cheesy Pronto Pups

Preparation: Easy
Cooking Time: 15 Minutes
Oven Temperature: 400°F

Serves: 8
Must Serve Immediately

1 (8-ounce) can refrigerated Parker House Dinner Rolls
8 frankfurters
8 (3 x ½ x ¼-inch) strips Cheddar or American cheese
3 tablespoons barbecue sauce
½ cup cornflake crumbs or cornmeal or crushed potato chips
Wooden skewers or sticks

1. Preheat oven to 400°F.
2. Lightly grease baking sheet.
3. Separate dough in 8 rolls.
4. Cut a narrow slit lengthwise in each frankfurter and insert 1 cheese strip in each.
5. Shape 1 roll evenly around each frankfurter, pinching thoroughly to seal.
6. Brush each with barbecue sauce; roll in corn flake crumbs.
7. Insert skewers into end of each frankfurter roll.
8. Place on cookie sheet.
9. Bake at 400°F for 15 minutes or until brown.
10. Serve hot with catsup and mustard.

Susannah Withers Frost

Peanut Crunch Ice Cream

Preparation: Easy
Cooking Time: 10 Minutes
Oven Temperature: 325°F

Serves: 12
Must Do Ahead

3 cups graham cracker crumbs
½ cup margarine, melted
½ cup crunchy peanut butter
½ gallon vanilla ice cream,
    softened
Chocolate syrup (optional)

1. Preheat oven to 325°F.
2. Combine cracker crumbs, margarine, and peanut butter in 13 x 9 x 2-inch baking dish; mix well and pat evenly over bottom of dish.
3. Bake at 325°F for 10 minutes. Cool to room temperature.
4. Spread ice cream evenly over crust; freeze.
5. Cut into squares to serve. Drizzle chocolate syrup over each square.

Carolyn Cathey Brinson

It took a Civil War, the circus and baseball to spark a national appetite for peanuts.
P. C. King, Jr., *The Chattahoochee River.*
Used with permission.

Fun Treats

Simple Sloppy Joes

A versatile and simple recipe for a child (or a busy mother!) to make. Keep some frozen in pint containers for a quick meal or for reheating when mother is away.

Preparation: Easy
Cooking Time: 10-15 Minutes

Serves: 4
Must Do Ahead

1 pound ground beef
1 medium onion, chopped
¾ cup catsup
2 tablespoons Worcestershire
2 tablespoons vinegar
1 tablespoon brown sugar
1½ teaspoons prepared mustard
1 teaspoon chili powder
    (optional)
¼ teaspoon salt
1 (16-ounce) can red beans,
    drained (optional)

1. Crumble ground beef into skillet; add onion.
2. Cook over medium heat until beef is lightly browned.
3. Drain off any grease.
4. Add catsup, Worcestershire, vinegar, brown sugar, mustard, chili powder, salt, and beans.
5. Turn heat to low; cook 5 minutes.
6. Serve on toasted hamburger rolls, on English muffins, in Pita bread, over baked potatoes, or over cooked macaroni or spaghetti noodles.

Micronote:
1. Crumble ground beef into covered casserole; add onion.
2. Cook on HIGH for 3 minutes; drain off grease and stir.
3. Cook on HIGH for 2 more minutes; drain again and stir.
4. Add remaining ingredients.
5. Cook on HIGH for 3 minutes; stir.
6. Cook on HIGH for 2 more minutes.

Dana Leigh Askew

Bacon and Egg Triangles

Perfect for breakfast, lunch, or supper. Those who don't fancy eggs have been known to eat this willingly.

Preparation: Easy
Cooking Time: 30 Minutes
Oven Temperature: 375°F

Serves: 4

1 (8-ounce) can refrigerated crescent dinner rolls
4 slices sharp Cheddar or American cheese
8 slices bacon, fried, drained, and crumbled
1 tablespoon finely chopped onion
½ teaspoon celery salt
½ cup milk
2 eggs, slightly beaten

1. Preheat oven to 375°F.
2. Separate crescent rolls into 4 large rectangles.
3. Place 2 rectangles in ungreased 8 or 9-inch square pan; press over bottom and ½ inch up sides of pan to form crust, sealing perforations.
4. Place cheese slices over dough.
5. Sprinkle with bacon and onions.
6. In a small bowl combine celery salt, milk, and eggs; pour over bacon and onion.
7. Separate remaining dough into 4 triangles.
8. Arrange triangles over egg mixture; do not seal.
9. Bake at 375°F for 30 minutes or until golden brown and filling is set.
10. Serve warm.
11. Can be made ahead, covered, and refrigerated up to 2 hours. Bake as directed. To reheat cover loosely with foil and heat at 375°F for 15-18 minutes.

Cookbook Committee

Rails split fo' bre'kfus' 'll season de dinner.
Joel Chandler Harris

Green Eggs and Ham

Dr. Seuss will love you for it!

Preparation: Easy
Cooking Time: 5 Minutes

Serves: 1
Must Serve Immediately

1-2 eggs
2 drops blue food coloring
1 tablespoon margarine, melted
Cubes of ham

1. Beat egg(s) and food coloring.
2. Scramble in margarine over medium heat.
3. Top with ham to serve.

Linda Wilson Edmonds

Blender Slushy

A super after-school treat! Or an instant "anesthetic" for a sore throat.

Preparation: Easy

Serves: 2
Must Serve Immediately

1 cup water
6 tablespoons (or 2 scoops)
    pre-sweetened juice mix
12-15 ice cubes

1. Place water, juice mix, and ice cubes in blender.
2. Blend on high until ice is a thick, slushy consistency. (If drink is too thin, add a few more ice cubes and blend again.)
3. Pour into 2 glasses.

Katy Darden

Peppermint Hot Chocolate

Just right for a quick warm-up on a cold day!

Preparation: Easy
Cooking Time: 10 Minutes

Serves: 4-6
Must Serve Immediately

1 quart dairy chocolate-
    flavored milk
½ cup crushed peppermint candy
½ cup whipping cream, whipped

1. Combine chocolate milk and candy in saucepan.
2. Simmer, stirring occasionally, until candy dissolves.
3. Pour into serving cups.
4. Top with whipped cream.

Darlene Cook Parrish

Peachy Banana Spoon Drink

Preparation: Easy

Serves: 4-6
Must Serve Immediately

3 ripe peaches, peeled,
    sliced, and frozen
3 very ripe bananas,
    peeled, sliced, and frozen
1 cup milk
2 tablespoons sugar
    (optional)
2 teaspoons lemon juice

1. Place fruit in electric blender jar.
2. Add milk, sugar, and lemon juice.
3. Blend on high speed until mixture is "slushy" consistency.
4. Pour into glasses and serve with spoons.

To make pops:
1. Spoon mixture into 6 (3-ounce) paper cups.
2. Insert popsicle stick in center of each cup.
3. Freeze until firm.
4. Peel away paper to serve.

Lavonne Palmer
Longboat Key, Florida

Yummy Pops

A tasty pop, sweetened mainly with natural fruit sugar.

Preparation: Easy

Yield: 6
Must Do Ahead

2 cups mashed bananas
(approximately 3 medium)
1 cup orange juice
¼ cup water
2 tablespoons sugar
1 teaspoon lemon or
lime juice
6 (5-ounce) paper cups
6 wooden sticks

1. Combine all food ingredients; mix well.
2. Pour into 6 cups.
3. Let partially freeze, about 1-2 hours, then push wooden stick into the center of each.
4. Return to freezer until firm.
5. Remove 5 minutes before ready to eat.
6. Tear away paper cup and enjoy.

Christy Michelle Harrison

Yippee Yogurt Pops

Cool, refreshing, and nutritious. Even so, kids love it!

Preparation: Easy

Yield: 10
Must Do Ahead

2 (8-ounce) cartons vanilla
yogurt
1 (6-ounce) can frozen juice
concentrate (apple, pink
lemonade, pineapple, or grape)
10 (3-ounce) paper cups
10 wooden sticks

1. In small bowl combine yogurt and thawed concentrate; stir to blend.
2. Fill cups ½ - ⅔ full.
3. Place in freezer until partially frozen, about 1 hour.
4. Insert sticks, freeze completely.
5. To serve, peel off paper cups.
6. For larger pops, use 5 (5-ounce) paper cups and 5 wooden sticks.

Katy Darden

Cereal Sticks

Preparation: Easy
Cooking Time: 8 Minutes
Oven Temperature: 400°F

Yield: 5 Dozen
Must Do Ahead

2½ cups flour
1 cup sugar
¾ cup granola-type cereal,
divided
¼ teaspoon baking soda
⅛ teaspoon salt
½ cup butter or margarine,
softened
2 eggs
1 teaspoon vanilla extract

1. Preheat oven to 400°F. Lightly grease baking sheet.
2. Combine flour, sugar, ¼ cup cereal, soda, salt, butter, eggs, and vanilla in large bowl.
3. Mix until well blended.
4. Pinch off small pieces of dough and roll between hands to form "sticks."
5. Roll each stick in remaining ½ cup cereal to coat. Place on baking sheet.
6. Bake at 400°F for 8 minutes or until lightly browned.

Judith Rankin Landers

Kissing Cookies

You thought nothing could improve chocolate kisses? Try these!

Preparation: Easy
Cooking Time: 10-15 Minutes
Oven Temperature: 375°F

Yield: 3½ Dozen
Must Do Ahead

1 cup butter, softened
½ cup sugar
1 teaspoon vanilla extract
2 cups sifted flour
1 (9-ounce) package Hershey
    Chocolate Kisses

1. Place butter, sugar, and vanilla in large electric mixer bowl. Beat at medium speed until light and fluffy.
2. Turn mixer speed to low.
3. Add flour; beat until well mixed.
4. Wrap dough in waxed paper; chill in refrigerator for 2 hours or overnight.
5. Preheat oven to 375°F.
6. Peel foil from all kisses.
7. Shape dough around kisses, using about 1 tablespoon dough for each one.
8. Place on ungreased baking sheet; bake at 375°F until "set" but not brown (10-15 minutes).
9. Cool on rack.
10. Store in airtight container.

Susan Leanne Oliver

It is a mistaken economy to deny young girls access to the kitchen on account of the loss of materials.

Mrs. E. R. Tennent, *Housekeeping in the Sunny South, 1885.*

Microwave S'mores

Guaranteed to make you want s'more!

Preparation: Easy
Cooking Time: 20 Seconds Each

Must Serve Immediately

Graham cracker squares
Chocolate chips or milk
    chocolate candy bars
Large marshmallows
Peanut butter (optional)
Sliced bananas (optional)

1. Place 1 graham cracker square on a paper towel or napkin.
2. Sprinkle with chocolate chips or broken bits of candy bars.
3. Top with ½ marshmallow.
4. Microwave on HIGH about 20 seconds, just until marshmallow puffs up.
5. Top with second cracker.
6. Repeat until desired number are prepared.

Variation:
1. Spread first cracker with peanut butter.
2. Top with several banana slices.
3. Add chocolate and marshmallow. Proceed as above.

Diane Hally O'Kelley

Moon Rocks

Preparation: Easy
Cooking Time: 2 Hours
Oven Temperature: 350°F

Yield: 2 Dozen
Must Do Ahead

    2 **egg whites at room temperature**
 ²⁄₃ **cup sugar**
    1 **teaspoon vanilla extract**
    1 **cup chocolate chips**
    1 **cup chopped pecans (optional)**

1. Preheat oven to 350°F.
2. Cover cookie sheet with aluminum foil.
3. Beat egg whites with electric mixer until stiff peaks form.
4. Add sugar and vanilla.
5. Continue to beat until glossy and stiff.
6. Stir in chocolate chips and nuts with spoon.
7. Drop onto cookie sheet 1 teaspoon at a time.
8. Place in oven and TURN IT OFF!
9. Leave there at least for 2 hours or as long as overnight.

Anne Bailey Catherine Durisch

Suckers

What fun! A recipe that has stood the test of time; five generations have loved it!

Preparation: Average
Cooking Time: 20 Minutes

Must Do Ahead

    4 **cups sugar, divided**
    1 **cup vinegar, divided**
    2 **teaspoons butter, divided**
 ½ **teaspoon baking soda, divided**
      Non-oil base flavoring of choice
    2 **shades food coloring**
 ⅛ **-inch diameter dowels, cut into 8-inch lengths**

1. Combine 2 cups sugar and ½ cup vinegar in saucepan.
2. Cook to hard-crack stage on candy thermometer (300-310°F).
3. Remove from heat. Add 1 teaspoon butter and ¼ teaspoon soda.
4. Add flavoring and 1 shade food coloring to desired intensity of flavor and color.
5. Working QUICKLY, pour onto COLD, buttered marble slab to form silver dollar-sized circles; press 1 dowel in each piece of candy.
6. Remove with spatula onto waxed paper.
7. Prepare second batch of syrup, as above, using remaining ingredients.
8. Pour onto COLD, buttered marble slab to form 4-inch diameter circles.
9. Quickly place each original candy piece, dowel attached, atop each larger piece, rounded side up.
10. When cool, wrap individually in clear plastic wrap; tie with colorful ribbon.

Hint: This recipe has two secrets for success.
1. Put on a sweater and work in a cold room, 50°F or less.
2. Marble must be very cold for suckers to set up properly. Place slab in freezer to chill before and between batches.

Ellen Bowers Wittel

Christmas Holly Wreaths

Preparation: Easy
Cooking Time: 5 Minutes

Yield: 4-6 Dozen
Must Do Ahead

60 large marshmallows
1 cup margarine
1 (1-ounce) bottle green food coloring
6 cups crispy rice cereal or cornflakes
Red cinnamon candies

1. Combine marshmallows and margarine in large saucepan.
2. Cook, stirring over low heat until melted; remove from heat.
3. Stir in food coloring until well blended.
4. Add cereal; stir well.
5. With buttered fingers pinch off small pieces of cereal mixture and shape into wreaths.
6. Place on waxed paper.
7. Decorate with candies.
8. Leave on paper 24 hours.
9. Store in airtight containers between layers of waxed paper.

Diane Railey Curington

A place that was ever lived in is like a fire that never goes out.

Eudora Welty, *The Eye of the Story: Selected Essays and Reviews.*
Random House, Inc., Copyright 1978. Used with permission.

Thumbprint Cookies

Preparation: Easy
Cooking Time: 20-30 Minutes
Oven Temperature: 300°F

Yield: 3½ Dozen
Must Do Ahead

¼ cup sugar
1 cup margarine
2 cups flour
1 teaspoon vanilla extract
¼ teaspoon salt
1 cup finely chopped nuts
Vanilla Icing or favorite fruit jam

1. Preheat oven to 300°F.
2. Cream sugar and margarine with electric mixer.
3. Blend in remaining ingredients.
4. Drop by teaspoonfuls onto ungreased baking sheet.
5. Indent with thumb.
6. Bake at 300°F for 20-30 minutes.
7. Remove to wire racks to cool.
8. Fill with Vanilla Icing or jam.

Vanilla Icing

1 cup confectioners' sugar
½ teaspoon vanilla extract
Water
Food coloring

1. Combine sugar and vanilla.
2. Blend in just enough water so that icing will drop from a spoon.
3. Stir in any desired food colorings.

Anne Bailey Catherine Durisch

Rocky Road Squares

Preparation: Easy
Cooking Time: 10 Minutes

Yield: 3-4 Dozen
Must Do Ahead

1 (12-ounce) package milk
   chocolate morsels
1 (14-ounce) can condensed milk
2 tablespoons butter or margarine
2 cups pecans
1 (10½-ounce) package
   miniature marshmallows

1. In top of double boiler combine chocolate morsels, condensed milk, and butter.
2. Cook over boiling water until ingredients are melted and well blended. Stir occasionally.
3. In large bowl combine nuts and marshmallows.
4. Fold chocolate mixture into nuts and marshmallows.
5. Line 13 x 9-inch pan with waxed paper. Spread mixture over paper. Chill 2 hours or until firm.
6. Remove from pan; peel off paper; cut into squares.
7. Store in airtight container at room temperature.

Millie and Laura McCranie

Oreo Parfaits

Preparation: Easy

Serves: 10-12
Must Do Ahead

1 (16-ounce) package Oreo cookies
½ gallon vanilla ice cream,
   softened
1 (12-ounce) carton frozen whipped
   topping, softened
   Extra whipped topping
   Maraschino cherries

1. Crush Oreos in blender, adding a few at a time.
2. Use electric mixer to blend Oreo crumbs, ice cream and whipped topping.
3. Place in covered freezer container; freeze until firm.
4. Spoon into parfait glasses; top with additional whipped topping and a cherry.
5. Return to freezer until ready to serve.

Becky Smith Dadisman

Fun and Games

Potpourri

A gift idea for children to begin during the summer with the gathering and drying of flowers and herbs.

Preparation: Easy

Must Do Ahead

1 quart dried rose petals
1 quart other dried herbs and
   flowers (lilacs, honeysuckle,
   carnations, geraniums, lavender,
   violets, mint, marjoram,
   lemon thyme, rosemary)
1 tablespoon orris root
1 teaspoon whole allspice
1 teaspoon whole cloves
1 teaspoon broken bay leaves
2 teaspoons dried chopped lemon
   and orange rind
1-2 drops each of one or more
   fragrant oils (available at
   pharmacies)

1. Combine all ingredients.
2. Store in sealed container in a dark place for 6 weeks.
3. Divide among smaller containers for use or for gifts.

Hints: This recipe is very forgiving of variations. Orris root is the preservative. As long as this stays in proportion to the total amount of dried ingredients, any combination which suits your pleasure will work. Most flowers or herbs will dry well if petals are separated and scattered over spread newspapers.

Susan Leanne Oliver

Play Dough à la Peanut Butter

Great group activity with pre-schoolers. What fun to eat what you make rather than having to "clean up"!

Preparation: Easy

Yield: Approximately 2 Pounds

1 (18-ounce) jar peanut butter
6 tablespoons honey
Non-fat dry milk
Cocoa (optional)

1. Combine peanut butter and honey.
2. Add dry milk gradually (and cocoa if chocolate flavor is desired) mixing with hands, until of commercial play dough consistency.
3. Store in airtight container until ready to use.
4. Children may wish to decorate their creations with raisins, chocolate chips, nuts, etc.

Joanne Ferrell Durisch

Silly Putty

A rainy day fun project. Needs to be stored in an airtight container.

Preparation: Easy

Yield: ¼ Cup
Must Do Ahead

¼ cup white Elmer's glue
2 tablespoons Sta-Flo liquid starch

1. Combine glue and starch. Mix well.
2. Allow to dry slightly until workable.
3. Use on smooth surface.

Judy Evans Harrison

Bread Dough Christmas Ornaments

Use this dough to make seasonal decorations. Create pins by placing a pin back (purchased at hobby shop) on decorations while baking (glue only if necessary). May refrigerate dough in plastic bag for 2-3 weeks.

Preparation: Easy
Oven Temperature: 300°F

Must Do Ahead

½ cup salt
¾ cup boiling water
2 cups flour

1. Dissolve salt in water.
2. Cool. (If colored dough is desired, add food coloring.)
3. Gradually add flour; knead until dough forms ball and becomes smooth. Roll to ¼-inch thickness.
4. Cut with favorite cookie cutters or create free-form shapes. (Small pieces of dough pressed through garlic press make great "squiggles" for decorations.)
5. Place on cookie sheets. If ornaments are to hang, use a large nail to form a hole at the top for hanger.
6. Bake at 300°F for 1 hour.
7. Cool on racks. Ornaments may be varnished or painted.

Violet Lee Nicholson

Suet Candles (Bird Feeders)

A good project for children's club group. Have children save milk cartons from school.

Preparation: Average
Cooking Time: 3 Hours
Oven Temperature: 300°F

Must Do Ahead

5 pounds suet
Wild bird seed
Sunflower seeds
Crunchy peanut butter
Red cherries

1. Place suet in covered roaster; bake at 300°F for several hours or until all fat is rendered.
2. Strain; measure, reserving 1 cup.
3. Combine bird seed with additional sunflower seeds.
4. Mix 2 cups warm fat to 1 cup seeds. Pour into 8-ounce cartons; refrigerate.
5. When ready to use, melt reserved fat. Peel paper carton off seed mixture.
6. Set each "candle" into an aluminum pan or other dish; pour melted fat around candle to secure.
7. Frost top with peanut butter and add a cherry for the flame. Garnish with holly sprigs and berries if desired.

Eric Benjamin Oliver

Creative Clay

A good substitute for play dough or ornament dough in school or craft projects. It can be painted with tempra paints and dries very hard and smooth!

Preparation: Easy

Yield: 2 Cups
Must Do Ahead

1 pound baking soda
1 cup cornstarch
1¼ cups water
Food coloring (optional)

1. Combine soda and cornstarch in medium saucepan.
2. Add water; cook over low heat, stirring constantly, until mixture resembles mashed potatoes. (Color clay by adding food coloring to water before heating.)
3. Remove from heat; cover with damp cloth.
4. When clay is cool enough to handle, it is ready to use.
5. Store extra clay in sealed plastic bag.

Judy Evans Harrison

Sand Painting

Preparation: Easy

Small bowls or jars
White cornmeal
Food coloring
Paper
Pencil
Glue

1. Pour cornmeal into each bowl.
2. Using different colors for each bowl, drop coloring into meal, stirring after each addition, to reach desired color.
3. Draw design on paper with pencil.
4. Spread glue on one part of design.
5. Sprinkle one color of cornmeal over glue. Let glue dry.
6. Slide extra cornmeal off paper.
7. Finish remaining design in the same way using different colors of cornmeal.

Sarah Catherine, John Kenneth, and Dorothy Dudley Nix

On Phyllo

Phyllo (or filo) is a tissue paper-like Greek pastry used extensively in Greek recipes for appetizers, casseroles, entrées, and sweets. All but the most accomplished purists will buy phyllo pre-packaged in the frozen food section of grocery stores or delicatessens. Using phyllo can be an easy, delightful, and rewarding experience, if the few simple hints below are carefully followed. Don't be intimidated by this wonderful means of producing gourmet treats.

- Phyllo is usually found in 1-pound packages. One pound equals 20 to 24 (17 x 13-inch) sheets.
- To thaw phyllo, place unopened package in refrigerator the day before using; then leave at room temperature 1-2 hours immediately prior to use.
- Remove phyllo sheets from their plastic casing and carefully spread out to full length. IMMEDIATELY cover sheets completely with slightly damp towel. (Sheets will shatter if they become dry.) Remove towel each time 1 sheet is removed; recover remaining stack immediately.
- As many sheets as desired may be layered and folded, wrapped, etc. around filling, but **each** layer must be brushed lightly with melted butter before the next is added. When layering or folding is completed, all outer surfaces should be brushed with butter.

- Unused phyllo may be re-rolled, returned to plastic casing, reboxed, and refrozen.
- To prepare phyllo appetizer triangles:
  - Place 1 sheet of phyllo on the cutting surface.
  - Brush with butter.
  - Top with second sheet phyllo.
  - Brush with butter.
  - Cut into 6 (13 x 2-inch) strips. (Pastry cutter works well.)
  - Place scant tablespoon filling in bottom right corner of each strip.
  - Fold pastry over in triangular shape, flag-style, until end of strip is reached.
  - Brush with butter, prick with toothpick, and place on lightly buttered baking sheet, seam-side down.

On Herbs

- Fresh herbs may be frozen or dried for later use. To dry herbs in the microwave: Place 4-6 branches between 2 pieces of absorbent toweling. Microwave on HIGH 2-3 minutes, until brittle and dry. Separate leaves; crush, if desired. Store in an airtight container.
- Snip herbs to desired size with scissors, rather than chopping or crushing them.
- Use 3 parts fresh herbs to 1 part dried herbs.
- Add ground and delicately flavored herbs late in the cooking period to preserve maximum flavor. However, firm herbs, such as bay leaves, require long, slow cooking to bring out their flavor.

- Release the flavor of dried herbs by crushing gently before using.
- Store dried herbs in airtight containers in a cool, dry place to preserve freshness. To determine freshness in dried herbs, crush a small amount in a mortar and pestle; a fresh aroma should be present.
- Easy herbs to grow in the home herb garden or in planters are basil, chives, dill, lemon balm, marjoram, mint, oregano, parsley, rosemary, sage, summer savory, tarragon, and thyme.

400 Herb and Spice Chart

	Basil	Marjoram	Tarragon	Dill	Thyme	Rosemary
Appetizers and Garnishes	Mushrooms Meatballs Fish-Shellfish Tomatoes	Liver Pâté Stuffed 　Mushrooms Meatballs Artichokes	Chicken 　Liver Pâté Cheese Spreads Garnish	Cheese Dips Fish Garnish	Fish Spreads Pizza	Sour Cream Dips Liver Pâté
Soups	Tomato Spinach Minestrone Chowder Chicken Fish	Stews Onion Tomato Mushroom Minestrone	Chicken Mushroom Tomato Pea	Stews Cucumber Fish Tomato Chicken	Cream Soups Chowders Fish Gumbo Vegetable	Pea Soup Stews Spinach Chicken Tomato
Salads	Green Salads Tomato Potato Egg Fish Chicken Dressings	Tomato Aspic Green Salads Chicken Herb 　Dressings	Chicken Potato	Coleslaw Potato Cucumber Fish	Beet Tomato Aspics Herb 　Dressings	Bean Tomato Aspic Fish Herb 　Dressings
Poultry	All Fowl 　Stuffings	Chicken Game Dressings	All Poultry	Chicken Pie Creamed 　Chicken	Chicken Turkey Duck Fricassee Dressings	Stuffings Duck Chicken
Meats	General Use	Meat Loaf General Use	Veal Sweetbreads	Broiled Meats 　especially 　Lamb 　Sweetbreads	Meat Loaf Veal Liver Venison	Lamb Pork Veal Beef Ham Loaf
Fish	Baked or 　Broiled Fish Shrimp	Baked or 　Broiled Fish Tuna Salmon	All Fish	Lobster Shrimp Salmon Sole Halibut	Tuna Scallops Crab Sole Croquettes Stuffings	Stuffings Salmon Halibut Poached Fish Spiced Shrimp
Eggs or Cheese	Quiche Scrambled Eggs Soufflés Cottage Cheese Cheese Spreads	Cream Cheese Scrambled Eggs Stuffed Eggs Omelets Soufflés	All Egg 　Dishes	Cottage Cheese Eggs, Scrambled 　with 　Cottage Cheese Omelets	Shirred Eggs Cottage 　Cheese	Omelet Scrambled 　Eggs
Vegetables or Fruit	Tomatoes Broccoli Eggplant Onions Potatoes Squash	Mushrooms Dried Beans Squash	Mushrooms Squash Potatoes	Cucumbers Potatoes Cabbage Beans Beets	Carrots Beans Tomatoes Onions Beets Broccoli	Beans Peas Cabbage Spinach Potatoes Tomatoes Cauliflower Carrots Zucchini
Sauces	Barbecue Tomato Spaghetti Orange Butter	Vinegars White Brown Sour Cream Hollandaise	Bernaise Tartar Verte Mustard	White Tartar	Creole Espagñole Spaghetti Barbecue	White Barbecue Tomato Pizza Spaghetti
Sweets or Breads	Herb Bread Croutons	Herb Bread Cornbread Croutons	Yorkshire 　Pudding Herb Bread	Herb Bread Croutons	Herb Bread Dumplings	Herb Bread Dumplings

Lemon Balm	Oregano	Sage	Ginger	Mace	Nutmeg	Mint
Fish Garnish	Guacamole Pizza	Sharp Cheese Spreads Meatballs Chicken	Pickles Broiled Grapefruit Rumaki Spiced Nuts	Spiced Nuts Meatballs	Spiced Nuts Liver Pâté Meatballs	Garnish
Stews Tomato	Stews Corn Tomato Green pea Minestrone	Fish Chowders Chicken Stews Vegetable	Chicken Onion Carrot Fish Chowders	Chicken Mushroom Fruit	Spinach Chicken Broccoli Oyster Stew	Pea Chilled Fruit or Melon Garnish
Fruit Fish Chicken Garnish	Green Salads Guacamole Tomato Bean Herb Dressings	Chicken Herb Dressings	Mixed Fruits Dressings for Fruit	Mixed Fruits Dressings for Fruit	Mixed Fruits Dressings for Fruit	Fruit Cup Melon Balls Orange Garnish
Garnish	Marinades Dressings	All Chicken Turkey Duck Stuffings Dressings	Grilled Chicken Stir-Fry Chicken Dressings Marinades	Chicken Turkey	Cornish Hens Duck Chicken	Garnish
Garnish	Meatballs Grilled Meats Sausage Lamb Meat Loaf	Veal Lamb Liver Pork Marinades	Pot Roast Lamb Steak Pork Chops Stir-Fry Meats	Lamb Chops Sausage	Hamburger Meat Loaf	Lamb Veal
Garnish	Shrimp Clams Lobster Stuffings	Steamed Fish Halibut Salmon Stuffings	Broiled or Baked Fish Sole	Trout Scalloped Fish	Creamed Fish Croquettes	Garnish
	Deviled Eggs	Omelets Cottage Cheese Egg and Cheddar Casseroles	Soufflés French Toast	Quiche Fondues Creamed Eggs	Quiche Cream Cheese Soufflés French Toast	Cream Cheese
Fruit Carrots	Eggplant Tomatoes Zucchini Cabbage Broccoli	Leeks Tomatoes Eggplant Lima Beans Peas Brussels Sprouts	Sweet Potatoes Carrots Onions Winter Squash Baked Beans	Squash Asparagus Broccoli Carrots Cauliflower Potatoes	Spinach Sweet Potatoes Green Beans Carrots Squash	Carrots New Potatoes Spinach Zucchini Garnish
	Cheese Tomato Any Italian	Cheese Herb Butter	Any for Pork, Veal, Chicken, or Fish Sweet/Sour Dessert	Cream Tomato	Cream Tomato Barbecue White	Mint
Custards Fruit		Dumplings Herb Bread	Custards Cookies Puddings Cobblers Fruit Dumplings	Custards Pancakes Fruit Dumplings Puddings	Ice Cream Cakes Custards Cookies	

On Substitutions

Ingredients called for: **Substitutions:**

1 cup all-purpose flour . . . . 1 cup plus 2 tablespoons cake flour

1 cup self-rising flour . . . . 1 cup all-purpose flour, 1 teaspoon baking powder, and ½ teaspoon salt

1 cup cake flour . . . . 1 cup minus 2 tablespoons sifted all-purpose flour plus 2 tablespoons cornstarch

1 teaspoon baking powder . . . . ½ teaspoon cream of tartar plus ¼ teaspoon soda

1 tablespoon cornstarch or arrowroot . . . . 2 tablespoons all-purpose flour or 4 teaspoons quick-cooking tapioca

1 cake compressed yeast . . . . 1 package or 2 teaspoons active dry yeast

2 large eggs . . . . 3 small eggs

1 egg . . . . 2 egg yolks (for custards)

1 egg . . . . 2 egg yolks plus 1 tablespoon water (for cookies)

½ cup butter or margarine . . . . ½ cup solid shortening plus ¼ teaspoon salt

1 cup sweet milk . . . . ½ cup evaporated milk plus ½ cup water or 3-5 tablespoons nonfat dry milk plus 1 cup water

1 cup buttermilk . . . . 1 tablespoon lemon juice or vinegar plus sweet milk to equal 1 cup

1 cup heavy cream . . . . ¾ cup milk plus ⅓ cup melted butter

1 cup half-and-half . . . . ⅞ cup milk plus 1½ tablespoons melted butter

1 cup commercial sour cream . . . . 1 tablespoon lemon juice plus evaporated milk to equal 1 cup or 3 tablespoons butter plus ⅞ cup sour milk

1 cup yogurt . . . . 1 cup buttermilk or sour milk

1 cup honey . . . . 1¼ cups sugar plus ¼ cup liquid or 1 cup molasses

1 cup tomato juice . . . . ½ cup tomato sauce plus ½ cup water

1 cup catsup or chili sauce . . . . 1 cup tomato sauce plus ½ cup sugar and 1 tablespoon vinegar

1 cup canned tomatoes . . . . 1⅓ cups cut-up fresh tomatoes, simmered 10 minutes

1 pound fresh mushrooms . . . . 6 ounces canned mushrooms

1 teaspoon onion powder . . . . 2 teaspoons minced fresh onions

1 clove fresh garlic . . . . 1 teaspoon garlic salt or ⅛ teaspoon garlic powder

1 tablespoon grated raw ginger . . . . ½ teaspoon powdered ginger

¼ cup chopped fresh parsley . . . . 1 tablespoon dehydrated parsley

1 tablespoon fresh herbs . . . . 1 teaspoon dried herbs or ¼ teaspoon powdered herbs

⅛ teaspoon cayenne . . . . 8 drops Tabasco

1 teaspoon dry mustard . . . . 1 tablespoon prepared mustard

1 ounce unsweetened chocolate . . . . 3 tablespoons cocoa plus 1 tablespoon butter or margarine

On Equivalents

1 medium lemon . . . . 2-3 tablespoons juice or 2 teaspoons rind

1 cup whipping cream . . . . 2 cups whipped cream

1 pound brown sugar . . . . 2¼ cups, firmly packed

1 pound confectioners' sugar . . . . 3½ cups, unsifted - 4½ cups, sifted

1 pound granulated sugar . . . . 2 cups

10 miniature marshmallows . . . . 1 regular marshmallow

8 slices cooked, bacon . . . . ½ cup, crumbled

1 pound mushrooms . . . . 5 cups sliced

1 medium onion . . . . ⅓ cup, sliced or diced

1 pound tomatoes . . . . 3 medium or 1½ cups chopped pulp

1 pound fresh lima beans . . . . 1¼ cups, shelled

1 pound potatoes . . . . 2 cups, mashed

1 pound uncooked stewing chicken . . . . 1 cup cooked, chopped meat

3 teaspoons . . . . 1 tablespoon

4 tablespoons . . . . ¼ cup

5⅓ tablespoons . . . . ⅓ cup

2 tablespoons . . . . 1 fluid ounce

2 pints . . . . 1 quart

4 quarts . . . . 1 gallon

(M) denotes Micronote

(M) denotes Micronote

(M) denotes Micronote

(M) denotes Micronote

(M) denotes Micronote

(M) denotes Micronote

(M) denotes Micronote

(M) denotes Micronote

(M) denotes Micronote

(M) denotes Micronote

M) denotes Micronote

(M) denotes Micronote

(M) denotes Micronote

(M) denotes Micronote

Perennials
Junior Service League of Gainesville, Ga., Inc.
P. O. Box 32
Gainesville, Georgia 30503
(404) 536-3616

Please send _____ copies of **Perennials** @ $18.95 each $ _____
Add postage and handling @ 2.50 each $ _____
Add gift wrap (if desired)* @ 1.00 each $ _____
Georgia residents add 6% sales tax @ 1.14 each $ _____
Total enclosed $ _____

Ship To:

Name: _____

Address: _____

City _____ State _____ Zip _____

Please make checks payable to: Charge to: _____ Visa _____ MC Account No. _____
Perennial Publications
Telephone _____ Expiration Date _____ Signature of Card Holder _____

Gift card to read _____

....

Perennials
Junior Service League of Gainesville, Ga., Inc.
P. O. Box 32
Gainesville, Georgia 30503
(404) 536-3616

Please send _____ copies of **Perennials** @ $18.95 each $ _____
Add postage and handling @ 2.50 each $ _____
Add gift wrap (if desired)* @ 1.00 each $ _____
Georgia residents add 6% sales tax @ 1.14 each $ _____
Total enclosed $ _____

Ship To:

Name: _____

Address: _____

City _____ State _____ Zip _____

Please make checks payable to: Charge to: _____ Visa _____ MC Account No. _____
Perennial Publications
Telephone _____ Expiration Date _____ Signature of Card Holder _____

Gift card to read _____

....

Perennials
Junior Service League of Gainesville, Ga., Inc.
P. O. Box 32
Gainesville, Georgia 30503
(404) 536-3616

Please send _____ copies of **Perennials** @ $18.95 each $ _____
Add postage and handling @ 2.50 each $ _____
Add gift wrap (if desired)* @ 1.00 each $ _____
Georgia residents add 6% sales tax @ 1.14 each $ _____
Total enclosed $ _____

Ship To:

Name: _____

Address: _____

City _____ State _____ Zip _____

Please make checks payable to: Charge to: _____ Visa _____ MC Account No. _____
Perennial Publications
Telephone _____ Expiration Date _____ Signature of Card Holder _____

Gift card to read _____